"ERNEST K. GANN
IS GRIPPING AS EVER!"
The Kirkus Reviews

"AN EXCITING, FACT-PACKED VOLUME
. . . The reader finishes A HOSTAGE TO
FORTUNE with considerable respect for Gann
both as a man and writer. His is a life which
had its share of joys and triumphs, defeats and
tragedies."
The Los Angeles Times

"A BOOK AS STIRRING AS ANY OF HIS
NOVELS!"
John Barkham Reviews

"SAILOR, FLYER, WRITER—A fascinating
memoir by a remarkable human being . . . by
the time the reader has turned the last page, he
will feel Ernest K. Gann a friend—a perceptive,
articulate, strong, wise, and humble friend."
New York Post

"MARVELOUS . . . A BOOK ABOUT FLY-
ING, DEEPWATER SAILING, WRITING,
AND JUST PLAIN LIVING!"
San Francisco Chronicle

Also by Ernest K. Gann
Published by Ballantine Books:

BAND OF BROTHERS

A HOSTAGE TO FORTUNE

ERNEST K. GANN

BALLANTINE BOOKS • NEW YORK

For the incomparable Kay Brown, who persuaded me into this . . . and my everlasting gratitude to Lisa Burden, Beverly Cobb, and Elaine Hines who deciphered my original hieroglyphics and typed their way through the more than two thousand pages of manuscript, and finally, to Bob Gottlieb, whose extraordinary editorial talent gave me heart for the job.

Library of Congress Catalog Card Number: 78-54908

ISBN 0-345-28401-1

This edition published in hardcover by Alfred A. Knopf, Inc.

Manufactured in the United States of America

First Ballantine Books Edition: March 1980

Part One

OVERTURE

THE TRAIN FROM PUERTO LIMÓN

As I boarded the train at Puerto Limón, the morning was benign, the sun's heat had not yet brought to a boil the humid air of that banana port, and the renowned brace of three-toed sloths in the city's palm-clustered plaza were wide-eyed awake. Like so many Central American seaports, the town itself is seedy, its environs barely one step ahead of suffocation by the surrounding jungles, and most of its buildings and streets are in disrepair. The population, overwhelmingly black, displays the heavy amalgam of gentle courtesy and lassitude peculiar to most humans existing in equatorial latitudes.

There was no air of purpose about the people passing through the mangy station. Making their way toward the cars of the narrow-gauge train, they boarded without salutation or farewell.

1

A small diesel locomotive was poised at the head of the train. It was panting softly, as if gathering strength for the day's labor. At eight-thirty, give or take several minutes, there would be a high whining from the locomotive's air compressor and the train would jerk into movement—one baggage car trailed by three passenger cars. By late afternoon we were to have traversed the two hundred eighteen extraordinary kilometers between Limón, Costa Rica's only deepwater port, and San José, the nation's capital situated high in the central mountains. Fifty-two stops were scheduled en route, some at what was no more than a grocery store squeezed into the jungle, a few just in the middle of nowhere. The route passes through fetid coastal swamps, squirms through pure jungle, and eventually emerges into the valley of the Reventazón River. Thereafter, the rails follow the river as long as the original engineers could contrive. Eventually the mountains are negotiated and after the continental divide is passed at a place called Cartago, there remains only a gentle slide downslope into San José. It is said that nearly six thousand men, mostly blacks and Chinese, died during the construction of this railroad. Their sacrifice is marked frequently by crosses along the right of way.

This morning the large majority of the passengers are black. Their language is an incomprehensible patois of Spanish and Creole rendered in a sing-along cadence of speech which reflects the ancestral speech of their Gold Coast Africa two hundred years ago. Also boarding are a pair of young American men awkward in their attempt to melt into the crowd; an impossible endeavor since their bounteous upbringing has blessed them with relatively enormous physiques. They are soon joined by a third American youth. All affect unkempt beards and wear the torn-dungaree-flop-brimmed-hat uniform of their culture. Their costume leaves the blacks, who have obviously taken trouble with their appearance before exposure to strangers, totally bewildered.

In almost total contrast, three older American tourists now commence searching for seats in the already crowded car. They are led by an elderly triple-jowled man wearing a ten-gallon Texas hat pushed back from his perspiring brow. In place of a tie he wears a leather thong fixed with a silver medallion, and a matching belt buckle of tooled

2

silver is centered upon his ample belly. He is heavily armed with cameras, the straps crisscrossing his chest as if he were a commando equipped for some desperate mission. But he is smiling at all the world on this steaming morning, and his eyes are alight with anticipation.

Trailing rather apprehensively behind the ten-gallon hat is a woman who bears a remarkable resemblance to its owner. Is she his sister or has their marriage endured so long that they have finally melted into a sort of common denominator? In their wake is a younger woman, perhaps thirty, whose mouth is creased as if she had just spoken the word "alas." Only her eyes succeed in brightening her mask of apology at troubling other passengers while she moves along the crowded aisle. Her eyes, like her father's or uncle's or whatever he may be, announce that she is brilliantly alive to the moment, a soul like all the rest of us bound upon some incomparably human business.

After some maneuvering and accommodation by those already seated, the American trio find positions near the middle of the car. Grateful to their neighbors, they thank them in their own tongue: "Muchas gracias . . . Buenos días . . . Muchas gracias." With the formalities over, for which I cheer them, they settle down to tinker with their photographic paraphernalia.

Outside my open window the brakeman waves his hand lackadaisically. There is a polite toot from the head of the train and the station starts to slide away. I have only to glance back into the car to be reminded how any journey can become as complex as the life of a man. For now, despite our moving into an environment quite different from the station, within the car all is the same. The Americans are as contentedly settled as a family of roosting pigeons. One of the trio of bearded youths leans against the platform doorjamb, staring into space. His two contemporaries are so slumped in their seats that only the backs of their manes are visible. The ancient Costa Rican hag who has taken the seat opposite mine continues her chewing on a sliver of chicory and spits gently into the aisle.

Nothing within this car has changed and yet all outside is changing ever more swiftly. Is it we who remain still while the landscape moves?

Leaning out the open window as the train gathers speed, I wonder if movement in which the body remains passive can alone create this heady sense of impermanence. Do we not begin to die the day we are born? As the seasons bloom and fade, as surely as day commences at midnight, man's metabolism and even his most rooted thoughts enact the continuous pattern of change.

There is more to this than the rhythmic swaying of a small and much abused railroad car. I must steer my thoughts away from the lush green landscape flashing past and the sensuous heat of the sun upon my bare forearm. This is a release into the unknown. Change now rules as the absolute. We, the travelers, cannot avoid it or even mitigate its force. We are all lost to change, for no man can know triumph unless he has known disaster, or recognize joy without knowing grief, or treasure health without having felt agony.

This kaleidoscope sweeping past my window can be more than the energy of light received in the visual cortex of my brain. My optic nerves inform me that there is a line of coconut palms marching across a luxuriant savanna and occasional groups of Brahman cattle grazing in the shadows. Yet without bothering to close my eyes, I can continue to receive the constantly changing scene both inside and outside the swaying car while simultaneously reviving totally foreign images. Like an efficient magic lantern I can superimpose across all that is now visible the delft-blue eyes and saucy swagger of Rikki, the Dutch girl who once rescued me from misadventure among Hitler's Germans, or I can retrace a moonlit walk in the Sudanese desert, or a brutal beating on San Francisco's waterfront, which only insufferable self-confidence allowed me to survive intact. There is the once-beautiful and vivacious face of Eleanor, who shared my name for so many years, until the ravages of disease overcame her; flashing just afterward, for some incongruous reason, the birdlike gestures of Mather, a military school professor, who channeled this would-be soldier into more productive enterprise. On command I can see a chalet in the geographical heart of Norway, a place called Ustaoset, remote as the moon, snowbound and shared with Dodie, who, I decided, had been fashioned by God himself to become my constant companion. There, before my eyes, is that natural nobleman my father, seated upon his horse, a proud and resolute man who eventually, as the last of his sight deserted him, took my arm to walk only a little way and in the doing at last learned humility. Still without abandoning the scene at hand, I can review the Pacific Ocean one dawning and watch it grow so terrifying that I yearned to weep for mercy, yet could not because others depended upon me for salvation.

And of course there were those buoyant times when acclaim was first won. I was now profoundly grateful it had come gradually rather than overnight. And just as certainly there were those loathsome, calamitous events which had caused me to forsake all previous faith and which even now I dare not think upon.

I know that all of these and thousands upon thousands of other images are available upon demand. They are registered and catalogued, although rarely in good order; nor am I always in command of their behavior. Certain of them have a way of appearing spontaneously, as if some mischievous genie would remind me of my inconsistency.

I guess our speed to be fifteen miles per hour, slow enough for me to count the coconut trees and attempt, idly, to estimate their yield. As the numbers increase beyond my limited arithmetical ability I reach into my shirt pocket for a round plastic computer, a heritage from my days as a pilot of the line. It is a simple tool which I still employ when flying my own aircraft. Now, this airman's abacus might serve as well to count coconuts as airspeeds, fuel endurance, vectors of the wind.

While the hag in the opposite seat watches suspiciously and spits ever more discreetly, I begin to twist the two plastic wheels fringed with numbers, and quickly they indicate solutions to simple arithmetical problems. But the coconut game soon palls and I fall into posing less immediate questions.

At first the questions are prosaic—how many days have I existed? Answer, if I have the present date correct: 24,455 days and nights, not counting time spent in the fetal stage. I find the figure incredible until reworking proves it fact. What then have I done with this gift of time, a bounty denied so many of my contemporaries? Determined to use only the most conservative numbers, I discover I have spent at least 750 of these days and nights physically removed from this planet. This, considering one of my professional lives, is believable, but how had such prolonged separation affected my view of the earth and of my fellow inhabitants? To my astonishment I next find that my heart has beat at least two billion times, and while still in awe my hand goes instinctively to my left breast. Yes, the rhythm is unbroken, which means the last figure is already inaccurate.

Now I am hooked. While the car dances along the imperfect roadbed the computer reveals I have read a mere 5,460 books and have copulated as many as 4,200 times. For this ridiculous comparison I know not whether to be ashamed or proud.

How can I possibly be still alive and breathing? A combination of numbers reveals I have smoked at least 292,000 cigarettes, even though I have never been a heavy user, and I have tried the patience of my friends while consuming a minimum of 5,160 bottles of wine. Now, having realized the bawdy cast of my basic character, I refrain from even attempting to estimate the total quantity of whiskey, rum, absinthe, gin, vodka, ouzo, tequila, and various brandies.

Caught up in a statistical frenzy, I ignore the American in the ten-gallon hat, who aims his lens in my direction and snaps a picture of the native shacks which have suddenly appeared alongside the tracks. Can it be true that I have known more than six hundred earthlings intimately, loved at least one hundred passionately, and hated only five?

I return the computer to my shirt pocket lest it further betray me. If what it has declared truly represents the statistical history of one man, then I am appalled. And there is much more which no computer could reckon.

The carcass which presently clothed the ephemeral mortal me had been sorely abused yet it rarely complained. Rendered down, it was worth almost nine dollars on the fat and gristle market, even though it had suffered during my occupancy rickets and most child diseases, two ribs, one arm, one collar bone, a thumb, a jaw, an ankle— all broken—a torn Achilles tendon, three collapsed vertebrae, and had had two thirds of its teeth knocked out. Other insults to this flesh had been a long siege of malaria, *a spell of pleurisy, a tonsillectomy, hernias repaired, prostate, hemorrhoids, wens and miscellaneous growths removed, while a hundred-odd stitches had held assorted wounds.*

Who could match such a dismal history? Perhaps the man in the ten-gallon hat, I thought, but not the crone, who spat more forcefully now that I had ceased playing with my computer. Not the young Americans, they had not the years; nor could any of the Costa Ricans, whose much poorer nation could not possibly have offered them the services of so many expert repairmen. If I had not so recently quit trusting an inexplicable God I should have whispered my gratitude and thus, conveniently, left the solution of such equations to the Almighty.

Now despite increasing distraction outside the window I find it difficult to defer this archaeological exploration of the native of a rich country who had enjoyed the fortunes of a prince.

So very little had gone according to plan or prediction. My earning capacity had confounded those who, having observed my youth, forecast early bankruptcy. Somehow I had earned over two million dollars and yet thought it proper to have unburdened myself of nearly all of it.

I had enjoyed two wives and sired four children. I had dwelt more or less extendedly in 37 man-made structures ranging from spartan military barracks to luxurious mansions. Among other tangible impedimenta I had owned nine horses, 300 head of cattle, five airplanes, 21 boats, 900 acres of land, and 26 automobiles. There was no estimating the multitude of shirts, ties, shoes, coats, sweaters, and other goods which had protected or adorned this flesh.

During all of this worldly accumulation and disposal I had never known an instant of poverty, nor of true hunger except for those few months when my multiple-fractured jaw was wired firmly together. Not having been born to a minority or having been even momentarily underprivileged, I held no true conception of social nonacceptance, and yet I had always known that arrogance was not within me. There were still prejudices lurking within my system as a consequence of my heritage, but whenever they insulted my intelligence by erupting, I immediately slapped them down. Except for their genius I had never

7

envied other men, and I still believed as I had been taught, that I owed the world a living rather than the other way around.

Now on this scrubby little train it suddenly occurs to me that I am a relic of a little-known culture and a survivor of a generation often misunderstood. At last I am part of a minority, for in spite of abnormal hazards I have somehow escaped destruction while participating in more than half a century of the world's most turbulent history.

The train slows and half stumbles to a halt at a place called Mary and Jesus. The settlement consists of a trading store open-sided to the railroad track and a cluster of shacks built of faded wood. They are perched on five-foot stilts, tin-roofed and surrounded by breadfruit and calabash trees. From a coconut palm a white-faced monkey regards the train without enthusiasm and I suppose he has witnessed its arrival and departure almost every day of his life.

The behavior of his human neighbors is exactly the opposite. It appears that every inhabitant of Mary and Jesus has been waiting for us. While the locomotive pants, they exchange greetings with the passengers now leaning well out of the windows. Child-peddlers climb on and off the cars shouting their wares in high anxious voices: "Helados! . . . Naranjas! . . . Leche! . . ." Their pitch is bold and resolute for they know they have no more than two minutes before the train will be on its way again.

Suddenly my attention is captured by a shack set a little apart from the others. It has no windows or even a door, but clean curtains flipping in the gentle breeze screen the dark interior from the outside world. A line of laundry festoons the spacing between the porch posts, and astride the porch railing is a small mulatto boy. His eyes are enormous and fixed as steadfastly upon me as if he were aiming a rifle. As the moments pass and his unwavering stare persists, I become strangely uncomfortable.

Very well, little friend, who will look away first? Come now, one of us must break it off, or smile, or at least make some kind of signal acknowledging our inspection of each other.

In that small brown face there is not the slightest change of expression.

Increasingly uneasy, I try to interpret his message.
"Who are you? . . . Where have you come from? . . . Why are you here?" Or is it simply my Anglo-Saxon façade that so bewitches the boy? Certainly he has seen others of my breed, and there are children hanging from the train windows who should interest him more.

I am determined not to look away until my little adversary first concedes the game, although now, with not even a blink on his part, I find myself wondering how long our liaison can endure.

No change, and I sense he is winning. *What is your name, small one, and how come you are there?*

In desperation I raise my hand, the beginning of a wave. Prompted by an overwhelming need to establish communication with such a solemn human being, I wiggle my fingers. *Declare yourself, small one. The train may pull away before we can gain a clue about each other.*

I flick my fingers once again. *Why are you trying to intimidate me? Come! Friend or foe?*

My instant of despair is canceled by a renewal of hope. For suddenly those huge and eloquent eyes are transmitting messages. "I am here because I am here," he is obviously saying. "I was born to this life in these circumstances which are neither very good nor very bad and here I will grow to manhood and probably die. It is the way of things. You have been where you have been and are what you are because that is also the way of things."

Now at last I detect a flash of indecision in his eyes. They are speaking to me of incomprehensibles. "Are we creatures of different planets? I am only beginning a life given me here on the fringe of the jungle, while you are history. Therefore you should examine how all of this came about, before it is too late."

The locomotive emits a toot, condescending in its brevity. The sound arouses the boy and his poise tumbles. As his lips part in a smile his white teeth are revealed one after another, then he raises his hand and moves it very slowly in gentle farewell.

The train jerks, and the hamlet of Mary and Jesus slips away, pulled offstage complete with small boy, never to be seen again. I cannot bear to look back at the settlement of Mary and Jesus. In those few minutes almost too much has happened there. Now my mind is invaded by other

9

scenes, remote and long ago, yet each as undeniable as the eyes of that small boy.

While the train gathers speed, the child-peddlers drop off one by one. Holding my breath for the sake of the last boy to leap from the swaying car, thereby proving himself the most daring, I suddenly find it imperative to return to another time, another place.

Warily, lest I uncover ugly artifacts and so sour my twenty-three thousand seven hundred and twenty-fifth day, I poke among the ruins of the long forgotten, and find there a boy who is not a stranger.

Chapter 1

About five thousand years ago Fu Hsi defined the cryptic logic of the universe. He pronounced *yin* as the centrifugal force and *yang* as the centripetal force. Fire is *yang* and its adversary is water. All phenomena are subject to this dual effect and only the intervening time varies. It requires but twelve hours to turn day into night, months for autumn leaves to replace spring buds.

It may take only seconds from ecstasy to anguish.

Thus, our lives from the miracle of birth to the mysterious instant of death are never stabilized. The story of every man is disjointed and, on cold analysis, chaotic. We plan, but our plans go awry; we systematize and almost invariably some totally unforeseen factor in the system falters, whereupon the whole scheme collapses. Fortunately, other unrecognized and apparently foreign influences often perform last-minute rescues of the situation, and this is true of nations as it is of men. And these busy forces also determine who is to live a long and fruitful life, and who is to be cheated of both material blessings and longevity. We are frequent witness to paradoxical injustices contrived by mysterious powers.

In this relatively enlightened era it is difficult to blame a trident-carrying individual with a pair of horns for the good so often gone unrewarded and the viciousness so seldom punished. But these perplexities did not always prevail. When I arrived in it, the world was not very much younger than it is now, yet in my new homeland, angels and the devil, not always dominated successfully by one almighty God, were still regarded as directly responsible for all things.

My first bawl resounded through a house in Lincoln, Nebraska, during a gloomy October afternoon. Perhaps Halley's comet, already months past the sun, still exerted some of its dubious influence, for my mother suffered such extraordinary birthing distress that the doctor sought a firmer surface than her bed for his assisting manipulations. He chose the handiest thing available, an ironing board. The despair of both doctor and mother at my refusal to emerge became so traumatic that no other children were born by my mother, and even after the initial deed was done the new American was declared deficient in both behavior and health.

In keeping with the eternal proclivity of mothers for infant feeding according to the latest fashion, the mainstay of my diet became a concoction known as Horlicks malted milk. The result, in spite of my mother's lavish and loving care, was disappointing. I howled so perpetually a hernia developed before I could crawl, and then a long siege of rickets retarded the natural development of my legs. Puzzled because she sensed she was being misled, my mother gathered courage to defy professional advisors and turned me out to natural grazing. Recovery began immediately.

My mother was a first-generation American, both her parents having been born and raised to maturity in Darmstadt, Germany. When they joined the throngs of immigrants bound for the promising United States, the presence of many other German hopefuls drew them to Burlington, Iowa. There they opened a hardware store which prospered far beyond their expectations. In time they bred and raised five children and had enough money remaining to send my mother to National Park, a boarding school for girls near Washington.

At seventeen, a stunning girl possessed of all the physical attributes, she precipitately married a young Southerner. Before the marriage was consummated, my mother's unrestrained enthusiasm for their union was written in that full-bodied hand which reflected her true nature: "My love, my life you are my all . . ."

The recipient of these sentiments was the eldest of three brothers born to a family of Scotch-English origins which

11

had immigrated to New England almost immediately after the American Revolution. In the early 1850s one branch (the Kelloggs) made their way by ship and coach to Newnan, Georgia, a small plantation settlement some sixty miles south of present-day Atlanta. There the young entrepreneur Moses P. Kellogg, a highly educated man for his time, started College Temple, the first school for Southern young ladies. During the Civil War the institution was used as a hospital, first by the Confederate Army, which paid in Confederate dollars and finally in promissory notes, and later by the invading Union troops, who did not trouble to pay in any kind.

During the terrible days of the Reconstruction, with the Battle of Atlanta still easily remembered, Kellogg's daughter Alice married Robert Gann, a shy farm boy from a place called Rough and Ready, Alabama. They lived in what was left of College Temple and in one of its spacious rooms my father was born. The event was remembered by an aged black I knew as "Sam." A former slave, he had elected to continue his life at College Temple and remained a highly regarded member of the family for more than sixty years.

Kellogg's passion for education was perpetuated in his grandsons and granddaughters. All went on to universities, my father, George Gann, graduating from Georgia Tech with a degree in chemical engineering. Already a man of very firm convictions, he believed any ambitious young Southerner was wasting his time in an atmosphere so heavy with tradition and in a society still numbed from the aftermath of a war concluded long before he was born. When he learned of a job opening at the gas works in St. Louis, he applied immediately and thereby became the first of his family to forsake the South. But St. Louis was only a way station for the young Southerner who had turned his back on corn fritters and magnolia. He wanted something more stimulating than a gas works, and telephones, just coming into general use, fascinated him. Here, he believed, was a marvelous means of quick communication; a whole new society could be developed from its potentials, and he intended, somehow, to be part of it.

As the first year of their marriage passed, long-established standards contributed to the ever-growing devotion between George and his bride, Caroline. She

12

discovered that his gentlemanly manners had not been temporarily assumed for the period of courtship, but were endowed in the man himself, a heritage of his meticulous Southern upbringing. Then, and until his final day on earth, he could not bring himself to remain seated if ladies or any person older than himself entered a room. It would have been unthinkable for him to precede his wife through a doorway, walk on the inside of the street from her, or fail to take her arm protectively at any crossing. He *always* raised his hat to ladies and tipped it toward men whom he respected. His verbal address to others was "Suh" or "Ma-am," chained to frequent pronunciation of their family names. First names were used only if he had known the person for a long time.

During the early years of his marriage my father's taste in apparel was absolutely conventional. No circumstance could ever persuade him to appear in public without being carefully groomed, and even in the privacy of his home he wore a tie, vest, and jacket. In the hot Midwestern summers the composition of his ensemble was sometimes relaxed by the omission of the vest, but regardless of temperature the hard collar, tie, diamond stick-pin, and watchchain remained a part of the man. A handwoven straw boater worn at a precisely level angle of attack completed the fashion plate. A certain amount of personal vanity unquestionably contributed to my father's sartorial habits and to his lifelong inability to pass a mirror without pausing for inspection. Along with most of his contemporaries he showed an unashamed pride in self, in family, and in his work.

Two years after their marriage a profound change came to the young couple who had previously led such simple and well-ordered lives. By dogged persistence my father landed a job in the enterprise which had so fascinated him. The telephone and telegraph company in Lincoln, Nebraska, decided they could use his enthusiasm despite his uncommon accent. He was employed as an assistant to the traffic manager, and almost simultaneously my mother discovered she was pregnant.

She was able to regard the forthcoming phenomenon with even more equanimity than is common to most prospective mothers. She had no qualms about introducing a new American to such a well-ordered world. For the aver-

13

age American there were no visible threats on the horizon and geographical isolation from older nations contributed greatly to the general peace of mind. The racial tensions which had prevailed for years after the Reconstruction had eased, and while the labor unions were flexing their muscles, there was sufficient food for most Americans and a bounteous supply for many.

Thus I was to be born into a tranquil era, into a nation at peace with itself and with the rest of the world. The future was bright, opportunity was everywhere, and the Western frontiers had barely been settled. And, as if reflecting the national mood, an inexplicable good fortune steered me to a happy and loving household. During all the years my parents were together, I would never be aware of the slightest friction between them. By the time of my arrival they were firmly established in a pleasant house with an ample and steady salary to provide most amenities and they were lavish in their gentle love for each other.

There was no reason for them to suppose that they had bred an *enfant terrible*.

Chapter 2

Every "good" mother and father is living proof of man's strange masochistic urge to punish himself by surrendering to the natural mandate of physical reproduction. The noble and instinctive giving to infants of our precious life time, the multitude of tribulations, the necessary separations between sire and dam involved in providing for the infant's primary needs, the frights of accident and the prolonged ironies of suspect development, the frequent erasure of romance, the loss of sleep and the physical confinement known only to prisoners, the physical and mental ordeals of birth and the invitation to death itself are exaggerated payment for those rare seconds when our beloved may gurgle preciously and smile back upon us. If we believe but one life is ours to live then the trials of parenthood are proof of our slavery to society and also of our innate madness.

Except for suffering more illnesses than average and as

a consequence providing more travail for my parents, I demonstrated no deviations from the biological anarchy which was my threshold privilege. Likewise by my fifth year of life the chrysalis was left behind forever and I became curious of things other than purely physical. My actual emergence seemed oddly coupled with my mother's renditions on the piano. Even now I can hear her singing in her soft clear voice: "Rings on her fingers and bells on her toes, elephants to ride upon . . ." Usually she played for my father in the evenings and apparently his favorites were "Beautiful Ohio," "Dardanella," and "Just a Song at Twilight," for they are indelibly engraved in my brain along with the summer night-humming chorus of locusts who accompanied the ceremony of being tucked into bed. I do not remember hearing Haydn or Bach, Handel, Beethoven, or any of the recognized masters in our house. We were not a musically intellectual family.

It was often said that everyone in Nebraska read books. The commentator, usually an Eastern sophisticate or a self-styled Nebraskan intellectual, would arch eyebrows and add snidely, "All the books of the Bible."

Yet in my family books were a very important part of our social life, albeit they were not very heavy going. Conrad, Stevenson, Dickens, and Melville were present, as were Hawthorne and Cooper, and all the works of Dumas, who particularly enthralled the armchair romanticist and adventurer in my father. He was also passionately devoted to Booth Tarkington and to Zane Grey and his cowboys, frontiersmen, and Indians, who swashbuckled across the Western ranges. I have no doubt my father's long devotion to Western novels eventually resulted in his latter-day career as a sort of glorified cowboy known as "Cactus Jack."

My father was a dignified businessman only during working hours. The moment he picked up a book he became the author's most romantic character. He was Ahab, Sherlock Holmes, Jeeves, Penrod, Micawber, or Sitting Bull. He spoke, walked, and talked in character until another business day obliged him to drop the mask.

During his early youth he had suffered a bicycle accident which cost him an eye. Much to his distress this handicap kept him out of active service in the First World War and frustrated his visions of leading a charge to

15

match the Light Brigade's. Yet his one eye served him remarkably well until the very last of his years. Even at the height of his career, when a briefcase full of reports, contracts, and all manner of business seemed to be chained to his person, he managed to devour at least three books a week. Once gone amok in his imagined surroundings he resisted going to bed. My mother, yawning at his side, would plead the demands of the new day, which nevertheless often arrived long before he agreed to close the covers of a new book. Even then he would gently admonish his wife with one of his favorite dictums: "Early to rise and early to bed . . . and you'll meet no interesting people."

If my father strained his good eye unduly there was no evidence of it. Until his late sixties he remained a crack shot with rifle or shotgun and often came out the high scorer in trapshooting meets. Nor did his rather prominent glass eye seem to inhibit his social life. At any gathering he was a great favorite with the ladies, his success a tribute to the marvelous and twinkling expressiveness of his true eye.

My mother was a much slower reader and more given to books she selected "to improve my mind." Her forte was painting, at which she was more than a talented amateur in both oils and watercolors. At her side I first learned to use a brush and know the very special joys of graphic creation.

Like so many Midwestern towns and smaller cities, Lincoln was both God-fearing and law-abiding. In spite of the severities of the Nebraska climate most residential areas now enjoyed the shade of planted trees, and where water had been brought to the surface, lawns and gardens were luxuriant. Most citizens did not trouble to lock their doors at any time. The residents of each block considered they owned their houses regardless of mortgage size and they knew all of their neighbors on both sides of the street unto the names of their children and grandchildren. They also kept well informed of each other's business. Our block, which was as absolutely flat as when buffalo grazed the same plain, was peculiarly distinguished because of the Polsky family. As Jews, they were a relatively rare breed in Nebraska and were treated accordingly.

My visitations to the Polsky house were regular and

obligatory since Bernard the son was my very first friend, and the bond between us was of the steel only little boys can forge. Spending lunchtime at his best friend's house was a very special privilege for either Bernie or myself and was usually granted upon a solemn guarantee of good behavior through the morning.

Bernard Polsky and I often vowed eternal friendship. We would have died for each other, and as soldiers in opposing armies, frequently did.

Romance was also available within our block. A few houses nearer the corner from our gray wooden house with its modest front porch there stood a similar dwelling which sheltered the Ridnoors. Their daughter Joan was my contemporary, a flaxen-haired siren with a recently complete array of permanent teeth. Her smile, dazzling in comparison with that of the other neighborhood girls, who could only display various maroon apertures between scattered teeth, was to be my undoing.

It all began, as do so many affairs, with a rendezvous in a secret place. During this period of American history vacuum cleaners were still to be invented and the cleaning of carpets remained one of the most onerous chores in a housewife's long list of domestic burdens. Wall-to-wall carpeting was almost unknown, for who would conceal the beautiful joiner-work in the parquet floors of the affluent, or hide the highly polished oak of the bourgeoisie? According to their finances, the average family walked on all varieties of rugs, from "oriental" (Persian) to Navajo, or hooked. With the arrival of spring each year, just as surely would the rugs be rolled up, taken to any convenient place on the lawn for airing, and then assaulted vigorously with a special wire rug-beater shaped like an oversized tennis racquet. The rugs were beaten until the winter's accumulation of dust and debris was hammered into the grass or carried away on the Nebraska winds.

One afternoon, with the cicadae serenading the Ridnoor backyard, daughter Joan and I crawled into the inviting tunnel formed by a rolled rug. There, in the semidarkness, hidden from every eye, even from friend Bernard, we chatted easily for a while, our voices subdued in keeping with the clandestine nature of our shelter. And in time as our conversation turned upon our devotion to each other and particularly my gallantry at her recent birthday party, we spoke only in whispers. The ends of our tunnel remained round orbs of sunlight, but within the rug the darkness contributed greatly to a new and acute sensation of being alone together. Soon I touched Joan and, gently, she touched me. Then slowly, inexorably compelled by something bigger than ourselves, our faces came together and we touched lips.

It was hot in the rug and airless and our skin was moist with the perspiration of excitement, yet from that magic moment I was Joan's slave. It was my first experience with the rapture and penalties of dalliance.

My pledge of undying loyalty to Joan was terminated when in keeping with my father's increasing prosperity he decided to build a house far removed from the scene of our secret courtship. The new house was sturdily built of wood and a white stucco applied in a style which left thousands of small peaks and craters across the surface. There was a garage for a new Buick touring car in the rear of the house and a flower garden which eventually flourished beneath my mother's hand. Here on the fringe of the city the land remained as it had been in buffalo times. There were no trees and the blazing Nebraska sun and withering winds remained untamed until long after we decamped.

The new house marked the true beginning of my life as a minor princeling. The common goods lavished upon middle-class white children had been both given and accepted by me as a natural birthright. I wore highbutton shoes, my garments were laundered and untorn, my cheeks fat, and my eyes bright with ample nourishment. Photographs of me in various regalia were dutifully handcolored by my mother. When I had survived one year she inscribed in the large record she kept of such matters: *Baby saw President Taft who was on a tour of the U.S. stopping off at Lincoln for two hours.*

The Christmas of my fifth year reflected the prosperity of middle-class America and did nothing to shake my faith in Santa Claus. In the already distorted spirit of the occasion his phantom sleigh brought me a complete cowboy outfit including hat, chaps, rope, gun, bandana, and fringed gloves. Since I also possessed an Indian costume from the preceding year (in which I had been photo-

18

graphed in the act of scalping a patient baby-sitter), I could now fight on either side. Additional booty included a fire engine, a toy grocery store, a coloring book, and a game board with a projecting clown's nose. Prior to the actual arrival of these items there had been a thrilling visit to Herpelsheimer's department store where the German traditions of Christmas were awesomely exaggerated. The displays of lead soldiers were almost unbearably exciting, although I had no idea that real German soldiers, real French, English, and Russians, were celebrating the same holiday season by dying in the mud of distant trenches.

The still underdeveloped character of the area surrounding the stucco house meant that playmates were non-existent until I found, about a quarter of a mile away, a bonanza of five children. For reasons never revealed to me, their family name was thought sufficient identification and no Christian names were given the juvenile members. They were simply known as A, B, C, D, and E. C, the scrawny middle son, was my special friend, but in no way did his mother match the fare served at the Polsky house. C's mother was a cheery and kind enough soul, but her idea of a sufficient midday meal for boys was invariably a few crackers spread with a tissue-thin layer of peanut butter. I pronounced my ingratitude by declining lunch at C's house whenever possible.

I knew, somehow, of a great war before I was taken to the Rialto Theater where I viewed a motion picture called *Hearts of the World*, which portrayed spike-helmeted German soldiers committing a long series of atrocities.

The room which had been my very own in the stucco house was decorated with a wallpaper frieze depicting cowboys and Indians pursuing buffalo through clouds of white dust. Every night I had dropped off to sleep thinking how fine a life it would be to join such a band of hearties. Now my ambitions changed as the glamour of a military life and glorious death inspired the imaginations of my new society. For with the discovery of a quite separate neighborhood beyond the slight hill behind our house I had acquired a squad of new friends. A, B, and C were supplemented by Howard, whose

19

perpetually running nose distressed my mother, Billy Roth, whose freckles were the envy of us all, and Junior Gooch, who lived in an immense brick house and was usually early wounded in our new war games. We therefore distrusted him if only because the more gallant of us knew the reason for his abandonment of battle and according to the rules there was nothing we could do about it. No more than the cry of "Charge!" was needed to see Junior halt and stumble, fall back a few steps, and then retreat in great pain to a dugout where we had established an advanced casualty station. Once arrived there, Junior would fall into the solicitous arms of the two neighborhood girls we permitted to serve as nurses with the troops. While the rest of us ran breathlessly across the open fields sometimes triumphantly bayoneting the enemy and sometimes dying heroically when ambushed by a hidden machine gun, Junior lay in the cool of the dugout, bandaged wherever he had been hit, overwhelmed with sympathetic caresses.

In time we learned to emulate Junior's brand of heroism. And soon after the start of every battle casualties mounted alarmingly. The dugout hospital was operating at full capacity, while there were almost no troops in the field.

Again my mother set the mood with music and lyrics reflecting America's growing involvement in the European war. "Keep the Home Fires Burning" was a sentimental ballad admonishing the home folks while the hero was away gathering medals, and "K-K-K-Katy" was an attempt to lighten the mood through a soldier presumably comic because of his stutter. "I Didn't Raise My Boy to Be a Soldier" and other tunes suggesting that war might not be all medals and heroics were still in the disillusioned future.

Fear of their own son ever playing at more than mock war was obviously not in the catalogue of my parents' worries. Almost immediately after the sinking of the *Lusitania* and subsequent developments which ended in the American declaration of war, I was taken to Camp Funtson, Kansas, where an officer friend of my father conducted us on a royal tour of the booming military establishment. As the cavalry clattered past my wide eyes and the dust raised by caissons drifted into my open mouth I thought surely there could be no life like a soldier's. Nor was I discouraged in this conviction by my parents.

While I received a star for maintaining a clean desk at Prescott School and enjoyed a dramatic triumph reciting something called "Caw-Caw Said the Black Crow," teacher Mary B. Hicks wrote in a fine Palmer hand:

My dear Mrs. Gann,
    Your little son's choice of words in his English work has been splendid of late. I just wish you could have heard his story yesterday on "Patriotism for Uncle Sam—!!"
    "Uncle Sam" would surely have felt proud had he heard him.

These were heady times and Santa Claus, whose actual existence I was beginning to question (with due caution lest lack of faith be penalized), clearly demonstrated his adaptability to national interest. My military arsenal was augmented by a large box of cardboard soldiers and a battleship. A wind-up train and a small Meccano set were regarded as mere dividends.

All gifts and possessions were reduced to uninteresting baubles upon the arrival of a heavy package wrapped in burlap. The moment I learned it had been sent by my uncle Archie who was fighting in France I became choked with emotion and watched in reverence as my father unwound strip after strip of the protective burlap. At last, revealed in all its camouflaged ugliness, was a genuine German helmet. It was the heavy "coal-scuttle" type and still smelled mightily of its owner's last labors and anxieties. Although it was several sizes too large for my head I wore it everywhere except to bed and thought it the most valuable treasure in the world. For a week I maneuvered beneath its wobbly steel canopy and spoke only in gutturals.

My family had none of the unity common to Italian, Jewish, or Scandinavian families immigrant to the United States. Holidays were not an occasion for a gathering of relations and visits among our relatives were brief and not particularly felicitous. Having once broken

21

away from his territorial heritage my father was not anxious to maintain anything more binding than the most tenuous connections and I was never imbued with enthusiasm for the clan. Likewise my mother was a firm believer in leaving her family life resolutely behind when she married. She carried on an occasional correspondence with her brother Ernest, for whom I was named, but they rarely saw each other. She was saddened by the death of her brother Bill, a sailor who in a moment of whiskey bravado dove off a thiry-foot cliff into less than three feet of water, yet her mourning was brief and his existence was never mentioned again.

One relative did bludgeon her way into our tight little family circle on several occasions and no effort on her part could stay me from cringing at the sight of her. My mother's Aunt Ethel was an extraordinarily formidable woman, wide of girth, enormously bosomed, thin-lipped, and ox-jawed. This imposing corpus was topped by a rat's-nest coiffure towering on high. I distrusted "Aunt Ethel" with every animal instinct at my disposal. I knew she could, and would, betray a small boy for the slightest behavioral deviation. Her condescending tone made me sullen and morose. Worst of all, believing that much in the world was not fit for young ears, she would start whispering the instant I hovered within yards of her loquacious presence. She was a gifted mistress of the whisper, setting the volume just loud enough to maintain communication with her immediate listener while keeping the substance of her monologue audible yet incomprehensible to the casual passerby. I hated her for her mastery of espionage and secrecy.

Once my father's parents came to gauge his progress among the barbaric Yankees and to observe at a wary distance what sort of addition he had made to the basic family. My grandfather, an austere gentleman ornamented with a brush mustache, bow tie, and an ill-fitting toupee, failed utterly in establishing any rapport with his grandson. He stood very straight, spoke most softly when he deigned to comment on anything at all, and regarded the world via a pair of almost expressionless blue eyes. Both as a doting grandparent and as a possible origin of gifts, I found him a shocking disappointment.

My grandmother was of totally different texture. She

was a small creature, possessed of sparkling eyes and a sense of humor which constantly came to the rescue of an otherwise imperious woman. She was marvelously intelligent, well-read, and gentle, despite her iron determination. In addition she was an artist of astonishing precocity; a splendid oil done by her at the age of fifteen still testifies to her talent. I wept when she finally climbed into a Pullman and thereby disappeared in a southerly direction to be gone from my life for several years.

About this time my genuine German helmet was augmented by a genuine gas mask in which I was duly posed for photographs. I was advised that the great war in which I fully expected to participate had come to an end, but my disappointment was eventually alleviated when I was taken to observe the returning American troops marching bravely along the main street of Lincoln.

Gradually the toys of war were abandoned and the inevitable changing of all things eased me into a sort of *Penrod and Sam* existence. Our fierce battles were stilled and our scarred and broken weapons laid aside eventually to disappear somehow from the face of the earth. Now, instead of limping into advance casualty stations, we played "Doctor-Nurse" when we played with girls at all. It was a game we found interesting according to our daring, for the operations often involved an innocent exploration of the patient's private parts, or to our astonishment if the patient was a female, their odd design. During this stage, suddenly overwhelmed by curiosity, I made a search of my father's dressing bureau during his absence and there discovered a loaded .38 revolver which fascinated me by its weight when pointed at my image in his mirror. I also found hidden beneath his handkerchiefs two small tin boxes containing circular rubber objects which after some experimentation I decided were balloons. I wanted very much to ask my father what he was doing with such fine toys, but instinct warned me he would not be pleased with my investigations.

———

The Ringling Brothers, Barnum, and Bailey Circus which had arrived in Lincoln paraded along the same

23

magic main street the victorious soldiers had once graced, and culminated their triumph by performing under a great tent erected on the outskirts of the city. Not far away from this hallowed ground where camel and elephant droppings could still be inspected, half an hour's hike along the railroad track, there stood a hill I had dubbed Eagle Mountain. There we had cached treasures of various worth, firecrackers left over from the Fourth of July, an army canteen containing a cherry-tasting liquid made by Billy Roth's mother, our frog spears, a BB gun, assorted fishhooks, a can of matches, a supply of corn silk for the manufacture of cigarettes, and several million dollars in play money which had been given Junior Gooch's sister for Christmas (I often wondered how this present affected his fiscal attitudes in later years).

This was the age of "Let's Pretend" and our skill at the game was so highly developed that no conceivable role or situation was beyond our immediate imaginations. We were pirates or their victims, Indian travelers or buffalo hunters, gypsy fortune-tellers, cavalrymen suffered the loss of a horse, or engineers at the throttle of the Overland Limited. My mother's cast-off dressmaking form, with certain alterations to the length of the torso, served to transform me into a knight in armor. My rather too bosomy foreside was further protected by a metal shield so decorated with escutcheons and heraldic devices it was hardly recognizable as the top of our garbage can.

In these and other guises we passed with the greatest of ease from the familiar world into others of our choice, lands where our deeds were always gallant and the good guys always won. We were the Huckleberry Finns, the Tom Sawyers, and the Penrods, those American boys later painted with such tender appreciation by Norman Rockwell. All of us carried knives, although their use as weapons never entered our thoughts. Our knives were for whittling and making things, the dissection of certain dead insects and animals, and, more importantly, the playing of "mumblety-peg." None of our games were organized; adults kept their distance until the summer's dusk when their voices could be heard echoing up and

24

down the street as they called for the immediate return of their progeny.

One glorious day a real knight in leather armor descended into a pasture on the south of Lincoln and began taking people for airplane rides. By chance I was among them; my first and unforgettable ascent from which I did not recover full consciousness until days later. This god of the wind and sun was flying a biplane of fabric and wood known as a Jennie (JH4D), and his name was boldly presented in white letters on the top wing and the underside of the lower wing: OMAR LOCKLEAR. Previously, at the Nebraska State Fair, I had witnessed a performance by another such superman and had been affected in the same mystical way. He had also been flying a biplane, but it was smaller, of much lighter construction, and the great man himself was easily visible sitting on a sort of platform projecting forward from the wings. When he passed between earth and sun the transparency of his wings was enchanting to behold and his name lettered in black was clearly visible when he performed his famous loop-the-loop: LINCOLN BEACHY.

Pretending I was either Locklear or Beachy was a simple matter of assembling enough sticks, boards, paper, and string to create a flying machine. My own vocal cords—trilling in vibrato and modulated according to effort of take-off or speed of each death-defying maneuver—supplied the power.

Amid so many demands upon my attention, the prospering of my father remained unnoticed by me. I was not at all interested in the arrival of a new Buick touring car and even less excited about its utilization on a trip to the Far West. I was reluctant to leave my neighborhood comrades, although the prospect of seeing real Indians lent me a status I found hard to deny.

All the roads west of Lincoln were unpaved and in questionable condition. Communication and transport by automobile over large distances was yet to be nationally recognized. (Even in the East, which was considered to be advanced in all things, U.S. Highway 1, connecting Boston, New York, Philadelphia, and Baltimore, as it had since Revolutionary days, was still only two lanes and ill-paved.) My father proposed to drive all the way to Estes Park in Colorado and to Yellowstone in Wyoming over roads still bearing the deeper cuts of pioneer wagons bound for Oregon. There were known to be long reaches wide enough for only one vehicle, and except for the Platte and Missouri rivers the road was devoid of bridges. Along the way there were occasional sod houses and less often a wide place in the road where the local inhabitants dared to identify a few wooden commercial structures as a town.

For hundreds of miles the featureless ocher plains baked beneath the cruel sun and hours would pass before we encountered another power vehicle. Desolate areas of alkali deposits dotted the terrain and even the hardy buffalo grass disappeared. At night there was never any light on the horizons except the luster of stars.

My father took precautions against the distances between the few larger towns by carrying ten gallons of fuel for the Buick in cans strapped to the running board and hanging from the opposite side a five-gallon canvas water sack for a possible overheated engine. In case of a serious breakdown the water could provide our very salvation. He also carried two extra tires and tubes against the twin threats of blowout or puncture. At least it was heartening to know that if any sort of breakdown occurred there was a reasonable chance that one of the often seen mirages would cease quivering and become a tangible vehicle complete with driver. If so he certainly would not hesitate to stop with an offer of assistance. Americans trusted other Americans all along what had only recently been a true frontier and the succor of those in need was not only obligatory but pleasurable.

The Buick was heavily loaded with camping paraphernalia including a tent which with some doing could be fixed to the car's canvas top and extended outward until it formed a reasonable dwelling. In this shelter we slept even as those only one generation before us had done while bound for a land of greater promise.

We were dressed for the expedition rather dowdily but most practically considering the lack of commercial housing along the way, the presence of rattlesnakes, and other creatures native to wherever my father decided to make camp for the night. Much to my amusement my mother wore breeches. Since I had never seen, much less expected to see, a female in pants, I covered my sense of shock in taunting ridicule. The cloth wrap-around puttees, a protective device worn by most Allied combat soldiers during the recent war, hardly improved our overall appearance. Only my father, ever the fashion plate, embellished his image by wearing a tie.

My post during all of the journey was astride the mounds of camping gear, plus antlers, rocks, and various impedimenta accumulated en route. Perched there above what would normally have been the Buick's rear seat I sang to myself hour after hour as I watched the great spare face of buffalo and Indian land unfold. Our speed varied greatly. According to the sharp contrasts in road conditions, we proceeded often at one to five miles per hour and very occasionally as high as thirty-five, which was near maximum velocity for the heavily loaded Buick.

Serious picture-taking began when the character of the land became more scarred and broken with mounds, sheer cliffs, and rock-filled streams to ford. My father's Kodak increasingly absorbed his attention. When a vista pleased him he would bring the Buick to a halt in the middle of the road, turn off the engine, and direct my mother and me in poses to suit the landscape. Finally satisfied, he would open the bellows of his Kodak, take a few minutes looking down at the image in the convex viewfinder and finally press the trigger. After closing the Kodak he would turn it over, flip up a narrow metal lid on the backside, and write the locale and date. When developed, this inscription later appeared on the negative itself.

On several occasions we saw other camping expeditions, but our sense of isolation was never broken by the necessity of sharing a campsite. The plains offered miles and miles of unfenced fields and the plateaus were populated only by gophers. Later the canyons and vigorous streams roaring down from the true Western mountains offered an endless variety of choice sites beneath their bordering trees. A few minutes' casting in the mornings brought all the trout we could eat to the breakfast table and often we would sight a bear, or a deer, or on the higher slopes the white butts of antelope. There were

27

times when we seemed the only people left on earth, and —without fears of any sort, lost in the bounty of a beautiful and still unspoiled land—we were profoundly content.

Chapter 3

Soon after the successful auto tour of the Far West my father achieved an even more significant triumph. Word of his energy and abilities had reached St. Paul, Minnesota, where the Tri-State Telephone Company had need of a general superintendent. The job and the much greater challenge (and a much greater salary) were accepted by my father with characteristic resolve. Recognized by his peers, he knew he was on his way toward satisfying his churning ambitions.

I was convinced that Indians, of whom I had seen only a few during our Western adventure, would comprise the principal population of Minnesota. Instead I found a true city much larger than Lincoln and filled with wonders. And in spite of the Arctic winters and steaming humid summers the climate seemed more benign than that of our former home.

Here in St. Paul where the prosperous city fathers lunched at the Athletic Club, belonged to Kiwanis or Rotary, actively participated in the great winter carnival, and picnicked along the shores of the many surrounding lakes, the so-called Roaring Twenties were just under way. Skirts and hair were very short and cloche hats standard. Bright red lipstick was heavily applied and most women rouged their cheeks. Long cigarette holders manipulated for emphasis like batons along with telephonic relations with the best bootleggers were considered badges of the sophisticate. "Fun" was the watchword for all not too severely affected by the minor depression under which the era began. The changes within the United States itself were anything but subtle. Like every American, regardless of age or station, I was influenced by the energetic excitements of the early twenties and in some measure molded by them.

Imagination remained the most employed resource of

28

our young existences. My dog Sparky was not merely pulling my sled along the snow-covered street in front of our house, he was a fierce king of the Arctic, a half-wolf negotiating treacherous ice packs and barren tundra. He reacted to my high thin cries of "Mush!" "Gee!" and "Ha!" as would any faithful sled-dog of a Royal Canadian Mountie pursuing his man. When both of us had performed our arduous police duty, and law and order triumphed in the frozen wastes, Sparky also joined me in my first commercial venture—the selling of *The Saturday Evening Post,* a magazine of enormous influence on the minds of its several million American readers.

Other times were devoted to my career as a Zeppelin commander and the serious troubles experienced during the bombing of London. I stood at the control wheel in the command gondola, stiff-backed and grim, my dueling scar pulsing as I strove to contain my inner excitement on sighting the city in the darkness far below. My orders to the crew were at first calm and reserved, appropriate to a bemedaled hero recently decorated by the Kaiser himself. Then as the moment of truth approached and I fought to guide my Zeppelin precisely to target in spite of terrible weather, my gutturals were pronounced with ever more anxious intensity. Finally I would raise my hand and lower it smartly.

"Eine bomben!"

Smiling in satisfaction I would hear the hiss of the first bomb exiting and make a slight course correction.

My hand rose again. *"Zwei bomben! . . . Drei bomben!"*

Hiss-hiss as the bombs fell away. Then suddenly a cry of despair from the crew working in the bomb racks. I leaned out to ascertain the trouble and above the roar of the eight Maybach engines heard the always dreaded warning, *"Der bomben ish schtucken!"*

Here aboard my beloved Z-105 I was faced with the terrible predicament of all Zeppelin commanders. A bomb stuck in the release mechanism and already fused, the perfect situation for a fatal explosion.

Quick now to the diving wheel, for seconds counted. Better a prisoner of the English than a flaming corpse tumbling from the night heavens. Yet there was a chance, however slim. I knew my ship and I knew my stalwart crew. In an exhibition of supreme aeronautical skill and daring, I brought the famous Z-105 safely to earth. Taps were played for those who had lost their lives while attempting to free the bomb which had so nearly caused the destruction of us all. In the fatherland the wild descent of Herr-Kapitan Ernst Heinschmidt and his gallant crew soon became legend.

There was a cupola extending from the attic of our house which served admirably as the Z-105's control gondola. A bicycle wheel was the perfect size for a diving wheel and my wooden wagon was plundered to provide a steering control. There were several rope pull and push controls for dropping ballast and the transfer of lifting gas, and a considerable panel of tin can tops told me immediately of speed, altitude, wind, and course.

In the same fashion I created a long superheterodyne wireless. In spite of a total lack of innards, the elaborate device enabled me to communicate instantly with all the countries in the world, and sometimes when conditions were right I gossiped with the people on Mars. The super-heterodyne served me well until my twelfth birthday brought the gift of a real crystal set. Using the springs of my bed as an aerial and experimenting carefully with placing the point of the delicate cat's whisker on the crystal, I was sometimes rewarded with the faint sound of "Tea for Two and Two for Tea" in my headphones.

There were many other stimuli to most young American imaginations. I discovered the *Oz* books, *Robinson Crusoe, The Swiss Family Robinson,* and most thrilling of all, *Treasure Island.*

The silent movies were approaching their zenith and held a particular fascination for me. While Westerns starring Tom Mix or Hoot Gibson were standard fare, my celluloid hero remained Douglas Fairbanks (Sr.) who portrayed the supreme heroes. The music for his films rendered by a pit orchestra inspired Fairbanks audiences to a near frenzy of excitement. I sat entranced through *The Thief of Baghdad* four times and *Robin Hood* seven times. I knew all of the titles by heart and every piece of action so well I resolved to compete with St. Paul's Rialto Theater. To that end I enlisted my friends in the gathering of the neighborhood's discarded

Christmas trees. We dragged them to the basement of our house and created Sherwood Forest.

"Once more then, dear friends, into the breach!" Robin Hood, Friar Tuck, and all the merry band performed to a capacity house, and dizzy with first success I had prompt answer for adults who inquired as to my plans when I grew up.

There is no logical explanation for the quirks of circumstance which at the time of early youth seem of little significance and prove, in later years, to be key factors in the progression from womb to maturity. They happen to all and are usually unrecognized. By such raw chance, or so it seemed, was my education now torn from formula and suddenly, with the bewildered consent of my parents, redesigned.

I had attended the Longfellow School for only one year when a committee of the faculty decided it was unnecessary for me to continue, finish the eighth grade, and graduate in company with my contemporaries. I was never made privy to their reasoning, but it is an easy thing for any parent to become convinced that their image is touched by genius, particularly if the hint comes from outside the immediate blood. If the dictum originates in a teacher, or worse a covey of educators, then the conviction may become overwhelming.

Thus, while still in short pants I was induced to turn my back on all that was familiar to me and enter a new and hostile world. As an "experimental student" I was enrolled at the University of Minnesota High School and persuaded (as if I had any choice) into a formidable curriculum. In September those educators responsible, undismayed that I wouldn't reach twelve years of age for yet another month, decided I should take Latin, during which I would read of a certain Caesar's adventures in Gaul, chemistry taught by a pipe-smoking professor who also taught college classes, algebra to keen my mind, English composition because it was mandatory, and as a sort of recreational snap—architectural drawing.

During the following two years I learned, without bitterness, how to be utterly alone and survive. The university students and those in the high school of normal age were not intolerant of the freak who walked their same halls and used the same toilets marked MEN; they

31

simply ignored my existence. I soon learned how a fourteen-year-old going on fifteen can look right through a twelve-year-old, and of the total self-preoccupation of college students. As an experiment, I was observed by educators at a safe distance and my academic deeds both dismal and brilliant were solemnly recorded for a purpose I never knew. No one said, "You have done this well" or "badly"; nor was I offered any assistance. I was simply observed, a case history to one day become a statistic in an educational paper.

Sensing rather than truly realizing my special status, my loneliness often became nearly overwhelming and I wept sometimes in self-pity as I struggled to conquer lessons designed for a more developed brain. The total effect culminated in rebellion and led to years of ignobility and mischief.

It was two years before all agreed that my precocity did not necessarily herald genius and that my education should proceed normally. Meanwhile I had joined the Boy Scouts and risen with startling rapidity through the various grades until I was nearly qualified for Eagle Scout. And yet . . . the forces of *yin* and *yang* once more took charge.

While at summer camp I led an after-taps expedition across the lake. On the opposite shore there were vacationing girls and I persuaded two of my troop that their presence should not go unobserved. Concealing ourselves outside their cabin until they undressed for the night we approached their window in the best silent Indian style and through the wire screen viewed the unclad female form. We were at first in awe and next delighted with our daring.

We giggled softly. Hair? *There?*

We were as yet too unknowing to be aroused. An hour later we encountered disaster in the vague outline of a man waiting for us at the shoreline. He proved to be our scoutmaster.

Next morning, before a true drumhead court-martial, I was stripped of all merit badges and ranks, and formally dismissed from the Boy Scouts of America. Although my companions were simply scolded and confined to their tent even my Scout belt was re-requisitioned.

As I packed my duffle I heard one of the camp counselors say, "Can't say I regret being rid of that trouble-maker." His words echoed in my frantic thoughts as I mournfully went about being returned to my family hearth.

Or so the leaders thought. Since it was only three days before camp closing I reasoned that any good Scout should be able to hide out in the woods until the official date arrived, then proceed home and appear as sched-uled. Thus, I departed the train at the first station, bought a supply of candy bars, cake, bread, and grape juice, and found a nearby promontory from which I could survey the difficult world. There I made camp and survived for two days until, overcome by loneliness, I made my way home. It was nearly a week before my story about the camp closing a day early was found to be not entirely accurate.

Chapter 4

There is a terrible time in the lives of all men and women, a simultaneous blossoming of the ego and the physique, which has not changed since the beginning of history. These are the colt and filly years endured to the utmost limits of their patience by both progeny and parent. During these perilous years, the young of the ancients sometimes murdered their creators because they were so wrong and stupid in all things, or simply as a seizure of power. Now hardware is rarely employed to correct the obtuse thinking of elders, but the tongue bloodied in defiance can be the cruelest blade.

This awkward era begins with the first rash of pimples and the intimate discovery of menstruation and mastur-bation. It rarely subsides before a score of years has been attained. It is a time of perpetual movement and fickle emotions; it is impossible to remain physically calm or mentally stabilized for more than a few minutes. We are sure of everything and yet woefully unsure. It is a time of whispered secrets shared with best friends, but never with elders.

Who are you today? At once a famous actress, then again godmother to all the abused in the world. Today a nun, perhaps, or a generous princess distributing alms to the poor. Tomorrow a poetess inscribing tender verses of love, and the next day the applause is deafening acclaim of your performance at the ballet.

The legs are overlong and spindly, the feet not always responding to intended agility, the breasts developing with such alarming speed are curious and embarrassing, unasked-for appendages. For girls the specter "I shall be just like my mother" becomes tantamount to a fate worse than death.

The burgeoning male may be even more positively uncertain, and the fires in his private purgatory are usually slower to cool. Where there was formerly a family system of desire and fulfillment, an estrangement begins; the young male is almost irresistibly driven to reject all that is offered except sustenance and shelter. While the more spirited becomes nearly uncontrollable, the alternate victim of dark moods and explosive exhilaration, the more passive youth is at best tolerant of his parents' overall imbecility. Mixed into these general behavior patterns are the brash challengers who, though their balls may not yet have dropped, choose to bait and argue with the old man, drawing him into a jungle of political and social discussion from which he cannot retreat in dignity. These are the most dangerous and provoking of male juveniles.

I was a little of all of these and as a consequence my father had extraordinarily clean hands. "I wash my hands of you!" was a phrase he uttered regularly. He accompanied this mental cleansing with a corresponding rolling gesture of his hands as if rinsing them in a soapy solution and his one good eye would fix on me with what I supposed *he* supposed was righteous anger. When the hand-washing was finished, I tried not to smirk too obviously in retreat.

When I had acquired fourteen years I also acquired a secondhand motion picture projector. It was only a toy, a tin box with a lamp inside, a cheap lens, and brackets for holding a fifty-foot roll of highly inflammable 35 mm. celluloid film. Hand cranking provided power to run the film past the lens, and while the resulting images projected on a bedsheet were far from brilliantly defined, they had a powerful effect on me. Short clips from certain films were available at a reasonable price, and a minute or two of Charlie Chaplin, Snub Pollard, Hoot Gibson, or Mary Pickford, repeated over and over again in a darkened cellar, were so exciting I at once forgot most of the available mischiefs. Earlier I had found that a magic lantern projecting post cards provided considerable enchantment, but the movement, the energizing of personalities, held me utterly enthralled.

In unconscious deference to the businessman in my father, I founded the Reel Film Company, naming myself as president and my friend Bud Geer as vice president. Our intention was to exhibit films in the company's theater christened the Reel Rialto. The entrance and ticket booth were migrant—either my basement or the vice president's family garage. Seats for Saturday matinees were always sold out in advance, but standees were always accommodated. If we were short of film, any sort of local talent was employed to fill out the hour of entertainment, and to the astonishment of our parents we prospered. Even more unpredictable was the duration of our interest and growing expertise. Instead of becoming bored after a few shows and going on to other endeavors, we continued to improve the quality of the performances and, because short films were difficult to obtain, resolved to produce our own. The decision was made with proper corporate solemnity and the prospectus presented to my father as the most likely candidate for financing.

There were times when my father was not washing his hands, but instead would be gritting his teeth in canine fashion and seem to be worrying a bone while he proclaimed, "You are as stubborn as a bulldog! You never let go." This act was usually inspired by my requests for money.

Apparently I had timed the business interview well, for there was no revolving of hands and my father's teeth were bared in an obviously beneficient smile. I think he was so delighted that his son would consult him about anything whatsoever, he was almost pathetically eager to help. I did not reveal that the businessman's jargon which graced our prospectus was deliberately chosen to stimulate his interest.

"You are premature," he announced with impressive dignity. By now he was a civic leader of such considerable note that I was obliged to admit he might not always be wrong about everything. "You are proposing to expand without sufficient capitalization and the result is invariably disaster. I do not intend to participate, because I work hard for my money."

This statement was not only a disappointment but obviously a subterfuge. Work hard? All he had to do was go down to a nice office every day, tell a lot of people what to do, then maybe look out the window for a while and have lunch at the Athletic Club. There was nothing in the way of work involved.

"However," he went on quickly, lest he lose my entire attention, "I know a man who runs a studio. Maybe . . ."

St. Paul, Minnesota was an unlikely place for a motion picture studio, but Ray-Bell, the largest commercial outfit in the United States, was housed in a stucco building on University Avenue. The use of films as a sales tool for industry or as an educational tool was still in its infancy, but railroads, insurance companies, and agricultural implement companies kept the studio reasonably busy.

I was hired by Reid Ray, a young sallow-faced man who had only recently bought into the firm and become the partner of Charles Bell. The two men could hardly have been more opposite in both appearance and personality. Ray was gregarious, very bright, and articulate. His partner, Bell, was a taciturn man with the leathery look of a cowboy. He was a thorough technician and the firm's prime cameraman.

Ray hired me with no attempt to conceal his lack of enthusiasm. He simply wanted a full-time boy to "turn the drums" and I could only work after school.

"Turning the drums" proved to be starting as far down the labor ladder as it was possible to go. And I began, appropriately, in the basement, where there were located several large darkrooms smelling of chemicals, and I came to love their acrid smell.

All of the negative developing was presided over by Charles Bell who moved about in the darkness with the ceremony of a high priest engaged in esoteric rites. The positive prints were developed in a separate and somewhat lighter room using a similar array of wooden racks and tanks. Here also, the film was tinted by dipping into

36

solutions compatible with the mood of the scenes, blue for moonlight, yellow for desert.

Bell did not trouble himself with positive development or the tinting and toning. He left that work to Davey, a husky and very tough young man who became my immediate boss and first genuine fellow worker. One look convinced him of my uselessness to society in general and since he was one of the most profane men I have ever known, he announced that he would goddamn well sure make a man of me. Little by little I was learning there was another world which did not speak the same language I heard at home or read in the *National Geographic* magazine.

Once the film was developed and fixed, it was taken to a third room to be dipped in tanks full of constantly circulating water which removed all chemicals. Then, thoroughly cleansed, it was brought into the lighted drying room where, under a gentle shower of water drippings and a cascade of invective and epithets, I did my best to please Davey.

Removed from the washing room, the rack of film would be secured to a wooden brace and fixed in the middle in such a way that it revolved freely. One end of the film was then led to an enormous drum of wooden slats; reaching for the spokes one after another I would turn the drum precisely at the speed prescribed by Davey. The film was thus unwound from the racks and wound on the open drum for drying, and Davey stood between rack and drum with a chamois called a squeegee which removed most of the excess water. The revolution speed I provided made things easy or difficult for Davey. That speed he seemed to judge by the wind, the stars, his sexual success of the preceding night, or the severity of his hangover. I could not always please him.

Turning the great drums was an excellent muscle builder, but the task was not exactly what I had in mind when I joined the glamorous movie business. Though I considered my labors in the basement as sort of a cinematic replay of *Oliver Twist*, I actually enjoyed the work and soon became conscious that Davey was doing his oath-laced best to teach me the fundamentals of film and, along the way, his lascivious views on life. Thanks to his innate sense of decency he did not laugh

37

when I slowed ever so slightly in my drum turning one day and told him I had written Cecil B. De Mille advising I would be directing films to match his own.

"You keep at it, kid," he replied without a single oath. "Maybe you'll make it and give me a job one of these days."

After weeks of drum-turning I was taken from the dank caves below and installed upstairs at a splicer. The machine was a hot-block type made by the Bell and Howell Company and capable of such injury to the operator that Reid Ray supervised while Davey instructed me in its idiosyncrasies. He was such a perfectionist, the mere joining of two ends of film together became almost a religious ritual to be accomplished in a certain way and only that certain way.

Seated at the machine I was flanked by two metal tables holding the reels. By moving two pedals with my feet two heavy plates were actuated up and down to meet or disengage from an electrically heated base plate. The film end from the right reel was placed on the right block and the perforations set into extending pins. The jaw was then locked by a hand lever and the whole section elevated out of the way by pushing the right foot lever. When eventually I became adept I could complete this initial phase in a few seconds. The virtuoso in Davey took over as he demonstrated the "right and only way." "Don't hurt the oathy film," he instructed as if it held the breath of life itself.

He held up one finger to be sure of my full attention, then delicately, as if he were spreading gold leaf instead of film cement, he made a single brush stroke across the width of the splice. "No more than *one* oathy stroke, for Christ's sake, or the oathy cement will smear and make an oathy blotch between every scene on the screen."

I was impressed with this meticulous procedure; its preciseness appealed to some unexplainable urging deep within me and I could hardly wait my turn.

"Now, if you like all your ten fingers and especially your middle oathy digit be extremely careful when you bring the right plate down," he cautioned. He moved his right foot back and I heard a satisfying *chunk* as the two film ends were slapped together. It was a heavy union between metal arms and I could see how a finger left

38

overlong could easily land on the cutting room floor.

The hot-block speeded the adhesion time of the film cement, thus a practical operator was expected to cut, scrape, cement, and have the reels whirling again in slightly more than a minute.

After an afternoon of practicing on scraps of old film I was given my first genuine production job and with it a further education in the ways and woes of mankind.

The studio had contracted with the U.S. Army for the rehabilitation of certain training films, which meant that every splice must be inspected and remade if even slightly suspect. Thus a more than ordinary viewing of the film was necessary and as I began to turn the first reel my efficiency deteriorated rapidly. For I could not resist stopping again and again to examine the closeups and longer views etched so vividly on the little frames of celluloid. I was stunned and unbelieving at what my eyes told me were the wages of sin. Halfway through the first reel I resolved to pay more attention to the Presbyterian Church on the coming Sunday and never, never to succumb to those certain urges which were beginning to stimulate me with increasing frequency. Scene after scene presented shock after shock, and as my eyes grew ever wide, Davey winked evilly and said, "It's enough to turn a man into an oathy priest, ain't it, kid?"

I nodded in wondrous agreement, for the films—of which there were fifty reels of a thousand feet each—had been made by the medical corps as a part of troop indoctrination. They portrayed case histories of soldiers who had strayed from the paths of righteousness and as a penalty contracted venereal disease. Each and every variety of the pox had been photographed from all angles, with the ravages of syphilis, gonorrhea, chancroid, granuloma inguinale, and something entitled Bubo portrayed by pitiful victims, all in advanced stages of dementia or decay. Every pustule, body rash, and lesion was sharply detailed. Bent men hobbled, many on crutches, forming a loathsome parade of cankered penises, swollen testicles, rotting lips, and half-decomposed noses.

After the first few reels I tried to look at only the splices, but my effort was only partly successful; each new scene drew my attention. This nightmare continued for more than a week and depressed me so completely I could not bring myself to reveal even to my school friends the fearful sights I was witnessing. They became my own dreadful secret and for a while, totally emasculated, I did consider the life of the cloth as a wise man's only salvation. I vowed I would never expose my own body to that act which I now understood brought with it a whole catalogue of horrible malignancies.

Splicing the Army film had such an extraordinary effect on my resolve that I maintained a holier-than-thou deportment until my fifteenth birthday. Soon afterward, in an unplanned liaison, I succumbed to the incomparable pleasures of the flesh and having somewhat to my surprise suffered no apparent ill effects, I joined my schoolmates in their everlasting hot pursuit of more.

Bart Foss, a tall, shy, and kindly man, worked in the same room with the splicer. Making titles creative and eye-catching was only a part of Foss's job; he was a cartoonist-animator who interpreted through line drawings whatever message could best be told through his laborious process. Because I had always been fascinated with any sort of graphic technique, I was drawn to Foss's board and later volunteered to assist him at the animation table.

There were many methods, tricks, cartoon connivances, and shortcuts, which Foss was at pains to teach me. He had watched my continuing education under the aegis of Davey with silent disapproval. A gentle man, he thought Davey's rough ways with me might discourage or otherwise misguide me. He tried to remain aloof, but the constant presence of a youngster with a spongelike interest in his craft was irresistible. Once among those who were convinced my enthusiasm for films would not last a month, he now seemed determined I should learn all I could absorb.

The most exciting area at Ray-Bell was the studio itself, a large barn-like appendage on the back of the original building. Here the sets were built just as they were in Hollywood and the equipment was much the same.

The single camera (only very rarely were two employed simultaneously) was always operated by Charlie Bell or a man named Frank who rarely spoke to anyone at all, much less to the kid who had apparently wandered in off the streets from God knows where.

Reid Ray himself directed the filming and I was rather disappointed at his failure to wear breeches, puttees, and eyeshade in the manner of the great De Mille. When my own turn came I certainly would conform.

My school grades suffered in direct relation to the time I spent at the studio, a development which anguished my mother and father. They blamed themselves for providing such unruly distraction. Yet by now I was obsessed with all facets of the film business and when summer came I begged for full-time work at the studio.

The making of prints from the negative film was accomplished in a small, dark, and stuffy box of a room off the main stage. Within it was the only motor-powered machine in the studio. It was as high as the average man and held two rolls of film, the negative and raw positive, which were juxtaposed momentarily while passing a light gate. The operator adjusted the amount of light to Charlie Bell's specifications by actuating a short lever centered in a numbered dial, a task of such little demand a full day in the printing room was said to drive a man mad. Davey saw to it that I relieved him frequently at this chore, and thus without formal planning I completed the full circle from laboratory to final exhibition printing. Later I benefited from my printing room presence in an unforeseen way.

My total preoccupation with the film business had a subtle yet persistent effect upon my family life and social relations. I left home early in the morning, covering the four miles to the studio by bicycle, or in bad weather by streetcar. I returned the tired working man at day's end, much too weary for ordinary juvenile activities. My friends, with the joys of summer at hand, drifted away. I was much alone except for my dreams, which were peopled with characters from the splendid films I intended to make.

Like most industrial establishments in the United States the studio worked five and a half days a week. At noon on Saturday the adult employees departed, with Davey usually the first out the door. Partly because of my voluntary exile from my own age group I chose to linger about the studio on Saturday afternoons doing odd

41

jobs for Reid Ray or Charlie Bell, who, as proprietors, fell to the paperwork which had accumulated during the week. They remained in the front office while I roamed the darkened studio and laboratory—for the space of an afternoon, all mine. Lost in reverent silence I studied everything at hand, from the manner in which the electrical junction boxes were rigged to the intricacies of the portable Acme projectors, which Davey had taught me to operate.

I investigated every cranny of the old building and one afternoon while prowling through a windowless closet came across a large wooden box. It was nearly buried beneath rolls of old electric cable, tin film cans, broken lamps, burned fuses, and miscellaneous junk. It was encrusted with dust, and when I wiped it away, I knew immediately that I had made an important find.

The heavy box was fashioned of mahogany and a fine draftsman had obviously worked on it lovingly. Best of all I discovered an opening in one end encircling a lens. Opening the side I beheld the inner workings of a motion picture camera.

Picking up my prize I ran as fast as its weight would permit to the front office.

Ray, his paperwork disturbed, frowned at my intrusion. "What have you got there?"

"I think . . . it must be . . ." I was nearly inarticulate with excitement and to my distress my voice cracked ludicrously. ". . . it was under a big pile of junk . . ."

"God," Bell said in wonder, "where did you find that?"

I set the box tenderly on Ray's desk and was disappointed at his lack of recognition or even interest. But Charlie Bell was smiling the smile of a man suddenly presented with an agreeable page from his past. He scratched at his brush of gray hair and said, "I haven't seen that relic for fifteen years or so. It was our first camera here . . . a German make. Called an Erneman. Used by the German signal corps during the war."

During the *war!* Visions of spike-helmeted cameramen braving enemy fire in Flanders fields flashed across my mind. I was now dizzy with the enormous value of my find. I caressed its varnished surface anxiously, as if it were a living thing, a creature needing only my loving attention to bring it back to health.

"Would it . . . could it be made to work?" I was almost afraid to listen to Bell's answer. What if he said this beautiful thing was only a piece of junk!

"Sure it will work. It survived a war and a lot of knocks around here—"

I cheered silently, but strove to contain myself, for already a scheme of wild ambition sparkled in my thoughts. I turned the crank gingerly listening to the smooth clicking of the Erneman's mechanism.

"If I had some film . . . could I use it?"

The partners glanced at each other and smiled. Then Ray said solemnly, "It's yours. Do what you want with it."

From that moment on I would happily have given my life for either man. And in a sense during that same moment I shook off the remnants of childhood; I was a young Roman with his first sword, an Indian youth who had killed his first buffalo. Adults were my comrades now and I longed for their approval.

The Reel Film Company now had a prime asset and its president determined to exploit it. At last we could begin producing our own films, a project of heady promise if certain vital components could be assembled within our limited budget.

The first was film, which was prohibitively expensive. Yet there was one solution, conceived during my times at Davey's side in the stuffy printing room, and I prayed he would have a bawdy Saturday night and a peaceful Sunday to recover, enough of everything he loved to soothe his unpredictable moods.

Both negative and positive raw film passed through the printing room. When at day's end Davey unloaded the 400-foot camera magazines there were sometimes a few feet left unexposed because the next scene would be too long and would require a new magazine to be placed in the camera. These were called short ends. They were clipped off the roll to be developed and thrown in a barrel. Later when enough had accumulated they were burned for their residue of silver nitrate. Likewise, the standard 400-foot or 1,000-foot rolls of positive raw film were often more than a printing job required and the short ends of ten or twenty feet would join the negative surplus in the burn barrel. If Davey would permit, I planned to rescue these short ends, splice them together in total darkness, and seal the rolls in my own cans until I had enough to make and exhibit the greatest motion picture of all time. Without the slightest difficulty I could see the billboards proclaiming its premiere—and in bold letters, the name of the director.

On Monday, after Davey had given me a lucid description of a certain Sally's privates and the superb dexterity of her tongue, I told him of my discovering the Erneman and broached the matter of the short ends.

"Why didn't you tell me you wanted an oathy camera? I knew that oathy old piece of oath has been back there ever since I first come to work here." Despite my spending all of Sunday oiling and polishing my beloved, I ignored his slander. Davey was obviously going to cooperate and I asked for nothing more.

After consultation with the other directors of the Reel Film Company and hearing the treasurer's report, I discovered that our total capital resources amounted to slightly under one hundred dollars. This gloomy financial statement put such limitations on my directorial plans for a feature-length motion picture that we decided to limit the production to one reel. To minimize extra cost I volunteered to prepare a scenario with the resounding title *Sweet Sixteen*. Since I was fourteen going on fifteen, this increase in seniority gave me a sense of superiority. Most people, we were sure, would believe we were actually sixteen, a magic year when American boy becomes youth with car or at least qualifies if he has a friend with car.

Sweet Sixteen was an original story with certain time-honored elements. A country boy was in love with a country girl. She went away to a fancy school and when she returned considered her former swain no more than a country bumpkin. By managing to survive through various embarrassments he won back his beloved in the last minute of film.

Because the Erneman held a 100-foot roll of film which could not be removed unless the entire camera was taken to a dark room, I wrote all the scenes as exteriors of very brief duration. I could only suppose the spike-helmeted war cameramen must have done their reloading at night.

I instructed Bud Geer, vice president of the Reel Film Company, in the operation of our precious camera, then chose Robert Devining as the star because he was by far the prettiest of us all with a face quite unblemished by pimples. The girl was an easy choice. In the best directorial fashion I recited a chain of promises and selected Rhoda Pierce, a dark-haired, ruby-lipped young lady with whom I was enjoying a still unconsummated affair. Since she played the cornet in our school band I thought her histrionic talents would certainly be revealed.

The country bumpkin's rival was also a natural piece of casting. Glenn Fuller had curly hair which he combed straight back in a pompadour, a certain sign of a talent for playing the sophisticate.

My mother in a moment of inattention, had agreed to the loan of her Ford coupe for certain scenes in the story. I did not trouble her with the fact that the windshield would have to be removed for most of the shooting.

A lawn party on a considerable estate was the setting for the "big" scene. My father spoke to one of the wealthiest residents of St. Paul, who agreed that his house and lawns were ours at no cost.

All of this was assembled and ready for shooting when the vice president quit in a huff. "Cassius and Brutus combined!" I thought, remembering my recent exposure to Shakespeare at the university high school. My friend's sudden defection was shocking. It became even worse when I discovered he now intended to move with all speed in the production of his own movie, and—still worse—was reported to be well-financed.

A race began which the newspapers were quick to discover and exploit. Any Hollywood flack would have been ecstatic over the reams of publicity throughout the filming of *Sweet Sixteen*. Harassed with production problems I was hardly aware the newspapers had created a homespun celebrity. My father, observing what he thought was a glimmer of new promise in his rapscallion son, carried the clippings everywhere, constantly obliging his friends to read of each new event in the race.

Sweet Sixteen took seven weekends to film, another month to cut and to refilm the most awkward scenes and create the titles. The total cost in dollars was two hundred, and in my grades at school, inestimable. My teachers, like most humans, were insidiously influenced by the newspapers and particularly by frequent repetition of a name they recognized. Yet the ordinary homage they might pay to notoriety was difficult to focus on a juvenile who sat vacant-eyed before them every day, and even more difficult to reconcile with his abysmal academic performance. Worse, because his name and photo were so frequently in the local papers, other students began to emulate his dubious behavior, a paradoxical situation since the culprit himself was doing his physical utmost to swagger along with his own heroes, the football players.

There remained the demanding business of exhibiting *Sweet Sixteen*, a problem I had almost totally ignored. I was advised to call upon one Eddie Rueben, who headed the sole theater chain in the area, Finkelstein and Rueben.

My prepared sales pitch was thrown into total disarray by Rueben's genial charm. He confessed to have heard of *Sweet Sixteen* and agreed to run the film with a view to its possible exhibition in his chain.

Rueben and I were alone in the projection room. When *The End* title appeared and the lights went up I held my breath, for the silence was excruciating. Rueben was a big and handsome young man and it seemed that a touch of his almost visible kindness had left him when he turned to me and said, "Well—well."

Oh God, I thought, let this great man smile again.

"I . . . I've been thinking about taking it to the Oxford Theater," I said, breathing the odor of despair. The Oxford was an independent theater, one of the few in the surrounding states. It could not be classed even remotely as competition for the Finkelstein and Rueben circuit, but at least mention of the name broke the stillness as Rueben rose from his chair. Yet I knew when he smiled so benignly that I had met with my first real-life defeat. "Yes. The Oxford might be a good place for it," he said. "I'm awfully sorry."

Fighting an almost irresistible urge to weep I vowed there would come a day when I would return in triumph.

The manager of the Oxford Theater lacked Rueben's charm, but for all I cared he could have been

Quasimodo. After only a few moments' suspenseful hemming and hawing he agreed to run *Sweet Sixteen* for two nights and pay the Reel Film Company fifty dollars. There was one condition. The principal characters must appear on stage and be introduced to the audience between the showing and the main feature.

There was a maxim which stated that only Jews or Irishmen could run theaters successfully. The manager of the Oxford was an Irishman who had not survived as an independent without long reliance on his wits. While he was visibly cautious in his enthusiasm for *Sweet Sixteen,* remarking how some of the key scenes appeared to have been photographed in a Minnesota blizzard although the actors wore summer clothes, he was keenly aware of the newspaper space already achieved at no cost to himself. More in touch with his patrons than the mighty Rueben, he reasoned that all the families unto the most distant relatives would make their way to his theater if their very blood would be celebrated on stage. To this end he took extra advertising space announcing: *See the original cast* IN PERSON.

The results were spectacular and so exceeded the Irishman's expectations that he booked the film and cast for the following weekend as well. His eyes sparkled and his puffy cheeks turned crimson as he watched the line at the box office form so early in the evening. By seven o'clock there was standing room only in the Irishman's theater. The newspapers pounced on our success with reams of free publicity. The Reel Film Company received another fifty dollars, which made up half our production cost. Most triumphant of all was a note of congratulation from Eddie Rueben who had apparently done some rethinking. If agreeable with me the Finkelstein and Rueben circuit would be pleased to exhibit *Sweet Sixteen* in eight of their major theaters.

If agreeable with *me?*

In spite of our obvious success, the performances at the Oxford had been trying. The audience reactions proved so unexpected I alternately looked for places to hide or to strut. The paying customers laughed uproariously at what I had considered a drama, remained silent when I had thought they would cheer, coughed, yawned, and stirred restlessly where I had been certain the suspense would have them hanging on their seats. This unpredictability of audience reaction was a revelation which I accepted in bewildered sorrow. Uncertain whether to be contrite or proud I borrowed a half-full bottle of my father's best bootleg whiskey to help me resolve the problems of success at fifteen going on sixteen.

The four hundred dollars received from Finkelstein and Rueben easily turned the movie into such a profitable venture that the Reel Film Company paid off all production costs and had capital remaining for future endeavors. Yet further artistic efforts were postponed because of overexpansion in work orders.

I was almost, but not quite, too busy to keep pace with my contemporaries. I wore bell-bottom pants of such fullness they covered my shoes. I smoked cigarettes, neither with enthusiasm nor from habit, but because others smoked. My father, like all Americans, then totally ignorant of cancer causes, offered me Camels from his own pack because, he said, "I'd rather have you smoking in the open here than behind someone's barn." Accepting a free cigarette I saw no reason to remind my obviously senile parent that there were no barns anywhere near our present fashionable locale, nor if there had been would I consider going near such dull places to conduct any sort of business other than copulation.

I read far more books than most of my teenage friends, but in formal schoolwork lagged far behind them. A part of my inattention was due to the fullness of my purse, much fatter than those of my classmates, and a lack of sleep which went together with such financial independence. The skills I had learned from Davey at Ray-Bell were beginning to pay off and I was much in demand as a projectionist for all manner of public gatherings. Churches and societies wanted scenics, travel, or instructional films as an extra added attraction to their regular meetings. To these occasions I lugged one of the heavy Acme projectors, which I rented from the studio at ten dollars, providing my services along with the machine and a screen for an additional twenty dollars. Somewhat to the surprise of my clients the shows always went off without a hitch and word of my expertise spread. Between showings, the Irish manager at the Oxford was always pleased to have me replace him at the ticket-taking job while he went about more pressing details. He paid me two dollars a night and I saw whatever movie was playing at no cost.

The ex-vice president of the Reel Film Company had attempted to produce a film he entitled *The Perfect Sheik.* I tried not to gloat when he discovered the novelty of juvenile films had been overexploited and he failed to repeat our success.

I continued to work when asked at Ray-Bell. There Charles Herbert, a famous Fox News cameraman, had temporarily established himself, and to his surprise soon found he had a shadow whether he pleased or not. Here, I thought, was a true hero of the lens and crank. If only I could have grown a mustache like his, then I would be well along the way to the cinematic deeds Herbert had performed all over the world.

"Just please don't follow me to the bathroom, kid," he finally sighed. "You won't learn anything there."

Herbert, of course, had the finest of camera equipment and his skills were more highly polished than those of my local mentors. In spite of my omnipresence he never lost patience with my adoration of him and my almost worshipful regard for his gear. He larded my brain with new knowledge and inspired me to new professional ways. Such was his encouragement, I dared to write Kinograms, a newsreel rival to Fox and Paramount, asking for appointment as their local representative. With Herbert's permission I used his name in recommendation, advised that I was equipped with a Wilart camera, and was ready and able to cover any local story they desired. Free-lance newsreel cameramen were paid one dollar a foot of film used, princely compensation I thought, and certainly enough to justify buying a Wilart. Innocent of my age, Kinograms appointed me their local representative, and delirious with confidence I promptly augmented my income with even further endeavors.

The Northern Pacific Railway had established a library of travelogue films which needed constant rewinding, resplicing, and shipping. Since the films were supplied to various civic organizations at no charge, there was considerable traffic, albeit not quite enough for one man at full time. I managed to satisfy the great railway by working two afternoons a week and once enjoyed the unique experience of preparing a scenic for my own school, which I now attended only often enough to remain a part of the official student enrollment.

I had pestered Eddie Rueben until he passed the word down I should be allowed to apprentice in two of the theater chain's departments. I went first to "booking" where I came under the aegis of a certain Ralph, a lanky, cigar-smoking, frenetic man, recognized as "the best booker in the trade." His work was more than a simple matter of assigning whatever film was chronologically available to the various theaters. He was sensitive to all events of possible influence, whether transpiring in Minnesota, North Dakota, or Wisconsin, obliging himself between hours of rapid-fire telephone conversations to read assiduously the latest editions of the newspapers and to listen carefully for items pertinent to the locale he intended sending a film. It was no good booking an Eskimo saga to a community just digging out from a blizzard; likewise a local heat wave would not encourage people to attend *Moana*.

There were endless variations to Ralph's theme. He played the theater managers as a master tactician, cajoling and persuading, heckling and debating until they accepted the show he thought best at the moment for their trade.

I hung on his every word, thereby, in time, persuading him to view me at least as part of the office furniture. Officially my pay was nil, but I considered the dividends well worth my time. I began to sense the debilitating effects of office politics, for Ralph's blunt ways did not endear him to his underlings or to other departments. I saw what regular attendance in an office could do to the energies of the most energetic humans and resolved to avoid such confinement or die. I learned new profanity from Ralph, for his imagination and vocabulary were both more sinuous than Davey's; he vilified with a lighter sledgehammer, and I learned there was more to the strange world of show business than a story and an actor.

My precious dessert was the occasional privilege of sitting beside Ralph in the projection room while he judged a new film.

"It is a seven-thousand-foot turd," he would declare after a few reels of a mediocre film had unwound. He would depart then, leaving me in lonely glory to bring him a capsule résumé of the remaining footage.

I did well enough at this task to be sent down to the advertising department. There I wrote one- and two-paragraph synopses of films to be exhibited in Finkelstein and Rueben Theaters. These literary efforts were sent to the local newspapers wherein they served as demi-reviews. I troubled no one with the grim fact that a school report card indicated my performance in English 3 was straight failure.

Now, impressed with the sight of my own words in print, it was I who kept and flaunted a sheaf of clippings.

Chapter 5

My father once tried to corner the New York market on cocoa and nearly succeeded without ever going within two thousand miles of a cocoa pod. That he nearly lost his all in the attempt was unknown to me at the time, but in a dubious way I shared his enterprise. In a desperate attempt to conceal the damage my various jobs were inflicting on my schoolwork, I contrived to remove a supply of blank report cards from a teacher's desk. Each month then I made out my own grades, being careful to keep the scores modestly high and without overdoing my brilliance in any subject. I presented the result for the signature of my parents, who were reasonably pleased with my progress.

The deception was Faustian in its inevitable consequences. I could not stop in midterm, nor could I retrogress to self-created failing grades and thus predict my certain doom. Each month I became increasingly aware that a debacle was imminent and yet I saw no hope of escape. My intestines roiled as by chance I one day saw my mother in solemn conversation with the principal. The ax fell swiftly.

It was decided a military school might have some beneficial effect upon my disgraceful behavior, and since I was hardly in a position to object to anything less than hanging, I was enrolled in an Irish-Catholic institution which stood handily nearby.

51

Trouble began the very first day, this time not of my making. Strangely, I liked the military discipline and drills and found unusual comfort in the wearing of a uniform. But I was neither of Irish descent nor Catholic, both terrible failings, and as soon as they became known I was a minority of one.

All of the faculty were priests total in their dedication to the most severe discipline. If a cadet even considered being disrespectful or was guilty of the slightest infraction of any rule, let alone being late for mass, his punishment was an automatic slap across his chops; and if his expression suggested defiance rather than abject remorse he could very well expect a priestly fist to knock him flat. No dutiful Catholic parent ever questioned this knuckle justice, nor for that matter did the cadets. One priest, a florid-faced sadist with a peculiarly soothing voice, often had trouble keeping his mathematics class alert. He had developed a solution for the rousing of any cadet whose eyes appeared to droop. Suddenly, turning his back on the culprit lest he be warned, he would reach within his robe, pull out a heavy bunch of keys, and in one flowing movement of cloth and body whirl and hurl the keys at the cadet. His accuracy was uncanny. I never saw him hit the wrong cadet nor did anyone ever receive the keys in his face, which could have caused very serious damage. Always the priest's favorite projectile would thump against chest or shoulder, or sometimes if the target sat near a wall, he would deliberately execute a perfect ricochet shot. Thus rudely awakened, the cadet was expected to retrieve the keys and return them to their owner with proper humility.

The pugilistic atmosphere was naturally reflected in cadet behavior, which itself was structured with extreme rigidity. Arguments of any kind were nearly barren of dialogue. The first was the gavel and there was no sympathy for the wounded. The rules were loose Marquis of Queensberry with kicking, gouging, and hair-pulling never attempted. The ever-present witnessing pack would have fallen upon a scoundrel who departed from their style.

Fights between cadets were constant, often two or three a day. The only temporary escape was when a cadet actually stood at military formation or inside the classroom.

Sooner or later cause to prove himself would be found for every new cadet. Then according to his prowess, victory or defeat, and his ability to suffer the spouting of his own blood, he was accorded a certain status. Fight he must and frequently to maintain his social position, yet actual bullying was rare; upper classmen, no matter how annoyed, did not assault younger and lower classmen.

Unknown, I entered upon this belligerent society and it was not long before I was challenged by one of the very few non-Irishmen in the academy other than myself. At least he was a Catholic. His name was Johnson and he stood three hands taller than me even when puffed to full rooster posture.

The newspaper notoriety I had so casually accepted made it impossible for me to slip quietly into the ranks of the cadet corps. Yet I did not realize how powerfully the urge to humiliate me might assert itself and was caught wholly by surprise when the ugly scene began.

The priests tolerated no interruptions of any sort when their classes were in session. No wary cadet ever attempted to leave their lecturing, not even for the needs of nature. The result was a mass retreat to the latrines, particularly after the last class of the day.

I was standing at a urinal when I felt someone shove me from behind. Thinking it an accident because others were waiting, I momentarily ignored the interruption. I was shoved again, the second time so forcefully I slipped partway into the urinal and soiled myself. Turning in anger I saw the leering face of Johnson, whom I barely knew except that we shared the same drill class.

Our eyes met and I heard a voice behind him say, "What are you waiting for, Johnson?" The tone was urgent, but Johnson seemed uncertain. All around behind him I saw a circle of cadets forming. They were silent as if gagged by expectation. Suddenly I knew I would have to fight Johnson and I was terrified, for I had never in my sixteen years exchanged blows except in play.

Beyond Johnson I saw a line of smirking faces, mostly, I realized, upper classmen.

I heard the same voice say, "Go ahead, Johnson," and knew there would be no escape. The line of sour-smelling urinals was directly behind me, the gallery formed a

53

half-circle around the solitary Johnson, who still seemed hesitant.

I reached to button my pants, an uncalculated gesture which diverted Johnson's attention. Instinctively, I lunged at him, first flaying wildly. Johnson fell back trying to defend himself, but I had gone berserk. I had no idea what I was doing, I chose no special target except Johnson's lanky uniformed body and his already bloody face. I heard shouting all about me, but it echoed only from a great distance and had no effect upon my savage efforts.

Johnson, bewildered by the ferocity of his attacker, kept moving away from me, a fatal mistake as I was later to learn from true fighters. I had taken the initiative and kept it through at least a hundred rights and lefts into the carcass of my antagonist, a shape I could barely see through tears of fear and passion. If Johnson ever hit me I never felt the blow, nor was I sure what finally made him go down. He sank to the cement floor halfway between the urinals and the line of stools. He collapsed in a square of pale afternoon light shafting down from the high windows and I stood over him grunting and sobbing as my fury diminished.

There was no question about my conquest. Johnson's puffy eyes were open, but they were fixed, and his body remained still. I waited momentarily, wondering if I had killed him. At last my deep whimpering became only a gasping for air and I stepped back. I saw an expression of hurt surprise come over Johnson's face and heard all about me subdued mutterings of approval.

I buttoned my pants without haste. Then, trying to still my ungovernable trembling, I turned away from Johnson and walked out of the latrine. During the balance of my single year at the academy I was never again challenged by anyone.

After a fruitless year at the academy, I chose, of my own accord, another school far enough away to assure me a fresh start. To my parents' wonder my choice was another military academy reputed to be one of the most restrictive in the land. In promoting the transfer to a new school I played down the frequent display of horses in the academy's advertisements and brochure, nor did I confess my continuing disappointment in my failure to excel in any athletics. Somehow I thought I might do better on a horse.

I was rather shaken on the day of my first departure from the family abode. Neither my mother nor my father displayed any sign of regret.

Culver Military Academy is located in the heartland of the United States, its environs spread over one end of Indiana's Lake Maxinkuckee. It has been a functioning educational institution for more than eighty years and its graduates have served with traditional gallantry in four wars. The architectural scheme has been followed faithfully since the erection of the first "Main" Barracks in 1895 and its martial design, featuring mortared brick, casements, turrets, crenellations, and false ramparts, set the prim style of later additions. Cascades of ivy cling to the sides of the older buildings, but even this natural softness barely mitigates the underlying serenity of a fortress and its fundamental purpose.

"Send us the boy and we will send back a man," was the school's unyielding creed, and all new cadets (known as "plebes") soon realized the authorities intended to make good their claim. If in the process an occasional young ego was shattered, the large majority of graduates did fulfill the academy's vow and went on to extraordinarily productive lives.

I had no idea my latest institution was of such unyielding philosophy. One hundred five cadets had once been dismissed for demonstrating against the expulsion of only two of their comrades who had broken regulations. I had arrived at the academy on a bitter January afternoon, been escorted to the tailor shop where I was provided with a basic uniform, and was temporarily assigned to a room by myself, a development I took as thoughtful recognition of my liking for privacy. I had no notion that my status was already established among those who would soon be concerned with my activities.

As my enrollment occurred during the middle of the year I would henceforth be known as a "half-ass," a caste in cadet society equivalent to a leper. Among my yet-to-be comrades, roommates had been assigned, friendships cemented, and cliques formed in September, the normal entrance time. Now, with the corps of cadets just returned from Christmas, I watched from a discreet distance as they immediately slipped into long-established routines

55

and joyous reunions with their particular cronies. The first night I found the library and read to relieve my loneliness. Did you just grab the arm of a fellow cadet and say, "Hi! I'm new here and need a friend"? I wished my uniform was not so obviously new and wondered how I could remove the telltale sheen.

I retired to my cell-like room early, already homesick for the easy and familiar. It seemed I had hardly slept when the report of a cannon aroused me. Still drowsing, wondering if there had been a boiler explosion somewhere in the building, I padded across the cold bare floor to the window.

There was nothing to be seen outside my window except cascades of rain as it swept down past a streetlight and drummed into puddles scattered across a glistening sidewalk. It was only five-thirty.

Confused, I stared at the dismal scene while listening to the faint sound of someone blowing a bugle in the distance. Considering the weather and the time, I thought the fool was tootling away with irritating zest. Then, vaguely, as I returned to the hard cot and slipped beneath the blankets, I heard someone shouting in the hallway outside my door. He sounded like an auctioneer determined to be heard against all competition and yet only a few of his words were understandable.

". . . shirts! . . . boots! . . . rain gear! . . . Sirs! . . . Sick call, sirs! . . ."

It was a singsong chant, rhythmic, strident, anxious in tone. I wondered only momentarily about the constant repetition of "Sirs," concluded that nothing I had heard need concern me, and tried to go back to sleep. As I hung halfway suspended between honest slumber and wakefulness I heard the hammering of an alarm gong, more bugling, then a raucous chorus of confused shouting and the pounding of feet. I was relieved by the sudden silence which followed. Apparently those responsible for the racket had come to their senses and returned to their warm bunks.

I remained pleasantly detached until the door was thrown open and banged hard against the wall. The bright ceiling light exploded into my widening eyes. I was no longer alone.

By this time I had developed a strong instinct which

warned me when all was not well, but I was ill-prepared for the apparition now frowning down upon me. From my prone position he appeared enormous, wide-shouldered, mighty-chested, a giant demanding tribute from the world. He was standing feet spread wide apart, fists on his hips, his head thrust forward like an angry mastiff. Rivulets of water slipped off his raincoat to break the uncomfortable silence with a delicate plonking into puddles on the floor. I was uncertain of his age, perhaps three or four years older than I, but there was no doubt about his displeasure.

"What are you doing in bed?"

"Who are you?"

"I happen to be Stillman, the regimental Sergeant-Major, and I repeat my question. Or am I disturbing you?"

"Well . . . I—"

"Are you sick?"

I shook my head. Suddenly I knew my first day at the academy was off to a bad start and I was sorry for it.

"No, I'm not sick, I—"

"No, *sir,* I'm not sick, *sir!*" The cutting rasp in his voice was unmistakable. "You are a goddamned plebe and a half-ass at that. From this instant on you will address all upper classmen as *sir,* and you will employ that *sir* after every three words when communicating with people other than plebes. Understand?"

"Yes, but—"

"*Sir!*" He was becoming very red of face and his eyes were bulging. "*Sir,* goddamnit! *Sir!*"

"Yes*sir!*"

I had had enough experience with cadet officers in the Catholic academy to know I must not be overly emphatic in my response or it would certainly be taken as sarcasm, a fatal mistake in any situation wherein the lowly offend the mighty.

"Get your ass out of that bed," he said huskily. "Get in uniform and while you're at it tell me you didn't hear the reveille cannon, *or* the bugle, *or* the gong, *or* the Caller of the Day. . . ."

I noticed he was so overcome with the emotion of the moment that his voice was beginning to break and I knew this was not a good sign.

57

Slipping into my new uniform as quickly as I could manage I reasoned that total silence would only be a confession of guilt. I must offer some reasonable explanation of my behavior since he was obviously a man devoid of humor and hardly, I thought, one to appreciate sloth.

I began with a careful portioning of remorse in my voice. "You see, sir, I just arrived yesterday afternoon. They issued me this nice new uniform—"

"New uniform, *sir!*"

"Yessir, they forgot, sir, to issue me a raincoat—"

"Raincoat, *sir!*"

"Yessir, and when I got up this morning and saw it was raining outside I thought it would be pretty silly to get a new uniform soaked—?"

I stole a look into the Sergeant-Major's eyes and saw he was shocked into momentary silence. His mouth was agape, he was breathing with difficulty, and he was examining me as if I were iodine in his wounds.

"Listen to me, Mister whatever-your-name-is," he intoned as he wiped droplets of water from the broken knob of his football nose. (I made a small wager with myself that he must be at least captain of the team.) "Listen to me carefully. The entire regiment is now standing in a pouring rain waiting for you. According to regulations the regiment cannot be dismissed from reveille formation until every cadet is accounted for. This means there are seven hundred men who have to stand in rank outside that window when they should be doing other things like brushing their teeth, shaving, showering, getting ready for the next formation. They have twenty minutes to perform these functions between dismissal and breakfast formation, which keeps them on the run. Now you, all by yourself, have just robbed them of ten minutes and maybe more."

"I'm sorry."

"Sorry, *sir!* Now put on your cap and follow me, and may God have mercy on your soul."

I trailed him at a respectable distance as he marched out of the room. I followed him at a double march down the steel-treaded stairway and out into the soggy darkness where I saw, to my horror, long lines of cadets standing in ominous silence. The only sound I heard was the peckling of rain on the hard visor of my garrison cap.

My escort showed me into a rear rank vacant slot and growled, "For now, you form up here." Then he marched away and I was left standing between two total strangers neither of whom turned their heads to recognize my existence. I knew better than to say, "Good morning."

The waiting was interminable. I looked toward what I hoped was the east, but could not discover even a hint of dawn. And all about me glistening in the streetlights were raincoats enclosing other boys like myself, yet I knew there would not be one to whom I could turn for sympathy in my terrible trouble. As my very real fears mounted I heard a high-pitched cry in the distance, a howl I remembered, like the sound of a lonely coyote on the Nebraska plains. The words were intelligible to everyone but me.

"Reg—i—mon . . . dis—missed!"

Instantly, I was surrounded. Wet raincoat after wet raincoat pushed its way to confront me and tap my chest, while from behind the dripping waterfall of each visor cap a voice intoned, "Report to my room after breakfast . . . report to my room after breakfast . . . report to my . . ."

They all used exactly the same phraseology. Since I had not the faintest notion who they were or where their rooms might be I remained rooted in place until the last raincoat had departed. Only during my time as a child student on the University of Minnesota campus had I felt so alone.

The lingering darkness only prolonged my desperation. Visions of terrible mutilations overwhelmed me as I climbed the stone steps to my room. The barracks itself seemed a madhouse of shouting, running cadets, warning bells clanging, and a continuing series of announcements by a very young cadet who stood stiffly at the end of the corridor. His eyes bulged with his vocal efforts, his chin was retracted until it seemed to melt into his neck, his arms were tight against his waist and the palms of his hands flat against the black stripe on his breeches. I had wit remaining only to notice the high polish on his shoes and leather puttees, his total lack of rank insignia, and his years, which I thought even less than my own.

"Attention, sirs!" he yelled with all the falsetto power of his lungs. "Mess hall formation, sirs! Five-minute warning! Sirs! Uniform, fatigue, garrison cap with cover, and raincoats, sirs!"

"Attention, sirs! Sick call, oh seven-thirty hours, sirs, form in front of Main Barracks, sirs."

"Attention, sirs! All cadets interested in gymnastics report to Major Whitney, Rec building, fifteen hundred hours, sirs!"

As cadets flew past me bound on apparently urgent missions, my regret mounted with my confusion. I was ignored by older cadets with stripes on their arms and by those with towels draped around their necks bound at a quick march for the latrine.

I found my way between and among them, waited for a vacant washbowl and finally managed a quick splashing of water at my face. The alarm bell was clanging again before I had half finished brushing my teeth. I heard the now familiar drumming of feet on the stairs and resolved to depart this nightmare as soon as I could persuade my father to send the train fare.

Joining the river of descending cadets on the stairway I was accosted at the bottom by an obvious upper classman.

"Where is your rain gear, mister?" I had never been called mister in my life and was not at all sure I liked it.

"I . . . they didn't give me—"

"*Sir!* You will begin every sentence with *sir—*"

"Sir. I just came here yesterday afternoon—"

"Shut up, mister! Get those shoulders back! Get that chin in. I want to see some wrinkles in your chops!"

I obediently took what I considered a stiff brace.

"Get that chin in more. *More,* I say! What platoon are you in?"

"I don't know. No one has told me anything—"

"You don't know, *sir!* When an upper classman asks you a question you will give him a direct answer."

"Sir, I don't know and I don't give a damn," I said, wishing instantly I could cut out my tongue. For temper had now gotten me into terrible trouble. I could see it burning in my superior's eyes as he attempted to recover from having been exposed to such an incredible statement. He appeared to be even more shocked than my earlier visitor, the Sergeant-Major.

"Go!" he choked, nearly inarticulate with scorn. "Find a place in the ranks, or if you can't, just follow us to the mess hall."

"Yes, *sir!*" I answered with a simultaneous salute.

"Never salute when you're inside! *Ever!*"

Nothing I could do was right. As I marched in the dawn of my first day at the academy I lost all hope.

Chapter 6

My agonies had barely begun. The vain and self-centered little savage, the thief, liar, the haughty little prick who had been so intolerant and careless of pain he might inflict upon others, was about to be redeemed and I could feel it happening. Divested of my habitual rights, I was being forced into the limbo of the unrecognized, and I squirmed in self-pity.

On this grim morning I did not know that contrary to opinion outside the academy's forbidding gates, the very large majority of the cadets had, like myself, enrolled of their own choice. They had come from all over the United States and a considerable number from South and Central America, Mexico, and the Philippines. Only a few had been sent by desperate parents who hoped academy life would rehabilitate their sons before it was too late. But now, all I saw were glistening masses of potential enemies moving mechanically through stone bastions, of which the mess hall was presently the most imposing.

I tagged along as best I could in the wake of a formation in which I had found a place. At least I had learned how to march in step at St. Thomas and was able therefore to remain almost as inconspicuous as I wanted. The "Hut . . . two . . . three . . . four. . . Hut . . . Hut . . . Hut!" was familiar and even reassuring as the ranks of raincoats jounced in perfect rhythm before me. In comparison, I thought with a sudden sense of belonging, the marching at St. Thomas resembled the retreat from Moscow.

We marched up a wide flight of steps and through the doorway without breaking step. Our heels knocked sharply on the mosaic tile floor as we marched into the great hall and continued to a section of tables. The same martial display was occurring at two other doors in the halls, as platoon after platoon pounded into the vast room. The heavy lock-step echoing completely dominated every other sound except the staccato "Halt! . . . Right face! . . . Left . . . face" of the platoon officers.

After less than two minutes seven hundred cadets stood rigidly behind their assigned chairs. Each table held fourteen cadets with a student officer or non-commissioned officer at each end. And each table was served by one of a small army of white-coated black men who stood in line near the huge swinging doors separating the kitchen from the main hall.

Suddenly there was quiet. Somewhere a raincoat rustled, but that was all. All about me cadets remained at attention, but now they bowed their heads slightly as a distant voice in the area of faculty tables invoked an unintelligible prayer of grace. After a moment another, far more authoritative voice cried a single word, "Seats!"

Then followed a common peeling off of raincoats and a raucous scraping of chairs as their owners slipped quickly into their places.

Since I had no raincoat to trouble me I was the first to be seated. The whole mess hall now reverberated with the voices of cadets telling eagerly of their Christmas leave adventures in the outside world. Yet about me, seated near the center of the table, there was a cocoon of silence. Hungry, I reached for the pitcher of milk, filled my glass, and leaned on one elbow as I relaxed to drink.

"*Mister!* You there!"

I glanced at the Corporal who occupied the nearest end of the table. He was a blond cadet with very pink cheeks and overlarge ears. The "you" he was pointing at was obviously me.

"Sit up straight," he said in a not unkindly fashion. "Take a brace and your elbow off the table."

"Yes . . . sir," I replied while making a half-hearted attempt to comply. I found genuine warmth in his smile and my hopes rose momentarily.

"You're a half-ass, aren't you?" he asked.

"I suppose that's the term."

"Term, *sir*. Now listen," he said patiently. "Look at your tablemates. They are all plebes. Until exactly one year from now you will never touch the back of your chair. You will sit in a brace. You will not touch the table with any part of your arms or hands. . . ."

He glanced at the black man who eased a great dish of scrambled eggs before him. "You will never under any circumstances order or request any food or utensil from Roger, our tableman. If there is something you need, ask me or Sergeant Bray at the other end. Do you understand?"

"Yes, *sir*." I was beginning to catch up with the style, but became more than ever determined to escape as soon as possible. Grudgingly, I admitted that the Corporal seemed to have taken pains to be pleasant.

"You may proceed now," he said smiling. "Enjoy your breakfast."

He ladled himself a generous portion of eggs with sausage and passed the plate to the plebe on his right. I watched in fascination as the plebe served himself without moving his torso perceptibly or allowing the sleeve of his blouse to approach closer than an inch to the tablecloth.

I was even more impressed with the amount and quality of the food, the sparkling silver bowls, pitchers, and tureens all engraved with the name of the academy. I listened in equal amazement at the polite conversational exchanges between the pink-cheeked Corporal and the four plebes flanking him. It was as if they bore him no resentment whatever; their "sirs" were frequent but neither insolent of tone nor sullen, as I had chosen to pronounce them. They were, I thought, either resigned to their servitude or, worse, content with it, and I wondered how that could be. It was then inconceivable that I would ever master the variety of pronunciation for "sir," the vast ranging of a mere three-letter word from subtle insult to challenge, to pleading, to cunning, respect, fear, and hatred.

Throughout the breakfast I sat in lonely isolation although the cadets on each side of me were only inches away. Yet they did not totally ignore me. One passed me a plate of toast, another asked me, without a "sir," to pass the schooner of jelly.

Sensing I was at least not actively disliked I was emboldened to ask, "Sir? Are there many other half-asses in the corps?"

Pink-cheeks considered the question while he carefully rolled his linen napkin and inserted it in a silver ring.

"I think there is one other this year. There are usually one or two."

So I had not only chosen a harsh existence but had doubled the lash by entering at midyear. Where in this mass of seven hundred was the one soul who shared my wretched station? Of course the plebes at my table did not object to my presence. From their own inglorious status they at last had someone they could look down upon.

Before I was half finished eating, a strident voice cut through the hubbub: "Att . . . ten . . . *shun!*"

I was several beats behind my tablemates as they scraped back their chairs and assumed a ramrod stance. Out of the corner of my eye I could now see a splendid assembly that had formed between the cadets and the tables where the faculty sat relaxing over their coffee. Facing the corps was the Regimental Commander, a tall, very handsome cadet made more imposing by a magnificent cape lined with yellow silk. His staff stood slightly behind him as his adjutant held a sheet of paper at arm's length and read a series of orders. His high thin voice echoed and re-echoed across the hall and I understood not a word of his oration except that cadet Lieutenant something-or-other was Officer of the Day.

Dismissal was as abrupt as the simultaneous heel-toe about-face of the beautiful commander and his aides. I managed to follow my tablemates into ranks forming in the aisle while still sticky-fingered from the last of my toast. Exiting the mess hall and returning to barracks was an exact reversal of our coming. Yet the rain had ceased and the hint of coming sun lifted my sodden spirits.

My wits were churning at high speed against the phrase "Report to my room after breakfast." It repeated itself with the regularity of a metronome. Whom would I first honor with a visit I knew would not be pleasantly social? According to the printed schedule on the bulletin board there would be thirty minutes between dismissal from breakfast formation and the first academic classes. Obviously I could not accept all my invitations. I decided to decline them all.

As I passed an open doorway on the way to my room I

was hailed by a cadet I recognized as having stood near me in the predawn ranks. Daylight had hardly improved his appearance. A pock-marked, overfleshed face now studied me from beneath heavy eyebrows.

"You there, half-ass. Come in here."

I stepped cautiously to the framework of the door, wondering if I should flee for my life. There were four other upper classmen with my host. None bore a smile of welcome.

"Close the door," the beefy face said. I complied in silence. A cadet moved behind me and I watched apprehensively as he pulled the curtains across the small window.

"What do you say, half-ass?" my host inquired.

"I'm sorry."

"Sorry, *sir!* Whenever you enter a room, address a member of the faculty or an upper classman, you will begin thusly: Cadet whatever-your-name-is reports his presence, sir. You will then remain silent until asked to speak. Let's hear it."

"The silence?" Alas, my errant tongue! I watched the eyebrows wigwag and my host's thick lips compress into a barely visible line. He glanced at his comrades and their eyes compounded my fears.

"So you're a wise guy?" He went to his locker and took out a bayonet. "Turn around. Bend over and get your butt in the air."

I could try to escape, I thought desperately, but I could not possibly open the door before I would be tackled. There were too many of them. I turned obediently and bent in abject humiliation. I thought of the sensuous pleasures I had left behind in the ordinary public schools: the girls, the beer, dances, intrigues, and always the soft comforts of my family home. It seemed incredible now that I had deliberately abandoned all those things for a life amid uniformed bullies.

I heard the slither of the bayonet as it was withdrawn from its scabbard and knew from tales at my former military academy, where thank God I had been a day student instead of a boarder, that I might soon expect the searing pain of its flat side against my backside. Waiting, I closed my eyes and vowed not to give my host the satisfaction of a whimper.

"Ready?" he asked.

"Go ahead." I tried to sound defiant, but my voice quavered with anxiety.

"Go ahead, *sir!*" There was a moment of silence, then he added, "This will teach you to make formations on time and maybe even keep a civil tongue in your head."

I heard a movement of feet behind me, then a whoosh of air. I was instantly struck hard on the buttocks, but I knew at once it was not by the blade of a bayonet. Another whack followed, I heard laughter followed by a command to turn around and stand at attention. With only a mild smarting of rump I was more than willing to comply.

My host was holding a broom and smiling tolerantly. Nor could I detect anything but amusement in the faces of his friends.

"You have a lot to learn, half-ass. I suggest you shape up fast. Do you hurt?"

"No . . . no, *sir.*"

"That's better. Now you can request permission to leave."

"May I have permission to leave, sir?"

"Granted. If I were you I wouldn't mention being here . . . to anyone."

"I don't intend to . . . sir."

To my astonishment he advanced and laid his hand gently on my shoulder.

"Let me know if I can help you . . . any time," he said softly. "Now, *out!*"

I turned quickly, hardly able to see the door through my tears. And I made a great business of rubbing fiercely at my nose as I marched along the corridor. I wanted no one in the world to know how the discovery of a friend in a lonely world could so wet my eyes.

———

Further rescue was also mine on this initial morning. While I debated accepting my many other invitations, Captain Gregory, a faculty officer, came to my room, introduced himself, and apologized for a mixup which had caused me to be left to my own devices since first arrival. He also explained that my application for the cavalry troop had been denied only because there was not a place available until the following year. However, if I wished, there was a vacancy in the artillery, which also had horses.

Gregory was a youngish, mustached, reserve officer of so kind a manner I thought he must have been dispatched directly from heaven. He was too young to have been in the war, but his Sam Browne belt gleamed with polish and his boots had been broken in with a proper stovepipe form. He explained he was the tactical officer of the artillery and would welcome me to his Battery B. If I wished to join his command he would help me move my still unpacked effects to Main Barracks where the two batteries were quartered.

I accepted without hesitation. As a faculty officer Gregory would provide protective escort against any of the local cadets who might feel put out because I had failed to call at their rooms, and removal to another area of the campus would presumably make it possible for me to melt into the mass until I could arrange a permanent disappearance.

By the time we reached Main Barracks, Gregory had taken complete charge of my future. He found me a room and arranged my academic curriculum, particularly difficult since I was entering at midyear. I did not realize how his charm had wooed me into the most recalcitrant outfit in the entire regiment, the home of cunning mavericks whose pride in their batteries was surpassed only by their accumulated demerits.

Gregory's attributes were common among the faculty officers, a quite different assembly from the militant priests of my former military academy. Nearly all of the academic members were of excellent caliber and once chosen for their posts remained until retirement. According to their length of tenure they were designated as Captains, Majors, and finally Colonels. They wore a brown uniform devoid of insignia and, while a few had known something of military life, the majority were career scholars of high reputation in their disciplines. Except for their uniforms, in which they always appeared uncomfortable, there was absolutely nothing military about their bearing or behavior. Their caps were usually worn askew, their manner was preoccupied, and they walked with professorial mien. Sometimes, lost in contemplation, they would return our salutes with their left hand or ignore the courtesy altogether. Two exceptions in the scholastic ranks were the language instructors, a French lieutenant who wore the powder-blue uniform and red-topped kepi of his regiment, and the Spanish captain who wore the khaki and wide-brimmed cap of his army.

A second category of faculty included the purely military officers. Some were on assignment from the Regular Army, true professionals, exceedingly smart in appearance. We admired and respected them although they managed to remain aloof from our personal affairs. Also in uniform were a number of reserve officers who served as "tactical" officers to the infantry companies, the two troops of cavalry,* and two batteries of artillery.

The almighty God in direct charge of all this was Rossow, the Commandant of Cadets, whose very being exuded the characteristics of a hardbitten cavalryman. The skin of his face had been peeled from a well-worn saddle and his jaw chiseled from the butt of a carbine. His baronial voice issuing from the bottom of his highly polished boots sounded like a flourish of kettledrums and the approaching *chink-chink* of his spur chains either sent cadets scampering for hiding or brought them to a quivering brace and a salute, which hopefully would catch an approving acknowledgment from his swaggerstick.

Rossow was stocky and very bowlegged, a powerful bull of a man who moved with the purposeful dignity of a Roman tyrant. Cadets breathed his name rather than enunciating it, lest his enormous power somehow penetrate into the secrecy of their barracks meetings. Most cadets were terrified of Rossow, nearly paralyzed in his presence, and I was a long time learning that his heart was softer than his charger's nose.

Supreme master of the entire domain was a delicately framed Georgia gentleman, Gignilliat. A brigadier general of infantry who had served with distinction in World War I, he combined all the attributes of a soldier-educator. He was so remarkably thin, he suggested a cardboard soldier, and his voice was so gentle it semed inconceivable he could ever have commanded men in action. Even as cadets we sensed that our General symbolized a vanishing aristocracy and we regretted his aging, for he had

---

* Known collectively as the Black Horse Troop, a famous unit which often appeared in presidential inaugural parades.

somehow managed the impossible. Without compromise, without the slightest bending of his straight-backed dignity, he maintained total devotion among seven hundred teenage boys many of whom were hardly model citizens. When the General spoke to his assembled troops, as he did only on important ceremonial occasions, we sat enrapt, fearful we might miss a single word. There was not a boot scrape, a squeak of a chair, or a tinkle of our accoutrements as his cultured voice told us of our place in society.

The splendid uniforms provided by the academy were designed for the rigors of the Middle-American climate, and there were so many variables that a high-ranking cadet resembled a Napoleonic marshal.

Everyday wear consisted of a heavy drill gray shirt decorated with the various insignia of class and rank, and breeches of the same material. Black leather puttees covered the distance from just below the knee to the black shoes. Artillery cadets were sometimes referred to as "red-legs" because of our identifying pants' stripes. We wore either puttees or heavy black field boots according to the order of the day.

We were protected from the biting winter winds by brass-buttoned greatcoats of dark blue. Great pains were taken in fitting our various "dress" uniforms. While the cadet was admonished to take a deep breath and hold it, the tailors marked and pinned until not a wrinkle was detectable either back or front. There was breathing room, and no more. As if carefully designed to perpetuate discomfort the neck of the blouse was board stiff and lined with a two-inch starched white collar guaranteed to keep the most weary cadet awake.

Full dress uniforms, worn for Sunday morning inspection, chapel, and special parades, were Graustarkian in opulence. The basic jacket was swallow-tailed and adorned with forty-eight brass buttons kept to peak luster by weekly polishing against a "button board." For all maneuvers in which a horse was involved the dress uniform would have satisfied a nineteenth-century Hussar. Booted, spurred, and sashed, we also draped from our left shoulder a woven cord of red if we were artillerymen and yellow if cavalry. A peculiar visored cap sprouting a pom-pom topped the display.

All of this panoply cost a great deal of money and there were no scholarships except in the band. As a consequence the average cadet came from a family capable of affording the expense, or if otherwise, the parental sacrifice was cruel.

There now began a new era in the life which was mine to employ, and in many ways the transformation was like a physical pounding of the flesh even though no one ever laid a hand upon me.

Everything was hard. Main Barracks was built of brick and concrete, the stairs lofting too the fourth floors were iron. The halls were of composition flooring as were the floors of our rooms. There was nothing to soften the scene anywhere except in the Memorial Building, to which we sometimes deliberately retreated that we might briefly sense the luxury of carpets, tapestries, curtains, and upholstered furniture. Plebes, much less half-asses, were not permitted decoration of any kind in their rooms. The walls were bare, the windows were bare, and the cots hard. Even upper classmen and cadet officers were denied most amenities. They could hang a school pennant on the wall, enjoy a record player during certain hours, and a throw rug beneath their chair. Nothing more.

Every cadet made up his own cot immediately on returning from breakfast. The gray blanket must be without a wrinkle, the upper sheet folded over it a precise eight inches. Pillows must be immaculate and undented, which was not difficult since they were extraordinarily hard.

There were backs on our wooden chairs, but no arms and no cushions. We studied at a desklike cavity in the center of our "wardrobes," tall wooden structures compartmented to hold our sundry uniforms, underclothings, handkerchiefs, and a Springfield rifle with bayonet. Our civilian clothing was taken from us on the day of enrollment and stored.

We washed, shaved, showered, and relieved ourselves in a common latrine, large enough to accommodate the cadets of each floor. It so stank that only the most tardy arriving cadets were assigned a room near it. We lingered in the latrine only for clandestine meetings with Louie, the black janitor of the barracks, a kindly, good-humored man

70

who sold us cigarettes or snuff at reasonable prices considering the risk he was taking.

The echoes in the hallways were harsh and continuous except during study periods at night. The clanging of bells, rasp of commands, and the strident announcements of the callers on each floor mixed with the chink of spur chains and the knocking of hard-heeled boots until we knew silence only as an ominous warning—someone had been caught in an infraction of the countless regulations and the culprit's fate was about to be dictated.

Plebes and upper classmen lived under a quite different set of rules and customs. Plebes never walked; wherever bound, they must march at the standard one hundred twenty steps per minute. Any change of direction must be executed by a "square turn," ninety degrees to left or right after a halt, only then to proceed onward. Shoulders must be hard-set, the back bar-straight. The chin kept hard in at all times.

Plebes made way for all others, at the washbowl, at the toilets, at doors, stairs, *any* situation which might conceivably give them priority over any other human being. The intent was to humiliate without breaking, to remove forever from the plebe's thinking any conception he might hold of personal privilege. He was deliberately reduced to a common nonentity for a year, thus in most cases successfully removing the corroding effects of parental indulgence and the natural cockiness of healthy youths.

No barracks-wise plebe would room with a half-ass lest some stigma be reflected upon himself. Thus I lived in solitude until Gregory at last persuaded a cadet to share his room with me, the regular roommate having failed to return from Christmas leave.

Under any circumstances the pairing of roommates was an extremely delicate affair: confining two young men and all their military and scholastic paraphernalia in a room twelve feet by twelve always invited friction and unhappiness. Strangely, there was little of either. The great majority of cadets were content with the youth who had chosen or been assigned to share their intimate lives, and change-abouts were rare. Usually a very strong affection developed between roommates, reinforced by a fierce loyalty. Even more surprising than this mutual tolerance was the almost total absence of active homo-

71

sexuality. All drives, discussions, and fantasies were devoted to the opposite sex and the mere sight of a female a hundred yards distant would make us randy.

We discussed copulation in all its aspects, our eyes glazed as some of the better raconteurs told of their exploits on leave or hinted of the wonders to be experienced in brothels real or imaginary. Yet the notion of making our bodies available to each other was rarely hinted at and would not have been acceptable.

Gregory had aimed his persuasive powers at a tall, resolutely lazy cadet whose real name was Woods. Except in ranks or class he was never referred to by his proper name, but according to his nickname, the Fop. In the battery there were, among many others, Bag Ears, Soapy, Balloon Butt, and Fox Face.

The Fop was so christened because of his fastidious regard for the civilian clothes which adorned his frame when he had entered the academy. Now, five months later, he had cause to accept his tactical officer's suggestion that he share his room with a half-ass, for he was already in deep trouble with the authorities. Perhaps Gregory thought a new personality might mellow the Fop's twisted and hopelessly impractical view of the military world. His philosophy was direct and simple: "Fuck 'em! They can't do this to me."

The Fop would persist in voicing his belief even while marching around the punishment quadrangle for hours under full battle pack, or when confined to barracks while the remainder of the battery went to the Saturday night movie. *They* had done this terrible thing to him for a crime of which he was always innocent, but *they* could not get away with it. Regardless of his sin he resolutely refused to recognize military omnipotence. *They* were dumb sons-of-bitches who invariably exceeded their legal authority.

The Fop's father was a judge, a factor which may have contributed to his stubborn reasoning, but, regardless, he had a multitude of opportunities to fall afoul of his superiors. Unlike the rest of us the Fop had a natural laziness that prevented him from making more than feeble attemps to cover the tracks of his violations. He therefore suffered endlessly. There were so many regulations and traps that not even the most namby-pamby cadet could expect to continue through an entire day without committing at least one petty offense.

Crimes ranged from such standard military taboos as refusing to obey an order (serious), to out of uniform as prescribed (medium serious), to ungentlemanly conduct (very serious). Every violation earned a cadet a corresponding number of demerits in increments of five to one hundred. An accumulated fifty demerits was worked off by five hours' parading the quadrangle, which in time became the Fop's personal territory.

Regardless of home training or habit we were all good housekeepers. Dust on a room radiator or anywhere else in our room was bound to be revealed by the inspecting officer's white gloves on Sunday mornings—and earn us five demerits each. A dirty window, spare shoes or boots out of line beneath a cot, brass or puttees not shined, shirts not aligned exactly on wardrobe shelves, food of any kind in the room, an unswept floor or soiled collar brought five demerits. There were times when the Fop, who lacked all sense of time and was never ready for the inspector's arrival, collected the lot.

Next to open mutiny the most heinous offense was the possession or use of tobacco in any form. The first offense resulted in an "order of the day" proclaimed before the entire corps. All athletic privileges were revoked for thirty days and if the criminal was a cadet officer or noncommissioned officer he was reduced to the ranks. A second offense within the same year brought instant dismissal from the academy without appeal. In spite of the severity applied to this regulation, smoking and the use of snuff persisted. It was hardly surprising that the Fop would insist on his right to smoke, the one enterprise which stirred him to superactive plotting, for the logistical problems were formidable.

Smoking in barracks was out of the question. The odor would have been detected after only a few puffs. The cadet officers rooming on each floor were comrades in the name of the unit only—they were still part of the establishment and obliged to report infractions of rules. The most mature usually looked the other way at minor offenses or merely handed down a warning, but smoking could not be ignored.

It was not the fragrance of tobacco, but the sweetness

73

of triumph over authority which drove the Fop, certain others, and myself to such enormous expenditures of energy and resourcefulness for a few puffs at a cigarette. While we were aware of the risk, like all devoted criminals we found the challenge irresistible, and of course we would never be apprehended. "Why, hell's bells," argued the Fop, "all we have to do is stash an entrenching spade down there and post one guy as lookout. If he sees anything suspicious on the horizon we quick bury our butts, and start looking for wildflowers. We're interested in the wonders of nature. Got it?"

I got it, but I was never too confident that our more suspicious officers would be so gullible.

Even the scene of our crime was of dubious security. There were almost no places of concealment on the campus, but the Fop had discovered it was possible to remain relatively inconspicuous between a line of heavy trees and a wooden building located near the lake shore. He lamented the placement of the building at approximately one quarter mile from our barracks. Timing was a critical factor since a period of only twenty minutes prevailed between dismissal from breakfast formation and the first academic period.

The Fop was tall, but also humpy and clumsy. Nor was he fast on his feet. But the urge to outwit authority drove him to several half-mile track records to and from his favorite asylum. Experience taught us we could enjoy seven minutes and twenty-five seconds for smoking; the balance of time must be spent in rapid transit.

"It's good training for football," the Fop would declare while panting. He did not think it odd that despite his size he had never shown the slightest interest in going out for the academy team, nor were any of us who shared his rendezvous likely candidates.

The only other possible time span for smoking was after military drill in the late afternoons. During a free period of about an hour many of us repaired to a network of trenches built for training in the Great War. The trenches had eroded with time and the several dugouts nearly collapsed, but they served as an ideal locale for our endless "bull sessions" and erotic discussions. Presumably the trenches, separated by a no-man's-land from the riding stables and the brick structure which housed our cannon and caissons, were too far away to invite official investigation. Once there, we knew we were safe.

As in all formalized societies, cliques were indigenous to the corps of cadets. And in spite of my ignominious station I eventually became a part of one, nameless, but nevertheless a unit within Battery B of the field artillery.

It was a loose collection with an uncertain coming and going of members, nor were we adverse to outsiders joining our gatherings in barracks or our occasional Sunday afternoon hikes into the surrounding countryside in search of relief from the military atmosphere, or as a bonus, the sight of girls.

In addition to the Fop, who was pitied rather than admired for his obstinacy and perpetual losing battle against authority, there was Bag Ears, a slight gravely-spoken cadet from Ohio. Balloon Butt was named for his posterior, which was overlarge. Since our common denominator was trouble, Fox Face was accepted into our little band despite his ability to make the academic honor roll. Once when an English examination on Dickens was due the next morning Fox Face approached the Fop, whose lethargy did not extend to books; he was an insatiable reader. "Tell me about this guy David Copperfield," Fox Face asked. "What's with him?"

The Fop recounted Copperfield's story in loving detail.

Next morning Fox Face, who had never troubled to open his book, received an A.

The Fop failed the examination.

Gradually, as I became an accepted member of our little enclave, my desire to run away from the heavy discipline lessened. And in time I acquired my own nickname: God. This curious appellation was explained to me by the Fop, who as my roommate suffered more patiently and knew me better than any other cadet.

"It is because you expect perfection," he said, assuming his favorite horizontal position on my bunk. If he reclined on his own bunk he would be obliged to the great effort of smoothing the wrinkles made by his one hundred and eighty pounds. Once in position on my bunk he considered himself a guest. And when quite comfortable he was often inclined to philosophize.

"I will tell you why you are so named. I fart and you complain of the smell. You expect ambrosia? If the eggs

75

in the mess hall are scrambled, you say it was not intentional. The cook really wanted eggs sunny side up. If there is saltpeter in the mess hall food, you claim there is not enough to keep us from being horny, or so much we'll be impotent for life. Yesterday, in the privacy of this room, I said Lieutenant Hood was a prick because he gave me ten demerits for failure to salute. You said he could not possibly be a prick because a prick has a head. . . ." He paused. "And last week at drill when Balloon Butt came out with his spurs on upside down, was it an officer who embarrassed him? No. It was you. Again, last week when we both grabbed five demerits for dust under the radiator, you gave me that look of yours—"

"What look?"

"That it's-all-*your*-radiator look. For Christ's sake, half of what's under our radiator has got to be yours."

"But we agreed if I did the walls and the ceiling and the window, you would do the floor."

"I did. But somehow I missed under the radiator."

"And we both got five demerits for it."

"Exactly. That just proves Lieutenant Hood knows half of what's on the floor which should not be is yours."

"I thought you said Hood was a prick."

"He is. Can't you see that's just it? He can't be perfect, nor can I. But you expect us to be. Therefore," he sighed while pointing a finger at me, "you are called *God.*"

Chapter 7

First Lieutenant Berg was in command of the battery's military activities and our progress toward eventual commissions. He was Regular Army, assigned to the academy along with several other career officers, both commissioned and non-commissioned.

Berg was a beautiful example of the professional soldier at his best and all of us revered him. He was lean, hard of jaw, and bore himself with just the right display of personal pride and dignity. Only his eyes, sparkling beneath the absolutely level brim of his campaign hat, compensated for his austere portrait. They were laughing eyes always denying the hard line of his mouth, as if he wanted to share some deep amusement with us, but dared not. Berg's uniform was always impeccable and his boots were the envy of us all. We did our best to emulate the creaseless stovepipes protecting his shanks, but were never quite successful.

Berg was a master equestrian, his seat relaxed yet his body poised, back straight, knees tight to the saddle, heels well down. His hands were firmly commanding with all horses, yet never brutal or flamboyant. When first observing me astride one of our battery mounts he declared over his chin strap, "You have good hands." I was prepared to lay down my life for him.

Riley, a dark-eyed, pompadoured artillery sergeant with a skin of burnt sienna, was our drill master. While Berg observed from a distance suitable to his magnificence, Riley, through our cadet officers, drove us for two hard hours a day. His announced intention was to make proper artillerymen of us. It was as if he had to prove he could triumph over such mediocre flesh.

The material of the battery consisted of four caissons and limbers. The guns were the famous French 75s (millimeters), which had made such a name for themselves on the Western Front during the First World War. They were each drawn by six horses, some of whom were older and ever so much wiser than the cadets who rode them.

While we did secretly envy the splendid black mounts of the cavalry troop, we found a certain pride in the power and general recalcitrance of our draft-type horses. They were all bays of typical government issue and temperament. Glamorous as the cavalry troopers might be, those of us assigned to mounted posts rather than riding, arms folded, on the caissons and limbers, were much busier than any trooper, and our jobs more demanding. Each gun or caisson unit required three teams, "lead," "swing," and "wheel." Each team was managed by a cadet riding the horse on the left while controlling the one on the right. The job was reasonably easy if the horses were well fed before departing on maneuvers and the battery was held at a walk. No one could predict the action when the order to trot or gallop was given. It often became near chaos because horses inspire each other. Excitement passes invisibly from one to another, sometimes compounding itself into a stampede. At a walk our harness gear and squeaking saddles produced an easy rhythm, a musical tinkling of metal chain soothing to man and beast alike. The horses nickered their woes to each other; unless on parade we were allowed to talk among ourselves and, joking of our own troubles, all was right with the world. Returning to the stables in the yellow evening, our red pom-poms dancing and the sword scabbards of our officers glinting in the last of the sunlight, it was easy to imagine we rode with the ghosts of a more colorful and innocent era.

While my academics languished, I did show some affinity for horses in general and, in Berg's eyes at least, appeared to control my lead pair with a minimum of rebellion. He therefore invited me to try for the polo team, of which he was coach.

The influence of adult mentors upon youths in their charge is inestimable. One phrase, one gesture, one apparently innocuous suggestion or rejection, can build or destroy the spirit of a youth, and sometimes, if all elements are in proper juxtaposition, forever influence the balance of his life. Berg released me from a growing sense of shame at my current inability to comprehend geometric theory, chemical formulae, and Castilian inflection. He guided me into a competition where I might at least achieve equality.

Everything about polo appealed to me. It is dangerous. It is one of the fastest games played on earth and brute physical strength is not of paramount importance. To excel, the player must join in a special alliance with horses, for the finest player becomes inept when poorly mounted and the intermediate player can far surpass himself when a knowing and cooperative horse puts him in the right place at the right time and behaves himself while the man on his back swings at the ball.

The game of polo is more than a contest between opposing teams. The elements of ball, horse, and man must all be brought together in perfect harmony, an exceedingly difficult combination when an opposing player is doing his muscular best to physically shove his opponent off a solid hickory ball the size of an orange. The action takes place while the opponents' horses may be traveling between fifteen and twenty miles an hour and the ball itself, propelled by the whip of bamboo mallets, may attain a velocity of eighty miles an hour. In many aspects the game resembles hockey although the speeds are higher and the playing field very much larger. A good polo player must ride his mount to the limit while concentrating solely on the elusive ball. He considers the actual management of his horse no more than a hockey player does his skating. He must become one with his mount. Now, with the impromptu whims of youth in full command, I suddenly found relief for my Tartar energies in the contest of princes.

The Fop was disgusted with me. Instead of girls I spoke only of horses, a passion he did not share. "I am not a gardener," he stated flatly, "and I do not need any more horseshit than already comes my way."

When the Fop believed I should be joined with others of our clan in the trenches for a leisurely hour of chain-smoking, I was devoting myself to a wooden horse situated in a large cage covered with chicken wire. There I swung at polo balls every afternoon, practicing the various shots until I rarely missed. The floor of the cage was so constructed that the ball returned to an approximately realistic position on either side of the "horse." It was far easier to hit the ball than in actual field practice, but the basic strokes, off- and near-side forehand and backhand, neck and tail shots, could be repeated until they became automatic.

Sometimes Berg watched me in the cage and offered a word of instruction or approval. Soon I was playing in real scrimmages, and envy, the prime element in youthful malingering, left me. I no longer needed to balance my athletic inadequacy with some display of defiance or petty villainy. I became secure, and as a consequence a thousand changes began occurring within me. If my courage failed, then my horse carried me into the heart of conflict anyway. In time I could not tell the difference between my own resolution and that of the horse, and began to believe whatever fragments of praise came my way. Believing, I was able to walk among my fellow players with new pride. All upper classmen, they began to teach me boldness and a disregard of physical damage to myself. Thus I came to love them and even found contentment in the stern regime of the academy. When my father telephoned inquiring of my progress, I made no mention of deserting this new life.

While Lieutenant Berg continued to mold our characters in the late afternoons, another diametrically different type of adult inspired the most engaging hour of my academic mornings. Known as "Major" Mather only because of his tenure and scholastic rating in the faculty, he was a teacher of English enjoying such clout that he had managed to make dramatics a full credit course on a par with chemistry, trigonometry, history, and the languages.

Mather was a hawk-nosed, nervous man, given to quick and jerky movements in perpetual revelation of his volatile temperament. His eyes were blue and small, ever-darting like a wary bird's, and frequently he would cock his head, rocking it to the left and right as if he heard some distant mating call. Even his walk was bird-like, a sort of running prance with momentary halts to tilt his head and survey the immediate scene. He wore the drab uniform of the academic faculty in a resolutely unmilitary fashion. In class, as his boundless enthusiasm for all matters literary heated his body, he was wont to remove his uniform jacket, an unthinkable relaxation for other members of the faculty.

Mather was a born actor given to emphasizing his points with miniplays of his own conception. Thus his classes were always alive and unusually hearty, with full give and take prevailing. There were no half-closed eyes in Mather's classes. Excitement prevailed from gong to gong and, with it, powerful stimulation among his fortunate students. Discipline in his presence was voluntary and as a consequence rarely violated. Every cadet admired Mather and some of us revered him.

I came under Mather's spell because I needed subjects to balance my wretched showings in the science and language courses. Since he could make even Thackeray and Wordsworth provocative, I had little trouble capturing marks rivaling and sometimes surpassing those won by the illustrious Fox Face.

Yet Mather was more than a teacher. His true love was the theater and his grand moments in this bastion of military code and protocol were those occasions when his cadets performed a play which he directed with the dedication and verve of the most important Broadway production.

It was not long before Mather recognized a willing

disciple, and I became heavily involved in his entertainments.

In the shadow of such obscure events are all of our early lives cultivated. My mother taught me to paint and would not have been displeased had I become an artist. My father insisted I should become a businessman. At the academy I was for a long while indeterminate, vacillating between my still-lively desire to become a director of films and a new, half-conceived notion that I might try for West Point. From my view in the rear rank, the life of a professional officer was not at all bad, particularly in the mounted services where polo was always available.

None of these careers came to pass. All of a man's life is patterned on chance and sometimes the more carefully contrived the planning, the more contrary and frivolous the result. The rules for predicting individual fortune have never been written and never will be, if only because they can be outraged by the most trivial event.

———

Two activities consumed my first summer leave from the academy. I had hardly shed my gray uniform when I voluntarily donned another—this time of the ill-fitting khaki standard to the U.S. Cavalry.

Fort Snelling, situated on a promontory above the Mississippi River where it winds between the twin cities of St. Paul and Minneapolis, is one of the original forts so vital to the development of the West, a complex heavy with military tradition and during that summer basking in comfortable middle-age. Its standard red brick barracks, stables, and officers' quarters were still in fair repair, and its vast green lawns were mowed regularly by soldier-prisoners serving out their various sentences in the stockade.

It was a world of its own, a feudal autocracy in which no one exerted himself any more than was absolutely necessary, least of all the commissioned officers. The 3rd Infantry, one of the oldest units in the American Army, endured the harsh Minnesota winters by remaining almost invisible on the frozen landscape and slipped into a leisurely, unruffled occupancy during the lush months of summer.

I entered upon the tranquil scene by enlisting in the C.M.T.C. (Citizens Military Training Camp), and in accordance with my fierce desire was assigned to the 14th United States Cavalry bivouacked at Fort Snelling for the summer. It was a mounted unit operating almost exactly as it did during the Civil War, the Indian wars, and the white man's ruthless conquest of the West. Even our sabers, issued to every trooper with an admonishment to keep them sharp and glistening, were relics of Appomattox, Bull Run, and the Dakota Territory.

Joined in this military anachronism we were two hundred troopers in all, not counting the regular commissioned and non-commissioned officers, who considered themselves designated by God himself to keep the spirits of Custer, Sherman, Jackson, and "Light-Horse" Harry Lee alive.

In comparison with the military academy I found the life of a cavalryman easy and the discipline soft. The horses were surprisingly fine animals considering their numbers, holding up splendidly under five or six hours of strenuous riding every day. Unfortunately, the unit was equipped with the invidious McClellan saddle and our butts did not survive as well.

By now my military sense of survival was well developed. I knew as habit the peculiarities of military logic which drive some men to Section 8 early in their enlistment, and when mastered allow others to lead a tolerable existence. While the phrase "never volunteer for anything" is ancient combat wisdom, in peacetime conditions certain exceptions are admissible and often bring special privileges. The trouble is in the customary refusal of officers to identify the need for volunteers. Will it be an agony, a bore, or a thrill?

"I need four men for a special detail. It will take about six hours and you'll be excused from all other duties."

Listening carefully to the inflection of the Sergeant's voice while remembering he is a master at guile, an astute soldier would probably not volunteer for this one. He would know the Sergeant might hint at its nature even with his granite eyes if it was going to be a holiday, or if it was going to involve arduous labor. Without appreciation of such delicate signals the soldier volunteer could find himself digging or cleaning latrines or, at best, six hours at shoveling manure.

"I need thirty men for a special detail. God knows how long it will last."

After quick analysis this one sounds promising. Thirty men is too many for household labors and the indication is that the volunteers will be going somewhere. The Sergeant's complaint of its doubtful duration means he is going along himself, which is a very good sign since cavalry sergeants display sheer genius at avoiding unpleasant duties.

By volunteering for our Sergeant's latter pitch I became one of the troopers assigned to protect Charles Lindbergh when he landed at Minneapolis after his flight to Paris.

At Fort Snelling we were quartered in four long wooden barracks which were considerably removed from the permanent installations occupied by the regulars. We were fifty troopers to a building, our cots and footlockers arranged in two long opposing rows. Visually it was a sienna world faded to various degrees and punctuated only by occasional glintings of metal accoutrements. All bathing and washing was accomplished at outside installations and the latrines were open to the elements, a blessing since they had been dug by trainees during the First World War and never rehabilitated.

Soon after selecting a vacant cot I realized that this new society was quite different from either of my military academies. Here my comrades were mostly from poor families, many had enlisted simply to assure themselves of ample food, some shelter, and at least a few dollars' pay for the six weeks of their encampment. I resolved then to keep my own counsel on many matters lest my much more fortunate circumstances separate me from the others. Many of the new troopers had no knowledge whatever of horses. I vowed not to parade my better knowledge or, more embarrassing, reveal the special reasons which had brought me to sleep and eat among them.

At last finding something in my conduct he thought worthy of honor, my indulgent father had bought me two fine polo ponies. Arrangements had been made for their care in the stables of the 3rd Infantry, whose officers were still mounted in historic style. In the autumn, riding to the hounds was their pleasure on Sunday mornings, with a dragged scent rather than a fox employed to set the course over the reservation. With free government mounts readily available and ample personnel to groom them, the officers also maintained a fierce polo competition against the teams of St. Paul and Minneapolis and other teams coming to the fort from afar.

As an ordinary private in the Regular Army it would have been unthinkable for me to play polo with "officers and gentlemen" regardless of any talent I might possess, but as a reservist presumably in training to become an officer, an exception could be made. My father's civic activities were also recognized by the soldiery, who tried to maintain a healthy relationship with the leading local civilians while secretly regarding them as no more than a necessary nuisance. It was politely understood that after my duties as a trooper were ended for the day, I could slip away to the permanent stables and work my ponies on the adjacent polo field. During the long northern twilights I had no trouble getting in two hours of practice and on Sundays, after parade, I was able to vanish completely from the khaki world and reappear on the field in whites, including a cork helmet across the face of which I had painted a skull and crossbones device. None of my 14th Cavalry comrades ever ventured near the polo field or its environs and my innocent deception was never discovered.

While the language and atmosphere of the weekend polo tournaments was reserved and even stiff at times, my daily service with the troop became the other part of a double life. That hoary phrase, "swears like a trooper," was based on long cavalry tradition and was in some ways the natural result of a cavalryman's relatively dangerous and often frustrating existence. Hardly a day passed without some trooper being thrown, kicked, or bitten, mostly because horses know instinctively when an inexperienced hand is theirs to try. And then there were our mules. None of us including our almighty career sergeants could bend our mule train to his will. I learned, amid ringing choruses of the vilest invectives, that there is no creature able to break a strong man's spirit quicker than a mule. There were only thirty then serving in the 14th Cavalry and each was an individual of tenacious independence. Twenty-two were to follow in our dusty wake carrying our four .30 caliber Browning machine guns, tripods, water cooling tanks, and ammunition belts. The remaining eight were divided into two teams for pulling our mess and supply wagons. Neither food nor guns ever made any of our rendezvous on time. While we troopers engaged in traditional cavalry maneuvers all morning, covering and cursing vast amounts of rugged real estate in the process, it seemed impossible for our mule train to travel only a few miles. Thus, the legend of the profane trooper. For sweetness and cajolery would not move a mule if he liked where he was standing, nor did the cruelest abuse persuade him onward if he preferred to stay. Only infinite patience made a true mule-skinner of a mere man and it took a rare personality to long tolerate the look of superiority on their bland faces. Mules serving their hitch in the United States Army did not give a damn about the course of battle, simulated or otherwise. Their attitude greatly enriched a trooper's vocabulary.

These days I wonder if my need for personal privacy is not in some measure due to the nature of a very public youth, and a later life nearly saturated with the close proximity of my fellow men. I spent two summers in the cavalry reserve where of course I shared nearly every physical function with two hundred contemporaries. The seasons between were spent in barracks teaming with the shouts, gruntings, sighs, and hard rapping footsteps of my academy comrades. I lived in a world of noise. Later, there were two wars which required an equal and close sharing of available necessities plus a moral mandate to share whatever at the moment might be comfortable or precious. Sometimes that obligation included a less than ample supply of spirit or of courage. There were also the years as a pilot of the line when the agreeable sharing of inches of space for long hours was absolutely necessary. Finally, there were the years at sea in vessels when solitude was always difficult to obtain and often impossible.

It seemed I was rarely alone except in my thoughts, which, almost as if some genie were prompting them, began transporting me elsewhere whenever I pleased. Upon my return to the academy for a second year, "Major"

Mather apparently recognized this still very uncertain promise and did his utmost to nourish it.

"There was a cadet here a few years ago," he said while assuming his favorite alert-sparrow pose, "his name was Josh Logan and he's already making a name for himself in the East."

Logan had obviously been a jewel in Mather's diadem and now he seemed to expect an equal performance from me.

I tried to please him with all that was in me, for Mather had become my savior within the hitherto impregnable academic fortress. He paced and postured, crossing his classroom at high speed to emphasize a point of poetry or drama as if the same point did not exist on the side of the room he had just departed. He whipped his glasses on and off his beak with a fierce gesture, his eyes blazing with enthusiasm, his voice hoarsening with emotion as he sought to lead us into literature. Never still for an instant, his arms and hands drew whole maps in the air while his busy eyebrows wigwagged hints of subplots, planted auguries of misfortune, and (wildly incongruous considering the immediate environment) spoke most softly as he played out tender nuances of love between man and woman.

Whether for cause or out of pity Mather aimed much of his erudition directly at me. And like a sailor marooned with a single plank for flotation I clung to him desperately. With Mather as my apostle I was well on the way to achieving distinction when the law of criminal averages took charge and calamity struck.

The Fop and a cadet called Moonbeam because of his fat, gibbous face invited me to join them for a quick butt between the last bugle notes of tattoo and taps. There was ample time for the expedition. We had only to remain at our books until the bell clanged official conclusion of the nightly study hours. We would have already slipped into our heavy sweaters, as the December night was cold and our window rattled against the high wind off the lake.

While the restful notes of tattoo drifted ever fainter on the wind we knew the other cadets would have some twenty minutes for informal visiting, brushing their teeth, making up laundry, and the necessary details of the self-sufficient before taps brought lights out. Instead of such dull business we intended to skitter down the four flights of iron stairs, then run through the night to the bushes near the tennis courts. Once arrived, we should have a full ten minutes for smoking a butt. Returning with all speed we calculated we should be back in our rooms by the final notes of taps—whereupon all would be at peace with the world.

The route was shorter via the sally port, but we knew the Officer of the Day would probably be in the vicinity and become suspicious of our unseeming haste.

We chose to depart our Main Barracks by the front entrance, rush past the cadet guard, who would still be walking his post, and continue across the dark parade. The guard, we reasoned, would doubtless be nearly frozen and only anxious to be relieved. He was probably an infantryman and would not report our swift passage. Any cadet other than a cadet officer forced into the position, who betrayed others to the authorities, committed social suicide. Even the most severe of the faculty gave cold welcome to tale bearers.

Our choice of route was right, but our reconnoitering was lax. We had just lit up when the beam of a flashlight froze us in position. Behind the approaching blob of light we recognized the worst of all eventualities, the face and figure of the Ferret, a faculty officer with a reverence for rule books. We were not surprised when he said he would cite us, nor did we attempt to get off with pleading. We would not be expelled unless caught with or using tobacco again.

"The son of a bitch had to be waiting for us," the Fop snorted in the darkness of our room. "An ambush! 'Woods,' the son of a bitch says, using the familiar without my permission, 'aren't you in enough trouble without *this?*' Did you notice how he practically ignored you and Moonbeam? *I* was the only guy there, for Christ's sake! I was leading poor you and poor Moonbeam astray. I should have told the son of a bitch we were smoking *your* cigarettes."

While the Fop continued with his endless woes I climbed into my bunk and worried for I knew Mather would not be pleased with this night's episode. He had me writing a play now, which was exciting work, and I did not want to disappoint him in any degree.

Lying in the darkness, listening to the window rattling and the Fop's vengeful railleries, I vowed not to smoke again until the school year was done.

It was typical of Mather to let weeks pass and my remorse nearly dissolve before he said, "For God's sake don't get caught again. I'm depending on you for the lead in *The Butter and Egg Man*. And for commencement we'll do your play."

Months passed in a sort of undeclared truce between authority and Fox Face, Balloon Butt, Bag Ears, Moonbeam, and God. I applied myself to Spanish with greater devotion, doing my best to imitate the lisping pronunciation so dear to the ear of Lieutenant Perez, late of the Spanish Army. Chemistry, long a bayonet in my scholastic ribs, continued to bewilder me if only because I knew my talent for it was nil.

My play, *Hate Island*, a direct steal from a *Saturday Evening Post* story, was finished. It concerned the plight of a shipwrecked freighter's crew and how a fierce stoker revived their will to live by making them hate him. It was grim stuff, not alleviated by the casting of our Cadet Regimental Commander (a ponderous enough fellow without my leaden lines) as the stoker protagonist. I was also meeting with Mather's enthusiastic approval for *The Butter and Egg Man,* with performances scheduled for the corps and their visitors during the Easter ceremonies. And true to my private pledge I had not smoked.

There are good fishermen who would rather catch one illegal salmon than twenty in season, and policemen who steal a fistful of cigars while otherwise faithfully upholding the law. There are professional con men who often reject a sure thing and instead attempt a risky venture which may send them to jail.

Some similar urge drove me to the use of snuff as a substitute for smoking. While I was well aware that snuff was a form of tobacco and thus subject to the same academy penalties, I had convinced myself it was a safe indulgence. I found a curious satisfaction in tapping the round tin box with proper solemnity, then removing the lid and forming a "bittle" with practiced manipulation of thumb and forefinger. But our true reason for using snuff was seldom recognized or admitted. It was defiance of authority and if it had been legal it is doubtful if any of us would have long continued our commitment to it. As it was, we paid Louie the barracks janitor outrageous prices for a can of Key or Copenhagen and risked far more in its possession.

Sunday mornings at the academy were always hectic if only because reveille was one hour later and the surfeit of sleep left us lethargic against the pressing demands which began immediately after the breakfast formation was dismissed. We had then but two hours until inspection of ourselves and our rooms.

The Fop's already sluggish metabolism languished even more on Sunday mornings. The closer the hour of inspection approached, the slower his movements became and there would be long spans of time when he would stand, polishing cloth in hand, simply staring out the window. When I protested the need for haste in making our cots, or polishing our brass, the floor, or our boots, or whatever was next in sequence, he would assume his most haughty air.

"Last Sunday they gave me five demerits for books out of place," he lamented. "Five demerits for three lousy inches away from where some prick says they have to be! Don't they know that books are the fount of all knowledge and cannot be kicked around just to satisfy some officer's measuring stick? *They* are not going to get away with it."

"Maybe," he added thoughtfully, "I could distract their attention by pissing out the window—" He flicked his polishing rag aimlessly at possible areas of dust around his wardrobe and added, "This is one hell of a life, I don't mind telling you."

While I tried to calculate how many thousands of times the Fop had not minded telling me this was one hell of a life, I carefully stowed one full can of snuff and one half-empty can in my cartridge case. These small patent-leather boxes with their polished brass academy insignia on the flap were issued to all cadets as part of their full dress uniform but were never worn by those in the artillery or cavalry troop. Thus in our barracks they had been assigned an inconspicuous space on our wardrobe shelf, far back, and inconvenient to reach. No one even paid the slightest attention to the boxes, which was why, after deep consideration, I had chosen mine as the ideal hiding place for a supply of snuff.

We were still polishing the forty-eight brass buttons on our dress blouses when we heard the Caller of the Day shouting from the end of the hallway. "Attention, sirs! General inspection in five minutes, sirs!"

Almost immediately it seemed the alarm bell clanged. An overwhelming and ominous silence fell upon the entire barracks. The Fop and I were still buttoning our blouses when we heard the hard pounding of boots approaching and the musical jingle of spur chains. Our door was suddenly thrown open and we heard the familiar voice of the battery First Sergeant.

"Tent . . . *shun!*"

The Fop and I smacked our heels together with a resounding double report. We took a stiff brace, shoulders back, chin in, eyes unseeing and unblinking. Standing at the head end of our cots on opposite sides of the room, we were expected to remain as if carved in bronze until the visiting inspectors departed. Usually it was not an unpleasant experience. We stood in a trance, our eyes glazed, our spirits abandoning all mortal matters as surely as if we had perished.

An instant after the initial call to attention by the First Sergeant, our Sunday morning visitors entered in full glory. The delegation was always the same, led by our Battery Commander, a dark and handsome cadet who was a winner in every aspect of cadet life. Various insignia proclaiming his achievements made him resemble a marching Christmas tree. As usual he was now accompanied by a faculty officer of the military category. I was dismayed to see out of the corner of my eye that he was the Ferret.

I moaned inwardly. There was no need to divert my eyes to see the Fop and I watched him blanch and purse his lips as the Ferret passed inches in front of him. He had forgotten his books in the last minute rush. The Ferret spied them at once.

"What are your books doing in your wastebasket?"

"I can't say, sir."

"You can't say? Who put them there?"

"I suppose I did, sir."

"You *suppose?* Have you any logical explanation for misplaced books?"

"Maybe the wind blew them off my desk. You see, sir—"

The Ferret turned to the First Sergeant, who raised his clipboard in anticipation. It was his duty to record the various discrepancies found during the inspection and note the penalties, if any.

The Ferret's voice was without anger, impersonal, and didactic.

"Five demerits for books out of place . . . five demerits for frivolous remarks while standing at attention."

Both our Battery Commander and the Ferret wore white gloves, which they now passed across our desk tops, shelves, windowsill, and radiator. Occasionally they would invert their hands looking for telltale smudges. I was grateful for our Battery Commander's sword. It kept him from kneeling gracefully. At a lower eye level he might discover much more than he, as basically one of us, would care to see. Other faculty officers would never forsake their dignity long enough to go sniffing about like a hound, but suddenly watching the Ferret I realized he just might.

He moved with abnormal slowness around the room and I thought, the son of a bitch thinks something is fishy and he's not going to leave until he finds it.

A chill passed from my unbelieving eyes to my locked-in-position feet. While I sought desperately for some diversion (I could faint from standing at attention too long), I watched the Ferret approaching my wardrobe, his head cocked inquisitively. He glanced at me, I saw what might pass for a faint smile cross his lips, and I was comforted in remembering how I had taken special pains with the alignment of my shirts, underwear, and handkerchiefs. Block to block, I thought, squared off to the exact millimeter; there was nothing he could find awry.

The Ferret was behind me now and therefore unseen. But I could hear him poking around and I became increasingly uneasy. Good God, was he going to spend the whole Sunday morning with us? Didn't he realize he had at least forty more rooms to inspect?

Normal inspections took only two or three minutes. I was sure more than five minutes had already passed.

Most animals have an instinct for impending disaster, a faculty shared by military cadets. The instant I heard something rattle behind me I knew the Ferret had come upon my cartridge case.

He came around to face me with it and I thought how this must be the first time in battery history any officer had shown the slightest interest in something he knew belonged on the tail of an infantryman. He studied the brass plaque bearing the academy insignia and made a faint humming sound.

"You haven't polished this for a long time." His voice was reserved, even kindly, but my pulse was thumping as if he held a time bomb.

"No, sir. We never use——"

I saw it happen as if I stood in a remote balcony. Driven by some instinct of his own the Ferret shook the box experimentally, then unclipped the lid and turned it upside down.

The two cans of snuff I had so cleverly cached fell to the hard floor with a terrible clatter, then rolled slowly across the room until they capsized against the wall. The ensuing silence was appalling.

The Ferret took his time retrieving the cans, which he held before my frozen eyes and asked, "Are these yours?"

"Yessir."

He opened one carefully lest its contents soil his white gloves. It happened to be the one half used.

"I'm sorry," the Ferret said as if he truly regretted his discovery. "I'm very sorry, but I shall have to take these with me. You are confined to barracks until the superintendent has a chance to talk with you."

Our Sunday morning visitors left without further inspection or word except from the First Sergéant, who said, "At ease," as he passed out of the room.

I crumpled to my cot, desolate with remorse. I knew no one could rescue me from a second tobacco offense. "I've let Mather down," I mumbled, all attempt to stay brave having left me.

"I'm going to miss you, God," the Fop said softly.

Chapter 8

Even as a departing cadet I realized Mather's influence would be with me for the rest of life. When I crawled away from the academy in disgrace he seemed to sense my secret tears and spared me his disappointment. Likewise my father's reaction on my arrival home. He grunted unhappily several times, but he refrained from his "I wash my hands of you" declaration. His tolerance, however feigned, made me all the more determined to redeem myself. To this end I devoted myself to honest industry and listened with new attention when my father spoke. This was not difficult since I had matured, and evidence of my father's worth was everywhere. He was by all normal indications one of the city's leading citizens, appointed to boards of directors, the chairman of this and the president of that. He was much sought after by charities, which discovered his driving energies brought record contributions for any campaign. Amid all this my mother maintained her serene calm and total simplicity. While she went along willingly enough with my father's ever-increasing extravagances, the phrase "a penny saved is a penny earned" still came frequently to her lips.

My penitent mood was so all-prevailing that I leaned upon nepotism to ease my shame. My father acceded to my request for work as a ditch-digger during the burial of a telephone cable beneath one of the city's major avenues. At night I worked as a ticket-taker for the Irishman who ran the theater where in happier times my film had played. When at last the ditch was nearly done I made application to enter summer school and determined to make such a record that my re-entry into the academy could not be denied.

The final result of so much remorse and retribution surprised everyone. My father regained his hope in me and my mother no longer changed the subject when inquiry of her son was made. When my application to reenter the academy was accepted I managed to behave as a model youth for nearly a week. Then I fell in love.

Troubadours never sing of love among elders. In the eyes of youth the chosen one is never weighed honestly, for what is the need of assaying the perfect? During the first flaring of youthful passion the thunder and lightning of revelation obliterates all else, discovery after discovery so stuns the participants they become nearly incapable of normal reactions and are sometimes described as "mooning." This advanced state of ecstasy endures until marriage or until one of the youthful pair comes to his or her senses. Minstrels never sing of this eventuality.

While still moving from disgrace to hope for better times, I became enchanted with Eleanor, a local beauty of great popularity. She was very bright, breathlessly vivacious, beautifully proportioned, and blessed with deep brown eyes and the olive skin of her French forebears. That she employed her lovely eyes constantly to attract the attention of all males was something I did not notice. Nor could I as yet recognize her iron will and great intrinsic courage.

When I departed for the academy once more, our parting became a six-hour melodrama. We vowed to write every day until—*until!*

Once I returned to the soldier's life, Mather again determined to keep me out of trouble. Scheming as my personal Merlin, he had grandiose plans for my future. He immediately put me to work on a new play; hopping birdlike about his little office he swore he would see me graduate with honors.* Thus, as the first rumors of a worldwide financial calamity shook the American stock market, I became once again a comrade-in-arms to the Fop, Fox Face, Bag Ears, and Balloon Butt.

The financial catastrophe which triggered the Great Depression and years of worldwide woe did not slow my father's enterprise. While others of his caste were moaning and economizing and a few obsessed with money jumped out of their office windows, my father continued to prosper. "Do what the other fellow is not doing," became one of his favorite phrases, and no one could argue that his thinking was entirely wrong. Ever the optimist, and firm believer in his country's basic soundness, he launched the first cable radio system and saw it reward him almost from the start. He bought while

---

* Which he did.

others sold and gave lavish parties while others wore social mourning.

Even as disaster upon disaster befell the American economy, my father found room to maneuver and negotiate. He was riding high and fast on the road toward a state he considered "success." All parties concerned applauded his arrangements for the sale of the Bell System of the very telephone company employing him and as a consequence he was offered an even more challenging position with a huge telephonic combine in Chicago.

Meanwhile an equally busy if not so financially minded Mather had so praised and overstated my abilities that the normal course of my education was again altered drastically from the norm.

"It would be a waste of time for you to spend four years in college," he insisted. As a member of the academy polo team competing against Eastern colleges and particularly West Point, I had already changed my mind about becoming a professional soldier. One look at the heavy gray bastions perched on the Hudson River promontory quenched all desire for another four years of uniforms and saluting. And Mather had re-inspired my yearning for the fame and fortune I thought successful artistic endeavor could bring.

"The place for you is at Yale with George Pierce Baker," Mather insisted. His eyes shone with such anticipation I thought he might be going himself. "Baker runs the Yale Drama School. He is incomparable."

Carried away with his enthusiasm, Mather ignored the fact that Baker's school was for postgraduates. Somehow he persuaded Baker and Yale to accept two students in a "special" category. By offering a pair rather than a single person he convinced Baker that an interesting project would develop. Arguing with negative persuasion, he held that if two military cadets with only high school diplomas could survive Baker's curriculum there must be something wrong with it.

After long deliberation the illustrious Professor Baker agreed to take a chance and once again I became an "experimental" student. Neither of us realized how far beyond our academic thresholds we had been propelled.

·Professor George Pierce Baker first established what he called his 47 Workshop at Harvard. There Eugene O'Neill and other writers of stature came to study under the great man. In time the 47 Workshop became so successful that Yale University offered Baker a chair of his own, the Yale School of Drama.* Yale so valued his talents that a magnificent theater was built for him. There he was free to instruct his students in comfort and produce whatever entertainments he pleased.

By the year of our arrival the nature of the school was well established and its reputation already the envy of all other similar schools. The physical facilities were superb, far superior to many commercial theaters, and the faculty of the very highest quality. Among other innovations, Baker invited those who were doing rather than teachers whose sole experience was academic. Thus no less a talent than the brilliant John Mason Brown taught us dramatic criticism, while Donald Oenslager instructed in scenic design. Constance Welsh taught diction and the finer nuances of oral English, while Frank Bevan taught costume. Elizabeth Elsen taught the dance, an obligatory course which I at first thought silly but soon learned to value. Stanley McCandless taught lighting and Edward Cole the physical mechanics of scene building and stage management.

All of these people were stimulating and creative professionals. They were also at a loss to know what they should do with two experimental students both of whom stood out like thistles in their academic garden. For some time we were at a loss to understand each other, a situation which contributed to my fellow ex-cadet's defection within the first year.

The faculty were not alone in their bewilderment at the two products of a harsh military background who had landed hob-nailed, straight-backed, and short-haired in their midst. Our considerable contrast to the other students was accepted with varied grace, but the reason for our presence was difficult to explain. Why were we not in college? How were we ticketed to move in their company? The majority of the students were aiming for a future as teachers in universities offering dramatic courses, or as directors of the many "little thea-

* A unit of the School of Fine Arts.

96

ters" scattered across America. Very few held any ambitions toward the New York theater, which even then was in decline.

The School of Drama was unique to Yale in nearly every dimension and those attending were considered freaks by the regular student body. Our association with the sports-jacketed, corduroy-trousered, two-toned gumshoe undergraduate was absolutely nil. Although their fraternity and club houses surrounded the theater they rarely attended any of the performances. Thus we drifted almost unnoticed in the middle of an ivy Sargasso whose regular denizens were masters at looking right through us.

The differences were hopelessly irreconcilable. Yale was still a university for the sons of rich men, while most of the drama students were extremely poor, barely able to afford the most basic shelter and nourishment. One, Elia Kazan, whom we knew as Gadget, wore the same threadbare striped shirt nearly every day. He could not afford more, and to save pennies he shaved only when absolutely necessary. Oddest of all to the hallowed halls of Yale was our co-educational status and our living off-campus. Real Yale men, confined to beer, bulldog symbols, and singing "Boola Boola" in their dormitories, told enviously of the licentiousness and depravities enjoyed by those artistic weirdos in the Drama School. They never knew how right they were.

While many of us did indulge ourselves in a sort of common effort to prove we were free souls bounded only by the precepts of Bohemia, there were as many to whom our frivolities were contemptuous. These were the intellectuals, the solemn, and the ponderous, all of whom took themselves very seriously, many of them as devoted to the works of Marx and Engels as to Molière, Racine, and Shakespeare.

Almost all of these more contemplative individuals were enrolled in the 47 Workshop, Baker's own course in the writing of plays. Not even Mather could thrust me into such an exalted sanctum since the absolute minimum requirement was a bonafide bachelor's degree. An additional qualification was a written play submitted the previous year and approved by the master himself. Similarly the specialized disciplines of costume design, scenic design, and lighting specifically required formal documentation from a recognized college.

Unable to qualify officially for anything, I came under the rather loose aegis of one Alexander Dean, an over-fat potato-sack body supporting a lean and hungry mind. Dean's forte was directing, which he taught throughout the mornings in regular classes and engaged in himself the rest of the time in the major school productions. His temper was mercurial, his compliments lavish, and his disdain searing. His voice was high and extraordinarily penetrating, and he sweated copiously as if the magnificent performance he gave each day was his final mortal effort. In all, Dean was a sybarite to the very roots of his flabbiness, an unashamed exhibitionist, often pouting childlike in his demands for attention. He was also devoutly in love with all aspects of the theater and a very great teacher.

If Dean's intentions were ever suggestive he never went further than to slap me playfully with his fat moist hand, nor did his great rolling eyes ever suggest more intimate relations. Rather, he took me under his tutelage as if in defiance of his colleagues he would prove beyond doubt that an ex-military cadet could excel in their tight domain. He also saw at least a temporary solution to one of his long-standing problems, for Mather had advised him that I had some talent for acting.

Serious students of acting or those who hoped to make a career of public pretending did not enroll in the Yale School of Drama regardless of qualifications. They chose the American Academy of Acting in New York. Both Baker and Dean discouraged actor applicants, believing it too ephemeral a profession, too dependent on chance for success, and not demanding enough intellectually. But their attitude proved self-defeating when it came to casting the very plays written in Baker's workshop and costumed, lighted, directed, and designed by the other departments of the school. The majority of the students flatly refused to waste their time acting, or, with a few exceptions, obliged without talent. The lack was particularly critical in the category of juvenile male leads found in so many plays, and as a result my prime activity was decided almost from my first class under Alexander Dean.

I had told him I had come to Yale with the idea of becoming a director, preferably of great outdoor adventure movies. "Nonsense, my boy." Dean smiled. "Movies are for peasants, a crass business, not an art. I see you young, strong, uncomplicated, and forthright as the juvenile in *People on the Hill*. We start rehearsing immediately."

I thought of my father's "do what the other fellow does not do," and agreed to try acting the part. Nervous, now that I was so acutely aware of my educational shortcomings, I was willing to attempt anything if I could avoid disappointing Mather again. I had already become uncomfortable among people who quoted from Dante, spoke casually of Drury Lane pantomimes, or of professional familiarity with Commedia dell'Arte. The recent peak of my own reading had been *King of the Khyber Rifles*.

For the next two years I appeared in a series of Yale plays. Although I soon became less than enthusiastic about making a career of acting, I was also aware of its qualities, particularly the constant visibility it afforded in an atmosphere where I was so hopelessly outclassed.

There were additional rewards. While commanding my onstage behavior, Dean was at pains to tell me precisely why he wanted me to react in certain ways, thereby teaching me much of his own profession.

I learned many of the actor's tricks—how to avoid being upstaged and how to upstage others. I learned how to steal a scene by making the slightest movement at just the right time, how to strengthen a few lines of dialogue by grasping any handy object of furniture, how to keep the voice in low key so there would be room for expansion as emotions raged, how to cadence and build a scene, plant seemingly insignificant visual cues which would later prove vital, and even how to dominate a scene when the character's actual lines were few. These subtleties, defensive trickeries, and dramatic understandings became invaluable when later I ventured into the tough and unforgiving theatrical world.

"Some day, dear boy," Dean said while lounging across the edge of the stage apron like a stranded whale, "the gossamer will be torn from your eyes. You will discover actors are fierce competitors, artistic cannibals who will eat you for dinner unless you know how to avoid the pot. You may begin as only a walk-on carrying a spear. Just make sure someone doesn't shove it up your ass."

Dean also insisted I read continuously. "Your eyes are only holes in your head, dear boy. You can never wear them out by pouring the oceans of great art through them. If you never let your eyes rest perhaps you'll gain some weight in your brain."

I was awash and sometimes near drowning in dramatic masterworks and found it a feat in incongruity to remember what it was like to calculate range, elevation, and trajectory of a French 75, much less marching by the mumbles. Where the physical had been so long emphasized I now found the mental far more prized and my own capacity strained to the utmost.

Most inspiring of all events, even beyond the improvisations, electric monologues, and wild posturing of Alexander Dean, were the twice-weekly lectures of George Pierce Baker himself.

The man was a paradox, a mystical genius in his way, possessed of schizophrenic powers. In appearance he was the archetype college professor, complete with graying head too large for a body of sedentary conditioning. He wore pince-nez and walked with monarchical dignity. He was a short man with narrow sloping shoulders, finely boned hands, and a babylike skin. His voice was soft, almost diffident, and if he had announced himself as the sexton of any New England Baptist church the congregation would have been comfortable.

When he took the podium a transformation occurred and almost instantly the mild-mannered professor became whatever the dramatic gods ordained. These character exchanges occurred with lightning speed when he read Shakespeare. He became alternately coy, fierce, pleading, commanding, saintly, and cunning, according to the scene of his selection. Man or woman, child or crone, it made no difference; Baker could at his will become Lear, Desdemona, Iago, Puck, Antony, Macbeth, or all the witches. Listening to Baker read any dramatic work was unmitigated magic. Listening to him breathe life into the fire and caressing words of Shakespeare was a haunting voyage backward in time to the most exciting days of the Globe Theatre. I have never heard an actor, including the Barrymores or Olivier, match the thrilling Shakespearian quality of the dumpy little professor.

While regular students at the Drama School fought a constant and usually losing economic battle, I lived shamelessly in relative splendor, beyond even that of the Yale undergraduates. I shared an off-campus apartment with Gaillard Fryer, the easygoing roly-poly son of a McGill University professor. Above us in even more luxury lived Barbara O'Neil, one of the girl students, who was without competition in charm and beauty. During a rehearsal an upright piano capsized while being moved from one side of the stage to another. I happened to be pushing on the wrong side of the piano and suffered many contusions. For days afterward Barbara O'Neil, who would one day become a famous actress, came regularly down from her loft to tend my wounds and needs. I regarded her as descending directly from heaven.

Of all this my father, now in direct command of a worldwide telephonic complex, took a sour view. He had moved to Chicago, establishing the family hearth in a huge apartment building overlooking Lake Michigan. He had furnished it with heavy furniture, crystal, precious bric-a-brac, several fine paintings, and his personal library of Wodehouse, Zane Grey, Tarkington, and Sinclair Lewis. (Even though he objected to Lewis's portrait of Babbitt.) Although the Great Depression was still deepening, he continued to give lavish parties with buckets of champagne and favors of expensive perfume for the ladies. Above all he wanted to provide comfort for my mother whose health was becoming more in doubt, a mysterious debilitating malady not even the most expensive doctors seemed able to identify.

While my father looked down upon the educational activities of his only son with such tolerance as he could muster, his digestion sometimes suffered during lunch in the executive dining room. There, as the great of the corporation gathered in wary bonhomie, he found it difficult to match the familial comments of his more fortunate associates.

"My boy has one more year at Princeton. Going into law, he says. . . ."

"Alice and I had a letter from our youngest just yesterday. He's doing very well at the bank. . . ."

"Hard to believe I'm already a grandfather with a boy who knows a lot more about the market than I do. . . ."

". . . mining engineer . . . geologist . . . he's with Dutch Shell Oil now. . . ."

Amid the obligatory congratulations and hearty hohos, it was trying for my father to enjoy his after-lunch Havana. Could he say that his son was studying for the stage, even considering becoming an *actor?* Everyone knew they were at best charming scoundrels, charlatans, and poor of credit rating. Unknowing, I had denied my father the ancient rite of braggadocio, and thus inflicted upon him the sorest of petty cruelties. His trials were far from over.

It was a time of telegrams. People sent telegrams indiscriminately, as a mark of prestige, as tokens of affection, as thank yous for a hearty dinner, to make appointments or confirm plights of love. There were two companies in the United States: Western Union and Postal Telegraph. Both offered excellent service and employed uniformed messengers to deliver the enormous harvest of their wires.

Major C.J. Herzer
Durham Building, Chicago
I regret to report that I cannot comply with the active duty orders issued me as business requires me to be in the East at this time. Kindest personal regards.
      Second Lieutenant Ernest Gann
      Five hundred and thirty-first
      Coast Artillery.

My years in military schools augmented by two summers in the cavalry had resulted in the official creation of yet another downy-cheeked second lieutenant in the reserve. Since there was not the slightest possibility of war, I saw no reason to serve in the Major's Coast Artillery unit* during summer training and prayed he

---

* The military machine was quite as illogical before computers added to the confusion. I had been trained as a field artillery officer with some cavalry service. Instead of being assigned to a similar unit I was slotted into the Coast Artillery, custodians of huge stationary (and even then

would believe my "business" so demanding he would classify me a "hardship case."

In my thoughts there was no subterfuge. More than a little of my father's philosophy had taken root in me despite my strenuous efforts to avoid it. Unconsciously, I was trying to please him and therefore described almost every endeavor as a "business." Now, gasping unhealthily for air while breathing my praises, Alexander Dean had persuaded the Cape Playhouse at Dennis, Massachusetts, to sign on an untried juvenile actor for the summer season. It was, considering that theater's prestige and my scanty experience, an almost incredible opportunity, for all the great of the theatrical world scouted Dennis and many of the theater's finest stars appeared regularly. I tried to coat the pill for my father by assuring him I would actually be paid for my services in this new "business." He doubted its worth. How could a self-respecting young man be paid honestly for pretending he was someone he was not?

The Cape Playhouse at Dennis was one of the first Eastern summer stock theaters. Raymond Moore, a tall, languid, unhappy man who drove a sixteen-cylinder Cadillac roadster, was the owner-manager. He set my salary at an impressive fifty dollars a week. He employed George Somnes as the director, a talented man who bickered constantly with his employer. Watching them and the weekly change of cast removed the first gauze of glamour from my conception of the professional theater. Fortunately for my innocence, there was no available competition for the juvenile roles.

All of the professionals who came to the Cape helped me most willingly and tried to improve my bumbling style. They knew and I knew that acting would never be my forte if only because my real-life emotional experience had been so shallow. Nor was I particularly interested in exposing myself to the banks of white blobs beyond the footlights, which on the few occasions I dared look became faces. I felt naked and uncomfortable. My

---

obsolete) cannons. Not too many years later as war loomed, the Coast Artillery took over anti-aircraft defenses. I attempted a transfer to the Air Force where I reasoned my considerable experience as a pilot might be useful. Request denied. Anti-aircraft officers could not be spared. Although I had never seen an anti-aircraft gun I could easily have viewed the war from a bunker while shooting at fellow aeronauts.

voice sounded as if it belonged to a stranger and frequently threatened to leave my control. Yet with sympathy and encouragement I was able to remain on stage without obvious panic, playing opposite such Broadway luminaries as Katherine Alexander, Earle Larimore, Spring Byington, Frances Fuller, Henry Hull, Ilka Chase, and Ruth Gordon. There were also Tom Powers, with whom I was destined to appear under more important circumstances, and a Hollywood starlet appearing under the saucy name of Freya Leigh. Her acting talents were as limited as my own, but our friendship, through a long series of apparently unrelated circumstances, proved to be of much higher quality. I could not then conceive of her as a real-life heroine, a beautiful woman who would demonstrate extraordinary courage in concealing American fliers downed in France during World War II. The French government would decorate her with their highest honors. Nor would I have believed we would rendezvous again during that same war or that her shelter and mercy would mean so much to me.

The summer of my first genuine theatrical employment left me uncertain of my ambitions, yet I decided to join my fellow troupers in a life of glamour and greasepaint. Anything, I thought, would be preferable to the alternative I knew waited in the telephone business. I wondered intolerantly at my father's patience with the steady, deliberate, and so-solid citizens who shared his business day. I longed to roam the world with the modish, the spirited, the charming, the impious, and the morally corrupt. I would become a mountebank and a scoundrel along with them if necessary, rather than die early in some business dungeon, my jailers selected from the ranks of executive respectability.

Chapter 9

The summer at the Cape Playhouse was deceptive. I mistook the seductive sound of vacationers' applause and the comfortably larded praise of the visiting professionals, who were themselves on a paid holiday, as guarantee of immediate recognition once my talents were displayed in the true arena. Hence, I decided not to waste another year at the Yale School: instead, in classic fashion, I set off to conquer Broadway.

Soon Broadway became like a familiar village with one invisible wall running along Sixth Avenue on the east, a seedy, decrepit area of pawnshops, filthy one-arm eating stands, and secondhand clothing shops. Rising above the surrounding rubble was an aging red brick structure known as the Hippodrome. Relic of the preceding easier century, it was already having trouble finding spectacles to fill its cavernous maw.

Carnegie Hall and Fifty-seventh Street were considered the northern boundary of Broadway, but only serious music lovers ventured so far; the real northern rampart ran along Fifty-fifth Street. Eighth Avenue, a wide street lined with weary two- and three-story buildings weeping for care and paint, comprised the western frontier. Madison Square Garden, not considered an honest part of Broadway, at least served as a prominent way post. Show folk who ventured farther west on visits to the home offices of Warner Brothers Pictures or Fox Films found themselves stalking the artistic prairielands, which extended from Eighth Avenue to the Hudson River.

The southerly wall of Broadway town was the famous Forty-second Street, already in decay, a street haunted by former glories, demoted in caste by cheap movie theaters, burlesque, tattoo parlors, and shooting galleries.

The very heart of Broadway was one half-block from the street itself, a lane cutting between Forty-forth and Forty-fifth Streets known as Shubert Alley.* The first thing a theatrical hopeful learned was the way to this hallowed strip of cement, there to speculate on the presence of the powerful Shubert brothers in their offices above the theater also bearing their name, there to dream of the surely coming night when he might stand in this identical location and observe his name illuminated on the marquees of the Morosco, the Imperial, the Booth, the Barrymore, or any of the surrounding theaters. From the area around this accidental epicenter, thousands of invisible tentacles reached out to what was left of real-

---

* Shubert Alley was unique and very real. (It is still there.) Tin Pan Alley, a honeycomb of frayed studios and offices, was only a mythical phrase employed to designate that general location.

life entertainment in America. All the shows intended for the road originated within a thousand yards of Shubert Alley and even the final decisions involving major motion pictures were made in the home offices of Paramount, Metro-Goldwyn-Mayer, RKO, and Columbia, all situated in Broadway village.

The professionals at Cape Playhouse had insisted that September was the month when casting for the winter's plays began. Not even the cauldron temperature and the dripping humidity of Manhattan could melt my enthusiasm and confidence when, with shocking disregard for artistic convention, I took up residence at the Army and Navy Club.

Day after September day the sun hammered upon the monuments of stone which housed and fed the bedraggled inhabitants of Manhattan. The rich were away in the country, not yet returned to their metropolitan pleasures, the commuters left work early, irritable and bageyed. Even the suburbs were swathed in heat. The unemployed, of which there were countless numbers, gathered at dawn in the food lines west of Eighth Avenue.

I saw nothing incongruous in my efforts to join a world of art while living in the flag-bedecked, regimental-medallioned atmosphere of the Army and Navy Club. I had returned to the womb I knew, sallying forth in search of work long before most of Shubert Alley had even considered awakening. At night, in a room even smaller than my very first at the academy, I wrote great plays, smudging the ink with frequent droplets of my sweat. I also wrote a continuous stream of letters to ease my loneliness and avoid thoughts of expensive carnal indulgence. To Alexander Dean I gave promise he would soon be hearing of employment, to Charles Mather a review of my successful summer and a plea to read my play when it was done. To Eleanor, in St. Paul, with whom I had not communicated for more than a year, I scribbled a fanciful report of my inability to find other girls to equal her charms. To my mother and father an equally imaginative prospectus on my immediate theatrical future and a forlorn description of my spartan surroundings, the debilitating heat, and my frugal ways. Touched, if disbelieving, they promptly sent me a check for one hundred dollars, most of which I as promptly spent on an ingénue whose invitational smile and Southern accent rendered me vulnerable.

Although many aspired, there were only a handful of true grandes dames in the city of New York, each scheming, maneuvering, and commanding in her own milieu. In the theater, Margaret Pemberton, a raven-haired, umber-skinned lady of ample proportions, reigned supreme. She was, as were all grandes dames, a powerful personality, always seeking to expand her empire, imperious and insistent, fanged to enemies and potential rivals, unstintingly helpful and generous to those she considered worthy. Margaret Pemberton's eyes were nearly black, sparkling with humor, intelligence, wit, and venom. She was in every aspect, except her championship of the young or troubled, far from beautiful. Her breasts sagged and her nose was too large for her face. She attempted to be a leader of fashion, but her taste too often approached the bizarre and she loaded herself with so much cheap jewelry she clinked and clanged like a gypsy wagon.

The Pembertons' East Side salon usually opened its gates between the hours of six and eight and all of the theatrical great were made welcome by the hostess. She was careful to include as many hopefuls as the already successful, thereby perpetuating her benign rule over ever more personalities. The number of fruitful meetings thus provided between job givers and seekers was incalculable.

A not-so-warm welcome was extended by producer Brock Pemberton, who regarded his wife's social affairs and nearly everything and everyone else with torpid disapproval. He was a shy man, introspective, thoughtful, caustic, and cynical. He was of medium build sliding toward paunchiness, baldheaded, and flat of voice. He did smile on those rare occasions when he was pleased, but what actually triggered the so temporary light in his washed blue eyes was difficult to identify. Only those who finally won his confidence realized he was possessed by his own devil of inferiority when surrounded, as he was day and night, by such obvious and exuberant glamour. He was a scholar, a verbal hermit who mixed ill with the chatter and posing and instability of those who came to his theater and to his hearth.

He was also in love with the remarkable woman who directed his many successful plays, Antoinette Perry.

For these and a conglomerate of his own secret reasons, Brock Pemberton often found excuse to absent himself from his wife's soirees.

Margaret Pemberton put her considerable powers to work in my behalf immediately after I arrived in her special grand duchy. Waving her pencil like a scepter she charged to the telephone and began a series of audiences with those subjects who were either indebted to her or afraid of her. I was stunned with her cavalier treatment of individuals whose very names were royalty in the legitimate theater.

"Theresa . . . there's a young man I want you to see immediately. He would be just right for *The Good Earth.* . . ."

"Jed! How are you, dear? Let me tell you about . . ."

"Gilbert, darling, what time can you see a most talented young man today? . . ."

My embarrassment at her wild descriptions of my worth, of which she was almost entirely innocent, faded as I weighed the hours and days I might have waited in the outer offices of such people hoping for at least a moment's notice. In less than half an hour she had arranged a sheaf of interviews and I set off blithely through the blazing sun, blind to those less fortunate who were spilling out of their brownstone ovens in search of relief. My own search was just beginning, I knew, but I had youth, superb health, and a certain dash which many mistook for confidence.

Not surprisingly my first appointment was with Brock Pemberton, who inquired acidly what the hell I thought I was doing play-acting when he understood I came from a nice family of considerable means. After grumping ominously, he listened to me read from his coming play, *Ceiling Zero.** I read the part of a young airmail pilot, totally unaware I would eventually be playing the role in real life. At the end of the reading Pemberton said he would see what he could see and would keep me in mind.

I knew the battle was lost before I escaped.

* Starring Osgood Perkins, father of Anthony Perkins.

The next appointment was with Jed Harris, renowned as the most difficult of producers. Wild tales were told of his idiosyncrasies and harsh language. Even many stars were said to fear the awesome Jed Harris,* but he was reputed to be a slight man and I thought at worst we might come to blows. He was also reputed to be a genius.

In Harris's outer office I was greeted by James Shute, an incongruously kindly young man, considering the reputation of his employer. He was almost a caricature of the cultured New Englander, his diction cautiously modulated, his suit and tie better suited to a bank official. He said automatically, but politely enough, "Mr. Harris is busy. Mr. Harris is always busy."

"But I have an appointment."

"Meaningless. Mr. Harris gives appointments to hundreds of people and ignores them all. I should say your chances might be better without one. If you drop around once a day for a year or so it is just possible you might catch the great man at the right moment. Do you live nearby?"

"At the Army and Navy Club."

Shute was visibly shocked. "For heaven's sake, what are you doing in a place like that? We are not hiring soldiers, or sailors for that matter."

Something about the way Shute said "for heaven's sake" combined perfectly with his quaint manner and sympathetic tone so I told him the whole of my story including my wish for a job as a stage manager rather than as an actor.

"That will take you a few years, friend. Come back tomorrow about this same time. The genius may fire me for trying, but I'll try to sneak you in somehow."

I returned the next day and the next until Shute finally ushered me into the genius's presence. There was no light in his office except an oval blob created by the single lamp on Harris's desk. He was in shirt sleeves, his hair wild and untamed, his jaws nearly black with several days' growth of beard. Feet on his desk, perched catlike on the edge of his tilted chair, he glowered at me as if I were an unpleasant creature emerged from some subterranean tunnel. His black penetrating eyes seemed to

---

* In contrast to *Sam* Harris, who was much admired.

express a special loathing of me as I ventured to mention his conversation with Margaret Pemberton.

"She's a bitch," he said carelessly. "I'd tell her anything to get her off my neck. What do you want?"

I told him while he fumbled and scratched at his crotch and half listened. Among the petty tyrants I had met I thought he had no match for boorishness. Then suddenly he held up his hand to interrupt my talk and in the blob of light I saw his teeth flash in what might pass for a smile.

"Have you got any money?" he asked as casually as if inquiring of my health.

When I told him I had enough to last out the month he smiled again, but this time in open disappointment.

"Go away," he said solemnly. "Right now I need money. Then I'll have jobs. Leave your name with Jimmie."

"How did the genius behave?" Shute asked when I returned to the outer office. I offered that he seemed to need money.

"Indeed he does. He always does. And so do I since the ghost hasn't walked around here in weeks. By the by, would you be interested in sharing an apartment? That club of yours is a bit stuffy, isn't it?"

I told him as soon as I found work my interest in moving would be more realistic. "Tomorrow I have an appointment with Gilbert Miller. Maybe something will come of it."

"You do get around for a beginner," Shute said, blowing out his cheeks. "Mind you, Gilbert Miller is *the* producer in New York, money coming out of his ears, lavish productions, the lot. A word of advice. Mention any social connections you might have since he sits up nights reading *Burke's Peerage*. And if you work for him, beware. I've heard he has a terrible temper."

Gilbert Miller proved to be a fat man, bushy of hair and high of voice. Although he was an American he affected a British accent and elaborately genteel ways. He was a devout sybarite, in love with England, where he had often produced West End successes. In contrast to Jed Harris's moldy office, Miller's was heavy with lush solidity and the admirable personal tastes of its proprietor. Fine oil paintings graced the walls, the carpeting was quiet and costly, and vases of flowers accented the beautiful mahogany furniture in the outer office. Miller's staff, overcorrect and politely crisp, reflected the anglophile in their employer.

He came out from behind his enormous polished desk, greeting me warmly, eyeing the conservative suit I had decided to wear in spite of the heat, and the club tie which I had bought only that morning. While he inquired of Margaret Pemberton's well-being, instinct sparked by Shute warned me I must use every advantage I might have to stand out from the double row of suppliants I had passed in the outer office. So I told him of my father and his activities in England (as if I knew what they were all about) and made mention of Culver Military Academy and of Yale, and particularly of polo, all of which I saw gained his attentive approval. It was a rank appeal to his known proclivities and I knew it was working even as I continued unashamed, for my target was a job.

Miller's eyes and manner warmed as the interview concluded, until he said there must certainly be something for me in his new production of *Firebird*, which would star Judith Anderson. "You could play the messenger boy," he said. "It isn't much more than a walk-on so you could double as assistant stage manager."

Firebird was produced at the Empire Theater, a gold-prosceniumed, flying-cherub-ceilinged, elderly theater actually situated on the street called Broadway. It was a critical success thanks to Judith Anderson's performance and the customary exquisite Gilbert Miller production. I found Miller pleasant enough to get along with and only once saw him lay his famous temper upon an underling. I enjoyed my job and the people about me; here I thought was a life of proper reward and excitement. I had developed a great affection for the lovely blond girl Whitney Bourne, who also played a walk-on, and such was my euphoria that I broke away from the confinement of the Army and Navy Club to share an apartment with Jimmy Shute. We went so far as to hire a cook manservant, a Chinese named Dak Sue who was happy to leave the Depression dole and accept free room and board plus five dollars a week.

111

The apartment was a split-level affair at Fifty-ninth Street and the East River. For fifty-five dollars a month rent we had a view of the Queensboro Bridge and a slice of the river. There we entertained in spite of a minimum of furniture. There were three mattresses, but no beds. We slept on the floor. We had bought one couch, punctured everywhere as if wounded by shrapnel. Four old kitchen chairs and a card table provided our dining arrangements. Dak Sue, whose command of English was almost entirely profane, served our guests with a flourish and a total disregard for spillage.

While most of the world slipped deeper into economic distress with consequent human woe we seemed to ride ever higher. Even Shute's paycheck was coming more regularly to his hand and I thought myself amply funded by Gilbert Miller at sixty dollars a week.

Winter came, with the snows as always softening the hardness of Manhattan. We were warm while much of America was not. Except for our vastly different tastes in music, with Shute devoted to Bach, Handel, Haydn, and Wagner, while I preferred the more contemporary works of Fats Waller, we lived in agreeable harmony, sharing all costs and yet each of us usually going his own way. Whenever our schedules did permit we enjoyed our developing friendship; I was always intrigued with Shute's intellect, his dry wit, and innate air of dignity. He was outspoken in his regard for me as a sort of muscular phenomenon whose sheer energy might someday overcome the conceits, calumnies, treacheries, and overall perils of Broadway.

This state of bliss continued for months until very suddenly *Firebird* closed and my salary ceased. In my innocence I had taken it for granted that *Firebird* would run for a year or more and had spent all as it came in. Now, overnight, I was flat broke.

I looked and scratched persistently for even a rumor of possible work while Shute supported us on his barely adequate salary. Regretfully, we told Dak Sue he must find other employers. He refused flatly and profanely to leave. Soon I fell into the habit which has afflicted and supported all show people since the first strolling players kept need at bay by maintaining that unreality was reality. Tomorrow and tomorrow and tomorrow the gods would smile. Tomorrow the abyss would close, some fluke, some twist of fortune, some wise and brilliant individual would provide before the unthinkable occurred; before the make-believe and the sound of applause, no matter how faint, must be abandoned for duller work.

Daily I explored and further learned the intricate pathways of Broadway. I knew the quickest way from the office of producer A to producer B, every curbing, every manhole spouting steam into the winter's blast, every doorway and stair leading to a source of hope. Passing the dreary apple-sellers, their ragged coat collars pulled high against the chill, I knew an occasional moment of empathy for their lot. I soon learned Shute's money would better fill my belly at noon by ordering soup at the Automat. The roll included in the price made a tasty sandwich when smeared with free ketchup. Once hungering near Fourteenth Street, where I had gone to investigate a job which proved non-existent, I slipped into the Bowery Mission for the midday serving. Before that ceremony I stood guiltily among the forlorn, the truly aching hungry, and the not-quite-drunk, singing "Throw Out the Lifeline."

My indigence was a sham, play-acting in itself, and I knew it. One telephone call to the grand apartment in Chicago would have brought me ample funds with the speed of telegraphy. Yet I could not bring myself, after such repeated declarations of independence, to hear my father say, "I told you so," or, worse, "I wash my hands of you." Even as I crossed and recrossed Shubert Alley day after day, I could see my father pursing his lips and frowning in righteous indignation. His one good eye would fix upon me accusingly, saying in its marvelously expressive way how I deserved all the anguish now mine because I had turned traitor to my caste and heritage. A theater person, indeed!

Along the way I met innumerable people, some helpful, many uncaring, and most in the same predicament as my own. Billy Rose, energetic and exciting with hardly more age on him than I could claim, was kind and fair and for nearly a week I was certain I'd won the lead in *Merry Go Round*. But eventually he chose another* and

---

* Elisha Cook, Jr., a much better actor.

once more hope was stabbed. It was as soon resurrected by agent Leland Hayward, who arranged a movie test with the same Southern ingénue I had once pursued. The test was made at a studio located on the west bank of the Hudson where Edison had first experimented with his revolutionary camera. Far more interested in the lights and camera equipment, nostalgic for my youthful excitements at Ray-Bell, my acting was distracted. It was possibly one of the worst movie tests ever photographed and deservedly came to naught.

At this appropriate moment David Lesan, a former student at the Yale Drama School, appeared on the scene, likewise discouraged and unable to find theatrical employment. He said there might be something open away from the watering hole where the whole zoo insisted on drinking. Chicago too had a theater of sorts and his dilapidated Ford would take us there if only we had money for fuel.

Shute, ever unruffled and generous, floated yet another and even more risky loan. He knew I was at last bound home to Mother, a defection which would obviously cause him great inconvenience, but he refrained from all but encouraging words. He saw us off into a raging blizzard, both of us wondering unhappily if we would ever see each other again.

Chapter 10

My father's one good eye caught the pall of discouragement wreathing his son almost from the moment I shook the snow from my coat and again entered his domain. He was properly sympathetic, even appearing to be interested in my theatrical tribulations, but his ultimate target remained unchanged.

"These are difficult times," he said while clearing his throat, making a church steeple with his fingertips, and squirming slightly in his chair, always a physical demonstration preceding an important announcement. "You should see what is going on in the world. I suggest a trip around it."

The arms of the clan were wide open in welcome.

"Now, suh, I will personally finance the trip since I

would not want it thought I had authorized such an exploratory expense in the company's behalf." (His associate executives, jealous of his power, would be delighted to catch him at financial nepotism.) "You should meet the people we know and work with abroad, and become as well acquainted as possible. However, we must be very careful they do not entertain the notion you might be some sort of spy from the home office." (His cronies in the executive lunchroom might find any protest from the overseas affiliates very useful in furthering their own ambitions.) "You should start in London with our man in charge of European operations, René Pleven. Who knows? You may find this business more interesting than you think."

The church steeple collapsed while my father lit a Havana and waited for agreement.

I had not yet learned the folly of underestimating my father, nor had I the wit to analyze how his determination and drive had placed him so high in the tribal councils that only one man, the legendary A. F. Adams, outranked him. Now he had not only sensed his son's disenchantment with all things theatrical, but had deliberately chosen the most intriguing of his associates to send me to. I was to learn that, unlike the dull fellows who seemed to me representative of the telephone business, Pleven was a connoisseur of fine art, a literary glutton, and a diplomat with a thorough knowledge of European financial and political affairs. He was later to become the French Minister of Finance, Minister of Defense, and for a time Premier of France.

I surrendered to the offer with mixed feelings of guilt and excitement. Suddenly, a comfortable post somewhere in my father's empire looked more inviting. I promised to write reports of my observations while being careful to explain I had no official connection with the parent company.

My father bade me bon voyage with a generous letter of credit and a full portfolio of introductory letters to the powerful in his world. As it happened, I was to spend too much of the money recklessly, on my own conception of a broadening education, gathering as if by plan a changing consortium of colorful harlots, pimps, thieves, and assorted rascals. The letter of credit failed me only once, a

115

surprise which taught me in minutes the artificial and tenuous value of money itself.

I was in Fez, Morocco, learning mainly of the entranced effect of Amer Picon when drunk in the company
of young French officers serving in the Foreign Legion.
After a night of carousing, which included a passionate
exhibition by buxom Oulad Naïl dancers, I awoke the following afternoon to find I had spent my last centime.
Hungry and repentant I descended upon the Bank of British West Africa to restore my finances. Presenting my
letter of credit I said a few thousand francs would do.

"But, Monsieur, it is impossible," the teller lamented.
He explained then how during the night, while my entire
concentration was fixed upon the revolving hips of a
young female from the Moroccan desert, the President of
my country, a Monsieur Roosevelt, had closed all the
American banks. Until they reopened, my letter of credit
was worthless.

The financial world I had thought so dependable, if
dull, had crumbled overnight leaving me a beggar in an
alien land. I offered my camera through the teller's window as security against enough money to eat.

The teller, a Moroccan who seemed genuinely shocked
at the specter of an insolvent American, said he was un-
authorized to negotiate. But he asked me to wait while he
consulted with the manager. Soon I was ushered toward
his tiny office in the rear of the bank.

Guthrie was a smiling Scot with cherry-colored cheeks
and perpetually amused eyes. He was short and stocky, a
formidable man with the heavy-fingered hands of a laborer. The teller had brought him my camera. He held it
out to me.

"I fear the Bank of British West Africa is not quite set
up for this sort of thing," he said solemnly.

I told him of my foolishness during the preceding night
and of my present raving hunger.

"You may become much hungrier because it may be
several days before the American banks reopen. There
is only one solution," Guthrie said checking his watch.
"I'll put you up until this thing blows over. The cuisine
at my digs isn't much, but—"

During the next week while the sensationally inclined
French newspapers raved of the impending American

revolution, of panic in the American city streets, Guthrie's constant solidity reassured me. "No bloody reason to flap," he smiled. "And no reason to abandon your tour."

From René Pleven in London and finally from my father in Chicago I received further encouragement to continue on as planned. Carried away with new self-importance and half-baked knowledge I began to take my mission seriously. From Guthrie's flat in the Medina of Fez, which had not greatly changed in two thousand years, I tried very hard to see the surrounding world through what I thought might be the eyes of my father.

". . . I have been fortunate in making acquaintance with several of Fez's principal merchants and had opportunity to talk business and conditions with them. . . . I can best illustrate the telephonic possibilities by telling of my friend the Sherif Amryni who owns a fifty-room house. His staff of slaves is considerable and he has one antiquated telephone in his establishment which he rarely uses. Why should a man bother with a telephone when it is so much more pleasant to talk business over a steaming glass of hot tea? Hence I believe you can dismiss the old city of Fez as a possible market. . . ." Although I knew my industry at reporting would please my father, I did not yet appreciate how much more avidly he would have read a chronicle of my night with the Oulad Naïl.

Now linked by financial osmosis to a great international cartel, I made honest attempt to join in spirit. The members of the telephonic companies known as the Group were the Strowger Automatic Telephones of England, Automatique Électrique de Belgique, and the tremendous Siemens and Halske of Germany. They operated under a Zurich Agreement which in essence bound them not to undersell each other in international markets. With the exception of Sweden's Ericksson Company, the Group had thus managed an iron grip upon the supply of telephonic equipment to the world and a considerable portion of its operation. Since the majority of contracts were made with national governments, the diplomatic and political aspects were quite as important as the technical.

The various American companies under my father's direct command were also party to the Zurich Agreement. Likewise were the subsidiaries in Italy, Portugal, the Philippines, China, and Japan. As a scion of such empire

117

I at least had the decency not to embarrass my father abroad, and when in the company of the innumerable consuls and plenipotentiaries scattered across the world I strove to maintain a suitable dignity. My favorite garb of corduroys and sweaters was long left behind and my wardrobe now reflected the basic theme. Carried in my considerable dunnage was my penguin outfit—white tie and tailcoat plus collapsible top hat. Nestling with them, a hammer-tailed morning coat and striped pants for formal daytime occasions, plus a black tie dinner jacket for ordinary evenings.

My traveling wear consisted of a heavy Scotch tweed suit for the northern climes, and a blue business suit of ultraconservative cut which served me well during obligatory visits to factories and offices of the Group. In addition there were two suits of white and a cork helmet for service in the tropics, or, as I apologized to the mirror, for elephant hunting. Finally, there was a portable typewriter for letters and reports, and as a wistful gesture to lost Bohemia a record player with music selected to relieve my pomposity. Outfitted to the nines, I moved about the world as minor royalty.

After Antwerp, where I tried to take a genuine interest in the Belgian works, I went on to Berlin where I learned more about the burning of the Reichstag and the carnal pleasures of the Kurfürstendamm than I did of Siemens and Halske's enormous electrical complex. Yet I was learning to mind my manners in the presence of the powerful, even though inner rebellion still scraped and pounded at the bronze doors closing upon my apparent destiny.

My impressive portfolio of introductory letters was but half presented to the addresses when I boarded the *Suwa Maru* at Naples, bound for the Far East. I looked forward to a month of personal adventuring without obligation to caste or system and the total abandonment of my role as a pseudo-businessman.

The *Suwa Maru?* The tangling of events and lives is not confined to human beings. During the Korean War when I was once again flying fodder to the cannons and returning with the torn remnants and the dead, we usually paused for a day of mandatory recuperation at Wake Island in the Pacific. Stranded on the south beach of that lonely atoll was a Japanese ship deliberately run aground during World War II when the crew thought they were being attacked by an American submarine. She was the *Suwa Maru,* a gaping hole in her starboard side, her red bones rusting in the blazing sun. While her hull was half submerged and listing some twenty degrees, her upper works were reasonably intact, all of her a silent witness to the bloody career of a minute but important atoll nearly lost in a gigantic ocean.

I swam out to the *Suwa Maru* and after some exploration found a way to her foredeck. From there I managed to slip aft along her upper deck far enough to peer into what had once been her main salon. I was instantly rewarded by visions of another time and faces still familiar to me because their images were still framed on my wall at home. We were posed in a group at the costume ball held somewhere in the Indian Ocean. There was the ship's captain, Takahashi, smiling bashfully from behind a life ring set on the floor as a centerpiece to the group, and Raoul de la Chevaleri, a charming Belgian, costumed as a maharaja. There was his son Guy as an Arab sheik, and Murdock and Conway, both English civil servants returning to India, one costumed as a Buddhist priest, the other as a gypsy. There was Count Sugimura, a fat and jolly Japanese dignitary who had boarded the *Suwa Maru* because as chief of the Japanese delegation he had recently walked out of the League of Nations and must return to report to his Emperor. Sugimura was wearing a fez he had bought in Port Said and was surrounded by his family and staff disguised variously as pirates, harem ladies, clowns, and incredibly, his wife in blackface as Aunt Jemima. There was also Randall, the editor of the newspaper in Kuala Lumpur who had invited me to stay with him in Malaya. And most fascinating of all in this moment of resurrection was Sugimura's daughter Kazu, an exquisite girl who had captured me completely. She is wearing pieces of Raoul de la Chevaleri's uniform and for some reason has blackened her beautiful face. I was standing on a chair in the last row wearing a uniform borrowed from one of the sailors, my hands clasped in front, my head tilted quizzically and a rather silly smile on my face. Perhaps I was a little drunk, which may have been why Count Sugimura and family always did their best to chaperone meetings between their precious Kazu and myself.

Enthralled with what I could see of the salon's ruins I wondered if it was in this life or during some other that I had danced across this very space of gently sloshing water. I had only to close my eyes to hear the band again, a mixed bag of musicians from the crew who somehow managed to inflict an oriental lilt with minor key half-notes into any dance tune they played. I could hear the laughter, I could hear the giggling of the smaller Sugimura children, I could hear the *Suwa Maru*'s great bronze bell tolling eight times at noon.

I could not reach my old stateroom. It was deep below the water's surface, visible but unattainable, occupied now by fishes instead of my extravagant dreams.

I was a long time exploring what was left of the *Suwa Maru*. Wherever I looked there was at least a minor link to another life of my own and another era for the world. Suddenly, standing waist deep in water, braced against the irregular surge of the sea along her canted deck, I realized I had died somewhere along the line, or at least a piece of me had, and what remained alive was now as if reincarnated, visiting the exact site of that other existence.

And sometimes now, when I pause to look at the small Japanese tori I caused to be built outside our house, the same haunting notion flickers across my mind. For hanging from the tori, now planted in the earth of my island farm, is the *Suwa Maru*'s great one-hundred-and-seventy-five-pound bronze bell. Below the name is engraved the year of her launching, 1914, and N.Y.K. for her owners. Inside the bell's mouth some long lost Wake Island Marine took brush in hand and painted: TO HELL WITH TOJO.

Still, inanimates do not always boomerang in such neat circles. During the same Korean War we were quartered temporarily in Tokyo. At first opportunity I took a taxi to the Diet Building, and then a few blocks farther until I became uneasy at my lack of familiarity with the area. I paid off the driver and using the Diet Building as a guide-mark sought my old street, Nagata-Cho 2 Chome, where, still under the aegis of my father, I had completed my telephonic education. I had rented a small house at the end of the street complete with two serving girls and for months lived strictly as a Japanese. It was a sublime other life, as I learned far more about the Japanese than of their need for telephones. Mrs. Kondo, my gracious landlady, gave me Japanese lessons each morning; her husband taught me the game "Go" every afternoon. As I sat writing in the little garden behind my house the serving girls would apologize for intruding upon my privacy, then dip water from a bucket and throw it against the surrounding wooden fence. They were cooling the air.

Late in the afternoon, when the sticky, humid heat of summertime Tokyo began to subside, the same girls would escort me to my bath. It was the usual barrel-like wooden tub, marvelously soft to the touch, but this facility was different from any I had seen before. Once I was fully immersed, only my head protruding like a jack-in-the-box, the girls would raise a sliding door and the special delight of my bath would begin. For the tub was equipped with small wheels and stood on a cement ramp. The girls giggled their amusement as they shoved me down the ramp and into the narrow street. My initial embarrassment was momentary. Almost to a man all of my neighbors had made a similar launching and now sat steaming, splashing, and gossiping in front of their houses. They welcomed me—round eyes, Ivory soap-skin and all. In time my Japanese became sufficient enough to remark on the weather and understand a few of their comments on the events of the day. My pride was very great when Mrs. Kondo told me my neighbors were pleased with my conduct and admiring of my efforts to live in their way.

I slept upstairs on the tatami, wished peaceful sleep by the same girls as they closed the mosquito netting about me. The same angels hung a different painted scroll in the alcove at the foot of the stairs every morning, complementing the painting with a different flower arrangement.

Living in the little house in Tokyo became one of the most rewarding and delightful experiences of my life. There I had learned much of the goodness of human beings and almost nothing of their evil. Because of my days in the little house I only reluctantly left Japan before I went completely Asiatic. My departure was observed in traditional style by my neighbors who joined me in maudlin rivers of tears.

While the cruelties of the Second World War shattered my affection for the Japanese man, there still lingered sweet pieces of the joys I had known in Nagata-Cho. Now, during Korea, less believing but still hopeful, I sought at least a momentary return to innocence, some physical reminder like the *Suwa Maru* to reassure me my memories were real.

Alas, I could not even find Nagata-Cho, much less 2 Chome (the second block). Nothing whatever was even vaguely recognizable. The Diet Building stood where it had always been, but behind it everything had been fire-bombed by my own flying comrades. Nothing remained, not a stick, a stone, a flower, a wooden tub, or a painted scroll. Mrs. Kondo was gone, and her husband as well. The servant girls had disappeared in fire and smoke. My neighbors were gone and the very streets obliterated. Nothing . . . nothing . . . nothing . . .

Chapter 11

Sixteen days out of Suez the aging *Suwa Maru* eased into Colombo, Ceylon, and the vibration of her engines ceased. I disembarked in white cottons and "pith" helmet, very self-conscious in assuming what I thought of as my part in the white man's burden. I had not read Kipling for nothing and even if Ceylon was somewhat removed from his territory, there were elephants to ride upon and a satisfying enough Pukka Sahib atmosphere.

I set about my own idea of further education by first hiring an interpreter and starting off for the island's deepest forests in search of a tribe of wild men rumored to be still in the interior. The search began along paved roads as far as Kandy and on the third day became a genuine safari consisting of a guide, six porters, and myself. We forded a river during the middle of the third day and trekked off through swamp and jungle past the ruins of ancient Anuradhapura, and thence into more than I had bargained for.

I had not really believed we would actually find any

wild men until a ranger in one of the government rest houses confirmed the stories I had heard of their existence. He was a taciturn Ceylonese, obviously with some recent British mixture in his blood, and thirsty for contact with the outside world. At night he took me wild boar hunting, which I found challenging after he warned me there was every possibility the boar would charge and I had best be quick and true of aim. This transpired exactly as he had predicted, and a sizeable boar with an ugly tusk projecting from his snout stumbled to his death almost at my feet.

Less than an hour later any sense of triumph I might have had was obliterated. Once again I saw the flash of eyes in the beam of the ranger's powerful flashlight. And once again I fired immediately to halt the charge of a boar; but this time I was horrified to discover I had murdered a fawn.

My self-disgust turned me away from the "sport" of hunting forever.

The following day further humbled my petty heroics. My original guide now confessed himself lost in this region and the ranger with hesitation took over. I thought his strange reluctance was a bid for a higher fee than I had offered and his dubious attitude part of an act to enhance his value in the forest. He kept saying the wild men, known as Veddas, were unpredictable, easily aggravated, and therefore dangerous.

As I slogged through the morning's increasing heat trailed by my original guide, whose eyes were wide with fright, and the four porters, who kept dragging back until we were strung out much too far, I nearly abandoned such a ridiculous expedition. I was by now certain of the outcome. At some point farther into the forest, perhaps after we had again sloshed knee-deep through yet another marsh, a halt would be called and the ranger would say we must return. He would regret that the wild men must have moved elsewhere and like searchers for the Loch Ness monster I would be left with the sense of a good try as well as a considerable bill. Then everyone could return to his normal pursuit and the legend would survive until the next sucker came along.

My conviction that I was the victim of a harmless fraud became so strong, I was thoroughly startled when a stranger slipped out of the bush and crouched before us. He was whimpering miserably, abject fear dancing in his tormented eyes. He was wearing a filthy loincloth and held a bloody burlap sack between his knees. His posture of supplication was embarrassing and I wished he would stand up straight. I tried to ease my discomfiture by reminding myself he had doubtless been hired to complete the safari show and was therefore on my payroll.

The ranger questioned the man for a moment. The man, somewhat more easy after his initial appearance, kept pointing behind him. I asked the ranger what it was all about.

"He's been poaching. That's a deer in his sack and he is afraid I'll take him in for lack of license. But these poor people have little to eat so I said he could keep the deer if he would tell us where the Veddas were."

And, I thought cynically, the poacher has carefully learned his lines. They went that-a-way.

We continued for another two hours in the direction the poacher had indicated. Simmering in my own sweat, scratching at innumerable insect bites, I had wearied of playing Doctor Livingstone.

The ranger said that if the poacher had told him the truth we should soon be meeting the Veddas. I decided one more hour would see us in full retreat.

As the sun finally moved past its scorching zenith we came upon a clearing and the ranger halted. A few birds screeched in the treetops, and somehow I knew, without being told, that we were being watched.

While our porters remained on the edge of the clearing, we walked slowly toward a great banyan tree which stood apart from the underbrush. Beneath the tree were two armless chairs of the type featured in mail-order catalogues and beyond the tree a line of brush wood huts. We waited in silence for any sign of life. For a few minutes all remained so unnaturally still that I could hear my own breathing.

Finally a child appeared, a scrawny creature with enormous eyes and the potbelly of malnutrition. Then another child, a girl I thought, but I could not be sure since both were frail and wore identical loincloths. Then finally a man came toward us from the edge of the forest, a short, stocky, bearded anthropoid I found difficult to believe was real. For his nose was spread wide across his face, almost as flat as an ape's, his nostrils were flared as an animal testing scent and his eyes were malevolent. He held a stone mallet at shoulder height, his hairy fist clenched hard about the wooden handle. I suddenly realized I had seen him before—in New York's Museum of Natural History as part of an exhibit portraying the earth in prehistoric times.

"Don't move," the ranger cautioned. I could not if I had wanted to, for the slowly approaching specter stunned my senses. *This* was my brother?

The man halted several paces from us, half challenging, half afraid. Before others of his tribe made an even more cautious appearance one by one, I had time to estimate the first man's pitiful condition. Like the children, his potbelly only emphasized his air of desolation and weakness. No matter his angry eyes or his little stone hammer, which might break a head if the victim cooperated in his own conquest. The poor savage was without claws or true fangs, barely able to defend himself against even a weak enemy. He stood looking at me as if I had arrived from Mars, which might as well have been so, and without saying a word or making a gesture, he mirrored my ancestors of millennia ago.

Now more of the tribe came toward us, moving hesitantly, cautious as wild animals driven into danger by curiosity. Somehow these creatures had survived without change through more than the known history of the world, yet instead of feeling superior I felt humiliated and confused. I saw very suddenly how artificial were our modern standards and how fragile our hopes. Here was the very essence of human survival, the not yet agrarian hunter so preoccupied with the pursuit of his next meal he had not the energy remaining to double as warrior.

In all there were only five men, three women, and a scattering of children who ventured into the clearing. If there were others in the tribe they remained hidden throughout our stay, but I think they all found our presence irresistible.

The tallest of the Veddas was also the oldest, and apparently the chief. He was somewhat over five feet in height and, unlike the others, sinewy and spare. A frazzled, graying beard covered his chin and his eyebrows were like thickets along the sloping terrace of his brow. His eyes were black holes, nearly dead of expression, and yet he seemed to look right through us. He moved with considerable dignity, obviously in command. Like the other men, he carried a bow, a fistful of crudely made arrows, and a stone hammer.

The ranger spoke to him softly, but there was no response or change of expression on any of the faces before us.

"They have their own language," the ranger explained. "I cannot speak it and I don't know anyone who can."

The chief pointed to the mail-order chairs, moved to one and sat down. He looked at me and indicated I should sit beside him. I supposed the color of my skin impressed him because the moment I was seated he reached out to pinch the bare flesh of my arm. I could not think how to tell him I was real.

There followed a prolonged and difficult silence while everyone in the clearing including the porters drifted toward our two chairs. Once a loose formation had been achieved, a further silence ensued, this time without the relief of movement. Now, I thought, what comes next? Obviously no one knew what to do to further the occasion and it occurred to me that all such exploratory meetings are planned up to the very moment of discovery and recognition and then collapse into uncertainty. When a blind mouse meets a dead rat nothing much is likely to happen.

I handed my camera to the ranger and asked him to take our picture. He faced the assemblage, fiddled with the mechanism until he found the trigger and pressed it.* I asked him to wind the film and take another. As he obliged, I looked at the chief, who was watching the ranger. Obviously the camera or even the idea of a photo was totally incomprehensible to him. Later when the photos were developed the camera revealed an absence of concentration in all their eyes, leaving only the vacant stare of a patient animal.

My own patience was leaking slowly away. We had hiked since early morning, not, I thought, just to sit in a mail-order chair. Apparently if anyone was going to spur action it must be me.

* The photo now hangs on my cottage wall.

I beckoned to the porter who carried the two thermos bottles and took one from him. I removed the cap and offered the chief a drink. I saw he had no understanding of the shiny thing I held before him so I took a drink in demonstration. He understood there was liquid in the container and repeated my gesture. Suddenly he jumped up, dropped the thermos, and trotted around to the front of the group spitting and coughing and wiping at his mouth as if the thermos had contained molten lead. The ranger frowned at me. "He's never tasted anything cold before in his life. He thinks you hurt him."

I promised myself to be more careful about future diplomatic overtures. My nectar was another man's poison. Yet perversely, I wanted more action, something to compensate for the effort and expense involved in visiting these people. I already thought of the first Vedda who had appeared as "Andy" (for Neanderthal), and having christened him felt the comfort of knowing him.

Now as if the chief sensed my disenchantment with his hospitality he muttered a few words to Andy who skulked off to one of the huts and returned almost immediately with a small drum. It was made of a short hollow log with an animal skin stretched across the mouth. Andy set his bow and stone hammer aside and sat down in the dust about five feet to the left of my chair. The chief remained directly in front of me while the rest of his tribe formed a crescent fanning out from the banyan tree.

The chief cleared his throat several times and spit into the dust. He continued to watch me as if assuring himself of my attention, and I thought: Good. He is obviously warming up for something.

Andy now began to slap at the drum listlessly with the open palm of his hairy paws. After a moment I saw his fierce little eyes soften and become glazed. Was the soul of a musician about to be released? There was no rhythmic pattern to Andy's drum-beating, rather he slapped erratically for a while until something prompted him to forsake his overture and get down to the main theme. He launched into it with the wild yell of a practiced attention-getter. Before his cry had faded, the chief sucked in his breath and topped Andy with a howl that reverberated against the ramparts of the forest and sent strangely uncomfortable shivers through my supposedly civilized brain.

Howling and whimpering, spitting and grunting, the chief began a slow undulating dance in the dust. Now there was a distinct rhythm in Andy's slapping, rather like the barbaric drumming I had heard in Morocco. The chief began to turn and twist in his shuffling and all of his movements became more dynamic. His feet pounded at the earth until a cloud of the fine dust rose nearly to his waist.

As Andy steadily increased the frequency of the drum beat the chief responded with ever more violent physical tumult until I wondered if he was an epileptic about to have a fit. And I knew a growing sense of alarm as his convulsive shuffling brought him steadily closer to my chair.

From the oval of dust where the chief first began his antics to my chair was some eight or ten feet, and the ground inclined upward at a slight angle. Now the chief gradually closed the remaining distance, lurching and dodging up the incline, turning, twisting, and hollering, poking his hands in my direction in a way I found very disconcerting. As my uneasiness increased so did the cadence of the drum-beating and the yelling of both Andy and the chief. As a further counterpoint the others of the tribe began a noisy series of encouraging yelps.

Soon the chief was no more than a yard away from me stomping violently at the earth, his cruel eyes now over-wide with frenzy. I wanted to get out of his way. Something was very wrong and I thought to leave without waiting for the rest of the program.

I had just firmed my resolve when the chief made a sudden rush at me and placed his hands on my shoulders. He dug his thumbs into my shoulders an inch or less from my neck and I thought I must escape instantly. Then I heard the ranger speak urgently above the din.

"Don't move, sir!"

I could not if I wanted, for the chief had pinned me so firmly in place that locomotion without actually striking him was impossible. As his thumbs dug deeper into the base of my neck the pain became nearly unbearable and although he made no attempt to choke me I seemed to be suffocating.

"Don't move, sir!" the ranger begged again and I wondered why he was so insistent.

Now I could smell the chief's rotten breath mixing with the turbid stink of his writhing body. I thought, if he doesn't let go in ten seconds I'm going to kick him in the groin and run for my life. Estimating that action, I glanced at his loincloth and saw to my dismay his penis in full erection.

At that instant, as if sensing the end of my tolerance, the chief jumped backward, turned, jumped again, and with an unearthly, agonized howl threw himself face down into the dusty bowl. There he writhed a moment, his bare buttocks rising and falling as he fornicated the earth, and at last with a final spasm of movement he lay still. Suddenly everything and everyone in the clearing became silent.

I had been so frightened I was unaware that Andy had ceased his drumming and there were some long minutes while I re-established normal breathing and heartbeat.

The chief lay in the dust like a crippled bird, apparently lost to everything about him. The members of his tribe were likewise silent, as if struck dumb by what they had seen. Trying to keep my voice out of tremolo I told the ranger it seemed like a good time for us to leave and in an equally nervous tone he agreed.

Rising with the careful discretion of a guest who prefers to depart unnoticed, I saw the rest of the tribe, including Andy, were not the least interested in my movements. Instead, they were staring at their still prone chief as if expecting further fireworks or at least an encore.

We left the clearing in complete silence and without even a gesture of farewell. One child followed us hesitantly, but after a few steps turned back to the herd. When I knew we were safely away I looked back once. I saw the chief still immobile in the dust and quickened my pace. The ranger, my original guide (who appeared to be beside himself with fear), and the porters all seemed equally anxious to be away from the strange clearing where events beyond our understanding had occurred.

The march back to the rest house was interminable, although somehow the discomforts of heat and the slime

129

of the intervening swamps did not now seem important. Walking in line and pausing only very occasionally we said little, and I was grateful for the resulting privacy, for I knew we were running away from something that had disturbed us profoundly.

Had we witnessed the removal of the superficial civilization of man, his total surrender to savagery, and found the sight unbearable? Had we, one half-breed Ceylonese, five pure-blood Ceylonese, and one American, glimpsed the origins of ourselves and beat a hasty retreat for shame? Was the chief's dusty orgasm some sort of welcoming ceremonial, indication of friendship, or a threat to our continued presence in his domain? Or had I, by chance, in this return through five hundred thousand years into the Paleolithic Age, encountered a gay pithecanthropus?

Chapter 12

One of the more important outposts in the telephonic empire now directed mainly by my father was China, a tremendous land then torn into the quasi-independent provinces of sundry rapacious warlords. There was an official although very weak government, but the warlords and nearly anyone else who pleased virtually ignored its existence. Even so, it supported a full quiver of bureaucrats stationed in Peking and Nanking, the two cities serving as combined national capitals. As if the internal strife did not supply sufficient fountains of blood and bottomless pools of human agony, the Japanese, in their desire for the riches of Manchuria, had bombed, stabbed, tortured, beheaded, and shot countless innocent peasants who happened to be in their way. Almost as an afterthought, they made a shambles of the ragtag, tennis-shoed, official Chinese Army.

The headquarters of the Automatic Electric of China plus a more modest group of associated enterprises was in Shanghai. Their affairs, which mainly consisted of keeping their only customer—the Chinese government—happy, were the responsibility of Cavell, a notably handsome, charming, and urbane Englishman.

I was committed to Cavell's tutelage and as a consequence of his sensitivity and lack of pomposity slipped even more deeply into the pattern of the Group. For Cavell was no ordinary businessman with a clock-bound mind and a warehouse of statistics ever ready to screen secret ambitions. Cavell was an adventurer at heart, out of Kipling, but not sired by the arrogant British Raj. He laughed easily and was quick of wit, an expatriate who knew the Orient thoroughly and thus moved always with his back to the wall. He knew that only one law prevailed in China, inexorable and observed with neo-religious fervor by oriental and white men alike. The law was Squeeze, and without it virtually nothing could be accomplished. All politicians practiced the art of Squeeze, a gentle symbol for extortion. All business was conducted under the rule of Squeeze and foreigners either complied or went bankrupt. There were no exceptions. The peasant practiced Squeeze on the wholesaler, who expected his bit from the retailer, who turned right around and squeezed the peasant again in one form or another if actual dollars were unavailable. Every imported product began with Squeeze at customs or the papers would never be in order, then the transporter from the ship took his tribute, and the "godown" (warehouse), and so on up the line unto the government official who had consented to order the product. It was a cheerful yet vicious round-robin which not only suited the oriental fondness for complication, but affected the very thinking of white men who had been resident long enough to be known as "old China hands."

Cavell was also keenly aware of my status as an unofficial envoy and from first meeting determined I should pass on his ideas and tribulations to the distant high command.

"I suppose I should jolly well cut down on my drinking and tend to business with you about," he smiled.

I reassured him according to the formula prescribed by my father.

"Right. Then I shall introduce you to the proper people . . . and some improper people. The potentials of China are tremendous, but we mustn't press things. Plenty of time to play." I could not tell whether Cavell had simply sensed my lack of zeal for serious business or had been forewarned of my activities by his peers in the countries I had visited previously.

After more than five months on the road I was physically weary, homesick for America, and suffering from a painful rash contracted somewhere in Ceylon. Yet Cavell and Shanghai itself soon revived my enthusiasm.

Shanghai was then unquestionably the most colorful and exciting city in the world. It literally reeked of evils: every depravity was readily available and much practiced, every sort of knave and villain waited like a hawk for likely prey, and the teeming city itself was so divided into national enclaves that any unity was impossible.

Some semblance of order in the core of the city was kept by the Chinese city police who were not given to the coddling of offenders. The wild mixture of traffic, autos, trucks, pullcarts, pushcarts, bicycles, rickshaws, donkeys, marching troops, and throngs of pedestrians were kept from chaos by huge bemedaled, bearded, and turbaned Sikh policemen, who relied more on their remarkable dignity than force to keep the situation in hand.

Except for the racetrack area along Bubbling Well Road, Shanghai was anything but a beautiful city. It was as flat as Chicago and in some respects similar. An imposing range of tall commercial buildings stretched along the Bund, the principal avenue along the waterfront. The Cathay, a luxury hotel overlooking the Bund, was the tallest building and among other amenities provided a penthouse restaurant where the salads were guaranteed safe for caucasian stomachs.* There one night I gave a party for no less than twenty-two local dignitaries— Cavell having made all the arrangements before even telling me about it.

Cavell had chosen an apartment for me in the same building as his own, situated directly opposite the Annamite barracks in the French section. He had also arranged for a rickshaw coolie to pick me up at nine every morning and pull me to his office. There were thousands of rickshaws on the streets of Shanghai used by everyone including the poor. But not the very poor. They were pulling the rickshaws.

Every morning I tried unsuccessfully to soothe my

---

* A rarity in China where human excrement was (and still is) used for fertilizer.

sense of guilt at being pulled along on the physical strength of another human being. I knew the puller considered himself lucky to be on charter, for it guaranteed him a full day's pay, yet as I sat back and enjoyed the gentle breeze created by our speed, I could never persuade myself that he was lucky. As we progressed I would watch the blotch on the back of his loose-tailed shirt enlarge, the byproduct of his sweat in my behalf. And gradually the odor of the man—acrid, like something fermenting—reminded me with every breath of the almost incredible differences in our fortunes. How could I tell the puller of my youth when his own was totally taken with a fight against starvation? What all-powerful authority dared make him the puller while I rode in solitary majesty? Like Andy of the Veddas he was presumably my brother, a principle mocked into nonsense whenever we arrived at my destination. He would lower the rickshaw's shafts to the pavement and I would step down with such dignity as I could manage, cool and relaxed in my tropical whites. He would straighten and turn to me, a question in his eyes. When? I would point to the sun, make a downward movement with my arm and place a finger on my wristwatch. Four. He would look as if he understood and as if it made any difference, for we both knew he would be waiting regardless.

After a week or so I realized I had never asked the puller his name. While I always did my best to greet him as an equal mortal and leave him in like fashion, the act was contrived. He remained just "the puller," an excuse for keeping him apart from real life.

To further my oriental education Cavell insisted I make the long overland journey to Peking, there to meet certain government officials on their home grounds, particularly the Minister of Posts and Telegraphs, a Doctor Yeng.

The train ride via the Paotow-Tientsin-Peking line passed through a China ravaged for years by warlords and still subject to frequent upheavals. With luck the journey required three days and two nights and sometimes the speed of the train was so leisurely I could jump off and run alongside my car for exercise. My folly was viewed with a total lack of comprehension by the ever-changing mobs of Chinese occupying the roofs of the cars.

Unable to find even standing room inside, they stared in amazement as an obviously insane caucasian left the comfort of a heavily guarded wagon-lit and exerted himself so foolishly. I was always aware of their presence above my head, jampacked with their precious bundles of possessions and fleeing from God only knew what terrors, and I could not understand why there were just as many refugees riding on the roofs of the southbound trains as on our own northbound. I did not then know of war's fifth horseman, Bewilderment, who rides in the wake of every Apocalypse. We who lounged so sedately in our wagon-lits, complete with white lace tablecloths, flyswatters, and chilled beer, existed in a different world from those only a few yards away, and I was not unmindful of the difference.

Peking was a huge, flat, ugly city of slums, ancient and magnificent gates, crumbling masonry, palaces, and dust devils swept down from the hinterlands of Mongolia. It was also an anachronism in Chinese national affairs since it produced very little and required a great deal as do all settlements dominated by bureaucrats. Most of the national treasures had been taken away for fear of capture by the still-threatening Japanese or the wandering troupes of bandits who infested much of the Chinese landscape. The once-magnificent palaces had become hardly more than empty shells in which I was usually the only tourist. I looked everywhere for inspiration and excitement and found none. Perhaps the heat and my general ennui were responsible for certain events skittering away out of my control, my shocking violation of protocol, and the abrupt termination of my stay.

The affair began innocently enough with a dinner party given by the Minister of Posts and Telegraphs, a man of considerable importance to the Group since he authorized major communications purchases by the Chinese government. My arrival in Peking was made known to him by lesser government officials and he, erroneously believing me to be of some importance, arranged a party in my honor. Or so I was informed by one of his emissaries. Later my ego was squeezed back to size when I realized the Minister would seize any excuse for a party.

The festivities began in an unpretentious restaurant

noted for its cuisine. It was situated in a narrow alley, on the second floor of a wooden building; a curious place, I thought, for even a semi-official function. I was ushered along a hallway happily enwrapped in the incomparable odors of fine Chinese cookery. I followed my escort up a flight of stairs and was ushered into a large private room already occupied by about ten middle-aged men. I was the only caucasian present and soon discovered that my escort was the only guest who spoke even elementary English.

There was a great round table in the center of the room now supporting rows of whiskey and gin bottles. Three waiters attended the guests, who seemed determined to see the bottles empty. They were all in fine spirits, perspiring, laughing, and enjoying themselves almost, I thought, too assiduously. They had already removed their coats, ties were askew, and their voices were overloud. Only three wore the more comfortable and traditional Chinese gown. The others, whose deference to one of the gown-wearers suggested they might be minor bureaucrats, were dressed in Western style.

I was introduced to the Minister, a tall, paunchy Chinese wearing a gown of aquamarine blue. He had a full-moon face, no hair on his head, and had obviously been hard at the whiskey. He took my hand gently in the oriental fashion, made me welcome in Mandarin, and patted his fat belly with gusto. He clapped his hands, yelled at the waiters, and almost immediately a glass was put in my hand. The Minister raised his own glass in a toasting gesture and after a moment I reciprocated.

Then began a spell of confusion as one after another of the guests approached and the business of toasting was repeated. The Minister appeared to be one of those hosts who best enjoys his own party. He was everywhere at once, laughing and guffawing, beaming with enthusiasm for the occasion.

At last, when I had nearly lost standing equilibrium, food arrived and we floundered into the empty chairs at the table. My escort had long forgotten about me. It made little difference. I was nearly incoherent with drink, as were all the others.

The decibel level diminished slightly as we fell to with chopsticks, but the whiskey-drinking continued as inexorably as the toasts. We toasted President Roosevelt, Sun Yat-sen, Confucius, Li Po, ex-President Hoover, the Minister, several generals I had never heard of (but not Chiang Kai-shek), the Automatic Electric Company of China, my father (who I thought would have been touched), the city of Peking, the bird's-nest soup, the bean cake, the chef and proprietor of the restaurant, and the makers of the various whiskeys before us. All of this took a very long time and I found myself joining the Minister in frequent naps.

After one of my mental departures from the scene I was awakened by a band of musicians who had apparently arrived during the interval. Their playing seemed to revive activities and particularly the Minister's sense of duty as host. He soon dispatched an aide with urgent instructions.

A nap or so later I opened my eyes to the sight of several singsong girls doing their best to enliven affairs. Their success was stimulating, but the girl who had apparently chosen or been assigned to me was by far the least attractive of the lot. In contrast, the girl seated beside the Minister presented a thrilling oriental image of porcelain, silk, and jade. She wore her ebony hair in a somewhat longer bob than I had seen before and it framed her perfectly proportioned features and her eyes as if she had stepped from an emperor's prized scroll. Her skin was a warm sienna, dark enough to contrast with her teeth and eyes, and yet not so subdued in tone as to become lost against the sapphire blue of her high-necked gown. She was alternately serene and vivacious, her change of mood signaled by the dangling jade earrings hanging level with the top of her collar. Unlike the other singsong girls, who were now doing their utmost to drink while simultaneously arousing their patrons, the girl beside the Minister sat erect, enjoying the antics of her sisters, but obviously not tempted to participate. She had a delicacy of manner and movement totally absent from the others. I found myself staring at her longingly, for certainly she was the most exquisite creature I had ever seen.

I watched the Minister, who gave her only occasional attention, and in my envy I resented his casual and proprietary air. Once he leaned to kiss her quickly on the cheek. The gesture distressed me so I gulped down all the whiskey remaining in my glass. What, I thought, is that baldheaded old potbelly doing with such a ravishing beauty? It is wrong and evil. She is less than half his age and something drastic should be done about it. If I am the guest of honor, then . . . ?

Brooding, watching, I drank still more, and when the party began to spread in all directions from the table I moved as close to her as what was left of my decorum allowed. As my original envy became anger at obvious injustice I sought out the aide who spoke English and pressed upon him suggestions to right this terrible wrong. She was a Mongol, he told me, which accounted for her features and her complexion. Her family, he went on, had once ruled the Gobi. We then, without my being at all sure of any commitments, fell into a financial discussion which became increasingly vague as I continued to gulp at my whiskey.

The evening wore on, the band played ever more enthusiastically, men and girls danced, disappeared, reappeared, blue swirled around blue, arms, hands, and laughing faces swam before my eyes, and momentarily, while all the others hooted and howled for joy, I posed for a flash-lit photo alongside the Minister, who was helpless to rise from his chair. The positioning and repositioning for effect to satisfy all brought me repeatedly in physical contact with the Mongol girl, and my excitement became nearly overwhelming. Then suddenly, as if time had been stopped and vision blinded during the interval, I found myself lolling in a rickshaw, slipping quietly through the night toward the Grand Hotel. Alone.

I came crawling upward from an abyss, my very bones aching with the effort and my skin seared by a blazing fire of source unknown. Then I turned and twisted and snorted and moaned softly as I gathered courage to open my eyes. I lay still finally, blinking at the splash of sun upon the white sheet covering my legs. My head was of marble and my eyes, hurting even in their inner muscles, gradually accepted the familiar furnishings of my room at the Grand Hotel. It is going to be another hot day, I thought, feeling the warm white

137

sheet and my baking legs. It is also likely to be a day of great pain.

Moments later I became aware of my reason for awakening at ten, according to my watch, much too early for one who had been an over-zealous disciple of Li Po. "These days, with all men behaving like drunkards, why should I alone remain sober? . . ."

Someone was knocking on my door, discreetly but persistently, and somehow I knew it could not be the boy whose province is one floor of every Chinese hotel.

After a clumsy search I found my bathrobe and shuffled, yawning, to the door. Waiting for me was a Chinese man I had never seen before and a Chinese girl who looked vaguely familiar. I gathered what dignity I could and waved them in. As I closed the door I apologized for the disorder of my room and my general dishabille. I had been late in celebration with friends, I explained, and asked them to sit down.

Scratching at my beard and hair, smacking my desiccated lips, I sank to the edge of the bed and after remarking on the heat of the day, inquired as to their business. I kept staring at the girl, wondering why she should look familiar. She smiled shyly.

The man explained in easily understandable English that he was merely making a delivery and would be gone as soon as the formalities were completed. There was something about his condescending smile which did nothing to reassure me, but I could not remember having bought anything at any of the several shops I had visited the day before.

"Well, well," I said. "Are you sure you have the right room?"

"Indeed, sir." He held out two one-hundred-dollar traveler's checks and I saw, unmistakably, my name upon them. "Last night," the man said tolerantly, "you buy this girl. You make down payment two hundred dollar American. You very clever. She make good girl for you and is ready to go now to America."

The ensuing long silence was broken only by the tinging of the bed springs as I sought a more comfortable position. I recognized the girl now—the Mongol of course. Even in the brilliant sunlight she appeared more beautiful than other Chinese girls I had seen, but there had been considerable slippage from her role as princess of my dreams.

"How much was the total price?" I asked uneasily. My wits were like mercury in a flat dish, elusive, fracturing when caught for only an instant, then coagulating without permission from me. More than anything else in the world I now wanted a cold shower, followed by a day of rest and contemplation. Romance was not in me.

"You agree one thousand dollar American. You pay now and everything is in order. She have very small baggage downstairs."

Vaguely, the substance of one of Cavell's lectures on Chinese current affairs echoed through my throbbing head. For centuries many Chinese had sold off their daughters, hoping the best for them, but usually willing to accept the highest offer. The purchaser was expected to take good care of them for the balance of their lives no matter how many further wives or concubines might come under his protection.

"You very clever. This girl the very best in Peking."

"Does she speak any English?" I sought frantically for some honorable escape from this bargain. A thousand dollars? I had barely five hundred remaining in my letter of credit, and while my father had instructed me to "bring home some souvenirs to remind you of your journeys," I doubted if he would care to finance the present delivery.

My state of shock was eased somewhat by a brief knocking on my door followed by the entrance of the floor boy. He penetrated my bewilderment sufficiently to make me understand I was wanted on the telephone, which even in so splendid an establishment as the Grand Hotel was down the hall. I followed him hoping for a miracle.

It was Cavell, faint of voice in faraway Shanghai, but unmistakably perturbed.

"What have you done?" he began. "I have had a call from the Ministry I find difficult to believe. Is it true you have bought a girl?"

"Well . . ." Cavell was not my confessor, but I hoped he might suggest the best way out of my dilemma. I explained the delicate situation.

"Delicate? You may well have set the company back

several years. That girl you bought happens to be the favorite of the Minister himself. He has been considering her as his number one concubine and you outbid him by more than double. He does not appreciate your abuse of his hospitality and his formerly favorable view of the Automatic Electric Company of China is now quite reversed. In a word, he is extremely angry."

Alas, I thought, I had always known I had never been cut out to be a telephone man. I told Cavell how I had offered far more than I could pay and expressed remorse for my lack of wisdom.

"And I daresay you're full of piss too," Cavell went on. "Now listen carefully. Let the girl keep your two hundred dollars, providing they leave the hotel immediately. There is a train out of Peking at two o'clock. Do not fail to be on it. It is imperative you leave the city as soon as possible."

Cavell was ordering, not suggesting, and the intensity in his voice simplified my reply when he further warned me, ". . . under no circumstances must you have anything more to do with that girl. Don't go within ten feet of her. Get back here to Shanghai where I can steer you into trouble we can handle. Meanwhile I'll try to pacify the Minister."

There followed one of the most arduous half-hours of my lifetime. Now I was obliged to unravel the knots of promise I had tied with such apparent determination, and the atmosphere in my room became ever more uncomfortable. The man, who I gathered was some kind of uncle to the girl, insisted I had made a contract and must abide by it. His translations to the girl produced a remarkable effect upon her beauty. I saw the thorns of hurt and resentment flower in her lovely eyes and knew she was taking my begging off as a personal rejection.

I was fast learning that the inscrutability of the Chinese was a Western myth. Old China hands knew the Chinese were high among the most emotional people in the world. Now I watched in horror as the Mongol girl's lovely mouth became set in a thin line and her enchanting eyes chilled with the fury of a woman scorned.

True gentlemen, I thought, did not involve themselves in such mortification, or if they did, they at least handled matters with aplomb. I could not seem to manage. While the heat in the room climbed with the sun, the

140

uncle lectured me on the qualities and qualifications of his ward and my wretchedness became nearly unbearable. Please, God, I thought, take them away with my head on a salver, and let my body decompose in peace.

At last some change of aim did come to my rescue. Suddenly convinced I either could not or would not accept the girl, the uncle agreed to cancel the agreement and depart in consideration of a further hundred dollars American. He declared that they had been put in considerable trouble, not to mention embarrassment. The girl had already informed her relatives and friends she was not going into the household of the Minister as planned, but leaving for America.

I paid the uncle gladly and swiftly, for I could no longer look into the girl's eyes. There was to be no lute playing in a pagoda for this naïve American. My radiant butterfly of the Orient had become a dragon lady.

Chapter 13

My loneliness in foreign exile peaked during the last of my stay in Japan and, returning, I longed for all that was familiar American. Thus urged, I sent a wireless from the ship to Eleanor Michaud, who I remembered was attending Mills College in California. We met soon after my ship docked, we drank wine and ate what my fast-dwindling funds could afford of San Francisco. Although I had not seen her for three years, I found her captivating and on the following afternoon vowed eternal love and asked her to become my wife. I was somewhat taken aback when she accepted, but was almost immediately caught up in the exciting logistics of transforming promises into fact.

On the following afternoon, a Sunday, I found a pawnshop open on Market Street and bought a wedding ring for seven dollars. Later I bought two train tickets to Reno where I had learned marriages could be accomplished in minutes. Finally I took the ferry to Oakland and there met my bride-to-be surrounded by several of her dormitory companions, who had actually eased her past the eyes of the headmistress by applying ladder to window in the

141

best traditional fashion. They escorted us to the train. My fright mounted with every giggle, and there were moments when I was appalled at what I had brought about. The notion of partnership was still in the future.

The train arrived in Reno at six in the morning. At seven, eight, and nine, my resolve fluctuated alarmingly, but by nine-fifteen in the courthouse, choice was gone for both of us. I heard what the Justice of the Peace said: "Two dollars for the witnesses, please." All else was a distant mumbling, and a sense of foreboding nearly scuttled my spirits. Yet I knew the girl-woman I had chosen was incomparable.

After composing a flowery telegram which I hoped would mitigate unfavorable reactions from either family, I spent my final dollars on railroad tickets for as far as the total would allow. Omaha, Nebraska proved to be the limit, and I reassured my bride, "I know a man in Lincoln who runs a grocery store. I'm sure he'll give me a job."

"But how will we get from Omaha to Lincoln?"

"I don't know."

That night as the train rumbled through the Rocky Mountains I reached down from my upper berth and caught Eleanor's hand. We held on to each other for a long time, desperately, two innocents begging for happiness in a world we suddenly feared. What had happened to yesterday and the day before, when the spirit frolicked, when the "we" was "I," and abundance was everywhere?

While he would have preferred a slower courtship and a more conventional wedding, my father was not altogether displeased. He telegraphed thirty dollars, enough to cover our trainfare from Omaha to Chicago, and concluded his message with: YOU HAVE GIVEN A HOSTAGE TO FORTUNE. Minutes after our reunion, he began, "You have responsibilities now . . . might as well face up to them."

Three months after arrival in Chicago I was snarling frequently at my ever-growing sense of entrapment. To no one's surprise, my father "found a place" for me at Automatic Electric Company.

"Fine bunch of fellows out at the factory. It will take you a while to get acquainted, but working out there is where the story begins. There are the fundamentals. It's not as dull as you might think."

It was worse. The Automatic Electric home factory was in an enormous old brick building on the west side of Chicago. My "place" was logically enough in the foreign department under Mr. Todd, a kindly minor official who had never traveled farther than St. Louis. Our desks were about a yard apart and set in rows so long they seemed to reach a vanishing point at each end of the great room. There were windows along the outer row of desks, nearly opaque with the grime of Middle-American industry. No one in the outer row ever looked out.

Todd's desk was directly behind mine but his gently paternal nature soon dispelled my fear of being under his constant observation. He was interested mainly in the health of his dear wife whose ailments were specified for me daily, and he was not even vaguely intrigued by what the big bosses, who worked far away in plush offices near the city center, intended for their sons. It was the position of the hands on the wall clock which counted, and his exits were timed to the second.

Our work was simple enough. The morning mail brought orders for equipment from the various countries using Automatic Electric products: a hundred condensers to Quito, fifty relays to Havana, and occasionally something or other for my friend Cavell in Shanghai. I viewed his signature with nostalgia.

We directed the orders to the proper stores or production departments, verified dates of shipment and payment, and wrote acknowledgements. By noon and often before, it was all over. We allowed an hour for lunch, which Todd partook from a brown bag at his desk, and then the long afternoon began. Todd sat staring into space and I drew cartoons.

Our conduct matched that of the hundred other white collars in the vast room, most of whom paced their work so as to appear reasonably busy throughout the day. This ingenuity was marvelous to observe; a meeting at the water cooler might consume fifteen minutes and the opening of a single envelope as much as five minutes if tactile fumbling had been truly mastered. A trip to the toilet could require an honest half-hour if the hands were cleaned meticulously. As a last resort against the disgrace of falling fast asleep at desk, there was always the telephone. There must be someone at the other end of ennui —otherwise just let it ring for a while.

I attended these ceremonies in the accepted uniform of the establishment, suit with vest and watch chain across same, white shirt and tie of subdued tone. A homburg hat topped the ensemble, and since it was winter I often wore spats. This departure from the norm aroused limited curiosity among my fellow desk-sitters and did little to separate me from the herd. They rarely looked downward, but frequently upward—at the clock.

The clock also became an obsession with me. Not long after I had reported to Todd I thought to test the system. As usual all the paperwork was completed by noon and I had returned to my desk at one. I toyed with my supply of paper clips for some five minutes, then wrote a letter by hand to Jimmy Shute in New York. I asked him to tell our old friend Dak Sue how much I had enjoyed his country. When the letter was finished and the envelope sealed, I stood for a time looking at my outgoing and incoming baskets, both empty. I drew a few cartoons on a scratch pad and finding little inspiration telephoned our apartment. I wanted to tell Eleanor I loved her and suggest we go out for dinner. There was no answer. As I replaced the telephone I found myself looking at the wall clock without really seeing the position of the hands. Had I then at last succumbed to the regime? Anxious, I took out my own watch, studied it a moment and found the two timepieces agreed exactly: 1:47.

I stood up and turned around to face Todd, who was carving the end of a pencil into a needlelike point. Every afternoon he took out the short gold knife which was fixed to the end of his watchchain, opened it with a deft movement of his thumbnail, and selected a pencil from the collection on his desk. Then he would sharpen it—gently, almost lovingly. One every afternoon.

I could see that he was totally absorbed in his creative effort, but I was irresistibly compelled to disturb him.

"Mister Todd? Could I ask you a few questions?"

He looked up at me over the rims of his glasses and as always his gray eyes were soft and benevolent. "Why, of course." He smiled. "What's on your mind?"

"First, have you anything for me to do the rest of the afternoon?"

"Why . . . no, not really. . . ." Todd's eyes began to fill with puzzlement. *Was* there perhaps something to be done?

"My orders are all taken care of and there cannot possibly be any more today. Is that correct, Mr. Todd?"

"I suppose it is. Why, yes."

"Then can you tell me what I'm doing here except consuming heat and light? Is there any reason why I shouldn't go for the day? Go home, to the movies, or just for a walk in the park? Is there any reason why I should have to sit here doing nothing whatsoever until exactly five o'clock and then put on my hat and remove my body elsewhere?—just because it's five o'clock?"

"Why!" Todd was aghast, but not angry. He sat motionless as if pondering the outcome of my proposal.

"Will the building burn down? Will the company go bankrupt? Will it make any difference except to the clock whether I leave now or three hours and two minutes from now?"

"Well, good heavens! Supposing everyone thought like that?"

"All right. Supposing everyone in this building who had honestly completed his work for the day got up and went home. Would it make any difference?"

Todd worked his mouth as if he had suddenly tasted something too heavily spiced. For a fleeting moment I regretted having troubled his patient calm with such cruel realities. But then he sighed and went back to his pencil sculpturing. I was sure he wanted to warn me away from such thoughts, perhaps even suggest I might avoid offering such notions in the presence of my father, whose daily work was never really done.

Yet there was only that forlorn sigh from him, a resigned exhalation I thought came as much from his heart as his lungs. Little sweet man, I thought, what caused you to surrender yourself to this tranquillity? What might have been your otherwise life, your unknown potential? A sculptor in marble perhaps, for your hands are strong and sure. A surgeon? A carpenter?

Go away, I knew he was saying to me, go away and bother me not with conundrums to which the answer is so obvious it becomes unspeakable. There is still a terrible depression lurking outside those windows. You are young and rich and so you would not understand.

I hesitated, then decided there was now no choice. Either the regime was going to break me or I must violate its basics. Even though he continued to scrape away at his pencil, I knew Todd was watching me as I closed my desk drawers, put away my pad of cartoons, and carefully aligned my own battery of pencils, all activities usually reserved for 4:55 on the clock. I went to the coat rack, slipped into my coat, and popped on my homburg at a slightly steeper forward angle than usual. Then without looking back, or to the right or left, I walked down the long row of desks to the end of the room and descended the stairs leading to the street. At a loss to utilize my momentary freedom I walked the three miles to the center of the city and, within the shadow of my hard-working father's offices, went to the movies.

Some remorse kept me reasonably docile for another week. I arrived at my desk at nine and left it at five plus ten seconds. And I scorned myself for lack of compassion in having taunted Todd with ridiculous questions he was helpless to answer. As recompense I listened with forced but true attention to the continuing saga of his wife's deterioration. Like a penitent Catholic I did my best to make amends for the blasphemies uttered while the devil was in me. But I was still his easy mark.

During the dreary and empty afternoons I had written a series of articles on the telephone situation as I had seen it throughout the world, which rather to my surprise and my father's unbounded pride were published in *Telephony*, a trade magazine. The recognition so achieved gave me unwarranted prestige along the rows of desks, and most of the resentment at my employment when countless family men were begging for any sort of work seemed to melt away. Higher officials delighted my father with hearty comments about a chip-off-the-old-block working for the company and predicted a brilliant future for his son within the complex of the Group.

One afternoon when my cartooning had palled and Todd's pencil sharpening seemed to become the metronome of our monotony, I left my desk resolved to explore the vast building from end to end. I had calculated that taken at leisure, the expedition might absorb several afternoons.

I began in the cavernous basement where innumerable huge reels of wire were stored. Eventually I came upon a separate room and entered. Only a single bare bulb illuminated the interior and the disorderly accumulations of dust-covered electrical gear, now obsolete and forgotten. Yet on the shelves there was a neat array of brick-sized leather boxes, row upon row, several hundred if my estimate was correct. I took one down and recognized it immediately as identical to the field service telephones we had used during training at the military academy and at Fort Snelling in the cavalry. They had been manufactured for use during the First World War and were beautifully made. For a moment I thought to take one home for a souvenir, then I had what I thought was an inspiration.

Todd was surprised when I laid the instrument on his desk. "Where in hell did you find that? Haven't seen one in years!" He fingered it thoughtfully, admiring its durable workmanship and the fineness of the leather case. I told him there were hundreds in the basement and asked if I might borrow one.

"Oh sure. They've been written off long ago. Bet they aren't even on inventory. No one would care if you took it home. Might make a good fishing tackle box."

That night, while my bride wondered at my industry, I painted the Peruvian coat of arms on the leather face of the box. Within a week the paint was dry enough to apply several coats of protective shellac. When all was done I took it down to the shipping room with instructions to wrap carefully and send fast mail to our men in Lima. I wrote a covering letter and waited impatiently through a long series of desolate afternoons.

The response arrived much sooner than I had hoped. The Peruvian military would be pleased to order one hundred of the field telephone sets at one hundred dollars U.S. Within two days I saw to it the telephones were on their way. Meanwhile I basked in small glory, the enterprising young employee who had turned company junk into money.

Alas, I was not content. Aware of the festering border war between Peru and Colombia, I reasoned the other side might be interested in improving their communications on the field of battle. This time I repeated the entire successful process, substituting only the coat of arms of Colombia. The model was sent off to our man in Bogotá and the military interest he found was identical, except only seventy-five sets were desired. And once more I saw to their immediate dispatch.

While I was mentally scouring the world for further customers a cable arrived from Lima. It was not directed to me, but to Todd, who paled as he digested its ominous message:

AUTHORITIES HERE HAVE DISCOVERED WE SOLD THEM IDENTICAL EQUIPMENT AS DELIVERED COLOMBIA THIS EXTREMELY EMBARRASSING FOR ALL CONCERNED. AUTHORITIES SAY WILL NEVER AGAIN BUY EQUIPMENT FROM AUTOMATIC ELEC. FOR CIVIL OR ANY OTHER USE. RECOMMEND IMMEDIATE APOLOGIES FROM HIGHEST GROUP EXECUTIVES OR ULTIMATE LOSS OF BUSINESS INCALCULABLE. OFFICE CLOSED PENDING YOUR ADVICE.

Todd cleared his throat several times, a usual signal for me to turn around and face him. My desk chair was of the rotating type and through practice during the boring afternoons I had developed a technique of whirling around one hundred eighty or three hundred sixty degrees and stopping precisely on target without manual braking. I knew the action was a pathetic display of my immaturity, but I could not resist it in this desert of pleasures.

This time as I swung to a stop I knew something was very wrong, for Todd appeared a man who had dropped an anvil on his foot. He handed me the cablegram in silence.

I did not mind the obvious calamity my junk business had wrought half so much as I minded the injury in Todd's eyes. For in my brief and cocky acquaintance with success, I had selfishly contrived to keep all credit to myself and neglected to tell Todd about the second order of phones sent to Colombia.

Now Todd's eyes told me I had betrayed him by detouring his authority and, worse, placed him in a fix where he must either take the blame himself or castigate the boss's son—neither of which he was inclined to do. I had troubled the equanimity of the foreign sales department

148

which he had sergeanted for over twenty years and he could see no end to the ramifications.

When I handed the cablegram back to him he accepted it between thumb and forefinger, held it momentarily as if it was contaminated with a hideous disease, then passed it uncertainly along the glass covering his desk, and finally set it down directly over the photograph of his wife smelling a flower.

He pronounced my name almost inaudibly, then shook his head and that was all. I waited in vain for more, but his attention to all local matters appeared to drift visibly upward to the high ceiling of the room and out through the grimy windows. I wondered anxiously whether he was dreaming of more peaceful times or whether, like some victims of instant shock, he had protectively severed all contact with the real world.

Viewing his overwhelming unhappiness I knew there was only one honorable rescue and I thought, with growing excitement, the time has come at last.

I asked him if I could take the telegram to Mr. Blomeyer, the chief executive of the plant and thereby one of my father's most valued associates. "Mister Todd, I'm sorry. It was my doing. Let me explain it."

He nodded diagonally and although I was not sure he had even heard me I took the gesture as permissive. He did not look down at the photograph of his wife when I slipped the cablegram away, nor did he seem to notice my going. Nor had I the heart to tell dear Mr. Todd, who had never been anything but kind and gentle to me, how very far I was going.

When my father had finished washing his hands of me —a proclamation he issued not because of my Peruvian-Colombian adventure but because of my resolve to resign from the company—I was not surprised. He considered that I had overreacted to a justifiable mistake and I knew it had provided a flimsy excuse for escape. I told him I never wanted to see another nine-to-five office as long as I lived.

The continuing Depression made my resolve seem even more reckless, and when she looked at our checkbook, Eleanor had misgivings about her own audacity of only five months past. After we had subtracted my trainfare to New York there was enough money to pay the rent for two months, keep her eating for about the same time, and no more. I was not at all sure how *I* would eat when I arrived once more to seek my fortune in New York, but I hoped I had enough friends to keep me going until I found a job in the theater.

I also had one special hope. As an antidote to my boredom with the telephone industry I had written and illustrated a book covering the more colorful events of my recent world tour. Calling it *Distant Pastures*, I held no illusions about its becoming a best-seller, but thought it might at least alleviate my financial problem if I could find a publisher. Fancying myself now as my own man, my confidence was unbounded.

My arrival in New York coincided with the worst blizzard since the calamity of 1888. The snow was knee-deep in the very heart of Manhattan and most of the streets were impassable. It was bitterly cold, the unemployed and WPA workers built great fires in the middle of ordinarily busy avenues, and commuter trains operated very late or not at all. The great and bustling metropolis I had counted on to further stimulate my spirits was in deep hibernation, yet I determined to set it afire. Now if ever, I knew, I was on test. I had walked out on a perfectly good job, rejected deliberately the protection of my clan and kind, and stood alone in an always difficult and sometimes hostile environment.

I took the cheapest room available at the Great Northern Hotel on West Fifty-seventh Street, where Fryer, my former classmate at Yale Drama School, was already established. His report on employment prospects in the theater was so gloomy I begged him to cease lest I lose all hope before even trying.

It went on snowing through the first four days of my rounds through the theatrical offices, none of which offered even future prospects. Fryer, Jimmy Shute, and sometimes Margaret Pemberton fed me. My book was in the hands of Miriam Howell, one of agent Leland Hayward's finest aides, and as theatrical disappointments mounted I pestered her for news of its fate. She tried to smile when she showed me the report by professional reader Bill

Fadiman. While he praised the illustrations, he vetoed the book as "jejune" and hardly a prospect for publication. Then I tried to smile.

Despairing of finding work with the more prosaic threatrical entrepreneurs, I had decided to heed advice long ago dictated by my father. He had said, "If you want action don't bother the office boy. Go see the boss." I waited so many days in the outer offices of a very great man his secretaries viewed me as part of the furniture.

David Sarnoff, Chairman of the Radio Corporation of America, was such a high cockalorum in the communications industry he could not be specifically identified with my needs, but he was certainly not an office boy. My calling upon him was equivalent to troubling the President of the United States for a job in a rural post office, and Sarnoff was about as available. Discreet and noncommittal lady receptionists and secretaries formed polite barricades between an endless stream of petitioners and Sarnoff, but my attendance at his outer gates was so faithful that toward the twilight of a nervous day I was finally ushered into his presence.

What Sarnoff lacked in physical stature he more than made up in charm. He smiled as he took my hand, said he understood I had been waiting interminably and apologized for the delay. All of the pat speeches I had rehearsed for so long now seemed fatuous in comparison with Sarnoff's simplicity and warmth. Before my eyes I saw a big man demonstrating how a genuine big man behaves. No foreign dignitary or chief of a giant corporation could have been treated with greater courtesy. I told him I would do anything, regardless how humble, if it involved entertainment. He listened attentively and within five minutes changed my life.

He made a crisp telephone call to a Mr. Van Schmus at the new Radio City Music Hall. He was sending down a young man. "Good luck!" was all he said, when nearly bursting with my good fortune I backed out the door.

I raced from the RCA building to the Music Hall and found Van Schmus quite as courteous as his superior. He was a tall man with snow-white hair, more reserved than Sarnoff and lacking his magic charm, but in my anxious eyes already striding through the Pantheon. After a few minutes he called in a younger man, Gus Eyssell,* and they discussed my future as if they really cared. At last Van Schmus made a telephone call and sent me into the bowels of the world's largest theater where I would find a Leon Leonidoff waiting for me. I was slipping down the chain of command, yet I was breathless with anticipation. For weeks I had been trying to see Leonidoff, who directed the huge Music Hall stage shows and had never managed to get past the guard at the stage door. Now I realized that my father's advice was sometimes worth listening to.

Leonidoff soon cooled my ardor. He was a short, extremely volatile Russian who ruled the backstage of the Music Hall. His thick, curly hair stood straight up and out from his head as if he had been struck by lightning, an event the more abused of his lower-echelon staff sometimes wished would hurry up and occur. Leonidoff was a tyrant, yet his charm was so very great—when he chose to use it—that he created a sort of masochistic loyalty among those who worked with and even for him. They were Russell Markert, who was in direct charge of the world-famous Rockettes, Vincente Minnelli,† who was responsible for the enormous scenic backgrounds, and Erno Rapee, who conducted the fine Music Hall symphony. Bill Stern, later a sports announcer, was the stage manager, and Dick Leibert played the world's most versatile organ. All of them recognized Leonidoff as a stager of spectacles equal to Salzburg's Max Reinhardt, if not more talented.

"You," Leonidoff said with a total lack of enthusiasm, "vill be my assistant. Vat is your name again?"

I told him, but he had already lost interest. He returned to his absorption in a revolving stage set Minnelli had created for the important Easter-time show. I thought he had forgotten my existence, yet in the middle of a passionate plea to Minnelli for more rehearsal time on stage he turned to me and said, "Your salary will be thirty dollars a veek. Dere is an empty office down the hall. Take it. Are you hongry? You better eat if you haf not. Tonight vee vork until **maybe** vun maybe two o'clock. Who knows?"

---

* Later, in its heyday, general manager of the Music Hall, a job he held for many years.

† Later a famous motion picture director and father of Liza Minnelli.

I did not know, nor was I ever again conscious of time during the months I worked as Leonidoff's assistant. The great stage shows lasted almost an hour and were followed by two hours of feature film. In the backstage areas of the Music Hall there were huge rehearsal halls capable of accommodating the entire ballet or the hard-working Rockettes. These rooms reverberated almost twenty-four hours a day with the clicking of dancing feet, the strident commands of the ballet mistress, the hysterical complaints of frustrated temperament, or the chanting of the Music Hall chorus. As many as five hundred people worked unceasingly in the numerous anterooms, corridors, and about the main stage itself. There were seamstresses for the costumes, electricians, scenic carpenters, and stagehands. There were whole bands of musicians tootling, plucking at their strings, and mouthing their trumpets. Property men built howdahs for elephants, and treasure chests for pirates. Wardrobe ladies were perpetually fitting, taking away, and refitting the spectacular costumes worn by everyone. Pandemonium, ever more excited by the presence of Leonidoff who pitched his voice to penetrate through all other sounds, was ordinary throughout this entire area. The countless demands of producing so many tremendous entertainments each year were awesome, and there were times when near-panic prevailed.

Leonidoff soon made it known to all his backstage crew that I was an assistant he did not need, shoved down his throat by the almighty authorities. Gradually, however, he did find minor chores for me and began, when it pleased him, to further my theatrical education. In this regard he sent me on weekly scouting trips to observe performances of every sort from burlesque to opera, all in the hope that I would find unique material for his endless needs. I wrote reports on what I had seen, and how the audience had reacted. (A few performances so recommended actually appeared on the Music Hall stage.)

Even Leonidoff's perpetual motion society was not enough to consume my inherited energies nor could my occasional humiliations long allay my spirits. While waiting for orders, I began, as I had in Chicago, drawing cartoons. The first efforts were casual illustrations I hoped might sell to *The New Yorker* magazine, but gradually the drawings began telling stories in the manner Bart Foss had taught me during what already seemed another life at Ray-Bell studios.

One day when Leonidoff seemed to have forgotten my very existence, I sent off a batch of cartoons to RKO Pictures, the parent operating company of the Music Hall. I could hardly believe the speed of their acknowledgment.

I stole away from the cavernous Music Hall during a performance of *Madame Butterfly* in which I had been more than normally involved. With the arias of Lieutenant Pinkerton and Cio-Cio-San still echoing in my thoughts I called on Ray Gillette, the bald, eager man who had seen my drawings. After directing the award-winning *Three Little Pigs* for Disney he had been hired to produce a cartoon series for RKO, *The Rainbow Parade*.

"I was wondering," he said, "if I could interest you in directing a few of the series. Unfortunately, I can only pay one hundred dollars a week."

I looked out the window which faced upon Broadway and the heart of Times Square. Early summer had come to Manhattan and the temperature was still ideal. That morning as I was on my way to the Music Hall, the pigeons who worked so endlessly at depositing their guano on Radio City had seemed to coo with particular satisfaction, and Leonidoff's mercurial temperament, subject to the yeast of a successful operatic production, had turned him into a jolly hail-fellow; a natural Kiwanian, I thought, is buried beneath those moods of Russian despair. On this day even the tugs plowing the East River, above which Eleanor was now established in a minuscule apartment, seemed to have developed a special saucy toot of their whistles. Now this man Gillette was offering me more than three times my present salary to do what I loved to do.

Leonidoff expressed polite regrets at my unheralded departure, but his eyes betrayed his relief. I wondered if his Slavic suspicion had made him question from the beginning if I had been sent to spy upon him. Later, when he at last became convinced there had been nothing devious about my arrival in his world of controlled hysteria, our relationship warmed.

My appointment as one of Gillette's directors was far more demanding and exciting. I was given my head with a professional crew and soon became convinced that I had found my place in the working world. The cartoon series was unique in employing live actors simultaneously with those drawn by the battery of artists under Gillette. He was a generous man, overflowing with enthusiasm and given to such self-harassment he sometimes forgot what he was about. As soon as he learned of my Ray-Bell experience he turned over the directing of the live sequences to me. Then, in the tight circle of New York filmdom, word soon spread that I knew how to handle a camera and crew. Outside invitations came my way to direct tests for several movie companies. Previously I had moved through life at a fast walk. Now I was obliged to run if I would fulfill all my increasing opportunities.

Gillette's *Rainbow Parade* for RKO-Van Buren were charming films and a success, but for reasons we never understood the series was terminated after six months of production. I was indifferent to my own dismissal since by that time I had more work than I seemed able to handle —in the feast-or-famine world of the theater everything now seemed to be coming my way.

The volatile, extraordinary Kay Brown, who would later become such a factor in my life, began by hiring me to direct tests for her employer David Selznick. Fox followed in her wake and soon afterward Mildred Weber at Warner Brothers. Ben Hecht and Charles MacArthur, having embarked on a movie-making schedule at Paramount's Astoria studios, offered a job as assistant director. I was about to accept when the Theater Union, a loose assembly of politically far-left young theatrical tigers, offered me one of the leading roles in a thrilling play about an Austrian Navy mutiny, *The Sailors of Cattaro*. The ham still lurked within me and I succumbed once more to the intoxication of audible applause.

The Sailors of Cattaro opened at the Eva Le Gallienne Fourteenth Street Theater to stirring critical approval and raucous rejoicing among the far-left of New York, then in minimal numbers despite still festering wounds of the Great Depression. Disillusion with the Soviet had not yet taken place, and the great god Stalin was still enshrined along with Lenin. The praises of both were sung backstage at the Fourteenth Street Theater, a chorus both Tom Powers, the star, and I refused to join. One Saturday afternoon both of us reported for the matinee only to be told that the balance of the considerable cast was in jail after a violent demonstration linked with a strike at Ohrbach's.

A prideful announcement of the mass incarceration was made to the audience just before curtain time, but no mention was made of the two defectors backstage. Cancellation of the matinee was received with dismay by Eleanor, who had chosen that afternoon to bring two wives of my father's more conservative friends. I thought it probably all for the best. At least they would not go back to Chicago and report how they had seen me leap joyously down from a fake battleship's gun turret waving a bright red flag and shouting to my crewmates about the glories of revolution.

My apolitical nature had more than enough of socialist theories by the time *The Sailors of Cattaro* rolled over and sank. I came to resent the constant preachings of my fellow employees, the cant, the self-righteousness, and the observation of every facet of life as if seen through the wrong end of a telescope. At the urging of others in the cast I tried to read Lenin and Spengler, and even had a go at Marx, all of whom I found boring beyond measure. My stubborn lack of appreciation for such saviors of society only seemed to stimulate the Fourteenth Street missionaries to greater efforts. They insisted my conversion was imminent, and to keep them at least temporarily at bay, I let them believe that my chains were all I had to lose. When the show closed at last, I sighed with relief.

The prosperity resulting from so much activity brought changes in our lifestyle with a few dividends. While my father took the expected view of my acting (fortunately he never attended the minirevolution on Fourteenth Street), he was somewhat encouraged by my total weekly income. He knew that it was considerably in excess of what I would be making had I remained under the benign eyes of Mr. Todd in Chicago. I did not explain the fickle nature of the theatrical world where one week's income may have no relation whatever to the next. My father thought as a businessman, in terms of "the long haul." Good, sound, sensible people could expect regular paychecks through the balance of their lifetime, with annual if modest increases every year. Because it was much easier to think his way, I proceeded as if a dependable merit and reward system also applied to my chosen field. In this endeavor Eleanor was pleased to help.

We forsook the cubbyhole on the East River and took an apartment in a brownstone on Sixty-third Street. I painted a mural above each of the two fireplaces and we augmented our previous lack of furniture with a couch, wooden dining table, benches, a drawing board, and a few lamps. Our further extravagances were beer and books, with frequent dining out nights on the town at the Zumbrauhaus on Fifty-fourth Street and Billy's Bar on First Avenue. All was well with the world—almost.

The lack of prudence in our marriage had apparently been of no consequence. Eleanor worked hard at transforming herself from a popular belle into the current version of the good wife. Because of her unique beauty other men were frequently attracted to her, an attention she fostered by harmless flirtations. The early years of marriage are more difficult and confusing for popular beauties than for the withdrawn and homely. Suddenly the attention of the crowd is not so openly realized. As a wife the beauty is considered reserved and sometimes she tries in strange ways to compensate for the general lack of attention.

The first time Eleanor fainted I rushed to her side with a cold towel and a frantic sense of helplessness. My God! I thought, suppose she is dying!

After a few moments her eyelids fluttered, her lips parted in a soft sigh and I found my own breath again. When her eyes opened at last I comforted her with sweet words and carried her in to the bed. She apologized for being so much trouble.

"Are you pregnant?"

"No."

"Sure?"

"Absolutely. I went to the doctor only two days ago."

"He could be wrong."

"Oh, not Doctor Phipps!"

There was a certain way Eleanor pronounced the word "Doctor" that should have hoisted a signal of trouble, but I failed to recognize it. The only trouble I could recognize was my beloved bride prone on the bed. She was smiling when she asked me to leave and let her rest a while.

About a week later, this brief melodrama was repeated with the performance being identical in all respects. Once again she denied pregnancy, but this time I insisted she visit Doctor Phipps on the morrow. Now her pronunciation of the word "Doctor" did strike me as odd, there was a sort of breathless awe about it, as a neophyte nun might announce the name of a Cardinal. Still, I recognized only beauty in momentary distress and though somewhat appalled at the thought of becoming a father, I was in no position to retreat.

The doctor said she was not pregnant. For reassurance I talked to him on the telephone. He could not explain her fainting.

Perhaps two weeks passed before Eleanor fainted again, this time to a slightly different scenario. Most evenings I spent at my drawing board, trying always to improve my drawing and speculating how I might turn the figures I created into monetary value. Suddenly I heard a thump in the bedroom and knew without looking that Eleanor had fainted.

I fought the urge to jump up and run for the bedroom. Instead I put down my pencil deliberately, then took my time going to the open doorway. En route I wondered if I had the nerve to carry out my intention. I had reviewed my own terrible shortcomings as a young husband, of which there were so many, and I had asked my conscience a thousand times if having torn this girl-woman from innumerable offers of better security I had any justification for doing anything but worship at her feet. But my resolve held.

Carefully and without actually stepping through the doorway, I leaned out until I could see more than half the bedroom. The light was on beside the bed and Eleanor lay face up on the floor. Her eyes were closed, her lovely mouth slightly open. All was as I had seen it before.

I hesitated, so undecided that my own steady breathing sounded obscene. I waited perhaps one full agonizing minute while I regarded the woman I loved evidently unconscious only a few yards away.

I waited, hoping to detect some fluttering of her eyelids, any evidence to make me abandon my terrible plan. I was reassured only by the very slight motion of her breathing. When I saw that its tempo was regular, I clenched my fists to toughen my faltering resolution, then turned deliberately and walked back to the drawing board.

Several minutes passed while I fiddled anxiously and ineptly with lines and circles. When I had nearly convinced myself I had made a terrible mistake, I heard movement in the bedroom. Soon afterward Eleanor appeared in the doorway. She looked at me inquiringly, then wiped at her eyes as if she had been asleep. She asked, "How goes the drawing?"

"Fairly well," I replied.

Eleanor never fainted again.

Chapter 14

Time conquers us second by second, hour by hour, and its victory is always total. Time envies our being, cuts short our joys and prolongs our agonies. Time permits no living thing to endure. Time is the villain of the piece, the seneschal of all things in the world, and even the stones must eventually submit.

Yet the strange illusion of permanence still persists. Who was this upstart striding at high speed through the nooks and crannies of the world's greatest metropolis as if defeats were unthinkable and permanent fame with fortune were already but a fingertip removed?

Now I had a spacious office in the Warner Brothers building on West Forty-fourth Street. I had been hired by Mildred Weber and Steve Trilling as a talent scout, an enviable job even for Broadway veterans. I went to all the first nights and usually sat in an aisle seat. Beautiful girls flowed in and out of my office all day, finding their way of their own accord or brought by the very agents from whom only a short time before I had sought to help my own cause. Almost unique to Broadway, I received my ample paycheck every week.

I had my table at Sardi's where I lunched every day except when directing at the Warner Vitaphone Studio in Flatbush. Vincent Sardi (the elder) greeted me warmly on sight, ushered me past the peasants who waited in line at the doorway, and bowed me always to the same table.

I tried to avoid an overdisplay of smugness as I signaled greetings to the truly great regulars who regarded my presence in their midst as either miraculous or an indication of the theater's rapid deterioration. Gilbert Miller's response from his special corner table was always approving, Brock Pemberton rarely favored me with more than a thin smile, Antoinette Perry took me to her ample bosom whenever I was alone and gave me warning of too early success.

All of this climbing toward renown went on nicely for more than a year. As if my duties at Warner Brothers were not enough, I wrote a play with Dickie Whorf and directed a semiprofessional play in Brooklyn. Eleanor worked for a time as a fashion model, a job she enjoyed until she finally did become pregnant. Our apartment was a clearing house of young actors, actresses, and all style of theatrical and cinematic hopefuls, who found the free beer and an atmosphere of prosperity pleasant relief from their lesser fortunes.

I was employed by a recognized entertainment giant and therefore possessed of precious powers unavailable to my contemporaries. Using the prefacing title of Warner Brothers I could telephone anyone in the profession who might be interested in reading a play or talking to an actor. I discovered the unholy power of "names" and how people trust the establishment no matter how unstable its nature; if the name has a building, more than a hundred employees, and the assembly is labeled "incorporated" then entrée is automatic.

Such was my growing reputation, I was often asked to make tests for other motion picture companies. When I was physically unable to fulfill so many offers I often recommended Charlie Mather's former pride, Josh Logan. His talent was obvious and he needed the work.*

My symbolic chariot glittered as I passed through Shubert Alley; the very streets and avenues so lonely and hostile only a short time ago were now miraculously inhabited by people who smiled and called my name. In my necessary haste, I knew how to cross certain intersections without pausing for traffic lights, how to cut distance by dodging through an alley. I knew hundreds of names and all of the chieftains and petty officers of the

---

* Yet I had never actually met Josh Logan.

little Eastern theatrical and movie world, and I strove continuously to make them know mine. Magazines and newspapers printed absurd stories of my multiple enterprises which included the production of a short film with Jimmy Shute. It seemed only a matter of time before Warner Brothers in Hollywood would recognize genius in their midst.

Eleanor, placid in pregnancy, took all these events easily. Manhattan, we thought, was nearly ours. We had never heard of *yin* and *yang* and, tremendously energized by continuous approbation, we ranged with the greatest of ease from squalid parties in Greenwich Village to black tie affairs along Park Avenue. A prominent national magazine, apparently desperate for candidates, named me the young man of the year and my father became nearly beside himself with pride.

Now sailing with a bone in my teeth, I knew the world was mine and nothing could deter my inevitable realization of fame and fortune. Thus unprepared, I bumped across the first shoals all standing. One harrowing day I was informed I had sired a son. Her doctor proclaimed that a normal birth would be hazardous and a Cesarean was performed. For Eleanor the whole enterprise was extremely difficult, and it permanently influenced her thinking.

The boy was named George after my father, and I was somewhat disappointed to observe that he looked much like any other baby. Once he had safely arrived and all seemed well, I returned with relief to the pressing demands of my profession and the numbing realization that without having made any financial preparations for a family life, there were suddenly a great many new bills to be paid.

Worse, I had allowed my ears to believe the pleasantries passed on by various sycophants and the gist of various complimentary articles, and to these blandishments I added the most treacherous ingredient of all—an abiding faith in my own talent. As a final foolishness I developed a tendency to take myself seriously. The total acceleration had been too rapid and trouble was inevitable.

Now, I was disinclined to make ordinary tests wherein the subject simply stood before the camera, turned both profiles, smiled sheepishly, and sometimes spoke a few lines. Instead I rehearsed my hopefuls in episodes from plays, or movies, running five or ten minutes. I fretted over their every gesture and word, saw they had the best of makeup, and with Jay Rescher, the Warner cameraman, took hours to light them favorably. I knew this was their big chance, perhaps never to be repeated again, and I was heavy with my responsibility to help them along their way. The Warner tests became known as "miniproductions" costing much more money than those given by other studios and as a consequence enthusiastically approved by agent and client alike. For my own part I hoped the powers in Hollywood would recognize directorial talent going to waste on the East Coast where almost no true production was ever scheduled.

Unfortunately, all Hollywood wanted was a look at whatever face and figure they needed, and nothing more. Jack Warner, the supreme chief of Warner Brothers Studios, wrote a scalding complaint at my efforts and for some days I wallowed in the self-pity of artistry unappreciated.

I was certainly susceptible to a pretty face or a voluptuous figure and only the illusion that I was working as an artist kept me from the obvious dilemma of being a young and vigorous man in a situation where he could affect the future of countless girls, most of more than ordinary beauty. They came from all over America to seek their fortune along legendary Broadway. No sultan ever presided over such a variable harem, and my immediate boss, Mildred Weber, was often at pains to remind me of my marital status.

In spite of this enviable employment I began to know a surprising sense of misplacement. My solitary attack on New York had been vindicated and my father appeased. We exchanged the most amiable letters and telephone calls. Still something was basically wrong and I could not identify it. Rather than basking in the Broadway atmosphere, I too often felt melancholy. I could not bring myself to converse in theatrical clichés, the frequent use of "Darling!" only embarrassed me, and "Okay, sweetheart" was worse. The constant employment of "terrific" and "sensational" as punctuation marks in speech was discordant to my ears. Everyone in the show business, it seemed, was too cunning. I found it impossible to say nice things about a play or a performance when my impression was negative and I found most theatrical cocktail parties, even at Margaret Pemberton's, boring beyond endurance. Instinctively, I knew something was missing, but I could not separate it as an element until Jimmy Shute and I made *Control Yourself*, a short film about flying. I chose to photograph much of the footage from the rear cockpit of a Navy fighter, a rather foolhardy endeavor since it required my standing up during the relatively violent aerobatic maneuvers. No one could understand why I so enjoyed the risk—including myself. Had I greater wisdom I would have seen the beginning of a cycle, or in a larger sense the further curving of the main ring. There followed a series of well concealed factors, each contributing to the pattern.

Who can consistently balance the influence of more subtle factors against the more obvious? Certainly there was nothing subtle about a statuesque blonde who called herself Candy, yet during our brief acquaintance I could not conceive she might have a very significant influence on my immediate fortunes.

Usually Mildred Weber escorted to my office whatever talent she thought worthwhile. In the case of Candy she merely telephoned from below, advising that the young lady was already en route to my aerie and indicating in unmistakable terms that I was to prepare her for a screen test.

"She's a lovely girl," Mildred explained, "somewhat short on experience but she should photograph very well."

Mildred Weber was a woman of enormous heart and keen mind. At Warner Brothers she had begun as a secretary and through devoted and unceasing work had made her way to become nominal head of the Eastern talent department. I admired her and, aware of her true taste, I was unprepared for Candy.

Candy came through the door decorously enough, no mean feat, since she was six feet of one of the most spectacular figures I had ever beheld, with every minute and second of physical arc displayed beneath a tight sequined dress.

Candy eased herself into the chair beside my desk where the brilliant light from the arched window emphasized her cleavage and the faint impasto of her makeup. She smiled hesitantly and I saw that her teeth would tolerate a closeup. Her facial features were almost too regular; I thought of Nero's wife Poppaea, who nurtured her skin with honey and the milk of wild asses, but watching Candy's blue eyes I sought in vain for any sign of character. There must be something wrong, I thought; this vapid creampuff belongs on a float in the Rose Bowl parade, not in a dramatic movie. Not a hair on Candy's blond head was astray and her carmine fingernails were the grace notes of her total portrait. I had never beheld such a perfect pastry cake and hesitated to cut into its interior. I began gently.

"Who sent you to Warner Brothers?"

"Someone . . . a friend."

"Where have you been acting?"

"Well . . . here and there." Her voice was so faint it was almost inaudible. She must be, I thought, terribly frightened and I began to feel very sorry for her.

"Smile, Candy," I said. "Smiles rule the movie world."

She smiled uncertainly and a dimple appeared as I handed her a speech from a play in which a young girl reveals anguish at the loss of her lover—standard fare.

One of the few things I disliked about the job was my apparent inability to get studio contracts for so many deserving young actors and actresses. I had only sympathy and an abiding respect for the talents of the achingly sincere young professionals who lived and breathed the glamour of the theater. I did everything possible to help them into jobs. If Warner's turned them down I hastened to recommend them to everyone who would listen, and with so much true talent left unclaimed, I had vowed never to waste time or film on the obviously hopeless. Listening to Candy's halting monotone I was certain a new nadir in histrionic expression had been reached.

"I think you need more experience," I said with practiced gentleness. It was a phrase I had overused and heard far too many times myself, but it had always seemed better than an honest, "Why don't you forget the whole thing and take up bookkeeping." A young actress disheartened, I knew, was a broken heart, and from the eminence of my desk whatever was said apparently became fire or ashes.

164

By now I was fairly certain Candy was the victim of a common cruelty. Some influential citizen had either enjoyed her physical charms or hoped to, and as reward had promised a movie test.

Candy rose and left without the slightest sign of surprise or disappointment. The zero in her blue eyes returned to zero, her generous mouth attempted a wan smile which I took for resignation. I escorted her mouth and eyes and nicely proportioned nose to the door in exactly the same manner I accompanied all visitors male or female. They deserved the courtesy and I had been left dangling in subservient retreat often enough to forswear ever watching a visitor depart while I sulked behind the rampart of a desk.

We said goodbye. I could not resist a sigh as I watched Candy sashay down the hallway. She flowed rather than walked, no girdles or other devices impeded the seductive grace of her movements. Her physical perfection still haunted me when I went reluctantly to my telephone.

"Mildred, how could you send that dish up here?"

"When are you going to make her test?"

"She can't read three words without stumbling, let alone act."

"You've got to test her."

"It would be a criminal waste of film."

"Work with her a few weeks."

"Stanislavski himself could not make the poor girl an actress."

"I'm telling you make the test. The Coast wants to see *Candy*, if that's any persuasion."

The "Coast" meant any executive at Warner's Burbank studio. While the purse of the movie industry remained in New York, along with the administrative offices, the Coast was the vortex of nearly all production. Hence we were subservient to the dictates sent by remote generals and their very distance created a sense of awe. I knew well enough how limited my own future must be if I remained on the wrong coast, and I longed for a chance to prove my worth in Hollywood.

I hesitated. Did I believe in myself and methods or was I simply an opportunist?

"I refuse. I can think of ten girls who deserve a test. Let me—"

165

"What shall I tell the Coast when they ask where is Candy's test?"

Some uninvited prude now took command of my tongue. "Tell them," I said slowly, "I was not hired as a pimp and do not intend to take up that profession."

Mildred was horrified. "You want I should put that on the teletype tonight?"

"No. Let me do it."

Two days later Mildred received a response from Jack Warner. She was instructed to discharge the test director immediately.

Kay Brown eased the immediate pain by hiring me to make tests for *Gone With the Wind,* but the actual work days were sporadic and the consequent income far below the regular salary I had enjoyed. Such had been my naïveté, I had not really believed I would be fired, and at first I experienced a period of relief—the balm of the disenfranchised is always the idea that they have been undervalued. It would not have surprised me if the Brothers Warner had invited me back, but no signal except the regrets of Mildred Weber ever came.

Was it my imagination or fact that my friends now seemed over-polite? I was back to the familiar hunt through the theatrical jungles, and whereas the routes were all too familiar and I thought to be wary of every opportunity, I could not make a kill. Everyone was helpful and kind and somewhat too jolly. Rather to my surprise I did not experience a total reversal of friendships simply because I was once again on the outside looking in. Encouragement was everywhere and as my funds approached exhaustion, the few I dared ask offered loans. A vaudeville agent, Jack Davies, who now had nothing whatever to gain of my favor, carried me through one financial crisis after another. It was an indulgence he could ill afford.

Try as I might, nothing came of my constant search for employment. I sold our short movie *Control Yourself* for just enough to cover our expenses and watched the wreckage of another hope float away. I wrote short stories at night and drew cartoons, but none ever sold. My father, suspecting all was not well, came to New York and found me still stubborn in resistance to his offers of aid. I would borrow from friends, but not from family. He thought my pride a foolish pose and told me so, to no avail.

"We enjoy being broke," I declared, while he hosted Eleanor and myself to a lavish dinner at his favorite Waldorf Astoria table. A thin smile passed between Eleanor and my mother. They knew I lied.

Each day I became more desperate. The precious freedom I had won had slipped away from me. My talents, I thought in an orgy of self-deprecation, had lasted about as long as a shooting star.

Although some evidences of recovery from the Great Depression were apparent, I was now one of the eight million Americans still unemployed. The government's WPA program did offer a few jobs of a theatrical nature, but somehow joining those dismal activities seemed an admission of failure. I thought it a justifiable salvation for musicians and artists, but no place for film workers.

Adding to my discouragement was the obvious transition from a way of independent life I had been taught was rightfully mine if I but labored, to a reliance upon other people as a national creed. My father, who vociferously disapproved of Roosevelt, the New Deal, and all its manifestations, was now inspired to address his son with one of his "You are as independent as a hog on ice" addresses.

While it is doubtful that he had ever seen a hog on ice, his dictum had certainly been the true culprit in my loss of a prized job. The proposition that I must rejoin the system and practice much more humility if I would continue to feed Eleanor and young George disturbed me almost as much as the unpaid rent. Yet much as I rebelled against the system, I had been raised a part of it. Total honesty, absolute personal integrity, and hard work were the high-sounding phrases first heard in childhood, repeated over and over by all adults with whom I came in contact and finally pounded home during the most impressive stage of youth at Culver Military Academy.

I was profoundly shaken. The pride which had carried me so easily before melted under the onslaught of repeated rejections everywhere. Nearly all of my classmates at Yale who had chosen the Broadway scene rather than academia were now on some form of government relief.

I could not rest for fear of succumbing to the same temptation. I borrowed and borrowed, a hundred dollars here, a hundred there, and never did any of the lenders press me for return. Their faith compounded my sense of urgency, but all work not already being performed by someone else seemed to have evaporated.

Eleanor reacted magnificently to our tribulations. Her grace and humor never failed and together we disproved the theory that financial distress was the certain lethal poison of young marriage.

––––––

One afternoon on Forty-fourth Street, while prowling the theatrical area in my daily search for work, I recognized a bottle-shaped man proceeding directly toward me. As always he was wearing a mortician's suit, slightly crumpled, and his tie had drifted askew. It was Jimmy Shute. Now his extraordinarily high forehead made him look more than ever like a visiting scientist from another planet, and I was again impressed by the incongruity of our friendship. Here was Shute, that almost total aesthete from whose pores flowed intelligence rather than perspiration, and I thought to drop my employment problem into the machinery of his wonderful brain.

As he poked his precisely wrapped umbrella at the sidewalk and conceded that he might have some suggestions, I was as always entranced with his Dickensian manner. "By Grace of God and most bounteous fortune I am now employed at a company known as the March of Time. Are you aware of its astonishing success?"

I knew it to be a documentary film company inspired by *Time* magazine. They released an exciting thirty-minute film once a month.

"As one of their writers office boy wastebasket-emptiers, I know we have need of a carefree man such as yourself. Did I say carefree? Alas. I had quite forgotten you married. How rude of me. I suppose I meant resourceful . . . or perhaps reckless."

I waited, knowing that Shute considered men who refused to wear rubbers on a gray day as reckless.

"We had a wonderful approach to a story which was to be called 'Inside Nazi Germany.' We were going to

168

show how the young people are indoctrinated in the schools and how Jewish children are ostracized and mal-treated. To our dismay, *Time* and anything to do with *Time* or its subsidiaries, have all been tossed out of Germany. In a word, the Nazis do not like our attitude. Here is the most vitally important story in years and my bosses cannot imagine how they are going to get the necessary film."

He traced a delicate pattern on the sidewalk with the tip of his umbrella and I thought how well he knew the weakness of my will when challenged with any enterprise that might be difficult or dangerous. And he also knew of my past employment as a cameraman for Kinogram's newsreel.

Still pondering the tip of his umbrella, he said, "Charlie Herbert dropped past the other day. He sent you his fondest regards."

I was delighted to learn that the redoubtable Herbert, who had been like a technical father during my youthful days at Ray-Bell, would even remember me.

"Well? . . ."

We smiled.

"A terrifying man named Roy Larsen is our boss. I can get you in to see him. What can you lose?"

It was several days before I was summoned to a gloomy red brick building on Tenth Avenue and granted an audience with Larsen, a man with too much to do. He was suspicious of my reliability, but the magic name of Herbert made him listen in spite of his conviction there must be something very wrong with anyone who would take such an assignment. He was frank in admitting he had hoped to obtain the film in a more orthodox way and he wanted to protect *Time* in case the Germans had a change of heart and said they could return. Even after I had finally convinced him I could enter Germany and come out with the needed film he hedged his gamble.

"If you get caught, don't bother yelling for help. We don't know you . . . we never heard of you."

I thought how the jackal, too, is brave when hungry.

The rest of our agreement would hardly be admired by any sensible businessman, much less my father. The March of Time would pay all my expenses to Germany and back to America. They would furnish me with an

Eyemo 35 mm. camera and special lenses to my request. They would also supply a thousand feet of 35 mm. film in one-hundred-foot rolls. When exposed the film would remain their property and I would be paid only according to the footage actually used. At two dollars a foot.

I remembered Shute asking, "What can you lose?" and I deliberately avoided thinking just what that could be.

Within a week I was en route to Germany.

Chapter 15

I had been in Amsterdam twice before, but under entirely different circumstances. Now, though it was the beginning of spring, there was only denial in the bitterly cold wind sweeping down from the North Sea. The room I had taken in the American Hotel was supposed to be heated, but I had found the only way to keep warm was by countined pacing. I had been pacing since early morning, trying to stave off intermittent chills and dissipate the rancid taste of defeat. For I had certainly lost the first round to the Germans, and the thought of Larsen's caustic greeting if I returned empty-handed unnerved me.

Now I realized how my initial plan had been based on an overenthusiastic assumption that the Germans were as thickheaded and myopic as our current news reports portrayed them. "We never heard of you." As Larsen's phrase kept tumbling through my mind I developed a new sympathy for all the real spies I had read about. I had talked myself into a situation from which I could not see any escape, and my bravado, so boldly worn when surrounded by my own countrymen, had almost totally evaporated.

I had crossed the Atlantic in the *Veendam,* deliberately choosing a Dutch ship because its passage ended at the threshold of Germany. I had thought to use Amsterdam as a base and enter Germany by a small boat near Terschelling or along the lonely beaches of the German Bight.

After a day on the Amsterdam waterfront I had reluctantly discarded this idea, because there were no boats available without the company of the boatman himself, which inevitably meant complication. And once inside Germany, I would need efficient transportation. A bold and open approach, I had decided, would best support my masquerade.

I began by ordering a box of printed business cards which designated me as President of the International Amateur Bird Photographers, headquartered at my home address on New York's Sixty-third Street. Although ignorant of the difference between a thrush and a golden flippet, photographing birds, I reasoned, left a great deal of room for maneuver. Presumably, following a bird I could point my camera as needed, and if no birds were handy when spectators became overinquisitive, I could always lament their sudden departure.

Next I bought two small American flags and rented a motorcycle. I lashed the flags to the handlebars in keeping with my honest purpose. After searching through several motorcycle establishments, I eventually found two saddlebags large enough to accommodate the Eyemo camera, lenses, film, and personal gear. On the morning of the fourth day I placed four one-hundred-foot rolls of film in the bottom of each saddlebag and covered the cans with dirty laundry.

The Eyemo camera and a special eleven-inch telephoto lens presented a problem until I gave up the idea of trying to conceal them. Wasn't I President of the International Amateur Bird Photographers? I placed the lens in one saddlebag and the camera in the other, cushioning them against my shirts and an extra sweater. I had loaded the Eyemo with one roll of film and left the last one with the hotel's concierge as a possible reserve. At last, in a mist which occasionally became true rain, I set off for Germany.

My spirits weakened increasingly as I progressed farther into the east. I was wretched with sudden loneliness, and every foolhardy aspect of the expedition arose to mock me. Along the bottom rim of my goggles I could see the small American flags fluttering in the breeze and I tried without success to take heart from their brave display.

During the late afternoon the sun broke through the

heavy overcast. Although it was only a pallid, ochre ball, it threw my elongated shadow far ahead on the brick road, jouncing the scarecrow which I recognized as myself in such a delightful way that I began to hum fragmentary passages from *Madame Butterfly,* the only music my tin ear would permit me to remember. Thanks to the all-dominating roar of the motorcycle's exhaust, my voice sounded almost on key. It was an English machine of very good manufacture and by the time I approached the frontier, riding through the soft and smoky hues of early evening, my enthusiasm for the venture had returned. I *must* succeed.

The Dutch frontier guards simply glanced at my passport and waved me through. In less than thirty minutes I had returned to them. For the Germans had not been influenced in the slightest by my simplicity of transport, the American flags, cards, or my exuberant pantomime of posing birds.

Jawohl! It was all right for me to enter Germany, although I must pay a small customs fee for the supply of tobacco and cigarette papers I carried. But such a camera, and so much film. *Nein!* Only with a special permit from Berlin.

I argued and searched the nearby trees for birds to convince them of my journey's innocent intent, but the trees, stark against the twilight, were barren of life. Four guards gathered to witness my pantomime, yet by the middle of the second act I knew the show was doomed to failure.

Now I had returned to zero start in the same comfortless hotel room I had left only the previous noon.

Outside the window I could hear one of the Dutch street organs piping and thar-rumping a march tune. Instinctively I fell into step with its musical beat, seeking in physical action new stimulation for my thoughts. Larson was in a hurry and two weeks had passed without his bumbling cameraman exposing an inch of film. Since I was obligated to try again, I decided to enter Germany a different way.

I descended to the hotel lobby where the concierge who knew everything there was to know in the Lowlands might help me. He was pessimistic, because, he said, the tulips were still dormant and consequently the season for renting cars in Holland had not begun. Yet after three funereal telephone conversations he finally directed me to a place with a name I thought rather odd for a car rental agency: Fireside Rental.

A taxi took me to the fringes of Amsterdam and stopped before a fat Dutch house with two curved windows extending like bosoms from its formidable façade. I regretted dismissing the taxi. Why was there no commercial sign identifying the place as Fireside Rental?

I lifted the brass doorknocker twice and waited. Somewhere within the house I heard a dog growling. The heavy door was pulled open and a middle-aged man stood glaring at me.

"Is this Fireside Rental?" I found it difficult to utter the name in a businesslike tone.

As he nodded his head I wondered if it could have been the man growling instead of a dog. He had dark hair, was of medium height, and needed a shave. Perhaps, I thought, he just has a terrible hangover.

"You do rent cars?"

"Yes."

"I would like a car for two weeks. The hotel called about me."

"Where are you going?"

"Here and there." I saw no reason to advertise my route to anyone and there was something curiously wrong about the whole place. In a moment of wild fancy I wondered if the hotel concierge had somehow learned of my true purpose and set me up for a permanent stay in Germany.

"Enter."

My sullen host led me down a hallway, then through a door on the right which might normally open upon a Dutch-style parlor. The room had been converted into a spartan office.

The Dutchman said, "The only car I have available is a Ford."

"All right."

"You must deposit one thousand guilders and settle the account each week." His attention drifted to the bleak leftover winter scene outside the curved window and he appeared to have forgotten my existence.

"Where did you say you were going?"

I hesitated, wondering how much I wanted him to know. "Among other places . . . Germany."

"Why?"

"A tour."

"At this time of year? You Americans are fools. It will rain all the time you are there."

Here, I decided, was the grand master of undersell.

"Let me see your international driver's license."

"I do not have one."

"Then I can't rent you a car."

"I'm willing to pay . . ." At the place I had rented the motorcycle they had never mentioned such formalities.

"Come back when you get a license. With good luck it shouldn't take you longer than a fortnight."

I told him I must have a car at once, and, now peevish, announced that if he were not interested in at least two weeks' rental I would find someone who would be. Two weeks, I thought, was about the maximum Larsen would finance his gypsy cameraman without actually seeing usable film. The Dutchman shrugged his shoulders, uncaring.

The parlor-office and what I took to be a dining room were separated by a curved wooden arch. Now, even though the arch was behind me, I sensed I was no longer alone with the moody Dutchman.

Turning I discovered a young woman framed in the archway. She was not beautiful in any orthodox way; there was a sturdiness about her trim figure and face which spoke of robust health rather than delicacy. Her nose turned up slightly in the classic Dutch line, her cheekbones were pronounced, and her lips full, but there the resemblance to a Vermeer model ended. Her eyes were a startling delft blue, and her smile was anything but enigmatic.

My desire to leave diminished. As she moved into the room I was instantly taken with her air of total confidence. She glanced at the man behind the desk, but I saw no message pass between them. Since both were of very dark complexion for Hollanders, I assumed they must be brother and sister. I was not surprised that the Dutchman failed to trouble himself with introductions since he had not yet been disposed to even ask my name, but when she turned to smile again at me, the sullen atmosphere, for which I could not possibly account, vanished immediately. "Would you like a cup of coffee?" she asked.

The Dutchman advised her coldly that I was just leaving. "He wants to rent a car without a driver's license. I have told him it is impossible, but he thinks I am telling him a lie,"

I had not for an instant, either by word or gesture, suggested he was lying.

"That is so," she said, still smiling. "I am so sorry for you."

I explained how I had assumed the concierge had settled the car matter and I had therefore dismissed my taxi. How could I return to the hotel?

My host pushed himself to his feet and his manner was strangely preoccupied, as if he could hardly bear waiting any longer to conclude our meeting. Something, I thought, which has nothing to do with me or the renting of cars is troubling him, and I wondered if it could be the woman with the delft-blue eyes.

"Walk to the tram head," he was saying. "Two kilometers only. To your right down the road."

But I hardly heard him. I saw that her eyes were assessing me, and I stood a little straighter, instinctively seeking approval.

"Nonsense," she said brightly. "I have an errand in the city. I will drive you. Wait two minutes."

The car was a Ford, which I presumed would have been mine had I the necessary papers. She drove expertly, although at a speed which I considered too nearly matching her dashing manner, and halfway to the city I realized she had renewed her frank examination of me instead of keeping her eyes on the road.

"Why do you not allow me to drive you to Germany?"

We swerved past a milk cart, missing it by millimeters, careened through a turn and plunged down a wet cobbled road. I became so absorbed with the chances of our skidding into the bordering canal that I wasn't sure I had understood her.

"You, drive me?"

"I do so every summer for tourists. Many people do not have the license. It is so stupid to take so long, but that is the way things are in Holland. Every person must put his little stamp on every little thing. We are a slow people."

"Not in a car!" I was reviewing the many reasons why such an idea would not work, when a truck carrying a load of manure challenged her for space on the narrow road. I covered my eyes, convinced a successful passing was obviously impossible.

"Also I can show you many things. Of course I speak German and also French and Flemish if I must. You will please excuse my English."

I heard a loud whoosh and I forced my hand away from my eyes. By some miracle she had managed to pass the truck. "If you're late for an appointment," I said unhappily, "don't go out of your way for me. I can walk the rest of the way. The exercise will do me good."

She laughed and I thought how only truly great women dare reveal themselves in a lusty laugh. Easing off slightly on the throttle she said, "If I drive you, the expense will not be much more."

There were, I thought, countless reasons to avoid this temptation, so at the hotel I deliberately made our parting formal and as cold as I could manage while looking into her challenging eyes. They seemed to be asking, "Why are you so timid?"

By eleven o'clock I was back to pacing the carpet in my room, but now my cadence had become erratic and savage, as if anger could clear my frustrations. Of course it would be an advantage having an interpreter along, particularly when the actual filming began, but a woman? How soon would she discover I was not utterly devoted to birds? And what might she do then—run off with our transportation, leave me stranded in Germany with nine hundred feet of hot film and no place to hide? If she wanted to be rid of me and incidentally pick up a fee, she could easily turn me in to the Gestapo.

The room telephone, a sort of small hunting horn contrivance, hung on the wall over the bed. I had passed it many times, frowned at it, reached for it—changed my mind. Now very suddenly I reached a decision. In my aloneness I had become a rabbit, wagging my ears at every hint of danger, conjuring up hazards which for all I knew did not exist. This super-caution was not the self I knew and I half ran to take down the hunting horn.

My tongue shied involuntarily as I asked to be connected with Fireside Rental. Almighty God, I thought, what a name.

Shortly I heard the dour grumble of the Dutchman.

"I understand you will furnish a car if it's plus driver?"

"Right."

"Do you understand the trip may take two weeks . . . maybe more?"

"Right. But you must make the deposit."

Maybe, I thought, his ulcerous disposition originated in finance, for money certainly appeared to be his only concern.

"All right," I said in my best damn-the-torpedoes fashion, "tell her to be here ready to go in an hour."

They arrived together and my second meeting with the proprietor of Fireside Rental was even more cryptic than the first. He took my deposit without so much as a thank you, sheltered a sheaf of papers from the wind while I signed them, and immediately hailed a taxi. He nodded at my new employee as the taxi pulled away and ignored me, behavior I found strangely satisfying. For I had begun to admire his uncompromising misanthropy.

Her name was Rikki. As she drove her personal Grand Prix through the lingering windswept Dutch twilight, we rarely spoke. I was lost in film planning and I hoped she was totally given to her chauffeuring. In much less time than I had thought possible we approached Maastricht near the frontier. Darkness had just enveloped the flat countryside and a moderate rain hissed against the windshield.

She glanced at me. "Do you want to go on to Germany tonight, or stop in Maastricht?"

"I want to go on. But first let's eat, and there are a few things I'd like to discuss with you." I had been brooding about a second attempt to cross the German frontier. The Eyemo camera and film were now together in a duffle bag stowed in the luggage compartment. I did not plan to declare them.

"Are you a rich American? I know a fine place to dine. You will like it."

"I am a poor American, but we'll go there anyway."

I was puzzled and disappointed at her choosing the railroad station, but it proved to house the finest restaurant in Maastricht. There were white tablecloths, potted palms, and a lively string quartet. While the food was heavy, the German wine was light and of pleasant bouquet, and it gradually dissolved the little formalities remaining between us.

While we toyed with an oversweet dessert the string quartet sawed bravely away at "Barcarole" and I noticed that for the first time Rikki seemed off guard. Watching her, increasingly aware of her tremendous vitality even when she relaxed, I thought I must tell her before it was too late how I was not the bird-watcher of my pretending. And yet, I must not reveal too much.

"You don't know anything about me," I began. "How can you go wandering off like this? I might be Bluebeard, plotting a murder."

She took up her wine glass and smiled at me over the rim. I became uncomfortable. She was laughing at me, gently perhaps, but it was there. "But you know nothing about me, either," she said easily.

"I know your brother is never going to become salesman of the year."

"My brother?" she asked. "I don't understand you."

"Your boss. The big chief of Fireside Rental."

"But he is not my brother. He is my husband."

I tried to recover what little composure remained to me. "Ah?" I choked. "Ah? Your, ah . . . husband doesn't mind if you go off for two weeks or so with a stranger?"

"No."

There was not a hint of invitation in her voice or of guile in her eyes.

"I know more about you than you think," she said, still smiling. "Most things you do in Amsterdam are known . . . if you do it in the American Hotel."

"What have I done to deserve so much attention?" I wondered if she knew about my misadventure with the motorcycle and if (a wild thought) there might be more to Fireside Rental than mere auto-renting.

"You do not behave like a tourist." The smile left her face as she turned her wine glass slowly back and forth. "It is very strange . . . every person is watching everyone these days."

I was now reasonably sure who had been watching me —my advisor, the hotel concierge.

"I am a tourist in a different way. I want to photograph birds in Germany . . . take movies . . . the cinema, you understand?"

"Of course . . ." I watched her eyes carefully, half hoping to catch her in suspicion. Now was the time to turn back if I must, yet for once her face was almost devoid of expression.

She listened politely while I told her I heard the Germans were very stuffy about taking cameras through the frontier . . . particularly equipment like mine, which was so special because of the birds. Finally I attempted to create an air of innocent mischief when I asked if she knew a quiet little place to cross the frontier, a place where the inspections were not likely to be overly strict.

"Is it not so that birds are just as interesting in Holland, or perhaps in France?"

"No." I tried to keep my voice as flat as possible.

"Then I know just the place."

Behind Rikki's head I watched the reflected rain dribbling down the black window, wondering how far I could trust the woman behind those remarkable eyes.

We drove for about half an hour in a direction I guessed was roughly north from Maastricht. It was raining very hard, which mellowed even Rikki's mania for speed. Even so, I was becoming increasingly uneasy, for I was convinced we should long since have reached the frontier. Yet Rikki seemed to know exactly where she was going, never hesitating as the narrow road made innumerable junctions, twisted over a series of hills, and then turned upon itself while descending into the marketplace of a dark and sodden village.

"How much farther to the frontier?"

"It is near now."

I had been watching her face for some indication of excitement or even apprehension, but found her apparently absorbed only in the business of driving. I tried not to dwell upon the wisdom of placing my immediate fortunes entirely in her hands.

We passed through the Dutch-controlled side of the frontier in only a few minutes. While Rikki spoke to the solitary guard in Dutch I watched in fascination as her volatile spirit rose to the occasion. Somehow she contrived to inject a flourish into her every gesture, a physical gallantry as if she were delighted in this reunion with a trusted comrade-in-arms. The guard responded with equal enthusiasm. He stepped back from the car window, the pounding rain creating a halo effect around his cap and glistening cape. After a hearty laugh he saluted smartly. Rikki rolled up her window, blew him a kiss, and we sped off through the night.

After about a mile, a red-and-white striped barrier appeared in the shafts of the headlights and Rikki slowed to a stop. There had been no visible habitation of any kind along the road, but now beside the barrier, I saw a small plaster building with an overhanging roof. Two windows faced the gravel road and the light from within formed translucent columns of rain between the car and the entrance. There were no guards outside the building and I could not detect any movement inside. When Rikki switched the engine off I found the overall quiet disconcerting. The only sound was the drumming of rain on the car roof.

Rikki clamped a beret on her head, buttoned the collar of her raincoat and held out her hand to me. "Let me have your passport."

I hesitated. Larsen's concise words echoed across my thoughts. ". . . we never heard of you."

My passport was the only thing I possessed to prove I had any rights at all.

"It will be much easier if you wait here," she said. "Do not get out of the car unless I call you."

How does *she* know it will be much easier, I thought. If the style with which she had found this dubiously remote place were her standard, it would seem that all the tourists she claimed to escort in the summertime had asked to cross the frontier at a "quiet little place."

I handed her my passport reluctantly and watched her run through the rain, then enter the building. Should she have paused to knock, or was she expected? By leaning far back in the seat I found I could see through the window. Framed in the relative brilliance of the light, I watched Rikki greet a heavy-set, elderly man in a green uniform.

I watched them converse a moment, then Rikki made a sweeping gesture with one hand. The man in the green uniform began nodding his head and I could even see the rumples of fat along the back of his neck enlarge and collapse. I squirmed around, trying to see if there were other people in the room, but the windowframe limited my line of vision.

In a moment Rikki laughed with the gusto I already regarded as her trademark. She clasped the man's arm and with the other hand I was astonished to see her slap his considerable belly. Now he tossed his head back and joined her in laughter. Strangely annoyed, I muttered aloud, "What is this . . . old home week?" I was not at all sure I liked the pantomime I was witnessing.

They moved away from the window, still laughing. For every joke there is a butt, and it suddenly struck me I might be wearing the clown's bells.

I waited unhappily, now searching the darkness all around the car, but always coming back to the lighted window. The rain was steady, dinning noisily on the car's hood, ploshing into a chain of puddles between the car and the candy-striped barrier. My window was becoming opaque from the heat of my breathing. Rolling it down, I discovered that the rain was as cold as my enthusiasm had turned for this whole endeavor. How had I come into this thorny detour from sanity?

I tried to ease my anxiety by telling myself Rikki had chosen the perfect frontier crossing. In ten short paces I could reach the barrier and slip beneath it, a considerable difference from the complex I had tried to pass on the motorcycle. Yet it seemed to be taking her overlong with the man in the green uniform . . . unless, I thought with some misgivings, they already knew each other.

Could he have been warned of our coming? Nonsense, I decided. The rain was depressing me. How could I have forgotten that March was one of the worst months in Northern Europe? Rikki's crazy husband had been correct when he said it would rain all the time. And with my powerful eleven-inch telephoto lens, rain photographed as a translucent gray wall, not exactly the sort of film quality Larsen had a right to expect. Jimmy Shute, I thought, why did I run into you on Forty-fourth Street?

Light played across the road and I saw Rikki appear in the doorway. She pulled the collar of her coat tightly around her neck and, sidestepping the puddles, ran head down toward the car. She was followed by a man, apparently the same man, now wearing a black slicker and a uniform cap. He shouted something at her in German then marched off to the barrier.

Rikki jerked the car door open and slipped quickly into her seat. She started the engine, wiped the moisture from her face, and flicked on the driving lights. I saw that the man was cranking up the candy-stick barrier and I glanced at my watch. It was twenty minutes until ten.

I rolled up my window as we started to move. Immediately Rikki reached across me and rolled it down again. She slowed almost to a stop as we passed the German and, smiling, made the gesture of blowing him a kiss. As he saluted she stepped on the accelerator and we were away. Incredulous, I heard her say: "The *pig!*"

"Are you referring to your dear friend back there?"

"Yes. All Germans are pigs."

Rikki was driving fast now through a black countryside. There was not even an occasional light from a farmhouse.

"Just how did you manage? The guard didn't look at anything . . . not even me." I tried to keep the tone of my voice much more casual than I felt. I was committed now, the man Jimmy Shute saw in me must be revived and directed to expel this other panicky newcomer who spied calamity behind every turn of the road.

"I told him we were on our honeymoon and you were sick with a cold and I had to get you to bed quickly. It gave him a chance to make many stupid jokes." She was silent for a moment, then her intensity grew chilling. "I *hate* Germans!"

The deluge persisted until we approached the outskirts of Cologne. Then abruptly, as if the ancient city itself supported an umbrella, the rain ceased and I saw a piece of moon. At two o'clock in the morning, after a high-speed ride through the deserted streets, Rikki pulled up before the venerable Palace Hotel.

The sleepy receptionist was mystified when I insisted on two rooms, preferably on different floors. There had been enough complications for one day, I reasoned, and I wanted to devote all my energies to the problems of filming under what promised to be very difficult conditions. It seemed to me unnecessary to go much deeper into Germany. One German child should do as well as another, so why not confine my filming to the Rhineland, choosing a few of the more picturesque villages for atmosphere? I had lost almost a week with the motorcycle fiasco. Now I needed all the time I could salvage for the planning of scenes and selecting of hidden situations where the wonderful yet temperamental eleven-inch lens could be used to full advantage.

We exchanged a quick good night and I warned Rikki that we must be up and away by seven in the morning. I told her of my intent to film around Cologne, then make southward along the Rhine for more open country and the smaller villages. I thought her "Sleep well" was dry and overly formal, although she had given me no cause to expect anything more.

My room was small, but it offered a view over the city and the magnificent cathedral of Cologne sleeping in the moonlight. Turning from the cathedral I found some comfort in realizing I had fulfilled at least part of my agreement with Larsen. I was inside Germany, in reasonably familiar territory, and, so far as I knew, still undiscovered. I was a successful Trojan with my horse parked in the hotel garage and though my nerves were still thrumming from the events of the previous day I was ready to begin my very special mission.

There was not a sound from the slumbering city below. I turned toward the bed and slipped beneath the huge German pouf, grateful for the peace of this innocent early morning. Vaguely I remembered it was the seventh of March, 1936, and the last I knew of it was a heavy bell's thrice tolling somewhere in the distance. I had no idea whatever how on the eastern flank of the Rhine, less than a mile beyond my open window, the elements of an apocalypse were gathering.

It was a chosen morning. Only Adolph Hitler and a very few German generals knew of an operation they called *Schulung*.

Chapter 16

Somewhere in my system there has always lurked a marvelous device, a special consciousness of time passage which has served me so well I've usually been able to estimate accurately the hour and even the approximate minute. Likewise, if it is necessary to awake at a certain hour, some restless genie will see that I do—five minutes before or exactly at the appointed time. Yet now in Cologne, where all unknowing I had been sleeping in the lap of history, the mechanism lagged and from oblivion I gradually became aware that someone was disturbing my peace. I opened my eyes to find Rikki sitting on the edge of my bed tugging gently at the pouf. She was fully dressed.

"I thought you wanted to be up at seven?" she said with a mocking smile. "The birds you want to film have been up for hours."

I glanced at my watch, saw it was already seven-thirty, and barely paused to consider the failure in my personal alarm system. My thoughts had been almost instantly captured by twin questions: who was this woman who so casually entered a near-stranger's room without invitation, and how had she gotten in, since I was certain I had locked the door? Too many things seemed remarkably easy for Rikki.

Still wondering at her boldness, and secretly yearning to trust her more, I asked her to leave. I would meet her in the lobby in half an hour. Rising, she cautioned me to hurry with my dressing since she had told the floor maid to bring me breakfast. "A large breakfast, much toast and sausage and cheese and coffee. All right?"

When she had left and closed the door I was troubled by a new sense of uncertainty. My needs, it seemed, were being almost too well taken in hand by a Dutch woman I had met for the first time less than twenty-four hours ago.

At the window I found the view across the city of Cologne more reassuring and traded my darker thoughts for appreciation of the magnificent morning. It would be a perfect morning for filming, and I thought to begin with some shots of children at play, which could later be spliced between scenes depicting their indoctrination with theories of the Nazi Party. Any handy schoolyard would do for this first background. As for Rikki, whose assistance as an interpreter might be valuable, I would explain how closely children and birds were related in the overall film story.

The sun had climbed halfway to the zenith before we found a locale which exactly suited my purpose. We had previously inspected two other sites farther removed from the center of the city and had now doubled back almost to the hotel. Only a few blocks from it, just beneath the western buttress of an iron bridge spanning the Rhine, we found a school play yard swarming with children as blond and Teutonic in appearance as any propagandist could wish. It was recess time and they were shouting, running, calling, tugging, and jumping all around us, the very sort of action I had hoped for. Deliberately hoarding my limited supply of film, I had loaded the Eyemo with a hundred-foot roll and brought no more lest I be tempted to use it. I wanted only about fifty feet of this unbounded energy, just enough to deny the portrait of German schoolchildren as sickly and half-starved, a view so many misguided publications had offered the democratic world.

On the far side of the play yard, next to the school, stood a few adults, faces upturned to the sky. I assumed they were teachers, hungry for the sun as were all northern Europeans at this time of year. They did not trouble themselves to ask what so engaged us. When the children first exploded from the school building, spattering in all directions like multicolored shrapnel, a few of the more observant were curious about two adult strangers with a camera, but Rikki had spoken to them in German and now, wholly absorbed in their playing, they ignored us. Which is exactly what I had been waiting for.

Now a few nimbus clouds formed overhead and began to play with the intensity of the light. I would be ready for a shot, a face poised just right, and the sun would suddenly become veil; then, frustrated, I would change angle and lens setting only to find the sun burning down again. It was difficult as always when trying to capture children unaware to assemble all the elements simultaneously, and the problems were aggravated by the deep shadows beneath the bridge where it seemed my most photogenic actors insisted on playing. I became so absorbed in the continuing challenges, I was only vaguely aware of a radio blatting on, or was it a portable loudspeaker powerful enough to dominate the happy screeching of the children?

"It is Hitler again," Rikki said in disgust. "He is always these days making the big noise."

As I worked she translated fragments for me. ". . . in this historic hour, when in the Reich's western provinces, German troops are this minute marching into their future peacetime garrisons, we all unite in two sacred vows . . ."

I found a face, just the right taffyhead among so many, which I knew would appear spectacular on any screen.

"Rikki! Ask that boy to move over this way a little. See if you can persuade him to look up at the sky." I pressed the button and felt rather than really heard the whirring of the Eyemo's motor.

". . . we pledge that now more than ever, we shall strive for an understanding between the European peoples, especially for one with our Western neighbor nations. We have no territorial demands to make in Europe! Germany will never break the peace!"

I wanted just one shot more. I swung the lens turret around until the three-inch lens locked in place and caught a fine closeup of the boy. Even as I admired his innocent features in the viewfinder, a new noise overwhelmed all the rest, penetrating through the children's shrill clamor like the fundamental throbbing of heavy machinery. "That's all I need, Rikki. We can go now."

To leave the play yard we were obliged to climb a metal stairway, green with verdigris from long exposure to the elements. While we climbed, I explained to Rikki how I proposed to combine the shots of schoolchildren with later material. Her expression turned doubtful, but she did not question me further.

As the jubilant squealing of the children sank away, the heavy noise from the bridge above became ever more dominant. We reached the top of an incline and paused by an iron railing which swerved gracefully downward from the bridge. I stood for a moment catching at my

186

breath after the climb, looking down at the play yard and then at the bridge's roadway stretching toward the east and the opposite bank of the Rhine.

Then, very suddenly, I realized my eyes were absorbing action I found difficult to believe. And I became aware that Rikki was also disbelieving. For marching straight toward us, snare drums hissing a soul-shivering beat, boots knocking hard and smartly on the pavement, was a long column of German soldiers.

I shook my head trying to convince myself it was a mirage, for I knew we were standing in the demilitarized zone of the Rhineland, the historic buffer division between France and Germany. According to the Treaty of Locarno, which the Germans had signed, no soldier of any nation was supposed to be on this side of the Rhine—much less, units of the German Wehrmacht.

"Rikki. Something is very wrong."

She stood in silence, her brilliant eyes strange and cold as if she were watching the uncoiling of a poisonous serpent.

Two armored cars flanked the head of the column. Gunners manned the turrets, staring straight ahead. They were not real, I thought, just figurines in some sort of daytime nightmare. I watched in awe until the sharp sound of their vehicles' exhausts ripped through my shock. Then I quickly wound the spring motor of the Eyemo, swung the turret so the two-inch lens was in place, and framed the column of troops in the view-finder. As I pressed the button I held my breath to insure a steady image in the camera. But the whole bridge was shaking under the impact of so much machinery; and so, I thought, was the world.

Now fully aware that I occupied a box seat at a historic event I became acutely conscious of my inadequate film supply. There remained only fifty unexposed feet in the Eyemo, barely enough for half a minute's viewing.

As the troops continued past us only a few yards away I forced myself to save twenty feet for closeups. Finally I swung the four-inch lens into place, selected a face here, a face there, and held down the motor button until I knew from the total lack of vibration against my fingertips that at last I was shooting with an empty camera. When I took the viewfinder away from my eye and saw the real world so close I could touch it, I was uncertain whether to cheer or weep for my luck. Reluctantly, I admitted it would be impossible to cross the bridge through the marching column, run to the Ford, reload the camera, and return in time to shoot anything more.

Now I saw there were not so many troops as at first appeared. Yet numbers were not significant. My own years in uniform had taught me the importance of caliber in any military unit, and I had never seen soldiers like those now passing in parade. I knew by the hang of their equipment, by the cadence and style of their swing, that here were true professionals. Regardless of their rank insignia I became convinced that every private was a capable corporal, every corporal a sergeant, and every sergeant an officer. Here were soldiers to frighten the senses, here were the prime legionnaires of a dictator, soldiers to crunch the soul. A battalion? Less, I guessed. It was hard to be sure because the form of their platoons was quite different from ours.

I held the camera at my side making it as inconspicuous as possible. I hardly needed an encounter with the Gestapo to teach me that a foreigner who happened to have a commission even in our reserve, and who also happened to have a camera, might not be welcome at these proceedings. Or would it make the slightest difference to anyone?

It made some difference to Rikki. I became aware that she had been watching me instead of the troops. And now I saw that her eyes were accusing, her lips poised in question.

"Why were you telling me foolishness about children and birds?"

Of course. How could I convince anyone not privy to the background of this venture that I had *not* planned to be standing on such a bridge *with a camera* on this particular morning? Rikki was obviously not going to believe me without some kind of proof, and I had nothing more convincing for her than I would have for any German official who might take an interest in my activities.

I met Rikki's frank examination, hoping for reassurance. There was none of the warmth in her expression I had seen over a wine glass the previous night. All of the agreeable mischief was gone from her eyes, her feet were spread wide apart, her hands jammed down hard in her coat-pockets, her whole body poised in challenge. Her eyes seemed to say she realized at last how easily she could ruin whatever project was at hand and, if she pleased, ruin even me.

A long uneasy silence stood between us. I dared not look away from her.

The sound of the drums and pavement-smacking boots merged and diminished as the last of the column passed onward. Finally Rikki spoke, her voice firm and faintly patronizing, as if she were addressing someone in whom she was disappointed.

"Do you want to take more pictures of birds?"

"No."

As I tried to estimate her thoughts I discovered a dimple above the left corner of her mouth which I had not noticed before. It deepened slightly now as a question seemed poised on her lips. I could not blame her if she was troubled by a multitude of doubts for which I had no ready answer.

The moment of waiting was a long one. Then suddenly she reached her hand toward my side.

"Give your camera to me. I will carry it behind my bag. It will be better that way."

The village of Ochtendung was gray, stolid, and a generally oppressive stucco hodgepodge of dwellings and crooked crevasselike streets. There was no formal hotel, but instead a sort of municipal bierstube doubled as a hostel where simple meals could be taken. Along the backside of the cobbled courtyard, over the stables, were four rooms available to travelers.

We came upon Ochtendung just after the gloaming had melted all the smaller local hills into a few greater silhouettes. Now openly in league with each other, Rikki and I had decided that Ochtendung's removal from the general stream of traffic through the Rhineland offered many advantages, and I hoped it would be a place where I could work without exciting more than local curiosity. For now I knew that regardless of Larsen's original conception of a film involving children inside Nazi Germany, the significance of the troops we had seen crossing to the western bank of the Rhine must overwhelm all other subject matter. Somehow, although woefully short of film for such an important change of circumstance, I must manage to combine the indoctrination of children theme with Hitler's bold challenge to the Western democracies.

Riding beside Rikki in the twilight, hanging on while she drove with her usual verve, I wondered if all would return to normal in the morning if the Western nations called Hitler's bluff. Had we just witnessed the first pawn moved in a new world conflict? Now how long would it be before Hitler decided Austria needed his sublime protection?

As we entered the village a loudspeaker truck parked in the center of the square was broadcasting the voice of Adolph Hitler. His declarations were interspersed with announcements of a National-Socialist meeting to be held in the town hall that evening. I was determined to attend and asked Rikki if she would interpret for me.

My doubts about her had been eased during the long afternoon ride down from Cologne, not so much by anything said, but more by the questions she did not ask.

She had made a statement: "You're not really photographing birds." And I had said, "No . . ." and that had been the end of it.

As the afternoon passed I became impressed with Rikki's willingness to become an accessory in something she must now be sure was at least illegal and might very well be dangerous. Either her hatred for Germans was such that she would do anything to embarrass them or she was one of those special women for whom adventure holds even greater appeal than for men. Or, a final possibility, which I now decided to dismiss—she knew something I did not know.

There was an extra charge for my room since it was the only one equipped with a stove. Now we sat close to it, our feet on the lip of the stove, leaning back in two rickety chairs and drinking a sourish wine, the sole variety available in the hostel. We talked for a time of the penetrating cold of the night and, as if fearful of deeper exploration of each other, we avoided personal references and spoke instead of the town meeting from which we had just returned.

Whereas the troops had impressed me, the Nazi meeting had been more like a fourth-rate vaudeville show. There had been several very inept entertainers presumably offered to put the audience in a receptive mood for the second act political propaganda. Even without full knowledge of the language I could sense that the meeting was not a success. The peasants laughed in all the wrong places, according to Rikki, and only a number of bull-necked, bland-eyed young men, obvious strangers to the locale, kept the audience from going home. Yet I knew such thinking was exactly the kind of complacency I must avoid. Too many people had regarded the Nazis as fools and found themselves behind barbed wire.

"In the morning you must find out what time the children leave school to go home. Then ask which streets most of them will pass through." I handed Rikki a hundred-mark note. "Buy a bag of candy . . . little pieces wrapped separately. I'll need it tomorrow."

Her yawn became a smile. "Nothing for the birds?"

"No. Just do as I ask for the next few days and when it's all over, I'll explain."

We drained our wine glasses and rose together. As we stood in a sort of momentary embarrassment I watched her eyes in what light the single bare bulb afforded. And I thought I saw there only loyalty and a silent agreement that we were not only in this venture together, but also two persons made to the same fundamental design. All suspicion of her left me along with a nagging sense of fear which I had thought a byproduct of loneliness. With Rikki at my side, I thought, only my own clumsiness might bring failure to a mission which through totally unforeseen events had changed drastically since first conceived. I must film more of children, yes; but other more sinister game must be brought within range of my camera.

"Now I must be the gentleman and offer you this room. It's warmer."

"I'm Dutch. I don't like heat where I sleep."

"Thank God. I do."

When she had gone I began the ritual act veteran cameraman Herbert had shown me long ago. I removed the face and side from the Eyemo, wiped it down with a special soft cloth and blew out any lint or possible dust. Herbert had taught me to keep a copper penny as the best tool for the final devotion of the ceremony. I scraped the penny all around the border of the steel aperture gate, thus without scarring the gate itself removing even the most minute foreign object which might hinder the free passage of film through the camera.

Later, as I tipped the residue of acrid smelling coal from the bucket into the stove, I was haunted by visions of the troops we had seen on the bridge at Cologne. If only I had been waiting on the bridge with a standard Bell and Howell camera, or a Mitchell, equipped with four-hundred-foot magazines! For a moment I wondered if I should send Larsen a cable asking him to consider changing our basic theme, and almost immediately decided against such a plea for reassurance. How could he respond without compromising me? And besides, Larsen had insisted he would not recognize any connection between us. I was in this alone—except, I remembered, for Rikki.

The thick smell of dung from the stables below rose easily through the rough flooring. Climbing into the high lumpy bed I debated whether the odor would be less or more if I opened the window. Already half asleep I remembered the temperature outside and chose the stench. It was, I thought, representative of the new and all too real Germany.

In Ochtendung the children went home for their noonday meal. They were obliged to pass along the narrow main street which bisects the village square and then twists some hundred paces toward the north where it straightens just in front of the hostel. Beyond, it starts twisting again and finally emerges from the village to blend with the surrounding fields.

All morning the village lay soaking in a cold rain, but before noon as if on order the sky cleared partly and a peaked sun became visible. It was neither winter nor spring, yet the cold was so penetrating the tips of my fingers turned white as I waited on camera station. I had made myself as inconspicuous as possible because I wanted to avoid the certain display of self-consciousness if the children saw they were being photographed. The camera site I had chosen was anything but comfortable and when filming actually began I would have no choice but to kneel in the cement gutter which drained the hostel stables.

I waited in a wooden shed which was actually part of the hostel. There was little chance of the children becoming aware of me unless they paused for a considerable time and looked directly at the shed. During the mid-morning I had experimented by standing in the street and found I had trouble locating the camera although I knew exactly where to look—a narrow slit between the wooden wall of the shed and its stone base. Although the separation was hardly three inches, there was room enough to sweep the scene and even some latitude for tilting up or down if needed.

The primary problem had been to halt the children at the right place for as long as required. To answer this need I had stationed Rikki on a small iron-railed balcony projecting over the entrance to the hostel. She was some fifty feet down the street from me. When the children passed she would throw pieces of candy into their group. I had cautioned her about a deliberate cruelty which I hoped was justified by the final intention of the entire film. Rikki was to throw her candies at any Jewish children in the group. They would be easily identified by the small black skullcaps they were compelled to wear.

As the bell in the church's tower struck twelve times I damned my lack of planning for the unforeseen. A heavy diesel truck came snorting up the street and stopped directly in front of my position. All the area I had intended for coverage by my lens was obscured. A moment later, even above the hammering of the truck's engine I heard the shouting of approaching children. As I sought desperately for an alternate position I heard the driver yell something in German. Then to my great relief the truck continued down the street. Beyond it, moving erratically toward me, small haversacks strapped to their backs in the European fashion, I saw my quarry. There were at least forty children, all in lederhosen and sweaters. Their bare knees were scuffed and red with the cold, and their shrill voices ricocheted continuously off the walls towering above them. The largest boy swaggered in the lead with a pair of ruddy-cheeked henchmen holding position close by his side. The rest of the company straggled along in clusters of two and three, their swirling progress as unpredictable as leaves blown before an autumn wind.

Viewed from a distance they came toward me like children bound home from school anywhere in the world.

Yet even as I framed them in the Eyemo's viewfinder, I discovered a difference. Three boys remained together at the very tail of the column, far enough back so they formed a second unit. Their apparel was much the same as all the others except for their tight black skullcaps.

As the children passed the area below the balcony I heard Rikki calling to them. In the viewfinder I saw them pause, look up, then suddenly swarm together and extend their hands. A piece of candy landed in their midst and the melee exploded. I was not surprised when the leader held up his fist triumphantly. The three boys in skullcaps had remained aloof from the first scrimmage. They were standing against the face of the building on the opposite side of the street, looking up at the balcony, waiting in exile without apparent hope or expectancy.

Rikki threw another piece of candy, but her aim was poor. It landed too near the balcony and only the boys in the front of the group scrambled for it. The others, seeing their chances slight, waited. Behind them, faces expressionless, somber eyes shouting their fierce inner torture, the Jewish boys remained fixed in place and I knew they were not expecting any bounty except the sight of the next candy sailing through the air. Holding on their figures I pressed the camera button, hoping Rikki would have their range at last.

Suddenly there was a moment of silence in the street. Two pieces of candy had landed almost at the feet of the Jewish children. I saw their eyes enlarge, their mouths open, and the one nearest me looked up at the balcony daring to smile.

The ominous stillness was broken by an astonished, protesting screech from the leader. *"Jude!"* he screamed and his complaint was echoed immediately by his henchmen. *"Jude! Jude!"* They began jumping up and down and pointing at the black skullcaps. Soon the others were chorusing, *"Jude! . . . Jude! . . . Jude! . . . Jude!"*

As the Jewish boys reached tentatively for the candies at their feet they were almost immediately overwhelmed by sprawling bodies. After a moment the mass broke apart and the three black skullcaps were once again back against the wall.

194

I was relieved to see the Jewish boys had not been physically abused nor was there any display of vindictive wrath from the others. The balance of the boys quickly returned to looking up at the balcony, which was beyond my line of vision. They kept repeating: "Do not throw candy to them! They're *Jews!*" There was a sort of exasperated patience in their tone as if Rikki had made a grave social error and would be forgiven only if she would observe the rules.

Once again the paper wrappers sailed across the street and landed in front of the black skullcaps. And again they were engulfed in a mass of bodies. The wretched pantomime was repeated exactly in my viewfinder. Again there was no evidence of physical revenge against the Jewish boys. After the scrambling subsided, the skullcaps resumed their places along the wall and the others resumed their protests to the balcony.

I thought to be more sparing of film now, for it struck me that the marvelous instrument I held in my hand, so capable of transmitting messages to millions of eyes, was utterly incapable of perceiving the true brutality of this German noon. I could because I had once been a boy and knew the ways of young savages. Not one of the Jewish boys had been hit or kicked. They had not had to defend themselves in any of the ordinary ways. They had not even been shouted at, directly. They were untouchables, not to be fought with or played with or rolled in the mud with. They were recognized only as existing, not as present, wherever they might be. I wondered if Rikki knew a child's hell is bound on all sides by indifference.

Now as more candies were lofted into the street I found it difficult to hold the Eyemo steady. Whether I was trembling from anger or cold was of no matter. The cruelty of man to man had been captured in the metal box I held and there was no need to repeat it further. Nor could I photograph apathy. Now the black caps did not even reach for the candy. They merely watched the others, and I could not detect any resentment in their dark eyes. Maybe, I thought, by some sort of national osmosis, even they had lost faith in their own right to be.

There was a final shower of candy and apparently Rikki left the balcony. The boys began drifting toward me. Through my narrow and private window I watched their bare legs pumping past like thin piston rods. When the first contingent of rods had gone there followed a moment of barren street, then three more pair of rods crossed my line of vision. From my humble position in the gutter, they looked exactly like the others.

Chapter 17

There is a heavy, bilious monotony about German skies in early spring, and for three days the village of Ochtendung huddled in melancholy while one rain squall after another soaked its streets. Between squalls I had been able to film a few scenes which I thought would be valuable in illustrating the final story. They had been obtained by subterfuge.

On a dark morning with the light from the windows weak and milky I had filmed a local schoolteacher in action. His face alone was a caricature of Teutonic firmness and his histrionic talents proved not inconsiderable. Permission to film in his classroom was granted when Rikki explained I was making a cinema on the schoolchildren of the world and wanted to show what a classroom was like in the true heart of Germany.

"Now if the dear Doctor Professor will be so good as to address his class with firmness, admonishing them to study harder, to think of their futures and the destiny of their country . . ."

His performance had been all I could have asked. His voice rumbled through the room as he warmed to the subject before his somewhat amazed pupils. Even the thick glasses failed to conceal the genuine fire in his eyes and I was fascinated to see the rolls on the back of his neck rumple in the best tradition. When he brought his fist down on the desk it startled me so I inadvertently shook the camera.

Success in the schoolroom had been balanced by complete failures when I tried to make certain filler shots which might serve as useful cuts. I wanted to show the village Jews relaxing on the special yellow benches in Ochtendung's tiny, uninspiring park. The lettering was prominent on the benches—*Jews Only*—but the instant the occupants observed me with a camera they rose and walked rapidly out of range. It troubled me to invade what little outdoor privacy they might have, more so as I began to appreciate why they were wary as deer. Although my rude intrusion upon them was inspired by a desire to tell at least partly of their tragedy, I could not possibly understand how they smelled their own doom.

By the evening of the third day in Ochtendung I entertained a few premonitions of my own. People in the village were beginning to stare at me with more than passing interest, and Rikki confirmed the increasing curiosity of their casual remarks. I knew it must be only a question of time before the police became interested. Then there would be inevitable questions about papers for cameras and other even more embarrassing matters. It was past time to change scenery.

I had also discovered an alarming development which I seemed powerless to stop. I was falling in love with Rikki. While I had never bothered to examine my moral standards, I had assumed they reflected the dubious hypocrisy of the times. Now, I wondered. Could a man love two women simultaneously without being struck by a thunderbolt? Was it an unnatural emotion, a betrayal of both women, or simply a betrayal of self? I was far from home and thus more than usually susceptible, but lust was not at all the driving power. Looking back, I realized that this new perplexity had made a stealthy approach while we had stood on the bridge at Cologne. When Rikki had volunteered to carry my camera, my loneliness in hazard had been annihilated. Rikki's apparently indomitable spirit made her an ideal comrade when my own resolve began to sag, and the ancient male-female relationship seemed to be taking on a different cast. I tried ineptly to catalogue the reasons for my growing enchantment. There was something continuously alluring about the challenging way Rikki tossed her head back and laughed, and the free-swinging movement of her body if she merely crossed a room. She seemed to know instinctively that I had no inclination toward a tawdry romance, and if there were capricious tricks in her behavior then I was already so blind I could recognize only a few.

There were several very sound reasons why this increasing devotion should be stifled before it took charge entirely. Most immediate was the hard demand of the filming and somehow smuggling the result out of a country which had double-locked the doors. I was becoming acutely aware that this was neither the time nor the locale for personal complications, and sometimes as we strode the narrow streets of Ochtendung together, swinging along boldly as if we had every right to be doing what we were doing, I found myself wishing there was a third musketeer.

I have always preferred to rise very early, treasuring every dawning regardless of the weather. It had always seemed each morning was like the beginning of a new life. Now on this German Sunday I rose in company with the sun. Roosters rejoiced in the courtyard below my window and even the pungent odors rising from the stables were nearly tolerable.

The deeper I became involved in this enterprise, the more aware I became of my amateurishness and of the certainty of my making mistakes. It was only a question of how many I could make without encountering very serious trouble. I had no training as an undercover agent nor had I ever any talent for deception. Somehow I had talked myself into a situation from which there was now no easy retreat. My sense of entrapment was increasing every hour; animal-like, I often found myself halting to assess the behavior of others before I made my next move.

The buoyant morning persuaded me that spring had come at last to middle Germany. To celebrate, I made more faces than usual splashing at the near-freezing water in the room's crockery basin. While shaving I reviewed the dubious status of my clandestine endeavor and knew once again a near-collapse of my resolve. How clumsily I had planned, and still by some miracle remained free to move about. Or was I merely allowed to continue under surveillance, a fly crawling about a web whose moment of apprehension would be fixed at the spider's leisure?

There were only four rolls of unexposed film remaining. Enough of pink-cheeked school children, I decided. Now I must attempt to reveal the present spirit of Germany. This day I must vary the hunt. Our isolation in Ochtendung had removed us from the main theater of action. Now we must drive to Koblenz on the Rhine itself and see if there was anything I could photograph which might emphasize the magnitude of Hitler's daring maneuver.

I thought it best to keep our rooms above the stables, since the distance to Koblenz was only twenty-two kilometers, and if we were to remain in the general area much longer, a return to the hostel at night might allay local suspicions.

The rolling fields on the way to Koblenz were accented with errant splotches of cadmium, cinnabar, and fawn. Where the earth had been freshly plowed, the rains had left the fields a metallic black, and parallel trails of mist still huddled in the deeper furrows. All of the countryside was embraced in languid easy air and the presence of any hazard seemed totally incongruous.

High on a hill commanding the lovely valley of the Rhine we abandoned the Ford and walked without aim or haste, reveling in the beauty of the morning. For a time I forgot we were not visitors, but intruders. We were strangely content. Before either of us were aware of it, Rikki and I were strolling hand in hand.

"When you return to America, what will you do then?"

"I don't know. I think I would like to fly for a living."

"Why not? You can be a good pilot I am sure." By her voice I guessed that Rikki now believed I had only to ask and the world would be mine.

"I have had only a few lessons and I loved it. But it is very expensive."

"You do not like what you are doing now?"

"Yes . . . and no. I worked at this sort of thing when I was very young . . . my first job in fact. When I was fourteen I worked in a commercial movie studio in Minnesota. We made films for insurance companies, scenics for the railroads, advertising cartoons . . . things like that."

"Where is Minnesota?"

"In the heart of America . . . like this is the heart of Germany. It is much colder though, in Minnesota."

"Were you born there . . . in that cold place?"

"I was born in Nebraska. It can also be very cold there."

"Is it cold everywhere in America?"

"Not in Florida or California."

"Your country is so big I cannot understand it."

We did not speak of love, but of uncomplicated matters, for we were each exploring the other. Soon we would be compelled into total honesty, but not yet, I thought; no intrusions of other lives should be allowed to spoil this enchanted morning.

It appeared that all of Rhineland Germany joined us in applause for the sun and the arrival of spring. The riverside restaurants in Koblenz were packed by two o'clock. The tinkling of beer and wine glasses everywhere provided a gentle and harmonious interlude between the bombastic renditions of the riverboat bands. The full-bosomed hausfraus and their thick, ponderous husbands were in a holiday mood. They were able to regard their beloved Rhineland with its grapevine escarpments and distant sleeping castles in the embrace of spring, and this mild Sunday they beheld an almost forgotten treat—the sight of German soldiers on what had so long been declared the "wrong" side of the river.

There were not very many soldiers and now, without helmets and equipment, they appeared less formidable. They promenaded along the river walk in twos and threes, rather ill at ease as they accepted the admiring stares of their fellow citizens. They offered no display of military arrogance, but instead were rather wistful, and stiff, and obviously lonely as young soldiers on Sunday appear everywhere.

One sat at the table next to ours in the Kaiserhoff restaurant. He was alone and his beer glass was empty. He was a private, although like all the others he had the bearing of a sergeant. He had been watching us carefully, as if the mere waiting for Rikki's smile was enough to entertain him.

"Rikki. Ask that soldier to join us for a beer. He looks thirsty and lonely."

He sprang from his chair, his eyes smiling with gratitude. He was very correct, very stiff of back, and very handsome. Unfortunately he spoke no English, a circumstance which would later contribute to our salvation. He proved to be a Bavarian from Darmstadt, his name was Franz, and he was off duty until eight o'clock in the evening. He was obviously entranced with Rikki yet he labored to divide his attention between us lest he seem to be taking over.

It was needless concern on his part. I had invited Franz to share our table because I hoped to use him in a way which I thought might give even Rikki pause. Now with my eyes alone, I tried to encourage her acceptance of him. I was delighted to see her smiling in spite of her antipathy for all Germans and it pleased me more when, as if on cue, she told him we were not married. So encouraged, Franz responded with increasing enthusiasm. His family were florists and the ensuing conversation about flowers was totally lost on me, but soon we were engaged in a sort of tripartite discussion of natural beauty such as the pouch-cheeked cumulus forming over the Rhine Valley. I managed to explain it had been my special joy to fly between and around such clouds and Franz said he would wait until he was an angel before he left the earth. Our good humor carried us through another round of beer and then another until at the end of an hour we were exchanging home addresses and the language barrier hardly seemed to exist.

Franz carried a small, cheap camera. I suggested a stroll while the sun was still high. Franz could take our picture and we would photograph him. I urged that we take our photography seriously and produce works of art rather than ordinary snapshots. We should include a colorful background to memorialize our new friendship, something typical of Koblenz and all of the Rhineland.

We began our Sunday afternoon diversion at the base of a great bronze equestrian statue of Bismarck. It was an imposing monument forged in the grandiose style of his day and now mottled with verdigris and bird droppings. Using Franz's camera. I snapped a traditional pose of Franz with his arm around Rikki.

"Gut! Smile!"

We laughed and exchanged places. After elaborate gesticulating and several revisions of our pose Franz finally declared himself satisfied. This one would be a masterpiece. I sighed with relief for I had been watching the descending sun and there was still much to be done.

"Now, Rikki. Tell Franz we want a picture of him with *our* camera. To remember him with . . . and of course I'll send him a copy. Not here. Up top. There's a platform of some kind up there and maybe we can see down the river."

We climbed the steps to the upper deck of the monument and emerged through a narrow doorway onto a rampart surrounding the massive statue. I regarded the heavy breast-high stone wall and made a solemn business of selecting just the right angle. ". . . let's see, now the river can be in the background from here . . . no, better this way . . . still the sun is much better over on this side. *Gut! Bitte* . . . Smile! Rikki! Franz! Smile! *Danke!*"

Laughing, now totally at ease with his new friends, Franz said he would pose all the rest of the day if he could keep his arm around Rikki. I wondered if she understood what I was doing.

". . . a little farther apart, Rikki. You're too close together. That's more like it."

I stood some twenty feet from them. An ordinary lens would include the whole valley of the Rhine visible to the south, a large part of the statue base, and a comparatively miniature German soldier with his arm around a girl. While we were wandering about the plaza below I had slipped the Eyemo's four-inch lens into position and now Franz's broad shoulders and fine Teutonic head entirely filled the viewfinder. Along one side of the frame I could still see the tip of Rikki's nose and a part of her cheek.

"Move your head a little that way, Rikki. I want the sun to hit your face just right."

I did not give a damn how the sun struck Rikki's face. I wanted her out of the finder. It was Franz's face I cared about—a closeup, staring toward the west, the yellow regimental numbers on his red collar tabs plainly readable.

"Now Rikki, ask Franz to look more like a soldier . . . tougher . . . he is better not smiling . . . ask him to look like his sergeant does when Franz has done something wrong . . . that's better . . . now tell him to look right at the sun."

It was working beautifully. No man can look at the sun without pinching up his whole face in an expression which can easily be interpreted as fierce determination. The Eyemo's motor was whirring. Franz, I thought, you are a good actor—better than you know. Your face is the new Germany, facing the west defiantly, waiting impatiently for the Valkyries to redeem your honor. Franz, you think this is a very expensive American camera and you are correct. What you do not appreciate is how this camera, like all cameras, can be made to lie. It just depends on what the ventriloquist wishes it to say.

"*Danke!* That was perfect!"

Directly across the river from Koblenz loomed the fortress of Ehrenbreitstein. In spite of its lofty situation there was nothing remarkable about it. It was actively manned, and our friend and hero for the day, Franz of a grenadier regiment, was one of its garrison. About four o'clock, with the sun already tipping the higher western hills and the Rhine itself becoming a deep swirling sienna, I began to have trouble maintaining my role of an easygoing American tourist with camera, a girl, and the problem of passing a Sunday afternoon. Looming over the landscape was something far more exciting.

Franz had confessed that his true passion was motorcars and lamented the restrictions of his army life, which prevented him from a Sunday afternoon ride with a friend in Darmstadt. At first his yearning left me totally uninterested, and now with sixty feet of his rugged features on film, his slightly fawning manners seemed rather insipid. I had even been considering ways to be rid of him.

While Franz and Rikki prattled on at much too fast a pace for me to follow, I found myself compelled to look up more frequently at the bold promontory which supported Ehrenbreitstein, and suddenly I saw as if superimposed across its bastions the egg-shaped figure of Shute tracing a design in the cement of Manhattan's Forty-fourth Street with the tip of his umbrella. You *knew,* you dome-headed Machiavelli, I thought. You *knew* such moments of temptation must sprout from this expedition and you *knew* how feeble must be my resistance.

I had thus far been bold in believing that if I were caught photographing children, or schoolyards, Jews on benches, or even troops marching across a bridge, I probably would not be taken very seriously if apprehended. I had easily persuaded myself that the most likely punishment would be confiscation of my equipment and expulsion from Germany. Yet not in my most optimistic moments had I held any illusions about my future if I were caught photographing military installations.

Here, brooding down upon me, inviting, was an opportunity which simply could not be refused. Here was reputed to be one of the strongest fortifications of the German Westwall. And here was a Sunday! Was there a military installation in the world not Sunday's orphan? At Fort Snelling in Minnesota, which I had known so well, you could steal the flagpole on Sunday.

"Rikki," I said casually, "ask Franz if he would like to go for a ride. Maybe he would like us to drive him back to his barracks."

She took a moment to recover from her shock and I knew well enough how renewed doubts of me and all I had intended must have troubled her. Here, at last, would be the real test, and I could not blame her if all I had told her seemed a series of lies. Watching her eyes I knew it would be impossible to convince her that this new idea of entering Ehrenbreitstein was any less a matter of chance than our timely encounter with the troops on the Cologne bridge. I knew she must believe that this fortress so high above the Rhine had been my true objective from the moment I first arrived in Amsterdam. Now her eyes were asking if I had merely used her, which I could not refute since it was partially true.

"Well?"

I saw the beginning of a little smile about Rikki's lips and I held my breath as she turned to Franz. She hesitated, then took his arm.

In ten minutes the Ford was on the ferryboat bound to the opposite side of the river. We posed along the rail and took more pictures with Franz's camera. Pathetically eager to repay our beer and auto hospitality with impromptu guide service, he was constantly plucking at my sleeve, pointing, "Here! . . . there . . . look! *Wunderbar!*"

I displayed as much interest as I could manage in his scenic delights, but I was far more devoted to the rusting sun and the heights of Ehrenbreitstein.

Ascending from the ferry landing, the road followed a serpentine pattern to the slanting plateau upon which Ehrenbreitstein was situated. Rikki and Franz were together in the front seat for I had insisted his ride would be more enjoyable beside her. I wanted the back seat for myself so I could bend down to the relative darkness near the floor and insert a new roll of film in the Eyemo. Apparently Franz thought the Eyemo was some kind of elaborate still camera, an illusion I preferred to maintain. He kept asking Rikki to remind me about sending him copies. Alas, Franz, I thought, it will be much easier for you if you forget this Sunday.

We reached the plateau and, following Franz's guidance, Rikki parked the car on a gentle grassy slope which became a sheer dropoff some five or six hundred feet away. The Rhine was now only a thin gray ribbon far below in the violet murk.

We stood for a moment supposedly enjoying the magnificent sweep of the Rhine Valley. I glanced at Rikki and once more our eyes met in silent understanding. I pressed my camera into her hand believing it would seem more innocent if carried by a woman, although for the moment at least, any precaution appeared unnecessary. There was not a person to be seen either on the plateau or about the surrounding ramparts. Sunday.

We ambled slowly down the plateau, pausing occasionally to appreciate the view, which under ordinary circumstances I would have found exhilarating. Yet I was becoming grumpy and my disappointment more obvious as we descended through the long, innocent-appearing grass. Of what photographic use was grass? I needed a longer shot with a suitable military background to complement the closeup I already had of Franz's face. Some sort of action should be transpiring in that background and Franz must be related to it visually.

As we moved farther down the slope I heard the unmistakable sound of a cement mixer and soon its metallic gnashing became mixed with human voices. Curious, I increased my pace slightly until we passed a line of grassy knolls and reached an area where the plateau declined very sharply. As a consequence the entire profile of the western ramparts was revealed, and there, as if staged by a master director, was the action I so desired. About a hundred men were working with pick and shovel along the brow of the rampart. Others, pushing wheelbarrows, would vanish into the rampart itself, then reappear. They all appeared to be about the same age as Franz, although their working clothes did not seem to be a standard uniform. Soldiers? Working on a Sunday afternoon?

Franz explained that the men were members of his

own company and if he had not drawn night duty in the message center for the past five days, he would certainly be among them. He also claimed he had been unhappy about his isolation until he had met us since his freedom left him with no choice but to wander the streets of Koblenz alone. His buddies were digging.

"I do not like to be alone," he said thoughtfully. "You Americans are so kind to be my friends."

Preoccupied with what must be done before the sun slipped below the western hills, I had hardly noticed that sometime during the afternoon Rikki had adopted my nationality.

"I want Franz alone this time. Ask him to stand right here and look at the sun again. Then leave him quickly and start back up the hill."

I took the camera from Rikki and walked about twenty paces away from where we had been standing. Now with the culmination of the whole venture so near at hand I was suddenly gripped by an oppressive foreboding. Something was awry and I could not identify it. It was as if I had been flying between thunderheads with remarkable ease and after rounding them all, discovered a line squall squeezing the final exit. I paced away from Franz as a duelist might, clutching my camera as a gun, counting my paces before the final fateful reversement when I must fire. Franz must be caught unaware to avoid the impression of a soldier posed. He was already becoming restless with being photographed and I was convinced he now regretted bringing us to the plateau. Still pacing away I set the exposure to accommodate the fast-weakening light.

I stopped, checked the focus on infinity, and turned. I punched the motor button immediately, hoping to shoot enough film before the soldierly image of Franz deteriorated into a self-conscious, lonely, German boy.

Rikki, bless her silent perception, had moved far enough up the slope to be out of the viewfinder. In it, alone and properly imposing, was Franz and behind him the busy construction activity. As I listened to the motor whirring I could almost hear *The March of Time* voice intone: ". . . as the Wehrmacht strengthens her bastions . . ."

Now I needed only one last shot and the Ehrenbreitstein sequence would be complete. Returning slowly to a position near Franz I fretted about an exposure change because the next scene would be a photographic gamble. The sun had mellowed, almost too much, and the lens I intended to use demanded more light than the others. Was the quality of the light troubling me so, or something else?

I carefully lowered myself into the grass and swung the six-inch lens into position. My concentration on technicalities was total because the lens was a dangerous tool; not only must focus and exposure be precise, but the slightest camera movement would be so greatly magnified, the film would become unusable.

I lay on my belly with my head and arms forming a tripod to support the Eyemo. In the viewfinder I saw how the magic of this lens placed me right among the working soldiers. Even the fringe of grass along the bottom of the frame should give an air of stealth and urgency to the subject matter.

I took a deep breath and held it as I pressed the motor button. Not even my breathing must cause the Eyemo to quiver. As I ran out the balance of the film I thought of Charlie Herbert and thanked him silently for teaching me his craft.

Regaining my feet I discovered that Rikki and Franz were walking back up the slope. They were already some hundred paces from me and my admiration for Rikki became boundless. Without any signal from me she had also sensed Franz's increasing discomfort in our presence. She had deliberately drawn him toward the top of the plateau where the car was parked.

As I started up the slope after them I saw a German officer moving around the car. I halted and remained absolutely rigid, momentarily incapable of movement. So this was the proof of my premonition? I watched the officer hesitate while he studied the car's license plate. His pause of a few seconds seemed one hour and I wondered if I should drop the Eyemo in the grass and move away nonchalantly.

Fascinated, yet still unmoving, I saw the officer discover Rikki and Franz. He was looking down at them, tipping his head curiously to one side. Suddenly he barked a command. Franz left Rikki and ran up the slope. Rikki stopped in place. It was like watching a distant pantomime with which I had no connection. My body would have made the perfect tripod for any telephoto lens, I thought. I had not made the slightest move.

I realized the officer had not seen me. I was much farther down the slope than the others and the sun was directly at my back. Even the suit I was wearing was a green-and-straw-flecked tweed which conveniently matched the surroundings. I considered dropping to the grass and lying prone again, then changed my mind. If I moved I might attract attention. And what was left of the sun was still enough to blind the officer if he merely glanced in my direction. Rikki also remained a statue although her elongated shadow reached almost to the officer's boots and he must certainly have seen her.

Franz reached the officer, snapped to attention and saluted.

Their conversation seemed interminable. Franz remained absolutely rigid while the officer paced back and forth slapping at his leg with his gloves, his every mannerism such a caricature of how a German officer was supposed to behave, I had trouble accepting him as anything but an actor in costume. I found it difficult to believe his boots would break just so, his gloves would be gray, his peaked cap visor would slice across his eyes, and his proconsul voice would be so cutting. Or that he could possibly have anything to do with me.

Suddenly I heard the officer's voice ring out in anger. Repeatedly I heard the epithet *"Dummkopf!"* Poor Franz. The thumping of my pulse increased as I wondered how long this could continue. For here was a foreigner without any credentials whatever, standing awkwardly in the middle of a new German Wehrmacht installation with a movie camera. And the timing? Just as the Wehrmacht was surging back to power.

To my enormous relief the tirade ended abruptly. Franz saluted and half ran down the slope to Rikki. The officer watched him a moment, then turned away. He stepped out smartly as if bound on some urgent duty and soon disappeared over the brow of the plateau. I was positive he had not seen me.

Franz was motioning to me and I started up the slope without enthusiasm. Wasn't there some easy way out of this? The Eyemo camera had suddenly become a huge chunk of machinery painted bright red.

Franz was obviously terrified and Rikki explained his near-panic as we walked rapidly toward the car.

". . . much trouble. The officer was very angry because no one is supposed to be in this place. It would be very bad, but Franz told him I was his sister. The officer is telephoning now to another place, I do not understand exactly . . . but Franz must report there."

Franz interrupted her. His German was rushed and thick as if he were choking. He had become very red in the face. Rikki translated. "He says we should take him down the road a little way and then keep going. And we are not to speak to any person about being here and especially about taking pictures."

This time Rikki and I occupied the front seat of the car while Franz climbed into the back. Rikki swung the car around and we sped down the winding road.

There was a clipped, hurried, conversation in German between Rikki and Franz which I could not have followed even if my thoughts were not so heavily engaged with the problem of concealing film and camera. Franz almost led me toward the most desperate solution. By chance I turned back to look at him just as he threw his own small camera out the window. Caught in guilt he tried to smile, but I saw he could not manage such deception and I regretted the trouble I had laid upon him this lovely spring Sunday. I knew his cheap little camera represented a considerable investment for any soldier and from the beginning Franz had seemed to hold a special affection for it. And I thought he must expect very serious trouble if he was willing to sacrifice it.

"That officer was not from Franz's company," Rikki explained. "There is some kind of guardhouse down the road where his regular officer will be waiting. We are to let Franz off a little before that place."

"Then what? What about us?"

"Franz does not know."

"Ask him."

They began what seemed an endless dialogue. "Franz says he is afraid they will soon know he was lying because his own officer knows he does not have a sister.

He will ask many questions and Franz does not know what he can say."

"Can't he just say he had one of the local girls out for a Sunday afternoon?"

"I suggested that. His officer will ask who the girl is and where she lives."

Franz's problems, I thought, were his to solve. Now, in a shameless yielding to jungle instinct, I was anxious to abandon him.

"Ask him again. What about *us*?"

"We should go away. That is all he can say. Go away from Koblenz very fast."

"Did the officer see me?"

More German.

"Franz does not know. We are very lucky it is a Sunday. If the Major were here the officer would have taken us directly to him. Franz asks us please not to come back here."

"Tell him he can depend on it."

About halfway down to the river opposite a grave of stunted trees, we let Franz out of the car. His *auf Wiedersehen* was mumbled and his eyes darted from one to the other of us as if pleading for haste.

As we pulled away, I turned to look through the rear window at Grenadier Franz Müller. He did not wave or appear to be looking after us. He just stood where we left him by the side of the road, immobile, facing the last of the sun, and I wondered if he was thinking of glib strangers and of how their temptations could ruin a Sunday afternoon.

By great fortune we found the ferry still on our side of the Rhine and she sailed almost as if she had been waiting for us, immediately after Rikki drove aboard. In less than thirty minutes from the time we had parted from Franz, we were across the river and speeding through the peaceful streets of Koblenz. Now aware that our immediate future depended entirely upon the whims and curiosity of an unknown German officer, I was delighted with Rikki's mania for high speed.

"The time has come," I announced with more bravado than I felt. "We leave Germany tonight."

We entered the narrow streets of Ochtendung with the very last of the sun and went at once to our rooms above the stables. Packing our simple bags took ten minutes, paying the hostel bill required another ten. We were very hungry, but still thinking in minutes I thought it best we be away from Ochtendung without delay.

Now discouraged, I saw how my amateur status in intrigue had finally propelled us into a trap from which the most expert would have difficulty in emerging unscathed. All during our flight from Ehrenbreitstein and our departure from the hostel I tried to visualize the sequence of events now occurring in or about the fortress and to match them against the racing hands of my watch.

How long would it take to locate Franz's regular officer? Fifteen minutes? Thirty? And then how lengthy his interrogation of his wretched soldier? Would Franz do some lying, which since he was not a cunning man would certainly complicate matters as I prayed and thus take more time, or would he be the boy scout and lay everything on the line from the beginning of our acquaintance? If he chose that ploy, I decided, and his officer were only half intelligent, the net would already be closing.

These unknowns formed a rickety basis for planning, but as an apprentice smuggler-spy I had nothing better at hand. At least I could be sure that even Rikki's wildest driving was no match for the speed of electricity and it was reasonable to assume that once the officer realized how his Franz had been duped, he would be at the telephone. How far his warnings and instructions to apprehend us might extend was another unknown.

Rikki, displaying the same jolly vivacity I had seen her use on frontier guards, persuaded the hostel proprietor to forsake his grumpy beer customers and man his fuel pump on a Sunday evening. During the long verbal interchange I heard Rikki reply to several of his questions with a sort of sly laughter which apparently disarmed his curiosity about our sudden departure.

Somehow, I thought, we must avoid the obvious. We had been caught red-handed and any offender would be expected to get away with all speed from the scene of the crime. The nearest exit from Germany meant Belgium along a fine road aimed almost directly west toward that frontier. The distance was hardly more than fifty miles, but I decided if I were trying to thwart the hurried exit of anyone from the vicinity of Ochtendung, that road and the towns through which it passed would receive my first attention.

As an amateur fugitive I was determined to avoid it.

Another choice was the somewhat longer route toward the southwest and the border of Luxembourg, but I rejected it for an even more devious route along an intricate network of minor roads almost directly southward. I noted with sorrow that it would be dark by the time we would be passing along the valley of the Moselle, but at least, I thought, we would be fleeing in style through a landscape producing one of the world's most noble wines.

As the sound of the Ford's exhaust echoed against the last buildings along Ochtendung's narrow streets, we did not bother to look back. Once emerged from the edge of town Rikki floored the throttle and we plunged into the fading twilight. I busied myself with the road map so Rikki might have prewarning of the way and partly to contain my nerves as the Ford was pressed to its utmost along roads designed for oxcarts. Soon there were moments when I secretly questioned the wisdom of trying to escape, at least in a car driven by a madwoman. Now two ugly visions of my teenage driving days returned. Once I had rolled a Ford roadster and miraculously survived. On a much more haunting occasion with another Ford I had struck a woman pedestrian so hard she suffered serious pelvic injuries. I have never been comfortable in autos since.

What conversation we had was clipped in cadence as if we sought subconsciously to speak in harmony with our speed.

"For God's sake, slow down!"

"Don't be nervous. We have a long way to go."

"From what I can see it's a long way to any hospital. Or the morgue."

"Don't be so pessimistic."

"I'm trying to be realistic."

"You are afraid of my driving because I am a woman."

"Leave sex out of this and for the love of God slow down," I groaned as we careened around a blind curve and soared over a one-lane humpback bridge. "I'm just not ready to die."

"I know from the cinema. All Americans drive fast."

"What are you going to do if we meet anyone coming the other way?"

"Very few people are out on a Sunday night. The peasants are in bed."

"It takes only one insomniac." In the faint light reflected from the gravel roadway I saw Rikki shrug her shoulders. And I also saw that her eyes were now all the more remarkable in total concentration, so very much alive and beautiful.

As the kilometer stones rushed past I saw that Rikki had been right—the countryside and its people were already asleep. One by one the little German towns were left behind, Mayen, Kasusesch, Gutzerath, all slumbering in the night and with only an occasional bright window relieving the darkness. Nor did we encounter a single vehicle until approaching Wittlich, a fair-sized town which I thought must certainly have police and a telephone.

We passed through without challenge and sped on to Bernkastel-Kues, a directional feint which required our turning back east for a time until we could connect with a series of indifferent trails on the way to Mühlheim and finally Neumagen.

"If I have the distances right we are now halfway to the goal posts," I announced, and instantly questioned if this could possibly be the same voice which in another era had cheered so joyously at the sight of a hickory ball sailing between two real goal posts. "Some day I must tell you about playing polo."

"I do not understand how you can play such a dangerous game and be afraid now."

"This Ford is no pony. Ponies are wonderful animals with a strong sense of self-preservation."

"Did your wife come to see you play?"

There we were again, the inevitable consideration. I told her Eleanor had attended several games, but long before our marriage.

"Ah? That must have been very nice. But I think it could not have been very long because you are not very old."

"I'm twenty-six . . . going on one hundred after this night."

"When you go back to America I hope you will not forget this night."

My urge was to assure Rikki there was little chance I could ever forget her, and several times I had actually considered never returning to my official home. But I veered away from the subject, taking refuge in my business with the map.

"The only big town between us and France is Merzig." Then yawning as if our words held no significance I spread my thumb and forefinger between where I thought we were and the delineation of the French frontier. "About fifty kilometers as the crow flies."

I closed my eyes as we zigzagged and swerved through a series of boxes and wooden barriers where repairs were being made on the road.

The road worsened and its demands kept Rikki silent. And somehow I had lost all heart for any further exchange between us lest the things we did not say take charge and ruin our fragile relation, or in misinterpretation become more important than what we did say.

It was nearly ten o'clock and I was hungry. My heroes had always been dashing fellows apparently without need of nourishment and yet here, in the midst of a situation begging for a most stalwart performance, I could hardly desist from thinking of my belly. Now that I had already proven I was not the strong and silent prince, I wondered if my preoccupation with sausage and bread marked a hopeless sybarite or merely a careless fool.

After we passed through Hermeskeil and then turned westward again toward Zepf, Rikki broke the long silence between us.

"Tell me. Do you have enough film now . . . of your birds?" The sarcasm in her voice was unmistakable.

"I really didn't plan to . . . well, the way things happened—"

"Of course. You almost made me believe you."

I noticed her emphasis on the word *almost* and knew it would take a major campaign to convince her otherwise. And by now, I thought, in a sudden excursion from sausages and bread, Franz's officer should have certainly done what he could to spread the word of two foreigners claiming to be Americans who should be apprehended. The final test would be the town of Merzig. If we managed to pass through it without being halted then it was only a few kilometers through open country to Silwingen on the frontier.

In a perverse way Merzig was a disappointment. At twenty minutes past eleven the town and every last one of its inhabitants seemed to be sound asleep. We slipped quietly beneath its occasional overhead streetlights, proceeding through a ghost town, until we were swallowed once again in darkness on its western approaches.

"Six kilometers to the border," I sighed.

We came to the German side of the frontier just after eleven-thirty with the fuel tank needle bouncing on empty. Again Rikki asked for my passport and this time I gave it to her without hesitation. "When I am talking to the guards you go away from the car," she cautioned. "If they see you they will open everything. Stay out of sight until you hear me call. I will tell the guards you are not well and must go to the toilet. All right?"

All right, indeed. We had not stopped for nearly four hours.

It was a much larger frontier post than the one through which we had entered Germany. We left the car together—Rikki to the brightly lit guardhouse siutated on a rise of ground some thirty yards from the barrier, while I made my way to an apparently unoccupied building on the opposite side of the road. I passed around it, found concealment behind a stand of brush, and groaned with relief.

The waiting seemed interminable and provided a nasty opportunity for considering my recent follies. As the minutes passed, recriminations crept so relentlessly out of the darkness I could not escape them. Escape? Somewhere far beyond this dank and lonely copse there existed a beautiful wife and fine son, dwelling in a world which if stubbornly difficult to conquer was at least familiar and had given me some token recognition. In spite of my defection it was most likely I might again find employment and there was always a father anxious to persuade me into the solid life. Why had I been so obtuse?

Now, somewhere in Germany, I was hiding like an escaped criminal, my companion another man's wife, and my funds barely enough to last out the week. I tried not to dwell upon the reactions of the German authorities if they confiscated my film and developed it.

All of this, I thought ruefully, the consequence of an imprudent vow made to a stranger who had carefully stated that any appeal for help would only result in his firm declaration he had never heard of me.

For these sour moments of self-pity, I realized, there was no one to blame but myself.

At last I heard a low whistle and stepped quickly to the corner of the building. Rikki was sitting in the car and the engine was running. There was no sign of guards, although the lights in their house illuminated the immediate area and the roadway.

As I crossed the road the few yards separating us became a great distance.

"What's the matter?"

"Nothing. Get in quickly before they change their minds."

"We're *through?*"

"Yes. They said they were sorry you were sick on your honeymoon. They looked at nothing."

We pulled away casually, as if reluctant to leave Germany. It was ten minutes until midnight of the finest Sunday I could remember, if only because it was less than four kilometers to the French border.

"Bon soir, Messieurs!" I was so happy to see the two French frontier guards I could barely resist embracing them. Before they could ask their first questions I rushed around to the luggage trunk and threw open for their inspection everything I had brought with me.

"Mais non, Monsieur! Vous attendez à demain!" one protested. Come now, I thought, here are allies—your friends. I am arrived in the spirit of Lafayette. You must know, Monsieur, how I value memories of Amer Picon in Morocco, of Le Dôme in Paris, of my long-time mentor René Pleven, of my residence on the Boulevard Raspail in Montparnasse, of my admiration for the better years of Graves, all which are to me mere particles in the exhilarating essence of La Belle France.

The guards, apparently doubling as customs inspectors, were openly reluctant to match my enthusiasm. With the inimitable finality of the French bureaucrat they were pleased to inform M'sieur-dame there would be no crossing into France this night. A duty must be paid on this camera and film, which of course, Monsieur, will be returned when you depart France. The official who must collect the fee is not obliged to be at his post on Sunday night and what is more, Monsieur, we are off duty ourselves this very minute because it is exactly twelve o'clock and will you be so good as to move your vehicle so we can lower the barrier?

"Mais . . . !"

"M'sieur—dame! It is impossible. Those are the regulations. Of course you must return to Germany. Where else is there to go?"

Pleading, I called upon them to consider our arrival as an opportunity to demonstrate French hospitality toward weary travelers. Rikki pleaded in much better French than mine but the result was the same . . . palms upheld hopelessly. I groaned in frustration. If we returned to the Germans, giving them a second chance, they would probably become more curious and discover camera and film. I thought how a man and particularly a Frenchman might be a philosopher, poet, saint, or the artful lover of countless women and beloved of all his children—it was all of no matter. Once he donned a civil service uniform he became transformed into a living negative.

We explained that the car was out of fuel or nearly so, and probably would not start. On cue, shoulders were shrugged again, after which in a surprising display of energy, the same negative shoulders were applied to the car. They pushed it away from the overhead barrier, which they solemnly proceeded to lower. They were going home to their village, three miles farther along the gravel road and nothing was going to delay them.

"Will you permit us to leave the vehicle here with everything in it and walk to your village with you?"

A long silence followed, broken only by their mutual mutterings of exasperation.

"We cannot disappear into the air," Rikki insisted.

Logic is the key to all Frenchmen. It undermines even the bureaucrat's worship of regulations. Since first acquaintance I had been convinced there was a comfortable percentage of crazy Frenchmen, but never had I met an illogical Frenchman.

"Very well, Madame. But everything must be left in the car. In the morning, you must return promptly at eight o'clock."

I felt an almost irresistible urge to embrace them. "What about a toothbrush for myself and Madame?" "D'accord . . ."

I ran to the car trunk and yanked it open. Rikki was at my side by the time I had opened my own bag. The eight one-hundred-foot rolls of film were in tin cans, each about the size of a hockey puck if somewhat thicker. With our heads inside the trunk we were able to move our hands without being observed by the impatient guards. I slipped two film rolls in the side pockets of my overcoat and squeezed two more in the pockets of my pants. I glanced at Rikki, my lips forming a quick question. She answered by reaching for the four remaining cans. She placed two in the side pockets of her coat, but the last two presented a momentary problem. I whispered for haste and saw Rikki tighten her coat belt as she deposited the last two rolls over her breasts.

We emerged from the trunk and slammed it shut. Then we hurried to join the guards and in our haste Rikki forgot to lock the car. It was our logical guards who protested such illogic, and in spite of their impatience, they waited while she returned to secure the doors.

We stepped out smartly for the few glistening beads of light in the distance which the guards identified as their village. Almost at once I made a frightening discovery and instinctively tried to walk on tiptoe. For every step of mine and Rikki's was accompanied by a dull metallic click. The rolls of film were not quite as large as their protective cans and now they moved rhythmically in accordance with our pacing. No logical Frenchman nor anyone else could possibly attribute such muffled thumping to a toothbrush.

I realized we must keep them talking rather than listening so I inquired persistently after the crops of the star-lit countryside, the terrible trials they must suffer in pursuit of their wintertime duty, and, surest of all, I asked for a résumé of their lives. It was of no matter that my French was inadequate; they prattled on continuously and soon I knew that only Rikki and I were aware of a strange and alien sound.

Later, in a pseudo-baroque room at the dingy village hotel, I searched desperately for a place to hide eight cans of film. I dared not risk carrying them back to the frontier in the morning since concealing them in daylight would be difficult. Finally, I stowed the cans in a Louis Napoleon chamber pot beneath the bed.

In the darkness I calculated what I hoped would be the last of our delicate timing. Back at the frontier at eight according to instructions. Through customs in half an hour, then back to this room to retrieve the film. Hang the *Prie ne pas Déranger* sign on the doorknob before leaving and take the key with me. Thus not even the most diligent chambermaid would disturb my peculiar treasures.

Next morning proved bright and cheerful with the first soft breezes of springtime caressing the French countryside. We accomplished the shuttle between village and frontier without challenge and by noon were on our way to Holland. Once arrived in Amsterdam I mailed the film to Larsen, spent almost the last of my funds settling the account with Fireside Rentals, and after our more than two weeks together, mumbled my way through an embarrassed parting with Rikki. Almost simultaneously a new and unexpectedly difficult problem arose and I found myself vacillating outrageously while guilt besieged my thoughts. Surely my recent record proved me a disgraceful failure as husband and father. What now of all that heritage of "duty—honor?" Why did I keep seeking excuses to postpone my return to America?

I sent a cable to Larsen asking for a further European assignment. While I waited for a reply, the alert Rikki learned of a great increase in munitions shipments from the port of Amsterdam. There was one roll of unexposed film remaining in the Eyemo so one morning I lay on my back shooting upward from the hold of a small freighter while various explosives were lowered toward me. The shipment was destined for Spain where the first rumbles of a civil war were barely audible and I thought the action might well be in keeping with Hitler's new arrogance.

When Larsen's reply finally arrived it was discouragingly noncommittal: UPON RECEIPT OF FILM CAN ADVISE IF FURTHER ASSIGNMENTS.

Even though I had been staying in a very cheap hotel called the Nassau, my funds were now almost exhausted and I realized immediate employment must be found or my departure was imperative. Both Rikki and I knew the ultimate answer without actually discussing the matter. If our regard for each other had become more than infatuation, a great deal of unhappiness would be our responsibility. For the time being at least, my place was with two other people on the opposite side of the Atlantic.

Rikki took me to the dock in Rotterdam where the overnight ferry sailed for England. I intended to see René Pleven in London before taking ship to America. It was raining hard when we arrived as if the sodden Dutch sky was determined to depress our spirits further. We talked of a future reunion without believing it would ever happen, and as the time of sailing approached we became strangely distant in voice and manner, struck almost dumb, I thought, by the apparent ease of our parting.

Finally Rikki took my hand, squeezed it gently, then released it. Simultaneously, a porter seized my bag and started through the ship with it. I called out to halt him, but he continued down a corridor and I seemed compelled to follow him.

Even as I left the deck I knew Rikki would be gone when I returned. The presumptuous porter was a convenient excuse which I accepted instinctively.

Returning to the deck only moments later I found the gangway deserted. The stone surface of the wharf was empty of life and the only sound was the peckling of rain into the pools formed by the cobbles. Everything was wet and dead.

In London, Pleven, who was far more knowledgeable on international affairs than most men, assured me there would be a European war involving his native France against Germany in three years. I did not believe him. And he handed me a cable from Larsen, who had finally received the film. I read it unbelieving, then crumbled in defeat. The careful inspections and cleaning I had given the Eyemo each night had failed to dislodge a microscopic speck of dirt on or near the aperture gate.

SORRY YOU ASKED FOR IT. WIDE SCRATCH THROUGH FILM MAKES MOST OF IT UNUSABLE.

LARSEN

There are times when only hyenas roam the earth and only buzzards glide the sky.

Part Two

FLYING

THE TRAIN FROM
PUERTO LIMÓN

Slow down, Señor Engineer, your huckety-buckety lit-tle train is going too fast through the jungle. The jour-ney will be over before I have time to untangle all the elements and fit them into a logical pattern. I must try to resolve where the pieces of yin *and* yang *fit into the mosaic.*

How about the little black boy, back in the more open country, and his gestured acknowledgment of my pres-ence in his land? What is his connection, however tenuous and fragile, between the life he has so recently assumed and my own, already threadbare from use? Why was I not born his father or more likely his grandfather who in matching chronology must have been surrounded by a vastly different life? Would I be a pro-portionately different person?

Of course! Economics aside, our total environment would have been almost as if we had taken up existence on two different planets. The other me, grandsire to the little black boy, would have gone to bed with the sun

222

and risen long before its heat. Instead, I often reversed that particular routine.

Most important of all is the difference in people we would have linked to ourselves—for it is people who fashion the lives of other earth citizens and sometimes the individual is nearly powerless to stem their influence.

The grandsire of the black boy would doubtless have known every inhabitant of the hamlet of Mary and Jesus and he might also have known the people who lived along the railroad track a few miles distant in both directions. But his active world would have stopped there, unless he happened to be a sailor, which in this banana culture would have been unlikely. He would have been influenced and his existence molded by the local saints and the local villains and if he obtained good and evil in equal amounts he might have attained the great human passivity. Then it is reasonable to suppose he is at relative peace with himself and would not be sitting on a toy train in a far off banana republic restlessly asking questions for which there is no positive answer.

Out of several thousand possible candidates it would have been inconceivable that my black counterpart would have met Mather, or Alexander Dean, artist Linford Donovan, or actor John Wayne—or cartoonist Hank Ketcham—all of whom for better or worse had some influence upon whatever sort I may be at this very moment.

There is a wooden card file in the little cottage where I do my actual writing and every time I open it seeking an address I am stunned by the number of human beings represented in such a small container. And it comes as a further shock to realize how a supposed loner in a lonely job has not really been alone, except for relatively short periods. The box is crammed with "influences," a touch here, a brush there, a nick, a deep cut, sometimes a hurt, and more often a hoist to morale by those persons whose names are within.

We do not make ourselves. It takes many years to create even an approximation of a complete human being and a great many artisans both skillful and clumsy combine to do the job. We have to die before people stop working on us. Therefore since two obviously different groups worked on the black boy's grandsire and on *me, we would today have very little in common except the influences of nature and even those, because of our widely separated native geography, must leave us strangers.*

Señor Engineer! Are you aware your train is now haunted by a multitude of faces unknown to you? A whole masquerade lurks beyond and between the hirsute young men in the seats ahead, with some individuals sitting beside the old hag across from me who is still chewing away, and others surrounding the elderly American couple with their battery of cameras.

There, for example, is Ron Dudman in white shorts, epauletted shirt, an automatic at his belt—he who was for a time my bodyguard during a strange episode in Hong Kong. From a photograph his face still looks down impassively from above my writing desk.

Now aboard this train there is Bigelow, big as life, his physique and especially his anvil jaw belying his delicate artistry. And Colin Hill, the walrus-mustachioed captain in the Royal West African Frontier Corps (or so he said), who flew with me out to Burma on a mission so secret he never confided it even when we were in our cups. Is he real, or a ghost? I've no means of telling because I've never heard from him since he said "Bye-bye" in his clipped modest way and disappeared into Burma for God knows how long.

Señor Engineer, halt the train and let some of these people get off. Those who are already ghosts should have no difficulty making their way ahead to Matina where I am told the vermilion gingers provide such a color thrill even the dead will be aroused.

I am become the sorcerer's apprentice with this toying at my flight computer. The game has taken charge of the player. Reed Chambers, for example. I am not at all enthusiastic about sharing this long train ride with him, much as I admired his courage as an ace in World War I and however grateful I may be for the encouragements he gave me. But he is here on board, and characteristically not to be denied. Also present if not accounted for is Paul Draper, the superb dancer who enchanted audiences wherever he performed; a great artist whom I heckled to our mutual amusement by appearing unher-

*alded at ringside tables in New York, London, Chicago,
and Rio de Janeiro.*

*And what is Wellman doing here, the feisty Bostonian
who joined the French Flying Corps and much later,
when my own ambitions to referee actors had melted,
directed two of my better movies?*

*All of these people, ghosts and mortals alike, contri-
buted to the pattern of this life which is still mine actively to investigate. There are hosts of others and, Señor
Engineer, I must warn you some may be heroes, but
many are rapscallions of the most treacherous breed.*

Chapter 18

Once returned to the United States I thought my fortunes
had reached their absolute nadir. I had no money left at
all and, worse, knew that I deserved the shock of failure; in a sense I had betrayed Reid Ray and Charlie
Herbert and all the others who had so patiently taught
me their craft. I had taken an unfamiliar camera into a
difficult task and frequently employed a powerful tele-
scopic lens in weather unsuited to its use. Although I had
been reasonably careful scraping the camera's aperture
gate with a copper penny at each film change, I had obviously not been cautious enough to discover the speck
of dirt which had brought defeat.

All the effort involved and exposure to hazard had
come to naught.

My conscience was erupting with uncomfortable
reminders of those recent times in the company of Rikki
when I had utterly forgotten my wife and son. Now I
found Rikki's presence had not just evaporated at dock-
side in Holland but remained insistently tempting. By
reminding myself that Eleanor had done nothing but try
to be a good wife while son George deserved more than
a fable for a father, I finally returned to reality.

When my brooding became chronic I wrote long letters to Rikki. And my inner turmoil feasted upon itself
as I realized how subject I was to the puritanical code
of my forefathers. Then suddenly, as if an overdue miracle had been waiting upon a moment of almost total
despair, a man I barely knew tracked me down in Chi-

cago and offered me a job as a talent scout for Major Pictures, an independent unit producing films for Paramount. The pay was beyond my wildest dreams, twice what I had received from Warner Brothers, and I was to be my own boss. I vowed to be in Manhattan the following morning and once again borrowed money from my father to finance the expedition.

The miracle man was Ben Piazza, a gigantic individual with a heartiness to match his dimensions. He had great banana-fingered hands which it pleased him to fold over his enormous belly while he laughed resoundingly. He was also given to hoarsely whispered confidences, which he delivered with satanic guile. He was capable of shifting from an uproarious Falstaff to a scheming Iago in seconds, and likewise from joy to despair over the continuous struggle between Paramount Pictures and his boss, Manny Cohen, who had once headed that company.

The contrast between Cohen, a diminutive, quiet-spoken Jew, and Piazza, a three-hundred-fifty-pound, explosive, devout Catholic, was nearly matched by the man they had chosen to share the suite of New York offices with me. He was George Palmer Putnam, whose sole task was the discovery of literary material suitable for transfer to film. At least twenty years my senior, he came from a publishing background of which I knew as little as he did of films.

Putnam was a pleasant man, guarded, and usually rather dull. In contrast, I always found his wife, Amelia Earhart, magnetically exciting, a personage of great inner dignity. Sections of her next-to-last and last flights were plotted on my desk. I was always much impressed with Amelia's ability to switch almost instantly from a rather pixie-ish hoyden to a charming and very feminine lady, and then, without missing a beat, turn into the serious aviatrix. I thought it would be very easy to fall in love with her and only the omnipresent Putnam kept me from embarrassing overtures.

Into this array, colorful even for show business and dedicated to the production of commercial films starring the likes of Mae West and Bing Crosby, I entered with gratitude and full determination to please my employers.

226

The stink of failure was still heavy upon me. It must not happen again.

Ben Piazza had once been a professional baseball player, but his consuming passion for commercial entertainment won out over all else. He knew circus high-wire performers, animal trainers, burlesque clowns, swamis and magicians, coloraturas and gangsters—all of the population in the heart of and along the murky fringes of show business. His instant recall of first, middle, nicknames, and wives' names, the morals or the pornographic and spiritual inclinations of nearly all who passed his scrutiny was incredible, and the comments torn from the vast catalogue in his brain were usually proven correct. Piazza ambled through his day's work like a friendly hippo, pausing to graze when his great nose caught scent of something interesting, encouraging the forlorn whose names would never appear in lights, and chiding those whose theatrical success threatened to overpuff their vanities. He was fond of and hence a believer in the young, and I prospered greatly in his company.

What had been a landscape almost devoid of light now became a glittering place of remembered delights. Once again I took my regular table at Sardi's and was assured of the better seats on theatrical opening nights. Again I directed tests for the effervescent Kay Brown and for other outside companies. My telephone again echoed the extravagant claims of agents and the hopes of the ambitious. My time was my own and my expense account was never questioned; therefore I endeavored always to give more than a day's work and keep my expenditures at a minimum. For the first time an efficient secretary graced my outer office, a luxury I found more of an embarrassment than a need and somehow, I thought, overpretentious. I admonished her to tell the truth always of my whereabouts and to admit anyone who troubled to find the way—for I had too often been on the other side of the barricades and sympathized with those still there.

With my income so generous and apparently ever-increasing, I repaid all my debtors with hardly a loss of stride. I brought Eleanor and our son to live in an ancient and lovely Dutch colonial stone house near Tappan. Such was our well-being that I suddenly found time for interests other than films and the theater, a certain sign that the horn of plenty was overflowing. I drew and painted and wrote short stories which I did not even bother to submit. Among these diversions was hidden a totally unrelated activity which seemed to revive that peculiar yearning for physical excitement I had known in polo and more recently in Hitler's Germany with Rikki. It was then impossible to foresee how profoundly this new endeavor would affect my life and that of countless others.

The Dutch colonial house stood across the Hudson from Manhattan, very near the spot where Benedict Arnold was hanged. Farther up the west bank of the Hudson was Rockland County, a peaceful countryside of rolling hills, fields, and forests, dominated toward its northern sector by a small mountain known as High Tor. Here, certain of my acquaintances had settled, since the area was essentially wilderness and offered handy retreat from city life. The playwright Maxwell Anderson lived in Rockland County and willingly shared his genius with those who passed his way. Nearby, actor Burgess Meredith built a new house for his bride, the former Margaret Perry.*

Almost centered in this retreat, favored by so many people in the arts, was a small stone-fenced field near the base of High Tor. Known as the New City Airport, it was a challenge to the most skillful pilots. A deep swale formed a depression in the middle of the field and a fringe of power poles and wires presented a high fence around its perimeters. Three of the most independent and recalcitrant citizens in the United States chose to operate this "airport." They were the Christie brothers, who rarely approved of anything, nor were they inclined to be overly genial when serving customers.

The total equipment inventory at New City Airport consisted of two dilapidated hangars, a fuel storage tank and pump, and a small shack with a windsock fixed to the roof. Because he was a direct descendant of the early Dutch who had originally settled the area, the Christies allowed one independent flight instructor to use their field, charging him only a small portion of his unpredictable income. He was Rosamond Blauvelt, known as "Rizz," a young man of such shyness he sometimes

* Daughter of Antoinette Perry.

228

seemed to be hiding behind whatever object was at hand. While the Christie brothers argued and assailed, Blauvelt would retreat into a neutral corner of the little shack, smoke, listen, and rarely make a sound. Yet his timidity was only social; once aloft or even near his beloved airplane he became an entirely different man.

Rosamond Blauvelt was slight, dark of complexion and eye. He was mischievous and subtle, devoid of arrogance, and, fortunately for his students, extraordinarily patient. We were of the same age and the difference in our backgrounds was soon enough reflected in our special regard for each other. He admired my ability to make money and I saw no cause to disillusion him with tales of my failures. I admired his independence of spirit and his mastery of a machine I little understood.

Only a few years previously, Blauvelt had taken the Ryan School of Aeronautics offer of free flight instruction for any student who would buy an airplane. He chose a Great Lakes, a small, handsome biplane built of wood, wire, and fabric. The yellow wings were swept back in a style seen only in aircraft of much later design, a feature which contributed greatly to its sweet performance in the air, but did make it relatively difficult to land. There were two open cockpits in the bright red fuselage, a bare minimum of instrumentation, and more than ample ventilation. A varnished wooden propeller pulled the Great Lakes through the atmosphere at a cruising speed of one hundred five miles per hour. Power was provided by an English inverted Cirrus engine of eighty horsepower, just enough for basic aerobatics, but barely enough to clear the wires and stone walls surrounding the Christie airport. The Cirrus engine was of four cylinders with the exhaust pipes pointed upward, all four barking a reassuring song of reliability once the propeller had been pulled through by hand and the usual sequence of explosions commenced. The throaty ballad was too often a deception. The Cirrus had a passionate appetite for its own valves, swallowing them at most inopportune times. I was not aware of this gluttony when I first engaged Blauvelt to teach me his art.

In the beginning I had two companions in this new pursuit. Paul Draper, then an enormously successful dancer, caught my original enthusiasm and also started lessons with Blauvelt. He would drive out from Manhattan in an enormous twelve-cylinder Mercedes-Benz roadster. Its powerful engine developed twice the horsepower of the airplane he was about to fly, made an equivalent amount of noise, and was, in the hands of Draper who was a wild man at the wheel of a car, driven at speeds the Great Lakes could not attain.

After several lessons Draper lost interest, claiming the flying adversely affected his sense of balance on the dance floor. Since he was capable of leaping nearly as far as Nijinsky and his routine demanded superb coordination, I could hardly blame him.*

Burgess Meredith also joined our innocent squadron briefly, but for some reason never explained decided he knew of better ways to die. I carried on, totally and absolutely hooked. Even so, I regarded the project only as a sporting amusement and had no thought of doing anything serious about it, *if* I ever managed to go aloft and return safely to earth without Blauvelt's assistance.

For a time it appeared such a day would never come. When I was able to break away from my very demanding duties at Major Pictures I made haste to New City. There my principal accomplishment often seemed to be the provision of new complaints for the brothers Christie. They claimed, with some justification, that my performance on landing and take-off was damaging the good name of their airport. They alleged that someone was bound to be killed because passing cars caused traffic jams as they halted to watch my insults to their terrain. And whatever did happen *was* of my own doing, for Blauvelt was a believer in students learning by doing. He was also utterly fearless and would touch the controls only to prevent a certain crash.

The effect of Blauvelt's teaching philosophy was thorough, but he did not kick me out of the nest alone until I had eighteen hours of dual instruction. Since the average American student soloed in eight hours I sought excuses for my laggardly record. A few were legitimate. The Great Lakes was far more demanding than the average primary instruction aircraft, and many of my take-offs

* Paul Haakon, another very successful dancer, also listened to my zeal and thereby caught the flying fever. He continued with it until he became most expert.

were aborted by engine failure before we left the rough Christie real estate. Others were soon terminated in a nearby cornfield for the same reason.

I did not inform my father that I was flying. Despite his pioneer efforts in organizing Northwest Airlines and his later work as one of its directors, he mistrusted airplanes and after his original promotional efforts in tri-motored Fords refused to fly. I knew he would remind me that Eleanor's father had been killed "fooling around up there with the birds."

As my aerial exhibitions became less breathtakingly amateur, the demeanor of the Christie brothers mellowed. One Christie even ventured a congratulatory smile when I passed the test for a private pilot's license. Because of Blauvelt's prolonged dual work I found the test easy, although applicants then were required to demonstrate much greater aeronautical skill than they are now. Every candidate was asked to execute at least one genuine forced landing. A simulation and pull-up before touching down was rarely accepted. The brave examiner who rode with the student throughout his ordeal would cut the engine at a moment of his choosing and the student was expected to put the aircraft gently down upon the most favorable terrain available. Spins were mandatory, two turns to the left, and the next time two turns to the right. The applicant was expected to come out of his spins exactly on the original heading. Side-slips and fishtailing for short field landings were also required and, at the pleasure of the examiner, slow rolls, loops, snap rolls, and "falling leaves" were added to the list. In contrast, the written test was cursory, requiring only a few minutes to complete. Since there were no radios except in airliners and military aircraft, their existence for communication or navigation was ignored.

Soon after acquiring my private license I bought an airplane. Like the Great Lakes, it was a wood, wire, and fabric biplane. It was also much slower—and much safer. Known as a Bird, it had a vast wing area for its size and a fine round Jacobs engine. The Bird cruised at such a slow speed I could often look down and watch cars on the highway leaving me behind. It landed like a baby carriage at forty miles an hour and was therefore ideally suited to the Christies' airport. In spite of its little

231

old lady flight characteristics, I came as close to falling in love with the Bird as a man can with a machine. It cost eighteen hundred dollars and I kept it in one of the dilapidated hangars.

Wearing a polo coat, breeches, boots, galoshes, mittens, and leather face mask beneath helmet and goggles, I flew the Bird all through one bitter winter. I flew almost regardless of weather; in snow, rain, and wind. If I could see a hundred feet up the sides of High Tor, I flew. Those who knew anything about flying predicted it would only be a matter of time before I killed myself. The Christie brothers told me to my face I was crazy.

They were right. I was carrying on a mad love affair with flight and nothing could stay me from it.

By the end of the first winter I began to sense that my preoccupation with the sky was more than an infatuation. I flew in my thoughts and even in my sleep. As the winds of spring gusted down the Hudson Valley, my beautiful Bird became ever more alive and pleasurable.

Then one day when I longed to leave Manhattan for the soft blue sky beyond my office window, Blauvelt called with sorry news.

My beautiful Bird was dead. Somehow the hangar had caught fire and there survived only the cremated remains of something I had thought of as more than a machine.

Soon I found a replacement for the Bird, although it was a surrogate of much less appeal. With the payment of insurance money I bought a Waco A, a biplane no experienced aviator would praise. There was only one large open cockpit which seated two persons side by side instead of tandem as in the usual designs. Thus it became a one-sided airplane for the pilot, who, if alone, sat in the eye of a hurricane. The round Warner engine was reliable but unpleasant company aloft since most of the exhaust fumes found their way to the overlarge cockpit.

The Waco A had two additional peculiarities, which probably explained why so few were ever built. While the cockpit was too wide, the landing gear was too narrow, a feature which increased its tendency to chase its own tail and ground loop on landing. Then some engineer of dubious talent had somehow decided to fight force with force by linking the brake system to the throttle.

If the pilot wanted more power he pushed the throttle ahead in the normal fashion, but if he wanted right or left brake (or both brakes), he pulled down on the throttle lever while simultaneously applying right or left rudder with his feet. The slightest error in hand or foot coordination brought trouble, and the resulting exhibitions were often ridiculous. Somehow I managed to avoid any damage before eventually mastering the technique. I was not surprised that the Christie brothers approved of the Waco A. They preferred the obstinate and unwieldy.

Despite its sometimes recalcitrant nature I flew the Waco A most joyously for over a year. One afternoon when less foolish aviators were keeping their feet planted firmly on the ground, I encountered a grandfather of thunderstorms over the Catskills, a region known since the earliest Dutch settlers for spawning fierce storm activity. I had then accumulated some two hundred hours, a dangerous era in any pilot's life, for it is then he considers himself invincible and is compelled to prove it. In keeping with current aeronautical style I wore an enormous wristwatch which I consulted ostentatiously, an overlarge pair of wings sprouted from the buttonhole of my business jacket, and to further establish my affinity for all things aeronautical, I salted my conversations with arcane lingo. Words like "dihedral," "negative stagger," "washout," and "angle of incidence" came frequently to my lips. Eleanor, refusing to brood upon her father's fate during an almost identical state of skill, gave me a white silk scarf which I was at pains to tie in such a way that one end fluttered in the slipstream. I wore it whether I was near an airplane or not. A leather helmet and goggles completed the portrait, but there was no way to exhibit the fundamental transformation I felt deep within me every time I ventured aloft.

On the day of the thunderstorm I had been in such a great hurry to leave earth I had departed with a known defect in the Waco which I considered of no consequence. A locking device had broken away from the throttle. If I took my hand off it even for a moment the throttle would retract, with consequent loss of engine power. A prudent aviator would have remained earthbound until the defect was fixed.

All went well until somewhere in the vicinity of Kingston I plunged into the slavering lower chops of the thunderstorm. While Blauvelt had taught me well in the manual command of an aircraft, his natural reticence had limited my acquisition of a prudent flying philosophy; nor was he exceptional in his verbal reserve. Most contemporary pilots of experience affected the strong and silent character. Even the most experienced pilots were still groping for more weather wisdom and very few flew in bad weather. Thus the neophyte had little chance to develop a philosophy of flight other than remembering to keep speed up and nose down in the turns. Unfortunately, a certain rudimentary code governed the thinking of many pilots. If in flight he encountered unfavorable weather, then the iron-man image was supposed to take charge. The leather-clad knight shoved his lantern jaw into the tempest, descended until his wheels barely cleared the terrain, and, with the help of road map, local knowledge, and God, carried on to his destination. The land was not as yet festooned with hungry spiderwebs of high-tension lines, and the airplanes were slow and very maneuverable. Hence the pilot had a reasonable expectation of surviving if his fuel held out and he could see half a mile ahead. A great many pilots were killed because the most important dictum, the 180-degree turn, had not yet been learned by all. Not one of my growing collection of high-flying princelings ever pulled me aside and said, "For all anyone knows, death may be disappointing. Since any slob can participate there is nothing noble about it. Even in an airplane death can hurt. So always keep your back door open. When in doubt turn around and go back where you came from."

Unknowing of such fundamentals and still obsessed with an uncommon urge to tilt with windmills, I was a prime candidate for disaster. And now in this line of thunderstorms I saw an undeniable temptation to try my steel. Ignorant of atmospheric power, I sailed straight into the fray, rejoicing in the crack of thunder audible even over the rumbling of the Warner engine, exhilarated by the magnificent display of fireworks all about me. *This* was flying, I thought.

My initial bravado was soon tempered by heavy rain. The better to see ahead, I pushed up my goggles and instantly regretted it. My eyes were stung by a thousand lancets, and my jaw smarted from a horizontal cascade of chill water. I hunkered down in the cockpit for protection and wished I had brought gloves since my fingers were already cold.

I entered a region of rough air, more turbulent than I had ever encountered before, and was alarmed to observe the antics of my compass, which gyrated until it was nearly unreadable. My concern mounted when I peeked over the rim of the cockpit and caught a glimpse of the battlefield I had so deliberately chosen. Murky trees were just beyond and a little below the Waco's wingtip. They hung in a dreary mist as in a Japanese sumi painting. Tendrils of cloud vapor swept down between their branches and occasionally I could detect the dark and brooding slopes of hills in the very near distance. Yet I dared not pull up. The bottom of the cloud layer seemed just above my helmet and, worse, was closing with the earth like a giant vise.

I yearned to climb away from the trees but one common principle *had* been handed down by my mentors. "Don't get in the clouds. They bite." I knew the airline pilots and a handful of the military were the sole and often lonely travelers through cloud.

With the compass dancing and the Waco requiring considerable stick and rudder to keep it anywhere near level flight, the battle I had joined with such heart soured rapidly.

The whole sensation of physical fear was unfamiliar to me and now against the ramparts of a thunderstorm I felt it, and found it extremely unpleasant. I was, I thought, a coward after all. My chill face flamed, my stomach roiled, and my arms tightened involuntarily. Worse, a sense of disorientation nearly overwhelmed me. How long had I been at this? Where was I? When would it end?

As the jouncing about a series of axes continued, I resolved to check my whereabouts, a superfluous decision against the very immediate demands of the rising terrain. It was an excuse to look away from calamity, I knew, yet I could not resist. Suddenly, instead of a leather-faced, steely-eyed pilot of the heavens, I had become a small boy trembling beneath the blankets. I wanted to hide and

I knew at last that physical courage was as tricky and ephemeral as mercury in the palm of a hand.

All the way since take-off I had kept the road map under my leg, but now I could not find it. I bent forward as far as I could without banging my goggles on the instrument panel and finally saw it wedged between the bottom of my seat and a longeron. I decided I might just reach it by loosening my belt, twisting half around in the seat, and extending my left arm to its full length.

The very first movement set fire to the fear which had only been smoldering. Since my right hand was more than busy enough with the control stick I instinctively reached to release my belt with my left hand. Almost simultaneously the throttle slipped back and the engine subsided to idle power. The loss of its comforting roar produced a relative silence interrupted only by awesome explosions of thunder. It was a long moment before I realized what I had done and placed my hand back on the frivolous throttle. After pushing forward on the throttle and feeling a reassuring surge of power I took a series of deep breaths while trying to reorganize. I was all too aware the Waco was proceeding in a generally southerly direction at better than one hundred miles an hour and apparently in a valley. And with valleys, I realized, there must always be hills.

Where was I indeed? If there were hills ahead, I was in serious trouble. What I could see of the terrain below was uninviting: trees, rocks, ravines, and round earth knobs offered little hospitality despite my confidence in putting aircraft in small places learned the hard way at the Christies' airfield.

Retrieving the map became an obsession with me, even though I knew it had no contour lines and its only useful information demanded the visual sighting of a road or town. There was no evidence of any civilization below me, not even a farm.

While I tried to settle the compass on a steady heading I became newly alarmed at the reading of my altimeter. It declared I was five hundred feet high, which my eye told me was a considerable exaggeration. My arduous training under Blauvelt wherein I learned to eye-measure altitude with surprising accuracy now served to convince me the Waco was no more than one hundred feet above the terrain.*

There now began a series of manipulations and vacillations both physical and mental which left me panting with fright and alternately chuckling like a madman. My hard breathing suddenly produced visible vapor. The rain became small hailstones which peppered my leather helmet with a resounding bombardment every time I ventured to move my head out of the direct protection of the windscreen. The empty seat beside me gathered a little mound of white petit pois and I wondered how soon the fabric would start peeling back from the wings.

Removing my hand momentarily from the control stick I tried reaching for the map, but found the intervening distance impossible to span unless I let go everything and stood on my head. I tried again with my left hand, heard the engine throttle back and the flying wires sigh before my seeking fingers were even near the map.

I returned to the business of maintaining at least some separation between my quivering buttocks and the state of New York.

As a momentary balm, I fell into cozy conversations with the God I thought I knew. In the time-honored style of all humans in trouble, my words took the form of appeals for relief from present stress. "Get me out of this terrible trouble immediately. I'm not ready to die." Castigation of self for creating the predicament is practiced only by survivors.

The Waco's overlarge double cockpit swallowed the elements with wide open mouth. Rain variously mixed with small hailstones swirled into the open space on my right and that half of me was soaked. I pushed my goggles up for a clear view of the situation overhead and wished I had resisted the urge. Though the deluge I saw great fat inverted balloons of black cloud blossoming with inner fires. Whore's drawers, I thought in a feeble attempt to revive my spirits.

Yet suddenly a transformation took place. I became a spectator rather than a combatant. I heard the rumbling of thunder followed by sharp cracks as an audience viewing a spectacle. I watched the tributaries of rain

---

* Few aviators then knew of the quick and sometimes drastic change in altimeter readings when entering a cold front.

spewing into the cockpit from innumerable sources. There was an interesting race between several lines of water over and around and underneath the windscreen, down across the glass facings of the instruments, with the finish line on my knees. I opened my mouth so dry with fear and collected a few droplets of moisture. Another attempt at humor: "I am a spawning salmon bound upstream . . . I am Captain Nemo in his submarine."

I knew I was whistling in the dark. I was over a forest now with the treetops barely below my wingtips. There was almost no forward visibility. I spared an instant to congratulate the Warner engine's manufacturer. As long as I held the throttle forward it continued sweetly on.

I ventured another look straight down and saw a railroad track, the shale roadbed black with water and the rails a polished gray-white. I cheered without sound and, in hope renewed, dismissed any further possibility of divine intervention. Here, I knew, was rescue—unless the track vanished into a tunnel.

I descended a few feet and without shame locked on to a sure thing. Several minutes later a station loomed out of the mist. I could not catch the name board approaching, but did read it clearly over the Waco's tail. GOSHEN. Then the station was gone again. I did not care, for I knew where I was.

Another twenty minutes and I had left the thunderstorm grumbling behind. The Hudson River flowed beneath my wings and once more I could pose as a leather-clad swashbuckler. Yet subconsciously I had discovered one of the primary truths of the aviator who might expect longevity. Prudence was necessary, but as in all things it could be ruinous if overdone. Elan was beneficial as long as it did not involve stupid sacrifice upon the altar of courage. Now I knew that the most priceless attribute of all was humility: regardless of training or equipment or time, we were all little men, self-pitted against forces often beyond human measure. Later, when my logbooks were heavy with hours flown all over the world, the lesson I had learned that tumultuous afternoon was many times confirmed: those who failed to recognize their true insignificance rarely survived.

Another afternoon in the same Waco led me to further contemplation of men who had been seduced by the mystique of flight—or had, for more tangible reasons, recognized that its inevitable impact upon all civilizations would exceed even that of the wheel. Unlike my wild matinee with the Catskill thunderstorms, this experience found me well in the clear, northbound from Baltimore toward Christie airport and home. I passed over the New Jersey swamps at four thousand feet, content beyond belief with my high station and the glorious spectacle on display all about me. It seemed I was a solitary audience, since there were no other aircraft in sight, a situation I regretted. More human beings, I thought, should revel in this show, if only to elevate their thoughts above the thousands of earthly mischiefs now transpiring in the depths below. Far away to the east stretched the Atlantic, black against the horizon with the fringe of the Jersey shore just touched by the late afternoon sun.

I looked west over my left shoulder and beheld great slanting pillars of radiance shafting down between distant thunderheads. Ahead, beyond the outline of the engine's speed ring, I saw the towers of Manhattan, a lustrous cake against a glowering northern sky. There, I thought, in momentary guilt at my theft of time, is where I should be laboring along with a few million of my kind; I am not paid to ride this wilderness alone, but for lesser things.

I was enthralled with the dramatic contrast between black water, sparkling city, and sense of my own minuteness against the western sky. Was this not the only true life for me? And as I passed over New York harbor and continued up the west bank of the Hudson River, I stared at the stone monoliths of the city and wondered more.

Now I was between the light and the city polished to a golden brilliance by the dying sun. Each of the towers was etched against the somber eastern sky and they seemed to quiver as in a mirage. The total effect was such that the entire island appeared to be floating in midair. Then, when almost opposite the middle of Manhattan, I saw an apparition moving toward me, southbound. I pushed up my goggles, unbelieving, for beyond my right wing and closing the distance rapidly was a monster from the upper world.

I forgot all else as the great Zeppelin slid through the airspace between me and the stone citadel. The very silence of its passage was stunning: its size created a sense of awe I had never known before. The damn thing is really alive, a lost whale, I thought.

As we passed, the huge shape, yellow in the sun, blocked most of Manhattan from my view. I could see the passengers in the windows of her belly and the name HINDENBURG painted in Germanic letters aft of her fat snout. And in my excitement I thought, there proceeds the ultimate glory of man in the sky; we are no longer so puny up here.

I also thought I had perhaps seen into the future, beheld a pre-vision of all those argosies the aeronautically imaginative were always talking about.

Moments later the great airship was only a blob beyond the Waco's tail. I entertained the notion of chasing after it, perhaps playing about its bulk, a fly in company with a monster from the heights. A cautiously executed loop around its circumference might be worth a year of ordinary flying, especially in this last light of a spectacular day. Then realizing the danger to others, I dismissed the idea with the contempt it deserved.

All the way to Christie airport and through eighteen thousand later hours of flying I held the vision. It was made all the more vivid and poignant when I learned soon after I had landed that fateful afternoon how the majestic *Hindenburg* had been destroyed. Lost in the same explosion had been an era of mighty airborne dreams—humbled by the elements.

Chapter 19

Since *yang* is the sunny side of the hill, then *yin* must ever be the side in shadow. Likewise all men, except the very sick, are optimists or they could not long survive the daily assault of bad news. A byproduct of optimism is a tendency to forget hard times, plus an ability to replace what damage may have occurred with renewed faith. Thus, in my general euphoria with flying and a fine job to support it as well as my family, I rarely looked back on leaner days. The correspondence with Rikki in Holland had languished, and while I was far from domesticated, the union with Eleanor was apparently able to withstand all shocks common to the young married. Never having developed any empathy whatsoever for those young husbands who foisted a wallet full of their children's pictures on helpless companions, I was now dismayed by my particular pleasure in my son George. He accompanied me everywhere except to the office. At Christie airfield he would wait patiently, sometimes for hours, while I cavorted aloft, and when I returned he smiled. He rarely talked and never wept. As a consequence, we became true companions. I spoke to him of many things and of puzzlements I would not have confided to anyone else in the world. And as devoted allies we never questioned the other's right to independence.

These halcyon days came to an abrupt end with the overnight collapse of Major Pictures. One day I was king of the mountain and the very next, without any kind of warning, I was unemployed. Ben Piazza went down with me, as did George Palmer Putnam and to a degree Manny Cohen.

I was stunned. It took a few days for me to appreciate the extent of the debacle. In my optimistic conviction that a good thing would last forever and even doubtless improve, I had not troubled to save a penny. For two years I had been given to quoting various sages on the insignificance of money; now, once again bereft of it, I was stuck with my own pomposities. Eleanor, with innate female practicality and ample justification, pointed out how easy it was to hold money in contempt when it was plentiful.

The first luxury to go was the Waco; then the car, then the lovely Dutch house, and finally, at last convinced I had been in the wrong locale all the time, I set off for Hollywood. The whole pattern seemed uncomfortably familiar. Eleanor and George returned once more to be sheltered beneath my father's wing, and his money financed my exploratory trip to California. I vowed as always to repay him and knew with a growing sense of guilt that he still hoped my frivolous days were past and that I would soon rejoin his commonsense world.

My mother's obviously deteriorating health worried us all. For my father, whose concern for her had never faltered, the capricious developments in his son's career were of comparatively little importance. "Blood will tell," he once declared flatly. "You will find out the kind of people you are."

I assumed he was referring to some of my theatrical friends, many of whom would have appeared quite out of place in one of his clubs or board meetings. His dogmatism infuriated me, but I held my tongue for I was again vassal to his purse.

The motion picture production industry did not hire people like other American enterprises. Separate employment departments were unnecessary, since innumerable candidates awaited like hawks to pounce upon the most ordinary jobs. Just to sneak a foot in a studio door was considered a victory. Then with cunning, patience, ruthlessness, and fierce devotion, there was some chance the employment could be made permanent—an enviable situation in an atmosphere of constant and meteoric change.

Under this system nearly all Hollywood jobs behind the cameras were secured by friends of the already employed, or relatives unto the sixteenth cousin of those in command. There were no exceptions to the rule and I had no friends within the formidable gates. And strangely, now that I was at last on the home grounds of the industry I had so long yearned to make my life career, it disappointed me. My attempts at job-getting were half-hearted and consequently unproductive. An agent arranged a screen test at Metro-Goldwyn-Mayer which mercifully I was spared ever viewing. It was the only time I was ever admitted inside any of the studios.

As the amount of time between exploring for jobs increased, so did my attendance upon newer endeavors. Before the collapse of Major Pictures I had achieved a commercial flying license and was therefore officially sanctioned to fly for hire. I knew there was no comparison between aeronautical and theatrical wages, but I found it increasingly easy to persuade myself that the sky was more my natural habitat.

I began to frequent Mines Field* and Clover Field,† testing the winds of possible employment, talking with men who made their living with wings and delighting in their acceptance of me, employed or not. At Burbank

---

* The present Los Angeles International. Mines Field consisted of one short cinder runway. It was surrounded by open countryside.

† Clover Field was an open pasture surrounded by assorted power wires. It is now an industrial area.

Airport where most of the airline traffic originated I finally found spasmodic employment with Lewis Air Service. There I instructed students and flew charter work in a cabin Waco. I soon became devoted to my employer, Lewis, a short, cigar-smoking pilot of relatively vast experience. The joy of working outdoors, of knowing exactly what was expected of me, did wonders for my morale in spite of woeful finances. I took home to the motel in which I lived three dollars for every hour spent at actual instruction and two dollars for flying charter. "Remember, you are building up your flying time," Lewis reminded me. Although my total pay was rarely more than thirty dollars, I so enjoyed the work I would have flown for nothing if I could envision some way to support a wife and son. To that end I devoted ever more energy and in the gaps between flights began writing short stories. Like so many thousands of others since the creation of pulp magazines, I convinced myself that writing was an easy way to make money in my spare time. Aware of my ignorance and lack of training, I aimed my stories at the pulp market served by such magazines as *Flying Aces,* and *Adventure.* Out of approximately fifty stories my total sales were zero.

In what was left of my spare time I redoubled my efforts to find what I had now become convinced was "honest work." I flew to San Diego where I applied for selection as an Air Corps cadet. My physical examination was nearly perfect and my application forwarded with high recommendations. Unfortunately, the Air Corps was cutting down on all flying activities. Even West Pointers were being turned away.

I tried Douglas Aircraft at Santa Monica where Johnnie Cable was considerate but obliged to remind me that the factory then employed several pilots at pounding rivets. Their flying experience was much greater than mine. Carl Squier at Lockheed was also most courteous, but his answer was essentially the same.

My remaining optimism carried me as far as the airlines, where, for the first time, I encountered caste in aviation. It seemed that wherever coveted jobs existed, compassion for the hopeful diminished. At United Airlines the stiff-lipped chief pilot took one look at me and asked, "Are you Air Corps trained?" When I responded in the negative he shook his head and said, "There is no use in your even filing an application."

At TWA the scene was repeated, albeit involving a different branch of the service.

"Are you Navy?"

A headshake, a regret. An attempt to explain how I had learned to fly the hard way and perhaps that effort should be of some value. My recitative was cut short by: "Sorry. We only hire Navy-trained pilots."

Western Airlines declared my flying time hopelessly inadequate. "Come back when you have more than a thousand hours and an instrument rating."

I had less than five hundred. Gaining an instrument rating would cost a thousand dollars.

Back at Lewis Air Service my optimism fluctuated with the gauge of activity, while my aerial confidence became ever more steadfast. This was the life I *must* have, somehow, somewhere in the world. Felix Jones, a United pilot who had tried without success to ease me past the military fixation of his airline, put me on to the possibility of flying trimotored Fords in Central America. I fired off an exaggerated resumé of my capabilities to Lowell Yerex at TACA, a hell-for-leather operation in Tegucigalpa, and received a promise of a co-pilot's seat "within the next six months."

Kalberer, another United veteran, had through an almost incredible chain of circumstances become a new friend and champion. But a champion who is himself in trouble is rarely a powerful aide. In an era when most aviators were sparkling with color if not beauty, Kalberer stood supreme in garish splendor. He was of medium height and stocky. His hands were powerful, his manner confident, while his voice and cadence of speech were unusually melodious and persuasive. His single bow to convention was his close-cropped almost hairline mustache, then the common denominator of a veteran pilot.

Kalberer's blue-green eyes captured all attention which might have lingered elsewhere. His eyes were startling in their vitality, wild and venturesome, ever full of the powerful urges which drove him so relentlessly. Not for Kalberer was the go to work at A, then fly to B, thence back to A and home for two days of family and working in the garden. In spite of his thousands of hours, which had included flying the airmail in open-cockpit De Havillands for NAT,* Kalberer was as passionately devoted to flying as the most recent initiate. He never blamed fate or the business of flying in general for calamity. It was always human error; the man had betrayed his trust through stupidity. Yet somehow Kalberer managed to remove any blemish of arrogance from his condemnations, perhaps because he avoided gossip in judging a fallen individual. Then the time came, as those who found his enthusiasms objectionable were delighted to proclaim, when he met his comeuppance.

On a take-off at Chicago he crashed only a short distance beyond the perimeter of the airport. No one was injured, but the aircraft was a total loss.

Kalberer was fired, but not, peculiarly enough, because of the crash. The official reason was "instability," a newly employed brand of airline terminology indicating the nonconformist. Among all the airlines, United was then particularly devoted to casting its pilots in a common mold, each—in the name of safety—flying in exactly the same way, and each conducting his personal life as a manageable, sedate, and solid citizen.

Everything within the complicated mixture of the man Kalberer refused to toe the company line. He was married, but declined any interest in family life. Instead of gardening or golfing he collected arsenals of exotic weapons. He read with lightning speed, often a book a day, on subjects ranging from technical treatises on the internal combustion engine or the flight envelopes of certain aircraft, to anthropological studies of African pigmies. He wrote stories and sold them. He was working on an enormous history of William the Conqueror, a project he blithely declared would take him at least ten years.

Most aggravating to his superiors and other pilots of the line who believed a low-key demeanor would further assure their precious jobs, was Kalberer's flair for the gaudy and expensive. His civilian suits, shirts, and ties were as wild as his eyes and he would have none of the ordinary cars in which other United employees transported themselves to the airport. Instead Kalberer drove a great Pierce-Arrow with tulip headlights flowering from the front fenders. In the company it kept when its master

* National Air Transport, a predecessor of United Air Lines.

was away on a flight, the huge limousine stood out like a circus wagon, and everyone knew it cost nearly as much as a Rolls-Royce. "Instability," they whispered. How could a man be so free with his money and be mentally sound enough to fly passengers?

There was another, more provocative reason for Kalberer's unpopularity in the eyes of his airline's officialdom. He was one of the original founders of the Air Line Pilots Association, a very devil's own union to airline administrators. Before the eventual acceptance of the union, an airline pilot's life was not a happy one in spite of his lofty view and relative independence. While the pay was adequate, a pilot could be fired on the whim of an official, for a minor infringement of a rule, or for a scratch on an airplane. If a pilot refused to make a flight because of bad weather or what he judged was a serious mechanical defect in an airplane, a dispatcher could say, "If you don't feel like flying the trip, we'll get someone who will."

As unions go, the Pilots Association was composed of a peculiarly intelligent, alert, and well-educated membership most of whom were as interested in the financial prosperity of their companies as any desk-bound executive. Hence, with the exception of Behnke the president, who *was* given to the suspender-snapping and name-calling and the common rhetoric of organized labor, airline executives had difficulty finding suitable red-necks among the opposition. Kalberer, who was an avid follower of the Dow-Jones averages and a total believer in the system, was a handy patsy if only because of his flamboyance.

My father, as unlikely a candidate as could be imagined for the defense of anyone who had ever been near a union, moved his not inconsiderable presence into the fray. During one of my periodic visits to Chicago a few months previously, I had, with some misgivings brought Kalberer to dinner. I knew my father viewed all pilots as reckless daredevils forever clad in helmet and goggles and perhaps even marked with a death wish. Most American companies specifically forbade their employees to fly on business, and nearly all life insurance policies were voided if the holder was unfortunate enough to be killed in an airplane. These rules were heartily endorsed by my father.

To my astonishment my father succumbed almost immediately to Kalberer's forthright charm. He listened in fascination as Kalberer related various of his flying experiences and, to my father's delight, asked his advice on market investments. Certainly my father found Kalberer refreshing in comparison with his blood son who had never asked his advice about anything, much less punctuated sentences with the frequent use of "sir." And as the evening wore on, he found him stimulating as well. For Kalberer was not only an authority on William the Conqueror, but spoke knowledgeably of Attila, Saladin, Hannibal, Scipio Africanus, and a host of other legendary adventurers whose deeds my father had lived vicariously. Kalberer was also a student of Mahan and Clausewitz.

While they discussed those military thinkers I saw my father's good eye light with a distant fire. I realized he was hearing drums and bugles and perhaps the subsiding roar of cannon as he marched triumphantly through defeated enemies. Watching and listening as Kalberer and my father consumed each other, I realized the joyous harvest of their meeting. Kalberer admired wealth and position and all the trappings he saw as a part of them. The second man in my father, a wonderfully independent and romantic soul, yearned for more excitements than annual reports: more of the blood of life than the practicalities of industry and the fawning of underlings. For the first time I understood how my own snide disregard of his accomplishments and my retreats into oversimplicities must have bewildered and even hurt him. Secretly, I vowed to wear a tie more often, evidence at least some interest in the performance of the stock market, and not run for cover when his purple Stutz hove into view.

As the evening progressed to brandy and cigars in the library and the two new allies had thoroughly discussed a fine set of dueling pistols my father had recently acquired, Kalberer mentioned his difficulties with United Airlines and his subsequent dismissal. He was simply responding to my father's questioning about his present flying route and had no idea how promptly his host would mount his charger; nor could I quite believe my ears.

"This is the most disgraceful thing I ever heard of!" my father declared. "Absolute nonsense. I am a stockholder in United Airlines. I'll call Patterson* in the morning and we'll get this thing straightened out. Damn stock has never paid a dividend anyway. Poor management somewhere, I daresay."

Kalberer explained patiently how the matter was closed and how he was already arranging an interview with KLM, who were anxious to hire experienced American pilots.

"Nonsense. We can't have a fine American like you flying for the Dutch. I've been to Holland. They are a dull people."

I wondered if my father would sustain his caveat had he met the vivacious Rikki and I also resolved to try KLM for at least a co-pilot's job.

True to his word, my father devoted the following morning to a lengthy "discussion" with Patterson and other United Airlines officials on the subject of a certain pilot and his abrupt dismissal. My father always launched his attacks from the platform of "reason," his voice calm and persuasive, his thoughts touching upon the lessons of history, and his remarkable memory supplying suitable quotations from the great philosophers. When his listeners began to fear a monologue, he would turn the tables on them by inquiring with sweet temper of their opinions and suggestions to remedy whatever problem was at hand. When he appeared to be listening in fascination to his opposition it was well to watch the wandering of his good eye, for having established himself as the most reasonable man in the world he would tumble the "discussion" and start hammering away on his original theme. In Kalberer's case he failed only because he came too late upon the scene, but the United officials long nursed their wounds.

I was sorry the decision was past the reversible stage, yet greatly heartened by the stalwart performance of my sire. There was, I knew at last, a very special man hidden behind the watchchain, vest, stiff collar, and the smoked-glass windows of a purple Stutz.

Kalberer did get a job with KLM, flying from Amsterdam to Batavia. I failed, again for the lack of flying time and an instrument rating.

* William A. ("Pat") Patterson, president of United and a fine executive.

Once more I assailed the studio gates in California, this time with a cast of puppets I had designed and built with a German woodcarver. They were two feet high and so constructed they could be animated into any desirable action. I wrote two short scenarios featuring the little people, but the efforts created little interest. Hollywood was preoccupied with much bigger things.

All through the thin flying days at Burbank Airport I held out hope someone might buy *Distant Pastures,* the book I had written about my adventures as a young telephone envoy. Then by great good fortune Max Schuster troubled to read it. He had little choice. He was one of a group of city-dwellers who went regularly to the B-Bar-H Ranch at Garnet, California. Three, in somewhat the same manner as members of Louis XIV's court engaged in month-long parties, a collection of people took names they thought appropriate to their holiday theme. They wore expensive Western outfits and went daily from horse to swimming pool. My father (Cactus Jack) and my mother (Desert Flower) were an integral part of the group, which included such luminaries as Walt Disney (Banjo Pete), Jack Kriendler, proprietor of New York's "21" (Pistol Pete), actors Ray Milland and Robert Young, Si Seadler, a vice president of MGM, and Max Schuster (Hard-Tack Harry).

Confined to the living area of the ranch, Schuster became easy prey for my father who "suggested" he read the book I had written and give thought to its publication. Schuster complied, but had the good sense to decline it for his house, albeit his letter of rejection was long and gracious enough for me to place him high among my special heroes.*

Eleanor and I were always invited as guests of my parents to these holiday affairs. Our pleasure amid such luxury was never complete because we both knew our still hand-to-mouth real life lurked just beyond the gently swaying tamarisk trees. In spite of the preponderance of people present who might easily have helped further my inclination toward a career in the arts, I never mentioned the need. It simply was not done.

One of my flying students was Lester Linsk, who was himself beginning a career in a Hollywood agency. An-

---

* Simon and Schuster later published many of my books.

other was Harmon Oscar Nelson,* also involved in an agency. We became a trio soon bound in friendship and the struggle to make our way in a difficult world.

Since the studios were steadfast in their refusal to recognize how difficult it was to get along without my assistance and the Air Corps still held me on stand-by, my only income was from flying charter and teaching a handful of students, none of whom were very regular or even very enthusiastic. Their lack of dedication was understandable. Lewis suddenly forbade me to instruct at Burbank since he had decided I was competing against him while using his airplane. He sent me to an open space in the San Fernando Valley about three miles west, a field empty of any other activity save for a few hungry jackrabbits and an occasional snake twisting between the mesquite. It was surrounded on three sides by high-tension wires while telephone wires marked the northern perimeter. These lethal fixtures were like spiderwebs to a fly and at least offered students the advantage of easy return to roost. "Just find a large square space between the wires," I told them, "and land anywhere in between. You'll be in the right place." †

In addition, the airplane Lewis made available was hardly exciting for students although it did provide more than enough stimulus for the instructor. Known as an Aeronca C-3, or "Airknocker," it was underpowered and slothful. On a hot day with two people wedged side by side into its little open cockpit it could barely be persuaded to leave the ground, a lethargy which obliged me to make all take-offs *under* the high-tension wires. The Aeronca's greatest disadvantage as an instructional device originated in its single set of controls. Thus the student was actually in command at all times while the instructor more or less went along for the ride. If the instructor wished to demonstrate a maneuver, he had to reach across the student's leg for the control stick while telling him what to do with his feet on the rudder pedals. This became difficult during borderline situations and sometimes deteriorated into a wrestling match if the stu-

---

* Husband to Bette Davis.

† The field was in approximately the same location as the present Van Nuys Airport—now one of the busiest in the world.

dent was inclined to be stubborn, or became so terrorized by promised disaster that he froze on the controls.

I did not like the Aeronca. It had no guts and no pride. Older, wiser pilots said I must want to fly very much indeed to instruct in the Aeronca. I could only reply, "I do."

The graceless Aeronca taught me the difference between working for a living and nearly dying for a living— at least twice a week. Even so I would have been temporarily content if it actually provided me with enough income to continue. To that end I made new efforts.

Somehow I managed to persuade two hundred dollars each from Nelson and Linsk. With such capitalization I engaged an oompah band and as a songstress hired Darlene, one of the waitresses at the hamburger stand where I occasionally took an indelicate luncheon. Before the Fourth of July weekend we proceeded to the Isthmus at Catalina Island where I had rented the meeting hall and rehearsed my troupers in a parody of nineteenth-century oleo shows. The audience, which I assured Nelson and Linsk would fight for admission, would sit at tables and drink beer during the performance. I rigged a trapeze so Darlene could swing out over the heads of the audience as she sang bawdily of her charms and dropped souvenir red garters to the bigger spenders. After frantic rehearsals and the thwarting of an embarrassingly passionate affair between Darlene and the bass horn player, I believed they could get through at least one performance without being arrested for lewd and lascivious display.

We were blessed with a full moon, a soft breeze, and the soothing whisper of wavelets along the beach. Darlene had sworn she had gargled only with mouthwash instead of gin for a change and had departed the bass horn player's couch momentarily satiated. Nelson and Linsk arrived in their capacity as "angels." I anticipated a thrilling and profitable opening night.

By the middle of the evening we could no longer postpone the performance, lest the fifteen impatient customers who had wandered in from somewhere beneath the moon beat the tables to kindling. Darlene sailed out over their heads with her first song. At once a new worry made me wipe at the perspiration along my forehead.

Very obviously Darlene had rediscovered her gin bottle and tipped it against her pert little nose once too often. With every swing of the trapeze she threatened to try her own wings. I estimated that the extent of her fall would not be more than ten feet vertically at peak, but had no way to calculate how much kinetic energy would be manufactured by her gyrations. I also noted that the bass horn player seemed bent on dominating the entire show —including the frail voice of his beloved.

What there was of the audience cheered uproariously. Led by actor Victor McLaglen, a renowned tosspot and true throwback to the days of the most rambunctious pirates, there was enough noise to create the illusion of success. The following night McLaglen brought more than a score of his friends, who made the hall quiver with their joyous approval. Darlene, blushing scarlet with gin and overcome with the applause her swing act created, deliberately dropped into the waiting arms of McLaglen's claque, knocked over the table and spilled beer and drinkers in a sort of mosaic pattern across the floor. For this, I thought wryly, I studied the theatrical masters under the great George Pierce Baker at Yale.

The following night was a Sunday and destined to be our last. McLaglen was again in raucous attendance along with his cronies and a full house of new customers who had been attracted from all over Catalina by rumors of the mayhem and debauchery to be witnessed for the price of a ticket and a few beers. Once again Darlene promised me she would avoid all gin until after the show, and once again she proved that a dedicated alcoholic is marvelously resourceful. Not until the following day did I learn that the atomizer she employed to spray her delicate larynx between songs was not filled with balm for her vocal organs, but with pure gin. At least this night Darlene herself could not be held responsible for her early departure from the trapeze. McLaglen, enjoying himself hugely, climbed on his table and taking full advantage of his magnificent physique plucked Darlene from her perch as if she were a true canary. I closed my eyes while the audience roared with approval.

No one could argue that our show was not joyful entertainment, if somewhat lacking in serious artistry. Alas, the first night of poor attendance reduced the whole to a financial tragedy. After the oompah band, Darlene, and all the other expenses were paid off, Nelson and Linsk received ten dollars return on their two hundred investment. There was nothing for me except a remorseful kiss from Darlene. My respect for successful entrepreneurs was compounded.

Nelson, having decided that the squaw man role with a famous and rather feisty wife was more than his gentle nature could longer tolerate, asked if I would like a free ride to New York where he intended to seek a new life. And I was also in need of renewal, having failed in everything I had attempted. Had it not been for the patient generosity of my father I could not have paid the rent on the little papier-mâché apartment I shared with Eleanor and George in North Hollywood. Worse, I had become an accomplished sponger. I had developed a distinct muscular deficiency which slowed my reaching for restaurant checks, a phenomenon matched only by my alacrity in accepting invitations of any sort as long as others were assuming the cost. I knew I was in danger of accepting the generosity of others as the natural way of things and was determined to change. Committed to one last detour around the telephone business, I rode to New York with Nelson and only hours after our arrival my dilemma began to dissolve. The unctuous self-apologies and temporizing which enable men to endure long periods of repeated disappointment, the secret promises of miraculous rescue on the morrow or the day after, had become so fixed in my thoughts that I accepted the change in my fortunes as normal. First, Kay Brown, at whose table I had so frequently dined that her husband could not refrain from making good-natured comments about "starboarders," arranged for me to direct a series of movie tests. Then I had not even time to fret about being right back where I had started when one of the few true geniuses I would ever know decided I would fill his need as an assistant. He was Norman Bel Geddes, designer, architect, artist, entrepreneur, liberal and libertine, inventor, bon vivant, and thinker.

Bel Geddes's energies were astounding and his talents so tremendous that his progress through an ordinary day was like watching the glittering trail of a rocket. In the morning he might be holding a conference on a trans-

Atlantic steamship designed to cruise at fifty knots, at luncheon he would solve the problem of hanging an entire building on cables, and in the afternoon immerse himself in the production of two plays, one * by a vital young playwright, Irwin Shaw.

Even Bel Geddes's contemporaries and sometime associates, Raymond Loewy and Buckminster Fuller, lauded his abilities while lamenting his nearly chaotic disorganization. Bel Geddes often worked at night, but never if opportunity existed for wild revelry. He was particularly devoted to bacchanals with his friend Max Reinhardt, who directed the Passion Plays at Oberammergau. On such occasions the distinguished pair would closet themselves in Bel Geddes's apartment for as long as three days, emerging cleansed, chastened, and with renewed energies for their noble works.

For mysterious reasons of his own Bel Geddes was, at least temporarily, under the illusion that I was just the person to bring order into his life. "I want you by me constantly," he announced. "You will have no hours. I may wake you at midnight and ask you to fly me to Boston, to Washington, who knows?"

It was typical of Bel Geddes that he never troubled himself to ask if I had an airplane.

Bel Geddes was stocky and of medium height, although he gave the distinct impression of being very tall. His head was overlarge for his body, as was his nose for his face. His eyes were small, almost piggish, and his chin was lost in a series of rumples which shook alarmingly in moments of anger. By any standards he could not be held a beautiful physical specimen and yet he exuded an air of beauty, conquering both men and women as he pleased.

Bel Geddes welcomed me to his professional estate, a brownstone house on Manhattan's Thirty-first Street, an unlikely neighborhood for the variety of enterprises boiling within. The top floor of the house was occupied by draftsmen and industrial designers with whom I had little contact. They seemed to work and live in a world apart

---

* The play was *Siege*, about the Spanish Civil War. Somewhat heavy and didactic, it revealed Shaw's considerable talents, but was not a success.

and were infrequently honored with a visit from the Master.

Bel Geddes's studio occupied the entire second floor of the house, an area sufficient to the nervous pacing and general physical exertions of Bel Geddes at work. The secretaries, bookkeepers, and others of his staff were crammed together in the windowless first floor of the building. Uncertain of my function, naturally suspicious of my apparent closeness to Bel Geddes himself, they gave me cold welcome. They would never believe my almost total ineffectiveness, a condition I too found increasingly hard to believe as the invigorating winds of Manhattan's autumn took on the bite of winter. Late at night, long after most of New York City had bedded down, the lights in Bel Geddes's establishment remained a brilliant relief amid the elderly houses of dark red stone. When at last the Master yawned over the whiskey he always asked me to share with him and finally departed to what he sourly referred to as "home," I walked the streets of mid-Manhattan brooding upon the day's events and wondering if I was indeed working for a genius or a personification of the Mad Hatter. Nothing balanced.

Bel Geddes paid me a handsome two hundred dollars a week—why, I was never to understand. From the first day it had been very obvious he was his own perpetually rotating circus and had no notion, much less intention, of allowing anyone to alter his domain. Even if I had an idea worth presentation, my awe in the presence of such artistic prowess left me gasping for air when I should have been lucid.

"Yes, yes! Of course!" Bel Geddes would exclaim and clap his hands. "Very good. Exactly!" Yet whatever happened to have stirred his approval or enthusiasm somehow always became lost in the blizzards of competing enterprises.

Bel Geddes was not one to spend his working day at a desk, although he had one which occasionally gained his attention either as something to lean against while pondering a problem, or as a handy place to stretch his length when his occasional hangovers overwhelmed him. My own desk was a steam radiator on which I could either sit or lay out whatever assignments Genius had selected for the day. It was an uncomfortable arrangement and left me feeling rather homeless, yet in practice I had little need of a desk since from early morning until late at night Bel Geddes dispatched me upon various errands about the city—"See if you can't find some cheaper spotlights over on West Tenth Street . . . take these drawings to the blueprinters and have them back by four . . . find out what type machine guns the Spanish Republicans used. I want to duplicate their sound exactly. . . ."

When I was not serving as a glorified messenger boy I took my post on or near the radiator and provided willing audience for Bel Geddes's endless repertoire of new and old projects. I had never been so stimulated and frustrated in my life, for Bel Geddes raved and ranted, was at times the most considerate of gentlemen and then again an outrageous vulgarian. Angered, he would shake his wattles and scream at whoever he thought was responsible for his momentary displeasure. "Goddamnit, man, I want more intensity on those lights!" he would yell at a man crossing the stage—only to discover he was yelling at the property man instead of an electrician. Yet almost instantly he would recover his dignity and laugh heartily at himself, a quality which compensated for his petty tantrums and made it impossible to hold a grudge against him. In spite of my radiator office and the very real difficulties in working so closely with such a human volcano I came in time to revere the man. He was royally generous in major items, a merciless skinflint in matters involving only a few pennies, almost totally unheeding of either the needs or sensibilities of others, vain, adamant, decadent in his way, rarely predictable, arbitrary, and sometimes cruel. Yet I loved the son of a bitch.

When the play *Siege* failed, it took heavy toll of Bel Geddes's money. With a characteristic corrective action he suddenly decided he could no longer afford an assistant who never flew him to the hundreds of rendezvous he had once thought important. Once again I was back in the streets, most regretfully this time, even more for the loss of a thrilling association than for the termination of pay.

Optimism is the son of confidence and extravagance is often capricious uncle of the two. Once employed by Bel Geddes, I had ignored the lessons of recent history and proceeded with habitual disregard for economics. Thus, the termination of my employment found Eleanor and George nicely established in a pleasant apartment on Beekman Place, even then considered precious Manhattan territory. One of the greatest actresses and certainly the most wealthy, Katharine Cornell, lived next door. Other theatrical greats including Noel Coward also found the neighborhood agreeable to their spirits. While I was impressed with their proximity, I took more pleasure in an awareness of the East River, which I could view simply by walking out the door into a small space between the adjoining buildings. I could not explain either to Eleanor or to myself the haunting effect it had on me, yet on each return to the apartment I went directly to view that muddy, odiferous stream surging through the corpus of a great metropolis.

This time salvation was so swift I hardly missed two weeks' pay. Margaret Pemberton's marvelous theatrical intelligence system advised of yet another famous entrepreneur in need of an assistant. In all of the American theater few men could offer greater contrast than Norman Bel Geddes and Vinton Freedley. While one was a genius, the other was a cultured businessman with a highly developed regard for the patrons of "baldheaded row." Freedley's record as a producer of successful Broadway musicals was unmatched, thereby, in such a tricky business, making him something of a genius in his own right.

Vinton Freedley was old school tie, suave, always impeccably dressed, and he always knew what he was doing. His offices were on the fifty-first floor of the RCA building in Rockefeller Center and reflected their proprietor's taste and habits. Fresh flowers were always in abundance throughout the suite, and Freedley's own corner office often overflowed with blooms of the season. His desk was a splendid antique with its complementary accoutrements all arranged and kept in precise order.

Physically, Freedley resembled Fred Astaire and Edward VIII, a wiry, lean, and graceful man who would look dapper in coveralls. Every day a fresh boutonniere graced the buttonhole of his jacket, a pleasant affectation which I found no difficulty in adopting. Freedley's manner and voice, unlike Bel Geddes's, were always controlled. The result lacked warmth, as did the man, yet his great personal dignity and a marked elegance of manner enabled him to look exactly right pouring whiskey from one of the crystal decanters which graced the sideboard in his office. He looked exactly right swinging down Fifth Avenue with his tightly wrapped umbrella marking the cadence of his steps. His derby sat just right on his rather small head, his ties were knotted as if taken directly from a display window, his shirts were initialed. He was a private man, given only to obligatory association with his employees. Except for actual financial conferences, he ignored the bookkeeper who had served him forever and who now greeted me coldly. There were two female employees, a receptionist, and a secretary. With them Freedley was always debonair, and I did not wonder at their devotion to him.

Freedley treated me exceedingly well and took me often into his confidence. When no more important company was available he often asked me to lunch with him at his Rainbow Club table, a gesture he would never have considered toward his other employees. Thus, our relationship flourished and I was much content. Musicals as pure entertainment had always fascinated me, and the excitement of rehearsals had already begun on a show called *Leave It to Me*.

The music was by Cole Porter, already so ailing he was obliged to attend auditions in a wheelchair. The stars were the same reliable pair who had made *Of Thee I Sing* a great success: William Gaxton, who gave Freedley close competition in gallantry and charm, and Victor Moore, a Broadway favorite and a performer of incredible versatility. Although he specialized in playing bumbling fools (Wintergreen for President in *Of Thee I Sing*), he was an intelligent and clever man unencumbered with the usual star complexes.

Freedley was in dire need of someone to relieve him of details, for he was attempting a dangerous theatrical gamble. He planned the almost simultaneous opening of two shows, a scheme which brought their rehearsals and production problems back-to-back. In addition to the musical, he was casting a play * which he intended to open and polish in Boston. One of my many duties would be to fly him from one project to the other.

As his ambitious season progressed, Freedley decided

---

* The play (a comedy) closed in Boston—fortunately.

I should be the General Manager of *Leave It to Me,* a position far more grandiose in name than my actual duties warranted. Once again I was somewhat confused about my status, although this time I did have a place to ask myself the now familiar questions. Unfortunately, the desk Freedley assigned to me was side by side with that of another of his staff, who, ever fearing for his job anyway, tried his utmost to pretend I was invisible. As time passed and Freedley kept adding to my responsibilities the veteran abandoned his see-no-evil strategy and began a not-so-subtle attack, with daily bulletins issued to our employer on all the things I was doing wrong. At first Freedley told me of the office Iago and, laughing, brushed his complaints aside.

"Only the silly nit-picking of a dull little man," he said reassuringly.

Later, when *Leave It to Me* became the greatest hit of the Broadway year, Freedley became more cool toward me and the invitations to join him for lunch ceased. I hung on for a few months because I so admired him and enjoyed the prestige of working in his shadow. But I knew I had underestimated the little veteran who spent most of his waking hours worrying about the security of his job. Even as the first seeds of trouble were planted by him my lifestyle had flowered and I had, to my immense satisfaction, achieved nearly all the objectives so long cherished. Not only was my father beginning to believe there was still hope for his twenty-eight-year-old son, but he passed through New York on one of his world tours and found himself a guest rather than an enduring host. He was delighted with his easy acceptance into the company of celebrities he had only read about, and the Beekman Place apartment was much to his taste. Freedley was at his most gracious when I introduced him. *This,* my father pronounced, was not the kind of show business he had envisioned.

All was extremely well. I had returned to the tight little world of Broadway where most of the citizens knew each other and where only one eternal subject overpowered all thought and conversation—the theater. I belonged, and at Sardi's, where my invisible lease on a back table was discreetly renewed, I again felt one of the privileged, and even Brock Pemberton smiled. I was able to host Antoinette Perry for lunch, who had in the past bought so many for me, and I found it amusing to realize I was privy to her gastronomic peculiarities. A great director, a most gentle person, and only incidentally a very wealthy woman, she invariably read the extensive menu and made a selection she thought would please either her guest or her occasional host. All waiters at Sardi's were trained to disregard whatever she ordered and bring scallops. No one ever saw her touch anything else.

Day and night I moved in the epicenter of the theatrical world, a lieutenant to one of its great Dukes, my cockade a boutonniere and my livery after dark, black tie and dinner jacket.

I did not then understand how chance acquaintance, the introduction of a total stranger into the scheme of things, could alter anyone's life beyond imagination.

The inevitable showdown came one Monday night while the whole East Coast was swept with wretched weather. *Leave It to Me* was playing at the Imperial Theater and as usual every seat in the house was sold. I was also, as usual, early at the theater, serving as Freedley's proxy for the many minor matters preliminary to every performance of a relatively complicated musical. I always enjoyed the general pre-curtain anticipation of such a large cast and unconsciously imitated Freedley's rather jaunty way of wishing them well for the performance or hearing out and promising to correct their problems, which ranged from replacing broken lights in the dressing room to making sure tickets for an uncle were waiting at the box office.

In addition to superb performances by Gaxton and Moore and Porter's incomparable music, one of the special enchantments of *Leave It to Me* was Freedley's daring selection of an unknown girl to sing a single yet very important song. His choice, ostensibly clothed only in a sable jacket, sat on a cake of ice and sang "My Heart Belongs to Daddy." The song became famous and Freedley's selection, Mary Martin, took the first-night audience in her hand and never let them go. In one of the most thrilling five minutes ever witnessed in the New York theater she became an instant star, and of course later continued to prove her enormous talent in a long series of Broadway triumphs.

This Monday night I found more than a minor problem backstage. The stage manager informed me that Mary Martin had not as yet arrived in her dressing room, nor had she telephoned to explain her delay.

I was not unduly concerned. There was still more than an hour until she was actually due on stage, and Mary Martin was of different stuff from so many other actresses. Sudden stardom had not affected her in the slightest. She remained a hard-working, conscientious girl whose idea of a binge was a quiet evening with her husband. The entire company paid her their highest compliment by considering her a thorough trouper.

With visions of a possible accident crowding my thoughts, I considered calling Bellevue or the police. As the dissonance of the orchestra tuning their instruments penetrated the asbestos curtain, a strange nervousness passed through the assembling performers. Instinct told them something was wrong, and the word was soon passed of Mary Martin's absence.

I telephoned Freedley to advise him of the situation, but was unable to reach him at his home. Then one of the girls in the ensemble who was particularly friendly with Mary told me she had left after the show on Saturday night and flown to Texas where her father was grievously ill. She intended to take the early Monday morning plane back East and had every intention of making the evening performance.

I thought of the weather and was certain her eastbound flight had been delayed if not canceled altogether. As the orchestra struck up the lively overture, I took up my customary station at the rear of the house where a broad aisle extended across the theater and tried to convince myself Mary Martin would make a last-minute entrance. When the crucial time came, the curtain parted to reveal the understudy perched nervously on the cake of ice. She began uncertainly, but gathered confidence and by the second verse was offering a reasonable if far from brilliant substitution for our missing star.

Watching, I became aware that someone had slipped quietly through the door leading to the foyer. It was Freedley, and I knew at once he was displeased. He glanced at me as if I were a stranger, then returned his frowning attention to the stage. I wanted to tell him I thought the understudy was doing a good job, but thought better of it. For the past few weeks our communications had become increasingly abrupt and cursory. While I longed for his approval and the sense of being his trusted ally which had earlier prevailed, I now thought that any favorable comment from me might have the opposite effect. I had reviewed my past record hoping to find some serious mistake to account for my fall from favor, but could find only minor failures. Then why had Freedley made my exile so obvious? I could not make myself believe he would allow the whispering of a Uriah Heep, as I had finally dubbed the veteran, to influence his judgment.

I kept my position along the balustrade until "My Heart Belongs to Daddy" was done and the understudy made her exit to mild applause. Several uncomfortable minutes passed while Freedley continued to watch events on the stage. I moved a few steps in his direction to assure him I was handy, but he seemed determined to ignore my existence. Then suddenly, breathless and disheveled, Mary Martin appeared in the darkened aisle. Her coat was sopping wet and in the reflected light from the stage I saw agony in her eyes. She went directly to Freedley.

"I'm so terribly sorry," I heard her say. "Oh, Vinton, *so* sorry! My father—"

He turned to her in cold anger, his voice low and bitingly crisp. Unbelieving, I heard the man I had so admired as a gentleman launch into a tirade on the show-must-go-on theme I had thought was only expressed in storybooks. *"Nothing* else matters!" he insisted. *"Nothing!"*

Perhaps it was simply the low barometer of the New York evening, or Mary Martin's stifled sob, or the ridiculousness of the scene being played out in the darkened aisle which suddenly triggered my own temper. I knew Freedley was right and I knew his protégée was wrong, but I also knew the reason for her failure to appear and I thought it of far more importance than a mere Broadway show. I moved in and gave Freedley my opinion and could scarcely believe the anger in my voice as all the hurts and frustrations of the past weeks exploded.

People in the rear seats turned away from the stage to watch the side-show in the aisle.

Later, I could remember little of what I actually said except a harsh suggestion that he should get down on his knees and thank God for bringing him one of the greatest stars he would ever know. He listened in silence, apparently stunned at a subordinate who would dare dress him down. I had no difficulty in recalling his icy response.

"You are discharged. The office will have your check in the morning."

I turned my back on Vinton Freedley. My face flamed and my whole body tingled as I pushed through the doors to the bright-mirrored foyer and walked its so-familiar length to the street entrance. In the cooler air I calmed down somewhat and the dampness softened my righteous indignation. For a very brief moment I considered returning inside with an apology, at least for accusing Freedley of being totally without compassion. But then I thought, no, I was right for a change. And he was very wrong. I will never go back to his world.

I turned down the street gasping in relief at the dank night air. As I marched into the relative darkness I felt no temptation to look back at the brilliant pool of light flowing from the Imperial Theater. Something had snapped within me. This Broadway I knew so well had taken on a different guise and I found it tawdry.

I walked all the way to Beekman Place, refreshed and wonderfully stimulated by the dripping night. Suddenly it seemed all I had so long held valuable was not of much worth. The ambitions begun in the days at Ray-Bell studios and nurtured for fifteen years faded and were wiped completely away as if the night itself held the power of cleansing. I did not care if I ever again saw a spotlight, a stage, a camera, an actress, or any of the world of make-believe. It was as if I had been born anew.

The next morning Uriah Heep presented me with my severance check, which I did not trouble to scan. He brushed invisible lint from his brown suit and, trying to smile, wished me well.

"The boss is busy or he would say goodbye," he said.

"Of course," I answered, staring at the closed door to Freedley's office. For a moment I wondered if there was any use in trying to tell the bookkeeper how grateful I was to him. For it was not my ambition, talent or lack of it, loyalty or faithlessness that was now initiating such a fundamental change in my life. It was this humble and petty man in a brown suit, this poor custodian of another man's numerals, a fellow creature I had never met before and would never see again. With pebbles rather than stones, he had brought down and killed one man in me. In the doing he had released another.

Chapter 20

Eleanor proved her great intrinsic courage when I advised her that my employment had again been terminated and that an immediate change in our lifestyle was mandatory. She refrained from the very obvious speculation—what is wrong with my young husband who can't seem to hold a job? She accepted my decision to abandon all forms of theatrical enterprise along with evenings at "21," the Beekman Place apartment, the first nights, the late mornings, the soirées at Margaret Pemberton's, the gay nights at Billy's Gas Light Saloon on First Avenue, and the beerily sentimental gemütlichkeit hours at the Zumbrauhaus on Fifty-fourth Street. All were now lost, I maintained— forever. We were selling everything we could, moving to the country, and starting a new existence.

The back-to-the-land expedition was begun with typical disregard for practicalities, but at least some regard for economics. For transport, friend Gordon Warren made a gift of his automobile, an ancient Ford with no top and no floorboards and due for a new license. I postponed the license formalities, loaded wife and son plus a fifty-pound bag of potatoes and a twenty-pound bag of rice upon its ravaged seats, and set out in bitter March weather for Rockland County. There, near the Christie airport, another friend, Marcum, had found a rental cottage at thirty dollars a month. I had calculated we could finance such an establishment for three months and from the balance of our capital keep healthy. At the end of the quarter, as my father was fond of referring to all financial plans, I foresaw trouble. I knew I must shortly succeed at one of two endeavors. In the event of failure I was now convinced not even nepotism in the telephone business could effect a rescue.

Once again I was determined to explore the world of aviation and to apply for every possible flying job no matter how paltry the pay. Between interviews I intended to write and draw a children's book. Marcum offered the back room of an unheated barn for my working headquarters, rent free. As I set about both endeavors my confidence wavered. Thus far, I knew, my record was extremely spotty and the time for accomplishment long overdue.

I set up a drawing board in Marcum's barn and borrowed a kerosene heater. It was usually so cold I could only draw a few lines between periods of warming my fingers over the heater, but I drew and wrote all day and the book progressed.

Now as if waiting in the wings was another stranger who would contribute significantly to the metamorphosis. He was D. K. Smith, an early-balding man of great heart. He also wore a great head at our first encounter and confessed he was suffering from a hangover. I came to him through the subtle machinations of George McCabe, chief pilot of American Airlines at Newark, the airport for the entire New York metropolitan area. After being rebuffed again at United Airlines' eastern offices, I eventually found McCabe in a ramshackle building which served American as a combination terminal and operations office. He proved to be a heavy gruff man with the face of a Roman centurion long on campaign and basso profundo vocal chords.

"How many hours do you have?" he growled.

"About a thousand," I answered in some exaggeration. "Do you want to see my logbooks?"

"No. They are probably full of lies like all the others. What kind of airplanes have you been flying?"

I decided not to go into my latest flying, the transporting of Vinton Freedley back and forth to Boston in a rather weary Stinson T. Somehow I thought McCabe would have difficulty understanding why the recent general manager of a very successful Broadway musical was so anxious for a co-pilot's job.

"Most of my time is in Wacos."

265

"Indeed? What design changes would you recommend to improve their performance?"

At once I recognized a keen mind behind McCabe's weary manner and rather bland blue eyes. For he had asked a trick question. Answered satisfactorily he had no need to examine my logbooks. If I had flown an airplane as long as I claimed then I should be able to offer an intelligent opinion on its characteristics.

"I would make the landing gear wider. They're not easy to taxi in a crosswind and have a tendency to groundloop on landing."

McCabe snorted and his eyelids dropped down until for a moment he resembled a slumbering turtle. But I sensed he had approved my answer and since he hadn't bothered to inquire if I was military trained, new hope rose within me.

"What is your opinion of Franklin Roosevelt?" he asked with his lids still curtaining his eyes.

I was shocked. Were pilots hired on the basis of their political leanings? Beware, I thought, as McCabe opened his eyes and stared at me. Something is not quite right here. I knew Roosevelt was still despised by many veteran pilots for his thoughtless cancellation of the airmail contracts and the tragic loss of young lives resulting from that action, but perhaps McCabe felt differently. I must somehow give answer.

"He has his good attributes and his faults," I said, as if I had actually troubled to follow the President's spectacular career, "but if a better man comes along I'll vote for him."

Later I discovered McCabe was equally apolitical. He simply wanted to see if I could think fast when surprised —a most valuable trait in pilots.

McCabe's eyes left me while he regarded his considerable belly and frowned. Then I saw him chuckle and the hope which had almost died returned. "You aren't worth a damn to us without an instrument rating. Even worse, if I send you out to our school in Chicago without any instrument time you won't last through the first day. But if you're willing to dig in and work . . . mind you, I promise you nothing . . . but if you are willing to gamble on yourself—"

Whatever he had in mind I assured him I had no fear of work.

Grunting, McCabe reached for his telephone. He muttered soft orders, hung up, and with a dubious sigh sent me to a nearby building where I would find a D. K. Smith.

If D. K. Smith had been less patient with have-nots or the least unsympathetic to my cause, then the whole project might easily have come to naught. McCabe, who was circumventing his own company's regulation against even encouraging prospective pilots who were without an instrument rating, could not order D. K. Smith to give me a hand. He could only suggest.

The phone call for Smith came at five o'clock, the end of the day for even the healthy, and the man I found was still paying dearly for his celebrations on the previous night. He told me he had been yearning for the hands on the clock to move faster. "I hoped I would be en route home by now," he sighed. "It's been a long, long day."

Before him, pathetically anxious, now stood a man he could only regard as an aerial ignoramus, as well as the cause of his having to endure another hour of work, unpaid, and on his own time. "Woe is me," he said, "but if McCabe thinks you deserve help that's how it will be."

He asked me what I knew of instrument flying and I confessed my total ignorance.

"Then God has been good to you."

He led me to the Link Trainer which had been his province since temporarily taking leave from flying the line. The device resembled a miniature airplane perched on a pedestal, and I listened carefully while D.K. explained its purpose. "Of course it doesn't fly like a real airplane, but the effect is the same. You can still kill yourself by doing the wrong thing. Fortunately you'll spill more sweat than blood."

I climbed into the cockpit and practiced flying it with the top open. Soon D.K. closed the lid and I was left in darkness except for the small spotlight on the instruments. Somewhere in the bowels of the machine there was a gentle whirring sound as if my new and very private little world was actually in motion. All the instruments confirmed that it was. I was greatly encouraged by the apparent ease with which I had mastered this esoteric art. There was really nothing to it.

In my headphones I heard D.K.'s voice. "Very good. Now make a three-hundred-and-sixty-degree turn to the left."

I moved the controls gingerly and saw the compass slowly revolve. Good enough. Then I noticed that the altimeter indicated a loss of height. I eased back on the elevator controls. Next I knew a queasiness in my stomach which had previously withstood violent aerial aerobatics without the slightest strain.

I rubbed at my eyes, now overbusy trying to make several instruments behave, all of which seemed to be working antagonistically against each other. My confusion multiplied. My hands were suddenly moist, and my cheeks became hot as I tried to ignore a fast-mounting sense of claustrophobia. Why was it so hot inside this thing? And it smelled: of my own fear, I decided.

I heard D.K.'s cautioning voice: "Watch your airspeed." As I tried to focus on the instrument, my limping brain accepted the information reluctantly. I had slowed to ninety miles per hour. I must shove the nose down, I thought with strange lethargy. But I could not descend because the altimeter already informed me I had lost all but a few hundred feet of altitude. This will never do, I thought, as near-panic took charge in this new little dreamlike world. It was a dream rapidly becoming a nightmare as vertigo spun my senses.

"Oh-oh!" I heard D.K.'s voice just as something inside the machine let go. I knew all too well I had somehow got the machine into a spin, even as would have happened in a real airplane. I fought a growing nausea as long as I could, then threw open the top. My senses returned to normal immediately as I saw the walls of the room spinning round and round.

"You are dead," D.K.'s voice proclaimed. "You leveled out two hundred feet below sea level."

For the balance of an hour D.K. led me patiently through the basics of instrument flight. He soothed my shame and mortification, assuring me my disastrous performance was not unusual for initiates. Finally, as he turned out the lights and led me to the door, he offered new hope. "The trainer is busy all day with our regular line pilots . . . booked for weeks in advance. But if you could come after five maybe I could work you in for an hour or so."

It was a thirty-mile drive in my unreliable Ford, but I vowed to be his humble servant every day. That freezing evening on the long way back to the cottage in Rockland County I ignored the cold air rushing upward through the space where there had once been floorboards. I was warm with the appreciation of two other men, who in spite of their exalted status had reached down to succor me.

Throughout the following month I made my daily pilgrimage to D. K. Smith's domain and not once did he display resentment for my intrusion on his personal time. Occasionally the trainer was still occupied by a tardy line pilot, or D. K. himself had been called away. I lost myself in his books then, manuals on the technique of instrument flight and all that pertained to the little boxes of aerial jewels which were already in the process of revising the human concept of geography. I had no idea how soon similar instruments would become a profound influence on the history of mankind.

At last both McCabe and D. K. Smith decided I was at least reasonably prepared to face the terrors of the American Airlines co-pilot school in Chicago. I was hired provisionally for a period of ninety days at a salary of one hundred dollars a month and given a pass to Chicago. I saw no reason to tell either of my benefactors of other troubles likely to be mine in Chicago, for now I would inform my father that I had, at last, found honest work.

"You are nothing but a bus driver in a fancy uniform!" my father declared. His ire might have been even more severe had I dared to reveal my total financial reversal since our last meeting, which had occurred at the height of my theatrical prosperity. Of that bounty he had at least been able to boast among his luncheon companions, but now—?

My employment agreement with the airline was standard for all new co-pilots. Out of the one hundred dollars a month I was supposed to support myself for the ninety provisional days and pay for my uniform. Its cost would be deducted from the regular co-pilot's salary of one hundred ninety dollars a month after the probationary period had been survived.

"You have chosen a profession which has a very limited future for anyone," my father lamented. "There is no way for a corporation to make any dependable profit if it must be at the mercy of the government. Why, we won't even let our executives fly and I don't know any sensibly managed organization that will."

Our painful reunion took place in the comfortable library of the Lake Shore Drive apartment. I considered the rows of inviting books, the separately lit oil paintings, and the superb oriental rugs which muted all sound. The smoke from my father's Havana was agreeable and momentarily signified the best of everything, and I saw my mother, now visibly ailing, drop a pill in her demitasse cup. Why was I so determined to forsake all this? I thought of the musty woebegone stuffy little room I shared with Robert Gay, another co-pilot aspirant. Like the majority of our student class we had chosen the Hyde Park Hotel, a decadent relic of the nineties on Chicago's South Side. Only the alms-house price of the rooms made staying at the Hyde Park worth enduring its overall air of melancholy.

"Be careful," was all my mother had to say on the matter of the work I had declared would become my life. For the rest of the evening she tried to pretend it had never happened.

Before I bade them good night and the purple Stutz transported me in style back to the South Side, my father mellowed enough to inquire of Kalberer, who was now flying to the Dutch East Indies for KLM. "Now *there*," he said, turning the palms of his hands upward in a favorite gesture meant to convey indisputable fact, "is a man who *should* be a pilot."

As I left the apartment and entered the polished mahogany elevator, my father refrained from either his "washing hands" speech or any references to independent hogs on ice. This time, leaving him, I saw his good eye moisten with tears and I knew with an almost overpowering surge of affection that I was not entirely on my own.

Next morning offered further reassurance. While white Anglo-Saxon Protestant American families are not nearly as clannish as the Jewish, or Irish, or Italian varieties, a complicated webbing of interrelation, based on environment and endeavor rather than blood, does exist. I was now to see it function in my behalf at a place and manner least expected. Before I was sent down to the school I was interviewed by Gage Mace, the manager of flight operations. He was a tight-lipped man, droll, soft-spoken. He studied my name on the application before him and asked, "Didn't you marry Eleanor Michaud? I flew with her father in the National Guard. I was flying near him the same afternoon he got killed."

This fragile link with a stranger and another man who was dead long before I married his daughter helped me believe that the coming battle would at least be fought on familiar fields. That afternoon the stern demands of the school pressed my inexperience unmercifully. Soon I knew that even the most minute scraps of encouragement were needed for survival.

My subsequent career as a co-pilot further convinced me I had at last found my life's work. Occupying the right seat in Douglas DC-2s, DC-3s, and the West Coast-bound DSTs (sleeper planes), I served a variety of masters—all, save a very few, proud men totally devoted to their profession. From some sixty different captains I tried to absorb the good and reject the bad and thus, as did my contemporaries, blend their various philosophies, tricks, and flying wisdom until we became a distillation of all of them. We were also that much better pilots in the end, for many of the captains had never flown as co-pilots and hence had less opportunity to learn directly from others.

I was so inspired and continuously fascinated by the new life, I never once looked back upon Broadway or Hollywood or any of their ancillaries. My new friends were pilots or others in the flying business. I never thought of Freedley's bookkeeper or all he represented, nor did I see any cause to tell of my more gaudy past. It was like shedding a skin; the transformation was as painless as it was complete.

The sheen on the backside of my dark blue uniform became obvious and the one and a half gold stripes on my sleeves lost their original luster. As I passed from assisting one captain to another—a unique master-apprentice relationship because of the long hours spent in the close confinement of the cockpit—I learned as

271

much of flying men as I did of flying. There were the true old-timers, survivors of the post-World War I era who had been trained by the military during the final months of that war to "save democracy" or had by sheer grit learned to fly in their youth. A few actually had taught themselves from their first ascension. These men were already aged for pilots, wrinkled about the eyes in the classical image of the aviator, and marked with the hairline mustache of their audacious brotherhood. They were, with some exceptions, mostly a profane lot, recalcitrant and fiercely independent, grand of gesture yet extremely frugal with their money. Some were given to endless tales of their aeronautical adventures while others spoke only when absolutely necessary and then in tones so low they were almost inaudible above the roaring of our nine-cylinder Wright engines. All of these men were rich with weather cunning. They knew every road, hill, forest, and dale of their routes as well as old-time river pilots were supposed to know the deeps and shallows. They knew, without ever having resorted to books, how Boston was likely to fog in if temperature and wind were in certain relation, and how, if it could be finessed at all, to sneak through to the easier side of a Great Lakes blizzard and get to Cleveland via the back door. They knew the Tennessee thunderstorms by the look of them, recognizing those capable of tearing their aircraft to pieces and those with bark worse than bite.

Because all of their flights were in the lower strata of the earth's atmosphere, where all difficult weather thrives, they had two choices: either cancel the flight if it promised to be hazardous or take whatever they encountered once in the air. They scorned "brave" men because every one of them had been frightened out of his wits too many times. They knew through the savage and often tragic experiences of their comrades how, once committed, there could be no surrender.

All of the true old-timers had begun their careers in leather helmet and goggles, flying aircraft of wood, wire, and fabric. Now they considered the fourteen-passenger DC-2s and twenty-one-passenger DC-3s, with their heated cockpits and several radios, as the ultimate refinement in a hard life made easy.

To a man this breed were stalwart American patriots.

While mostly apolitical like McCabe, the majority were inclined to the conservative. Their America had enabled them to eat well enough to enjoy excellent health and even to grasp some measure of higher education, although college graduates were rare among them. They had been taught frugality by their own early hungers, when as barnstormers, leaping from pasture to pasture and village to village throughout rural America, they lived off the not always provident land. Even though their being hired by an airline meant a steady job flying, their paychecks had not always been so regular because, like themselves, the original companies were accustomed to living from hand to mouth. Until the middle 1930s the various American airlines were in every respect far behind the government-sponsored European lines; then very suddenly the reverse became true.

The old-timers had been the muleteers and the scouts of the American skies; now still in command, fathers and even grandfathers, they believed first in God, next in themselves, and finally in their country. They were not delicate men and their speech often violated formal tense and grammar, but they rarely lied and never boasted and haughtiness was not in them. Those very ancient in seniority, which included pilots with as much as eight years with the line, usually took the night trips because of the extra pay. They were rewarded with as much as nine hundred dollars a month. Co-pilots were paid only according to length of service and regardless of duty. Their salaries were raised by twenty dollars every six months. A co-pilot of two years' seniority was paid two hundred fifty dollars per month and like all crew members received a small per diem when away from home base.

As I joined the line, a second breed of captains had already been in command for several years, having served their own apprenticeship under the old-timers. Most of the younger men were ex-military, joining the line after training at the Air Corps's Brooks or Kelly fields, or the Navy's Pensacola, and then completing the active service to which their government-sponsored aerial education had bound them. The majority of these men were in their midthirties or early forties. All were excellent pilots, more severe than the old-timers, but also in-

273

clined to give their co-pilots more landings and take-offs. Nearly all were married, many to former stewardesses. They lacked the color of the pioneers, and were much more inclined to be aeronautical and social conformists. D. K. Smith was one of these men.

Into this specialized society I entered, awkwardly stumbling and nearly bereft of confidence, for the tales of our ordeal, once we were to take a place on the line, had the two months of our initial schooling in which to fester and putrefy.

Such was my preoccupation with this new professional and social world, I ignored for the time being those far more important developments which would not only affect my puny affairs, but ultimately change the social and geographical designs of the world. Yet the blinder the bliss, the shorter its duration. Like most Americans, I was now well aware of Hitler's rampaging behavior, but of more immediate importance to me was the airline's decision to leave Newark and move to the new La Guardia Field, a visionary airport concept most critics hailed as an enormous boondoggle with a capacity far beyond need. Anxious to be handy and thus called for every possible flight, I had moved Eleanor and George from the country cottage to a small apartment situated only a few hundred yards from the end of the northwest runway. We settled down pleasantly enough with a view over Flushing Bay and the newly commissioned Pan American terminal built to accommodate the arrivals and departures of the huge Boeing flying boats. There, our contentment was increasingly disturbed by the continued reminders of the imminent European disaster. The press was full of Hitler's Napoleonic triumphs and each evening Edward R. Murrow radioed his mournful and ominous observations from bomb-torn London. Former flying student Harmon Nelson had been drafted and sent me his photo in a World War I-style tin hat. Lester Linsk was about to be drafted and was simply marking time along with the majority of young Americans.

Charles Lindbergh, who could normally have persuaded pilots to accept his word that the moon really was a wheel of cheese, had no success whatever with us in his campaign to keep America out of the war. We believed what he said about the quality and might of the

German Luftwaffe, but no more. Pulling on the opposite arm, the repeated urging of Roosevelt to commit the American people even further than they already were, aroused little public enthusiasm.

I was particularly riled by Hitler's increasing persecution of the Jews, a continuation of the evils I had first seen in company with Rikki. Unlike my father, who had in all his work life been associated with only one Jew, my theatrical life had brought me into the daily company of a very great many. I knew they were no different from any other Americans, although on the average possibly more intelligent and much more honest. One of my proudest moments had been that day in California when Lester Linsk's mother pronounced me her "fourth son" and sealed the pact with a bowl of her superb borscht.

Yet it was not really a consequence of Hitler's outrageous racism or even concern for his military adventures which compelled me to call upon René Pleven's wife Anne when she came to New York on behalf of the beleaguered French government. I begged her to help me join the Free French Air Force. She demurred when she listened to my halting French, realizing better than I how a misunderstood command might endanger others. Fretting at my supernumerary status as a commercial airline co-pilot in such increasingly dramatic times, I next went to Quebec City where I explored the chances of joining the Royal Canadian Air Force. They welcomed me, but not as I wished. For once I had too *much* flying experience. They would not think of promising overseas duty, but wanted to make me a sergeant-instructor at a new base near Toronto. Racing pilot Earl Ortmann stayed me from accepting. "If you want to spend the rest of your days popping up and down in a Tiger Moth while someone else has all the fun, then join the RCAF. But I have something better."

Ortmann, a persuasive man and excellent pilot, recommended the trans-Atlantic ferry service being operated, incongruously, by the Canadian Pacific Railway. They paid pilots handsomely for flying American-built bombers across to England. The job was considered hazardous and held a certain air of the clandestine about it, a combination I found impossible to resist, particularly since the railway had established a hiring agency on my Manhattan threshold.

The place was the old Murray Hill Hotel on Park Avenue, just south of Grand Central Station, and into this architectural ghost of America's Gay Nineties I entered clad in the armor of my own innocence. Like the majority of young men since the beginning of history I knew nothing of the realities of war. I did not need band-playing or even the beat of a drummer to inspire my martial spirit, nor could I at all understand those who contrived to escape the draft. I had never seen the battle-mangled or the dead, the plagued, the starving, or the tears of abandoned children. War was excitement and adventure; I wanted to take up my lance, which was an airplane, and boldly disperse the enemy.

I had now been four times frustrated in my attempts to join the grand fray. At the Navy recruiting office in lower Manhattan a lieutenant-commander had been delighted with my flying credentials while sparing me any snide comments about my second lieutenant's commission in an Army anti-aircraft regiment, no longer valid because I had failed to continue reserve training. He promised the Navy would welcome me for transition training at Pensacola and I could doubtless then apply for carrier service. His single "however" was devastating. The United States was not yet officially at war with anyone, yet, according to the game rules laid down by the War Manpower Commission, mine was an essential job of the highest category. A formal release was required from my airline before my application could be considered. I knew the answer before I asked. American Airlines had already lost several pilots with active commissions to the services and more were expected to be called soon. The airline held me as surely as if I had taken an oath of allegiance.

Karl Day, one of our dispatchers and a reserve colonel in the Marine aviation, was already back in green uniform. I had become friendly with him and believed a rumor that the Marines were going to Europe. Day's letter attached to my application was my fourth disappointment. ". . . nobody in the Army, Navy, or the Marine Corps can touch you unless you first get a release from American Airlines . . . *with your release in hand*

276

present yourself. . . . . I can't imagine anything that would stop your application *if* you get the release."

The Canadian Pacific Railway, I had heard, did not stand on such niceties. Their suite was on the third floor of the Murray Hill Hotel and I was dismayed at the number of young men who seemed anxious to fly the Atlantic. I joined a roomful of applicants, eventually stated my piece to a polite but obviously bored man of middle age, and departed with yet another disappointment. I would hear from him in about a month, he thought, when a new increase in pilot needs was anticipated.

I could not know how fortunate the timing of my interview had been. Had it been a month earlier I would have been immediately pressed into service and the tarnished magnificence of the old Murray Hill Hotel might well have been the first gateway to my tomb. A disproportionate number of the Canadian ferry pilots were killed within the year.

Now new developments in my own little flying territory greatly eased my sense of being left out of greater things. I had obtained an air transport rating, the highest license available to American pilots, and a mandatory step to a captaincy. Then I had successfully passed the rather severe test for a multi-engine rating, also required for captaincy. And recently I had been assigned to fly with "check pilots," men selected by the airline for their executive as well as their flying abilities. And ever more frequently I was offered the left seat, my mentor in the right seat now become critic and examiner. It was the final seasoning, I knew, and if the attrition rate to the armed services continued I thought my chances at a captaincy within a few years might be a reasonable hope.

Chapter 21

Like so many flatland Middle-Americans, my first sight of the sea had been a profound experience. I read ravenously of the sea and went down to it whenever I could; the sight of any vessel large or small excited my admiration and desire. Like my romantic father, I never thought of vessels as merely manmade contrivances capable of transporting men or goods from A to B. They were receptacles of dreams and proud symbols of adventure, commanded by larger-than-life men, a combination I found irresistible.

In a smelly estuary of Flushing Bay, hard by La Guardia Field, I found an ancient Friendship sloop named *Uncle Sam.* Now with my finances slightly improved I bought her from a beached sailor named Fennimore, who had created a small shipyard out of scrap wood and assorted gear hauled to the fringes of the tidal mud.

Fennimore was a delightful pirate complete with tattoos and cursing parrot on his shoulder. The price of the *Uncle Sam* was two hundred dollars with one hundred on deposit and monthly payments of twenty dollars, an arrangement I thought compatible with my co-pilot's pay.

The *Uncle Sam* was forty feet long, an unusual length for a Friendship sloop. What was left of her running gear was frayed and tasseled almost beyond redemption and her sails would not withstand a healthy sneeze. Her engine, a venerable pile of iron salvaged from a Dodge truck, stank even when unused for weeks. It gave off an odor of its own, a combination of tired metal, overheated oil, and scabby paint which mixed richly with the pungent sourness of her rotting hull. Overall the *Uncle Sam* displayed an air of nautical peasantry ill-used and condemned, a condition I was determined to remedy. If she seemed to sigh in exhaustion when asked to do my bidding I always found it easy to forgive her, for I was truly a man in love.

The *Uncle Sam* kept me out of serious mischief until more harsh demands took charge. Eleanor, whose marital policy was based upon the silken chain, joined me in unnatural devotion to this near-derelict. Between flights we scraped and painted endlessly.

In time, the purist in me insisted the stinking engine must be thrown overboard, an act we performed with proper ceremony. Only the frugal Fennimore, who saw a functioning piece of machinery sink into the mud, was distressed. My son George, now able to get about by himself, evidenced a particular interest in all matters concerning the *Uncle Sam* and spent many happy hours assisting in her transformation. I saw in him a definite bent toward the sea and did all I could to encourage his interest.

While the *Uncle Sam* made it easier to maintain my role as a good husband and a firm yet playful father, I knew my continued attempts were a sham. Try as I might I could not bring myself to be domesticated; and secretly I feared it. Eleanor endured my schizophrenic wanderings, mad schemes, and the almost perpetual motion resulting from my yearning to draw ever more from each hour and each day.

As if my airline career was not enough I was now enjoying some slight success with my writings. The book I had drawn so laboriously in Marcum's freezing barn had been doomed from the start. No publisher in his financial wits would even momentarily consider publishing a children's book in so many colors, even if the text had been literary jewelry, which it certainly was not. Yet eventually the book found its way to McIntosh and Otis, a distinguished if rather eccentric literary agency. There was only one copy of the book in existence and I had nearly forgotten what it looked like when a Mildred Lyman tracked me down by telephone at American Airlines. "Your book has a certain charm," she said, "but sale prospects are now nil. Do you think you could write a book about modern aviation for young people? We have an interested publisher."

It took me less than an hour to present myself before Mildred Lyman, who in turn presented me to the two senior partners of the agency, Mavis McIntosh, a forthright woman who somehow suggested a brave missionary teaching gospel to savages, and Elizabeth Otis, a diminutive redhead of extraordinary literary wisdom. They had only to mention John Steinbeck as one of their clients to speed my instant signature on their contract. Awed at the notion of even passing through the same portal as Steinbeck, I vowed to produce a book within two months.

I had at least some reason to believe I was capable. Desperate to gather more than the pittance the airline had been paying, I continued to write the kind of stories which had helped pass the hours while waiting for flight students in California. To my joy a few had sold. *Popular Mechanics* magazine bought two and the flying magazines took others. While I had no thought of forsaking flying for writing, these petty triumphs had at last convinced me writing might provide pleasant extravagances such as the *Uncle Sam*.

And still my energies were overflowing. If I was not flying at night I retired to the "studio" I had installed in the laundry room of the apartment building. There I produced innumerable drawings and oil paintings, always certain the next one would be a masterpiece. (All were far from it.)

All of this made me an increasingly absentee husband, feckless and sometimes inconsiderate. And yet who among most young husbands does not resist taming?

Here was a man just turned thirty who it seems had never been a youth but had passed directly from childhood to adulthood. He still bore the bumps of immaturity, although the profession which now possessed his spirit was based on a heavy sense of responsibility for the lives of others, and errant or frivolous thoughts while on duty were despised by all concerned. A careless or clumsy doctor might kill a patient, but a pilot in much less time could murder more than a score and bring incalculable woe to hundreds of others.

Eleanor had married in the then common expectation of financial security, in which promise I had failed her consistently. She had entrusted her future to one she presumed would be her protector, ever-faithful lover, and proud escort through the pleasures and perils of middle-class American life. In these assigns I was also imperfect.

These expectations were just reward for the gift of her beauty, her encouragements of my projects, and the care and feeding of my person. Because of our almost identical backgrounds she was also reasonably sure I would never embarrass her in public, strike her in private, or display undue emotion of any sort. Verbal communication between us was also easy because of our original environments. Therefore misunderstandings did not occur; a word, a gesture, a mere glance were sufficient to express the inevitable hurts, rages, yearnings, and satisfactions normal to any male and female humans in cohabitation.

Eleanor understood my restless spirit and even claimed that a more stable husband would not improve

280

her marriage. I had much greater difficulty understanding her ever-increasing preoccupation with doctors, all aspects of physical frailties, and the pharmaceutical world, which seemed to fascinate her.

"The bathroom looks like a drugstore," I complained one evening, and almost immediately wished I had not. For I was at once audience to a flashing lecture on the worth of the various esoteric pills and potions she had assembled. She pronounced their Latin derivative names with the fluent skill of a trained medic, and worse, I thought, she argued the need for each prescription with an authority I found nearly incredible.

"I didn't know there were so many things wrong with you," I said lamely. And I wondered, as I had before, how many of those afflictions, some of which I could not even pronounce, were real.

Man born of woman, what is the honest decree? What real effect did the sum of my unwitting cruelty have upon her ultimate destiny? I excused it then on the grounds of Eleanor's self-confessed urge for exaggeration, a heritage, she often claimed, of her French ancestors. If when I was away on some cause or other a man should chance to smile at her, then in later relation to me the incident became a very near rape. If a faucet leaked so much as a trickle, then the room was "flooded," and if George bruised his knee then he had probably broken his leg and should be rushed immediately to the hospital. As long as Eleanor's exaggerations concerned her children I put them down to natural maternal concern, but it became ever more difficult for me to hear that she had smashed up the car and upon examination find only a scratch on a fender.

These distortions of fact reached full flower in matters medical. In Eleanor's mind no one ever had a simple cold, but lingered on the brink of pneumonia. A headache was always "migraine" even if in fact it had been acquired in overindulgence with the grape. Tooth cavities were described as volcanic craters and bellyaches became a passing bout with appendicitis. Yet except for this single frailty, which transported her more and more into realms of unreality, the woman I married was remarkably without fault. Such was her grace, courage, and capacity for giving, I privately dubbed her Public Angel Number One.

I also thought she had chosen ill company in which to spend the balance of her life.

The Canadians never called me to ferry aircraft across the Atlantic, but my sense of being left out of major events was soon eliminated. One year and ten months after my first school day in Chicago, I was made a captain of the line and on that auspicious day became the father of boy and girl twins. Since childhood I had devoted at least a few moments of every day praying to the God of the Christians, a habit I could not reasonably explain since both my parents were most casual Presbyterians and had long ceased attending church. On my own account I had a special loathing of the trappings of all formal worship. I could not bring myself to believe that the supreme being who had created such a total system of wonders would necessarily be pleased because at an appointed time each Sunday a number of his creations genuflected in the general direction of another being who signaled them to do so. Yet every man needs some kind of God, some focus of his admiration and appreciation of the blood still pounding through his veins. Without some target grand enough to absorb man's second oldest emotion (the first being survival of his existence), the human being commences his own self-destruction.

As a consequence of these reactions I had developed a pseudo-religious style of my own, a sort of pagan worship of trees, mountains, oceans, clouds and sky, and a profound affection and respect for all animals of the land and creatures of the sea. I confirmed this attitude by establishing an easygoing relationship with "God," whoever or whatever "he" might be. I found it quite natural to express my gratitude for the song of a bird, the majesty of a mountain range, or the fury of a sea. These declarations were usually made silently in my thoughts, but sometimes I spoke my appreciation aloud as if to give pleasure to that being I had decided was in charge of earthly things. It was therefore easy on the day of the twins and my captaincy to announce my thanks to the deity who was obviously responsible.

"Thanks, God," I whispered as I looked through the

282

nursery glass at the twin issue of my loins, and "Thank you very much, indeed," I murmured when I took my uniform coat to the tailor's with instructions to sew a new pair of gold stripes on the sleeve, both to be of the same dimension.

Eleanor agreed the boy child should be named Steven Anthony, his second name derived from the novel *Anthony Adverse,* in which the hero suffered and triumphed over repeated vicissitudes. As in most twin births one is the weaker and the boy promised within a few days to endure quite as many tribulations as his fictional namesake.* In contrast the daughter twin was marvelously healthy and was christened Polly Wing, since, I maintained, wings had paid for her flawless Cesarean arrival and presumably from this all-important day on, wings would support her to maturity.†

The true war was not yet upon us, yet everywhere there were increasing evidences of a nation girding itself for an inevitable conflict. The fast-growing national involvement was recorded in the press as regularly as the fever and pulse of a hospital patient. The occasional brushes between American ships and German submarines plus the lend-lease program just getting in gear were visible signs. But the real signals of a much deeper and prolonged engagement were constantly multiplied in the throbbing veins of the American transportation system. It became ever more difficult to obtain a seat on a train. Our airlines, flying half empty only a year before, were now sometimes filled to capacity, a development we found reassuring because our paychecks were better insured. The spectacle of all fourteen seats (or twenty-one, depending on the aircraft type) being occupied was so exciting, we usually left the cockpit sometime en route, and went back to convince ourselves what the stewardess had told us was reality. Very soon it became necessary to establish a system of priorities for airline seats, with the military of course taking preference. Those who could prove they were engaged in the business of war were also given preference, and as a consequence there was great abuse of the term; everyone it seemed who wanted to

* He did.
† They did.

283

make a journey became automatically vital to the national survival.

About this time my father fell suddenly from the favor of that sedate court he had so long overseen. The metamorphosis was abrupt and merciless in the style of all the machinations of his one boss, A. F. Adams. My father's head was marked for the block because company executives all over the world, mistaking his steady progress and increasing responsibilities as indication of invulnerable station, had pledged to his banner and even some of the supreme council in Chicago were convinced his balding head would soon wear the crown. As a true dictator, A. F., whose own bent and tarnished crown had always been worn at the careless angle, found he could no longer tolerate competition from his deputy. Yet one minor thorn delayed him. My father's contract had several years yet to run and the annual stipend was heavy. The situation obviously called for cunning.

One frosty morning when the tremendous vitality of Chicago was just beginning to gather itself, my father entered upon the Persian rug splendor of his office, removed his overcoat and homburg, tugged gently at the jacket of his double-breasted blue suit, and twitched at the throat of his hard collar, lest from home mirror to office mirror the movements necessary to the journey had forced his tie askew. Thus prepared for the day he was ready to address himself to the affairs of the considerable empire he managed.

He moved into position behind his great carved mahogany desk and for a moment surveyed a plateau of simplicity. The polished surface of his desk was barren of papers, all quite usual since only government bureaucrats and file clerks worked amid stacks of papers. An executive was a poor manager if he allowed papers to accumulate; he doubtless lacked strength to make decisions, and was probably incapable of taking the broad view. Papers were the business of secretaries, who, as would Pat, my father's now strangely absent secretary, were expected to bring before him a nicely tooled leather folder containing the latest dispatches, contests, projects, and problems.

When Pat failed to appear after half an hour, my father left his office and inquired if the other secretaries had seen him. He was first concerned for his safety, for he was very fond of Pat, and second for the proper disposal of a multitude of corporate matters he knew required attention. Pat's colleagues knew nothing—or so they said.

My father went back to his office and eased himself into the large leather chair. Had the men in the outer office greeted him just a little too heartily—and familiarly? Or was it just his imagination?

While he toyed with his Havana he frowned at the two telephones, fine instruments used all over the world. Vital communications deciding the fate of nations, the hour of assignations, the wails of the lonely, and even the dispatch of an airliner flown by his son, were all transmitted through these devices. Now the telephones were silent. He reached into his vest and took out his wafer-thin Patek Philippe watch, a gift from his own father, who had returned from Europe just before Hitler's Polish rampage. Ten o'clock. It was going to be a long morning.

As time passed, everything my father observed further convinced him he had seen it all before. Lindsay, an executive charged mainly with the banking aspects of the corporation and therefore more independent of position than the others, dropped by. He was a hearty man, if somewhat ponderous, and a special confidant of my father. After the mandatory morning pleasantries my father went directly to his concern. He described the peculiar situation since his arrival. "Do you think I am in the doghouse?"

"I wouldn't know. A.F. doesn't confide in me unless he needs several million dollars."

"What can I do about it? Things will go to hell."

"No, they won't. You can be sure A.F. has already appointed your successor, if indeed you are persona non grata."

"Do you think I should go see A.F.?"

"He doubtless hopes you will. Possibly your anger will so undermine your judgment you will resign."

During the lunch hour in the executive dining room, a function never graced by the presence of A.F., my father did not need anyone to tell him his tumbrel was already rolling. Like the husband betrayed, he was apparently the last to know. All gathered, the luncheon assembly usually included several middle-status executives, bringing the number to twenty if all were in the city. Now the news was relayed in their eyes and voices. The more secure were a shade too solicitous, the uncertain and the ambitious were careful to avoid my father's good eye.

That day my father left his office in midafternoon and took a taxicab home. During the ride he tried to count his many blessings, but found it impossible to shake off his melancholy. No one, he thought, since the beginning of history had ever been inclined to feel sympathy for a rich man. Rather, they delighted in his troubles, measuring their joy against the weight of his woes. Therefore, he decided, for lack of outside interest, I shall feel sorry for myself.

Within the week the pattern was set. My father went faithfully to his office every day, where he read the bible of his culture, the *Wall Street Journal*, and made such phone calls as his personal business required. His considerable paycheck was delivered on schedule, as he knew it would be. He accepted the blank envelope with a thin smile. The very lack of address was indicative of his labors. He was nothing. He did not exist. Now, stripped of his shoulder boards, he was a visible ghost, visited by the brave and avoided by many he had personally lifted from the ranks. A.F. Adams, as always, remained aloof. It was a waiting game my father determined to win.

"There is nothing in my contract," he told Lindsay, "which says I must spend my full day on the premises."

By the time A.F. had calculated that his ex-deputy would beg word with him, my father was launched upon a full-scale campaign to display a surface enjoyment of his new leisure. He bought a fine saddle horse which he rode daily along the extensive paths bordering Lake Michigan. He gave lavish parties and always included at least a few of A.F.'s better spies to carry the news. And in all gatherings, regardless of their size or nature, my father was careful to speak only praise of A.F. These words too, he knew, would get back to the enemy and further confuse him.

It was an uncompromising inter-class war which might have destroyed two lesser antagonists during the months of maneuvering, but my father never lost his resolve. Pride, he decided, could be preserved at least temporarily, in the acid of nonchalance. He prayed the enemy would taste it.

As a special thrust he booked a trip around the world, and by letter advised A.F. of his pleasurable anticipation. ". . . it has been a lifelong dream. Of course if there is anything I can do for you while pausing in those various foreign ports outlined in the enclosed itinerary, I shall be pleased . . ."

At last it was A. F. Adams who surrendered. He sent for his ex-deputy, offered a generous settlement, and my father's flowing signature acquired an extra flourish as he signed the peace agreement.

While that action rewarded him financially, he knew it also committed him to permanent exile. It was not in the code that the once-fallen mighty would be rescued by offers of a similar position in other organizations. And a man of pride did not step down. Many high executives subject to similar isolation soon withered and died. My father had no intention of doing either. He was still packing for his world tour when Hitler invaded the Low Countries.

"That scoundrel!" my father declared in a tone of deep resentment. "The rascal has gone to war again deliberately to spoil my trip around the world!"

To assuage his disappointment he bought a twenty-two-acre estate in Pebble Beach, California, and named it El Retiro—the place of rest.

Chapter 22

In spite of my efforts to join various combat units, my capacity for belligerence has always been very low. I apologize to a fly before murdering it. Inversely, I seem to have maintained a penchant for playing around the fringes of hazard and as a natural result often meet more of it than I intended. If the capers of boyhood were only ordinary then the continuation of this strange indulgence becomes all the more suspect. There have been times when I have asked myself if I am deliberately trying to depart this life. William Sloane, a publisher friend of particular brilliance, deplored my weakness for jeopardy. "When will you learn there is nothing distinguished about getting yourself killed?" he wrote. The excitement of polo, where minor injuries are few, my rapture in acrobatic flying, my enjoyment of the mounted hunt until I wore a cast in the shape

287

of a crucifix, the thrill of skiing until a wheelchair became my only locomotion for three months, the cliff I decided to climb in the California desert, and a forty-foot fall off a Norwegian mountain—all combine to suggest a regrettable lack of prudence. The habit of speed in a car began with a two-seated racer which I somersaulted after owning it less than two hours, and I continued to speed until another capsize broke my jaw in thirteen places. These unhealthy dispositions coupled with a willingness to volunteer for almost anything may mark a certain gusto, but when there has always been so much to lose must also raise the question of my sagacity.

There are two compensations attached to this Humpty-Dumpty syndrome—both certainties. Never is life sweeter than when almost lost. The other certainty may be argued, but I have always believed that the caution-bound have rarely fulfilled their gift of life.

My new airline captaincy and the simultaneous arrival of the twins obliged us to leave the small apartment adjacent to La Guardia Field and find larger quarters in the country. We returned to Rockland County and rented a two-story frame house of rather fragile construction. There for a time we were content except for the boy twin who demonstrated an alarming tendency to protest. At night, while his sister slumbered peacefully, he would beat his head on his mattress so continuously and with such ferocity his wooden crib would walk across the room. When the chandelier hanging from the ceiling below began to swing with the force of these exertions we would go upstairs and attempt to calm him. We were not always successful, even though sometimes these performances extended far into the night. Likewise the boy twin was subject to constant infant ailments while his sister matured in placid bliss. He had his appendix removed before he was two and upon returning from the hospital began such a commotion he burst the incision. I held him in my arms, trying not to look at his protruding entrails, while Eleanor drove us back to the same hospital.

Perhaps my father's environment, which was always open to me, influenced my regard for older men. I always enjoyed them immensely and sought their mature company whenever I could. It was therefore natural that Reed Chambers, third-ranking ace of the First World War, should occupy a pedestal in my private pantheon. He was aware of my repeated efforts to join the Navy or the Marine Air Corps, but in his wisdom was not entirely sympathetic. When Rickenbacker fell ill, Chambers had taken command of his squadron;* after the war he had started the first United States scheduled airline,† and was now a very wealthy and influential man because he failed. Crashes of his own aircraft put him out of airline operations; seeing the same fate overtaking his contemporary pioneers, all of whom flew without insurance, he decided to provide it. He was a tough, resourceful man, politically to the right even of my Republican father. He had learned survival against Richthofen's flying circus and his philosophy had not mellowed since. "About my second flight over the lines a Jerry‡ jumped me before I really knew what was going on. I was all over the sky until I got away from him and had time to think things over. The bullet holes in my Spad didn't really worry me so much, I decided. It was the incendiary tracers I saw going past . . . maybe one in ten bullets. When I got back to our airfield I told the armorer to make mine *all* incendiaries. If they scared the hell out of me then the same should hold for the Jerries."

The moral, he explained, was to be found in the use of fright as a weapon in any battle. He aimed a thick forefinger at me as if it were a machine gun. "You don't scare easily and that is a very bad habit in combat," he growled. "While you're feeling cocky in the sky, along comes some amateur you didn't bother to watch. He gives you a fifty-caliber enema and it's all over in two seconds. I've seen it happen."

The walls in Chambers's luxurious lower Manhattan offices were almost solid with one of the world's greatest collections of air combat photographs. He escorted me to several where he said "it was happening" and in his beguiling fashion outlined what he considered a more productive adventure. "What do you know about South America?" he asked.

I thought of my disastrous manipulations with surplus

* The 94th Aero Pursuit Squadron.
† Miami–Havana in flying boats.
‡ American World War I term for German pilots. The British referred to them as Huns or the Hun.

telephones and for a moment saw the doleful face of my mentor Mr. Todd again. Fortunately, Chambers once launched on any project obliterated early opposition by charging right through it, this time including any answer I might have given.

"You will soon know more," he insisted, "and this is why."

Along with Laurance Rockefeller and William Burden, Chambers had been named by President Roosevelt to a new government agency—something called the Defense Supplies Corporation. Among its principal assignments was the elimination of the German airlines operating in Brazil and Colombia. Many of their pilots were Luftwaffe officers in training. Their presence, combined with various ethnic organizations and consequent political power, posed a very real threat to the Panama Canal if and when the United States would actually declare war on any other nation. If all Europe fell and then England, a definite possibility if not a probability, Hitler's lust for *lebensraum* must inevitably lead him to another and nearly defenseless continent.

German dominance of the South American skies had long ago been accomplished. "We're going to run the bastards out of there," Chambers announced with a sweep of his hand. "How's your Spanish?"

I recounted the number of years I had failed Spanish and the despair of Lieutenant Perez at Culver Military Academy, who nearly wept every time he heard what I could do to his beautiful language.

"Never mind. In Brazil they speak Portuguese anyway."

I was forthwith given a lesson in sheer power. When I suggested that American Airlines might not applaud one of their ever-scarcer pilots going on leave except in obedience to military mandate, Chambers grunted ominously.

"Never mind," he growled. "I'll call C. R."*

The next day, and without further ado, Boyd, who was American's chief of flying, advised me I was on leave of absence.

"Whether I want to be or not?"

"Well . . . you don't *have* to go."

* C. R. Smith, renowned and much respected president of American Airlines.

Boyd was not only a superb pilot, but a master of innuendo. He knew the sound and cadence of an order issued, but not expected to be obeyed, and he knew unto the most delicate nuance the request that was a firm order. ". . . you don't *have* to," in translation from the original Boyd, meant "you had damn well better if you know what's good for you."

Months before Pearl Harbor, Washington was already exploding with the apparently boundless energy of the nation it supposedly served. As France surrendered to Hitler's legions and England was choking for want of supplies and might, Washington replaced New York City as the center of the surviving free world. It was suddenly overwhelmed with young women who in various capacities were finding employment with the federal government. There had also arrived a mixed bag of "brains"— brilliant citizens from necessary worlds, called to Washington by direct request or plays upon their patriotism. Simultaneously, there arrived a host of opportunists, scoundrels, and chauvinists of every known category. To this mongrel crowd were added the true patriots like Chambers who sincerely believed his country was right however it might be wrong, batteries of high-salaried executives who found both satisfaction and prestige in volunteering their services at a dollar a year, assorted misfits and knaves who hoped to escape the draft or at least serve in the safety of Washington, various freaks, goons, merchants, and more than enough harlots to serve them all. They alone failed to prosper quite as expected. Wartime morals were already the rule; the phrase "who knows if we will live through this thing" was uttered perpetually in every conceivable place of rendezvous, and the new amateur libertines far outfornicated the professionals.

Before setting off to join this questionable crowd I called upon another veteran of the First World War, a contemporary of Chambers, but of totally different composition. José Mifsud was a Maltesian with a genealogy extending back to the Crusades. Although his ancestors marched upon the Holy Land with Richard the Lion-Hearted, only his speech retained a hint of English culture. Otherwise he was utterly Phoenician, and in my eyes the epitome of a gallant bachelor. He maintained himself in a Park Avenue penthouse to which I retreated as often as possible and always found welcome.

José Mifsud, like most natives of his fortress island, was of swarthy complexion, his mustache was clipped short in the style of many British Army officers, and his straight black hair was brushed tightly against the contours of his skull. His eyes were enormous, gray-green, and always alive with emotion.

During the Russian revolution, Mifsud was one of the British officers assigned to facilitate the escape of royalty who foresaw their fate as the Red Army approached the Crimea. While engaged in that endeavor, he met a young lady-in-waiting to the Dowager Empress Maria Feodorovna. He subsequently married her and before divorce tore them apart they begat two children, Paul and Tanya. Both were less than ten years old when I first knew their father and thus were almost ignored when they came to visit from their home in England. Yet Tanya kept turning up in my life like the key spoke in a revolving wheel.

It was always difficult to conceive of José Mifsud as ever having been even temporarily domesticated, and his way and manners had a powerful effect upon my own dubious career as a faithful husband. He was, first, a traditional gentleman and therefore refused to speak ill of anyone no matter how distressing that person's behavior, and he was always a most gracious host. Although he was nearly old enough to be my father, the age gap seemed non-existent, which further encouraged my imitations of his style.

While I held men like Bel Geddes and Freedley and certainly Chambers in great respect, Captain José Mifsud was my secret hero. Therefore, when Chambers called me to Washington I went to José and when settled at his bar said, "As you know I have one wife and three children. I can stay flying my regular route in safety or I can try this thing in South America. What should I do?"

José fixed his gray-green eyes on me only momentarily and one heavy eyebrow ascended slowly. He touched ever so gently at his clipped mustache, then reached behind him for the decanter of Scotch. He poured a drink for me, then one for himself, allowing the gurgle of liquid and the clinking of ice to fill the silence between us. Finally he raised his glass and surveyed me in such a way I thought for a moment I had somehow offended him.

"But of course, old boy. There is no choice. How could you think otherwise? You must go."

I knew my way to the proper oracle and I knew before asking what his verdict would be. Now, as we smiled over the rims of our glasses, I knew the sweet relief of finding another to blame.

The South American caper, as I came to label it, temporarily satisfied my need for challenge. I was at first astonished at the independence allowed me, a mixed blessing in the end, but an assurance I would not become utterly lost amid the vast and complicated American machinery now revolving at ever-increasing speed.

On the surface the project was simple: fly brand-new Lockheed Lodestar aircraft from the factory in Burbank to Rio de Janeiro and turn them over to Pan Air do Brazil, the national airline. The Brazilians were to accept them as a gift from their affectionate Uncle Sam, who asked nothing more in return than the cessation of all cooperation with German agencies and the dismissal of employees who might be overly sympathetic to the fatherland and the Nazi cause. The pattern is now standard procedure for powerful nations desirous of influencing the future of have-nots, but as in many endeavors then originating in Washington, someone had forgotten to do his homework.

The first omission was more diplomatic than technical, but, as experience proved, quite as potentially lethal. Chambers was already heavily involved in trying to increase the supply of rubber from Brazil to the hungry United States war economy, and the relatively small effort involving the delivery of airplanes soon took a low priority rating. Perhaps his preoccupation with greater affairs was the reason the two of us scheduled to do the actual flying were so naïve about the South American scene. We thought the governments as well as the natives would be grateful for the donation of beautiful new airplanes. We were unaware of the strong Germanic orientation all through the great southern continent and of the antipathy with which so many South Americans, particularly in Bolivia and Brazil, viewed Yankees. Their reasoning was realistic. For generations German influence had been a powerful factor in the development of South America. Many of the intelligentsia were German-born immigrants or the offspring of German parents. Likewise, the employees of the airlines and associated enterprises were mostly of German heritage or openly pro-German because their jobs depended on it. Even Pan American employees native to the land wished they could be similarly engaged by German management.

We were soon to discover Americans could do no right.

This situation prevailed in Bolivia, Ecuador, Peru, and Brazil. And with all of those nations we would have some sort of flying relations. We were supposed to ask people who managed a better-than-average survival, in lands where jobs of any kind were treasured, to resign or accept dismissal without show of resentment. The naïveté of such a program could only have been conceived in the fantasy land of wartime Washington. But until its course brought me into actual peril I tried to believe it would work.

Since in effect our little enterprise became a sponsored arm of the State Department, Pan American Airways rather grudgingly agreed to service our airplanes along the way.

Otherwise left to my own resources, it was like starting an intercontinental airline with one employee—the pilot. The first need was to locate South America more accurately than a nod in the general direction of the Potomac from Chambers's office window. I finally located a supply of topographical maps in the hydrographic office and supplemented those with the excellent charts of the National Geographic Society. In spite of the large areas marked UNEXPLORED the total accumulation of paper became a pile almost a foot thick. In many areas it was of dubious aeronautical value.

I was somewhat appalled at the distances between indicated airports, but fortunately was unaware that the neat red circles representing fields often existed only in rumor, were overgrown by jungle, or were otherwise unusable.

I spent days plotting and scheming routes of conquest, calculating not only magnetic courses and flight times, but points of no return, alternate destinations in case of foul weather, and even alternate procedures if things went wrong mechanically. When I finished this interesting if highly unimaginative chore I was satisfied there had never been a prettier display of straight lines, arrows, numerics, and significant circles. I had been taught by a long series of masters how to think ahead of my airplane and from the air-conditioned comfort of the Washington offices the whole show appeared child's play. My innocent concept of the flying was based on my experience with a well-run domestic airline.

Fortunately, my first two flights to Rio did not depend entirely on my office-bound labors. Enter now Parks, a tall, shy Texan wearing a ranger's hat to protect his bald pate and a tight fatalistic smile when the odds were against him. He was lean, hard, and laconic—most closely resembling a Winchester repeating rifle long used on the frontier. Remington painted his counterparts on horses, Bret Harte wrote about them, and—I easily lost my momentary disappointment at having to serve as his co-pilot. My dreams of sailing off in my own command through equatorial skies were postponed, for Parks had previously flown Lockheeds while I had never been near one. A superb pilot, he taught me well of the Lodestar's peculiarities while we both learned further lessons in aeronautical survival.

I was never sure why Parks chose to fly to Rio via Central America, thence down the west coast of South America to Lima, Peru, and finally across the stark and forbidding Andes to Brazil. Perhaps he was more comfortable over arid country and flying the more benign weather of the western slopes. Parks was not one to elaborate on anything, his intentions, his hopes, or his despairs; nor was adversity likely to reveal him more. I was unhappy flying at 18,000 feet without supplementary oxygen and unless Parks was a superhuman with the lungs of an Inca he must have suffered equally. But if he did it was not in his very private nature to confide in his co-pilot. Regarding him sitting in a purple haze less than two feet from the tip of my left shoulder, I only saw him squint in concentration as he surveyed the overpowering mountains, which even at our altitude towered far above our pitiful little machine. All of the altitudes at which it was our new business to operate were humbling to our kind, and, combined with the unpredictable weather, more humiliating still. There were no current weather reports available from any source and as a consequence no gauge with which to set our altimeter accurately. Thus we never knew exactly how high we were actually flying or even stood upon the ground. What statistics we had been able to gather indicated that Quito, Ecuador was at 9,000 feet, presumably then on a level with the dusty, rock-strewn airfield at Cochabamba in Bolivia. Then the pass between Lima and Bolivia was supposed to be no more than 18,500, while the enormous Bolivian altiplano stretching for hundreds of miles was said to be 12,000, give or take a few. And the airport at La Paz was apparently 13,000, plus some indeterminate hundreds. We had heard how the Germans, whom we would presumably replace, flew the Andes regularly at 20,000 feet without supplementary oxygen except for their passengers, and even sometimes at 22,000. If true, then they were indeed supermen, and any competition was certain to fail.

Once aloft in South American skies there were further indications that our enterprise might classify as another Washington folly, and our preoccupation with being goodwill ambassadors changed to a special wariness. It soon became obvious we must return to the earliest type of barnstorming, which had been based almost entirely on a pilot's local knowledge. In this respect our score was nil. We were strangers above these lands, obliged to learn by doing.

When we took off we rarely had any idea what the weather would be at our destination and were likewise ignorant of the flight conditions en route. Only Quito, Lima, and Rio had the familiar radio ranges for approach and even these erratic stations were frequently shut down. As navigational aids we were supposed to take bearings on various direction-finder "homer" facilities situated along the way. The vast majority of these stations were silent when we needed them most and in a few instances seemed to have been shut down deliberately upon our approaching. The total effect was disheartening when flying in clouds, particularly in high mountainous areas.

Attempts at radio voice communication between our aircraft and ground stations were never successful. We tried; we became a voice heard only by the wilderness, plaintive until at last we tried no more. Thus we flew on hour after hour on solid instruments, blind to the whereabouts of other aircraft if there were any so foolish as to inhabit the same high regions, and too often uncertain of our own position.

Bereft of all contact with the outside world we flew in a state of almost total unreality. Were we actually moving? While the steady pounding of the engines persisted and tiny droplets of moisture coagulated and slid across the windshield, all beyond our cockpit windows was dirty gray or blinding white, a suffocating murk smothering all indication of movement. We could, for reassurance, regard the instruments and discover a quiver in the various needles indicating our airspeed, altitude, rate of climb, or descent. Yet frequently they seemed to bear false witness. Then if, as sometimes happened, we saw the rusty-iron side of a mountain looming out of the mist and observed how it reached to altitudes far above our level of flight, was our altimeter lying or did the map mistake the true height of the mountain?

And what of the winds? Did they blow for or against us, to or fro? Without benefit of local knowledge we were as mariners cruising in strange tidal flows. We knew the elements were not still, but whether they were to speed or delay our time of arrival remained a mystery.

It was comforting to look at Parks, because in spite of his reticence I knew he suffered human tribulations and was therefore dependably real. His nose was sunburned and tiny flakes of overdone skin made a lace line across the division of exposed nose and the upper part shaded by his ranger's hat. He smelled of tobacco and nervous effort as did I. Usually we needed all the oxygen our lungs could gather and we spent it cautiously. So there were long silences between us. During these periods when it seemed we were in a space capsule far removed from earth we secretly cherished each other's company. We were man and man, a wonderfully powerful combination when respect is mutual. I knew it would be wretched flying alone in these regions.

Sometimes, in good weather when we could enjoy our lofty view, we would look out upon the mighty mountains, the vast deserts, and the fetid carpet of jungles which stretched to infinity, and we would wonder aloud what the hell we were doing wherever we were. There were other times when I thought wryly of my certain disappointment should life be terminated by such a fruitless venture.

Soon after I left Parks to his awesome terrain and chose for flights of my own command the eastern route via the Caribbean and the northeastern hump of South America, I wondered even more at the extravagance of war and the apparent hopelessness of our mission.

Soon it became obvious that I had made a questionable trade in choosing the eastern routing. We spent much more time over the open sea without so much as a life jacket aboard, let alone a raft or emergency supplies, but my faith in Pratt and Whitney engines was unbounded and with only water below I could choose the most benign altitude. I rejoiced in the sunlight and the sea and even in picking my way through the oceanic thunderheads which usually blossomed like gigantic mushrooms all along the way.

My satisfaction with the oceanic portion of the route was made all the easier by Gillette, a resourceful man from my own airline who in a rare moment of abandon had agreed to serve as my co-pilot. If Parks was frugal of speech then Gillette was a verbal miser. He spared himself remarks in agreement or negation by nodding his head. He sought the absolute minimum of words to convey all exchanges between himself and human society and yet, magically, by the intonation of his few words, or combining them with gesture, he was able to transmit his most complicated thoughts. A further talent for transmitting greatly enhanced Gillette's contribution to our rather haphazard aerial voyaging. He was fluent in Morse. By tapping the wireless key strapped to his leg he was occasionally successful in establishing contact with the earth people and was several times able to determine the weather at our destination. Not that it greatly mattered other than to provide a certain subtle lift to our morale. It was as if someone cared—momentarily. The Lockheed's maximum cruising range was often very close to the total distance between decent airports and usually we were obliged to proceed onward and land regardless of weather.

Our aircraft was sabotaged in Belém. Someone decided to do something about these Yankees who were threatening his job security. So that someone put water in our engine oil, knowing the heat of operation would create steam and the resulting pressure would cause something to blow. When it happened we should be over the jungle and that would be that. The jungle was unbroken and the trees very high. Even if we could manage a crash landing and somehow slip to the ground, walking to civilization was impossible.

"Took off and assumed a southeasterly heading," the report would read if anyone bothered to make a report. "No further contact." And that would be the end of it as the someone must have known.

But the someone who hated us so, bungled, or was frightened away with his job half done. While the right engine blew oil all over the wing and fuselage soon after we leveled out after climbing, the left engine continued smoothly. We turned in immediate retreat and Gillette did a masterly job taking us back to Belém.

At Barreiras, a godforsaken field in Brazil, there was sometimes a traffic problem with the mountain lions who found the runway a pleasant place to nap. There was also a cockatoo in residence, known as Doctor Max, who did not seem to resent our mini-invasion. He was more talkative than Gillette, and I thought he was as well informed as anyone concerning our future now that my country was officially at war.

One steaming afternoon, not long after Pearl Harbor, Gillette and I landed at Paramaribo in Dutch Guiana. What should have been a normal landing rapidly developed into a wrestling match as a tire blew on the landing gear. When I had somehow brought the Lockheed to a halt without damage except to our nerves, we discovered the construction crew had left an iron reinforcing rod protruding almost four inches from the asphalt. The American fighter pilots who used the runway knew the approximate location of the rod and were thus able to avoid it. Not that they cared. While we waited for a new tire we learned they no longer cared very much about anything. They were lost souls, ghost heroes, thousands of miles from any possible action. The overtaxed logistic system in Washington said they were supposed to be guarding a nearby bauxite mine. Just what they might do with their P-40 aircraft against any intruders had become an obsession with them because the obvious answer was nothing. While yearning for the true and violent combat according to the gospel of all fighter pilots, they stared at only empty skies and a hole in the ground which the most determined aggressor could not possibly move. They presumed their enemy would be of Teutonic origin and landed from a submarine. Yet an *Unterseeboot* could scarcely carry more than thirty men in addition to her crew, and the mine was far from the sea. Who or what then was their reason for existence? Honed to perfection in their trade before they had left the United States, they were without an enemy and therefore frustrated to near-madness. To assuage their boredom they sometimes went aloft and shot at each other. Thus far they had refrained from taking careful aim.

I told them of our logistical incongruity, but I saw they didn't entirely believe me. With the nation now fully at war and airplanes our most precious projectiles, not even the mad logistical machine in Washington would send brand-new glistening Lockheeds to Brazil. Or so it would seem. Yet we were bound in the wrong direction.

"No passengers? No generals or even VIPs? Just you two guys? Don't try to kid us. You're on some kind of a spy mission."

I wondered about the true value of our flights even more than the forsaken fighter pilots and was much relieved when the project was finally terminated.*

As a final consequence of this dubious campaign I was cursed with malaria and suffered its vicious attacks periodically for several years. During recovery from my first surrender to that terrible disease I thought my delirium might have become permanent, for Kalberer turned up to relieve my wretchedness. Pearl Harbor Sunday had caught him in Java where he was still flying for KLM. Within days the Japanese had descended upon Indonesia, but if they hoped to capture the likes of Kalberer they should have advanced even faster. As usual, he had performed a nearly impossible feat and I was very proud of him. Not only had he contrived his own last-minute escape, but in the finest swashbuckling tradition had managed to bring a beautiful Indonesian lady with him. Now, back in brown uniform, he ranked as a

---

* All of the Lockheed Lodestars we gave to Brazil were lost in crashes.

mere first lieutenant. I wondered aloud how soon he would be court-martialed or running the Air Force.

All of South America was so remote from the war scene, I had difficulty adjusting to the profound change which in less than a month had overcome my native land. After completing the final flight to Rio de Janeiro it had been my frivolous mischief to fill the moist hand of the maitre d' at the Copacabana Hotel with cruzeiros, thereby assuring a ringside table at the evening's dinner show. A poster in the lobby had informed me that Paul Draper was the star performer, and knowing his routine I longed to make him fault his first tremendous leap into the spotlight. Once in Chicago and once in Boston I had rattled his famous aplomb similarly, and in far-away Rio after more than a year without any communication between us I anticipated the perfect coup.

All went according to plan. After the usual fanfare of trumpets Draper started his run through the darkened ballroom, rose like a gazelle and landed with consummate grace in the center of the spotlight. He looked up from his crouch to see an all too familiar face hardly four feet from his own. I had practiced an elaborate yawn, which I held through the duration of his astonishment. When he recovered and began his marvelously intricate dancing I was deeply satisfied. Sure enough, I had seen his normally perfect timing falter. The world must look after itself, I thought. These were the exquisite moments when the gods smiled upon friendship of man with man and enhanced his life forever. Later we drank a bottle of champagne each and laughed together until nearly dawn.

The following day, just beginning to feel the chill paw of malaria upon my shoulder, I started the return for Washington. Although Pearl Harbor was hardly older than a month as history, I was shocked to find my countrymen apparently gone mad. Alternately freezing and sweating in a hotel bed I had great difficulty separating my malarial deliriums and the fantasies now playing all about me.

When my fevers permitted I reentered the real world and found it unreal. If this was the true nobility of war, I sorrowed, then I had indeed been long deceived.

Historians who were not even alive during the first

months after Pearl Harbor may record that some sort of magnificent spirit swept the nation, causing the American people to rise above themselves, volunteer great sacrifices, and eventually lay down their lives for what they believed must be the salvation of mankind. For a few dedicated souls it was so, but the vast majority of Americans inaugurated an orgy of self-justification and indulgence. American politicians of every category and persuasion garlanded themselves with self-importance and made unctuous speeches they hoped matched the national mood, even while they remained silent at the monstrous evil of throwing American-Japanese into concentration camps—after first, conveniently, appropriating their legal property.

Rising to the tremendous demands of the time, Roosevelt responded with an air of magnificence and began to match Churchill in status as a leader. The vicious Japanese attack had removed any need for him to explain or retract a campaign vow which had been important to his reelection: "I shall say it again and again and again. Your boys are not going to be sent into any foreign wars."

While a minority of stalwarts did volunteer for the armed services, there was no apparent shame whatever in young men striving to avoid the draft—or if caught by the inexorable (and fortunately indiscriminate) numbers, they together with their families tried every conceivable measure to wheedle a safe berth in the military. This concern was understandable if somewhat shocking to those Americans long indoctrinated with the sacrificial gallantries of Washington's Revolutionary troops, the Confederates, the bluecoats of the Civil War, and the jolly band-playing esprit of the First World War. Young Americans already in uniform were treated with respect and smiles of encouragement, but as yet they were not regarded as heroes, and men in civilian clothes were rarely insulted as was common during the First World War. This was one heartening reality swimming like a lovely amoeba in a pool of chauvinism. For some of the most courageous deeds of the entire war were accomplished by men who never wore a uniform.

As soon as my fevers subsided I passed the necessary physical examination and returned to regular line flying, mainly along my old route to Cleveland via Syracuse,

Rochester, Buffalo, and Erie, but with frequent diversion along other routes to Boston, Chicago, Cincinnati, Nashville, and Memphis. Thus I was able to observe my countrymen in an important section of the nation and much that I saw was hardly inspiring.

During the first months after Pearl Harbor the American people behaved as if they moved in a trance and I joined in the general disregard of fundamental truths. Ironically, now that we were officially at war, my desire to hurl myself at the enemy diminished. I was sorry to see my flying comrades who held active reserve commissions called away one by one. Too many would be flying a desk and we could not conceive of a more lamentable fate.

I made little progress explaining this view to my father, who, still mistrusting airplanes, brought my mother East on the train in hope of finding better medical analysis of her failing health.

"I do not understand," my father said while employing his purest tone of reasonable inquiry, "why it is you are still flying. It's dangerous. Every week I read about another crash. Surely you should have worked your way up to an office job by now. Good executives are always hard to find. I would have supposed that by now you would be well on your way to a vice president's desk." When he made a church steeple with his fingertips and skewered my attention with his good eye, I knew I must try to sound as if I really had given a moment's thought to leaving the cockpit. Deciding to appeal to his monetary sense, I wondered what he would think if I told him I sometimes felt guilty being paid so handsomely for enjoying myself.

"Well, sir. At the present time a vice president of American Airlines receives less pay than I do. He works all day every day and rarely breathes fresh air."

"But vice presidents do not get killed. You are our only son."

"They die in other ways. And I have time for writing, which you'll admit is not going too badly."

Any reference to my writing was an unfair diversion which I was learning to employ whenever conversation between us became sticky. For of all the disappointments and aggravations I had given my father, the minuscule success of my writings had been more than compensation. The original effort launched in Marcum's freezing Rockland County barn had now resulted in three books.* All were about aviation and aimed at the general reader. They were hodgepodge and awkward, riven with high-sounding phrases, and thin enough in bulk to avoid scaring away potential readers. Their one virtue was a comprehensible introduction for every man into something he had apparently been wondering about. The sales mounted far beyond the publisher's or my own expectations.

My father was certainly the prime customer, buying copies by the dozens for his friends and never missing an opportunity to plug their dubious quality. He haunted bookstores, badgering the managers about any display failing to feature the works of his son and admonishing them to order more. If one of my books was buried beneath others or hidden behind a Steinbeck or Hemingway, he would await his chance and surreptitiously reverse the order. He kept both reviews and advertisements in his coat pocket handy to bore any listener who might be even remotely interested. Worse than a stage mother, he demanded to know why the publishers had not taken full-page advertisements in *The New York Times*, not to mention the *Wall Street Journal*, which "*everyone* reads." I could never convince him such expensive flamboyance was considerably beyond the measure of my books.

This visit was the last time I saw my mother in reasonably good health. A strong protective instinct keeps us from realizing our parents will actually die and be out of our lives forever. Thus armed until the very last, we are able to complain secretly of their frailties or even bemoan their addled interference with our preferred routine. We resent and openly reject their wisdom, we are sometimes cruel, and even at our best are inclined to be patronizing. This callousness is as natural as its complete reversal when the death of a parent is obviously near; then whimpering in fright, we are brought up hard in the realization that our youth is over. Among normal American families, our last days' solicitude becomes genuine

---

* *Sky Roads, All American Aircraft, Getting Them into the Blue,* all published by T. Y. Crowell & Co.

and often agonizing. It is a shocking experience to grow up after thirty.

Now I saw my mother's once-lovely face sagging with more than the ravages of the years. The circles under her eyes, which had always been prominent and interesting, had become heavier and darker and she moved as if always in pain. Her eyes were still luminous and often shared her very private amusements with me, but there were long times when an overwhelming melancholy seemed to possess her, and I knew somehow that whatever ailed her was invincible.

To compensate, we pretended. I took my mother to my basement studio and showed her the drawings and paintings I had done. She had taught me the joys of mixing oils and smearing the results on canvas, a single gift of the multitude I owed her. As we discussed my crude work, which was at least sincere, we pretended all was well; it was only yesterday or the day before when I had begged her to stay at Bernard's, my childhood Jewish friend's, for lunch. His dark-haired mother promised rice and curry again. Now, not so much later, unless I looked too long into my mother's eyes, I could smell the fresh mud and the new spring buds in the narrow passageway between Bernard's barn and fence. After we played there I would run all the way home to find this lovely person playing "Just a Song at Twilight," and later, after she had tucked me in for the night, the locusts would buzz in the trees and the Nebraska wind would whisper me to sleep. This gentle person first taught me other arts—mumblety-peg, and how to fix roller skates to the bottom of a board thereby creating the world's fastest scooter. And teasing as if we were equals, she was the first to chant "Ernest's got a girral . . . Ernest's got a girral . . ." She was the same soft shield to cover me and turn my screams into sobs when I fell from that tree and broke my arm, my confidante when my youthful ambitions demanded to be told, and a discreet mediator when sheer stubborn maleness threatened anger between father and son.

"Do you sing any more?"

"No. I've forgotten how."

"I remember your singing something about 'rings on her fingers and bells on her toes . . . elephants to ride upon—' I used to think you would look very beautiful sitting lotus-fashion in a howdah while you sprinkled jewels upon the populace."

For an instant the twinkle came back to her eyes. She smiled as she always did preceding mischief and asked innocently, "Didn't you know I often did?"

Lester Linsk, one of my first flying students from the little Aeronca days, was drafted. For once the military did not assign a cook to drive a tank or even vice-versa. Linsk went into the Armed Services Radio Unit, bravely labeled the Yellow 69th by its multitalented troops. Later, in Iceland, North Africa, Europe, and Burma I would see the marvelous effect this highly specialized battalion would have upon overseas morale. No one resented those comfortable heroes whose front lines were Broadway and the MGM studios and whose mess halls were Rueben's, Romanoff's, or the Brown Derby.

Boyd, the chief pilot who had first introduced me to DC-3s, was called back into the Air Force, and Coates, who had helped me in the earliest airline school days, soon followed. Bigelow, a friend who would volunteer for crucifixion if asked in the right way, had been accepted by the Navy. Word from Kalberer informed me he had already been promoted. And still the bugles sounded unusually faint for me.

Much of the indifference which had replaced my former eagerness was due to the comfortable status I had at last achieved. I had emerged from a long diet of humble pie and found it very satisfying to slouch in the society of those who had until recently moved in a world far removed from mine. I had been a co-pilot for one year and eleven months, for that time, in company with all other co-pilots, remaining as nearly invisible as living men can be.

The duties of a co-pilot in our airplanes were well defined. On command he raised and lowered the landing gear and flaps. He nursed the temperamental heating system and made routine radio reports. He made out the flight plan and flight log, which, if approved, his captain would sign. He loaded and unloaded the baggage and mail and flew the airplane when his captain decided to take his lunch or dinner or visit with the passengers. Whatever the stewardess brought forward in the way of food or drink was first offered to the captain, and then, if she was of generous mind, she might remember there was another human being in the cockpit. Not a real human being, of course—a co-pilot who would one day break out of his cocoon and become a butterfly with two gold stripes on his sleeve instead of one and a half. All co-pilots understood the plight of India's untouchables and were likewise resigned to perpetual humiliation.

No one, except in jest, ever made openly derogatory remarks about a co-pilot. His status was too low for controversy; he was protected by his own total vulnerability to every hurt. Mechanics ignored co-pilots and unless they were bachelors stewardesses looked right through them. If in the operations office a co-pilot stood with a group of men, he occupied air-space and nothing more. Remarks were never addressed to him, nor would the sound he made with his mouth if he ventured a comment be heeded. He did not exist except as an extension of the flying machine in which he served and he was expected to behave accordingly, static except in actual flight. This human conditioning did marvelous things to the inner character of a man, and for a time sublimated the most obstreperous ego.

The same caste system applied in the social life of pilots. Captains went fishing or played golf with other captains. Parties rarely included a co-pilot and his wife, nor was a captain's wife likely to have lunch with a co-pilot's wife unless a very unusual relationship existed between their men.

In effect both husband and wife were adjudged by a seniority number which was tattooed on the brain of every pilot from the day he went to work. His route, his base, and his pay all started with his personal number. Thus when I finally made my first flight with American Airlines I was given the number 267, which afforded me a perfect view from the absolute bottom of the list. During my term as a co-pilot various factors including a war caused the airline to hire more and more pilots until there were now some four hundred, with all those above 267 junior to me. The view from here was much better, I thought. In the glory of my captaincy I could afford to smile benignly upon the peasants whose numbers were higher than mine and even signal my sympathies when they worried about their survival against so much competition.

Now it all seemed so easy. While serving as co-pilot I relearned the humility I had once been obliged to practice in military academy. The social denial was of no consequence whatever to either Eleanor or myself. We had a wide variety of friends and acquaintances, a mixed bag of show people, sailors, and fliers, and only rarely associated with pilots of the line.

There were a few exceptions and one in particular. He was Keim, an irascible man who frequently had been my captain and had taught me much. In the air and on the ground his acid tongue uttered a constant series of searing remarks on my obvious lack of flying ability, my overall level of intelligence ("Once a co-pilot always a co-pilot"), and the various disasters I was certain to endure unless I mended my ways. Keim's heavy jowls shook as he despaired of my aerial future, and the freckles on his red face seemed to bloom individually as he bemoaned my lack of financial thrift. "What the hell do you need a boat for? People drown at sea."

Nothing I did was ever right with Keim until I became a captain and then, according to him, it was only because of his patient instruction that I had made the grade. Our badinage became more intense and polished with the years, and our perfection of insult brought about a friendship which endured until his death.

With the balance of *yin* and *yang* so much in my favor I was thoroughly enjoying my new life as captain. The inner excitement of command and the general recognition of my peers was enough to satisfy my basic yearning for action. I had left the ghost of a co-pilot behind and now swaggered with all but the true old-timers, who, weathered by a thousand suns and storms, bore themselves far more humbly. "Two things frighten me," Keim snarled. "A new airline captain and a second lieutenant of infantry with a map."

Among airline ground employees a pleasing amount of recognition also followed in the trail of my books, and since we were purely a domestic airline, my South American argosies brought special respect from even the most veteran captains. Relaxed in the beautiful and vital world immediately about me, I temporarily managed to ignore the war.

This apparent hesitation withered before a succession of developments which clearly indicated I was not going to sit out the war shuttling between Eastern cities. We began flying with young military officers as our co-pilots who were presumably learning our way of doing things. We flew as targets for anti-aircraft searchlights, mostly spotted along the west bank of the Hudson River and thereby making a fine show. Then several of us, some very senior and others of my still lowly rank, were invited to learn celestial navigation. Rumors compelled me to instant acceptance. We were going to lead bombers across the ocean. We were going to lead night bombing raids on Germany.

The classroom for this enterprise was the roof of the American Airlines offices at La Guardia Field and the instructor was McIntosh, the very same man who had lamented my stupidity when I first attended the line school in Chicago. "Oh God," he moaned on sight of me. "Oh God. Not *you*."

Later McIntosh confessed he was not very far ahead of us when he introduced us to the stars above: Arcturus, Spica, Sirius, Dubhe, Polaris, and the planets were only recently so familiar to him. He showed us how to identify each one, which took some doing; I kept seeking in vain for the mythological serpent, lion, and bear designs I remembered seeing on a fortune-teller's astrological chart. With weary tolerance McIntosh explained the difference between astrology and astronomy and ventured his hope I would not depend upon the twelve houses of the heavens, the ascendence of my house star, or the zodiacal compatibility of Libra and Taurus to set course for far destinations.

Once having learned the principal navigational stars, we were supplied with octants (the aerial version of the sextant), and began practicing the measurement of various celestial bodies above the horizon. The sun was easy to bring into place and fix in the small bubble which floated somewhat nervously inside the viewfinder. Stars and planets were ill-behaved at first, dodging and disappearing from my field of view when most needed. There were times when I mistook one star for another, leading to the embarrassment of fixing my position in Zanzibar when I knew very well I was on the shores of Flushing Bay.

Before McIntosh despaired and drummed me out of his star-gazing seances, I made company with my dauntless neighbor Bigelow who knew something of such divinations and also had a remarkable ability to learn what he needed to know about anything in a very short time.

Bigelow was also a fine mariner who found that the Navy welcomed his application for seagoing service. (His war record, mostly in command of a destroyer escort, was outstanding.) Later, when the war business was done, I found it difficult to believe that my damn-the-torpedoes friend was being stoned and arrested for participating in Tennessee freedom marches, and thrown in the Honolulu jail for his protest sailings into forbidden atomic test areas.

Standing in my backyard, where the sky was much darker than when viewed from the city, we progressed from A to B in the art of celestial navigation. Then suddenly Bigelow went off in a blue uniform and still I lingered. My logbook now recorded more than four thousand flying hours, the majority in heavy aircraft, and an unusual amount on instruments. I knew the services rarely sent pilots with equivalent experience where I wanted to go. They instructed or flew a desk.

Abruptly, without explanation, our class with McIntosh was canceled. We went our separate ways for a month or more and all inquiries to our superiors brought similar answers. "I don't know . . . might just as well forget it . . . we haven't heard a thing."

Now, throughout America, it was a time of secrets. The understandable anxiety created by loose talk giving clue of various sailings to German submarines had been manifested by all who considered themselves privy to confidential information. "I've gotta secret" was played to a ridiculous degree and in countless ways. Although the nearest enemy was more than three thousand miles distant, frowns or the suspicious eye were the reward if anyone asked whither a train loaded with cannon and tanks might be bound. Even the weather map in our airline operations office was labeled a "restricted area." Officious guards now challenged us as we reported for flights, demanding to see our new identification buttons, which any three-fingered spy could have fashioned with ease. Beyond the doors so zealously guarded there was absolutely nothing new except the faces of the most recently hired stewardesses and they too were questioned as if they were so many Mata Haris. An ancient adage again covered the national behavior: the farther from the zones of true danger, the harder the game of war must be played. While the newspaper headlines told of Doolittle's Tokyo raid, the importance of women in the war effort, MacArthur's latest polemic, and the fall of Corregidor, the President of the United States publicly insisted there must be no violation of the forty-hour week. Our own pilots' union, of which I was a rather dissident member, rejected any suggestion that we might alleviate the shortage of pilots by flying more than eighty-five hours a month.

On the home front in America it was not a noble time.

Chapter 23

Already certain factors were at work which would ultimately affect the rest of my mortal days. The lively sense of euphoria created by my work aloft had rendered me almost immune to personal worries.

One very real air emergency had recently been my lot, and what might have killed us all became instead a powerful stimulus toward my early promotion to captain. Flying out of Nashville one winter night with Hughen, veteran of a thousand nights aloft, we encountered heavy ice in the vicinity of Knoxville. The rate of accumulation was incredible even to Hughen, who had seen far more of that evil than most pilots. Soon the burden of extra weight combined with the aerodynamic distortion of our DC-2 to make the aircraft nearly unmanageable.

In minutes it became apparent we were in serious trouble. At Hughen's command I went back to the cabin intending to inform the passengers as gently as I could of our difficulties.

"It may be we will have to make an emergency landing. Please take off your shoes, glasses, and loosen your collars. Cover yourself with this blanket and hold a pillow over your face. The stewardess will give you plenty of warning."

This awkward speech was hardly the whole truth. Unless a miracle happened we would certainly go down somewhere in the Cumberland Mountains, but it would hardly be just an "emergency landing." The stewardess, already terrified out of her wits by the noise of the ice banging against the fuselage and the unusual gyrations of the aircraft, might or might not know just when to give final warning.

I managed to appear calm and properly resolute—mainly because true fear had not yet caught up with me.

It struck me full force when I returned to the cockpit and absorbed some of Hughen's very grave concern. In spite of the temperature, globules of sweat covered his bald head, and he yelled above the frightful racket, "I've almost lost her a couple of times!"

The airspeed indicator had long ago iced up and become inoperative; Hughen was flying by altimeter, turn and bank, an artificial horizon behaving sickly, and the seat of his pants. We were going down and down and were now uncertain of our position.

Hughen instructed me to backfire the engines by alternately cutting their fuel mixture and then restoring it—a dangerous and spectacular means of removing the ice forming over the air intakes. It was very hard on engines already straining at full power, but we were desperate.

For the next three hours I continued the process and when there was time took innumerable bearings with our hand-cranked direction-finder. Snow static and antenna ice had rendered our other radios utterly useless. All through the everlasting night Hughen had all he could do to keep the DC-2 from stalling out, a superb job of airmanship. Later, for a brief period we did manage to establish a very erratic series of communications with our New York Operations office. We were not heartened by their advice that every airport along the East Coast was enveloped in heavy fog. Our only alternative was to turn back west toward Cincinnati where the weather was reported as "improving."

Reviewing those terrible hours together later, neither of us could find logical explanation for our escape from disaster. Somehow, frequently lost and confused, often below the levels of the terrain, we floundered blindly through valleys and between hills, seeking refuge and finding none, until at last we broke out above a solid overcast and there was the dawn.

Our ordeal was not quite done. Our uncontrollable trembling matched the debility of the DC-2, and we were every minute more anxious about the quantity of our remaining fuel. With only thirty gallons remaining and about fifteen minutes more of flying, exhausted of strength and spirit, we finally found our way down to a wild landing at Cincinnati.

I thought Hughen a great man for his performance of that night, but as we sighed together and rubbed at our sore eyes and the overwhelming weariness of salvation replaced our hidden fears, I supposed it would be just another night during which we had both earned somewhat more than our salary.

Hughen was not simply content to let it be. He went to Boyd and to McCabe and Braznell, all influential in the careers of pilots, and spoke so well of my behavior at his side that my promotion to captain followed soon afterward.

Now God was in his heaven and I flew in the celestial suburbs, a man proud and content with his reason for existence. I was treated everywhere with open respect, a sensation unknown to me in the theater or elsewhere in my various attempts to make a place in society. The butcher and the baker and the plumber and even the man of business all regarded me as an interesting specimen, addressed me as "Captain," queried me constantly about life in the skies, and frequently expressed wonder that I should voluntarily engage in such work when I now had a family to think about. Even with the war in full swing I was often asked what poor Eleanor would do "if something happened." My response to such concerns was a canned lecture on the safety of air transport and a secret conviction that I was, after all, quite a dashing fellow.

Time and prosperity had contributed to my blindness and too casual regard for those to whom I owed my devoted attention. While son George and I were still unusually close comrades, my involvement with the twins was confined to half an hour's pre-slumber gooing and ah-ha-ing if I happened to be at home. I had been neither pleased nor displeased when Eleanor announced she was again pregnant. Having long forgotten her peculiar faint-

313

ing spells, I assumed her current medical infatuations were part of having another child. I ignored the continuous and worshipful repetition of "Doctor this" and "Doctor that" in our household. And I went on about my flying.

My indifference to Eleanor's pattern of behavior was a grave mistake. Had I had the wisdom and compassion to recognize the first apparently insignificant flashes of lightning as dangerous, I might have been able to rescue my wife from the thunderstorms which finally devoured her.

A fetus bears a haunting resemblance to the great galaxy of Andromeda, and its design is kin to the shape of the Milky Way. In similar style many of the molecules and amino acids comprising our physical structure are found in nature. This interrelationship of ourselves to innumerable natural phenomena is well recognized, but unlike the cyclic fates of natural things which can be most accurately predicted (the blossomings of springtime, the witherings of autumns) the progress of our own transformations remains erratic and our destinies, until the very last, unknown. Some women age graciously and retain their beauty long past reasonable explanation while others are already hags in youth. Some men of seventy are more alert and alive than others of forty and no one can analyze why such outrageous ratios should happen to be.

We can only be sure of death, but when and where, how and why, remain unforeseeable. We can calculate with marvelous exactitude the positions of the stars and planets during a certain night one thousand years B.C. or in the year A.D. two thousand, but we cannot offer an approximate schedule for our own departure. This acknowledgement of indefinite mortality places a heavy burden on the human spirit, but not so intolerable as it would be if we knew the answers.

Neither the mystique of religion nor the exhortations of the occult, nor any other power can satisfy our yearning for explanations of the unexplainable. Why should a two-hour-old male perish just as the first breath of earth life became natural to him? God wanted him? A nurse gave him the evil eye? He was not born dead, which would have seemed more of nature's clumsy doing, but he lived and died all in the space of two hours—even before he could be given a name.

Who was to say it was a blessing or a catastrophe? Both Eleanor and I were ill-equipped to withstand such shocks to what had hitherto been a sheltered existence. We were, except for minor economic troubles already forgotten, not accustomed to woe.

The war soon erased my sense of loss. Eleanor never fully recovered.

In May of 1945 four of us posed in a line while someone snapped our picture with the little Minox camera 1 carried all through the war. It was against regulations, but since we had actively been violating several regulations a day for three years I saw no reason to make exception. Thus, without actually intending to, I contrived to preserve several rather grainy hints of our gypsylike existence during the time we were caught up in various degrees of hazard without actually being shot at.

The four of us who posed were Dewitt, a true veteran of some eighteen thousand flying hours in comparison with my own now six thousand five hundred seventy-two and eleven minutes, and Burns, another patriarch of the air, who had learned to fly in World War I; I stood between them; next to Burns, the only one of us without a tranch coat draped over his arm, was Hay, a tall, fair-haired, red-faced pilot of great gentility.

Our brown-green uniforms, vaguely resembling naval aviators', were particularly natty on this morning, while Dewitt and Burns had taken particular care to trim the traditional hairline mustaches which marked them as pioneer airmen. We were smiling thinly, obviously well-rested, and we posed as if we knew very well we were participating in yet another act of history. We all stood at momentary ease, but as if expecting an earthquake or rough seas my feet are spread wide apart, a habit displayed in other photos taken in various theaters of the war now over. For the Germans had surrendered, the cleaning-up operations were now said to be well in hand, and it had become our unique duty to facilitate the greatest military triumphs since the Caesars.

The background in the photo is Orly Field, Paris. We are part of the flight crews assigned to a special and presumably honorable mission. Four mighty generals, laden with the booty of victories and accompanied by their satraps, body servants, and assorted minions, would be lofted this fair French morning toward destinations over the horizons. There they would be celebrated in a series of processionals and ceremonial fêtes of tremendous magnitude.

The four generals were Eisenhower, Bradley, Patton, and Mark Clark. Because of his colorful nature and because his ovations were scheduled for Los Angeles, where it was rumored the returning hero would be greeted by hundreds of movie starlets, all of us wanted to fly Patton. My own enthusiasm was somewhat blunted when I learned our honored passenger would be Mark Clark, the questionable hero of the Italian campaign. The flights would be long and tedious and without crew changes, hence Burns and I would fly as co-captains.

General Clark's grim business had been to land on the Italian peninsula, take Rome, and make conquest of Hitler's "soft underbelly." Unfortunately, there was nothing soft about it. Clark found his inadequate troops opposed by crack German divisions determined to throw him back into the Mediterranean Sea. Eventually, Clark had been victorious, but not until a terrible bloodletting had occurred. We preferred to believe that Clark had done the best job he could under the circumstances, although it seemed the losses in young manhood were far out of proportion to value received.

One of our aircraft (a C-54) had been especially prepared for each general. Since we would be at least twenty-two hours en route from Paris to Chicago, a brass bed had been installed in the forward part of the cabin and the area made discreet by an arrangement of green curtains. The night before the photo was taken, Clark's batman, a genial black professional soldier, had seen to special commissary supplies and all stood ready by early morning. When a group of assorted full and lieutenant colonels plus a smattering of majors arrived and stood about splendidly in their clean uniforms, we were assured the great man was about to arrive. Would we be so good as to take our positions on the flight deck since the flight must depart precisely on schedule? The General, a West Pointer, liked things on schedule.

All transpired according to the time sheet we had been furnished. I caught a glimpse of Clark as he saluted his staff and preceded them through the cabin door. He was a tall, beak-nosed man of impressive military bearing. As the flight engineer and I started the engines, I was somewhat disappointed that no one had thought to introduce the General to those who would be responsible for his life during the next twenty-odd hours, then scorned myself for such petty self-importance. One hoped the General had more pressing matters on his mind.

There were still a few unfilled bomb craters off our wingtips as we taxied across Orly Field, but all else had changed so remarkably since I had stumbled into what became the Air Transport Command, I had momentary trouble concentrating on the business at hand. Later, when we were bound westward toward our first refueling stop in the Azores, I was intrigued with the outward transformation of ourselves. Even as we passed over St.-Malo and leveled off at cruising altitude we kept our uniform coats buttoned and our ties pulled up. We were bathed and shaven, our hair combed and our shoes shined. Was this all for a man who wore four stars on his shoulders and had only a few years ago been just another obscure soldier? I tried to rationalize the tremendous cost and effort involved in the entire project by telling myself it was not the individuals being so honored, but the multitudes of the quick and the dead they represented. It was a comforting thought, if difficult to keep in mind during the exhibitions soon to follow, but I certainly had no cause for bitterness. My limbs and eyes, stomach and genitals still formed a functional unit which was much more than could be said for hundreds of my westbound passengers during the last two years. It was a part of war I had never really considered when Chief Pilot Davidson hailed me into his office one afternoon in the time of a different world.

"How would you like to go to Presque Isle?" he asked.

If Davidson had asked me to fly to Venus I would have supposed it possible and assented, for I was growing more discontent with the familiar challenges of flying back and forth to Cleveland when there was so much activity beyond further horizons.

"Sure." I was ashamed to confess I had not the faintest notion where a place called Presque Isle might be. "How long will I be gone?"

"About a week."

Davidson's week stretched into more than three months and provided enough excitement to suppress any regrets I might have had at being left out of things.

Presque Isle was not some lovely atoll in the Caribbean as I had half hoped it might be, but instead proved to be in the opposite direction, a bucolic, drowsy little town on the northern border of Maine. The locals had been mainly interested in the cultivation and price of potatoes until the presence of an airbase made their tranquil area a temporary gateway to Europe and the war.

The same ten of us who had been selected to study navigation with McIntosh were sent off to Presque Isle, quartered for a time in a tourist camp, and then in a musty hotel which offered a mellow nineteenth-century atmosphere, strategically placed spittoons, and superb New England boiled dinners. None of us was prepared for our coming task; we arrived in light summer clothing and were as unsure of our status on the ground as we often were of our position in the air. We did suspect something very big was happening and our presence seemed to be important to whatever it was.

Flying a military version of the aircraft we normally flew on American Airlines, we had no more than landed at Presque Isle than some of us were sent even farther north. A weary lieutenant behind a counter in the operations office handed me a sheaf of papers and, yawning, said I should carry on to a place called Goose Bay in Labrador. Then he showed me where it was on a wall map while I thought wryly how I seemed strangely involved with flying over areas marked UNEXPLORED.

Finally the lieutenant handed me a chart for my very own, plus a crudely mimeographed approach plate for Goose Bay. He wished me godspeed and disappeared behind a door marked OFFICERS' LATRINE.

I turned to Johnson, my co-pilot, and in the best imitation of Davidson I could manage asked casually, "How would you like to go to Goose Bay?"

I was not at all surprised when Johnson raised one eyebrow and said, "Where in the goddamn tarnation hell is Goose Bay? Aren't we near enough to the North Pole already?"

Johnson was a Southerner, taffy-haired, blue-eyed, and pink-cheeked. He appeared to be in his late teens, a problem to him when he wanted to buy a drink, but a considerable advantage when in his best winsome way he sought the sympathy and comforting of the opposite sex. He was known as "Cotton," and I was delighted to have him flying on my right for he was a natural as a pilot, devoid of nerves, and pleasant company.

I waited until the yawning lieutenant returned, then asked, "This place Goose Bay. Are there landing lights on the runways?"

"I don't know. But who cares? At this time of year it never gets really dark. And I hear there is only one runway so you can hardly miss it."

While the logic of his last statement escaped me I thought: Of course. If you question, you betray your ignorance and further convince this paper warrior you are an intruder. Looking at Cotton Johnson I became even more aware of a sense of not belonging. We wore our blue American Airlines caps, light cotton shirts, blue uniform pants, and jodhpur shoes in the current fashion of airline pilots who could afford them. Our conversational exchanges were woefully lacking in "sirs," and our only concession to the unusual was a standard leather flight jacket issued by the Army. It replaced our uniform jacket, was without insignia of any kind, and offered some protection against the temperature, which was falling with the twilight.

"I guess we might as well go," I announced with vigor more suitable to the launching of a hundred-plane armada. I wanted the lieutenant to clearly understand we were professionals, unconcerned about taking off on a three-and-a-half-hour flight to a destination unknown to us. The lieutenant must perceive that our civilian status did not necessarily label us as faint-hearted. "By the way, how's the weather up there?" I asked as if fine or terrible would be all the same to me.

"Good."

"Thanks."

The lieutenant slid a paper forward for my signature, thus committing me to the responsibility of one military aircraft. "Bring it back," he said. "It belongs to the General."

"Really? You mean he bought it himself? Right out of his own pocket?"

"Don't be a smart-ass. General Giles loaned us his personal plane because we're short of aircraft and this stuff has got to get to Goose Bay."

"What stuff?"

"It's all listed on your cargo manifest. The papers I gave you. Don't scratch the General's airplane. He'll have a fit."

"So will I."

I made my mark on the flight clearance form and, wondering why I was content with a groundling's weather report consisting only of one word, made what I hoped was a departure suitable to the dignity of an airline veteran. Johnson, to whom dignity came with even greater reluctance, echoed the lieutenant's yawn as he eased himself out the door.

This petty performance occurred at the very beginning of what would become a gigantic worldwide operation, the Air Transport Command.

We flew northward in the thickening dusk, following a leg of the radio range station at Presque Isle for a while, listening to its fading whine in our earphones until there was only silence. We removed our earphones and listened to the steady rhythm of the magnificent Pratt and Whitney engines, which were new to us since American Airlines had been long committed to Wright engines. Although the Wrights were reasonably reliable, they vibrated so much more than the P and Ws it was said you could always identify an American Airlines pilot even out of uniform. Long exposure to shivering Wrights brought on an inconvenient weakness of the bladder.

We flew as in a dream, as if we might be the last two men alive bound on a hopeful expedition in search of other survivors. Once we had left the St. Lawrence River behind we slid easily through the chill smooth air with nothing but a wilderness of small glacial lakes, rocks, and scrub trees below. I descended until we were less than a hundred feet above the terrain and found it forbidding in the gloom, yet fascinating in its peace. We held on very low for nearly an hour, rousing up great squadrons of birds, gasping with delight when we saw a fish jump in ponds no man had seen before, climbing and descending a hundred-odd feet either way as the earth rose and fell beneath the aircraft's blunt brown nose. I thought this would be a bad place to become lost or go down for any reason whatever, and resolved that if there was to be another such flight I would bring along some kind of emergency kit—a few chocolate bars, matches, and a hatchet. "And mosquito repellent," Johnson said. "And a bottle of my grandpappy's bourbon."

Just before we took off from Presque Isle, a G.I. had thrown two parachutes aboard. I inquired if he thought we might be shot down and he smiled tolerantly and said, "I guess not, sir. But it's regulations. You got two souls on board. You got two chutes."

I thought they might make fine tents.

There were no landmarks on the chart north of the St. Lawrence and all the land below looked exactly the same. We were moving, the land rumpled by at high speed like an endless carpet, but we were not making any progress. Our view of half an hour before was identical to the landscape a half hour later. The sensation of being poised in space while the earth turned below was eerie and increasingly discomforting as fuel and hours passed.

We are spoiled, I thought. We were only flying a distance similar to that between New York and Chicago, but here our solitude aloft was not once broken by advice or interrogation from the ground. Our altitude was chosen as we pleased and our course depended entirely on the small magnetic compass hanging in the V between the windshields. We were back to sailing ship days, and remembering McIntosh I searched the sky for a star. Above I found only a wilderness as desolate as the one below. There was too much light in the heavens and a high, thin overcast would have hidden even the brightest planet. It really made no difference. There was no octant in the airplane, or chronometer to be sure of the time, or navigational tables; only a navigator who, given all the tools, might have further confused the situation. I made a note to find an octant somewhere and renew my practicing.

So we held on, unhappy only with the behavior of our magnetic compass, which displayed an increasing tendency to swing slowly toward the west and then back toward the east as if doubtful of itself.

"What the hell's wrong with our compass?" Johnson wanted to know.

"We must be near the magnetic pole. If I have things right we're about thirty-eight degrees variation."

"Wow." The way Johnson groaned made me wonder if his trust in me was deteriorating.

My own confidence might have leaked away with our fuel had I not held in reserve a hoary trick practiced by cunning barnstormers. I had learned it on hazy days flying out of the Christie brothers' little Rockland County field and practiced it on much longer flights in South America. It was a crude ploy, yet I knew it worked—always. The procedure was simple enough: if no navigational or positive landmarks are available, avoid flying a course directly to the desired destination. Aim to the left or right of it, the number of miles depending on weather and the value of your doubts. Then, when the proper time has elapsed and the destination is still not in sight, you will be spared what could be a fatal decision. You will not debate whether to turn left or right and risk a fifty percent chance of making the wrong choice. You will know on which hand the target lies and can proceed thence with little overall delay.

One feature was marked on the chart with some confidence. It was the Hamilton River. Though sketchily interpreted by a faint dotted line to the west, it was boldly drawn eastward to a great inlet and the sea. There, close to the river, was Goose Bay. Since I had deliberately set our course a few degrees to the west of rhumbline and knew from the smooth air and observing our lack of drift that there was little if any wind, we had only to turn east and follow the river once it came within view. I climbed for altitude now that we might sooner identify it.

Awed by the new perspective, Johnson said, "There sure is one Godawful amount of real estate out there." He scratched at his curly blond locks, playthings stewardesses had found irresistible in spite of his co-pilot status. "Can you tell me what the hell we're doing up here?"

I also had been wondering. As far as I could decipher from the manifest, which was mostly numbers, we were carrying various parts of a radio installation. There were also two cases of shotgun shells, which I thought might be rather ineffective against any military attack, several cases of lubricating oil, a bundle of nuts and bolts, and ten boxes of groceries and milk. It seemed a long and expensive way to haul such things, and if this was an example of the way the war was being run then both Johnson and I would be very old men before it stumbled to a halt.

This grubby service was not at all my idea of going to war. Where were the banners and bands, the uniforms glittering with medals, the evil enemy, and my sword? I had always envisioned myself as in Napoleon's cavalry, not part of the pack train.

My brooding lasted only minutes before the mystic enchantment of the Arctic summer night captured me and dispelled discouragement. Nearly on the horizon, a thin sliver of dull steel against the gloomy terrain, was the Hamilton River.

Johnson had been toying with the radio. "Listen," he said. "Hell, they even have a range station up here. Just like downtown."

I put on my headphones and heard a Morse repetition of the letters *y* and *r* every thirty seconds, the identifying signal for Goose Bay. I was disappointed. Somehow, I reasoned, it would have seemed more heroic if the muleteer of this pack train had been obliged to find his way via a trail of scattered breadcrumbs.

Soon afterward we swooped down over what had once been pristine forest and landed gently on a strip of gravelly sand. A huddle of men were waiting for us to shut down the engines, and I saw, to my delight, two familiar faces. One was Boyd, who had first introduced me to the very type of aircraft I now commanded. I had not seen him or heard of his fate since the Army had recalled him. Even from the height of the cockpit I observed the gold leaves on his shoulders and was not surprised he was already a major. If Boyd was in this desolation, I thought, then perhaps the pack train could become interesting. I was further cheered by the sight of Clark, a red-faced, red-headed, brilliant man, formerly a captain of our line. Now he was also a major and I thought only the face of God had steered me away from being at their side. My role as a muleteer still held promise and freedom of choice. They were stuck far from any action and, having sold their souls and bodies to the government, there was nothing they could do about it.

The third officer was an aging, barrel-chested, lieutenant colonel. His voice boomed across the night and echoed through the silent trees as he called up to me, "Did you bring any whiskey?"

"I don't think so. But there's some milk back there."

He made a face and I saw him shake his head forlornly. "Jesus Christ!" he moaned. "Milk is for babies."

Later, he took my hand in forgiveness and squeezed hard with his considerable paw. "Never mind," he grunted. "We have enough whiskey to carry us until your next trip. If we mix the damn milk with enough whiskey we can avoid being crippled up with calcium deposits."

He banged me on the back with his fist and nearly sent me sprawling. Then he invited Johnson and myself to his quarters to test the formula. He was "Fish" Hassel, the pro-tem commander of Goose Bay, a pioneer of Arctic flying, and a very great man.

Our new life aloft was like telling a preacher to tear up the bible and indulge himself in all the licentious pleasures his imagination might conjure, while promising him immunity for his sins. During the next three months we enjoyed the lush pleasure of flying as we pleased and with utter disregard of the rule books. Our letters of marque were clear. All the military asked us to do was deliver what they put on board to destinations of their choice. The doing was left entirely (and unbelievably) to us. We knew the operation was highly irregular and often unsafe. The military knew it also and looked the other way as we broke and scattered established traditions across the North Atlantic Ocean. I rejoiced in this return to aerial swashbuckling.

The airplanes were not designed for what they were now being asked to do, but we flew on to wherever it was without hesitation. It soon became routine to fly the relatively short distance between Presque Isle and Goose Bay, but almost immediately the flights were extended to Greenland and then on to Iceland. On the domestic line the CAA (now FAA) had authorized these same aircraft to be flown at a maximum of 25,346 pounds. Now we were flying at 31,500, which meant they would go down willy-nilly if we lost the power of either engine. And the ocean was very cold. We made night take-offs in zero-zero weather, a near-hopeless combination if one engine suffered even a minor loss of power.

We frequently started across the ocean without knowing either the weather en route or at our destination. Communication all along the North Atlantic route broke down frequently and sometimes days passed before our arrival or departure was known at the other end. Thus we were sometimes obliged to make descents and approaches in weather which would certainly have called for the cancellation of a commercial flight and sometimes with only the crudest radio aids, if there were any at all. In the air we cruised for long hours on solid instruments without the slightest idea where other aircraft might be, yet miraculously no one collided. Rather, a sense of utter solitude prevailed; we knew that at least half of our little group was in the sky somewhere, and little more.

Many of our flights were of considerable duration, a few of mine enduring longer than fifteen hours without landing. We had no other choice but to reach far ahead when the weather at our expected destination went completely sour. We had about sixteen hours' fuel until dry tanks, and I learned twice how the clock can tear at a man's nerves. We slept when we pleased, usually at the end of a flight, but if exhausted we spelled each other at the controls while one pilot went back to doze atop a packing case or a pile of parachutes.

During the first months of this quasi-military operation, our navigation was extremely sketchy. It was not helped by the peculiar behavior of the sun, which not only lingered in the sky until nearly midnight but hung so far in the north that our senses of direction, oriented to more southerly latitudes, often became confused. The disorientation was exaggerated by zones of relatively enormous magnetic variation and the listless behavior of our compasses. It took firm mental discipline to deliberately fly for hours on a southeasterly heading when we knew very well the destination was to the northeast. My own directional instinct, heretofore most reliable, was sometimes nearly lost in bewilderment and I spent as much time agonizing over our position as at the controls.

When I rose from my seat Johnson would pull at his golden ringlets and groan, "You're not going to leave me up here alone *again?*"

Actually, he was no longer to be left quite alone. Once we extended our flights to Greenland and Iceland we were provided with radio operators who were lodged in a small cubbyhole just behind the captain. Sommers, a balding young man with a rich vocabulary of expletives, became a regular member of our crew. There were no windows in his cubicle and he saw very little of the outside world. Even his earphones often forsook him. On some flights he would tap away his dit-dah queries hour after hour, become morose with the world's indifference to his challenges, and, pouting, cradle his head on his arms and sleep a while. Or sometimes he would rage at the lack of response: "It's the goddamned northern lights! They fuck up the atmosphere!"

Now we also carried a flight mechanic since there were none of his kind in most of the places we flew to, and few of us had either the wit or skill to right the simplest mechanical wrongs. Tetterton, an ex-racing car driver, flew regularly with us and also Ulbrich, another expert from the line. In flight they had little to do and would keep Johnson company if my seat were empty.

The exchange of position pleased me. Alone in the cabin I could make and, I hoped, correct my horrendous navigational capers without destroying the confidence of those who believed I knew what I was doing. Higher authorities than those doing the actual flying had caused a navigation table to be built over our extra fuel tanks in the cabin. It was knocked together with plywood and was large enough to plot the maneuvers of an entire naval engagement, but we blessed it since its length made a perfect bunk. There, if I was fortunate enough to calculate a believable position, I would shove the navigational tools aside and ease my weariness. The others too found the table a convenient refuge and sometimes I had to move someone's leg or arm to mark an X where I had finally decided we might be. Or had been. In the beginning it took me so long between shooting the stars or the sun to calculate the results and plot the fix, that we were already a hundred miles beyond it.

When Johnson would ask, "Where are we?" I would assume the look of a confident man and ask if he really cared.

"Not really."

"Then we are somewhere between there and here." Nodding to the gloom ahead and pointing to a star if any were visible I would add, "Just follow the three wise men."

"Who the hell are they?"

"Winkin', Blinkin', and Nod."

The long logistical chain of needs was the cause of my going to war, not on a glamorous charger as I would have preferred, but upon a heavily laden donkey and later on a ponderous elephant.

Originally, before the bombers and later even the fighter planes came, we were very few and our survival equipment almost nil. Eventually, there was time for someone to remember we deserved a fighting chance if we went down in the wilderness and they put emergency rations and two shotguns aboard our aircraft. Next they added fishing gear, a life raft, and even life preservers, which they recommended we wear when flying over water. None of us did, but it was nice to know someone cared.

We were chosen as heralds for the advancing horde because our bad-weather flying experience was great and presumably we could find our way without much help. Once, surrounded by foul weather and thwarted for position by a mix-up in the signal code being used in Iceland, I was obliged to make a nerve-wracking descent at night to within fifty feet of the ocean. Even Johnson paled, and Sommers, who held his hand on the trailing antenna "fish" to make sure it hit the ocean before we did, swore magnificent oaths to cover his anxiety. Not until later when the lights of Reykjavik made a joyous appearance along the black horizon did I balance the importance of our mission against the frustrating risk of our lives. Our load was office files and wastebaskets for the pencil-pusher military, but there were also many boxes of toilet paper.

When finally we landed and saw the toilet paper safely off-loaded, we trudged to a nearby quonset hut and lay down fully clothed upon the rumpled bunks left by a preceding crew. Thirty hours had passed since our last sleep in Presque Isle and we had come a long way without seeing much of anything except the gloomy fjords of Greenland and at the very end of the journey, the heartening lights of Reykjavik. We were too weary for hunger, our mouths were stale, and our eyes sore from tobacco smoke and too long concentration on instruments. Yet we were so grateful for our timely deliverance from a dangerous situation we still could not sleep.

As we entered the quonset, leaning against the hard Icelandic wind, the gray of dawn was already more than a hint. Inside it was dark and a stinking oil stove was so hot its sides were a glowing pink. We turned down the stove, flopped like gaffed fish onto the nearest bunks, and stared at the curvature of the hut which arced above our grubby faces. The stove tinked continuously as it cooled, and listening to it I assessed what we had accomplished since leaving our peaceful little town in Maine. Office files, wastebaskets, and toilet paper? It might have seemed easier to risk our necks and accept fatigue if our burden had been howitzers, ammunition, or bandages to mend the torn. Or would it have been? Smiling at the corrugated metal arc above, I said with due solemnity, "This is war, men."

The winds of September drove us from the longer flights over the Atlantic, not for lack of human resolve, but because once east of Greenland, our little aircraft simply could not return against the equinoctial gales, or loaded to even a fraction of efficiency might not survive the increasing presence of ice aloft. A handful of us then were called back to New York and almost immediately sent off to the airbase at Smyrna, Tennessee, for transition training in four-engined aircraft. It was typical of war's complex untidiness that the best way to deliver us to our destination was by slow train.

The novelty of surface travel palled after only a few hours and the journey took nearly two days. Our training took one. None of us had ever flown a four-engined aircraft before, yet except for a certain ponderousness because of size, we experienced little trouble in making the transition. "An airplane is an airplane. Lead me to it and I'll fly it."

We left Smyrna in high spirits, comforted in the thought we would now lose only twenty-five percent of our power rather than fifty percent if one engine failed. This ratio was akin to a bank account and we preferred to be rich men. What we did not realize was that our training had been in B-24 *bombers*, in fine weather, and their brute strength did not lead us to suppose that the type would fly much differently with heavy loads. Somehow we missed any chance to fly the B-24s at night, much less shoot a few landings.

It would not have made a great deal of difference. The four-engined aircraft we were soon to fly to and from the war were C-87s, a sick relation of the B-24 Liberator. An old saying held true—"An airplane flies like it looks." When loaded, the C-87 bore a haunting resemblance to a harpooned whale.

Afterward I had some days to become reacquainted with my family. My son George and I tried to repair the countless signs of neglect about the *Uncle Sam*. It pleased me greatly to observe George going about the little tasks assigned him as if the boat's survival was his sole concern, and I told him he would one day be a great sailor.

The twins had hardly missed me because of Eleanor's faithful devotion, but I saw now how deeply the loss of our baby had wounded her. She was shockingly thin and complained of arthritic pains in her hands. I thought unwisely, if it pleases her to extoll again and again this doctor's opinion and that doctor's brilliance then I will listen, at least for the little time until I fly away again. Yet I complied with only half one ear. Winter had come to the North Atlantic. All except my body had already left to join it.

Chapter 24

The blizzards came down from Hudson Bay and northern Quebec with stunning ferocity. These storms are living things with a stubborn inclination to sashay between Maine and Labrador, dawdle along the very courses we were obliged to fly, and make our bases as different from what we had known in summertime as rocks to butterflies. I pitied the mechanics who worked on our aircraft. With the temperatures hanging from zero to fifty below, they suffered grievously. They could work for only minutes at a time, then would come into the warm operations office where we stood easily sucking nicotine and caffeine to pass the time; they would arrive from the frozen white world outside bundled in various garments which made each man appear thrice his natural girth and they would rub at the frozen mucus around their nostrils and touch speculatively at their flaming cheeks and noses, testing for frostbite. I never heard one mechanic complain of his miserable environment, although many of us in the flight crews, spoiled beyond cure, were sometimes given to bitterness. The language of both parties was impolite, the weary, overabused, descriptive adverbs and adjectives of muleteers in any war.

"They forgot to put the fucking crew lunches aboard on my last flight. . . ."

"The goddamned heaters were never designed for these temperatures. . . ."

"The goddamned toilet got stinking so bad on the last trip I wanted to bail out. Twenty-seven guys back in the cabin, all ate something that must have been still alive. . . ."

We soon developed a profound respect for the Maritime provinces in winter. Our bases at Gander and St. John's * were not nearly so cold, but were frequently wrapped in heavy fog and were thus poor refuges when we needed them most. Our usual choice then was to the north and into the extreme cold. There, at least, we usually found better flying weather.

While we all sympathized with the mechanics, we couldn't resist speculating on our own miseries if by rotten chance we were forced to land short of our destinations. If it happened over the sea we knew the answer and therefore the possibility was discussed only in jest. It would be nearly impossible to make a successful ditching of our clumsy aircraft on the usual North Atlantic waves. The hours of actual daylight were now very few, thus decreasing our chances of passing a miracle. Yet good pilots are born with self-confidence and there was always

* Stephenville on Newfoundland was not yet fully operational.

pure human hope to spur our imaginations. We carried life rafts now and assorted emergency equipment the pessimists said was not worth the penalty of its weight. The optimists thought if all went well after a ditching in even a moderate sea, healthy men might last two or three hours. The pessimists said we would never get out of the airplane before it sank.

When we had nothing else to distract us, we also wondered about our chances if we went down in the winterland wilderness—providing we survived the landing. One of our still-few company found out.

During the first days of February 1943, men were fighting and dying in relatively small areas of the earth. The RAF was doing its utmost to obliterate German cities, but American bombers had not yet arrived to assist in any force. After heavy losses in North Africa, American troops were finally on the offensive with the British Eighth Army against a retreating Rommel. The Russians were slaughtering the remnants of German divisions that had marched to freeze in the rubble of Stalingrad. Our flying mule train had brought up an infinitesimal part of the manifold military needs in England, but worthy or not, our attention was almost totally absorbed in outwitting the constant challenges of Arctic winter, and we were discovering the even more vicious *sub*-Arctic weather.

In appearance and personality O'Connor was almost a caricature of what a veteran pilot was supposed to look like. His gray hair was a bristle brush and his pale blue eyes sparkled beneath a pair of bushy gray eyebrows. His face was ruddy and well pickled by some twenty thousand hours' exposure to the elements aloft and there was a hint of County Cork in his hearty speech. He laughed easily and frequently, presenting an irresistible father-image to stewardesses and passengers alike during his domestic airline days. Despite his relatively great age and seniority, which would have enabled O'Connor to remain in a comfortable flying assignment throughout the war, he had been among the very first to join our unique pack train. Only his innate fondness for petty intrigue kept him human and us from planting him on too high a pedestal.

The villain was a storm originating in the very far north, beyond those vague territories over which the meteorologists were so fond of drawing prophetic swirls. The mass of air came down through the Belcher Islands of Hudson Bay and from Cape Sandy, deployed its awesome forces along the Great Whale River, and soon overwhelmed untold thousands of miles of frozen tundra and lakes, a wilderness disdained even by Eskimos.

O'Connor had taken off from Presque Isle bound for Bluie West 8,* our northernmost base in Greenland. His flight, in one of our few mechanically healthy C-87s, would require eight hours. He would deliver goods of the highest priority to Bluie West 8 and return with seventeen passengers, most of whom were sick or injured.

The flight north was routine and after flying all night O'Connor and his crew were entitled to a rest. Later, we could not understand why they chose to linger only long enough for a hot meal, then loaded, refueled, and took off for Presque Isle. O'Connor was a stubborn man and as tough in spirit as he was soft in heart. Perhaps he wanted to prove that his age was no deterrent to his endurance, since by the time of actual departure from northern Greenland he had already been on flight duty for at least twelve hours. Unlike our primitive C-47s, there were no places for rest in a loaded C-87 even if O'Connor had felt the need. Once airborne on the return flight, he faced another nine or ten hours of demanding duty.

Perhaps O'Connor had been advised of the approaching storm by a wary meteorologist at Bluie West 8, or being weatherwise had smelled its approach and intended to outflank it. Perhaps the condition of one of his passengers appealed to his sense of mercy and influenced his judgment. Whatever the cause of his action, O'Connor, who had always thought himself indomitable, was about to be given a lesson in true might. His weapons were few, and those most handy were not to be trusted. As yet none of us knew very much about the behavior of a C-87 in bad weather. By the time O'Connor met his antagonist both he and his crew were weary, a serious handicap to even the most expert warriors.

O'Connor's radio operator, a man who had left the Merchant Marine because he had been twice torpedoed and thought our operation safer, got off a single plea during the afternoon that was already night. The message

* Now Sondre Strom Fjord.

was garbled, but ominous: ". . . am picking up ice . . . turning northwest . . ." Then there was nothing more.

Northwest? If O'Connor was anywhere between Bluie West 8 and Presque Isle, then flying a northwest course would take him to the beginning of nowhere. There was only a tremendous wilderness unexplored by any man. In fact, having once locked with his enemy, O'Connor had no other choice but immediate retreat. The only exit lay behind him.

Boyd, with yet another promotion, was now at Presque Isle. He called us to him just after one glorious winter dawn, for during the night the storm had only brushed across the lands south of the St. Lawrence and left the sky unsoiled. We came from the old hotel a few at a time: Thomas, who looked hardly old enough to be a co-pilot let alone in command of an aircraft; Catchings, baldheaded and audibly out of place with his marked Southern accent; and Wynn, a dynamic pilot from Chicago whose natural restlessness had wrenched him from the comfort of the domestic line and brought him to our frozen aerie. Bundled in leather and fur, laughing at Catchings's amazement at hearing snow squeak beneath his flying boots, we entered Boyd's overheated office. There, since he knew us from the line, he greeted us carefully by name and told us O'Connor was down ". . . somewhere. Apparently he iced up and turned northwest."

"Where is somewhere?"

Boyd pulled down a large roller map and we gathered around him while Vaughan, a major with more knowledge of the Arctic than any of us, speculated on O'Connor's problems if he was still alive. If he had survived a landing, then where was he? Certainly, we agreed, he would not continue on a northwest heading until he ran out of fuel or nearly so. Calculating backward from his time of departure from Bluie West 98 and the time of the garbled message, he would still have more than four hours' fuel remaining. What would *we* do given the same unpleasantness? We were all of a similar opinion; we would head for the sea as soon as possible, let down over the warmer ocean air, and hope to melt away our load of ice. Even if the temperature at fifty or one hundred feet were freezing, and the ice refused to leave, the C-87 would fly better at very low altitude. A few feet above the sea there would be nothing to hinder flight, not even an iceberg since it was out of season for their migrations. And the German submarines presumably had more important targets than faltering C-87s.

Thus, full of confidence, secretly excited at this break in our routine, we took off into the cut-crystal morning bound for the Maritimes, where logic told us O'Connor must have landed unless he was so unfortunate as to be down in the sea. If that were so then yet another of our clan would be lost forever.

We were four aircraft flying in loose formation until we came upon the Maritimes. Then we spread out to give us greater coverage of the rugged terrain below. It was nearly noon, the pallid sun was at our tails, and the visibility unlimited. The temperature at our altitude was only fifteen below zero and the air of such unusual clarity for the Maritimes I thought when we came upon O'Connor we would actually be able to see the details of his face.

The sun passed its timid zenith, which was no more than thirty degrees above the horizon, and during the time we had flown over areas where O'Connor might conceivably have gone down we had "found" him several times. Yet each sighting had proved to be a copse of wood similar in shape to an airplane, or a gash in a hill, or a formation of stones deceptive to our eager eyes.

Then a message came from Presque Isle telling of a new and somewhat garbled announcement from O'Connor:

AM ON A LAKE FIVE MILES LONG APPROXIMATELY FOUR HUNDRED MILES NORTH ST. LAWRENCE ON A COURSE OF THREE HUNDRED THIRTY DEGREES. ALL WELL. NO INJURIES. URGENTLY REQUIRE FOOD AND SUPPLIES.

Our ecstasy at learning O'Connor and his crowd had survived was soon overcome by shock. O'Connor had indeed flown his aircraft into the middle of nowhere. Our charts of the area were blank of any feature except the word UNEXPLORED.

334

Catchings checked our remaining fuel even as I banked our little C-47 toward the northwest.

"We can give it a try."

"How long to dry tanks?"

"Another seven hours, possibly eight. We should be able to make it where he says he is and back to Montreal ... just."

Just? Yet there was no hesitation in our going. We did not trouble ourselves to even discuss postponement. Night would soon be upon us, O'Connor's second night in the wilderness. In the back of our airplanes were all the things he needed. No other compulsion was necessary, nor did heroics enter our heads. The finding of O'Connor immediately became an irresistible challenge to all except an Army captain flying one of the other aircraft. On the radio he pleaded a shortage of fuel for such an extension of our enterprise and we waved him away without regrets since he was not truly one of us.

Greatly encouraged by the weather, we flew off the charted areas and by midafternoon had slipped into the unknown. Then little by little, hour after hour, as fuel and time expired together, we began to realize the size of our task. Nothing was as we supposed it would be.

Eventually we came upon a considerable range of mountains, sheer white and rumpled beneath the snow pack. They extended across our course from horizon to horizon; lacking any indication on our charts, we drew them roughly across the blank area where we thought we were and named them the Wynn Mountains after the pilot from Chicago. One bold and particularly bald peak we named Mount Catchings. A frozen cascade became Boyd Falls and a river was dubbed Cotton Blossom Creek after Johnson, my co-pilot. We were solemn about the printing and drawing of these details on our virginal charts, abashed at the notion that we must be the first human beings ever to look down upon this frozen world. O'Connor, we decided, must have been on instruments at night when he passed the same way and we wondered what sort of Irish luck or divine miracle could have led a blind man beyond these mountains without smashing against them.

We continued on another hour, holding low lest we fly over O'Connor without seeing him. Once beyond the

Wynn Mountains we watched the feeble sun turn pink while the sky above remained cobalt. Their reflected light transformed the gigantic snowscape below into an elegant carnival of subtle coloring, the treetops nearly orange and the thousands of frozen lakes between a submarine blue. Again and again we thought we saw the shape of an airplane, but always the cry of "There! . . . There!" became a despondent, "Ah shit . . . no."

We knew O'Connor's radio must still be functional so we sent out frequent warnings of our approach and asked him to build a smoking fire. We listened also for his small hand-cranked "Gibson Girl" emergency transmitter, hoping if his main batteries were down, we could at least take a bearing on him. From plane to plane we gossiped laconically for fear our own transmissions might blanket any word from O'Connor.

"Heard anything?"

"Nope."

"The outside air needle is against the peg."

"So is mine. I thought it was broken. That's forty below."

"What course are you flying?"

"God knows. The compass goes right around while the nose stays put."

A long silence imperfect only because of the steady rumble of our engines. Then, as if to seek reassurance from the presence of another plane, "How's your fuel?"

"Getting down there. We can't stay much longer."

Again the silence, not even a crackle of static in our headphones.

"Hear anything?"

"Nope."

A twilight that should have been a pure and glorious show now became a session of nervous responses to all the local news. Where were we? We really did not know. Multiplying airspeed by time we could make a guess at our distance north of the St. Lawrence, but we had only a vague count on the wind. How high? Our eyes told us we were *about* five thousand feet above the ground, but with no setting for our altimeters we could be off a thousand feet either way. Or, considering the temperatures, perhaps more. Our course? We had tried with all our will to fly three hundred and thirty degrees, hoping to follow O'Connor's track as closely as possible, but our compasses had long gone crazy. We wandered, relying on instinct, although we knew the human instrument was not to be trusted. There was nothing else.

"Hear anything at all?"

"Not a sound."

Another of our planes turned back for want of fuel. There remained the two of us holding on just a little bit longer. Just.

"If I have our fuel figured right, we should give up now."

I looked at Catchings, his face bronze in the last of the light and his nose purple with the cold. Although operating at full blast our heaters were totally inadequate to the temperatures outside and even within we guessed the cockpit was near zero. Immobile as so many stuffed quail we found our clumsy sheepskin and leather poor protection against the gnawing cold. We shook sometimes as if we had the ague, yet visions of O'Connor, possibly without any heat at all, reduced our complaints to almost nil.

We looked until our eyes ached, trying very hard to scan every lake below. But there were thousands of lakes scraped away by million-year-old glaciers, and most appeared "about five miles long." When we were not looking out and down we stole quick glances at the fuel gauges and remade estimates of our endurance. We persuaded ourselves termination time would come simultaneously with darkness, a risky estimate we knew, contrived in hope that a signal would come from O'Connor at the very last instant.

Our sense of minuteness in unlimited space became ever more acute; we were such puny little creatures fluttering like moths across this enormous frozen snowscape.

At last, after mutual lying and self-deceit concerning our fuel, came agreement. Very well, we must turn back. The sky was still luminous and a few pallid stars were visible if not yet twinkling, but the earth below had already been shaded in the night. I banked in a wide turn for Montreal and climbed to a higher altitude, hoping to avoid hitting mountains no one had apparently known existed. All of this, I thought as we reached to join the stars, for a war that must be waging light-years away and upon another planet.

After refueling at Montreal and warming our bones we set off again for Presque Isle where we landed soon after midnight. We reported our failure to Boyd and listened sullenly while the Army captain who had long ago deserted the hunt expressed his theories on the whereabouts of O'Connor. To us he looked warm and bathed and overfed, but we were too weary for argument. It is the theorists who will inherit the world, I decided. We had been in the air almost fifteen freezing hours and had nearly forgotten when last we slept.

Soon after the following dawn we wriggled into our ponderous armor of fur and leather, and stomped across the packed snow to our aircraft. The weather held fine if incredibly cold, the few reporting stations along the St. Lawrence recording sixty below zero. Wherever O'Connor was, we knew it must be colder. Now bound at least for a specific area, we again named new natural features for various of our crews and were pleased we did not have to include the Army captain, who, this time claiming a mechanical difficulty with his aircraft, aborted the mission. In the late evening we returned to Presque Isle empty-handed.

We were trying to explain to an anxious Boyd how random our searching had been: ". . . none of us knows where the hell we've really been. Our compasses go wild once we get beyond those mountains, which aren't even supposed to exist. We just kept going as long as we could, never heard a sound out of O'Connor, and came home."

Home? This dreary military base locked in a hard winter had now become home? Most of us were sitting on the floor, our backs to the pounding radiators, trying to recapture warmth for our blood. Boyd, who because of his thoughtfulness we now considered as sitting on the right hand of God, had furthered the process by providing us with paper cups and a bottle of whiskey. Our bodies melted to its stimulation, but our frustration remained.

"There isn't anything you can get an honest fix on up there. It all looks exactly alike. After five hours' flying we could be fifty miles either side of the target and never know it."

While we were grumbling and speculating, the message

came. O'Connor had been found alive! Watkins, a handsome man who had shared life in the Chicago co-pilot school with me and who would soon perish against a rocky hill in Newfoundland, had been searching due westward out of Goose Bay. In the last of the evening light he had stumbled on a lake and there was O'Connor sending up flares. He had just time to drop supplies and with the very last of his fuel beat a hasty retreat to Goose Bay.

We were excited beyond measure until Boyd brought out the cruel twist in the message. Watkins frankly confessed he was ignorant of his actual position when he found O'Connor. He was just so many hours and minutes west of Goose Bay. Remembering what we had seen of the territory, we thought O'Connor might as well be on the moon.

The next morning we took off once more bound for the same vague destination, although our spirits were higher in the knowledge that we were looking for living friends. Our most optimistic calculations allowed us only an hour over the search area before we must turn away for civilization. The only available C-87, the airplane we needed the most because of its longer endurance, was on a lake with O'Connor.

We returned from that day having failed again. Watkins, still operating out of Goose Bay, retraced his flight path, to no avail. He could not find where he had been.

We were now convinced we might pass right over O'Connor and fail to see him unless he built a great fire and poured oil from his engines into the flames. We wondered if oil would become a solid at such temperatures. Our own engines were behaving with nerve-wracking unpredictability. Despite the absolutely clear air they would gradually lose power and in such cold we could not raise enough carburetor heat to cure the trouble. We hand-pumped alcohol to the carburetors, a job normally assigned to co-pilots if only to keep them humble. Now we were all pleased to take over the labor. The exercise was warming and the pungent aroma of alcohol somehow seemed to warm our lungs.

The next day the same, but now a new and frightful development compounded our discouragement. Another great storm came screaming down from the end of the world and we had a hard flight home. The blizzard struck Presque Isle during midafternoon and by the time of our late-evening arrival the visibility was less than half a mile and the runway was covered with a foot of snow.

We thought O'Connor's Irish luck must have run out, for the tempest persisted three days, obliterating everything on the northeastern part of the continent including. the very shape of most airports. We fretted and swore and watched the horizontal lines of snow sweep past our hotel windows. I fiddled with the oils and brushes which were not my off-duty solace, but succeeded only in ruining what had promised to be a reasonably good portrait of Dunn, one of our original ten captains in the North. My thoughts along with those of all the others were with O'Connor, who must be suffering terribly in winds with a chill factor of eighty below or more, and possibly starving. We were not very optimistic about his chances of survival.

As the weather cleared, a C-87 arrived for our use. By chance I became its commander and with Wynn and Beattie as extra pilots we urged the aerial pachyderm into the air and turned north. Late that afternoon we picked up a signal from O'Connor on the direction-finder and homed on it until directly ahead we saw flares ascending and the faint blue smoke from a fire.

I was appalled. O'Connor's C-87, belly deep in snow, had been of familiar dimensions in my mind's eye. Now the vast panorama reduced it to a gnat, a pitiful little insect which on its own would never have caught our eyes. Even in descent, homing straight toward it, we had trouble picking it out against the shoreline of the lake. And now we knew how very wrong O'Connor had been in reporting his position originally. He was two hundred miles farther north than he thought.

We gave O'Connor and his charges a low pass, climbed in a steep chandelle, and began calling in all the other search aircraft. In less than an hour they were swarming over the lake and supplies were raining down on the castaways.

Captain Fred Lord of Northwest Airlines decided to land his C-47 and begin an evacuation. It was a brave but fruitless attempt. We watched while his aircraft glided down to the lake and disappeared in a cloud of snow. Moments later we heard Lord's voice in our earphones. "I'm stuck!"

Now there were more mouths to feed.

We turned away, content in accomplishment. Now, we agreed, it would be merely a matter of dropping enough equipment to make a runway on the ice. Since a considerable number of Canadian as well as American aircraft had been assembled, we were sure O'Connor would have enough to keep him going.

Whether from weariness or overconfidence, something went wrong with our resolve on the following day. Once again the C-87 was mine and we hovered over Presque Isle while a covey of loaded C-47s took off to follow in our wake.

Although the morning appeared benign from the ground, we were soon disillusioned by an extraordinary natural phenomenon. Hardly had we reached cruising altitude when we encountered rougher air than any of us had ever known. The violence present between the snow and the grudging sun was difficult to believe. The twin tails of C-87s always twisted back and forth in even minor turbulence and it was often our fancy to jest about their alleged strength, but now humor was shaken from us. Flying at a slow enough speed to remain near the C-47s, the bigger aircraft became an almost unmanageable beast. I dreaded wrestling with it for the next ten hours.

The first to turn back was again our redoubtable Army captain. We were snide about his departure, but were soon ourselves considering retreat. Normally in very cold weather and under clear skies the air is smooth, or nearly so; now we were flying in a bubbling cauldron of fierce up-and-down drafts of even greater vertical velocity than the thunderstorms of Tennessee and Ohio. For the first time since I had been flying, I became concerned about the structural integrity of an aircraft.

The wind saved our faces. By the time we had the St. Lawrence in sight we were able to calculate its unfavorable effect upon our cruising range. We could not reach O'Connor against such a blast and return with any margin of fuel. We turned back sheepishly and somewhat bewildered. We, who had strutted so arrogantly through years of atrocious weather, now turned tail and ran for home on a perfectly clear day. Boyd was understandably dismayed at our early reappearance. Had his shock troops been poisoned by a mere Army captain whose timidity record had always irked him? I avoided Boyd's eyes.

My shame stimulated me into greater effort if only because I had nursed a secret which I had not the courage to share with the others. The fateful flight to Bluie West 8 had actually been scheduled in my name and we were disappointed when O'Connor had exerted his seniority and taken it away, leaving for us only a short trip to Goose Bay. In a childish temper I had left O'Connor a note he could not fail to see before take-off. "Thanks for the bone, you old bastard. Have a nice long trip."

Had I put some kind of a curse on him? A long trip, indeed. My displeasure and envy had cooled in the very air that might now be freezing a fine flying man. Now I fretted continuously over our helplessness.

We were still by no means confident we could find Lac O'Connor again, even though we plotted the general area with what we hoped had been some degree of accuracy. The trouble was in our long cruise north and our inability to hold an honest course. The few visual fixes we had established were too similar and sometimes obscured by cloud. Thus our position en route, whether to the right or left of course, was always in doubt. Daylight was another factor, rather surprisingly adverse. The smoke from O'Connor's fire had been very difficult to see in broad daylight and his flares lost brilliance against the sunlit snow. We had drawn a crude outline of the lake on our empty charts; the problem was rediscovering it.

By now McIntosh's teachings had matured and we had considerable practical experience in celestial navigation. I found the whole ceremony of employing the heavens fascinating, and had taken some good-natured gaff from others because of my addiction. Simply by practicing at every opportunity, I had become reasonably accurate in plotting a small triangle based on my observations and could thus with some consistency fix my position within five miles. If I cheated just a little I could make a very pretty triangle indeed and it always gave me a strange thrill to tap the crossed lines of position with a grubby finger and announce, "There, by God, right *there* is where we are." The stars and planets and the sun had become my confidants and I thought of them fondly as of dependable friends.

I was somewhat miffed at my comrades who rarely shared my trust; therefore I went to Boyd in trepidation. "If we went up to O'Connor at night I could make continuous star fixes all along the way and maybe stay on track. If we planned to arrive just after dawn we could see his flares much better. . . ." I told Boyd how with any luck I could put us within five miles of any location.

"With luck and a little judicious fudging you might be able to tell whether you're over the Pacific or the Atlantic. You're crazy, but I'll show you what happens to volunteers."

The following night I found myself leading a formation of four airplanes, the others manned by friends more willing than wise.

My prayer for a miracle was answered on schedule. Just after dawn we saw flares rocketing up from the gloom ahead and our direction-finder needles were homing steadily on O'Connor's emergency transmitter. We had him hooked now. We knew where he was and where we were. For this lucky affair and later involvements some of us were bonged with a medal. As often happens in such cases, we were possibly the least deserving.

O'Connor had done a magnificent job getting his airplane down unharmed and afterward preserving his crew and passengers against final disaster. He kept them together and nourished their morale while they lived on chocolate bars and owl soup and fought the agonizing cold. Later a runway was cleared across the ice, O'Connor and his people were evacuated, and Lord's aircraft flown out. Nearly a month after O'Connor's perilous night landing, Wynn flew the C-87 out and back to civilization. It was undamaged and subsequently saw service over the Hump between India and China. So also did O'Connor's luckless radio operator. Flying the Hump with Hunt, one of our veteran pilots, he was obliged to bail out of a C-87 and after landing in the wild mountains hiked for days through jungle to civilization. Hunt himself was even less lucky. After ordering his crew to jump, he chose to ride his ship down. He landed in a rice paddy, smashed against a dike, and was killed. I dedicated my first novel to his memory.

Chapter 25

Soon after O'Connor was rescued, I was assigned as an instructor in four-engined aircraft. I was chosen only for want of better candidates since my total experience in such aircraft amounted to barely a hundred flying hours. The incongruity of my appointment was exaggerated by the status of my students, nearly all of whom were airmen senior to me and of vastly greater flying experience. The classroom was a C-87 operating out of La Guardia Field, with many of our exercises taking place over Long Island and sometimes Manhattan itself. Looking down at Broadway while my students went through the rather demanding drill of cutting first one engine and then a second on the same side, and various other emergency procedures, it was impossible to believe I had ever had anything to do with the lighted marquees below.

As long as my nerves held out the work was easy— usually no more than four or five hours aloft each day with arms folded while giving advice and criticism to my betters. If my instruction was at night I would have the next morning to myself and I promptly made up for lost time in both pleasure and accomplishment. Part of my energies went into the writing of a novel about the rescue of a downed aviator and his crew in the Arctic, a not too difficult feat of imagination since my fingers still chilled at the thought of the locale, and in real life I was frequently encountering many of the principal characters.

When the book was finished I displayed a singular lack of invention by entitling it *Position Unknown*, then took it to McIntosh and Otis, the agency which had placed my first three nonfiction efforts and which handled Steinbeck. Mildred Lyman of the agency took the novel to Viking Press where a Hungarian named Pat Covici presided as editor. It was a natural connection since Covici was Steinbeck's editor.

"Don't worry," Elizabeth Otis said. "If it doesn't go

344

at Viking we'll try another publisher." While I worried I changed the title to *Island in the Sky*.

The novel went no farther than Viking, which paid me three thousand dollars in advance. Covici did not think any changes in the manuscript were necessary.

Overwhelmed by new prosperity we took a house on the water at Old Greenwich, Connecticut, and moved the *Uncle Sam* to an anchorage visible from the front porch. What war? Only the local butcher reminded us of the distant conflict. To impress him I would often make a low pass over the new house with all four engines at full throttle. Although my pull-up altitude was approximately one hundred feet and my more conservative students were inclined to squirm, the neighbors never complained.

At home there were interesting developments, although my parental behavior was extremely casual. First, daughter Polly pushed her twin brother out of the second-story window. After bouncing off the slanting porch roof he landed shaken but undamaged on the front lawn. A few days later Steven pushed his twin sister out of the same window with identical results. The same week, with only son George, now age seven, aboard, I ran the *Uncle Sam* aground when I failed to heed his advice. I was finding the home front bristling with difficulties.

There is a fine line between foolhardiness and dashing into the breach with any real expectation of coming out the other side. Likewise, as my father was fond of insisting, "Some people just don't know when they're well off."

Since I had not thus far been responsible for any damage to a type of aircraft everyone agreed was a beast, I could presumably have stayed at my instructing for the duration of the war. Except for the occasional thrills when something went awry, it was thought "nice work if you survive."* Conveniently, at this time in my flying career I had reached such a euphoric stage I even doubted my mortality.

I also presently discovered that it was tolerable to play

* Until the use of ground-fixed simulators in large aircraft training, almost every conceivable emergency had to be practiced as in real life. The resulting loss of pilots' lives was out of all proportion to other air calamities.

the family man, and for the moment at least did my best to excel in the role. Eleanor, whose wisdom in certain matters was nearly clairvoyant, was not convinced I would long remain domesticated and she was proven right. I made no protest whatever when I was ordered to give up instructing and transfer to Natal in Brazil. There, I knew, was the promise of action.

Natal was geographically significant because it is situated like an ugly mole on the fat hip of South America, thereby representing the closest point to the even plumper butt of Africa.

Our clumsy C-87s were transferred there because they could not stay in the North Atlantic sky once the winds of winter blew. We discovered soon enough how their vaunted Davis wing would not carry enough ice to chill a bucket of champagne.

The South Atlantic between the bulges of Africa and South America is a benign ocean, an empty expanse of bland winds and almost continuously amiable weather. Ascension Island, conveniently about halfway between the continents, provided an ideal refueling stop. It is a volcanic rock, uncared for since discovery, adored by all whose weary eyes spotted it after a long night suspended between stars and ocean. It is not very big, but the word was, "You can't miss it because it's the only thing out there."

American engineers turned the rock into a fine refueling station and thereby made our African flights possible. The routing was simple and the flying placid after the North Atlantic.

Normally, a crew took off from Natal in late evening, which was not so easy. Part of the problem was the C-87's inborn reluctance to leave the ground when heavily loaded, part the necessity for instant transfer to solid instrument flight once the last runway light slipped beneath the nose. For beyond the perimeter of the airfield there was not so much as the flicker of a candle nor would there be, we knew, for at least thirteen hundred nautical miles. At less than a hundred feet over the Brazilian jungle with all four engines ripping the black night apart, we could expect to engage a high decibel rain squall. Given the morguelike hue of our primitive cockpit lights these moments were humbling and it was not uncommon for the entire crew to strain upward against their seat belts in an attempt to shake the lethargy from the altimeter needles. Very fortunately the surrounding area was flat, and not far beyond lay the ocean.

My own crews were cursed with an additional mental hazard. I loathe wasting time and have always been nearly incapable of relaxation in the usual sense. I cannot lie on a beautiful beach in the sunlight for more than three minutes without trying to accomplish something and, recognizing this fault, have always tried to compensate. I have never been bored in flight, but once returned to earth I inevitably commence an embittered counting of wasted minutes. As a distraction I had bought a concertina, which eased my own barracks boredom between flights, and my performance with it soon became part of our flight procedure. After the regular take-off checklist had been run through I would render an appropriate few bars of "Scots Awa'" or "Home on the Range." If I finished without a mistake we fancied the flight would be routine; if I faltered then something was certain to go wrong. During the long idle hours en route we managed to twist the facts until the relationship seemed half true and by the time we reported to Natal even my crew felt reassured at the sight of the leather box just aft of my left rudder pedal.

"Can't you just put the box there and not really play it?" navigator LaFrenier pleaded. In reply he received my best pearls-before-swine look.

Out of Natal for Africa we were usually five in the crew. Captain, co-pilot, navigator, radio operator, and engineer. The two pilots sat side by side with the fine view forward obscured only by the C-87's great brown snout. The roof was clear plexiglass, but our view upward was limited. The harsh tropical sun had already turned the plexiglass a tobacco-juice yellow, and grease, tools, dirt, sand, and mechanics' shoes had contributed to the overall cobweb of scratches and left little of the original transparency. Since we had no expectation of attack from any direction we rarely looked up.

The navigator worked at a small desk directly behind the captain. Opposite the navigator was the radio operator's position—a tiny esoteric region the rest of us avoided because all radio operators were regarded with a bewildering mixture of affection and awe. Lost in capacitors, diodes, and resistors, their utter failure to communicate with ordinary human beings was accepted as a fact of aerial life. We only prayed they would maintain communication with the earth beneath us, especially when we needed vital information.

The engineers were chosen from the ranks of mechanics at the lines' peacetime bases, young men of relatively little experience, but with compensating eagerness and will. Their position was in the corner of the flight deck behind the navigator. The good Catholics among them hung a crucifix over their jumpseats, which sometimes caused us to wonder if they knew more than we did.

With such willing support I persuaded a C-87 to leave the earth at Natal one black night, our take-off marred by a total blackout of the sickly blue cockpit lighting at the exact instant we became airborne. I should have taken at least some cue from the name painted along the C-87's nose, *Gremlin's Castle*.

I never knew what kept the *Gremlin's Castle* in anything near a straight-line climb while co-pilot Bigsbee, whom I had warned to keep his flashlight handy, twisted and turned and fumbled in the total darkness.

"Hurry! Get some light on things!"

I was holding firmly to the control yoke as a matter of habit. At least I was doing something while this so-called flying machine charged into the void like a bad-tempered rhino. Outside it was absolutely black—inside it was the same. It was as if I had suddenly been struck blind with all other senses left intact. By their sound alone I knew the engines were in fine agreement but I longed to know the two most important bits of information attendant to any take-off. How fast? How high? It was vital to know if we were climbing too slowly, a possibility denied by the sweaty seat of my pants. We must have *some* altitude since we had thus far failed to collide with anything. In the "nice-to-know" category was our flight attitude: were we in a bank and turning?

"I can't find my flashlight!" Bigsbee sounded ready to cry, but I did not yet know that the real mourners would be the rest of us in the crew after enduring far too much of Bigsbee's awkward assistance.

After some very long minutes a light blossomed between Bigsbee and myself, flittered wildly across the darkness, and settled on the instrument panel. It was Hogarty's, the engineer's flashlight, which he had dug out of his flight kit.

"Thank you," I said in a tone intended as much to restore my own confidence as to reassure the others. Now the instruments told me we were in good shape, climbing through four hundred feet with one hundred and forty on the airspeed. Bigsbee was still at his contortions, looking for his flashlight.

With enough information to hold things for a while and helped by the sight of a few stars ahead I told Hogarty to use his light in search of the basic trouble. Almost at once he found a guilty circuit breaker and the flight deck came alive again. Now with the maximum illumination available Bigsbee found his flashlight in the metal box beside his seat—right where it should be. "But I looked in there . . . first thing," he said.

If the incident had occurred two weeks later I would have thought: Of course. Anything necessary to the daily chores of flight, officer Bigsbee runs away and hides. If it is a razor, Bigsbee will try to cut down a tree, and if it is a map of Africa he will be looking for Tokyo.

If there had been the slightest repentance in Bigsbee's voice then we might have jested with him and forgotten, but Bigsbee took himself very seriously and his manner usually suggested that he was performing a favor by gracing us with his company. He was, on first meeting, a pleasant personality, although his youthful beauty was somewhat tarnished by a pot-belly, the fleshfolds of self-indulgence about his jaw, and a tendency to perspire abnormally.

The flight should have been a plum and we were much envied by other crews. The entire cabin of the *Gremlin's Castle* was stacked to the roof with Chinese money wrapped in heavy oilpaper packages: payment for Chinese troops and guerrillas who were at this time still engaged in desultory and not very successful operations against the Japanese. My assignment was beautiful in its simplicity. Deliver the money. How, by what routing, and when, was mine to resolve. It was like giving a drunkard the key to the saloon—or should have been. I dreamed of diverting to some undiscovered paradise and settling down as the big chief.

The flight from Natal to Ascension Island and thence to Accra on the Gold Coast of Africa took seventeen hours and seven minutes. We took off at night and arrived at night, having known during this flight only one aeronautical anxiety, part mechanical, and part meteorological.

With usual ugly-duckling grace the C-87 settled to the runway at Ascension Island soon after dawn. The weather had been beautiful once we were away from the South American coast, the stars and galaxies so brilliant their reflections were visible in the black sea below. I congratulated LaFrenier, our navigator, on his night's work. Only a few degrees of course change had been necessary the entire way and we had arrived within two minutes of flight plan.

While the *Gremlin's Castle* was being refueled we brushed our teeth and shaved in the nearest latrine, then went to the mess hall for a breakfast of "battery acid" (canned grapefruit juice), lukewarm "shit on a shingle" (chipped beef on toast), and Force Ten coffee.

Hogarty left the table early to measure the fuel in the tanks with a long stick, since the glass tube gauges on the after bulkhead of the flight deck were notoriously unreliable. On first meeting I had advised Hogarty that I was a very poor swimmer and had no desire to improve.

At breakfast, Bigsbee, who had been notably silent during the night, regaled us with tales of his social and educational background, which, we were led to believe, had been of a distinctly higher caliber than our own. Drowsy from lack of sleep we listened with only half an ear and I wondered how Bigsbee could alone be so exuberant.

The runway at Ascension Island was a marvelous engineering feat, a cut straight through a considerable promontory which extended into the sea. It did have one drawback which gave first-timers moments of near-panic because the degree of slope at the center of the runway was enough to seem outrageous, and all airplanes groaned and grunted and gathered speed with agonizing slowness until reaching the crest. The situation reversed itself as the aircraft started down the far side. Acceleration was so rapid the effect was exhilarating.

According to my custom of sharing take-offs and landings with the co-pilot, I told Bigsbee that this was his moment of glory. Only two years out of the right seat, I had no difficulty remembering the inner joy I had known when my captain announced the take-off would be mine. I was puzzled now at Bigsbee's behavior. His cockiness had evaporated and he seemed preoccupied. "Let's go. It's going to be a long day."

Bigsbee took a deep breath, wiped at the bubbles of sweat which had suddenly appeared above his heavy eyebrows, and eased forward gently on the throttles.

"Go ahead. Kick her in the ass. She's not going to exactly leap in the air anyway."

Hogarty, after a glance from me, placed his hand behind the throttles and with a surreptitious shove got them all the way forward. The *Gremlin's Castle* began to stagger up the slope without the slightest enthusiasm. Although the engines were making a satisfying racket, very little was happening and a half minute passed before we gathered any appreciable speed. Meanwhile Bigsbee was coming unraveled.

One of the many peculiarities of the C-87 was its free-castoring nose-wheel. It turned easily and there was no provision for locking it. Consequently, it took a certain amount of harsh dominance to keep the airplane on a reasonably straight line down the runway. The C-87's obstinate insistence to aim its snout right or left was magnified in inverse proportion to the speed; the slower the pace the less the rudders affected the action, and until the pilot resolved he was the boss, the greater his frustration.

Now, halfway up the slope with hardly thirty miles of airspeed, Bigsbee was leading himself into ever deeper trouble. The take-off procedure for heavily loaded C-87's had been developed after those of us who first flew them had nearly despaired of their ability. Balancing the handicap of propeller cavitation against the dubious nature of the beast, we decided the best and safest way to persuade a C-87 into the air was to stand on the brakes until all four engines were confirmed as giving full power. During those noisy fifteen seconds the C-87 would lower its snout and seem to paw at the earth, a sign we mistook for readiness to fly. The brakes were suddenly released, full rudder control was available thanks to the hurricane blast over the tail surfaces, and the C-87, if not exactly ready to lunge ahead, at least charged off in the desired direction.

Bigsbee had not stood on the brakes long enough and, like the sorcerer's apprentice, was now trying to make amends. The *Gremlin's Castle* sashayed from one side of the runway to the other, defying Bigsbee to make it behave like a real airplane. Since the runway was unusually wide I let events take their course until we reached the crest. In keeping with my code of the good instructor I believed in allowing the student to make his mistakes and then offering help in their correction.

Just before we curved over the hump and started down the other side, Bigsbee was heading full tilt for the right side embankment. All the way up the incline he had been trying to catch up with the C-87's meanderings, using his throttles instead of his legs and unless I did something immediately the results were certain to be catastrophic.

Until this moment I had sat with arms folded, feet on the floor, the customary silent-instructor posture signifying that the other man had full control. Now I slammed my foot hard against the left rudder pedal, easily overpowering Bigsbee. Once over the hump the *Gremlin's Castle* hustled gratefully downslope and apparently, after deciding Bigsbee was not going to do anything except rest his hands on the controls, took off by itself. We began a sickly climb for altitude, then to my astonishment Bigsbee started a gentle right turn toward the west.

"Hey. We're going to Africa." I waggled my thumb over my left shoulder toward the east.

"I know."

"Then why are you turning toward Natal?"

"To gain some altitude."

"Wouldn't it be just as easy to gain altitude aiming in the direction we're going?"

Bigsbee changed his turn to the east, sulked a moment, then said he had turned west because that way he could keep the runway in sight if we had to land immediately; Ascension Island was dominated by a high peak in the center and the way we were now going, he explained, would necessitate our circling the island completely should we suddenly be obliged to land again. I was about to lecture Bigsbee on the value of fuel conservation versus air miles yet ahead and the long day we faced before we sighted Africa, when Hogarty muttered in my ear, "The goddamned right landing gear is not all the way up."

Had any normal pilot been handling the controls he would have noticed the drag created by a hanging gear, but not Bigsbee. At last established on an easterly heading he appeared immensely satisfied with himself and the morning. Good God, I thought, if we do have to go back because of the gear, no one will ever convince Bigsbee his loony theory was wrong. It would not be possible to make Africa with one gear hanging down.

I suggested we might try recycling the gear and Hogarty obliged immediately by slamming down the gear lever. As always in a C-87 there followed a tremendous commotion as if it had just spewed its very guts all over the sky. When the hissing and rumbling had ceased and Bigsbee had barely managed to keep us from falling out of the sky, Hogarty reported the gear down and locked.

"Retract it again."

Hogarty complied. The rumbling and grunting were repeated in reverse order. After a look at both sides from the cabin windows and climbing into the snout for a look at the nosewheel, Hogarty returned to report all components of the gear were up and properly secured. "Gremlins, I guess," he said.

Something, an inner sense developed over the years perhaps, told me that this flight would not be routine. Yet I was reassured by the sight of Parker the radio operator already tapping at his key and LaFrenier the navigator laying out his charts and tools neatly and precisely, the mark of a good navigator. It was a good crew, I thought, easy to get along with and competent in their work. As for my counterpart, who evidently had no idea how a precious few gallons of fuel might be wasted by turning in the wrong direction, I began gloomy speculation as to who would bring the *Gremlin's Castle* back to earth if I were suddenly incapacitated.

Eastbound, the day went quickly. If Johnson had been along as co-pilot I would have gone back to the cabin, found a place to stretch out on a few million Chinese dollars, and returned with strength renewed for the greeting I knew awaited us along the coast of Africa. After watching Bigsbee allow the *Gremlin's Castle* to wander five or ten degrees off course before he made correction, I decided to doze in my seat.

Although my slumbers were occasionally interrupted by a high peeping sound from Parker's radio gear and the whine of the auxiliary pump as Hogarty transferred fuel, I remained "off-duty" for more than two hours. By then our speed plus the earth's rotation had put the sun behind us and afternoon was already in command of the scenery. To every horizon the view was the same, a brilliant cobalt sky overhead and flocks of little puff-ball cumulus hovering three thousand feet above the water. The air was smooth.

I told Bigsbee to go back to the cabin for some sleep and he disappeared immediately. When he was gone, Hogarty took his seat and leaned across to me. "Boss," he began hesitantly, ". . . would you mind not giving him another take-off?"

"He'll improve." Like it or not, Bigsbee was second in command of this aircraft and I had to be careful to spare him ridicule. To change the subject I countered with a question in Hogarty's own department.

"How are we doing on fuel?"

"We're fat. I figure we'll have better than two hours' reserve when we get there."

Turning back to LaFrenier, I asked him about the winds aloft.

"As advertised. Nothing . . . light and variable."

We agreed that the gentle South Atlantic was the only place to fly.

Evening came swiftly, first a purpling of the eastern sky, then a final ocher brushed across the western slopes of the clouds, and suddenly, in keeping with our equatorial latitude, it was night. We had dawdled over our box lunches provided by the mess hall at Ascension Island, a duplicate, except for a banana, of American military box lunches found everywhere. The spam sandwiches became delicious if consumed while concentrating on the rations issued to combat troops.

Bigsbee slept until I sent for him. I did not need any navigational aids to advise of our closing with the African

354

coast, for ahead, all along the black horizon, great bon-
fires suitable to mark the gates of hell were blossoming
and fading and exploding continuously. This magnificent
display was courtesy of the thunderstorms off the Gold
Coast, a permanent feature of the region. They were still
more than a hundred miles distant when Bigsbee stumbled into his seat and rubbed at his eyes. I thought to
stimulate him by pointing at these impressive pyro-
technics.

"Some show."

"We're not going through *that?*"

"We can't go around it, over it, or under it. Let's hope
it's not as tough as it looks."

Every American pilot of the line is familiar with the
thunderstorms of the Middle West, Texas, Mississippi,
and Tennessee. They are vicious, can be extremely dangerous, and are not to be argued with. Sensible pilots
avoid them entirely whenever possible, by retreat or
sneaking between them during the early morning when
their tempers are relatively subdued. The same policy
applies to the summer storms over New York State,
which can be rambunctious if not quite so lethal.

The storm line barricading the African Gold Coast is
quite another sort of antagonist if only because it seems
to be a permanent condition, peaks at night, and covers
such an immense area there is no detouring around it.
About ten miles before actual contact with the line, my
own resolution always wilted and I longed for a place to
hide. Now, the heavens were on fire while fat and gro-
tesque clouds bulging with muscle were illuminated from
the inside so continuously they appeared to be transparent boilers furnishing heat and light for the end of
the world. We transgressed upon the glowing columns,
caverns, and battlements, and as the *Gremlin's Castle*
penetrated into dense cloud, the rain seemed to become
almost solid water, a deluge fit for Noah. I said to Bigsbee,
whose eyes had become the hard marbles of a man transfixed in fear, "Just pretend you're in a submarine."

The only place to hide was behind the C-87's instrument panel. With shameless alacrity I lowered my seat
as far as it would go and turned up the morgue lights to
maximum. See no evil . . . know no evil, I thought, quite

aware how men afraid are inclined to silliness or silence according to their basic nature.

The noise was awful; we could not make ourselves heard above the rain without yelling. Someone had aimed a firehose at us and rivulets of cool water began dripping down everywhere. Lightning blossomed on all sides as we passed through an endless cannonade, and, strangely, the color of the lightning was not arc white as in our own thunderstorms, but brass yellow and sometimes almost bronze. I was grateful there was so little chain or forked lightning, for despite all the theoretical assertions that lightning does little serious damage to aircraft, it is unnatural for a humanoid to be in a position where he can apparently reach out and grab a lightning bolt by the neck.

Such conversation as we could manage over the roar of the rain was typical of men waiting uneasily for something unpleasant to happen.

"They say nothing will happen even if we get hit in a fuel tank."

"Who is 'they'?"

A conversational silence while the elements go heavy on the tympani.

"I have a brother who is scared shitless when he sees lightning. It must have got to him when he was a baby."

"You sound like a psychologist."

"If you could see my brother you'd never believe he could be afraid of anything. Right now he's in the Navy."

"Flying?"

"No. He teaches gymnastics. Exercises. He can do more than a hundred push-ups."

Another silence, longer this time. I care about three things. Altitude, even though the African coast hereabouts is low. We couldn't hit anything since we are now at seven thousand. Airspeed, now deliberately slowed to one hundred and seventy as a precaution against turbulence. But there is very little turbulence—just the deluge and lightning. A similar display in America would usually shake things up outrageously. I feel a moment of homesickness, as if worrying about structural failure was something to be missed. And I care about our course, which fortunately was well established before we entered this cataclysm. Now the needle of the automatic direction-finder, well behaved for the past two hours, pointing faithfully at the Accra beacon, executes a series of pirouettes, nodding like an electronic strumpet at every invitation from the surrounding thunderstorms.

"I can't understand why the air isn't rougher."

"Don't complain."

"Can we get a shower in Accra?" The query from Bigsbee whose voice sounds unnatural, as if he were choking on something. He smells. We all smell—a pungent mixture of sweat, tobacco, and mosquito boots of poorly cured leather. We also smell of poor diet, fatigue, all laced with the most subtle of odors, anxiety.

"Climb out on the wing. You'll get all the shower you want." Hogarty will not relent on Bigsbee and I have something new to care about. An unhappy crew can turn a flight deck into hell encapsulated and can also become a dangerous flight hazard. I make a mental note to warn Hogarty about dissension and the safety of his own neck. But not now. God is giving a virtuoso performance on his kettledrums.

Accra is ahead somewhere in the night. It has a radio range which, once audible, will take us by the nose and lead us to the airport, unless of course Accra is also beleaguered by thunderstorms. Range reception is so subject to the electrical energies released by thunderstorms that the valuable high-pitched whine of the beam is sometimes nearly obliterated.

I am growing very weary and long to empty my bladder, but if we should encounter the violent turbulence normally associated with such gaudy meteorology then how would Bigsbee manage things while I am back smelling chlorine, aiming my private member, and trying to hang on to the C-87 at the same time? Better to think about other matters and stay put. I inquire of Parker if he has contacted Accra lately.

"No. I can't hear anything with all this—" He makes a sweeping gesture across the surrounding sky leaving his reply suspended. He is unable to categorize "all this—"

We persist because there is nothing else to do. I am thirty-three years old and should not be frightened of thunderstorms, but in the midst of several hundred incendiary bullies I feel outnumbered and lacking in élan.

All the swagger of which I have been guilty when safely on the ground is gone out of me.

Perhaps my suddenly acquired humility is seeping through to Bigsbee whose moody silence has returned. I know very well how fear can pass from man to man, so quickly and feverishly the exchange is almost visible; but to be abashed is not the same as to fear.

I must be careful about Bigsbee. The power vested in me as captain can destroy a man. Who knows another man's inner torment until full confession? And even then the victim may not recognize the devils within himself.

We bounce through illuminated caverns and I manage to find a series of tunnels leading in the general direction of Accra. This is a gambling game which I sometimes lose. After twisting and dodging for perhaps ten minutes I bank around an enormous cloud and discover we are trapped in a dead end. There is no choice except a complete course reversal which would never get us to Accra.

"Into the valley rode the six hundred . . ." Why should I choose to mumble that line now? I am reaching instinctively for the comfort of something poetic while at the same time trying to prove I am unafraid of anything. Of course. At last I know what I am doing here. This is my war and the enemy is in full attack. I am our experienced trooper, canny, resourceful, and an expert with my weapons. Therefore I will conquer. For me the whole conflict is this interminable hour off the African coast burdened with money to pay soldiers for killing and dying on the other side of the world. It is as simple as that.

We plunge into the wall of cloud and for some ten minutes endure the most brutal shaking-up. We slide awkwardly into a spectacular display of St. Elmo's fire. All of the C-87 we can see—the wings, engine cowlings, propellers, and bulbous snout ahead—is glowing with an iridescent light that builds and fades and is sometimes so brilliant it seems we are flying inside a second, much larger aircraft.

"They say that stuff brings good luck."

"Who is 'they'?"

"Anyway you got to admit it's pretty."

"Are there any whores in Accra?"

"There are whores everywhere."

"Not on Ascension Island."

"Or Greenland."

"I'd like to take your bet on that. How about the Eskimos?"

"Did you ever actually meet an Eskimo?"

"No. We never got down to Sukkertoppen or any of those Greenland villages. We never had time to leave the base."

"Then how can you bet they have whores?"

This is my war presently transpiring some seven thousand feet above the Atlantic Ocean and not very many miles off the coast of Africa. Far to the west and north where it is still daylight Eleanor must have sent the kids off to school by now. And even farther to the west my father is worrying about my mother. She is in the hospital and when last I talked with her, more than a month ago, she was not doing well. Something about her kidneys. I have written, but there has been no response. Since I am a pray-er and still believe, I will now present a double request to higher authority. Please help my mother recover, and please get this aircraft to Accra in one piece. Soldier at war? No, just a little boy from Lincoln, Nebraska, whistling in the dark.

Suddenly the last cumulonimbus shakes us like a mastiff harrying a bone, then opens its maw and spits us out into the darkness beyond. The air grows smooth, the direction-finder needle swings to indicate Accra is almost straight ahead, and in the void below I think I see a few dim lights.

Chapter 26

This was war? A great smiling black man greeted us in the morning and overwhelmed us with suggestions for our further comfort. Breakfast at any time we named and whatever fresh fruit we desired. Polish the boots? Already done. Later, we met more of the locals and I was almost beside myself for time to draw their magnificent features, and try, if I dared, to somehow convey their open friendliness, pride, and total lack of artificiality. The permanent military personnel at Accra were on to a good thing and they knew it.

The following morning I urged the *Gremlin's Castle*

into the humid air and turned east over the jungles for a place called Kano in the interior of Nigeria. Just under five hours later I saw the weird towers of the historic caravan city. The airport was close by.

As we descended I saw the runway was long and being further lengthened by several hundred workers. With the weather fine and the wind light, I thought all factors favored giving Bigsbee the landing. He accepted the assignment as if I had struck him between the eyes with a hammer.

We were about two miles from the end of the runway, wheels down and locked, flaps at fifteen degrees, with Hogarty waiting apprehensively to add more when asked.

Bigsbee had done a reasonably decent job making his turns to line up with the runway, but he seemed to have lost contact with the real world now that he was in position.

"You're too high."

Bigsbee pushed the nose down hard and the *Gremlin's Castle* immediately gathered an overabundance of speed.

"You're too fast. Relax."

Bigsbee ignored my comment. He had both hands on the control wheel and from the look of his knuckles was apparently trying to squeeze juice out of it.

"Put one hand on the throttles."

"Why?"

"Because I say so. You may need more or less power ... and quickly."

Bigsbee placed his left hand on the throttles, but did nothing with them.

"You've got to lose some speed."

"You said I was too high."

"Right. Ease off on the power or we'll land in Ethiopia."

I glanced at Hogarty who translated the disapproval in my eyes as permission to pull back on the throttles. I saw him ease the levers back slightly and our speed decreased. Bigsbee, transfixed by the runway ahead, seemed conscious of nothing else. We were only half a mile from the end of the runway, sinking overfast in the hot dry air.

There now began one of the most spectacular aeronautical exhibitions I had ever witnessed. I had spent so many hours instructing in C-87s, I was convinced there was no wrong I had not seen, no clumsiness without formula for rescue. The ways of the C-87 were awkward, but there was nothing vicious about its temperament, and I still believed that anyone's grandmother could manage a reasonable landing if coached on the way down. In a series of compounding events during the next twenty seconds the hapless Bigsbee was about to prove me wrong.

Approximately a quarter mile from the end of the runway and while still two hundred feet in the air Bigsbee decided to make his landing. Suddenly he pulled the power all the way off and the nose up, a combination attempted only by experts when the wheels were inches above the runway.

The C-87 dropped like a grand piano thrown out of a window.

"You're way too high!" I yelled while slamming the throttles halfway forward. Simultaneously I shoved the nose down. The *Gremlin's Castle* came back to life as it swept down and across the runway threshold. At approximately one hundred feet and with enough speed to avoid a disastrous stall, I thought it safe to once again remove my hands and feet from the controls. Just behind me I heard someone say, "Jesus Christ almighty."

There was still plenty of runway ahead. No problem, I thought. Bigsbee had to learn someday. Give the man his head and his sense of self-preservation will do the rest. Good old self-preservation, the ally of both student and instructor.

I glanced at Bigsbee, trying to gauge his understanding of the situation. The C-87 was aimed at the asphalt, it was rising fast and yet he had made not the slightest movement of any control.

"They seem to be lengthening the runway, but it does have an end."

No action.

"Of course we could go to China by boring a hole in the runway, but that's the hard way."

No action. It was getting late. Seconds remaining.

"Better start your flare."

No action. I grabbed the yoke and pulled back the throttles just as the nose wheel and main gear contracted the runway. Too late. The C-87 ballooned upward some twenty feet, faltered, and started to sink again. Now I kept my hands on the controls, hoping by physical suggestion to make Bigsbee do the right thing.

"Fly the airplane. Don't let it fly you."

Another ricochet off the asphalt, the dry Nigerian landscape tilted to the right and disappeared momentarily beneath the nose. Shades of my first checkout in a DC-2 with tough old McCabe! My own disgraceful performance on that precarious day was near perfect compared to this wrestling match.

"Let me have it!"

Bigsbee took his hands off the controls in obedience and I was grateful we were now low on fuel. Our relatively light gross weight enabled me to accomplish a reasonably respectable landing and stop while there was still runway ahead.

No one spoke as we taxied toward a man in shorts and a cork helmet. Even Bigsbee, who normally became a chatterbox once he was out of the sky, kept his silence.

What do you say to a trombone player who should have been an insurance salesman?

That evening I watched with special interest as squadrons of buzzards wheeled and chandelled over the ancient city of Kano. The soft breeze brought the odor of offal, excrement, and a mixture of pungent aromas locked for centuries in a settlement too long inhabited. I heard camel bells tinkle, a man coughing until his very guts must have tangled, and a long spasm of dogs barking, then suddenly everything was still again. The twilight faded into night as uninvited memories kept invading my thoughts. Where now were Fox Face and the Fop? Rikki, silent for years, must certainly be in the Dutch underground if she was alive at all. Mother . . . Freedley . . . Bel Geddes . . . and Jimmy Shute? Kay Brown? Faraway ghosts of this night. I was here in Africa because of a man we casually referred to as "that son of a bitch Hitler," as if he was just another human being. Or was he really responsible? By chance I had witnessed his first machinations, yet I had never met the son of a bitch. Then what about the tricky influence of human beings upon each other? With some exceptions, I decided, we are not even pawns: events make us, not the contrary, and events are initiated by others, often strangers. Bigsbee too had somehow been included in the invisible net which had willy-nilly brought us to this exotic waypoint in the long caravan trail to the Eastern deserts. Although I had not asked, I assumed he also had a family to concern him, certainly some obligations and ties beyond the last light on the horizon. Now I realized he was utterly incapable of bringing the *Gremlin's Castle* safely to earth if for some reason I became incapacitated.

We had a long way to go. I resolved to teach Bigsbee at first opportunity how to land a C-87. Unless I did, he might be the innocent instrument someday responsible for the destruction of Parker, LaFrenier, Hogarty, and . . .

The haboob is encountered only in the desert areas of central Africa, which is a very good thing for the rest of the world. Soon after our lift-off from Kano I was surprised by the disappearance of the horizon, and in a very short time everything else.

We had acquired a passenger at Kano, Captain Colin Hill of the Royal West African Frontier Corps. He was a very tall and tawny Englishman straight out of Kipling, with a proper regimental mustache, an air of immense dignity, and a delightful sense of humor. When he came to me in the morning he was wearing shorts, a bush jacket with three pips on the shoulder straps, and a cork helmet. He explained he would like to hitch a ride east and asked how far we were going.

"To China."

"Really? Smashing. Could I come along?"

"Hop aboard."

"Just like that? Don't you need papers and et cetera?"

"The airplane is full of paper."

He studied me a moment and I knew he was wondering about the travel authority of a mere pilot. I tried to put him at ease. "We just kind of tootle along on our own. God willing, and if that flying machine holds together, we should land in China in about a week."

"As loose as that?" he said in wonder, for which I could hardly blame him. At least once an hour I marveled at how I had become sole master of a flight more than half-way around the world, not to mention several millions of dollars when the total in my wallet was thirty. Would someone in Washington suddenly come to his senses and realize what was happening?

"One way or another we'll get you there," I said as if I really believed it.

I offered Hill the freedom of the flight deck where he spent much time looking over our shoulders and sharing his vast knowledge of central Africa.

"Bloody awful, these haboobs. The wind picks up the desert dust of a million square miles round and sometimes carries it all the way out to sea. Goes on for days. Most depressing."

I wondered about our engines swallowing so much fine dust. If it continued long, the wear on moving parts was certain to cause trouble. Hoping to minimize the damage I climbed to thirteen thousand feet. The dust was thinner, but still there. Above we could see only a suggestion of blue sky, below there was a sickly brown pall. We flew on for more than two hours before emerging into the clear and I pitied the few scattered souls far below whose life was to cover the same geography on a camel.

Six hours out of Kano we descended in the thin desert air toward a place called El Fasher. Our chart showed its elevation as five thousand feet and I thought it a handy place to spend the night since the British had long ago established an airport near the town. With Hill aboard to interpret and resolve those subtle differences between Americans and Englishmen, I hoped for a pleasant interlude.

My hopes were more than fulfilled. At the north end of the runway the prewar British had established a fine rest house for Imperial Airways passengers and now with the staff still present and anxious to justify their continuance, we enjoyed all the amenities, including a ration of warm gin. Later, we sat in the sand and watched a movie with the small garrison of RAF personnel who maintained the airport and its facilities. Innumerable soft-spoken Sudanese also appeared momentarily between us and the brilliant stars, then sat down quietly in the sand while Roy Rogers made love to his horse.

Early the next morning, bathed and refreshed, we climbed into the *Gremlin's Castle* eagerly—our next pause, Khartoum. After the first two engines were turning out their throaty melody, the gremlins came running out of their castle. The number-three propeller refused to turn a millimeter.

I shut down the two running engines. We abandoned the C-87, already like an oven, while Hogarty and a pair of RAF mechanics removed the number-three cowling, hunting for trouble. They found it soon enough. The starter was broken beyond repair and the nearest replacement, the British assumed, would be Accra, California, or England.

After five days waiting for a replacement I found myself walking the runway measuring its usable length pace by pace, trying to convince myself that a three-engined take-off was possible. I had become overly weary of Bigsbee's platitudes and loquacious opinions; he seemed to become more effervescent each day we spent on the ground and, alas, all the more arrogant.

Colin Hill was my personal savior. His wit and intelligence never wore thin and he guarded only one subject, although I did not press him. Where was he really going . . . and why? He seemed not the least distressed at the delay, and now, with my own finances entirely depleted, financed our nightly "sundowners."

After seven days of waiting for a starter, impatience took such full command of my reason I fixed upon a scheme from which, once activated, there could be no retreat. I would ask the British to drain all but one hundred gallons of fuel from the accursed *Gremlin's Castle*. Then they must keep the fuel truck standing by. Our crew would unload the Chinese money. We would clear everything else out of the airplane—life rafts, flares, tools, axes, and God only knew what other paraphernalia stowed here and there as emergency equipment.

One hour before tomorrow's dawn I would start the three operational engines. I would be alone—one hundred sixty pounds of flesh and bone plus six hundred pounds of fuel, a mere seven hundred sixty pounds above the C-87's empty weight. In the cool of the dawn I would taxi to the extreme end of the runway, hand the C-87's tail over the end and finally ram on full power. The result would be a gamble of little concern if attempted at sea level and with a long runway, but El Fasher had everything against it. The result here would be in my hands with a considerable assist from the Almighty, who I hoped would approve. Once in the air, by employing the force of the slipstream to turn the propeller I should have no trouble starting the number-three engine.

Next I would land, reload money, fuel, crew, and passenger with the number-three engine still turning. Then at last, say an hour after dawn, before the sun became a blowtorch, we would be off and away for Khartoum.

All of the seventh day I fretted over my intended take-off. I was planning a definite risk and I knew it. While I persuaded myself the odds were heavily in my favor, I could not psych the C-87 off the ground if there was not enough power and runway length. There were no helpful figures or test pilot calculations to confirm my belief that I could make it, yet . . . ?

I will never know whether the following dawn would have marked a minor triumph or the end of my days. Just at evening, an American B-25 dropped out of the mauve sky, bringing a starter which had been held in Accra until someone came our way. Hogarty had it buttoned on the *Gremlin's Castle* within an hour. I knew a strange mixture of liberation and disappointment. I also knew, but could not understand, a genuine sense of loss, for I did not as yet appreciate how risk tears the wormwood from man, fills him with gusto, and afterward in victory loads him with satisfaction.

Three hours and one minute after we rose to meet the morning at El Fasher, we landed in Khartoum. New gremlins now took over from those already overbusy, rendering our main fuel transfer pump nonoperational and our direction-finder capricious. As we swept over the Nile in the blazing noon we discovered the landing gear nose-wheel would not come down unless Hogarty again climbed into the wheel well and kicked at it with all his strength. None of these items could be repaired in Khartoum.

Deciding the *Castle* was sorely in need of fumigation, I set course next dawn for Gura in Italian Eritrea where a large American maintenance base had been established. Within two and a half hours after taking off from the cauldron of Khartoum I brought the *Gremlin's Castle* down to a cool green fairyland where we at once became willing to believe that all good fairies had been truly assembled. For Gura was almost six thousand feet high in the Eritrean mountains with a beautiful concrete runway and a vast storehouse of parts. The mess hall stunned us with its opulence. It glistened everywhere with cleanliness; soothing music prevailed over the spotless tables while the long counters offered fresh salads and cheeses displayed against shovelfuls of real ice. We were like children given run of a fancy ice cream fountain, trying everything.

If they had taken a week to put our aircraft back together, we would not have minded in the least. I had to pinch myself to remember that war was hell. Yet, perverse as usual, the *Gremlin's Castle* allowed itself to be made airworthy that very night. Next morning, lacking excuse for more delay, I was obliged to continue eastward. We set course along the baking shores of the Red Sea and came down regretfully at Aden in the Arabian Protectorate. Here I was determined Bigsbee would learn to make a landing that the rest of us might conceivably walk away from.

I sent Hill and the others into the seedy, flyblown city of Aden and told Bigsbee his sightseeing must be postponed in the interests of aeronautical science. "Now," I began with what I hoped was an encouraging tone, "I will operate the gear and flaps for you and we are going to prove to ourselves how well you can handle a C-87."

The runway was a long stretch of gravel with perfect approaches from either end and there was no other traffic. We were light on fuel and a pleasant sea breeze was enough to slow our touchdowns if spare room was needed. Only the heat and Bigsbee's air of condescension suggested that our practice session might not be a total success.

During the next hour Bigsbee made eight intentional landings and approximately twenty which could be listed as unofficial and unexpected. He did try, very hard indeed. The sweat gushed from him, miniature fountains spewed moisture all over his face and even his curly hair dripped with moisture. As we rose up and came down again and again, each time in violent abuse of the poor C-87, I grew to admire Bigsbee's almost incredible absence of shame in his performance. When at last I decided the *Gremlin's Castle* did not really deserve such punishment and my own shock tolerance had been violated almost beyond endurance, I called a halt to the affair.

"I knew all I needed was a chance to practice," he

volunteered as we taxied drunkenly toward the ramp and finally squeaked to a nodding halt just before knocking down the small operations building.

"Yes," I lied. "You're improving. Maybe we'll have another chance someday."

If there was going to be another day with Bigsbee at the controls, I resolved, then I intended to be far away in another airplane. Meanwhile, in response to my own strong sense of self-preservation and the nerves of the others riding in the *Gremlin's Castle,* I would do all the flying, unless we were several thousand feet in the air.

All wars become very little wars to the troops involved. We were aware of Roosevelt's summit meetings with Stalin, Churchill, and De Gaulle. We had read of the Pacific campaigns, but naturally felt much closer to the continued fighting in North Africa and the bubbling kettle of armament which would one day be spilled over Europe. Yet these concerns were for politicians, generals, and admirals. My present little war was not waged directly against the official enemies, but against Bigsbee—the man who always came to life as soon as his feet were on solid ground—and the *Gremlin's Castle.* Both, it seemed, were quite capable of killing us all.

From Aden we flew eastward another five hours and descended upon a wild place called Salala on the southern shore of the Arabian Peninsula. Ever since leaving Ascension Island, the *Gremlin's Castle* had evidenced a peculiar vibration which originally I had attributed to the "automatic rough" engines usually acquire when over water and past the point of no return. Sure enough, the roughness had apparently cured itself while flying across Africa, but just to remind us the gremlins were still aboard it returned occasionally. Now between Aden and Salala the vibration became more substantial. Ten minutes out of Salala the number-two propeller ran away and set up a raucous howling before we could shut down the engine and feather it. When all was relatively quiet, I sighed. The loss of one engine was not serious since we were light on fuel and already in descent, but there were just a few too many things wrong with the *Gremlin's Castle* and my faith in it was almost gone.

As we turned into the final approach it was Hogarty's turn to sigh. After the usual commotion created by lowering the landing gear, he announced, "The goddamned nosewheel is stuck again."

Hogarty's honest eyes were unhappy and I could not blame him. Once again he would have to crawl into the C-87's nose, confront at least part of the tremendous blast of our slipstream, and kick hard enough at the nosewheel to make it fall away. He must worm his way into a very small space and hang on with a love for life lest he launch himself into space.

"So long," Hogarty said simply, and disappeared.

"I'll circle until you come back." I knew a heavy sense of guilt. As captain I belonged where I sat, particularly with Bigsbee as the only alternative, but I thoroughly disliked someone else standing in danger without sharing the risk.

All of our various tribulations had been observed without comment by Colin Hill. Not once had he evidenced the slightest concern.

Now I looked at him standing just behind me, a nonflier who readily confessed his total ignorance of airplanes. "Are you sure you want to go on with us?" I asked. "You might get there faster on a camel."

"What happens if the nosewheel does not come down?"

"Then we all get on a camel. I am bound to put a few scratches on things. From what I can see below this is hardly a repair base."

"My obituary is already on file with the *Times*," Hill said, and I treasured him for his nonchalance. I had nearly completed the first circle when I heard the nosewheel go down and lock with a thump. Next time we came within range of a bar I intended to buy Hogarty a drink.

It took all morning to repair the propeller governor, and then we were eastbound again along the parched shores of Muscat and Oman with Karachi our destination. It was a six-hour flight of little event except the total failure of the automatic direction-finder. I was more annoyed than concerned, since even Bigsbee on his own could hardly avoid our eventual arrival over India.

Hogarty kicked the nosewheel down again as we descended toward the cluttered metropolis of Karachi. The *Gremlin's Castle* proved it was by no means entirely subdued. This time on final approach the flaps refused to go all the way down and I was grateful for the long runway, since our touchdown speed was relatively high. Inured to repeated disappointment, I took solace in the fact that at least the brakes held.

Next day we flew across the wizened face of India for another six hours until we came to Gaya. I told Hogarty it was time to punt again and he descended to the nose-wheel well. During refueling I talked with a covey of Northwest Airlines pilots, who, far from home, were trying to herd the first Curtis C-46s toward the Hump. Their maintenance woes were even greater than ours, and like us they had found few places along the way capable of any but minor repairs. Their complaints encouraged me to carry on that same day, before the *Gremlin's Castle* collapsed beyond repair and left us stranded somewhere nearly in sight of our goal.

Thus, four hours later we came down at Chabua in Assam, where despite the straitened circumstances of the American air encampment and the hectic twenty-four-hour-a-day business of keeping a continuous stream of supplies flying over the Himalayas to China, we were overwhelmed with hospitality. A part of our welcome was due to the red-faced, quick-witted Harry Clark, who had, in what already seemed another life, first briefed me in Goose Bay, Labrador, on the best way to find the right fjord in Greenland and survive.

To our disappointment the Chinese money was transferred to another aircraft and went its way. Colin Hill likewise disappeared. His final destination and purpose remained his secret to the end.

While a dedicated maintenance crew did their utmost to make the *Gremlin's Castle* fit to fly, I took a load of ammunition to China in another C-87 with, incongruously, two machine guns in the nose. No one could explain their purpose. The relatively few Japanese fighter pilots charged with harassing Hump operations were hardly stupid enough to linger in front of our cumbersome aircraft unless they were committed to harakiri.

Once back in Chabua, we received orders to return the *Gremlin's Castle* to Natal immediately and after ten days' flying we descended once again through the humid Brazilian night. Yet even the familiar heat could not warm my bones, for I was shivering so miserably I had to be helped from the *Gremlin's Castle*. I was escorted at once to the military hospital where I endured a raging attack of malaria.

Were my nightmares real or the result of my fever? The terrible vision of what had happened during our return from the Hump kept repeating itself; proof again that wars are all-encompassing and capable of destroying people and things totally unrelated to the principal conflict.

Each time my fever subsided and reason returned I knew that what I had envisioned in delirium was true: I had very nearly become responsible for destroying one of the seven wonders of the world, a crime I would have previously considered unthinkable. The possibility of such dubious distinction haunted me long after I beheld the exquisite beauty of the Taj Mahal, and terrified me when I thought how I had held the serene beauty of another man's love in my sweaty bare hands.

Agra is one of the hottest places in the world, and we had arrived just after noon, the hottest part of the day. Circling to land we looked down upon the Taj Mahal, and all of us exclaimed at its design as seen from above. I noted as habit, but with no special interest, how the runway at Agra was aimed almost directly at the Taj. Then we descended into the boiling heat and I was mindful of the effect of such temperatures on the aerodynamic efficiency of any aircraft. Departing, I knew, we would need a lot of runway.

Because our forthcoming flight to Karachi would take only four hours, I ordered the refueling crew to put aboard just enough for the flight with a small reserve—a thousand gallons total. Longing to hide from the searing sun, I left them to their work and made for the terminal where I hoped to find a cool drink.

When we returned to the *Gremlin's Castle* the refueling crew had done their work and gone. We were in haste, wanting the quickest possible release toward cooler altitudes. It is always unwise to hurry the business of flight. The airplane was loaded with salvaged parts from crashes on the Hump operation where losses of men and flying hardware were appalling. Some of the parts were obviously very heavy, but no one, including myself, knew their actual weight. The custom was to load any aircraft until it looked full.

At Agra in the heat of the day I did not expect the *Gremlin's Castle* to behave like a gazelle, and I was not disappointed. I waited until the four engines were developing full power before I released the brakes and waited unhappily while the misbegotten aircraft gathered speed with agonizing slowness. A third of the distance down the runway we had achieved a mere fifty miles per hour with the *Gremlin's Castle* displaying no tendency whatever toward levitation. I should there and then have retarded the throttles and brought matters to a halt, for there was still ample room to stop and think things over.

Halfway down the runway I had time to reflect: By God the old bitch is going to test me today! But only an instant more remained for choosing. I let the precious instant slip by and it was gone.

The airspeed needle quivered at ninety miles an hour. There was not enough room left to stop without smashing into the grove of trees at the end of the runway.

Approximately a thousand feet from the trees, the *Gremlin's Castle* staggered off the asphalt. We rose, then sank, in spite of my manipulations of the controls. I saw we were certain to sink into the trees and thought: Well, at least we'll hit flat-ass and maybe walk away from it. The *Gremlin's Castle* was trembling in an incipient stall even as Hogarty retracted the gear.

I dared not turn a degree either to the left or right lest we lose a single mile of speed. The huge and cumbersome landing gear, which retracted sidewise and never with the wheels in unison, took forever to become tucked up in the wings. Individual leaves on the swiftly moving carpet of treetops directly ahead were clearly visible. I waited helplessly for the first sounds of impact.

The trembling eased when the left wheel finally stowed itself and my hopes rose as the *Gremlin's Castle* took on some feeling of true flight. The separation between the treetops and ourselves became almost tolerable. We held our breath, and all except Hogarty, who stood just behind the control pedestal, strained at our seat belts as if the physical effort would help our climbing.

Not a word passed between any of us. There was only the angry snarling of the four engines.

Seconds passed, then I beheld a vision which would be forever imprinted on my brain. Almost directly ahead stood the Taj Mahal. We were considerably below the level of its glittering dome and the four delicate minarets embracing the main structure. I wanted to blind myself to its swift approach. We were obviously going to knock it down.

We left the trees behind and sank in the descending air blanketing the river. I could not understand why by now even the *Gremlin's Castle* was refusing to fly. "Christ almighty . . ."

We crossed the river still in line of sight below the Taj. Now it appeared that our left wing would miss the main structure but would certainly slice through the adjacent minarets. We can turn and die, I thought.

Desperate in the seconds remaining, I made a wild decision. I doubted if anyone had ever tried it in a C-87, certainly not this close to earth. Speed was our vitality— without it we fell. We could not descend to gain speed and the engines were already doing their utmost. Yet what I intended would unquestionably reduce our speed.

"Hogarty!" I yelled the first command since we became so tenuously airborne. "Give me full flaps!"

Hogarty complied instantly. The result was nearly as unnerving as the vision ahead. The *Gremlin's Castle* seemed to mush into a solid wall as the flaps came down. I had no time to react in any way as the fat brown snout ballooned upward. We rose almost straight up, as if on a fast elevator. The whole plane shook angrily as we ascended just above the level of the trees.

I could see the repair work that was underway on the Taj Mahal. I could see the bamboo scaffolding which had been erected between the minarets. I could see the reed thongs holding the uprights and the parallel platforms together. I could see the astonished eyes of the workmen, their teeth as their mouths fell open, the twist of their turbans, their hands paused in wonder as a roaring monster passed only a few feet above their heads. Every one of them was frozen in position. There was not the slightest movement of anything anywhere except ourselves.

Then, like a page flipped in a book, we were past and already sinking in final stall. I shoved the nose down, for the terrain immediately behind the Taj was flat and barren and should have some lift from the heat. I told Hogarty to ease the flaps up a little at a time.

We gathered speed, a few pitiful miles during the next half minute. Gradually, teasing the *Gremlin's Castle* with invitations to fly, I managed to persuade it into a genuine climb. It was like cajoling a drunken hag into attempting a staircase she had just fallen down.

When at last we had straggled to a thousand feet I turned the *Gremlin's Castle* toward Karachi. Only then were we sufficiently relieved to explore the reason for our near-demise and I found it curious how, as always when death had knocked and gone without prize, we avoided mention of his passing. Instead we talked about the scaffolding on the Taj and the expression on the workmen's faces.

In Karachi we discovered the true cause of the *Gremlin's Castle's* extraordinary behavior. The fueling crew had misunderstood my request. To the fuel already aboard they had *added* one thousand gallons, resulting in an overload of three tons plus whatever unmeasurable load of junk was cargo.

The combination of such stupidities, with my own leading the parade, very nearly occasioned the worst single artistic desecration of the second great war. In the hospital at Natal, tormented by my malarial fevers, my role as candidate for number one barbarian compounded my delirium. And the dreadful specter haunted me for years.

Chapter 27

Something went out of my war when the C-87s were replaced by real airplanes designed for the work at hand. No one really wanted to see them go, but not even the most junior of us yearned for further association with their tricky dispositions. Their passing coincided with a change in the status of the European war itself; although D-Day had not yet been launched, it was obvious to the informed world that Hitler was in very serious trouble due to his Napoleonic excursion into Russia, and only a miracle could reverse the ultimate defeat of his legions. Despite the casualties expected of any Continental invasion there was a remarkable lightening of the atmosphere at home, in Africa, and even in a United Kingdom now newly plagued with buzz bombs and assorted hellish hardware dispatched by the increasingly desperate Germans. This overall confidence in Allied might and eventual victory was now reflected in the glistening aluminum of many American aircraft from the swiftest of fighters to our new transports.

As muleteers we were no little impressed with our new wagon trains, and rather shyly, as if to match their elegance, began a voluntary sprucing up of ourselves. We were more careful of our uniforms' neatness and ever so much more assured, for confidence was easy after only a few minutes flying our new birds. These were the C-54s (later, as civilian aircraft, DC-4s), low-wing, four-engined transports built by Douglas Aircraft. They proved to be superb in every respect, so efficient we at last believed we were contributing our fair share to winning the European conflict.

With the arrival of the C-54s, our whole flying life changed from a highly individualistic and rather haphazard endeavor to a relatively routine operation of vast dimension. Our aircraft now flew around the clock and spent little time on the ground. Our bases in Africa and in the U.K. were expanded, the better to accommodate the increasing flow of military traffic in both directions. We were beginning to bring home some of the baby-faced pilots we had transported to England in our more spartan aircraft. They still wore their 50-Mission caps jauntily, but the bounce had gone from their movements and their eyes were vague, as if they were still appalled at what they had seen. Though only a year and sometimes less had passed, they were no longer babyfaced, nor did I ever observe the slightest evidence of celebration at their survival. Instead they were somber and most of all humble, a complete transformation from the cocky youngsters who had been our most feisty passengers.

We used the Azores more frequently now as a refueling and crew transfer point between both sides of the Atlantic. The runway was perforated steel matting, noisy and very rough, but except for occasional torrential rains the flying weather was usually very good. There, while waiting to take over a C-54 from an incoming crew, we lived in tents, dined on Spam in all its various guises, and were sometimes able to indulge ourselves in the excellent Portuguese wines to be found in the town of Lagens das Flores.

In contrast to these occasional pleasures, we knew still certain anxieties and tribulations. Watkins, Hunt, Miller, and Charleton, all captains of my line, were killed in various crashes. I survived two serious incidents which left me wondering about any man's fate. In one instance I had a fire aboard our C-54, a disturbing situation in any aircraft made more so for us because at the time of discovery we were on solid instruments seven thousand feet above the inhospitable terrain of Newfoundland. Worse, emergency reports we received promised no clear weather for more than six hundred miles. A miracle and the marvelous C-54 proved our last-minute salvation. The appearance of a hole six thousand feet deep with Stephenville airport centered at the bottom of the misty well was either an unaccountable freak or a true miracle. The ability of the C-54 to be stood on its ear while spiraling down through an opening very little larger than itself and thus permit our feet to touch earth before the fire took complete command, made me ready to kiss its aluminum backside.

I was similarly inspired when an overeager engineering team caused an experimental-type spark plug to be installed in three of the four engines of a C-54 I was scheduled to fly to Scotland. The aircraft was fully loaded with cargo and fuel at New York's La Guardia Field. Unaware of the experimental plugs, I took off in normal fashion and when barely clear of the runway experienced alternate total and partial power failure on three engines. The result became what may be the shortest round trip ever made by a four-engined aircraft—four minutes, take-off to landing. I did my best to make the flight even shorter, but Rikers Island, a low hummock approximately fifty feet high, was in the way and I was obliged to circle it while being maintained aloft by the one good engine, very occasional bursts of power from the other three, and the urgent prayers of my crew.

When finally we were down, landing willy-nilly on the first runway I saw over the nose, it took much longer than the flight to shake my terror. And longer yet to soothe my temper when I learned that we had served as involuntary guinea pigs.

Soon after this affair I took emergency leave and went to California where my mother was dying. She was brave beyond comprehension and in spite of her agonies contrived to smile frequently and even accept distraction in the painting I attempted beside her hospital bed.

My father's anguish during these terrible days nearly overwhelmed both of us. After his withdrawal from the affairs of a great corporation and the infighting of telephonic nobles, he had mellowed greatly and had totally engaged himself in those pleasures that were to his taste. These were not the usual golf and bridge amusement of his retiree contemporaries. He alternated his vicarious life of cowboy Cactus Jack with that of the country gentleman at his Pebble Beach estate.

Now even the thought of losing his beloved companion in all his activities was incomprehensible to him. He sat dazed in the hospital corridor, fingering the silver ornament which joined the thong around his neck, his false eye veering off independently from his good. I could not persuade him to leave the hospital or to eat or drink. He was utterly lost, pathetically unwilling to recognize the limitations of wealth, for he had gathered teams of the finest doctors in the land to ease my mother's pains and rescue her from the inevitable. But they were as helpless as he while doing their utmost to fulfill his demands.

When at last she went, I was holding her hand, weeping not for her, but for myself and the man who was still denying that her end could possibly be and who remained outside the room until she was gone. Then I brought him to the bedside and left him there alone. He loved her so utterly that there was no conceivable finish to their tryst. And for that I loved him mightily.

Outside, in the hall, I could not control my own sobbing. Here, witness to the mortal ending of a lifelong sharing of love, I learned for the first time how difficult it was to weep with dignity—and of the inexorable balancing of *yin* and *yang*.

———

Between 1939 and 1945 there were as many wars as there were millions of individuals involved. As in all major human insanities, privilege prevailed and the meek were trampled into the mire. There were many true heroes who never wore a uniform and who received little or no reward for their valor. There were many villains wearing the uniforms and the military baubles of all the antagonists, and while countless humans perished in concentration camps or were brutalized, maimed, and torn to pieces by the jaws of the military machinery, there remained as always those who through chance or natural cunning contrived a far more luxurious existence than they had known prior to the conflicts.

Waiting, for prisoner and captor alike, is one of the minor and more insidious curses of war and our waiting time was when we were not airborne. If things were going badly we sometimes waited for days until an airplane arrived and the crew disembarked to do *their* waiting. Relay fashion, we would then become active units contributing, however insignificantly, to the ultimate victory.

Normally, our stations of waiting were Goose Bay in Labrador, Prestwick in Scotland, Casablanca or Marrakech in Morocco, Accra, the Azores, and Stephenville in Newfoundland. Our activities at the staging areas depended largely upon our weariness, the local environment, and personal urges.

My paint box proved my own salvation in Casablanca and Marrakech; I was enchanted with the color and semitic mystery of North Africa and only regretted my inability to capture it with a brush. Scotland was also a favorite haven, where to my astonishment I rediscovered Tanya, daughter of my Maltese friend José Mifsud in New York. Now an enchanting young woman of spectacular beauty, she was married to an English submarine officer and had mothered two children. She also served in the local Red Cross, where I found her, and at once began to brood about the incredible reappearance of certain people in the pattern of our lives. Was it true there were only a few thousand people in the world and they all knew someone who knew someone who knew—?

Waiting, for most air crew members, was a dull business. Thus playing cards became a major preoccupation and the games were almost continuous. Such was the concentration of the players that they made little noise and the exhausted could sleep nearby.

I had never been much intrigued by parlor games and knew that to mix with relatively expert gamblers would certainly include a financial penalty, and I secretly wanted to exclude at least one traditionally recognized sin from my personal catalogue. Thus, I always declined to gamble and instead engaged in a still riskier gamble by attempting to write a second book.

I wrote *Blaze of Noon* in ordinary school notebooks, sitting at the same table as my gambling comrades, sometimes half listening to the subdued chatter of the players and often not hearing them at all. Once aware of my endeavors their reaction was generous.

"Shut up. He's writing a book."

"For Christ's sake, can't you see he's thinking?"

If there had been any other place to go I would have left them in peace, but most of our bases offered little or no refuge and writing out of doors was usually impractical. Only Stephenville offered a one-room library where I worked in great content.

After the invasion of Normandy our sense of worthiness increased very rapidly. For a while we had carried the tools of war and the men to deploy them eastward; the return flights now became the real war. In one of the most humane efforts that ever emerged from military channels, our C-54s were converted into "litter ships." As flying hospitals they were complete with medics, nurses, basic surgical apparatus, and, most importantly, the young and bleeding carnage of battle. They were carried to us often directly from the field still splotched with mud, smelling of excretion and the sweat of their fears, groggy from opiates and bewilderment at "this has happened to me?" The only way most troops are persuaded into combat is through the conviction they will emerge undamaged. It must be understood that the hurt will happen to someone else. When the protective rule fails, the shock of surprise is overwhelming—if there is anything left to be surprised at. The men who were brought to us, most horizontally, a few limping, were still in deep dismay. Their sense of having been betrayed locked their eyes and lips until our actual take-off. Then little by little, realization of their deliverance came upon them.

"We're gonna be home by tomorrow? You gotta be kidding."

Home. Home . . . home? "We're going home?"

The effect was magical. The eyes of even the most grievously wounded brightened remarkably and their smiles were almost continuous. Flight after flight, the medics and the nurses confirmed the obvious. The so-called air-evac flights which removed a man from the toils of war became almost immediately of the greatest encouragement to troop morale: the mere thought of being actually homebound often provided the extra fire to save their lives.

I always went back to the cabin with assurances of our progress and invariably found my reluctance to join the stink and misery at once overcome by the spirit of these young men whose luck had nearly run out. Questions floated into the aisle from all three tiers of litters. "Where are we?" . . . "How fast are we going?" . . . "How long until we're home?" My cynicism, a byproduct of too much brooding on the worldwide waste I had unavoidably seen, evaporated before the onslaught of such human tolerance and sheer courage. By rough count I flew some fifteen hundred young men out of hell. Not once did I hear complaint or a crying out for pity. If there was anything noble about war, I decided, then it could be found in the roaring, stinking confines of a litter ship.

Wars make a terrible mess, and I lingered on, engaged in one aspect of the cleaning-up process long after the Germans surrendered. We brought the great generals home and saw them celebrated, then we went back again and again to the United Kingdom, France, and North Africa, bringing home the men and such pieces of machinery as anyone thought worth directing against the Japanese, or fancied worth saving for a peaceful day. It was an anticlimactic time for us with the world held in suspense wondering how staggering a debt would be paid in casualties when the compulsory invasion of the Japanese main islands began.

At last the ultimate bombs were dropped on Hiroshima and Nagasaki, and the totally unnecessary war which had begun in lunacy ended in insanity. The world, bleeding like a hemophiliac from countless wounds, ran amok for barely twenty-four hours before it seemed to lie down in exhaustion. Then came bewilderment.

Now our shuttling back and forth across the Atlantic Ocean became routine. The spartan bucket seats in our aircraft were replaced with reasonably comfortable airline seats and elementary amenities were offered our passengers.

One night of fair moonlit weather I watched the silent parade of dull silver dumpling clouds between my exalted seat and the black ocean. We were halfway between the Azores and Paris and all about me prevailed such a sense of peace and well-being that I slipped into reverie. What had the war done to friends I had not seen since it began? Bigelow, my neighbor in Rockland County who had joined me in the backyard learning of celestial navigation, was now a full commander in the Navy with two hard years in the North Atlantic skippering a destroyer escort. Nelson and Linsk, my first two flying students, had spent the war in the Armed Forces Radio unit, where through their very special talents they had contributed greatly to the morale of Allied troops on every front. Fox Face had vanished—someone said into the OSS. Surely, with his feline cunning and marvelous alacrity he must still be alive. Kalberer I knew was listing heavily to port with decorations for his exploits, which included the first fateful Ploesti raid, a triumphant attack on the Italian fleet, and finally command of B-29 squadrons over Japan. He was now a brigadier general. Likewise Boyd, my mentor on American Airlines, and C. R. Smith, its former president, who had all along encouraged my writing. René Pleven, godfather to my twins, was now the French Minister of Finance, and Dorothy Lee—Freya-Leigh-Tartiere—had been decorated by that government with the Légion d'honneur for her part in the Resistance.

Rikki had vanished, and knowing her hatred of the Germans I held little hope of her surviving four long years of occupation.

My own fortunes had prospered, in some categories far beyond my wildest expectations. Except for my continued absences, Eleanor and the three children had hardly been aware that a war was in progress—a *yang* for the *yin* contributed by the loss of my beloved little sloop *Uncle Sam*. The day after the 1944 hurricane struck the Connecticut shore, I flew over *Uncle Sam's* anchorage and saw only her masts protruding above the water. Even from the air I knew she was a total loss.

On this fair night with the moonlight's reflection on

the engine cowlings and the nether world below my window so tranquil, I wondered if I was finally wearing down. Would I ever make a straight daytime flight again or was I condemned forever to this all-night vigil followed inevitably by a feeling of grubbiness at dawn and then a fuzzy day of trying to recapture lost sleep? The same old instruments were now relaying the same information I could gather at a glance, and I knew the way to Paris or Scotland or North Africa as surely as the streets to our shoreside home in Old Greenwich.

I wondered if flying, my true wife for so long, had not aged rather badly. The excitement was gone except for occasional displays of temperament and, strangely, I had little faith in our future together. "If you are smart," I had advised my crew, "you'll start looking for another job right now. With the war over no one in their right mind is going to cross the ocean in one of these things. They'll be going back to steamships where they can have some comfort."

For this jewel of wisdom and foresight I paid dearly in later times.

In another hour or so I knew we would bear witness to a new dawn, developing quickly because of our speed toward the sun. The haze which always seemed to hang over western France would obscure the coast until we were nearly upon it, then soon afterward we would start our letdown for Orly Field. And, protruding from the early morning mist, there would be the Eiffel Tower, and another flight would be nearly done. The yawning then and stretching and the putting away of things—LaFrenier's navigating tools in his briefcase and the octant in its black plastic box. The engineer would make his final notations in the logbook and the radio operator would close up his little shop, remove his headphones, and doze, for we would be in voice communication with Orly Field. Finally, we would swoop down through the golden haze passing swiftly over the French farmhouses and our night's work was done.

Now, because I was becoming too comfortable amid such familiarity, I began to contemplate other futures. I took out my pocket calculator, which I regarded as a combination crystal ball and Ouija board. My ability to master its simple ways was, in view of my abysmal lack of mathematical talent, still a triumph. Using a series of very hypothetical figures I discovered to my pleasure that at least six people in the world must at this very moment be reading one of my first three books for youngsters, or the novel *Island in the Sky*. Was this only the beginning? Recently, the Morrow Company had taken my novel about the early airmail days, *Blaze of Noon*, and had paid a whopping five-thousand-dollar advance. I juggled the calculator discs around until they revealed a few hundred thousand more readers to whom I would presumably give some enjoyment, and I knew a sense of considerable satisfaction.

Next I was tempted to review the most recent bonanza. Only three nights before this flight the wonderful Kay Brown, who had somehow remained my guardian angel through all my rejection of her show business world, had presented me with a check for fifty thousand dollars for the movie rights to *Blaze of Noon!* I was still recovering from the vision of that Paramount Pictures check with my name on the "Pay to—" line. It was unbelievable. A total of fifty-five thousand dollars already received for a book not yet published?

I slid the calculator wheel around until I came up with the number of people who might possibly see the movie. When I became lost somewhere in the millions I put the calculator back in my shirt pocket before it got me into more trouble. *I* might be even partly responsible for the entertainment of millions? Wow.

This was heady stuff, and with consistent lack of prudence I spent the rest of the round trip plotting how to get rid of so much money. On my return from Paris a kindly yacht broker, recognizing my childlike passions, came to rescue me from indecision. He hardly needed to exert himself, for the first boat he took me to see was obviously ordained by God himself for my acquisition. Incredibly, across the fat schooner's stern was her gold-lettered name *Story II*. Since *Blaze of Noon* was my second novel and would pay for her, I had no trouble whatsoever in rationalizing the twelve-thousand-dollar price. Who would dare, I thought, refute such a significant omen?

I left for my next overseas flight with new reluctance and some frustration. During the six days spent at home,

I had bought everything the family needed and there was still a small fortune in the bank. More would be coming, it seemed, since the publishers now advised me that *Blaze of Noon* had been selected by the Dollar Book Club. Money, I was suddenly discovering, could be a very burdensome blessing. From the time of my elevation to captaincy I had thought us very fat on only my flying pay. Now my purse was bursting and I could not be comfortable with it. I telephoned my father with this stirring financial news and found him wistful in spite of it. His loneliness, I knew, was all-powerful.

Uneasy in new affluence I continued to fly as if it had all never happened. Nor did I confide in my fellow airmen lest such ill-gotten wealth divide me from them. Yet change was manifesting itself in many ways, and each return from a flight found Eleanor with a longer list of messages. The English rights to *Blaze of Noon* and *Island in the Sky* had been sold. More money. Likewise the paperback rights for both books. A Mr. William Sloane of Morrow had called several times. *Liberty* magazine had awarded a prize to a short story I had written—plus a bonus of one thousand dollars. Would I fly to Hollywood for a discussion of the Paramount movie? All expenses paid of course.

I kept shaking my head. The fifty-foot Alden schooner was still in Essex, Connecticut, waiting to be sailed— somewhere. I was scheduled for a flight to Iceland, thence on to Prestwick, and no one knew exactly where from there. Peace, I thought, was wonderful, but more demanding than war where most of the thinking was done by higher authority.

Other affairs were also falling into disarray. To my disappointment (and that of many others), my airline was showing little interest in continuing international operations and the thought of returning to the routine flying of DC-3s from New York to Cleveland or Chicago did not appeal to me. I went to Davidson, the splendid chief pilot who still governed our flying lives, and asked for a leave of absence. It was granted so promptly, my notion of being needed was severely shaken. It was difficult to admit that times had changed, and that the proprietary jealousy I had acquired during the more difficult years over the Atlantic was a little silly.

Chapter 28

Where I had once been a pariah among the dateless palms, I now arrived an honored guest. The guards at the studio gates I had been so anxious to enter in the long ago, now directed me to a parking place of middle status in spite of their open contempt for my vehicle. It was a battered Model A Ford I had rented for a hundred dollars because I still could not believe Paramount would long continue paying me four hundred dollars a week just for "advising."

The term "advising" originated in the man Paramount had chosen to produce *Blaze of Noon,* one Seton I. Miller. Based on the Hollywood stories fed regularly to the press, and my own disastrous experience with Jack Warner, I now expected the worst, and for several minutes thought I had found it in producer Miller. After his secretary had studied me long enough to be sure I represented no immediate danger to her boss, she opened the door and shooed me into his inner office.

I was taken aback by the sight of a bald head apparently decapitated and lying on the edge of a large desk. After a moment the head rolled to one side, then rose slowly to reveal a pair of thick glasses screening eyes of indefinite color. The rest of the face was hidden behind an oxygen mask I recognized as exactly the type we had used during the recent war. I thought, well, well, at least the man has style. His intention is to greet me with something familiarly aeronautical.

I heard a muffled greeting from behind the mask and a hand waved me to a huge upholstered chair. It was ten o'clock in the morning. Miller removed the mask, closed the valve on an oxygen bottle behind him, chuckled merrily and held out his hand.

"Excuse my image for which there is no excuse," he laughed. "I have what is known as a frightful hangover. Welcome to Hollywood. You may now remove that large chip I see on your shoulder."

At once I liked the man and never had reason to alter my opinion. He was almost totally un-Hollywood and therefore unguarded. His apparel was small-town banker and his mind marvelously inquisitive. He was over-fat for his age and so nearsighted he was obliged to hover only a few inches above a printed page to accomplish his voluminous reading. A veteran of the old screenwriter's school, when dallying for days over a page of script was accepted practice, he was in no hurry to start on *Blaze of Noon*. Instead, he interrogated me for the rest of the day on all phases of the aviation business, which fascinated him. That evening I met his lovely wife Anne, who to my amazement proved to have been a young actress I had once tested during my time with Warner Brothers.

The "advising" for which I was paid so handsomely was ridiculously simple. I would have been ashamed to take the money if greed had not already begun to rot my standards. Here a great studio, of which I had dreamed since a boy, had paid fifty thousand dollars for my story and was now gilding that booty with a further four hundred a week as sort of pin money. All this for very occasional reporting to Miller's office where eventually, after all other possible subjects had been chewed to pieces, we got around to mentioning *Blaze of Noon*. I knew something had to be done to keep my sanity and therefore disdained the temptation to set myself up in a bachelor apartment complete with legendary Hollywood amenities. Instead I rented a room in a small North Hollywood bungalow.

My landlords were Jim Gainer and his wife Jane, both of whom I had known when flying into Cleveland. Then, before anyone of us had even thought of war, it was my humble co-pilot's duty to hand the passengers' baggage from a DC-2 to the local agent, Jim Gainer. He worked now in a similar capacity at Burbank airport.

Gainer was a huge man as big in heart and humor as in physical dimension. His wife Jane was petite, very Irish, and vivacious. She was also, in accordance with her heritage, feisty and devoutly Catholic. It was her sworn ambition to "persuade" her easygoing husband into the same faith. They loved and argued and laughed together without reticence in spite of my being in their midst, a degree of acceptance I found most endearing.

Any true privacy in such a small bungalow was difficult to achieve and I did my best to become invisible, but their home became mine also and at least I was prompt with the rent. The title Uncle Nuggie was conferred when I was caught raiding the icebox, thus establishing myself as a true freeloader. Retreating from the unreality of Hollywood to such straightforward Americana, sharing my troubles and triumphs with people who never displayed the slightest sign of envy, kept me in place and I have been forever grateful to the Gainers.

One night I came home late, nearly exploding with the preposterous events of the day. I had spent the evening with Linsk, Nelson, and assorted starlets around a magnificent swimming pool—all in true Hollywood fan magazine fashion. Celebration was in the night's soft air and now I wanted to share my most recent coup with my landlords.

I parked the Model A in the street, hoping the thrashing sound of its engine would rouse no more than a few of the neighborhood dogs, then made my way to the bungalow's front door, pleased with the realization that the overhead light had been left on for me and reminding myself to turn it off. The cost of burning one light might not be extravagant for such a rich man as myself, I thought, but airline pay for ground personnel obliged them to count pennies.

I opened the front door with my own key and shut it softly behind me. I switched off the outside light and, turning, saw that the door to the Gainers' bedroom was ajar. A bar of light passed the door and lit my way as I tiptoed across the living room. Good, I thought. They are awake and I can share my extraordinary news.

I was about to call out, "Hey there, sleepyheads, let me tell you this before they put me away in an institution—" when I halted suddenly and stood in awe. For in crossing the room I had detoured around the coffee table and so changed my angle of perception. Now I could not avoid seeing into the bedroom and the scene within drove all other thoughts from me. Jim's long frame was stretched beneath the bed covers, his head propped on a pillow. He was reading a book. A quart bottle of beer was nestled against his side, half consumed. Jane Gainer was on her knees beside the bed, her nightgown making her seem as small and frail as a newly hatched bird. Her head was bent in prayer and her hands, holding a rosary, were clutched on the edge of the bed.

I could hear no sound until Jim sighed heavily and reaching out with his free hand felt the air above his wife a moment, then lowered his hand to pat her gently on the head. Not once did he glance at her. Then, never breaking his concentration on the book, he retrieved his hand and searched until he contacted the beer bottle. He raised it to his lips, took a sip, returned it to its place, and finally reached out to pat his Jane again.

I tiptoed away, passing through the kitchen in darkness until I came to my little room at the back of the bungalow. And I thought I should have been ashamed of my Peeping Tom conduct, but I was not.

Rich man? Yes I was, just in being able to tiptoe past my good friends' marvelous treasury.

In comparison, my own affairs seemed almost tawdry when reviewed on the following morning. At breakfast I told the Gainers I had discovered where the rainbows ended.

". . . there I was resting my elbows on the keys of the piano in the man's office, trying to tell him about my next book. After I had been blabbing on for too long he called in another man and then Hap Miller came in and they all just sat listening. I'm not even sure what I was rambling on about, but every time I got stuck I would lean back with my weight on the piano keys and the discords gave me time to think what might happen next in the story . . .

". . . when I was finished the boss man said it sounded as if it would be a very good book and should make a good movie and would I be interested in giving Paramount an option to buy it for fifteen thousand dollars . . ."

"God," said Jim, "has come through again. Bring on the dancing girls. It's steak and champagne tonight. Maybe now you'll buy a secondhand car of your very own."

"Maybe I should raise Uncle Nuggie's rent," Jane said, clapping her hands in delight. "Or I suppose now you're too good for us. You'll go live with a blonde in a penthouse like all the rest of the Hollywood types."

And Jim said I made more in one afternoon than he made in two years.

My own gaiety was somewhat modified in the morning light. I had realized that not even Paramount Pictures was distributing such honey without a binding invitation to enter the comb and produce more. And in this case it meant I would have to write another book.

I dismissed such logic almost immediately and began thinking of ways to be rid of this latest bonanza.

Soon after Paramount's latest offering was secure in my purse I went north from Hollywood to see my father. Still lost in loneliness for my mother, his solo occupancy of the considerable Pebble Beach estate was leading him into ever deeper melancholy. We joined each other in the library for a Scotch and soda before dinner. My father, as always, wore a tie, vest, and jacket for this hour of the day, and I knew my relating of recent events gave him considerable pride. We talked briefly and carefully of my mother and of Eleanor who was now calling at doctors' offices ever more regularly for causes she could not seem to define.

We were about to have a second drink when the telephone rang. It was Esther Hutchinson, a lady I remembered from my youth in St. Paul because of her extraordinary vivaciousness. Accompanied by her daughter, she was just passing through Pebble Beach, had found my father's number in the telephone book and wondered if he knew that her husband had died recently. After the proper condolences, my father insisted she join us for dinner and within thirty minutes a boisterous reunion was in progress. While I talked to the daughter Jean of her mother's remarkable physical resemblance to my own mother, the two elders gossiped continuously about all the others of their now widely dispersed tribe. For the first time in more than a year the great house rang with laughter. And before the evening was done I was pleased to hear my father making plans for his guests' further entertainment on the following day. It was easier to leave him for my own bailiwick knowing he would not be entirely alone.

When I returned to Connecticut I discovered Eleanor's ailments had become very real. She was, unaccountably, suffering from mild attacks of arthritis which worsened in cold weather. With the schooner *Story II*

389

ever inviting, money apparently falling off every tree I stood under, and the approach of winter, it was simple enough to persuade myself into an ideal solution. Near Nassau in the Bahamas, I rented a fine house at Lyford Cay. The house stood only a few yards from a magnificent and nearly always deserted beach of dazzling white sand, and the waters everywhere were green and azure blue in breathtaking combinations. The house belonged to a local entrepreneur whose piratical demeanor I thought well suited to the region, and with his help I hired a cook, a maid, and a handyman. The situation appeared as near-perfect as could be, and I envisioned Eleanor soothing her hurts in the sun while the children romped and swam in the crystalline waters. It seemed I had chanced upon a paradise exactly suited to our needs and I was soon beside myself with plans for our migration.

There was one disadvantage to the house which I thought in its favor. It was fifteen miles from Nassau and almost completely isolated. The only nearby dwelling had recently been the scene of the famous and still unsolved murder of Sir Harry Oakes. Now that I was an author, I assured myself, solitude was mandatory, for here I intended to write my third novel.

The logistics of our departure and arrival in the Bahamas were complicated and pleasingly expensive. Leaving Eleanor to the complex business of enrolling three American children in a pseudo-English school, I returned north to pick up the schooner. There I gathered a scratch crew which included Marcum, who had let me write a book in his barn during an almost forgotten winter, B. Allen Mays, who had occasionally flown the North Atlantic with me as co-pilot, and LaFrenier, who had been my navigator on countless flights. We set sail from New York on a bitterly cold day, bravely into the Atlantic with a fine little vessel, better provisioned with foodstuffs than experience. Now half my leave of absence from the airline had elasped and I had not written a word of the new book. But soon all would be well, I thought. It should not take us more than ten days' sailing to the Bahamas.

One month later, weary and disappointed after a voyage that was anything but a lark, we sailed into Nassau.

The fifty-foot *Story II* had proven herself a fine little sailer when she had the chance, but it seemed her luck was questionable. When there was no wind, her engine, a small three-cylinder diesel, performed flawlessly, but only if the sea was absolutely flat. The slightest wave action brought it to a coughing halt. The voyage was nearly over before we discovered that the fuel filters had been installed below the engine itself, and any rocking action caused an air lock.

We ran aground twice between the Jersey coast and Norfolk. The incidents, both the fault of *Story's* master, were more embarrassing than serious. In contrast we encountered very heavy weather below Cape Hatteras. As the little schooner labored through the wild night she developed such a leak her floorboards were soon awash and her buoyancy greatly diminished. She wallowed like a dying whale. The engine, predictably, refused to function under such duress, with the consequent loss of our mechanical pump. By dawn, already worn with our all night's desperate search for the cause of the leak, we set to with the large cast-iron hand pump on deck. The gale was still moaning in the shrouds, but daylight always reduces the image of peril, and we managed some optimism as we spelled each other, heaving and hauling on the heavy pump handle. Then, incredibly, just as we were making some progress against the water level, the cast-iron pump mechanism broke into several pieces. We were sixty miles offshore and in very real trouble.

All that day and into the night we sailed for the beach, hoping at the very best to strand the *Story* somewhere along the Virginia shore and make our way to safety. Although we formed a bucket brigade and worked desperately hour after hour, the water level rose steadily below. Our inevitable exhaustion could only mean we were going to the bottom. We had abandoned further attempts to start the engine. Fortunately as the day dragged on, the wind diminished enough for us to set full sail.

By midnight it was raining hard, yet the wind held fair. Despite the queasy motion of the *Story II* and our almost overwhelming fatigue (I had not stretched my length for twenty-four hours), we saw there was some chance of making Charleston before actually sinking, so we pressed on. At two in the morning we spied the light on the end of the Charleston breakwater and made for it with the very last of our vessel's and our own energies. An hour later I deliberately ran the *Story* onto the mud in Charleston harbor. At least, we thought as we celebrated a second dawn without rest and LaFrenier's birthday, we will not sink. That afternoon on the shipyard ways we discovered that the keelson had been constructed in two pieces. The schooner's heavy laboring during the gale had forced the lamination apart enough to admit too much ocean. The fault was repaired four days and nine hundred dollars later and never troubled *Story II* again.

As a final vexation to this luckless cruise, the normally dependable LaFrenier fell swooning in love with a girl cook I had mistakenly hired on reaching Jacksonville. For the balance of the voyage both were rendered absolutely worthless; I could not trust him to keep *Story II* on course during his watch nor her to prepare the most elementary nourishment.

At last arrived at Lyford Cay, I found all was not quite perfect in paradise. While Eleanor enjoyed the beach and the swimming, she surprised me with a totally new racial conscience. Most of all she objected strenuously to the attitude and arrogant behavior of the local whites toward the blacks. By now, including the wonderful Coaglie I had just hired as boat tender, we had four servants and were very apparently respected by them for our respect of them. I reminded Eleanor how most of the white locals with whom we had come to live had been following their ways for many generations, and though their bigotry was revolting it was hardly our diplomatic business to start out by trying to reshape their standards.

"I don't care!" Eleanor said with increasing vehemence, "I'm not going to bring up my children in such an environment!"

I countered with the obvious fact that they were also my children, and I thought relationship with blacks under any conditions was better than none at all. As husband and wife we had never quarreled, but now on this subject the debate became so heated I asked a question as silly as the argument. "If we were in a burning building and somehow you had your chance to save the children or me, whom would you choose?"

Eleanor replied without the slightest hesitation, and along with all other young husbands I finally learned exactly where I stood.

"The children of course," she said.

Now, with but two months remaining of my leave of absence and the drain on our finances somehow increasing every day, I set to work on my third novel. It was the story of a man I called Benjamin Lawless, a pilot by chance and a born rover who could not force himself to stay home and behave the good husband and father. His fictional distractions were hardly competition for my own.

The Bahamas and particularly Nassau itself had become a harbor for all sorts of colorful characters, many of whom had made their fortunes in recent years and decided to leave wherever it was they had been so well rewarded. The older white Bahamian families, said to be descended from those freebooters who once made the islands their base of operations, were inclined to perpetuate their heritage. When I sought to invoke the clause in my rental lease which clearly stated I could buy the house whenever I pleased, the proprietor blandly advised me that the house was no longer for sale.

"But we have a contract."

"So? I have changed my mind."

"I could sue you."

"I wouldn't if I were you. The judge is my brother."

This cavalier attitude prevailed throughout the local merchant community and among the white officials who had secured all power in their iron fists. Winter tourists and the few extremely wealthy American families who owned houses on Hog Island were to be only gently exploited so they would return another season. Immigrants who thought to take up permanent residence, however, were plucked at mercilessly, until, either bankrupt or utterly discouraged, they went away forever. White Bahamians wanted no new participants in their private plundering. The blacks, existing on what scraps fell from the festive table, were easygoing and gravely polite. They were numb with generations of having very little to say about anything.

Despite my landlord's repudiation of a formal contract, I thought he at least had style and my strange fondness for piratical men and women allowed me to enjoy living and trying to work in this nest of brigands. Eleanor, however, grew ever more discontent with the atmosphere and found it difficult to mold her principles to the local standard. She was thus very lonely for the kind of feminine companionship she understood, and I could not blame her. Swashbuckling is for romanticists and she was ever a realist.

I wrote every day from early in the morning until one in the afternoon. Then I would have lunch and afterward work on the schooner with Coaglie or attend whatever affairs were immediate. At the bank I found our once-more-than-ample funds melting away at an astonishing pace. But of course I was writing another bestseller and soon, in spite of the local pirates, my treasure chest would overflow once again. Then, I thought, we might move to one of the outer islands where it was said that life was much easier.

My confidence was based on wishful thinking and was short-lived. One afternoon I strolled the superb beach, lost in plans for our future, but troubled with a growing apprehension of the new book's merit. Whatever gave me the idea I could write? Except for the single play at Culver, odd magazine articles, and a love for books, there was nothing in my background to suggest I might interest others in what I put down on paper. I was barely half-educated, knew little Latin and no Greek. My classical knowledge was fragmentary and mostly self-acquired; I knew nothing of style and even less of the literary graces. The ecstatic reviews which had hailed *Island in the Sky* had been only slightly less enthusiastic for *Blaze of Noon,* but still . . . ?

Stalking the fine yellow sand with my head bowed and my eyes disregarding the magnificent seascape, I wallowed in this depressive mood and soon convinced myself that the only possible virtue in the first two books came from flying, the subject matter I knew so well. *Benjamin Lawless* was also heavy with flying and certainly I must have exhausted the whole subject.

394

As if on cue, the solitude of beach and rustling of waves was broken by the sound of aircraft engines. I looked up instinctively and saw above the scattered trade wind clouds a DC-3 humming sedately westward. He's bound for Florida, I decided, then perhaps north along the coast, and I knew almost exactly what the pilots would be doing in the cockpit and how they would be squinting against the afternoon sun. Suddenly, I felt hopelessly inadequate to the task I had set myself and I yearned for the camaraderie and familiarity of the air.

I found it easy to supplement my depression by reviewing Eleanor's health. If anything, her arthritis had worsened since our arrival in the Bahamas.

"I'm a pilot, not an author," I muttered. "To hell with this. I'm going back to a real job while it's still there."

———————

Three days before my six-month leave had expired, I reported back to American Airlines. There I found the red-faced Clark of Labrador, Greenland, and Chabua in Assam. Mustered out of the Air Force, he was now chief pilot and had the grace to welcome my return. He rode beside me on one check flight to Cleveland, then turned me loose on my old route. Eleanor and the children once more moved into a small rented house in Rockland County and after a taste of fame, a brush with Hollywood glamour, and temporary exile, we settled back to the routine life of a professional pilot's family.

There was one major difference, which I thought of little consequence at the time. I now had a publisher who considered me as a property of some value if I could be polished bright enough to overcome my literary clumsiness. He was William Sloane, a tall, thin, pipe-smoking, martini-drinking man of great intellectual ability and literary integrity. He had broken away from Morrow, the publisher of my second novel, and joining with Keith Jennison formed William Sloane Associates. He contracted to publish *Benjamin Lawless* on the basis of an outline as vague as the one I had given Paramount, and thereby enriched my worth by another five thousand dollars.

If Sloane was not the world's most astute businessman, he easily qualified as one of its best editors, and if anyone in the literary world could teach me the techniques of writing it was he. He was patient, marvelously tolerant of my awkwardness, and inspired me continuously with encouraging words. He became a major influence in my life and so stimulated my efforts that *Benjamin Lawless* began to live. I wrote furiously between flights, unaware that Sloane was watching me like a matador studying the habitual hooking movements of a young bull, letting me have my head until every faulting had been revealed, at which time he would step in with his cape, teasing and persuading me toward acceptable performance.

Chapter 29

There now entered upon my life another individual who held my everlasting respect and affection. He was Sloniger, a man who had become legendary to me even before we met and whose reputation I would further enhance by writing of his qualities. Sloniger had flown the mail mano-a-mano with Lindbergh and on my airline his seniority number was One. Our first encounter had been when we were both flying the North Atlantic and I bowed happily before his enormous charm and genuine humility. For here was a master airman who had survived almost everything that can happen in the sky without a scratch on his carcass or smear on his natural nobility.

Slonnie could have passed for a riverboat gambler, for he was swarthy of complexion and easily mistaken for a Latin when he removed his cap and revealed his glossy black hair. His dark eyes were engaged in a perpetual dance, absorbing all that transpired about him and much that others failed to see. His voice was deep and well modulated and his rather delicate hands flew along with whatever he had to say—which was mostly of flight, its perils and pleasures. I revered Slonnie as did nearly every other pilot of our line, and was therefore honored when he telephoned me from San Francisco with an offer I found irresistible—live in San Francisco and fly to Honolulu with a thousand dollars a month guaranteed by his new employer, the powerful Matson Steamship Company. If Slonnie could sacrifice his unassailable seniority number for this new venture, how could I hesitate over the possible loss of my measly number 267? I went back to red-faced Clark, who only a month previously had welcomed me back to the fold.

"You want another leave of absence? You just came back from one."

"You have more pilots than you really need. If I go, someone at the bottom of the list will have a job," I said piously.

"And you are thinking of his wife and starving children. . . ." I recognized that Clark had made a statement rather than forming a question. Our eyes met and held steadily.

"Of course."

"Bat shit. You are bored. You're like all my other clowns around here who flew the ocean. You want to go back to big airplanes and big distances."

"Admitted."

Clark refused to authorize another leave until I had seen Dunn, the newly appointed chief pilot of my area. A big and jolly man, he lolled back in his chair, folded his hands behind his head and stared at the ceiling.

"I can spare you. Plenty of people are panting for your job, but I think you're making a mistake. The government isn't going to allow a steamship company to operate an airline to Hawaii because Pan American won't like it. And Juan Trippe can make the government think his way."

"All I want is six months to give it a try."

"I hope I don't see the day when I rehire you as a co-pilot at the bottom of our list."

The next morning I stood beside a hospital bed where my dear friend and former captain, Auggie Keim, lay fuming and bruised. He had brought his flight in from Chicago about midnight and had offered to drive his co-pilot and the stewardess home. After he dropped them off, a drunk driver had smashed against Keim's car, he was catapulted out and struck his head against a curbing. In Keim's long career he had never scratched an airplane and was noted for his conservative ways. "If my ass gets there, so will the passengers'," was his favorite dictum, and now he appeared more furious than subdued by the interference of an unpredictable event.

For lack of bedside chatter I told him of my intent to leave almost immediately for San Francisco. "You're out of your friggin' head," Keim growled. "A steamship company won't know how to run an airline. Go sail your boat if you have to have salt water."

Keim was a devoted pessimist and accomplished fault-finder. I knew his surliness and caustic manner were an affectation worn to protect the softness of his heart and my suspicions would have been roused immediately if he actually approved of anything I did. He winced as he shook his head.

"Once a co-pilot always a co-pilot," he moaned in despair. "I once hoped you would become a reasonable man, but that is now obviously an impossibility."

Sloniger and the airline inaugurated by the Matson Steamship Line proved to be the Valhalla of airmen. During the service's brief existence it became what was possibly the finest airline ever operated in the world, an impression confirmed by the enthusiastic response of our passengers. Matson, unhampered by the lingering pinchpenny ways of various domestic airlines which had managed to survive since the airmail days, lavished the same attention on their passengers to and from the Hawaiian Islands as was customary on their fine steamships. The cuisine under Degorac, former chef to the king of the Belgians, was superb. The wines were exemplary. After being plied with free champagne or whatever their thirst demanded, passengers sat down to a long table where repasts never before seen aloft awaited their attention. During the Christmas holidays the menu featured a roasted boar with the traditional apple in its mouth. Pheasant under glass, squab, and guinea hen were offered among other fowl; Scottish smoked salmon, sturgeon, California crab, and Hawaiian *mahi-mahi* pleased the fish-lovers. Only the most select cuts of tender beef were served by the two stewardesses, and the wine steward quite properly draped a napkin over his arm and wore the classic chain of a sommelier.

Our flight crew uniforms were identical to those of the Matson Steamship officers, with the addition of gold-braided wings to the anchor device. With four gold stripes and white-topped caps we were all quite gaudy in comparison with personnel of other airlines. (At this time captains on domestic airlines wore two stripes and other flight officers one and one half. Pan American flight crews wore no designation except small metal wing devices and were known as pallbearers because of their black uniforms.)

There were two sittings at the long table, with the captain taking the first and the first officer taking the second. The stewardesses who graced these ceremonies were chosen from hundreds of applicants for their beauty and intelligence and wore uniforms especially designed for them by the world-renowned Mainbocher. The flight-deck door was always open and during the early hours of the flight the crews invariably held an informal open house. All of this was available to passengers at no higher cost than other airlines charged, with the added opportunity of flying one way and taking one of the Matson ships the other. A Matson band met the aircraft on arrival in Honolulu and the passengers were nearly smothered in free leis, courtesy of the local Matson hotels.

The ecstatic reaction of the island traveling public brought an immediate and outraged series of protests from the other airlines, particularly Pan American, whose arrogance toward their paying customers was an unfortunate heritage of their long monopoly. Every Matson flight was filled to capacity with waiting lists in reservations. Pan American, arriving at Honolulu almost simultaneously, was often only half full. The consequence, which nearly all of us refused to recognize, was inevitable.

The treatment of Matson flight crews under Sloniger spoiled us forever. I took a taxi to the Oakland airport at Matson expense. In Honolulu we were lodged at either the Moana or Royal Hawaiian hotels with a private room for the captain. The pleasures of Waikiki Beach were ours during the twenty-four-hour layover, and on the return flight to the mainland Matson always arranged to place a crate of fresh pineapples aboard to be divided among the crew.

With Sloniger in command, flight standards were of the very highest. During the entire operation not a scratch was put on an airplane despite mechanical growing pains during the early months. We kept pinching ourselves.

Such was my own joy and affluence I bought a fine old San Francisco house on Washington Street. It was a tall and narrow dwelling located in the heart of the plush Pacific Heights section where the wealthy city fathers had long before established themselves. The house reared itself four stories high and was perched on a stone pediment which afforded a fine view of the Golden Gate and the bay from the upper floors. A tranquil garden court backed the house. There was more than enough room for our tribe with separate rooms for George and the twins, plus a bedroom and bath for Mary, a two-hundred-and-fifty-pound black lady Eleanor had hired in New York. She had taken over the care of the children and those housekeeping tasks Eleanor no longer could perform. In our eyes she was a member of the family.

As a refuge and place to continue my writing of *Benjamin Lawless,* I had part of the top floor converted into an office-aerie. The expansive view, I thought, would similarly inspire my mind and minimize my growing suspicion that heaven might have a few thorns. I tried to enjoy looking at Sausalito across the bay through binoculars, for there I could spy the masts of my beloved schooner, *Story II.* Having brought her around from New York on the deck of a steamer at great expense, I now sailed her in the fresh bay winds whenever I could scratch up a crew. Yet the time I stole from writing troubled me increasingly.

Thanks to my flying salary I was just able to make our monthly expenses, which included ever-increasing amounts to doctors. I had not much faith in their ministrations against arthritis, and, indeed, Eleanor seemed to deteriorate month by month, but her brave fighting deserved every auxiliary and her devotion to doctors had become neo-religious. While they gave her at least some mental comfort, I continued to pray for a miracle.

It was not forthcoming. There were days and nights when Eleanor was apparently as healthy as anyone and wonderful moments when her former vivacity returned. Then there were periods when she rarely ventured from her bedroom and her crying out in the nights became almost unbearable. During these dread spells I did my utmost to comfort her. I had little success.

There were further problems as the *yins* splattered the fat, contented faces of the *yangs*. All of the money I had received from *Island in the Sky* and *Blaze of Noon* had now been squandered. Worse, the book *Benjamin Lawless,* with which I hoped to recoup, was going badly. I had sent Bill Sloane several hundred pages, almost two thirds of the book, which he returned with the suggestion I start all over again. There followed a six-page letter outlining my literary sins in such embarrassing detail that there seemed no hope for the book or its bumbling author. It was all too obvious I could split an infinitive at any range and my assignment of thoughts to various characters bore little relation to what they might actually be capable of conceiving. "Now we will start from page one," Sloane had written, "and learn how to say what we want to say."

I had no choice. Sloane was undeniably right in all his assertions and as he removed the blinders from my eyes every flaw seemed to jump up from the pages. For months thereafter, he tried to teach me the fundamentals of the craft I presumed to follow. His letters always began with a half-page description of the cold with which he was perpetually afflicted, then a paragraph on the queasy financial condition of his new publishing house, and finally the lesson would begin. He taught me the importance of "means of perception" and how the viewpoint must never be changed in the same scène lest the reader become confused or jarred out of his involvement in the story. He taught me how character builds story rather than the other way around, and he taught me how to avoid the prosaic and cut the turgid. And countless other things.

I was deeply grateful to Sloane for his generosity and kept assuring him in my replies, ". . . some day you will be proud of me."

It was a guarantee I was not at all sure I could fulfill. Now I strove to rescue a book I prayed would at least spare us from shame.

The final verdict came while I was still flying for Matson. The reviews were much kinder than the book deserved, but the public in its wisdom bought a mere three thousand copies. There would be no further royalties due me and, worse, I had contributed my share to the demise of Sloane's publishing house.

The distractions of my flying job detoured me from the overpowering and unique despair known only to authors who realize they have produced a bad book. Fortunately, Matson Airlines' growing pains did often make heavy demands upon our patience and sense of humor, thereby keeping me from overlong preoccupation with literary failure. Until we eventually found the trouble and expensive solution, one of our aircraft persisted in misbehaving. One night, bound for Honolulu, just after reaching cruising altitude, we were suddenly bedeviled with the unnerving problem of all four engines cutting out. There was a great scrambling around the flight deck as we attempted every conceivable remedy. I had immediately turned back for Oakland and our descent was willy-nilly whether we liked it or not.

While I preferred to believe my reactions to this strange situation were properly stoic as befitted a resourceful commander, I suspected my actions were more like a symphonic conductor with a rebellious orchestra. Fortunately all four engines did not quit simultaneously; yawing hither and yon with intermittent surges of power I managed to hold us in an acceptable descent toward the Golden Gate. The spasmodic commotion also allowed us time enough to discover the engines would keep running handsomely if we used full mixture and nearly take-off power. Otherwise they took on a convulsive belching, farting, and spewing of blue flames into the night sky which I knew must be disconcerting to our passengers regardless of free champagne. On the flight deck we were too busy to be terrified.

Ten interminable minutes after reversing course we saw the towers of the Golden Gate Bridge poking through the coastal fog, but the city of San Francisco and all of the Bay Area were still hidden beneath a golden mist. Having so recently left Oakland and climbed through the same overcast I knew we must now make an instrument approach before landing. Obliged to use an extraordinary amount of power to keep the engines functioning I managed to make the approach at speeds varying between two hundred and two hundred forty miles per hour, possibly the swiftest ever attempted. Sloniger met us. When he saw my nerves had untangled, he passed his hand across his slick black hair and, sighing, said, "Well . . . that's what you get paid for, not just to sit up there and look at the pretty ocean."

The recommended fixes to the outlaw airplane became as many as the experts involved. No one, including the sages from Pratt and Whitney who manufactured the engines, dared conceive of the true cause. We did prove with certainty that the engines would run without the slightest discontent and at normal power if we cruised at altitudes below four thousand feet. Thus, while the experts consulted, and toyed with their slide rules, the aircraft was permitted to continue in business.

It was my lot to fly our maverick aircraft from Honolulu to Portland, Oregon, on another night. I took the precaution of planning the flight at three thousand feet. One of the crew members was new to me, a blond stewardess named Hilda whose proportions, I thought, would certainly keep our male passengers from undue concern about our low altitude. Just after we passed the point of no return, Hilda came to the flight deck and announced that one of the passengers was having labor pains. Perhaps, she suggested, it would be well to radio ahead and arrange for an ambulance to meet the aircraft since the frequency of the pains was increasing. I turned to Vaclavick, the radio operator, and asked him to tap out the necessary request.

Before she left the flight deck, Hilda paused long enough to tell us a joke which I thought was rather raunchy considering her innocent appearance. About an hour passed as we drummed along steadily through the night. I was pleasantly surprised at the smoothness of our progress despite the low altitude. Then Hilda appeared on the flight deck again to tell me the woman's labor pains were increasing in frequency. How long would it be before we landed in Portland? I advised that it would be at least another three hours and was struck by Hilda's sudden indifference to the time. She seemed to have forgotten why she came forward until she braced herself against the support post behind my seat and began another story, even raunchier than the first. Then, laughing, she disappeared into the darkness aft of the flight deck. When I was certain she had returned to the cabin I leaned across to the co-pilot, who seemed to know Hilda, and asked him what he thought of her deportment. Had I become prissy at my advanced age of thirty-five?

He reassured me. "She's really a nice girl, but once in a while she gets into the vodka back there and turns into a real firecracker."

I knew now the peculiar glaze in her eyes was not just the dim light reflected from the instrument panel.

We had determined the cause of our previous engine difficulty with this aircraft was the plumbing system. It was not designed to provide enough fuel to the new type engines at higher altitudes. Yet the coast of Oregon rises boldly from the sea and I had intended raising our flight level to four thousand feet an hour before closing with it. That altitude was not high enough to approach the coast under instrument conditions, but the whole area had been reported free of cloud and the coming dawn should allow the final hour of the flight to be made in excellent visibility. I knew the several entries through the coastal range where relatively low altitude flight could be maintained in perfect safety as long as visibility was unobstructed. Considering the established reputation of our engines for tantrums above four thousand feet I had no intention of flying higher.

Vaclavick received a reply to our request. An ambulance would be waiting on our arrival. I telephoned the cabin and recognized Hilda's voice as she answered. Her acknowledgment was slurred and her reply well suited to her mood. "Okay, honey. Don' you worry 'bout a thing. We got everthin' under control back here."

How nice, I thought, as I cut the connection. Yawning at the first sign of dawn, I thought there were times when wartime flying had been relatively easy.

A final fix before the stars faded placed us almost exactly on flight plan. Although it was still clear over the ocean I climbed to four thousand feet on schedule. The day, hastened by our speed and higher altitude, announced itself with a serene sky of viridian green cooled with cobalt and touched fancily with bronze upon a few high wisps of cloud. It was going to be a beautiful morning, and I worked my dry tongue over my lips in anticipation. Scratching at the overnight grit of my beard, I vowed, as I had upon hundreds of other drawings, to quit smoking forever. The engines rumbled on smoothly. I watched the two whirling propellers over my left shoulder and saw them create a circular flashing pattern as the first rays of the sun struck their blades.

Half an hour later the loom of the coastline darkened the horizon and I swore softly as a new challenge presented itself. A bank of cloud hung over the coast and extended as far as I could see. Very obviously we could not top it at four thousand feet. Five or possibly even six thousand would be required to remain in the clear.

I waited until we were nearly upon the barrier which with any other aircraft I would have left easily several thousand feet below. Then reluctantly I told the co-pilot to climb. He obeyed with the expected lack of enthusiasm.

At four thousand three hundred feet the first jiddering began in the engines and all of us watched the instruments in a kind of apprehensive fascination. I reminded the crew that we had plenty of fuel remaining, enough if necessary to operate again at full rich mixture and nearly full power if the engines behaved too badly. As alternatives we had Crescent City, California, and Astoria, both at sea level. Thus there was no real emergency even in prospect, but the coincidence of problems on this flight was straining my now well-developed posture of serenity in the face of trouble.

At four thousand five hundred feet there were occasional backfires, muffled protests which the four engines seemed to have divided among themselves. At five thousand feet the overall commotion became so pronounced, I resorted to the full rich mixture and nearly full power. At once the engines smoothed, we easily surmounted the cloud bank and, full bore, sped toward Portland. I found some comfort in the thought that we might at least beat the stork.

Perhaps it was my frustration with the altitude limitation of a long night's flight, perhaps it was relief from tension, that led me to mischief, for now I reached for paper and scribbled a message. Vaclavick's Morse key enabled him to communicate directly with the San Francisco high seas station. They would telephone any message received to the addressee. Sloniger, I knew, would still be asleep. It was time to interrupt his enviable bliss.

ONE STEWARDESS DRUNK. ONE PASSENGER HAVING A BABY. FOUR ENGINES QUITTING INDEPENDENTLY. WHAT DO I DO NOW. QUESTION MARK.

Vaclavick smiled as he took the paper and began tapping at his key.

The froth of waves crashing against the Oregon rocks passed below and immediately all else was lost in the overhanging mist. We continued in brilliant sunshine, high above the black peaks which jabbed through the overcast.

Vaclavick moved both headphones over his ears. Listening, he wrote down Sloniger's reply.

DO WHAT YOU ALWAYS DO. PROCRASTINATE.

I folded the message carefully and tucked it in my pocket. It was a souvenir I hoped to keep forever. Now along the horizon I saw the Cascade Range clearly outlined. We were aerial sailors with port nearly in sight. Smiling at everything in the new-day world, I thought of Sloniger's pith and the certain play of muscles about his mobile face as he composed his message. And I thought of how he had turned my attempt at humor into an expression of absolute faith. For it had ever been the custom of fine airmen to underreact and make light of their troubles aloft. To suppose even briefly that I was one with Sloniger was satisfying tribute indeed.

———

When my first six-month leave from American Airlines had passed, I had requested a further six months. At the end of the year I wrote Dunn a letter of resignation which he had the decency to accept with regret. Only a few more months passed before we knew that our new and supposedly powerful employer was in serious difficulty. Pan American, grievously wounded in the Hawaiian trade by true competition, ran for succor to the Civil Aeronautics Board. Matson, like the Grace Steamship Line to South America, and the Santa Fe Railroad, were surface carriers and therefore were violating the law by engaging in air transportation. The battle was all Juan Trippe's from the start, and soon we were limited to only a few charter flights a month. In a last-ditch attempt to save a fine organization we began the miserable business of "slave flights" between New York and Puerto Rico, becoming hyenas scraping at the very bottom of the airline trade. All of the luxury was gone as avaricious agents paid by head count persuaded and pushed as many bewildered Puerto Ricans on our aircraft as there were life preservers. And sometimes more.

Just before the Matson airline limped through its very last flights, I brought an empty DC-4 nonstop from New York to San Francisco. It was to be sold. The only passenger was a puppy Keim had given me, a lop-eared hound I christened Solo.

We took off from La Guardia Field just at dawn, banked to the southwest, passed over the Statue of Liberty as the sun splashed her crown with gold. There was not a wisp of cloud in the sky and our visibility was unlimited. We climbed to ten thousand feet and settled down to what I had thought must be just another long day's grind across the country. Yet over New Jersey with its neatly arranged farms and cloistered little towns a new sense of special privilege asserted itself and I longed to share my thoughts with the crew.

I wondered if they would become uncomfortable if I suddenly asked such aerial veterans to look below and watch the carpet of an unsuspecting nation moving slowly beneath our wings. For now it seemed to me I had spent my life viewing the earth from on high, searching like some aging pelican for a pleasant place to die. Below, I knew, injustice often prevailed over justice and folly over reason. Somewhere below a male was being murdered, a female raped, a child beaten. Copulation in all its varieties was being practiced even at this hour of the morning, and youths still groggy from their slumbers and not yet out of their beds were furtively masturbating. Hidden in the graceful hills, the insane were confined by people whose own wisdom might very well be suspect, the sick neglected and the suicidal encouraged in their purpose. Somewhere below adulterers were joining, and respectable housewives still abed were fantasizing a liaison with their favorite movie idol.

Yet there were other threads to the pattern. Below in

the same geography, now invisibly divided by a line which insisted that one side was New Jersey and the other Pennsylvania, the Appalachians were no more than wavelets on the surface of my native land. They were mountains of such insignificant dimension they barely deserved the name, yet nestled in their shelter and beyond in the lusher hills to the west, some devoted wife was waking her children and assuring herself that her lifetime mate went off to his labors well fed and clothed. And there were some Americans below who would pass the morning in hunger, though fewer than in other lands which had unfolded beneath my wings.

There were multitudes of ordinary Americans below, neither saints nor psalm-singers, but earnest citizens who took on the woes of their fellow man as sympathetically as their own. Mixed in with the thieves and burglars, pimps and frauds, were many more of my countrymen whose belief in God was a nebulous mixture of fairy tale and self-conviction, but unswerving. They also believed in the unsteady pillars of democracy and tried as best they could to practice their own versions of the creed. In Pennsylvania, its grimy face scarred forever by the depredations of mining men, there was a concentration of new Americans who believed that any system here, however faulty, was superior to what they had abandoned.

These things I thought to share with my crew, but because I was the captain they would be obliged to display at least some interest and I knew such gratuitous attention would only be embarrassing. They had been long from home and were engrossed in their own dubious future with a dying airline.

As our progress toward the horizon continued and Ohio slipped easily below, I found myself wondering why this flight which should have been forlorn was so different from any other. Everywhere the sky remained unblemished. There was no smoke, or haze, or surface fog, and the clarity of detail below was further enhanced by the brilliance of the sun behind our aircraft's tail. I had never seen the earth so clearly defined anywhere in my ten thousand hours aloft, but the sense of belonging I knew had little to do with the weather. What I saw below now should have been only real estate, postal-card-pretty Ohio farms rampant on fields of green. Yet there was more to this morning's contemplation while I sailed through the earth's envelope. I did not care if the fashion now was to scoff at patriotism. Why should I be anything but proud of being an American?

As we passed along the shores of Lake Erie, then crossed the great inland sea of Lake Michigan, I wished there were some way to share my lofty perch with all Americans, and fix forever their admiration and affection for our mutual home.

To Vaclavick the radio operator, whose duties on domestic flights were minimal, I said, "Do you happen to have a soap box?"

"Why?"

"Because I want to stand up on it and yell, 'I love you.'"

Vaclavick, who was occasionally given to aerial philosophy, turned to his crewmates and said, "You would think by now I would know better than to fly with certain pilots. It must be the lack of oxygen over the years, or the vibration, or too long staring at gauges. You can tell when they start losing their marbles."

Part Three

WRITING

THE TRAIN FROM PUERTO LIMÓN

The train from Puerto Limón has now contrived a total change in our environment. I think the Señor Engineer must be lost. Somehow, while I was lost in that other life he must have also become sidetracked, because the passing scenery is not Costa Rican, but Swiss. The mountains are steep-sided and the air has become cool and relatively crisp.

With the heat of the jungles now bubbling in the valleys far below, the appetites on this train are thriving. Everyone seems to be eating.

I take down my rucksack with the intention of extracting the dubious-looking sandwich I have brought from the hotel, and once again there is Switzerland. How can this be? How dare my vagrant thoughts leapfrog over two

410

wars, a whole flying career, and a considerable part of a continuing literary adventure?

It is the rucksack, of course, that efficient trapping I once carried up and down the mountain at Verbier, Switzerland, where in a small chalet I had, among other efforts, incongruously written a book about the San Francisco police department.

Are the thoughts of all men subject to such frivolous departures? When we propose to think chronologically, how long do most people hold the line? Do they also divert a few thousand years in real time simply because of the passing scenery or the fumbling with an old kit bag, or any other real item which might have served them in another era? It is of such capricious mental traits that time confusion is born. We say, "It took me one year to do this or that," or "It has been five years since we have met." Our hopeless inaccuracy of such measurements is bound to aggravate what is already chronological deception. How convenient to believe that every year is the same length, and upon a certain day rejuvenate the hypocrisy by throwing away our calendars. Unless we are in prison, not one year of our lives is even remotely identical to another. Some years are so throbbing with excitement and joy they become the past long before we are willing to accept their events as history. Other years drag on interminably and become almost totally forgotten as having a beginning or an end.

I am on this train because the profession I finally came to allows me to work just about any place the local government will pass me through their frontier. I can afford to work where and when I please because chance meetings with a series of individuals obliged, perhaps even forced me, to become reasonably adept at my profession.

Chapter 30

No one, not Sloniger or general manager Schmidt, or even any of the powerful Matson chieftains, could put our humpty-dumpty airline back together again. My nonstop flight across the United States with the puppy Solo as the one passenger was concluded with a sentimental circling of the Golden Gate Bridge and a lingering vision of a vast land revealed without the modest adornment of a single cloud. It was my very last flight under the magnificent Sloniger, and it would be a long time before I flew again.

The demise of the Matson airline led to a series of difficulties, but the end of the *yin* was still invisible. The abrupt cessation of flying pay demanded an immediate change in our way of living, a metamorphosis Eleanor found difficulty in accepting.

My own adjusting would have seemed even more absurd if our sudden need for cash had not been so very real. A friend recommended that I should apply for unemployment compensation, a resource I had not even considered because I so firmly believed in personal independence; I should take care of the government, not it of me. I had noticed the deductions from my paychecks, but thought it just another way of milking the citizen-producer and had successfully ignored it. Now I was told I could retrieve some of my money if I could prove need, a requirement I found not as easy to fulfill as I had been told it would be.

The unemployment offices were in the ferry building, and I stood in line for just under an hour before a case worker waved me to a chair beside his desk. From the start I saw it was not going to be an entirely lucid interview, but I was determined to see it through.

"What kind of work have you been doing?"

"Airline pilot."

"Ah? And what has been your salary?"

"One thousand dollars a month."

My host rolled his eyes in disbelief. "What are you doing here? We don't have jobs available like that."

"I've come for some of the money I paid in."

"But . . . but . . . why after earning so much do you need money?"

"I have to pay our maid."

When the case worker finished shaking his head in disbelief he asked, "Would you accept similar work if we can find it for you?"

"Certainly. I'll run to the nearest prospect."

"I doubt . . . we don't have much call for pilots."

"I didn't think you did. When do I get my money?"

"There will be a three-week waiting period. If during that time you find employment . . ."

The first Christmas Eleanor bought a twenty-foot tree to grace the high entrance hall of the Washington Street house. Impressed by its proportions I inquired its cost and Eleanor replied gaily, "The Christmas tree man told me he had been saving it for the Bank of America lobby, but they decided it was too ostentatious and expensive, so he sold it to us at a discount."

The great green tree was perfectly complemented by the staircase of the Washington Street house and the mahogany bannister, complete with three laughing children who used it as a slide. Beyond was a mirrored dining room and glittering candelabra. Mary, smiling and chuckling in the spirit of the festive season, maneuvered her two hundred and fifty pounds around the table, where a goose was about to be served. The scene was better suited to the family of a prosperous San Francisco merchant rather than an unemployed pilot and would-be author whose latest book was a disaster and who seemed suddenly unable to write anything the magazines wanted to buy. It is always easy to elevate a style of living, but extraordinarily painful to start a descent.

The first atonement was the departure into other hands of my beloved schooner. She brought a much lower price than if I had been able to wait for a more enthusiastic buyer. Soon afterward, Mary left amid torrents of mutual tears. I wrote assiduously and at last made a sale to *Redbook* magazine. It was a story aptly named "The Money Tree," and it kept us in groceries for another month. Yet I knew we could not long continue without steady income; proof of how habits deform judgment, since it never occurred to me to divide the considerable sums I had made at writing by the number of months involved and thereby discover a steady income.

The elaborate studio I had created atop the Washington Street house had to be justified. Thus, every morning I rose at dawn and within an hour was hard at writing short stories which I thought would bring the quickest return. I wrote until midafternoon with a brief pause for lunch and soon discovered that the creation of short stories for the commercial market was an extraordinarily tricky profession. Moreover, the ambitious writer had better live in

413

New York City where easy and frequent meetings with editors could be arranged. All major periodicals except *Esquire* magazine were headquartered in Manhattan and the attitude of their editors was naturally influenced by personal contact. San Francisco was still a long way from anywhere, although a few editors did understand it was no longer necessary to send rejection slips around the Horn in a sailing ship.

There was no predicting the income of a free-lance writer, and as a consequence my hardiness was tested regularly and Eleanor's morale rose and fell with every latest response to my efforts. A story called "The Horse Latitudes" sold for the staggering sum of seven hundred fifty dollars and immediately sent us both on a buying spree. We were temporarily sobered by a story called "Square Sails," for which *Rudder* magazine paid only thirty-seven dollars. Then *Collier*'s bought "Nice New Pair of Wings" for eight hundred fifty dollars and added an additional thousand dollars when it won a literary prize. Something called "Mid-Latitudes Gal" brought eleven hundred dollars, but a story on the San Francisco pilots brought a mere thirty-six dollars after two weeks' hard work.

Other bits and pieces kept us tantalizingly afloat, but the scratching was constant and the financial rewards bore little relation to the time spent. Compared with flying, I soon learned, writing was coolie labor. Once I received a check for seventy-five cents, my share of the English royalties from my first novel *Island in the Sky*. Six months later I received another check for twenty-four cents. These returns might have looked better were it not for the percentages involved: twenty-five percent to Viking Press, ten percent to an agent in England, and ten percent to my American agent. I thought fifty-five percent to the author of a book rather poor pickings and became increasingly discouraged with the profession.

As time passed and the last of our savings evaporated, it became obvious we could not continue payments on the Washington Street house. I made plans to leave—among them, half-hearted attempts to return to flying. As I had suspected, the wartime surplus of pilots, coinciding with a general slump in airline activity, caused job openings to be almost non-existent. Both Dunn and Keim had been proven right. I had given up my precious seniority and once lost there was no possible retrieval. Now it seemed that the system I had so long railed against in my long-held belief that one man could not necessarily do a job as well as the next, and that every man should be judged on his ability rather than on the day and hour he happened to be employed, was taking revenge. I was a hyena sniffing everywhere for scraps.

My inclination to return to the flying world diminished still further when I learned that Sloniger, also unable to find a job to match his more varied qualifications and much greater experience, was now working as a postal clerk. A sorry fate, I thought, for a man who had made history flying the early airmail in open cockpit De Havil-lands.

Other factors now were combining to drive me into different ways. The physical inaction of a writer's life brought an almost uncontrollable restlessness upon me. I was short with the children and shabby with Eleanor, reminding her too frequently how much better off she would be if she had married any one of the businessmen suitors who once sought her attentions. I could hardly believe my hollow behavior during these times, much less that financial matters which had never interested me should now seem to dominate our household. As if it were happening to another man I watched helplessly as the one-time stalwart with a boundless appetite for high adventure became a mercenary with a mouth full of oatmeal. For this fall from grace I blamed the matrimonial institution, and as a protective device Eleanor began not hearing me.

At this critical moment Paul LaFrenier, my wartime navigator, arrived in San Francisco and made his way as if guided by one of his Catholic angels to the house on Washington Street. Once our boisterous reunion was over, we retired to the fourth-floor aerie, there to rehash more exciting days together and our present discontent. La-Frenier was at loose ends, uncertain of his ambitions, but as always charged with enthusiasm for any project. It was inevitable that within a very short time we should find something to renew our zest for conquest.

Loneliness no longer burdened my father. The tradi-tional father and son premarital dialogue was reversed when he felt obliged to ask my approval of his union with Esther Hutchinson. I found his bashfulness on the occasion touching and, taking the pose of a patriarch, first inquired if he realized the responsibilities of marriage and then urged him to proceed forthwith. Later I sent him a telegram including the same phrase he had once telegraphed to me: ". . . you have given a hostage to fortune."

When an invitation came to visit my father in Pebble Beach it was always in the nature of a command performance. We loaded into the jeep, fasted on the morning of departure, and charged off toward a different world. Now, having accepted my father's financial aid so many times, I could not bring myself to even hint at further support. I was thirty-eight years old, had conducted my affairs regardless of his advice, and brought myself and family only to shabby gentility. Yet I saw no reason to reject his bounteous hospitality once we passed through the grilled gates of his opulent domain. There, with my new stepmother now at his side, my father maintained the life of a well-funded country gentleman. Always in appropriate costume he wore tweedy jackets, although he never forsook tie and vest. It pleased him to be called Cactus by his son and he was so addressed by many of the local gentry, nearly all of whom were very heavy of purse.

When visiting my father it was usually our pleasure to ride together over the miles of well-kept horse trails and occasionally, when Dick Collins (who managed the stables) would lend me a willing mount, I would have at the Olympic hunt course which wound through unspoiled forest and opened alternately upon meadows spreading to the sea. It gratified my father's appreciation for the spectacular when I rode through his outer gates one afternoon, then urged my mount across the courtyard and passed between the enormous three-inch-thick, iron-studded, double doors of the main house. I clattered through the foyer and continued to the inner courtyard where I tethered my mount and joined my father in a glass of fine brandy. If he wanted to live like a Spanish grandee, I thought it my pleasurable duty to enhance the atmosphere.

Cactus was a munificent host and delighted in giving lavish parties. We had been invited to participate in a Spanish fiesta and were requested to attend in costume. Eleanor dug into a trunk and found my Culver uniform, which became entrancing on her, if oversize, and I intended to make do with the boots, breeches, shirt, and kerchief of a cavalryman. Cactus, predictably, wore an elaborately decorated outfit he had bought in Spain, and suffered good-naturedly the numerous accusations of having given the party so he could wear it.

El Retiro was the ostentatious culmination of all my father's dreams, admired by his contemporaries and respected by all who could catch a glimpse of its environs as they passed. It was a reflection of prosperous and self-made America during the years after the Second World War. Geographically isolated from the mainstream of American life, it remained a refuge equally aloof from the undercurrents of social change becoming more evident in every American day. For Eleanor and myself and our children it became a sort of fairyland where we could escape from the realities of wresting a livelihood from a world I was finding indifferent to my attentions. We were still eating three meals a day, but all frills were long gone and our outstanding bills far exceeded our resources.

Deer roved the grounds adjacent to the main house at El Retiro, peacocks strutted through the dappled shade beyond the formal gardens, a Chinese chef prepared the most sumptuous meals, and his wife attended the great polished table in the dining room. An elevator transported my father to the upper floors because he had been warned about his heart. I was embarrassed by such luxury and, ungratefully, often made light of it while secretly enjoying its every provision.

For his Spanish fiesta my father invited two hundred guests and imported a mariachi band to liven up the gathering plus a small dance band to take over while the Mexicans rested. Three burros roamed among the guests throughout the evening. Emboldened by too much fine whiskey, I mounted one and was promptly tossed through the air, landing almost upon a stocky little man who assisted me to my feet. He introduced himself as Fred Holmes and I remembered that during the guest list briefing my father had explained he was a sheep-rancher from Northern California. If so, I thought his appearance was most deceptive, for he was short, almost rotund, and jolly. Nothing about him except his eyes—clear and blue and far-seeing—suggested a man of the open spaces. His manner was extraordinarily simple and his voice so deep he seemed like a friendly bullfrog comfortably enthroned on a lily pad. After sharing a hearty laugh at the burro's humbling gesture I suddenly found the man's magnetism and warmth were like an open hearth and I clung to him almost desperately as someone who might be sympathetic to my nonconformist ambitions. After only a few minutes I was pouring my troubles onto my new-found friend. He listened quietly as I told him of my latest hope—to buy a fishing boat and farm the sea. The world needed food and those who provided it could depend on ample rewards. With millions of new mouths to feed every year, was it not obvious something must be done?

"I guess a limited number of idealists can't do the world too much harm," he said while his eyes left me and seemed to be studying something on the ceiling. Finally he rolled his cigar between his heavy fingers and regarded it thoughtfully.

"Tell you what," he grunted. "Whatever money you can raise to buy a fishing boat, I'll match. We'll be partners."

Later I learned he owned one of the largest sheep ranches in the world, but he managed to keep another matter his very private business for almost a year. The man whom I came to regard with near-adoration was suffering from myeloma, a terrible form of bone cancer which must soon bring him death.

The juxtaposition of events now became almost incredible. After a weekend of the high life with my father and Esther, we returned to San Francisco where a letter awaited me. I read the brief message through twice before assuring myself I was awake. My namesake uncle in St. Louis had died, leaving me a legacy of six thousand dollars. Since the estate was now closed, a check would be following shortly. I deliberately collapsed to the floor and let Eleanor discover me prone, but clutching the letter very firmly. Thus began the Western Ocean Fishing Company capitalized at fourteen thousand dollars. I conned the unsuspecting LaFrenier into parting with thirty-five hundred dollars to match the sum I thought I could invest. Fred Holmes matched our combined funds with a few good-natured croaks of surprise at the speed of my financing, and our enterprise began.

At this early stage I thought it would be unwise to

advise my father of our plans, fearing that his almost certain disapproval would result in discouragement. I should stick to writing, he had insisted on the morning after his successful fiesta. At the party he had been talking to Ray Milland, the actor, who had read one of my books and thought it excellent. And his friend Walt Disney had similarly responded to a copy of *Benjamin Lawless*. There! Was that not guarantee of a vastly successful future?

I barely heard my father. I wanted a life on the bounding main.

LaFrenier and I went directly to Seattle where we knew that the best fishing boats were for sale. And that was almost *all* we knew of the fishing business. Besides a brief education in a dragger out of San Francisco I had made a few trips long-lining for black cod with Tunisan, an Irishman of very great piscatorial skill. He had spent most of his lecture time trying to discover what a man of my background was doing at the heavy and unrewarding labor he had known all his life.

"You tryin' to hide from the police or somethin'? Did you kill somebody?"

Long-lining for black cod in Tunisan's *Northwest* did provide an excellent refuge from the civilized world and all its accoutrements. We worked twenty-eight miles offshore and had no company of any kind. Among the inhabitants of San Francisco fishing society, Tunisan alone was skillful enough and hungry enough to spend eighteen hours a day fishing black cod. While we bounced our brains about on the briny, smart fishermen stayed in port repairing their gear for the salmon and abalone season, which at least paid enough to keep a very good fisherman from living off his relatives. American tastes had changed and we were fishing for cat food.

Neither LaFrenier nor myself had any experience with fish buyers and had great difficulty in believing they were real when we actually came to deal with them. With a single exception, they were caricatures of evil, pasteboard individuals straight out of *Daily Worker* cartoons wherein the paunchy capitalist was always depicted with his boot on the poor laborer's neck. The majority were of Sicilian origin; they wore diamond rings, which they pleased to flash at the sun, two-tone shoes, huge cigars, gaudy shirts, and sports jackets of the wildest coloring. Their chariots, parked far enough away from the weighing scales to avoid possible anointment with fishy water, were Cadillacs with whitewall tires. Sometimes they lent money to fishermen, thereby securing their very souls in bondage, and if they were relatives the chains were all the more binding.

Western Ocean Fishing Company was launched by two idealists who had only a very sketchy idea of those who might buy their products. That there might be some problem in even producing something for sale, we easily ignored in our self-confidence. We knew the sea. We knew how to handle a boat and we were expert navigators. Alas.

We bought a new boat in Seattle, forty feet of Alaska cedar planking on oak frames, for twelve thousand dollars. She was a pretty little vessel and we promptly christened her in the masculine gender, *Fred Holmes.** We brought her southward, surviving a frightening tempest with maximum winds clocked by the Coast Guard at one hundred ten miles per hour. In our innocence we entered the salmon fishery out of San Francisco and by almost pure chance, occasionally caught one and sometimes two after a full hard day at sea. It soon became very obvious that the Western Ocean Fishing Company lacked know-how.

We sought help from more professional fishermen and found them surprisingly willing to share the wealth of their experience; what appeared to be a simple matter of baiting hooks and dragging them from dawn to dusk behind a seaworthy vessel was laced with secrets, instinctive reactions developed over years of practice, and a willingness to live just above the poverty level. Yet commercial fishing had one great attribute which redeemed all of its faults and left us, in spite of continuous discouragements, believing we had at last found the only remaining life for independent men who would avoid the entanglements of desk, paper, and telephone. The profession involved some of the most colorful, generous, and stubbornly brave men we had ever seen assembled. Joining their company was deeply satisfying, and soon our weary bodies were nearly as tough as theirs. "Look," I said to Eleanor during one of my rare overnights at the Washington Street house, "look at my paws." I held out my calloused hands for her

---

* She is still fishing the Pacific and doing well.

to touch. "There you see a *man's* work. Why haven't I been doing this all my life?"

We did not discuss financial reward for my calluses because thus far there had been none. Every "trip" (fishermen never used the word *voyage*) cost us more in fuel, ice, gear, and groceries than we brought back to port. LaFrenier, a bachelor of very simple tastes, was living aboard the *Fred Holmes* and still whistling merrily. He had indeed found a new life and had made a host of friends up and down the waterfront. His ability to converse for hours with others and his genuine simplicity made him a favorite among those fishermen whose homes were their boats. I was entranced with life on the wharves where I knew the wheeling seagulls were screaming over a permanent battle of men against the elements. Every trip was a fight for financial survival and many resulted in the fierce battle of little men temporarily obliged to conquer the sea. That they did not always win only added spice to the fray. The fierce individualism of fishermen appealed to me, along with their very special camaraderie, a quality known only to those sharing a common danger.

Soon my home was the wharves, where I could inhale the pungent odor of tarred piling, fish guts, diesel smoke, and the heady perfume of a great ocean rolling through the Golden Gate. I swaggered shamelessly in rubber boots and oilskins, and for several nights, as my contribution to a protest strike by my seagoing friends against the buyers, patrolled the docks with a two-by-four. My heart was not where it should have been—in the house on Washington Street.

One fisherman came early and heartily to our technical aid; Bill Kincaid, buccaneer, freebooter, powerful oak of a man who I decided must be the reincarnation of Sir Francis Drake or possibly Henry Morgan. Kincaid's irrepressible spirit exerted its wonderful magic on men, women, and children alike. His physical energies were tremendous and his huge banana-fingered hands were an extension of the powerful bull-man whose muscles rippled beneath his bosun's shirt. As if his physical strength were not enough, he was handsome without prettiness and his air of joyous dash was soon transmitted to all who kept his company.

Eleanor, in an almost instant revival of her former self,

sparkled in the presence of Kincaid and fell more than slightly in love with him. I could not blame her. He needed comfort in his loneliness, she said so frequently that I could not disillusion her by drawing attention to the crowd of women who felt the same sympathy. When Kincaid parted with his official wife, who had finally given up trying to domesticate him, a legion of hopefuls rushed to assuage his supposed loneliness. Such was the press, he was sometimes obliged to put to sea simply for rest and recuperation.

Kincaid was multilingual, speaking fluent dog, cat, bird, and child, and all these species revealed their delight in his attentions. Aboard his boat, the *Dolphin,* where he lived most of the time, he cooked fine meals for all who came and he washed the dishes afterward with skill and dispatch better suited to a devoted housewife. Yet beware and damn the eyes of those who might be deceived and consider Kincaid a tamed and simple soul.

Even Kincaid's expert counsel could not make success-ful salmon fishermen of us in a single season: somewhat abashed at our pitiful catches, we turned to the less com-plex, but much farther-ranging albacore fishery. It was said anyone could catch an albacore tuna if the fish were in the mood and could be found. Smart fishermen waited for someone else to do the exploring. LaFrenier and I set out boldly to discover the schools, and after twelve hun-dred miles' searching and twelve days, we caught two albacore, albeit the first of the season. Thereafter we cruised the eastern Pacific from below Baja California to Oregon, working fifty to one hundred miles offshore in all kinds of weather. It was a rough life with the trips lasting as long as our ice held out, usually about ten days. By autumn, when the albacore had fled to their mysterious refuge over the horizon, we had found our sea-legs and had slightly more than hurting hands to show for our efforts. My share of six trips between late July and early October amounted to $654.31. Eleanor suggested there was an alarming discrepancy between our income and expenses. Rollicking as the life of a sailor-fisherman might be, some-thing had to be done.

Heavy storms assault the Pacific coast in November and most fishing is curtailed. Like so many other boats in the fleet, the *Fred Holmes* earned little enough at sea, but tied to the dock she gathered only barnacles. I viewed this combination as intolerable inefficiency and set about correcting it by consulting with my mentor Kincaid, who had never entertained a pessimistic thought in his forty years of life. I told him how I would now take the lead and guide him into greener pastures. "Ho! Ho!" he cried rubbing his banana fingers together so enthusiastically I thought I could hear the hard skin of his palms scraping across each other. "Ho-ho! You've a capital idea there, my friend! It's time someone showed the goddamned buyers we're not as dumb as they think we are."

My scheme originated in the odd contrast of lifestyles between Eleanor and me. With the very last of my inheritance she had managed a surprising continuance of her role as a Pacific Heights matron. She wore spotless white gloves and a stylish bonnet when lunching with her ex-Mills College friends, most of whom were now married to prosperous merchants, lawyers, or corporate chieftains. They were open in their declarations that Eleanor was a very brave lady to tolerate the antics of her "difficult" husband. And my conscience was responding to the half-hidden pressures of the social stratum in which I was supposedly acceptable even if nothing else within me was willing to pay the dues. What right had I to go sailing off over the horizon in pursuit of a fortune I now suspected had never existed, while my good wife fought to maintain the kind of respectability she understood? Certainly she was half in love with Kincaid, but her enthusiasm soured when she became aware of his episodic financial crises and of our rambunctious celebrations when our seafaring fortunes turned for the better.

The arena for these more than occasional bouts became the Shadows restaurant on Telegraph Hill, a sawdust and checkered tablecloth establishment so situated it commanded a superb view of San Francisco Bay and, almost directly below, the shipping along the Embarcadero. We chose the Shadows because the German soup was superb, and the sausage and red cabbage were of incomparable quality. At no extra charge, sourdough French bread was heaped on the table and did much to satisfy our enormous appetites. The price of a full belly was less than that of any other restaurant within hiking distance of the wharves, and yet these were minor inducements compared to the air of warmth and welcome always extended to us by Carl Rebmann, the overfat, red-faced proprietor, who was being driven slowly crazy by his Hungarian wife. Whether Rebmann sensed something of himself in our rebellious behavior was of little matter; he always forgot to charge us for our drinks unless the cash register eyes of his Hungarian wife were upon us, in which unfortunate circumstance he charged only half. In return, it was our pleasure to arrive out of the night bearing as big a fresh salmon as we could catch and, to the wonder of the much better dressed customers, slap the great twenty- or thirty-pound beauty down on the copper bar and announce it was the chef's to do with as he pleased.

Now my triple life on the wharves, Telegraph Hill, and Washington Street brought enterprise from an unlikely source. The Pooles, visitors from the East, paused for an evening at the Washington Street house. Since they were true representatives of the establishment to which Eleanor still clung, I looked forward to a reunion, for their company had always been interesting, which would make it easier for me to avoid the irresistible yawning which now plagued me every time I joined a "proper" social evening. Here was opportunity to ease my remorse by playing the agreeable host and thus, in turn, make some amends to my long-suffering wife.

In fact Kincaid was the invisible host. From his line of traps outside the Golden Gate he gave me enough of the succulent California crabs to offer a meal I could not otherwise afford. The evening was therefore a gastronomical success and Ed Poole lamented his inability to order such a delicacy at either of his favorite restaurants, Chicago's Pump Room and New York's "21." I assured him the Western Ocean Fishing Company could fill this lack, and wondered privately what Jack Kriendler (close friend of my father in his dude ranching activities) would think of Cactus Jack's son entering through the kitchen door.

"Ho-ho," said Kincaid next day, "the buyers won't like this but now we will have vengeance. Damn my eyes, won't we!"

And we did, after an organization was assembled. Kincaid brought in the crab, usually with the assistance of LaFrenier or myself. Then all of us, including sometimes my stepsister Jean, set about the complex business of getting the crab from sea to our very special customers. We found a fifty-gallon oil drum, cleaned it thoroughly, and filled it with sea water. Then we built a fire under it wherever we could operate in semiprivacy, since we had no illusions about our popularity with the local crab-dealing Sicilians if we were known to be invading their preserve.

At first it was easy enough, because our two customers were experimenting and ordered only two dozen crabs at a time. Determined to make them order more we packed the crab in fresh seaweed, and added a chunk of dry ice for refrigeration. I drove this special cargo to the airport in a borrowed truck. For one dozen fine crab delivered on the East Coast only one day out of the Pacific Ocean, we charged a mere eighteen dollars.

The reaction was almost immediate. "21" doubled, then tripled their order; likewise the Pump Room, and soon Philadelphia's Ambassador Hotel was added to our list. Supersalesman Poole sold our crab wherever he happened to dine and a totally unforeseen problem soon presented itself. Kincaid simply could not catch enough crab to fill our orders, and the cooking was taking all day long. Worse, the waterfront was a small area; news traveled rapidly, whether it was a rumor that Freckles Lavella had chanced upon a ten-thousand-dollar pod of ambergris floating alongside his boat, or confirmation that foreigners of obviously North European origin and probably Protestants were muscling in on the crab market. We were beginning to receive dark looks from strangers who now gathered around our cooking pot, asking, as if it were their right, where so many crabs were going.

We raised the prices of our crab sufficiently to give us a decent profit and yet the sum of orders increased. Still other troubles followed directly upon prosperity. After the first euphoria of success had passed, we discovered none of us bore a merchant's heart.

"Who will cooka-da-crab today?"

"*You* cooka-da-crab."

"No *you!*"

All of us were willing to endure cold, rain, and rough seas to go after the crab, but none of us wanted assignment to the ordinary work of cooking and shipping.

Then someone must have decided we were in their way.

Chapter 31

It had been one of those increasingly rare evenings when Eleanor felt well. Year by year her arthritis had progressed until now her once-lovely and delicate hands were beginning to show signs of the disease. There had been many days and nights when she could not force herself from bed, and our bathroom was crowded with vials of medicine and cannisters of pills, all intended to alleviate her pain. I had also installed a remedial apparatus over the bedroom door which allowed her to hang by her chin and, by stretching her neck and back, make movements easier after half an hour's suspension. A series of doctors had done their utmost to help Eleanor without much success.

On this night, inspired by a yearning for Italian food, we made our way to a simple restaurant on Telegraph Hill. The cuisine was excellent, the wine palatable, and the atmosphere exactly as we wished it. We were almost two hours at table, chatting like new acquaintances with a thousand mutual ties to explore. We spoke of Manhattan and of how little we missed it and of the Bahamas, from which, we at last agreed, we were better gone. We spoke of my father and his continuing impatience with my flying and of his peripatetic traveling around the world with bride Esther at his side. For this happy evening we spared ourselves mention of our declining fortunes, and—worse—the hint of incompatibility which seemed to have risen between us.

"You follow your star wherever it may lead," Eleanor had once said, "and I'll tag along behind."

These, I thought, were very strange and welcome words from a woman as strong in will as Eleanor, and I was again reminded of her unpredictability. There were times when I felt I was married to two women, one as jolly and giving as any man alive could wish. This was also the

426

woman offered to the outside world, the striking beauty and gracious lady I had once named Public Angel Number One. The other woman, more rarely revealed, was resolute beyond belief and given to delusions of grandeur. I could tell which of the two Eleanors was present for the day by the sound of her voice and her phraseology as she spoke to others on the telephone. But bigamist or not, I was still very much in love with the woman I had kidnapped from a school across the bay, and I knew it would take a very powerful force to break our union.

I remembered Eleanor's faith in me now as I tried to forget the numerous times I had failed her. Watching her across the checkered tablecloth I saw that she had lost very little of her youthful beauty, her deep brown eyes were for these moments devoid of suffering and her lovely mouth was alive with the pleasure of our companionship.

We ate passionately, as we did all things together, and I envied no other man his wife.

When we had eaten our fill we decided on a short stroll to settle the fettucini and lasagne. We had walked hardly a block when I saw a bar on the opposite side of the street and suggested we have a nightcap to finish the evening in style. The bar was called "Tony's Place" and from the outside appeared to be just another neighborhood tavern. I opened one of the double doors and bowed as my smiling wife stepped inside.

The interior of "Tony's Place" was typical. A long bar of polished wood extended almost the full length of the room, but at the street end the bar curved and joined the wall at a right angle. There, a middle-aged man wearing a hat sat alone with a full beer glass before him. About six other stools for the accommodation of patrons were aligned along the front of the bar. They were now unoccupied, a situation I supposed was due to the hour—that pause between customers who stopped to quench their thirst after work and the later type of serious drinker. We had entered in the very last of the twilight, and outside the street had been nearly deserted.

I pulled back a stool near the center of the bar for Eleanor. She mounted it and peeled off the mink coat she was wearing, a legacy from my mother. She draped the coat across her lap and we agreed it was overly hot. I nodded to the bartender, a small man, who appeared to be dozing with his back against the cash register drawer, his arms folded across his belly. He did not return my salutation or in any other way acknowledge our arrival.

I removed the trenchcoat I was wearing, crossed the few steps between the bar and the opposite wall, and hung the coat on a standing rack. There were no other coats visible and it appeared we were the only customers, save for the middle-aged man at the end of the bar.

On returning to the bar I noticed a second man at the opposite end of the bar. He also wore a hat, and was middle-aged. I had no reason to take any note of his face, although I did observe he was wearing steel-rimmed glasses. I saw that the bar area in front of him was empty, but thought nothing of it. I was anxious to resume the pleasant exchange Eleanor and I had begun during our stroll.

I took the stool beside her, sat down, and—suddenly at a loss, since we rarely drank anything after dinner—ordered two beers. We both laughed at my choice since I was not fond of beer and neither of us could remember when we had last tasted the stuff.

The bartender roused himself enough to draw the beers and push the glasses toward us. Then, without a word, he folded his arms and went back to his dozing. Eleanor and I seemed to have lost the essence of our street rapport and our conversation became a desultory review of our troubles, which were increasing daily. Our voices became unnaturally subdued, although it was unlikely the two other customers could have heard anything we said, much less, I thought, be interested.

I glanced at the juke box which stood in the corner, considered dropping a few coins in it to liven the atmosphere, then decided against it. One beer would certainly be enough and we would be gone in a few minutes.

The middle-aged men at each end of the bar, apparently strangers to each other and absorbed in their private thoughts, ignored us. I assumed from their hat styles, ties, and ordinary-looking business suits that they were "paisanos," members of the stolid and usually hard-working Italian immigrant element that inhabited Telegraph Hill and the adjacent areas. Yet I was only vaguely aware of their presence; not once did our eyes meet or my attention focus on them. I was only interested in recapturing the mellow mood Eleanor and I had been enjoying in the street.

Probably some fifteen minutes passed before I laid a five-dollar bill on the bar. The bartender came to an approximation of life again, counted out the change without making a sound, then retired into his private cocoon once more. I slipped off my stool and held Eleanor's coat while she eased into it. She would need it during the drive home because our only car was the open jeep. She passed me, walked to the street door, and went outside. I turned, took the few paces to the standing rack, and reached for my coat. I put an arm in one sleeve and had my hand in the other when I felt the coat being yanked down. Simultaneously I was propelled forward so fast that I knocked over the rack and collided hard with the wall.

Before I could react in any way something struck me hard in the left kidney, then the right, and I was spun away from the wall. To my bewilderment I now saw the two middle-aged men swinging their fists across my line of vision. I tried to cry out, but the hammering blows choked off my voice. I tried to raise my arms in defense, but the trenchcoat held my arms at waist height. I was absolutely helpless as they pounded successively on my stomach and chest, yet deliberately avoided my head. My astonishment was so total it was as if this continuing punishment was being laid upon another man. I felt the repeated pains, yet could not believe my own body was their host.

As in a nightmare I saw the faces of the two men assaulting me. They were older than I and shorter. They appeared utterly unruffled as their arms swung in unison. The one man's glasses remained in place, their hats remained exactly level, and their expressions utterly removed from the violence they were inflicting. Beyond them I saw the bartender watching my ordeal with mild interest. The attack continued for some twenty seconds of unreality before my instinct for survival asserted itself.

I managed to twist away momentarily from my assailants. I was just able to hoist my coat high enough to raise my arms protectively, and then they were upon me again. The pounding went on, punctuated by their grunting. Retreating before the ceaseless blows I tried to strike back at their heavy faces, but was unable to pass their flying fists. They knocked my arms aside and their pounding took on such force, I was moved backward in unnatural jerks, like a puppet tangled in his strings.

My back hit the street doors. Suddenly I was on the sidewalk stumbling backward toward the curb with the two men hard after me. Then suddenly they stopped and, apparently not in the least affected by their exertions, turned their backs. Not a word had been exchanged between us and they had not once touched any part of me above my neck or below my waist. Now as I reeled with pain they vanished inside "Tony's Place" as if they had not really existed. I saw the doors flap closed behind them.

I stood in the street gutter coughing and retching beyond my control, yet nothing rose in my throat. I gasped for wind, sucking desperately at the crisp night air while I looked about for Eleanor. The street was deserted.

Soon I recovered enough to stagger away from the area in front of "Tony's Place." Still breathing heavily I made for the cross street where I had parked our jeep before dinner. By the time I reached the corner my breathing had eased and I was relieved to see Eleanor waiting beside the jeep.

"Get in," I said taking her arm. For some unexplainable reason I was trying to behave as if nothing abnormal had occurred, but even in the semidarkness Eleanor could see that something was wrong.

"What's the matter with you?"

"Nothing." I managed to circle around the back side of the jeep and climb into the driver's seat without wincing.

The jeep was open and to protect my hands from the cold of the night I carried a pair of leather gloves beneath my seat. I pulled them on now slowly, thinking only of what had just happened.

"Are you sure you're all right?"

"Yes. I'm all right." I started the engine and drove away conscious of a new strength which somehow the leather gloves seemed to have given me. The drive to our home on Washington Street took some fifteen minutes, a time space as unreal as the attack itself had been.

During the ride we did not speak and I rapidly recovered. Conversation in the noisy jeep was always fragmentary at best; what the sound of the engine failed to obliterate was swept away by the wind. Eleanor, I knew, would not consider my silence unusual. It would have been better if we had both made a determined effort to revive our earlier happiness, for something terrible and quite uncontrollable was boiling within me, overcoming all my hurts and transforming me from a rational man to a murderous animal.

Instead of parking the jeep in the garage I stopped the car directly in front of the house entrance and told Eleanor to go inside. As she started for the entrance stairway, she turned and asked where I was going.

"I'll be back in a little while." I heard the edge in my voice and, fearing Eleanor would try to delay me, slammed down the throttle and roared away. I was obsessed with a single desire and utterly blind to any consequence. I knew only that it was imperative I return to "Tony's Place," and now well-gloved and refreshed by the night's air, fall upon my attackers with all the surprise on my side. They were stocky, but I was half a head taller, much younger, and in excellent physical condition.

En route I had only one moment of self-doubt. Had the single beer been too much on the half-carafe of wine I had taken with dinner? I thought, not at all. And certainly on other occasions when I had had too much alcohol, I became anything but belligerent. Even with a first drink, in any society, I began loving all the world. Yet now, driven by some irresistible impulse, I knew that this ugly rendezvous must be consummated. I had suffered a wanton attack and had lost. Every bone and muscle in my body cried out for release to physical passion. It was as if I were standing aside and watching a stranger expose himself to jeopardy.

I stopped directly in front of "Tony's Place" and jumped out of the jeep. I ran to the door with both hands extended. The doors were locked. Furious, I beat on them with my fists and, that availing nothing, pulled on one of the four brass bars which crossed the face of the door horizontally. The bar came off in my hands and I threw it aside.* I heard it clanging along the cement, then the sound of someone inside working the lock.

The door opened inward and the two innocuous-looking

* As of 1975 the bar was still missing. The other three were still in place.

431

middle-aged men came toward me. I heard one of them say, "What you tryin' to do, fella, make trouble?"

Then they were upon me. But this time things were different. I was free-handed and went at them with all the pent-up fury in me suddenly released. For a moment it seemed I might actually be the victor, but my confidence was soon destroyed. As they forced me backward into the street with their steady pounding I found it next to impossible to hit more than their guarding arms. Suddenly I realized that they were a pair of professionals, and fear replaced my anger.

Still they avoided my head, but their hammering at my body increased in ferocity. Now I wanted away, desperately, but I was already too weak to run. My middle-aged enemies had not changed facial expression or spoken a word since the blows first began.

The combat moved up and down the street. After the first collision I ceased to be the aggressor and lost all hope of victory. The sudden realization that I might be fighting for my life spurred me to a frenzied punching, but I was no match for the two professionals who were laboring, but showed no sign of fatigue.

In less than a minute I had retreated to the corner where I had originally parked the jeep. Then suddenly my adversaries were screened by khaki cloth. Two huge soldiers, both more than a head taller than any of us, had apparently risen up out of the cement sidewalk. One was white, the other black. They simply moved between the middle-aged men and myself, caught their flailing arms, turned them around, and propelled them rapidly away from me. There were no blows exchanged. The odd quartet left me isolated in the darkness, the change of situation occurring so fast I could not believe the battle was over. I was still gasping for wind and bent with pain when the soldiers returned.

I thanked them with more sincerity than I had ever expressed before in words and asked how they happened along so providentially.

"We're just lookin' over the town . . . just cruisin'. We been up the street a ways and there's nothin' doin' there."

I asked why they had interfered and assured them there had never been two men I had been happier to see.

"We just didn't like the look of them two jumpin' on one guy. You know 'em?"

"No. I never saw them in my life before tonight."

As we walked together back to the jeep I offered to buy them a drink. They accepted and I drove them to a bar on Union Street. There, they soon lost interest in me in favor of the several available females within range and after additional thanks and laying the last of my cash on the bar to finance a second drink we shook hands and said good night. The black soldier, who had hardly said a word throughout our brief acquaintance, now laid his heavy hand on my shoulder. "I wouldn't go back there if I was you," he said softly. "They was *mean*."

I had no trouble in confirming that I would not return to "Tony's Place."

Driving back to the Washington Street house I wondered why it had never occurred to me to call the police after the first assault. Still aching with pain and the whole wretched affair now reversing itself in my thoughts, I knew that my shame at succumbing to savagery would long outlast my physical hurts. Why had I gone back? What loathsome measure of violence had so displayed its fangs and had now withdrawn—I hoped forever? My behavior was unaccountable to all reason. It seemed obvious that the men were not after any money I might have had with me. And why had they so skillfully avoided my face? One blow had apparently been misdirected or glanced off my shoulder, because the soldiers had told me my ear was bleeding and I had stopped the flow with my now bloody handkerchief.

I slept hardly at all that night, racked with as much mental as physical anguish. The next morning, barely able to walk, I called my good friend Rudy Webber at the FBI and asked him if he could think of an explanation for such an unprovoked attack. I described the entire prelude to entering "Tony's Place" and the balance of the evening in detail. He listened carefully as he always did and because he was a born cop asked several pointed questions. Finally he said, "It sounds to me like it might have been a case of mistaken identity. Those individuals were undoubtedly professional hit men and were probably waiting for someone. You walked in and happened to fit the description of whoever it was, and they simply went to

433

work. Maybe that's why, when you were stupid enough to go back, they asked why you wanted to make trouble. They didn't want any part of you."

I tried to join his laughter, but my sore ribs had no sense of humor.

"On the other hand," Rudy continued, "it might have had something to do with your present activities. Some of those individuals down around Fisherman's Wharf are not about to welcome competition in their territory. Maybe you'd better change your name to something more Sicilian."

"How would they know I was going into 'Tony's Place'? I didn't know it myself."

"The second man with the steel glasses, the one you didn't notice at first, could have come in the back way. He could have been tailing you. They don't call it Telegraph Hill for nothing. Those individuals have their own communications system."

_____

After my brutal night on Telegraph Hill, I wondered if Rudy Webber had been right in suggesting we had invaded territory where intruders were not tolerated? All of the fishing business out of San Francisco was dominated by Italians, mostly of Sicilian origin, who knew only too well that money from fish was made on the dry land, not at sea. Most of them, of course, were hard-working, family-loving men, but their rules were their own and generations of tough going had compelled them to fierce self-preservation. There were countless tales of the nasty punishments suffered by transgressors, and certainly the severe caste system was obvious for all to see. Along Fisherman's Wharf you were a fisherman who owed money on everything including your seaboots, or you were a buyer who loaned money to fishermen and therefore received not only the best of the catches, but avoided paying a fair price. You were never both. To hold a job ashore, whether wielding a filet knife, icing fish, or owning the sales company itself, blood relationship was mandatory. Everyone on Fisherman's Wharf was cousin to everyone else, and beware the Anglo-Saxon who had the audacity to challenge the bloodline.

Yet one buyer, Tom Gargenella, was unique. He was as honest as his scales and as forthright as the best of the fishermen who treasured his presence in an atmosphere of suspicion and betrayal. One afternoon, still sore from the beating on Telegraph Hill, I was sitting in his wharf-side office. Sunlight sprayed through the dirty windows, catching the humps and bumps on his fine Etruscan face. His air of simple dignity was further enhanced by the dolorous quality of his eyes and the rasp in his voice which suggested his breathing was impaired. I suspected he was not a well man. Gargenella knew me only as a fisherman who liked to drop into his office for a talk about the market and of course complain of the pitiful price we received in comparison with what we saw on sale in the stores. In this habit I was joined by innumerable fishermen of all nationalities, for Gargenella was renowned as the one man they could trust. I had thus far avoided informing him where I lived. He would not have understood how a fisherman came to be living in a house on Washington Street.

My original intention had been to ask Gargenella what he thought of the beating I had received, but once within the scrutiny of his sad eyes I abandoned the idea. If indeed the attack had anything to do with our crab venture, then Gargenella in his unswerving integrity would be obliged to confirm what he would certainly know. It was not worth the risk of forcing him into the role of informer just to satisfy my angry curiosity. Perhaps, I thought, he will volunteer enough warning to keep me safe, if warning is needed. For Gargenella knew everything.

I waited while he folded his liver-spotted hands behind his head and stared at the mewling seagulls beyond the windows. He smiled as if pleased with his thoughts.

"That chair you're sitting in is very special to me," he said finally. "Fella used to drop by to see me most every day. Used to keep a bottle of whiskey right here in my desk drawer. You're sitting in his favorite chair."

Looking at the chair I saw nothing special about it, but held my peace. We all knew Gargenella had his philosophical moments and if he chose to make me privy to his current observations, then I was more than willing.

"The fella wrote books," he went on. "Good ones too . . . at least we all liked them . . . and him. Name was Jack London. Ever hear of him?"

I nodded although I was not at all sure I had actually read any of London's books except *Call of the Wild.*

Gargenella allowed his eyes to drift away from the seagulls and settle on me for a moment. "I been thinking about you from time to time. You're different from most fishermen. You got some education for one thing and I been thinking, why don't you write a book about this crazy business."

I caught my breath. The people of Fisherman's Wharf were not book readers. For an instant I assumed that Gargenella had somehow discovered I had already written six books. Then I knew better, for Tom Gargenella had not a devious thought in his soul and if he knew of my writing efforts he would have challenged me directly.

"Well . . .?" he asked with his lamenting eyes. For the first time since our acquaintance began, I wanted to part with his company. Here was a beloved and sincere man asking me a question which to him must seem simple and reasonable. According to his code, a man fortunate enough to have an education did not deliberately take work where formal learning was unnecessary. That would be waste. In Tom Gargenella's honest eyes, books were sacred repositories of knowledge he and all his relatives had been unable to acquire. I troubled him. Even in his great tolerance he viewed me as a traitor to my fortune, a man who was rejecting his blessings.

I picked at one of the calluses on my hands while I sought some way to tell Gargenella why I had chosen exile from a world which, for a time at least, had been nicely won. How could I confess to this man who regarded me as someone of special value that my escape from writing had been an act of cowardice? At first sign of failure I had lost confidence and run off to sea like an immature boy unable to face reality. Of course hauling fish was easier than hauling words, and the fatigue at the end of a working day at sea was a sensuous pleasure compared to exhaustion at the end of a writing day. I had dared, and failed once, and quit when everything stopped going my way. Yet even now I equivocated.

"Maybe I shouldn't try to do a six-cylinder job with a one-cylinder brain."

"Balls. You can do it. Jack did it. Just don't get too fond of whiskey when you're rich like he did. I been

436

around the wharf most of my life and there's a lot for a fella to write about here."

I tried to deny any special feelings about the chair I was sitting in. Jack London, if the tales about him were only half true, must have been my kind of man, but was that any reason to suppose I might write even a single book in his shadow?

By late spring our catch of crabs fell far below the orders we had at hand. To supplement the supply we imported the crustaceans from Eureka, but scarcity had brought higher prices and we lost money. We advised our customers there would be no more available until midautumn.

As an alternative we went salmon fishing and had no sooner made a fair catch than the fishermen's union called a strike. The hold of Kincaid's *Dolphin* was nearly full, yet we could not sell a fish. We knew something had to be done before our catch rotted, and the buyers knew it even better.

Two days passed. Our ice melted with ever-increasing rapidity. The buyers sniffed the air for the first aromatic signals of spoiling fish. Obliged to find a solution to our dilemma, Kincaid and I hit upon it the very next morning in Sausalito. We began by borrowing a few cast-off yards of fish net and draped them at random over the superstructure of the *Dolphin* now moored alongside the municipal float. We borrowed a few signal flags from a local yachtsman and tied them to shrouds and stays, making her a rather jaunty portrait bobbing gently up and down upon the glittering waters of the bay with the fairyland profile of San Francisco in the distance.

At ten in the morning we took a dollar each in dimes, established ourselves in the two telephone booths in the corner drugstore, and started dialing. Kincaid took the first half of the Sausalito telephone book and I took the second. We selected names at random and with minor variations repeated our announcement.

"Good morning, ma'am. This is the captain of the fishing vessel *Dolphin*. I thought you'd like to know we have just arrived with a fine catch of fresh salmon. Some are still wriggling. If you'd like to give your family a treat tonight we're selling at only thirty-six cents a pound

. . . that's eight cents under what you can buy it for anywhere else. We'll be at the municipal float all day."

Although we called at random our plan had been carefully considered. By ten o'clock, we reasoned, the housewives would be finished with their early chores and ready for outside relief. We interspersed our pitch frequently with lusty ho-ho's plus a smattering of salty talk which we hoped would establish an air of adventure and a more exciting than usual trip to the market. We had also convinced ourselves that the hour was right for the initiation of morning gossip-over-coffee calls between housewives. I was certain each call would multiply itself ten times.

The two dollars in dimes was very nearly the last of our funds, but when we emerged into the brilliant sunlit morning we were much encouraged. All of the housewives had sounded interested and not one had resented our calling. We strolled down to the *Dolphin* and waited.

We waited expectantly until two o'clock in the afternoon. Not a housewife came near us. One aging man came down the float ramp to inspect our display of salmon we had so carefully set up on deck, sniffed suspiciously, and made his way back to shore. To keep busy and conceal our despair from each other we rearranged the display, decorated the crushed ice beneath the fish with bits of seaweed, honed our already sharp knives, fiddled with the scales, and stared at the empty street which the flooding tide had rendered almost level with our eyes.

At two-thirty a pair of women came down the ramp and confirmed that they had talked with one of us on the telephone. They began to inspect the fish as Kincaid turned on his charm. Ho-ho-ing in his most dashing manner he slapped affectionately at the bellies of a few fat salmon. After his initial paean to their freshness and beauty Kincaid went into a stirring address which held the two ladies spellbound and convinced me he had lost his wits. I thought he was deliberately driving away our only two customers. Holding up a banana finger he said, ". . . but I'm not going to sell you nice ladies even a small cut of this beautiful fish unless you promise not to ruin it in the cooking. None of your frying . . . it's an insult to this marine jewel. With that understanding between us, ladies, I'll be happy to make you a nice cut."

Only Kincaid could get away with such an approach, I realized, as he responded to their puzzled looks with detailed recipes for cooking salmon. I shook my head in wonder as the ladies carefully repeated his directions and glowing with anticipation bought two large chunks.

I wrapped the fish in newspaper for the ladies and minded the cash register, a biscuit tin now containing our last five dollars in coins. When the two ladies departed there followed a long pause while we stared at the empty street again.

"Not to worry," Kincaid said with his eternal optimism. "Ho-ho! We'll run out of fish before we run out of customers." Looking at the barren street I decided reluctantly that my partner was crazy.

Apparently we had miscalculated the schedule of Sausalito's housewives as well as the length of time required for them to exchange vital information. At last a third lady arrived, then another started down the ramp, and by three o'clock a line of five persons, male and female, faced the *Dolphin*. Kincaid never paused in his joyous tales of the sea, the succulence of the ocean's fruit, his appetizing instructions for cooking fish, and his suggestions for complementary dishes. Listening, I became so intrigued I frequently made wrong change, and usually in the customer's favor. As the line became longer I joined in the spirit of things with my own contribution. "Make sure you're back here next Friday. We'll be here with a fine load . . . salmon, cod, crabs, anything to suit your tongue and at the same bargain prices you just paid."

I had no idea where we would be next Friday, but I saw no harm in pre-advertising. By four o'clock Kincaid was unable to handle the slicing and weighing alone. The line of customers stretched from the boat to the top of the ramp and we were selling fish so fast we lost all track of poundage. I had emptied the biscuit tin twice into one of Kincaid's socks, which had somehow found its way unlaundered to the pilothouse.

By five o'clock the line extended along the float, continued up the ramp and as far as we could see down the street.

"Ho-ho!" cried Kincaid, slicing like a madman.

"Ho-ho!" I repeated, cutting my thumb. At once two

housewives expressed sorrow for my wound and concerned themselves with its cleansing and repair beneath a series of Band-Aids.

As dusk softened the steep Sausalito hills we continued to cut and admonish and I was once emboldened to discipline a customer who said she was not interested in our cooking advice and was damn well going to fry her fish because that's the only way her husband would eat it. "Very well then, madam," I said, focusing an abused look upon the other customers in line, "I will not sell you any fish whatever. We simply cannot tolerate this beautiful fresh salmon being ruined. If you want to duplicate the taste of a rubber boot may I suggest you go straight to the meat market where they have salmon of dubious age for sale at forty-four cents a pound. Next customer?"

As the lady turned on her heel and trotted angrily away I heard a murmur of approval from the line. Since none of them joined the recalcitrant one, I assumed they agreed with my action and in remaining were proven knowledgeable and superior.

Just before dark we had sold every fish in the *Dolphin* and still there were people in line. Kincaid nearly brought tears to my eyes as he told our unrewarded customers how deeply we regretted their tardy arrival and warned them to attend earlier on the following Friday if they wished to enjoy the bounties of the seas.

Later, when we had cleaned the decks and cutting blocks, we looked up at the hills of Sausalito where a thousand lights glittered in the night. The evening breeze tumbling from the hills brought us the aroma of cooking fish from every direction and as we counted the money in the sock and biscuit tin, and gulped hungrily at our cups of rum to allay our exhaustion, we agreed that at last we had found a way to make money in the fishing business. For we had sold our catch without betraying our fellow fishermen and at more than twice the price any buyer would have paid us.

The next Friday we were back on station and comply sold out by five in the afternoon. At least a hundred customers left the float carrying only our promise to return on the following Friday with two boats. As we kicked off our seaboots and lazed back with our rum we shook our heads in disbelief. This time, unable to catch enough salmon, we had substituted ling cod, which we offered as "Farallon cod" because we thought the name more appetizing. After Kincaid had insisted it be cooked his way, in milk, onions, and bay leaves, it sold nearly as well as the salmon.

"I wonder what the poor folk are doing," he sighed and smiled upon the cardboard box containing our day's take of more than six hundred dollars. Including the Farallon cod we had sold almost a ton and a half of fish. And still the rest of the fleet was on strike.

The following week we brought both the *Dolphin* and the *Fred Holmes* to Sausalito and were sold out by nightfall. People were beginning to come from all over the Bay Area simply to buy truly fresh fish direct from the men who caught them. Or so we allowed our customers to believe; the truth was we simply could not catch enough fish to supply the demand, and long before Friday's dawn we had been obliged to compete with the Chinese buyers on Fisherman's Wharf for the skimpy loads brought in by nonstriking drag boats. We made up the balance by odd-lot purchases from whatever fish boats we could find.

By the third week we had built a clientele of regular customers who often called us by name. I noticed with amusement how some of the ladies lingered long after their purchase had been completed, watching Kincaid's histrionic performance. And in the eyes and manner of several I saw the telltale sparkle of trouble and could too easily mark the fundamental cause; for against the clouded image of their gray-flanneled commuting husbands, Kincaid—in his boots and bos'n shirt, with a watch cap tilted defiantly toward one eyebrow, and his voice ringing with zest and masculine vitality—must have appeared a hero right out of a *Cosmopolitan* magazine story.

I did not realize how much trouble was heading our way. Two more weeks passed with such success that we sold from our boats on Saturdays as well as Fridays, bringing hordes of new customers from the black population of Marin City. Although the local grocery and meat merchants had laughed at our first appearances, they were soon of a different mind as they watched their fish products go unsold. They dropped their prices to match ours and still people preferred to buy directly from a boat while listening to the incomparable Kincaid. The situation worsened when we began to vary our stock with clams, abalone, and crustaceans—people were spending their money at the waterside rather than in the shops. Quite rightly, the local merchants ran to the city council pleading for protection. They complained we had not troubled to take out a sales license much less share in the local taxes. We were described picturesquely and correctly, I thought, as "pirates and brigands whose effect on the community was of doubtful benefit." Our troubles had only begun.

It was frustrating to see solid customers, many of whom we knew by now, arive at the float only to find us sold out. Reluctantly, I agreed to operate the market while Kincaid ranged the bay and the ocean outside the Golden Gate for more fish. We hired an ex-Air Force B-25 pilot who still wore his leather jacket to help me slice and weigh and we chartered a third vessel, a gasoline-powered near-derelict named the *Cynthia*. She leaked outrageously and I was never sure she would make it between Fisherman's Wharf in San Francisco and Sausalito without foundering. I was also unsure of our reception without the presence of my glamorous partner.

Three more weeks passed under this arrangement, while I did my best to satisfy our customers and explain Kincaid's absence to nearly every other female who came to the waterfront. Whether or not they were simply being loyal to his ghost I could not guess, but at least our sales volume did not diminish, and there were even a few ladies who took on an inviting shyness when I handed them their change. Yet in my heart I now knew that this minor success was doomed before it was really established. Kincaid was not a merchant; he was out fishing. I was certainly not a merchant and too often seemed incapable of even making correct change. We were bound for the same disintegration our crab-shipping business had suffered, and for much the same basic reason.

Then Kincaid returned to relieve me for one weekend and disaster was guaranteed. One of our regular customers, a lady of particular energies, had from first sight decided that Kincaid was the answer to her frustrations. I was not aboard *Dolphin* during their reunion or I might have urged more discretion. For I knew she had a husband, a complication of which Kincaid was innocent. The budding romance was discovered, the husband roused the locals to the evil presence of these interloping "pirates and brigands," and it was later reported there had even been talk of tar and feathers.

Kincaid—the lover, not the fighter—realized that a period of cooling and adjustment was needed. That very night, with a hasty farewell to me, he put out to sea and vanished for weeks. I managed to operate the next market without the *Cynthia* sinking beneath my boots, much less being lynched myself, but my heart was gone from the Western Ocean Fishing Company. The modern independent, I was discovering, was rarely given rest.

Thereafter, on Fridays and Saturdays the locals and the crying seagulls no longer flocked to the empty Sausalito float.

Chapter 32

That great enterprise, the Western Ocean Fishing Company, sank slowly before our eyes, disintegrating like an unloved ship in need of repair. Fred Holmes, the true heart of our little company, died, at last relieved of his terrible agonies. We took some solace in the knowledge that we had at least given him brief periods of interest and amusement by radioing reports of our catch from sea to his hospital bed. We lied outrageously about the abundance of our catch—"We are sinking the boat . . . up to our hips in fish"—and he knew we were lying and therefore laughed with us merrily in spite of his searing pain. LaFrenier went off to sea as skipper of the *Fred Holmes,* and for one season I fished our newly acquired ex-sharker the *Mike.* My son George went along as "puller." Our very hard labor was not a guarantee of financial well-being and eventually the *Mike* was taken over on a share-of-the-catch basis by McDowell, a lanky easygoing man with an innate ability to catch fish.

I tried a brief reunion with my typewriter, with little success. Lester Linsk, long standing in the wings as my "Hollywood agent," kept trying to sell *Island in the Sky* to the movies. While thought of his exertions always cheered me, I never believed he would succeed.

A curious flap now occurred which amused everyone in the publishing business except the staid officers of Little, Brown and Company, a house noted for its rather austere image. They liked a manuscript sent to them from an author in Ohio and promptly sent him a healthy advance. He had titled the book *Position Unknown* and given his box number as a return address.

Most new books are reviewed for the trade long ahead of time by Virginia Kirkus's very highly regarded service and there was something about this book that haunted her from the first page. Before she was long into the galleys her suspicions were confirmed. The manuscript, word for word, comma for comma, had been previously published as *Island in the Sky*. It then became Virginia Kirkus's dreary duty to shock Little, Brown with the news of their unwitting partnership in plagiarism. On the basis of enthusiasm for their new author, salesmen had already taken orders from bookstores all over the land. The final galleys had been printed, advertising allotted, and official publication dates set.

Little, Brown was having some trouble arranging personal appearances for this extraordinarily shy author whose box number proved to be the Ohio State Penitentiary, where he had been confined for armed robbery. He had borrowed *Island in the Sky* from the prison library and simply changed the title.* An ambitious man, he had already arranged a new advance from Little, Brown for his second book. With the first he bought a new typewriter and sent the balance to his mother.

The Eastern press had a field day with the story and called me in San Francisco for a reaction: "I admire his taste and will send him another of my books wrapped around a sharp file. An artist of his caliber does not belong behind bars."

Such minor distractions, together with an overlong preoccupation at making a living from fish and crab pots, kept me from viewing more important events, which were again proving that the world was a most dangerous place to live. Like so many world citizens I assumed that a lasting peace would follow the end of World War II's hostilities. While many of my friends had flown the Berlin

* Coincidentally, the identical title I had first used: *Position Unknown*.

444

Airlift, I, like most Americans, had simply accepted the "cold" war with Soviet Russia as a natural burden of the times, and the persistent hammering of radio commentators and other pundits on the subject roused little personal concern. The average American seemed to accept the possibility of another holocaust with a shrug of the shoulders. Then North Korea invaded South Korea and President Truman assigned General MacArthur the job of correcting the situation. Like all wars, this one had a far more significant effect internationally than anyone in charge seemed to have considered. Truman and MacArthur proved once again that history is often made at an unexpected time and place.

Except for a week in Antung during my "educational" tour of the world, I knew little about Korea. I was actually surprised to find myself once more in uniform, this time wearing a gray outfit with four black stripes on the sleeve, a pair of metal wings, garrison cap, and device to match. A company known as Trans-Ocean Airlines, founded by former United Airlines pilot Orvis Nelson, had won one of the several contracts to transport men and hardware to the new and very distant war.

From the first day I was haunted by the notion, this is where I came in since, like a rerun movie, all was the same. We took off from Oakland and used the identical hangars once occupied by the far more splendid Matson Airlines. The airplanes were DC-4s of the same type we had flown during the last years of World War II and also for Matson. Now they appeared to be sagging with age. Their windows were grimy and patches of engine oil here and there about wings and cowlings gave evidence of their long labors all over the world. Everywhere there were dents and scratches where innumerable mechanics had removed and re-installed various pieces of their outer skin to make repairs. While the flight and navigational instruments were functional, the flight deck seats were worn and lumpy from supporting untold numbers of airmen's butts. Only the faces of the cast had changed, although essentially their basic attitudes, manner, and abilities were the same as during that already forgotten war in which the majority now present had performed the same services.

The routing was fixed and rarely offered variation.

From Oakland we flew to Travis Air Force Base to the north of the San Francisco Bay Area and there picked up our load of mail, guns, butter, or personnel from the massive accumulation brought from all over the United States. We flew westward heavily burdened, passing directly over the now deserted Sausalito wharf and next over the sea between the Farallon Islands and the Golden Gate, the very waters where I had so recently been engaged as a fisherman. I hoped Gidley was doing well somewhere in the fog below, and I wondered if I had come full circle.

We proceeded thence to Honolulu and lay over in a muggy and crowded crew house where we rarely enjoyed uninterrupted sleep. When the next aircraft was reported en route from the mainland we roused ourselves, whatever the hour, groomed as best we could, and after a nearly indigestible breakfast took off for Wake Island. It was usually an eleven-hour flight made to seem longer by the monotony of the relatively fine weather at all seasons and the sameness of the sea. When at last we would pick up the radio beacon at Wake and make for it with full assurance, I often thought of the brave Amelia Earhart, who had, in another life certainly, graced the Manhattan office in which Ben Piazza had so long ago installed me. And I thought I knew why she had never reached her destination, Howland Island, for Wake, like so many Pacific atolls, could be easily missed if only one rain squall stood in the way.

On Wake we were quartered four or eight together in screened huts protected against the rain by tin roofs. The majority of airmen who spent any time on Wake eventually found their way to the Japanese ship still stranded on the coral along the south beach of the island. During one of my first flights into the island I was urged to visit the ship by an Englishman, William Oliver,* presently employed by Trans-Ocean as a flight dispatcher.

It was Oliver who presented me with a sun-bleached skull he had acquired during one of his island explorations. "Alas," he said, "I know he's not Yorick but I can only hope he's Japanese. Whoever he may have been, he is my way of thanking you for writing *Island in the Sky*."

---

* He eventually became the island's "oldest inhabitant"—after eleven years!

Since Oliver had read the book during his tour with the RAF in England this reminder that I had ever done anything but fly an airplane came as further confirmation that one factor in this vagabond flying life had changed for me. To my astonishment the majority of my flying comrades seemed to have read at least some of my writings and I had thus become some sort of a minor celebrity. Although I relished their enthusiastic approval, I was not at all sure I liked the subtle separation that followed. Too often a seat was held for me at wherever we shared a common meal; I was waved into the best bunk wherever we slept and when I sat down to read a book or merely write a letter, men passing were inclined to lower their voices. All of which made me nervous, especially the rumor that I had become very rich.

I treasured the skull all the more when I decided what must eventually be done with it.

Even from a distance I noticed something familiar about the wrecked ship. Perspiring in the sun I stared at the *Suwa Maru* as if she were the very bones of my youth revealed. Once again I fancied I could hear the makeshift band trying to play caucasian dance music on that humid night as the *Suwa Maru* plowed through the Indian Ocean. Since then, Japan had endured the most frightful bombing ever devised, bent like a reed before the humiliating winds of occupation, and paradoxically became our ally against a new enemy.

"Don't even attempt to find the answer, old boy," Oliver said later. We were watching the sun descend over the lovely lagoon near the place where the American Marines had made such a valiant stand against our new allies. He smiled and pulled at his long nose thoughtfully. "You bloody Yanks had best stay out of Asia, because Kipling was right."

We usually lay over a day or two in Tokyo, quartered in a sleazy hotel, and fed standard military fare in the downtown officers' club. I excused myself as often as possible to enjoy a reunion with Japanese food, wallowing in delicacies which caused much frowning and puckering of lips among the few airmen I could persuade to join me.

Japan was still under U.S. military rule and we regarded our visible "representatives" with a mixture of pride and awe. If nothing else, MacArthur knew full well the value of face to orientals and he saw to it that our own was never caught in disarray. Certainly he displayed the most gorgeous soldiers since the Praetorian Guard, splendid-looking fellows, big and straight, immaculate in their uniforms the same dull brindle worn by their older brass helmets, white puttees, and brilliant throat scarves. While I understood the need for such panoply, I could not ignore the parade of other young Americans we were bringing to Japan. Their helmets were not brass, but dung-colored steel. Their leggings were combat boots and their uniforms the same dull brindle worn by their older brothers only ten years previously on the way to death, maiming, or dubious glory. Most haunting of all were their faces; only a very few remarkable, the others melting into a common denominator of hidden fears, a vague loneliness, inner bewilderment, and an outward show of bravado to prove they were not personally affected by such emotions. It was always the other guy.

Every flight renewed my own sense of *déjà vu,* but my attempt to revive another happier time in Tokyo met with total failure.

I directed my taxi driver first to the Japanese Diet Building, which appeared to be unchanged. But when I told him "Nagata-Cho . . . Ni Chome" he shook his head negatively. His puzzlement was so obvious I finally paid him off and walked. I knew very well where my old house was: just behind the Diet Building was the district known as Kojimachi Ku and within it a relatively small crowded area called Nagata-Cho.

I walked with great confidence in the same direction I had walked so many times before. Then little by little my pace slowed. There was the Diet Building, big as ever and right where it should be, but where was the street leading down into Nagata-Cho?

I continued ever more uneasily. Nothing was familiar and yet I knew my direction was true. After half an hour's vain attempt to find anything recognizable I halted and stood staring at the Diet Building, for without it I would have been hopelessly lost. Now I knew I must be standing within a hundred feet of my former house—the angle and perspective were exactly as I remembered the view. But there was no natural bowl—I stood on a flat street teeming with traffic, jostled occasionally and without apology by the hordes of pedestrians, an unthinkable act in the Japan I had once known.

I wanted to weep, not in disappointment or frustrated nostalgia, but because I knew again the bitter aftertaste of war. This whole district had been firebombed by my own countrymen. There was nothing left—absolutely *nothing* when the ashes had cooled. There was no house, no Nagata-Cho or Ni Chome, no delicate Mrs. Kondo and her dignified husband. Nothing. The servant girls, the neighbors with whom I used to bathe and whom I would amuse with my puerile Japanese, the fish-peddler with his special signaling flute, the little garden where I tried to write, and most importantly one of humanity's most beautiful cultures had all been incinerated. "Goodbye, Mrs. Kondo," I whispered. "Sayonara, Mr. Kondo. Sayonara to all of you who were once my friends."

I walked back to our dingy hotel without realizing the passage of time. There was too much readjustment to be made in my thinking. I had to persuade myself that mankind was not utterly insane, and yet all I had seen since leaving the Washington Street house argued otherwise. My countrymen were now fighting a war more than ten thousand miles from our natural frontier. To further this idiocy I had, while en route to the scene, personally controlled the flow of more than six thousand four hundred gallons of fuel and would repeat the expenditure on my return. Twelve thousand eight hundred gallons gone forever. The cargo we had brought with us would not make anything but broken bodies or produce anything beneficial, unless a flow of blood could be deemed so. The nonproductive items I had brought were to be thrown away—presumably in the direction of the enemy. For this inane performance I would be paid out of the pockets of people who were making and growing things useful to mankind.

I attempted a smile which refused to come. Way back in my earliest flying days it had been my boss Joe Lewis who said, "You brood too much. It's bad for the customers to see."

Oliver, who had flown to Tokyo from Wake for his annual R and R, was waiting for me. "What's troubling you? You look like you've seen a ghost."

"I have. Several millions."

Soon the entire pattern of life I had known from 1942 until 1945 began to repeat itself. Once the combatants in Korea had been led to each others' throats, we began bringing back the kid brothers of those we had carried away from the bloody fields of Europe. Our litter ships had a much greater distance to fly and were somewhat better equipped, but the exhausted khaki-bound bodies were the same and the shocked young eyes were the same. This time, however, a new task had been added. Now we sometimes brought back the flag-draped remains of the fallen in battle; fortunately not in the same airplanes with the merely maimed.

While military exigency required us to make occasional reroutings via Guam, Saipan, or Manila, it seemed that whatever our course or destination, we spent considerable time on Wake Island. Again I found card-playing uninteresting and the perpetual discussion of women and flying all too repetitive. Sitting on my bunk, scribbling in cheap notebooks, I began writing a novel about commercial fishing along the Pacific Coast. I called it *Fiddler's Green* and tried very hard to follow the dictates laid down by Bill Sloane.

Soon afterward, Sloane arranged for his publishing house to pay me four hundred dollars a month to complete the work, and his continued faith restored my shaky confidence.

The juxtaposition of events during the life of every man seldom forms a significant pattern unless the various factors responsible for those events are examined in full perspective. While one trip to Pebble Beach resulted in a fiesta and ultimately a fishing business, another visit brought a rude calamity which came very near being the end of everything for me.

The dinner party at my father's house had been as usual, loud and gay and graced with superb food and splendid wines. My father, content in his new marriage, delighted in his role of Padrone—particularly as long as his grandchildren were well-groomed and well-behaved. To this happy condition both Eleanor and I devoted ourselves, and to assure peace during the important hours of cocktails and dinner we arranged for son George and the twins to be fed early. As further guarantee, my father provided a baby-sitter to soothe their natural vitality.

When they had finished eating he patted them each on the head, offered a few words of wisdom which passed unheard, and saw them safely tucked into their rooms. The adults' evening then progressed at high decibel.

Esther's son Don and daughter Jean were also visiting, and as always the accumulation of an audience and the exquisitely prepared food compounded the conversational exchanges and greatly pleased my father, who believed noise a true signal of his guests' enjoyment. When, after dinner, coffee was to be served in the library I declined, offering instead to take the baby-sitter home. Don said he would keep me company and the three of us climbed into my jeep. It was a lovely mild evening and we all found the air refreshing.

We dropped the baby-sitter at her home in Carmel then turned back for Pebble Beach. It was approximately two miles from the main gate along the famous Seventeen Mile Drive to my father's gate.

There was no traffic once we had entered Pebble Beach and the long twilight softened the lush beauty of the hedges and trees along the winding road. I knew its meanderings well and drove at good speed, but casually. Don and I shared approval of our parents' marriage and I told him of the striking physical likeness between Esther and my own mother.

The twilight was deepening and I thought to switch on the headlights as we came to a curve I had negotiated innumerable times. Suddenly I felt the right front wheel slip over the edge of the asphalt. I corrected with a quick turn of the steering wheel and instantly knew a sensation of weightlessness. I had nothing in my hands . . . all was confusion.

There was a hard explosive sound. For an instant I saw the dark asphalt skidding beneath me. I was flying. I stretched out my arms to stop the asphalt and saw death.

I collided with the asphalt at awful speed, knees first, hands, and then chin.

It seemed only a moment before I was able to gain my feet. I saw the jeep some fifty feet back, upside down and smoking. Don stood on a green lawn which fringed the road along the last half of the curve. He was staring at the jeep. I called to him. "Are you all right?"

"Yes. Okay."

"So am I." I limped slowly toward the jeep. One wheel spun slowly to a stop and watching it I thought, oh hell, now we'll have to get help and put the thing back on its feet or wear out our own walking to Cactus's.

A few minutes later I was repeating the same phrase to Jack, the sheriff I had known ever since my father had moved to Pebble Beach. And more minutes later I became stubborn as several people forced me into the back of an ambulance. I told them I did not need assistance but would like a ride to El Retiro; it was dark now and the people there would be worrying about us. The ambulance door was slammed in my face and somewhere above my head I heard the moan of a siren.

An attendant in white sat across from me. He was wearing a white jacket and staring at the floor. I told him I knew very well I was all right and he should open the door and let me out.

"You're all bloody," he said, keeping his eyes on the floor.

I looked down at my sweater and saw he was right. It was a favorite sweater of pale blue green and I was very distressed to see it so soiled.

"I think I'm going to be sick," the attendant said.

"Why? What's the matter with you?"

"It's not me. It's you. All that blood."

"I'm fine. A little blood shouldn't bother you of all people."

"This is my first trip. I just got the job this afternoon."

I spent the rest of the journey to the hospital comforting the attendant.

It was not until they pushed me down on a table in the hospital emergency room that I went into shock. The damage list was not nearly as bad as it might have been. All of my once-fine teeth were loose. My jaw was broken in thirteen places. I was covered with bruises and abrasions. And I had ruined my favorite sweater.

Don had fared much better. He had also flown through the air, fortunately not in formation with me. He had landed on the green lawn and except for a shaking-up was unhurt.

My care and feeding during recuperation from the daring adventure of returning a baby-sitter to her domicile was supervised by Eleanor. It was not an easy time for even the most good-hearted friends because a broken jaw is high on the list of frustrating injuries. Two-way communication with the victim is extremely laborious. A steel pin was driven through my jaw from one side to the other and all of the broken pieces, including my tumbled teeth, locked together with wire. Except for grunts and a sort of singsong whine emanating from my throat, I was obliged to practice the art of listening. I could express approval or disapproval with a nod of my head, but more complex messages were beyond me. I ate three meals a day through a glass straw inserted in the vacancy left by a front tooth which had never been found, and the same gap served as entrance for two glasses of blackstrap rum and water which I sucked at from five until six each day.

I made one attempt to dine with the family, but was compelled to leave the table after only a few minutes. The sight of other humans chewing became so unbearable I departed in a river of my own tears. I retired to my high aerie and did not reappear in the lower region of the house until the day my constrictions were to be removed.

The forced confinement enabled me to forego easier and more enticing physical temptations and write. I completed *Fiddler's Green,* rewrote it twice again under Bill Sloane's precise whip, and was rewarded with news of its selection by the Dollar Book Club, a paperback sale, and, even before it was published in the United States, offers of foreign translations. None of the amounts were large, but they were enough to cover my advance and have a few thousand dollars left for the business of living.

Thus was our Washington Street life temporarily prolonged.

Chapter 33

Throughout these many vicissitudes Lester Linsk had remained my friend and professional champion. In a moment of self-aggrandizement I had once appointed him my agent—although for what and of what neither of us could be sure. Reviewing one section of my past it seemed he might find me a job as a film director, but his recommendations brought little interest from Hollywood studios. Then he tried to sell me a writer, with similar results. Linsk's Hollywood acquaintance was wide and many of his close contacts powerful, but any enthusiasm they might have had dwindled when he explained that his undiscovered genius refused to work within the Los Angeles area. "He claims he can't think in the bright sun," he apologized, and saw only scorn in a prospective employer's eyes.

Even so, he managed to sell *Island in the Sky* to independent film-makers Stanley Kramer and Robert Stillman, a totally unexpected bonanza which triggered several trips to Hollywood. There were innumerable other hopeful notions and schemes which I thought, or Linsk thought, demanded our personal reunions, and since my funds were always over-spent before received from whatever source, I inevitably became his guest or his brother Joe's. Both Linsks were popular bachelors. Finding their sybaritic way of life much easier to endure than my own domestic woes, I became a sort of artist-in-residence. Not wishing to offend their true sense of hospitality I considered it my obligation to share their expensive whiskey, their food, and their more attractive guests. I saw just enough Hollywood to convince me I was right in my belief that it was no place for a writer who hoped to be taken seriously. The problem remained whether or not that is what I should attempt.

"Meanwhile," Linsk said with the pointed understatement which was so much his trademark, ". . . meanwhile, maybe you'd better keep on flying."

Yet it seemed the tide was finally beginning to turn. As if he had not already done enough to rescue his wandering author from falling on his pen, he sold *Fiddler's Green* to Universal Pictures. Still not satisfied, he persuaded the producer, Aaron Rosenberg, that I should write the screenplay wherever it pleased me to work. And yet more. The filming would be in San Francisco and the two fishing boats owned by the Western Ocean Fishing Company were to be chartered by the studio as major props. It was one of the very first "package deals." My cup ran over . . . temporarily.

As the recognized author of *Fiddler's Green* I sometimes found my status along the waterfront rising to disconcerting heights. Buyers smiled upon me. Highline fishermen, hitherto condescending, greeted me with respect. I was besieged with applications to appear in the movie, and the "dock committee," a band of footloose winos who infested the wharves night and day, were constantly at my heels. George Sherman, a diminutive director whose charm and talent far exceeded his net weight, cooperated beyond my fondest hopes. He hired the men and the boats I recommended, and for the duration of the filming I was a waterfront hero.

The movie, eventually released as *The Raging Tide*, starred Shelley Winters and Richard Conte. It turned out to be a reasonably exciting drama and I was displeased only with the title—the creation of some studio executive who believed the public would not understand *Fiddler's Green*.

At last I was solvent and had reason to believe that my days as an aerial freebooter were done. Trans-Ocean, the brave and sporadic airline whose letter of marque had sent me all over the Pacific, was now, as Matson had been, in the final throes of collapse. Orvis Nelson and Bill Keating and all their formidable crew had been unable to carry on profitably against their own antagonistic government agencies (mainly the CAB) while simultaneously fighting a competitive war against long-franchised airlines. I was very sorry because the ill-kept flight decks of their airline had become my home, and the off-again-on-again scheduling of flights and my own status changes from captain to co-pilot and back again, according to the current need for flight crews, had become a way of life which suited well my natural restlessness.

Now while my own fortunes seemed to bloom, my comrades at the airline were barely hanging on and were quick to approve when I volunteered for "indefinite leave of absence."

Even the Western Ocean Fishing Company was at last profitable, but with Fred Holmes gone forever much of the heart left our little adventure. LaFrenier and I decided to sell both the *Mike* and the *Fred Holmes* before they once again became a liability.

Yet the forces of *yin* and *yang* were relentless. While all should have been serene in the Washington Street house, disarray prevailed.

My years of repeated departures from my own hearth were the standard routine of any airline pilot, but there had been a large number of absences for which I manufactured excuses. Even so, the thought of divorce never occurred to me. Eleanor was not only my wife, she was an institution, and our union the natural result of two people knowing each other since early youth. We were almost the same age, we spoke exactly the same brand of American English, we knew or had at least heard of each other's friends and relatives from our first meeting; our tastes in food, drink, opinions on religion and politics, our manners, most of our principles, our appreciation of the arts, and our disregard for physical danger were all the same. It should therefore have been a marriage made in heaven. That it was not to be so was only further proof of the unpredictable and unforgivable perverseness of humans.

While I castigated myself for my repeated absences from Washington Street, I could not seem to change my ways. My conscience berated me for cruelty, nagging perpetually at my full life when, as often happened, I should have been at my wife's bedside. I endeavored to ease my shame when I was at home by continuing the same little attempts at comfort I had now employed for almost twenty years. When Eleanor was down, I brought her breakfast on a tray complete with flowers and news of the children's latest discovery or verbal sally before they went off to school. I tried with all that was in me to bridge the awesome gap between my bouncing health and her understandable preoccupation with each day's new affliction.

I had thought I had always been, at least, a man of courage. Now I was discovering difficulty in maintaining that illusion.

Even more insidious developments moved stealthily across the uneasy scene. While all who are cursed with arthritis experience good and bad days, Eleanor seemed to follow a particularly erratic pattern. There would be days when she would rarely leave her bedroom and others when she became almost wildly energetic. These were usually followed by morose depressions when she became uncomprehending of the world about her.

The ranks of pill bottles in the bathroom multiplied. The monthly bill for drugs became, even in our new affluence, a very considerable subtraction. The list of consulting doctors increased.

At last I went secretly to the one I trusted most and heard him confirm what I had long suspected. Eleanor's arthritis was very real, but controllable at least for the foreseeable future. If the disease were taken by itself there was no reason she could not lead a normal life and take only mild medication. Her most damaging enemy was psychological, and by simply being myself I had in a large measure contributed to it.

I wondered how a man can change himself.

Success was withering even before it had fully bloomed. If I practiced the most artful hypocrisy, could I share the life my wife preferred during her healthier periods and thereby, hopefully, make them permanent? Her league was composed of "nice" people, well-educated, well and regularly salaried, charitable pillars of society. They went to church on Sunday mornings, read the *Wall Street Journal* during the week, and knew the names of their friends' children. They were generous with their time and content with their accomplishments. They were gentle people, cautious of speech and manner . . . and they bored me almost beyond endurance.

In the years since we had come to San Francisco, Eleanor had become a public heroine. During her lucid periods she remembered the birthdays and anniversaries of people I had a tendency to forget on sight. She had even developed a special telephone voice which was warm and mellow, with the flat *a*'s of her heritage softened toward the broad British pronunciation. During the difficult periods when she had given herself over to extra medication, her face became flushed and slightly bloated, but the only other outward evidence of her suffering was that her once-lovely hands were now somewhat distorted, and at the worst times awkward to manipulate. Otherwise she had remained a strikingly beautiful woman, jovial yet dignified, and in all respects a lady's lady.

My own dark hours were becoming increasingly uncomfortable. Too often I recognized myself as a heartless villain and I could easily imagine what the world of nice people thought of me. My instinctive reaction to a growing burden of guilt was a determination to excel as a father, a task I found rewarding and much easier than I had supposed. The girl twin Polly was almost perpetually joyful and of a most giving personality. The boy twin Steven was a natural clown even in his solemn moods and we laughed much together. George, the eldest, was developing into a handsome lad blessed with his mother's dark coloring and invested with my passion for the sea. Since our earlier days of sailing together in the old *Uncle Sam,* his nautical interest had mounted and his skill in building model boats was considerably beyond his age. Like any father I was beginning to have thoughts for his future; anxious to give him choice, I decided he must soon learn to fly since he already knew how to sail. We discussed his future not as father to son, but as two friends, a relation now well established. My subliminal propagandizing obviously steered George away from office-bound careers, but much of the rejection was his own and I was content because I believed from observing his daily behavior that he was not gregarious and therefore unlikely to find happiness in the corporate world. George had a few young friends, but I saw how basically he was a loner and I understood his preference well.

Discipline at Washington Street was fundamental and very informal. It became harsh on only one occasion when George, in a rare display of juvenile savagery, struck a neighbor boy of much smaller size. After the screams of the offended child subsided I ordered George to his room and followed him. There, I stood before him and demanded he look at me from the top of my head to my shoes. "Now," I said, "I look very big to you. Right? I am twice your size."

A half-sob escaped George and my resolve almost collapsed. I decided against using my fist and struck him only with the open palm of my hand. The blow knocked him backward and he hit the floor with a thud. He looked at me not in tears, but in amazement.

"Now," I said as I crossed the room and lifted him to his feet, "now you know what that little boy felt like when you hit him."

Only a few years later, in another locale, I felt obliged to deliver the same lesson to son Steven for exactly the same reason. It was a mistake. They were very different young people and while George often laughed about the incident and as a consequence maintained a loathing for

458

all bullies, later developments suggested that Steven came to the conclusion that *I* was a bully.

Despite my absences, I spent by far the majority of my time as the active head of my family, and it was usually a happy situation. During the winter we all went skiing together at various California resorts and at Alta in Utah and Aspen in Colorado. Because of her health Eleanor abstained from taking to the slopes, but we enjoyed our mornings and evenings together. From a distance we appeared an extraordinarily close and happy family, which was true in every sense but one. Entering our lodgings at the end of the day, red-cheeked and comfortably weary after a day on the mountains, I could not look upon Eleanor without a deep sense of shame. The phrase "How are you feeling?" came automatically to my lips and I listened as willingly as I could pretend to the usual list of ailments. She is very brave, I thought again and again, very brave, and I am not brave at all if I leave her side even momentarily for my own pleasure. And yet life was slipping away little by little, like water leaking from a well I knew was not inexhaustible. I felt trapped and kept silently repeating my marriage vows. As a wife Eleanor had rarely behaved indifferently; she was indeed a private as well as a public angel and her often expressed desire was for her husband's contentment. "I don't feel up to it, but you go ahead and enjoy yourself," had become my constant verbal passport. Yet I found it difficult to enjoy anything with that phrase ringing in my ears. It became a shadow across my every endeavor and I became ever more lonely trying to ignore it. Not surprisingly I formed a near-reverence for physical wellbeing.

I sought and found some escape in work and physical activity. I thought nothing of walking the three miles to the Embarcadero wharves. Mornings began with twenty minutes of hard calisthenics, the same routine we had been obliged to follow at Culver Military Academy. Then it was down to make breakfast with the children, each by now his own chef and adamant in his requirements. If Eleanor was awake I would take her breakfast to the bedroom along with the morning paper, then I would be off to my aerie for the morning's writing.

As if to reassure myself that I was a practicing author

I took up pipe-smoking and contracted an even sillier habit—working by the clock. At my desk soon after eight I would read an author I admired for half an hour, then on the rebound attack my own work. I assumed various positions to aid concentration, sometimes sitting on a high stool with my typewriter supported on a Dickensian accounting desk I had found in a secondhand shop. In other moods I would place the typewriter on a metal stand, tilt back in an old-fashioned oak office chair, and rest one leg on each side of the typewriter. So positioned, feet in the air, I could just reach the keys and when stuck for a phrase or word could tip back my head and stare at the ceiling. I wrote very rapidly, as many as ten pages a day, using the "touch" system I had learned at the military academy.

Every hour I would halt, pace the room for five minutes, do a series of push-ups, and after ten minutes resume the attack. I was both driven and haunted; a sense of outrageous presumption became my only company. How dare I presume total strangers would trouble to read my words? What had my ordinary mind to offer in a book, against the competitive price of a bottle of good whiskey? Time and again I told myself this was madness, the writing of books was for intellectuals, graduates cum laude of Harvard, Yale, Oxford, and Cambridge. I had barely squeaked through military school. I toyed repeatedly with the pocket flight computer which had served me so long in the sky. It told me there was no reason to continue, for very obviously an astonishing number of people preferred what I had already written to another expenditure and they must be oblivious to the lack of letters trailing my name.

If I cheated and took an extra minute away from the typewriter I either made it up at the next break or for the rest of my day felt as if I had committed larceny. Work continued in this fashion until precisely one o'clock, whereupon I would quit as if an iron gate had slammed between the typewriter and myself. I then descended to make my lunch and Eleanor's, if it were one of her less good times.

The afternoons were devoted to as many pleasures as I could uncover. Perhaps Bill Holcomb, a rawhide ex-sea captain of great charm, would be working on his schooner and I could help him and in the doing gather new knowledge from his vast accumulation of nautical lore. Or I might go for a long hike along the misty headlands of the Golden Gate, or pick up George after school to join me in exploring a surplus store where marine treasures were sometimes to be found.

Nights, if my head was not too thick with wine, I read so voraciously I soon felt the need of glasses. Still inhibited by the image of an eagle-eyed airline pilot I donned them sheepishly and often "forgot" them.

Seven mornings a week the battle would again be joined in the arena of blank paper. Once engaged I would start by rewriting the work done the day before, a sort of leap-frog process which I hoped both improved the rough original and allowed me, like an athlete, to warm up. Sometimes if I had been redundant or turgid or common-place during the preceding session, or as often happened all three, the rewriting would take the whole morning and leave me in near-despair because I knew there would be at least three more rewritings to go before I could expose my clumsiness to a publisher.

The dismal failure of *Benjamin Lawless* had almost totally destroyed my confidence and as a sop to my ego I tried to discover why it had turned out so poorly. I made a list of contemporary successes in literature and the stage, trying to compare their merits against the faults of a disaster I knew all too well. As a consequence I developed a loose series of checks and balances applicable to any form of entertainment and while I knew it was im-possible to forecast outstanding success, I believed I knew how to avoid total failure.

Now I tried very zealously to apply these maxims to my present work, for time was against me. The money realized from *Fiddler's Green* had somehow evaporated. This time I had not even myself to blame, for, backed into a corner, I had spent nothing on frivolities.

As if on cue Lester Linsk came charging through the breach with the sale of a new movie option on *Island in the Sky*. Only a few weeks after Kramer-Stillman dropped their option, Twentieth-Century Fox studios took a similar chance of five thousand dollars.

"I hope no one ever gets around to actually making

the picture," Linsk said. "If they do we'll lose an annuity." *

On Washington Street we breathed easier, but I was beginning to wonder how long I could stand such hand-to-mouth ways. In a frenzied attempt to nail down survival I began writing an additional two hours every afternoon.

Soon I learned that one of the unconquerable fundamentals of authorship was fatigue. At the end of two hours I became physically weary, at three hours I was thoroughly tired, and after four I nearly reached total exhaustion. I could not understand why it was all I could do to rise from my chair at the end of a day's writing, why I was more physically expended than after sixteen hours' fishing in the rough open ocean. I blamed my own mental inadequacy; my intelligence and ability were both overtaxed. Only after a few hours of distraction did my strength seem to return and once again I would return to the tight and incredibly demanding world of blank pages. I was beginning to understand why so few of the thousands of books published every year were worth the reading.

Clinging tightly to my homemade maxims. I took care to review them at the beginning of each day's toil.

First, the story must have "sweep," a term I thought expressed a locale not easily available to the ordinary reader. It was much easier to make a story exciting if it took place in a palace or in a great wilderness rather than in a one-room apartment with kitchenette. I reasoned that too many readers were already in kitchenettes and they wanted removal to places they could only dream about.

Next, I must avoid soap-boxing, while still having something to say. Otherwise the frame of the story was on tricky ground and could easily collapse before the end.

Then, character must rule, for I was convinced that believable characters made any good story and not the other way around. In this respect there must be at least one character the reader could root for.

As an offshoot of character development I knew there must be the element of love; but that emotion could be wide-ranging and encompass not only man for woman or

* Fortunately, they did not. Fox lost interest and dropped the option after one year.

vice-versa, but man for man as in Damon and Pythias, or men together in hazard, or perhaps the love of man for his principles. I determined to include sexual overtones if and when they came naturally into the story and to portray all such interludes as simply and honestly as I was able.

I was convinced of the value of suspense and considered the many ways to create it in any story. Suspense and conflict go hand in hand; an evil force opposes an admirable force, thereby posing the question, who will win? Likewise, the loss of something at the beginning of a story, the searching for it throughout, and the finding in the end makes for certain suspense. The loss may be of a treasured object, the key to a prison, the formula for a terrible bomb, or a man's honor. It makes little difference—loss and recovery become a literary machine working faithfully for the author.

Comedy is the handmaiden of suspense because readers need relief lest their attention drift and interest in what might happen fade.

I decided uniqueness was an important factor, both unappreciated and too often overlooked. Taking a reader backstage whether in a hospital operating room, a diamond cutter's workshop, or the flight deck of an airliner, sparks his interest and through special knowledge lends him a warm feeling of superiority. Yet beware the author who would attempt to fake technical jargon or specialized practice unless he knows the drill perfectly. Phony authenticity emits an odor readers can smell pages away.

While I was at it I made certain new vows. Never would I regard any of my words, sentences, or even pages, with the fondness a father might feel for a newborn child. I would cut mercilessly toward the clear and simple, and if an editor presented good reason for further cutting then I would consider him a person of perception rather than a rude barbarian.

Finally I resolved to bear always the conviction that writing was the most self-revealing of all the arts. It is possible to paint the most delicate flowers and yet be a powerful man of brutal nature and raunchy desires; a musician can interpret the most sublime pastoral, though he may be mean of heart and the worst of scoundrels; but an author had better look frequently in the mirror and ask his eyes to reflect only his personal integrity.

So armed, I set apprehensively to work on a novel about the flight of an airliner from Honolulu to San Francisco. I populated the aircraft with people I had known and based the major suspense on an incident which had happened on one of my own flights for Matson. Long before, I had thought of a title—*The High and the Mighty*—but now it sounded too exalted. I was afraid people would think it a religious tome.

While I was still fretting about titles for an unfinished book, our funds ran even thinner and finally vanished. Eleanor's affliction could withstand no compromise. I sold the house on Washington Street within a week, simply by asking less than I had paid for it. With the paltry residue we moved to a small tract house next to the highway at Newport Beach in Southern California. The rent was cheap and a small muddy canal passed in front of the house, which at least suggested that the sea was not too far away. But need is not always harmonious to creation. Reprieve came at the very last of our cash resources. Trans-Ocean Airlines, in a final spasm of activity, called me back for flights of military dependents to Tokyo, a pair of flights to Manila, and flights of fishermen from San Francisco to Naknek, Alaska, a place I was never really able to see since the ceiling was always below two hundred feet and the visibility but half a mile. It was uneasy flying, but I knew my business thoroughly—and it paid well.

When there was time between flights, I wrote, but there were new difficulties. The incomparable William Sloane had become a casualty of the publishing business. Now with a book half finished I could have gone to him for enough advance to complete the work, but Morrow had taken over his imprint and Sloane himself had retreated to Rutgers University Press, hardly the ideal publisher for any work I might produce. Thus, as a sort of hand-me-down, I became technically a Morrow author. Although I knew no one at the establishment, I hoped someone there might remember me from *Blaze of Noon,* which coincidentally Morrow had published years previously.

When all except the last few chapters of *The High*

and the Mighty were finished, I sent the manuscript off to Morrow and entered the classic purgatory of all authors waiting for a reaction. During this period of uncertainty, my father, rightfully concerned about our future, decided he could no longer enjoy his opulent life, or a proposed cruise around the world, while his only family lived in what he described as "precarious circumstances." Still unhappy at my flying career, he thought he saw a chance to end it agreeably by proposing an almost unrefusable gift.

He made a special pilgrimage to Newport to outline his plan, which he approached with all the resolve and persuasiveness he had once employed in maneuvering great corporate affairs. He placed himself in the center of our tiny living room and took a moment to frown at the peeling paint on the ceiling. He looked at the canal and sniffed disapprovingly. I explained that it was low tide, which sometimes exposed a few rotting objects, but I saw he did not hear me.

"I have great faith in your writing," he began forcefully as he sat down. I hoped the professionals back East would soon declare themselves of the same mind.

"Everywhere I go, Brentano's in New York, Kroch's in Chicago, Newbegin's in San Francisco . . . I discuss your books. They are waiting for a new one. . . ." A heavy truck passing on the highway behind the house obliterated most of what he said about the future of books in general, but I gathered he was optimistic.

"If you will quit trying to make a living flying . . . remember I warned you years ago airline stocks were no good . . . I am sure you will eventually do very well with your pen. Now, there is a fine house in Pebble Beach, just on the market. Ideal, I believe, for you and your family. You could work there and I would tide you over until it becomes obvious you are in the right or the wrong business. . . ."

I had instant and terrifying visions of an ex-pilot whose name might be Faust and who, having sold himself out, was obliged to join the telephone company and there died of ennui complicated by shame.

"I will buy you the house and it would be yours . . . lock, stock, and barrel." My father made the usual church steeple with his hands as he always did while waiting for an answer he believed was predictable. "Well . . .?" he said, fixing me with his good eye.

The room suddenly seemed full of nothing but hands. Eleanor, listening quietly, now began to flex her misshapen hands. I found I was involuntarily clenching and unclenching my own. I was agonized with indecision. Most of all I thought I knew what my father would say if I refused such generosity. For the first time in years I might hear that scathing phrase, ". . . I wash my hands of you."

Certainly, if I refused, he was more than justified in his disgust. Yet a multitude of reservations assailed me. First, I wanted no man's charity, parental or not. I had earned a proud living for too long and abhorred debt of any kind. Then, of all places on earth, I thought Pebble Beach the most unlikely for a working man. The stunning beauty of the area made it a playground for the rich, a holiday never-never land enclosed in total security and the preoccupation of resident inhabitants with bridge, booze, and gossip. There was even a clause in the deeds of land sold within the gates forbidding ownership by any descendants of "the Ottoman Empire"—a roundabout way of excluding people of the Jewish faith. I thought of a weekend Lester Linsk and I had spent at El Retiro and of my father's strong affection for him. He had taken Lester along on his daily rounds introducing him everywhere as "my friend from Hollywood." Lester chided him later with, "Why didn't you introduce me as your *Jewish* friend from Hollywood and touch all bases?" My father took the rebuke with a hearty laugh. His lack of prejudice was exceptional, for the society in which he lived was nearly medieval in social concepts.

Pebble Beach was also inhabited by many ex-military people who knew easy living when they saw it, and the Mediterranean climate held many of the socially inclined. How could a budding misanthropist fit into another atmosphere where the "nice" people, to whom Eleanor was so devoted, were dominant? And yet here at last was some kind of security for her; a stable atmosphere, a place she could confidently call home. I knew it was selfish to hesitate and I accepted as graciously as a man who feels events closing in on him can manage. I had little choice, for Trans-Ocean had again put me on furlough and in view of their own difficulties it seemed obvious that this release would be forever.

We were not prepared for what my father had discovered in Pebble Beach. Instead of the stuffy semimansion we had envisioned, we came upon what is undoubtedly one of the most beautiful situations in the world. The house was really a cottage, small and simple, but airy and light and opening upon a breathtaking view of Carmel Bay, Point Lobos, and the swirling green heights above. The sparkling blue Pacific extended to the horizon and the soft rustling of the waves upon the distant beach was plainly audible. There was a guest house with three bedrooms, exactly right to provide a separate room for each child.

Although the house stood technically on the Seventeen Mile Drive, it was surrounded by six acres of brush and trees, and privacy was absolute. A writing man who could not work here, I thought, must be demented.

Even my fears about two related households existing within hardly a mile of each other proved unnecessary. My father never imposed on our activities, nor did he once by word or act hold us hostage to his magnificent gift. Here amid the most tranquil beauty I made a final effort to complete *The High and the Mighty*.

Chapter 34

I walked down the steep and curving driveway to the entrance gate where with some ceremony I fixed a sign to the overhead crossbar: ISLAND IN THE SKY. A fitting name, I thought, for a perch of such high and commanding view, isolated in the midst of such plenty. Now it seemed a whole new era had begun for all of us, as if the mere change of geography had triggered totally different fortune.

The head of Morrow, a man who introduced himself as Thayer Hobson, had telephoned to say he had read the manuscript of *The High and the Mighty* and liked it. He would be pleased to send me an advance of five thousand dollars. I was exhilarated in the discovery that I hadn't failed in producing a book that at least was publishable.

There was more to rock my equilibrium. Lester Linsk had been playing golf with William Wellman, a famous and notoriously truculent movie director. Wellman had flown with the French Air Corps in the First World War, receiving the Croix de Guerre with palms among other honors, and had directed *Wings,* a tremendously successful film of its time. Linsk thought he might enjoy reading the perennial *Island in the Sky* and gave him a copy which he "just happened to have with him."

Wellman's enthusiasms were as wild as his hatreds. Next morning as they met for more golf, Wellman, with characteristic disregard for details, berated Linsk for not showing him the book before. "You son of a bitch!" he demanded with his usual delicacy. "Why have you been hiding this story from me? It will make a great movie!"

Wellman's voice boomed over the fairways and his self-inflamed enthusiasm mounted with the sun. As he raved about what he would do to put the story on the screen, Lester Linsk, the grand master of the negative sell, prodded him. ". . . I didn't show it to you because it hardly seemed like your dish. It wasn't a number one best-seller. . . ."

Explosions of near-rage from Wellman as he poses a totally unnecessary defense of his air story record and disregard of best-seller lists.

". . . There are no women in it. You can't make a film without a love story."

Wellman runs his strong hands through his gray hair in frustration. "To hell with women. This is a man's story."

"Then it will die at the box office."

"It will make millions."

"Who would write the screenplay? The author is crazy and won't work down here."

"I like crazy people. They're the only kind who make sense. I'll make the bastard rich."

"He already is." (A considerable distortion of fact.) "He lives in Pebble Beach."

"Jesus! He *must* be rich. Does he play golf?"

"No. Hates it."

"You must be right. He *is* crazy."

By the time the golf game was finished Wellman had

convinced himself that *Island in the Sky* would become the greatest motion picture ever made. Linsk solemnly agreed to give consideration to any offers he might submit. The next day, Wellman carried his enthusiasm to, of all people, my one-time employer Jack Warner, who had fired me because I had declined to film-test a long-forgotten blonde. Evidently Warner had also forgotten my name since he approved a transfer of money to an independent company formed by actor John Wayne and producer Robert Fellows. Within days, my bank account bloated with a down payment of five thousand dollars, I set off to meet Hollywood on a new basis. This time, they wanted me.

"You son of a bitch!" Wellman cried before Linsk had time for even a brief introduction. "Do you know you've written a great book?"

I denied that the book should be so highly classified and, with what I thought becoming modesty, determined to keep credit where it belonged instead of, as so often happened in Hollywood, transferring it to wherever it might do the most good. The story, I explained, was mostly true and I had simply interpreted it. I also expressed the hope that Wellman wouldn't give it the Hollywood cosmetizing.

"Jesus Christ. *Me?* I have been fighting these bastards ever since I can remember. We'll tell that story exactly as you wrote it. We won't change a goddamned thing."

I noted how Wellman employed the "we" and wondered if the use was editorial, or just habit, or did he mean to collaborate on the screenplay? I began to study his face while he ranted on about his defiance of anything Hollywood, about the book itself, his plans for filming, his admiration for John Wayne, who had the guts to start his own company, the First World War, his encounter with General Pershing in a Parisian whorehouse, the perfidy of all major motion picture producers, his rebirth as a Christian gentleman after years of heavy drinking, his love for his wife and ten children, his former wives, and the idiocy of avant-garde film directors who were using camera angles he had used and discarded years ago.

There was elegance and dash about Wellman and it seemed to me he might have fitted in very well as one of Napoleon's dragoons or as a Dumas musketeer. He was of medium height, broad of shoulder, wiry and hard; a sense of great physical strength emanated from him in spite of his affliction with arthritis. When he began a long complaint about it I told him of Eleanor and he nearly wept in sympathy for her. I was beginning to realize that Wellman was an emotional child, mercurial in temper and unreasonable to the brink of arrogance. But he was also exciting and inspiring and capable of true humility. Soon, his voice alternately booming and plaintive, he so captured my own enthusiasm that I agreed "we" were about to father a film masterpiece.

Though I insisted on working in Pebble Beach, I seemed to hear Wellman even in my sleep. He telephoned constantly to rehash points we had already chewed to shreds, beginning his tirade with paragraphs of fulsome praise, then, his voice reverberating as if he were in an echo chamber, he would fret and stew over scenes we had agreed upon weeks previously. There were times when I thought Wellman was the most talented man I had ever met and other times when I became convinced he was crazy and was dragging me into his private asylum.

When the first draft was completed, actor-producer John Wayne joined our meetings and I received another lesson in Hollywoodese. Already a cinematic legend, "Duke" Wayne was the most popular and best-known actor in the world. I shared the common impression that he was of very limited acting ability, probably an easygoing, agreeable individual, and the sort I would want on my side if the Marines were unavailable. Hampered with this press-agent conception, I was totally unprepared for the real John Wayne.

Even Wayne's physical dimensions are somehow reduced on screen, for he is an enormous man with arms like the limbs of a great oak and a trunk to match. While many actors are dull fellows out of makeup and nearly inarticulate without someone to supply them words, Wayne is eloquent and as deceptively naïve as an Andalusian bull. His on-screen "aw-shaw" pebble-kicking is carried over into real life, thereby creating a fateful stumbling block for those who might think they are dealing with just another actor. To further confuse those who would seek to outwit him, he employs the most devious

470

counterattack of all; he says exactly what he thinks and in matters financial he is absolutely honest. Both tactics are socially unacceptable in Tinsel Town, and, to many employed there, incomprehensible.

Wayne's suggestions for *Island in the Sky* were few, but unerringly right on target. Instead of trying to increase his own part in the classic fashion of most stars, he showed us how the whole film would benefit if certain of his own scenes were eliminated. I worked furiously and happily to complete the final scenario; soothed by Wellman's flatteries and impressed by Wayne's sincerity, I found Hollywood much more satisfying than I had thought it would be.

Wellman decided I should take on the chores of technical director, an appointment normally considered as inferior in status to the peasant who unfolds the director's camp chair. A technical director is a person hired for his expert knowledge of whatever is to be filmed and who is usually ignored, from the first cry of "Roll 'em!" until the on-set party celebrating the shooting of the film's last scene. On pain of exile from the sound stage he is expected to be available at all times, but never under any circumstances is he to speak unless spoken to. It would be a breach of manners and tradition to consult him on any subject whatever.

Wellman was of a different mind. It gave me immense satisfaction to call upon Trans-Ocean Airlines, of which I was such a recent alumnus, and contract with them to carry out the considerable flying necessary to the production. Thus Keating, Word, and a number of the same men with whom I had shared flight decks were employed to fly four rather beat-up DC-3s we had found in a Kansas surplus dump. Thus, in a special Beechcraft, along with ace cameraman Bill Clothier, I found myself directing my own aerial armada and duplicating as exactly as we could a series of events which had happened more than a decade previously.

We found snow and the desired bad weather in the northern Sierra Mountains and began the re-enactment of the search I had been a part of during a long-ago February. The effect was haunting. I led our little squadron to areas which were almost facsimiles of the Canadian wilderness where we had originally flown. Even the weather was similarly difficult. Watching the other planes working their way through snow squalls, skimming mountain ridges by only a few feet, and occasionally disappearing for too many seconds, I found myself calling words of caution into the microphone. "For Christ's sake, let's not carry this realism quite so far!"

Yet I knew my anxieties were unnecessary. Day after day some of the finest fliers in the world were caught in Clothier's lenses, and as a result we captured ten thousand feet of very exciting aerial film. Wellman was ecstatic in his approval, and I was greatly relieved to know that the depiction of a great adventure once endured by men who were still my friends would not be insulted. There would be no fake Hollywood hocus-pocus in *Island in the Sky*.

Wellman, flaunting tradition with his customary gusto, decided that his technical director should be responsible for all scenes which would demand authenticity. Therefore I found myself directing Andy Devine, Lloyd Nolan, Jim Arness, and even Duke Wayne in several scenes where they were supposed to be actually flying. From Wellman and Wayne to the whole production crew, everyone seemed anxious to duplicate conditions as they really were. The result was an excellent movie, a rare combination of critical success to soothe our egos and enough of a financial success to solidify Wayne-Fellows Productions as a most promising independent. With Wayne's honesty ruling the bookkeeping a miracle occurred. Part of my sale contract called for a "share of the profits," an unusual accommodation at that time for a writer. Ordinarily, this "share" would have been a meaningless sop since movie companies' bookkeeping habits are convoluted. Cost and income from successful films are mixed with losers in such a way that the nuisance of sharing "profits" with creative people is rarely necessary. But with Wayne in the saddle I actually received money for my small share of *Island in the Sky*.

In the press of writing the screenplay, directing the air scenes, and commuting to Pebble Beach, I had almost forgotten a book called *The High and the Mighty*. I was reminded of it when Hobson of Morrow telephoned with a Virginia Kirkus advance review. She praised the book and since she was almost invariably the bellwether of success or failure, we were greatly encouraged. I told Linsk he might as well show the manuscript to Wellman as a possible movie since presumably he was now free to read.

A week later Hobson called to tell me the thrilling news that *The High and the Mighty* had been chosen by the Book-of-the-Month Club. Success was so obviously imminent I immediately bought a small sailboat, the *Thetis*. She was only twenty-eight feet overall, yawl-rigged, and of excellent workmanship. I went back to sea like a homesick lemming and it was several days before Linsk could find me.

Wellman had reached new heights of hysteria on reading *The High and the Mighty* and had persuaded Wayne-Fellows to make what sounded to me like a princely bid. Linsk asked in his deadpan voice what I wanted to do.

"Take it, for God's sake . . . before they change their minds!"

Soon Wellman and I were working together once again and in exciting harmony, for among other provisions of the sale, I was to write the screenplay. Once again I settled down to the same writing routine I had kept at the Washington Street house, but now desperation was gone, and after work the amenities were abundant.

I was able to ride through the Del Monte Forest frequently, often accompanied by my father, whose pride in his son rose in direct ratio with the number of times he read my name in newspapers or magazines. Now he employed a clipping service and a part-time secretary to assemble considerable piles of pap in scrapbooks. My lack of interest in this project distressed him: I was not at all sure I liked being even a minor celebrity and became uncomfortable when strangers recognized my name, or had the kindness to say they had enjoyed one of my books. Publicity embarrassed me and yet I was humbled by the thought of so many people willing to spend their time reading my words. I kept shaking my head in wonder and asking the forest, the ocean, and the sky how this could happen to a man who knew so little.

At least I now had a private shrine where I could stand in wonder and try, however unsuccessfully, to follow the raveled threads of one man's destiny. Bill Oliver of Wake Island had sent me a gift, so unusual and of such personal significance I could hardly believe my eyes. It came packed in burlap and enclosed in a wooden box—the great one-hundred-and-seventy-five-pound bronze bell from the stranded *Suwa Maru*. Twenty years before, its resonant tones had summoned me to lifeboat drill.

I had caused a stout Japanese tori to be built, painted it the traditional red, and placed it at the entrance to Island in the Sky. The bell was hung from the arch and I invited special visitors to examine what some besieged Marine had once painted along the interior of the bell's mouth: *To hell with Tojo*. Then I advised them to ring the bell for a share of the good luck it had apparently brought me.

My son George, who had already soloed an airplane, was debating between the sea or the air as a career. After the usual congratulations I gave him a present of the skull Bill Oliver had found on Wake Island. All too aware of the cockiness natural to beginning pilots once their confidence was established, I longed to keep my first-born son from hazard until he passed from the caution of unfamiliarity to the caution of experience. Across the forehead of the skull, just above the gaping eye cavities, I had printed words I hoped he would heed:

> *I can fly through any kind of weather ...*
> *When I buzz my girl's house I go low enough*
> *to count her beautiful teeth ...*
> *Damned if I didn't forget to check the fuel*
> *before I took off ...*

I placed the skull on the locker at the foot of his bed and said, "Promise me you'll say good night and good morning to Yorick until you have five hundred hours."

About this time *The High and the Mighty* was published and was greeted with astonishing reviews. I whispered softly to myself, "Come on . . . it *can't* be that good." Yet there must have been something very right about it, for the book climbed rapidly on the best-seller list and remained number one for nearly a year. My only regret was for Bill Sloane who had worked so hard with me and was not reaping his rightful share of the bounty.

As if we had not so recently known adversity I now led my family on the familiar parade of expenditures. There was a new sedan for Eleanor and two new doctors to consult. On his sixteenth birthday George received a car. I added a highly volatile Austin-Healy to the stable and, when the movie *Island in the Sky* was finished, took Eleanor in grand style to New York and thence to Europe. I employed a secretary to type my flow of words. To keep track of the booty as well as my careless expenditures and the lurking tax procurers, I needed an accountant. I avoided fancy firms and chose an independent, perky, young Chinese-American named Walter Joe. He conducted his affairs on Grant Avenue in the heart of San Francisco's Chinatown and there I opened a "branch office" as refuge from the stuffy rectitude of Pebble Beach.

Now Thayer Hobson, an ex-jam salesman who had somehow become the head of Sloane-Morrow publishing house, took charge of my literary fortunes both artistic and financial. He did not trouble to formalize the arrangement, but simply moved in and was suddenly always there. He was a jolly man, keen of intellect, and shrewder in business than I realized. He was afflicted with a frightful cough, the consequence of a gas attack during his service in World War I, and I liked his cavalier disregard of the further damage his chain-smoking might inflict on his single lung. Coughing his way through my activities he seemed in charge of everything. I was more concerned with gathering the utmost from life than with reading dull contracts, and royalty statements were simply tossed into the ever-growing piles of mail from all over the world. When asked, I simply signed on the bottom line and according to requests scribbled my initials here and there throughout reams of paper. This carefree policy proved unwise.

Once I completed the screenplay of *The High and the Mighty* I was puzzled to observe a strange aloofness fall upon Wellman. Suddenly I was not made privy to his production plans; I was shunted away from casting meetings and any suggestions I might have had for even the smaller parts were unheard. I could not account for such an about-face since all concerned expressed their satisfaction with the screenplay.

This time Wellman did not ask me to take over the flying scenes. Instead he suggested I recommend a technical director, and, somewhat miffed, I named Bill Benge, a flying comrade from Trans-Ocean. The same company was given the contract to perform the flying sequences, but I was not invited to participate. I did manage a minor coup in choosing a stewardess to keep the action and characters in the cabin honest. She was the much-beloved "Cup-Cake" who had flown with me on Trans-Ocean and who during the course of the production proved not only her technical value, but in her unspoiled manner captivated actors and crew alike.

Then one day, just before production began, I saw the covers of the newly typed script. I had labored hard and long on both the book and scenario—not a word of either version was written by anyone else. The story, based on a true event, was part of my flying life. Now, in bold letters I read:

WILLIAM WELLMAN'S
THE HIGH AND THE MIGHTY

I knew then the chilling ways of Hollywood and left town immediately.

My disillusionment with Wellman was so complete that I had no trouble staying away from the production of the film. In the worlds I had so far known, only the fish buyers had been ruthless. The script, with no sign of my name anywhere, not even a "written by," waved like a wind-torn banner across my thoughts; no matter how I tried to rationalize and even ridicule my childish pique I could not accept such blatant dishonesty. I sulked aboard the little *Thetis,* muttering, *"Sic semper tyrannis."*

By chance I encountered the movie company during the filming of a street scene in San Francisco. I stood about for a while watching Wellman directing the superb actress Claire Trevor. During a pause in his directing Wellman turned to greet me, but he maintained a strange reserve and asked after my health as if I were a distant relative come to see the movie people at play. I inquired after his arthritis and listened patiently to the details of his woes. During his oration a photographer took several pictures of us together and when he was done, Wellman was done. He went back to his directing and I wandered off to Chinatown, where with Walter Joe I enjoyed a succulent lunch of lichee nuts and boiled chicken feet.

The silence between us was broken only by our slurping

at the wonton soup. Walter Joe, a graduate of the University of California and a man who spoke better English than most citizens, liked to employ the patois many Americans thought characteristic of his ancestry. "You velly sad," he said sympathetically. "You no laugh and scratch. Think-um much trouble in heart belong you."

I confessed that for reasons unknown I had apparently lost a friend and, worse, one whom I greatly admired. I explained all that had happened since *The High and the Mighty* had begun and told him of my shock at discovering that Wellman had assumed sole proprietorship. I also apologized for my present snit, which I knew was unworthy of me.

Walter Joe, a Certified Public Accountant with the heart and soul of an ancient Chinese philosopher, rubbed his fist along the brush of his black hair and said, "Maybe you too smart . . . go too close to throne. Velly bad. Man who bring emperor present sometime get head chopped off."

The High and the Mighty had two premieres, both with the old-style hoopla. One was in Los Angeles and the other in San Francisco. My father, positively jubilant with pride, made a special trip with all his entourage to the Los Angeles event. I tried to attend the San Francisco opening but was disheartened when I saw the marquee lights and lobby displays hailing: WILLIAM WELLMAN'S THE HIGH AND THE MIGHTY. Some other time, I thought, when I have nothing better to do, I'll go see what happened to a story I still believed naïvely was mine.

I *was* included in the guest list of a crew party given by Duke Wayne when the film was finally completed. I attended as Cup-Cake's escort and had a thoroughly enjoyable evening. Wellman did not choose to join the celebrants.

The High and the Mighty was nominated for several Academy Awards* and soon held the same number one position at the box office as the book had scored on the best-seller list. Although I made by far the least money of any principal involved in the movie, my grapes were anything but sour. Thanks to Wayne's unique honesty I considered myself well rewarded.

The puerile brooding which had infected me like a sick-

* *On the Waterfront,* a movie directed by former Yale drama mate, Elia "Gadge" Kazan, won the Oscar.

ness disappeared completely under the impact of a new project. It was of a nature much more to my liking, a project for a man who preferred to work alone and had always been fascinated by the exotic. After playing the polite Pebble Beach resident for as long as I could bear the role I suddenly realized I had forsaken one profession for another even more demanding. An author without a book in work becomes an unhappy fellow, no matter how fiercely he defends his escape from creation. I was discovering art in any form to be a jealous master and, although still not quite resigned to my servitude, realized my freedom was already in chains. Therefore I proposed to make my labors more than drudgery; wherever in the world I assumed there might be a story worthy of telling, I would seek it out.

Quite to my amazement I found that very little had been written about one of the most colorful cities in the world. Rudy Webber of the FBI put me in contact with a Commander Cornell, just out of Hong Kong where he had served in Naval Intelligence.

"You must see a man called Gingles," Cornell insisted. "Gingles is the key to the Hong Kong you're looking for."

"Would you give me a letter of introduction?"

"To Gingles?" A wry smile crossed Cornell's stalwart face. "No. You'll be better off with Gingles if you never heard of me."

Gingles? The name itself was enough to send me off at once in his general direction.

Chapter 35

René Lim held daily court in the vast lobby of Kowloon's Peninsula Hotel. Here there were the usual accoutrements of any world-famous hotel, but a large area was set apart for tables where drinks could be ordered from the squad of white-coated attendants who knew many of the steady customers by name. Although "Hong Kong" was the all-embracing name of the New Territories colony, the newer city of Kowloon on the mainland was rapidly becoming quite as important as the venerable Victoria, which was situated on an already overcrowded island. The Peninsula served as the epicenter of much of Hong Kong's social and financial life. Here were gathered the old China hands —American and English businessmen, many of whom had been interned by the Japanese during their World War II occupation. Not welcome in the Peninsula were those who constituted the more visible population of the two cities—the untold numbers of street hawkers and hookers, shopkeepers in the shade and dance-hall girls under the neons; nor were the rag-tag remnants of the army Chiang had left behind, the Parsees, Sikhs, hordes of coolies sweating along the wharves, the armies of child-beggars, and the legions of thieves and pimps who roamed the streets and infested the waterfronts.

Frequent ferries crossed the short water distance between the city of Victoria and Kowloon, and the Peninsula Hotel was situated a short walk from the ferry landing. Thus communication between the two locales was easy and many people who would not otherwise leave the city made the crossing simply to meet someone at the hotel or be seen. There was no comparable establishment on the city side.

René Lim, the unofficial empress of the Peninsula lobby, was the daughter of a pioneer Chinese aviator who had flown a bamboo-and-wire biplane from Oakland to Salinas, California, before World War I. Now his daughter echoed his dash and bravado, adding her own vivacious good humor. Educated in California, she spoke American English without a trace of accent.

The habitués of the hotel's lobby lounge formed an unorganized nodding club and tried to stake out their claim to a table early in the day, thereby assuring themselves of a headquarters for business, pleasure, various mischiefs, or the gathering of information of possible importance to their sense of belonging and their pocketbook. René Lim served as a daily catalyst to these people, her remarkable memory for names and details enabling her to recognize and greet people she might not have seen for years. They were a heterogeneous collection of heroes and scalawags unlikely any other place on earth. There were still a few Pukka Sahibs crisp and white under the overhead fans, there were merchants from Malaya, airline pilots in hula shirts from everywhere, exporters from Japan, manufacturers from the Philippines, and ranchers from Australia.

479

There were rich Chinese and struggling Chinese and an occasional White Russian who invariably claimed to be royalty or of royal descent. René knew the pedigree of nearly all the Peninsula regulars, the state of their health, marriage, love life, and prosperity. She achieved her respected status because of her great heart and perpetual interest in helping others solve their problems. Her personal empire ranged far beyond the Peninsula Hotel, extending to the most remote regions of the Far East. I had expected to meet a Dragon Lady and found instead a young and utterly charming oriental woman.

On our first meeting René Lim apologized, "I speak Mandarin and Cantonese, of course, but not the other Chinese dialects. If you really want to know Hong Kong it will be best if you have a versatile interpreter."

René recommended her uncle, a former general in the Chinese Air Force, and a graduate of Yale University's Sheffield School of Engineering. "My uncle speaks seven Chinese dialects as well as French and German," she said. "He isn't doing anything just now and I'm sure you would like him."

I hesitated, questioning if I could afford a man of such obvious worth for as long as I intended to stay in Hong Kong. "He is also a gourmet, an expert on Chinese food, a connoisseur of oriental art, and a philosopher." She laughed quickly. "And he can use the money."

"How much would be fair?"

"I'm sure he would be happy with twenty-five dollars a week."

René explained that her uncle was one of the many abandoned when Chiang fled from the mainland to Formosa. Only the young of his armies were allowed to accompany him; the aging, the crippled, and ill were left behind. Her uncle, responsible for the building of many Chinese airports during World War II, had been too old. "He's past sixty now."

I agreed to hire René's uncle sight unseen and next approached what I had been led to believe was a more difficult matter. "This man called Gingles. How do I go about meeting him?"

René looked at me a moment, her dark eyes scrutinizing me carefully. She seemed to hesitate for the first time since I had entered the lounge bar.

"Do you know Gingles?" I pressed.

"Of course. Very well. Why do you want to see him?"

"I'm not sure. I just thought he might help me find a Chinese junk." My almost hopeless inability to lie convincingly now found reflection in René's expressive eyes. I wanted to laugh and accuse her of being inscrutable, but feared being overfamiliar at first meeting. And I thought it might give her the wrong impression if I told her Gingles was one of the known agents through whom Chinese in America sent funds to relatives behind the Bamboo Curtain. By the time Gingles took his cut, I had heard, very little of it ever reached the relatives.

"Why do you want a junk?"

"I'm not sure of that either. I've always wanted to sail one and I thought I might take my paint box along and do some exploring along the waterfront."

"Well, you can't explore very far or you'll be in Communist waters and you won't come back."

"Really?" I asked. Almost simultaneously a tiny, hopeful light flickered across my thoughts. "The Communists would hold an American citizen against his will even if he was only making a painting?"

"The Red gunboat crews are not art buffs. Right now there are several Americans who wandered across the frontier and they won't be back for a long time."

Another flicker of light. Supposing a young American found himself captive in China . . . and someone had to find . . . and rescue him . . . ?

"I'll take you to Gingles's Place, but he probably won't be there, since he's been ill recently and he rarely comes to town. He has a nice house in the country. I'll get in touch with him, but it may take a few days."

That evening we went to Gingles's Place, a checkered tablecloth restaurant and bar with a boisterous international clientele. René knew many of them, particularly the pilots, who acted cheerfully as her multiple liaison with people throughout the Far East and who seemed to have made Gingles's Place a second home. My attention was often distracted from René's encyclopedic dissertation on the locals' social status, the value of face, the art of squeeze, and the pitfalls awaiting the innocent by the activities of the two bartenders, one of whom doubled in a nonchalant way as a sort of maitre d'. Both men were middle-aged, tattooed about their powerful forearms, and of formidable appearance. They greeted René warmly and confirmed that Gingles had been ailing and would not be honoring the joint with his presence this evening. Without too much chance of error I thought I could identify the pair as alumni of the United States Marines, a not surprising association since my dossier on Gingles described him as an ex-Navy chief petty officer who had decided the Hong Kong New Territories was the place to make his fortune.

The next morning I met René's uncle in the Peninsula lobby and forever after called him "General." He was very tall for a Chinese, and straight as a guardsman. His face was structured in soft planes, but there his oriental heritage appeared to have been altered. Behind his steel-rimmed glasses his eyes were gray-blue, direct, and sincere. His manner and gestures were abrupt and resolute in contrast to the flowing, gracefully lazy movements common to Chinese in hot climates. He was wearing a tan cork helmet, an immaculate white shirt, and tan shorts. Long white socks covered his legs from the knee down and his loafers were newly polished. He carried a cane jauntily, as if it were a swagger stick, and certainly seemed in no physical need of it.

We exchanged smiles, shook hands, and found a table where we ordered tea. A momentary silence fell between us because I could not think how to begin. How dare I presume to offer this dignified gentleman only twenty-five dollars a week when I was not even sure what I wanted him to do?

We slipped into a brief discussion of Yale and New Haven, which he had not seen for forty years. "I am sixty-five now," he said, "and I'm sure there are great changes back there . . . as there are in me."

I explained how I had never been an undergraduate at Yale, but had slipped in and out of the back door and hardly knew one building from another.

When we had exhausted this subject, which seemed of little lasting interest to either of us, I knew the time had come to explain somehow my presence in Hong Kong. "Maybe," I faltered, "I might try to write a book about this area."

"What might the book be about?"

I avoided the question in his honest eyes for only a moment, then decided to drop all pretense.

"General . . . I haven't the faintest idea."

He smiled with such mellow warmth I knew we would understand each other. "Then," he said, eyes twinkling, "you are ideally adjusted to write something worth reading. Preconception is the enemy of knowledge. It's much easier to write on a clean slate than a messy one. Do you like to eat?"

I was aware of the General's trim figure, so spare and lean without a trace of fat, and wondered if he might actually be hungry? Yet there had been nothing ravenous about the way he chewed the cookies which had come with the tea.

"What has eating to do with writing?" I was surprised to find myself already regarding him as my mentor.

"You will see much and must clear your thoughts. Mystics fast and are frequently guilty of cloudy thinking. I assume you would prefer that people understand what you write. Proper food is not a soporific, but a stimulant to the brain. I have found it so."

"General," I said, delighted with the man, "where are we having lunch?"

Thus began my unique education under the almost constant and careful tutelage of General George C. Lim. According to the General's choice we dined on the food of Hunan, or Szechuan, or Peking, Shanghai, Canton, Mongolia, or any of the Chinese varieties resulting from a five-thousand-year national preoccupation with eating.

The General's unique curriculum was devoted to food only twice a day; the balance of our time together included long lectures on the several Chinese ethnic cultures, and what I called "art appreciation interludes." We spent hours in the finer shops, while he lectured on the qualities and faults of the paintings and sculptured pieces on display. On other occasions he would take me to temples where he could explain the history, symbols, and ceremonies, or the raucous traditional theaters where he would translate the dialogues.

After a week, my brain was spinning with so many new impressions I longed for relief. I found it by sometimes deserting the General, in a shameless return to steak, french fried potatoes, and apple pie. Other times I would take René to an American movie, one of which turned out to be *The Raging Tide*.

René held court as usual in the Peninsula lobby, and I encountered her nearly every day. She kept assuring me I would soon hear from the elusive Gingles.

After almost two weeks René's prediction was confirmed. Word was passed from Gingles's country retreat: he would condescend to meet me at his "place" on the following noon, but I must come alone. I asked René why she had not been invited. She said only that Gingles was known for his eccentricities.

I spent the morning with the General in the Yau Ma Tei district of the waterfront looking at junks and trying without success to find one suitable and with an owner willing to charter. The General, in spite of his open disapproval of the idea, proceeded nevertheless to do his utmost. Day after day I had watched his tall and erect figure marching across the narrow catwalks connecting the junks with the shore as he talked with owners about the possibility of chartering. The problem, he kept insisting, was more than finding a junk not already engaged in trade, for all of the better-kept vessels were under shipping contracts, or so crowded with the owner's brood there was simply no room for additional bodies. I considered solving the problem by buying a junk, until the General told me that all of the seaworthy craft were the lifetime investment as well as the homes of a family and assorted relatives—the Hakka people, who were born aboard, were living aboard, and would die aboard. As a consequence they were extremely expensive.

"And I can't let you go along with just any captain. Many of these chaps would not be above sailing away and holding you for ransom, others just might be caught in Communist waters and you would be a long time getting back. We have to find someone we can trust."

I knew from the General's eyes he was not warning of pirates and Red gunboats just to make his work more interesting. His genuine concern was impressive, but then so was my growing assurance that in this kind of an atmosphere there must be an exciting story.

It was twelve o'clock. I smoothed the red-checkered tablecloth at the small table for two I had taken, and in my little sketchbook made a small drawing of the salt and pepper shakers and glass of toothpicks clustered with the sugar bowl. I was the only customer in Gingles's Place.

One of the Marine bartenders had approached me soon after I sat down and asked politely enough what he could do for me. I told him I had an appointment with Gingles and would wait before ordering. There was not the slightest change of expression on the bartender's face as he returned to his bar and began a desultory twisting of a towel around some glasses. I watched the tattooed snake on his right arm undulate as he manipulated the towel, but when he caught me at it, decided to mind my own business. It was very quiet in Gingles's. The only sound was the street traffic outside.

Twelve fifteen. No sign of Gingles or any other customers. I had completed the drawing and was not pleased with it. Still-lifes had never appealed to me. Where was everyone? Was Gingles's closed for lunch on Thursdays? Then I remembered René had told me it was a dinner-only establishment. Another ten minutes passed.

Impatient, I left the table and walked over to the bar. "Do you think Gingles will be along fairly soon?"

The bartender halted his glass-polishing long enough to favor me with his full attention—and, I noticed, a thorough inspection.

"He'll be along."

No more. He looked up at the collection of model aircraft hanging from the ceiling and apparently found them fascinating. I watched the snake on his forearm undulate a few more times then asked the location of the washroom.

"Over there," he nodded toward the far side of the room. I drifted away, checked my watch once again, and entered the washroom. The urinal was on a raised stone step. Just above it at eye level was a small window screened by wooden louvers. I mounted the step and stood feet apart, my mind wandering vaguely in the normal fashion of males relieving themselves. Beyond the louvers I saw a narrow passageway, open to the sky and flanked on both sides by plaster walls. I assumed that the wall on the right concealed the kitchen since a ventilating fan was mounted just beneath the roof eaves. Another blank plaster wall about seventy feet distant terminated the passageway, but to the right a splash of brilliant sunlight indicated an opening. All of the passageway was in deep shade and seen through the louvers, I thought it no more than an interesting composition in light and dark, until a man turned in from the sunlight and entered the shadow.

Had I somehow been asleep for weeks and awakened in the men's room of a Hollywood studio? I had the greatest difficulty convincing myself the man I saw was not some actor in a B movie. For approaching me, head bent until the brim of his straw hat covered his face, wearing a rumpled white suit and leaning heavily on a malacca cane, was the composite of all the devious and dangerous characters who populated Grade B melodramas—"Surely," I whispered to myself, "Sydney Greenstreet in the flesh." Yet I knew it was Gingles and I knew he could not see me.

I watched his slow progress along the passageway and saw that he must indeed have been ill, for there was considerable hesitancy in his step, and once when he raised his head slightly I saw he was wearing very dark glasses. For a moment I thought he might be going blind, yet he used the cane more as a physical support than as an aid to sight. He had obviously been a big man, but now the white suit hung loosely upon him as if he had lost considerable weight. He passed within inches of the louvers, but my elevation was some two feet higher than the floor of the passageway and I could not see his face. He disappeared off to the right, beyond the visual limit of the louvers. I assumed he had entered into what I thought would be the kitchen.

I returned to my table and waited, expecting Gingles's momentary arrival. Nothing happened and I grew ever more impatient. It had been nearly three quarters of an hour since our scheduled appointment. The bartender, I noticed, had disappeared.

I was tempted to leave in a huff, but then I remembered René had gone to considerable trouble arranging a meeting and I resolved to wait another ten minutes. Almost at my time limit Gingles appeared from the kitchen door, ambled slowly across the room, and halted before me. The bartender appeared behind him.

Gingles ignored the chair directly across the table from me and hooked another with the crook of his cane. He dragged it into position on my right and sat down heavily. He was still wearing his hat and dark glasses, and I now saw a rather large nose protruding from heavy jowls. Come on, Sydney Greenstreet, I thought, get out of costume. I know you.

Gingles folded his big liver-spot mottled hands atop the cane and pinched his lips tightly together. I gathered a distinct impression that the eyes hidden behind the black glasses did not like what they saw.

"I'm Gingles," he declared finally. "What do you want to drink?"

I explained, lamely, how I preferred not to drink in the daytime, not wishing to curb the pleasant thirst which developed so faithfully toward sundown.

"You got to drink something," he said more as an order than as an invitation.

"All right. I'll have a Coke."

"For Christ's sake, what kind of a man is René sending around here? I thought she had better judgment. What do you drink at sundown?"

"Rum . . . if I can get it."

Gingles turned his head approximately one quarter inch in the direction of the bartender. "Bring him a rum."

I did not want a rum or anything else which might impair my thinking. By now I was almost certain Gingles disapproved of me and yet I still hoped he could help me.

We sat in silence until the bartender set a glass of unwatered rum before me and one containing liquid of a lighter hue before Gingles. He raised his glass halfway as if initiating a toasting gesture, then appeared to think better of it. He took a long swallow of the drink then put the glass down and asked, "What do you want from me?"

"I was hoping you could help me find a junk."

"What for?"

I hesitated—later, I thought, probably fatefully. For

here I was faced with a query I could answer only in the vaguest terms. How, I wondered, could I tell a man like Gingles that I was feeling my way toward a book—of what kind I was still uncertain. I hedged toward what I hoped was more easily understood, a detour, which was possibly my second mistake.

"Well . . . I would like to do some painting along the waterfront and much of what I want to paint is impossible to see from the land. . . ."

I knew I had not sounded at all convincing and was not altogether surprised at the ensuing silence. The orbs of black glass remained fixed on me, the lips pressed tighter. "Bullshit," Gingles said flatly. "You work for the U.S. government."

"I do not. What gives you that idea?"

"What gives any of the U.S. government agencies the idea they can send some guy like you over here to check up on Gingles? This is British territory and you people can't do a goddamned thing about anything. Now you go back to Washington or wherever in the hell you came from and tell them that. Tell them they can goddamn well leave Gingles alone."

"All I want to do is paint a few pictures," I repeated almost indifferently, since it was so very obvious that Gingles's mind was set. Now I remembered when Rudy Webber's friend had told me Gingles was the most valuable contact Naval Intelligence had in Hong Kong, he had not told me why. Obviously someone had offended Gingles and I had run into the recoil.

Gingles pushed down on the cane and rose. He eyed me in silence for a moment, then said, "You better stay away from junks or you could get yourself in a lot of trouble. Go back home where you belong."

Without further word he turned his back and shuffled away. Chagrined, I took a sip of the rum to test its quality and found it dreadful. I left nearly a full glass when I stood up and departed Gingles's Place with such dignity as I could muster.

––––––––––

The next three days were spent in further and frustrating search for a junk. I could not explain even to myself why I considered a junk so important to a project not yet even half conceived, but, like a child denied, the satisfaction of acquiring became more important than the object itself. Through one contact or another, René could arrange almost anything under the oriental sun, but now she confessed she had exhausted every lead. "I know Gingles could have fixed things if he wanted to," she said unhappily. "I think his illness has made him a little senile."

A strange division had somehow come between us. She did not ask why Gingles had not been more cooperative, and for some totally incomprehensible reason I did not want to repeat the details of our fruitless interview. There were even a few moments when I wondered if René herself disbelieved my identity as a writer and had somehow convinced herself, and possibly even Gingles, that I was some sort of government agent. I managed to be rid of such ridiculous suspicions in short order, but they contributed to my frustration. The General, stalwart throughout, finally learned of a junk in a shipyard on the Victoria side of the harbor. We made to her at all speed and found her to be an ocean-going junk and therefore considerably larger and more formidable than the local variety. She also carried a dividend in color, for her decks supported four ancient muzzle-loading cannon, presumably to repel pirates. They were squatting on tracks and rigged with rope tackles exactly as junks a hundred years previously must have borne the same caliber of artillery. Beside myself with pleasurable visions of swashbuckling through the South China Sea, I knew she would unquestionably pay off in a story.

As the General began to haggle for price, he soon discovered a more insurmountable difficulty. This junk, unlike so many of the locals, had an engine, now broken down and waiting for parts to be shipped from England. She was in the shipyard for good reason, requiring extensive repairs to her hull, and would not be seaworthy again for an estimated two months. Crestfallen, I lingered about the shipyard most of the day photographing the junk and her crew. Dutifully, the General photographed her captain and myself squatting alongside one of her fat old cannon.

Next morning in my room at the Peninsula I had just completed my breakfast when the telephone buzzed. The instrument hung on the wall near the head of the bed and it was the General's custom to call on his arrival. The day's research was about to begin and judging from the stagnant haze over the harbor I knew the day was going to be a hot one.

I crossed the room, took the phone off the hook and said, "Good morning, General." As always, I knew there would be a brief exchange of pleasantries, his wish for tranquillity in my sleep, and mine for his good health. But it was not the General's carefully modulated voice on the telephone. Without so much as a please the voice demanded raspily for my name. I gave it.

"This is Gingles."

I caught my breath. Bless his gruffness, he was going to come through after all. "Well, well . . . good morning, sir."

"I thought I told you to get out of town."

"Yes . . . I assumed you were just not feeling too well. . . ."

"You've had three days. That's enough. There's a Pan American flight leaving for Manila at two o'clock this afternoon. You better be on it. There's a ticket at the airport in your name. I say again if you like your good health be on that airplane."

"I'm not leaving Hong Kong for you or anyone else—" I protested, but a click in the receiver cut me short. Whatever I was about to retort I knew Gingles would not be hearing. I hung up the receiver and walked slowly back to the window where I finished the last of my tea standing up. I watched a few junks maneuvering about the harbor, sliding over the yellow water as if painted on gauze, almost transparent against the reflected light streaking through the morning haze. And I knew a sensation I had not known since the last time I had been in trouble in an airplane, the sneaking sense of fear created by something still unrevealed, a prickling along the back of my neck, disturbing but not altogether unpleasurable. Of course if I were so persistent about being in the right place at the wrong time someone eventually was bound to take a cut at my neck.

The more I warned myself that Gingles undoubtedly meant what he said, the less inclined I became to leave Hong Kong with my tail between my legs. Who was Gingles to dictate my destiny?

Then, for an unpleasant moment I remembered the beating I had taken in San Francisco and my resolve lessened. How much was a book worth, especially a book of unknown nature? Never mind. The book was not the important thing now. The character of the man who would write it was being challenged and he must not twist away.

The phone buzzed again. *That* would be the General. Going to it, growing all the more stubborn en route, I knew it was going to be a much hotter and busier day than I had imagined.

Chapter 36

The T-Lands police station was situated on a promontory a short walk from the Peninsula Hotel. It was built like a fortress with a great supportive embankment of rock. Here, a contingent of British officers, the majority of whom had matriculated through the London Metropolitan Police Force, were quartered with a much larger contingent of Chinese police. The building held a small jail, which smelled ripely of disinfectant, for the temporary detention of suspects and the offices and quarters of the Hong Kong water police.

René's friend Chelsey Debbs commanded the water police and because of her he received me most graciously. He was very proper and very British, a crisp, compact officer who listened patiently as I told him how I came to be in Hong Kong, of my search for a junk, and all the details about Gingles from our first meeting to the morning's phone call. When I had finished my story, which sounded even to me like a plot for a cheap novel, Debbs said he was not surprised. "Of course we've known Gingles for years, although generally he keeps shy of us and we have no reason for direct contact."

"Do you think he means what he said?"

"Quite." His voice was flat and there followed a pause I found uncomfortable. I was an American citizen in British territory and rightfully my troubles should be taken to the American consulate, if anywhere. But I did not believe the people at my consulate were in a position to deal with the likes of Gingles, even if they wanted to.

"I assume you're not going to take Gingles's advice and be on the Manila plane . . ." Debbs was saying, but I only half heard him. He had smiled thinly, then motioned to a young Chinese who had been standing quietly behind me throughout the interview. Debbs said something to him softly in Chinese and he left without making a sound.

Debbs said, "I'm going to do something a bit out of the way and I may have to answer for it, but I shall sleep much better if you have a chaperone during your stay."

Debbs rose as the Chinese man reappeared followed by a stocky, dark-haired, young man in white shorts and short-sleeved shirt. After an exchange of good mornings, Debbs introduced him. ". . . Inspector Ron Dudman. If you don't mind, he'll look after you. Perhaps you're a blessing in disguise. At last I've found a way to keep him out of the dance halls."

Dudman smiled shyly and offered his strong hand. We were of equal height, but he was even broader across the shoulders, a block of a man who exuded strength and confidence. I was then introduced to the Chinese man who had hovered in the background throughout. "You may notice this chap nearby most of the time," Debbs explained as he gave his name. I better understood an additional identification. According to his badge number, he was addressed verbally as "Twelve-oh-Three." Yet Twelve-oh-Three did not display a badge or any other item which might differentiate him from thousands of other young Chinese who populated the streets and waterfronts of Hong Kong. He wore the usual black, loose-fitting coat and pants, a funeral outfit contrasting strangely with his warm smile and sparkling black eyes. I was careful not to squeeze his hand as with another caucasian, but his hidden strength was very evident even in our brief clasping of flesh.

During the next half-hour I learned much more of the Hong Kong waterfront and eagerly accepted invitations to explore places I had not known existed. Among other matters I learned Dudman would not wear a uniform in my company, nor would he alter the unarmed tradition of the British constabulary. ". . . but just in case something unfortunate occurs," Debbs smiled wryly, "Twelve-oh-Three carries Ron's gun for him."

Twelve-oh-Three raised the bottom of his jacket and

displayed two guns, one for Dudman and one for himself. I was impressed.

"Now," Debbs said, "off with you and good luck. Drop in for a chat when you feel like it."

I left the T-Lands police station with Dudman at my side, the pair of us swinging along freely, bound for the Peninsula where the General joined us and led us to a Mongolian restaurant where the *Huo Kuo* was reported as superb. On the way I glanced backward twice. Both times I saw Twelve-oh-Three following at a discreet distance. Even Gingles, I thought, would hesitate to attack this formidable array. And such was my pleasure in our tight little company that I nearly forgot its true purpose.

After a few days it was Dudman who offered a possible solution to the junk problem. He banged his fist against his handsome head and said he should have thought of it much sooner. There was a junk captain he knew who could be relied upon. Not only did he detest the Red Chinese and was certain to avoid any contact with them, but he was a Seventh-Day Adventist and known to be a thoroughly honest man.

After another day we found him not far from where the General and I had first searched, in the Yau Ma Tei typhoon shelter. He was Captain Po Chee, a small, wiry, middle-aged man who was at first hopelessly bewildered and even a little frightened by our sudden intrusion. While the General explained our visit I had time to examine the junk which I had already decided to christen after the Chinese poet, Li Po.

The junk was nautically unimpressive. She was not as big as I had hoped for and was already overcrowded with Captain Chee's numerous children, who followed me about the decks expecting, I decided, some sort of caucasian miracle. I counted also the Captain's wife, a gaunt sad-looking woman, and another man who looked like the Captain and if not his brother was undoubtedly related. Their quarters were beneath the high poop with entries and exits via two doorless cavities on each side. Between them I saw a Christian cross made of copper stripping and nailed to the after-bulkhead. After a brief tour within, conducted by a pair of solemn black eyes in the peach-round face of the smallest daughter, I knew sleeping on board would be impractical. The ceiling was so low I could not stand even in a stoop and I wondered how the floor area accommodated even the usual number of bodies. A number of mats were rolled in one corner and the area appeared spotlessly clean.

The sails were collapsed * on their booms and from what I could see appeared to be in an advanced state of rot. Likewise all the running rigging, which was of the coarsest sisal, and her standing gear, loose and frayed. The three masts—main, mizzen, and a stump mast in the bow I thought of as a bowsprit—looked stout enough to stand without additional support. For mechanical aid there was a wooden drum winch operated by hand and when necessary by walking on the arms.

After a long and apparently delicate discussion with Captain Chee, the General advised me that the junk could be mine at one hundred dollars per week, with the exception of three days at next full moon when the Captain had a previous commitment he did not trouble to reveal. The pact was set with a nod and we agreed to sail on the following morning. But the General asked to be excused. The sea and his belly, he explained, were mortal enemies. Although Dudman was not a sailor he spoke enough Mandarin to make his wants known, and Twelve-oh-Three would also be aboard, hence I anticipated no difficulty and would rely upon my own observations should Captain Chee have a change of heart and approach Red Chinese waters.

On the following morning the *Li Po* caught a light breeze and sailed out of the crowded Yau Ma Tei shelter. Captain Chee put wife and children to work at a pair of enormous sweeps to speed our exit and I stood at the tiller, an automatic borrowed from one of Dudman's colleagues slung from my belt—the dream of every little boy pirate at last realized.

I was disturbed on this first day's voyaging by the presence of two new men who had not been aboard the *Li Po* when our charter agreement had been resolved. Moreover, they were sullen, rascally-looking fellows who gave a hand hoisting sails and then retired to the bow where they squatted and smoked for most of the day.

---

* A junk's sails cannot be furled in the usual fashion known to caucasians. Because of the many battens they are collapsed like a venetian blind.

Counting the Captain's brother, we were now outnumbered, but by late afternoon, when we came about and headed back to Yau Ma Tei without incident, my wariness eased.

So began two weeks of sailing throughout the archipelago of the Hong Kong New Territories and westward as far as we dared toward Communist-controlled waters. Once the atmosphere of suspicion had time to drift away, Captain Chee and his mixed-generation crew seemed to understand what I wanted to see and do, but I could not tell them of my continuous and secret satisfaction with all that transpired. I chuckled privately at the *Li Po* herself, a floating basket held together apparently by the strength of the gilded warlord who graced the bow as a small figurehead. She soon proved to be of unstable design, capricious, and even dangerous in disposition. I saw how her gallant Captain so mistrusted her stability in any sort of breeze he kept one of the new men constantly at the main halyard with instructions to let go immediately if the junk heeled beyond some ten degrees. Considering the number of junks lost through capsizing every year I could hardly blame him, but I wondered if our sails would blow out long before any wind would give us trouble. For the *Li Po*'s "sails" were a sight to behold: the mizzen was rended and holed as if a shrapnel bomb had exploded close by; the main was a sewn hodge-podge of flour sacks, coffee bags, burlap, and flax of twenty different textures and weights. The "water" sail, a lumpish thing draped from the bow mast, looked like the wrappings of a badly preserved mummy.

Yet, despite her grievous lack of smartness, the *Li Po* moved along handsomely enough in the lightest of breezes, a quality enhanced by her mere five feet of draft and almost flat bottom. The great arm of teak which served as her tiller was activated by a heavy tackle, in my opinion a totally unnecessary assist since her rudder was grated in the style of all junks and except when running in a full gale the tiller could be moved with the most gentle pressure. When there was no wind at all, wife, children, and the two men alternated in groups of four at the long sweeps. Under such propulsion we glided along at approximately one mile per hour. They eased their not very strenuous exertions by continuous giggling interspersed with occasional soft chanting.

I had my own amusements and certain times for laughter at myself. Now I noticed how easily I had fallen into the habit of standing with my feet spread wide apart and my fists punched hard against my gun belt, my back somewhat straighter than usual, and even my voice affecting a new resonance. I laughed because a little Nebraska boy was revived and on the loose again, his imagination ruling with every new sensation of sight and sound, a self-appointed reincarnation of all the swashbucklers who had ever sailed the China seas.

Dudman and Twelve-oh-Three rarely left me alone except when I returned to my room at the Peninsula, where we agreed any intrusion by Gingles's assistants seemed highly unlikely.

There came the approach of the full moon and Captain Chee advised us he must honor his previous commitment. I told him we would not rejoin him afterward since I also had other obligations. We parted friends, the more so, I thought, because on the last day I had brought an armful of presents for the children, and through Dudman the Captain made it plain our presence aboard had pleased him more than the mere fattening of his purse. Our sailing together had been relatively serene; we had surmounted no great dangers nor repelled so much as a single pirate, but leaving her I knew I was half in love with the *Li Po*, frowsy as she was—the junk was still a vessel of great charm. I was saddened to realize I had seen the last of her and her Seventh-Day Adventist crew, but junk life could now offer little more than repetition, and my escort of Dudman and Twelve-oh-Three could not continue much longer. My satisfying times in the *Li Po* had convinced me that the hero of the book I was now determined to write must certainly own at least one junk.

Thus inspired, I left the *Li Po* in the dazzling noonday sun. Sure now of my story, I began serious preparations for the return flight to the only place I could identify as home. Dudman, restless with his assignment to me, nevertheless suggested I delay. "There is one thing you must do before you leave and I can fix it for you," he said. "You should go along for a day on one of our Home Defense gunboats and watch their patrol."

Delighted with the prospect, I asked him to make the arrangements as soon as possible. Meanwhile, during these last days I would make some attempt to repay the innumerable kindnesses granted me by so many people of Hong Kong and Kowloon. I began with René and the General, and went on to Chelsey Debbs and others of less eminence. Finally, there was Dudman himself to be repaid, for he had gone beyond mere duty from the very beginning and we had become close friends. Twelve-oh-Three's lack of English made a similar closeness more difficult, but an unquestionable bond now existed between us and I treasured his quiet presence. I thought to please Dudman by holding our farewell party in his favorite dance hall. That decision probably saved my life.

As usual when celebrating, I drank with overenthusiasm on the night of Dudman's farewell affair. And carried away with love for fellow man and woman while all the world became aglow, I forgot the intensity of my hangovers. The next morning, overwhelmed with such wretchedness as I had not known since the long-ago morning in Peking when a Chinese girl was delivered to me, I whimpered as I opened one eye and saw the sun already high.

The phone above my bed in the Peninsula rang a long time before I gathered strength to reach for it. I groaned what I hoped passed for a good morning.

"Ron here. Good morning to you. Are you ready?"

Ready? Ready for what? For the hospital perhaps or even the morgue, but certainly for nothing else. I realized the sunlight was creating blinding shafts of light across the room, and the bed screeched as I made a slight movement, but little else mattered. "I'm waiting in the lobby," the telephone said, "we'll have to trot right along to make it."

Dudman's voice. Trot along to what? How could he be so goddamned cheerful after the night we had shared? "Oh, God," I moaned. Then in a faint whisper I begged to be forgiven for my sins.

"They can't wait for you and it's already eight o'clock."

Suddenly I remembered. On the way to his party Dudman had told me all arrangements had been made for a voyage in P1323, an armed one-hundred-ten-foot Royal Naval launch. She would sail from her berth on the Victoria side at 9 A.M. and I would be most welcome aboard. What was left of my reason knew we could catch the ferry and just make the berth if I leaped out of bed instantly and ran all the way.

"Ron . . . I—" I found that neither my jaw nor thick tongue would obey and remorse was heavy upon me. I was about to miss a rare opportunity and be rude to my potential hosts. "Ron . . . I just *can't* make it. I'm sick. I am probably dying. I just hope you can arrange another invitation. Please forgive me."

I heard a soft chuckle in the telephone, but I knew he was disappointed in me. Not half as much, I thought, as I was in what remained of myself.

"If you can set it up for later in the week I'll stay over."

"I'll try. Go back to sleep."

For a while I managed, but self-loathing finally triumphed and I spent the rest of the day floundering about the room, going frequently to the window for a possible sighting of either the patrol boat or the *Li Po*. I could not bear even the thought of venturing into the blazing sun or the slightest physical activity. Throughout the interminable day my principal occupation was the recitation of vows never to let alcohol touch my lips again.

At seven o'clock that night the phone rang. It was Dudman again.

"Ron here."

"I'm terribly sorry—"

"You've heard then?"

I told him I didn't know what he was talking about.

"The 1323 was shelled by the Communists. One hit was in the wheel-house and the other was in the engine room. Seven men aboard were killed. A petty officer brought her home from the Pearl estuary. There's going to be an awful stink about it. . . ."

There was a long pause, then Dudman said, "I should think you're a very lucky chap. If you like I'll come round and tell you more about it."

Lucky? Lucky to have a hangover which had rendered me nearly helpless. Certainly as a guest aboard the 1323 I would have been either in the wheelhouse or the engine room, and if so would not now be listening to Inspector Dudman. "Ron," I said evenly. "Come by. I think we should have a drink."

The wanton attack on the P1323 was inexcusable for she was merely going about her routine patrol in recognized territorial waters. The local and British newspapers were furious and the Red Chinese, as usual, silent. Her tragic voyage and the utter futility of her dead left a heavy mark upon the story I now believed I was ready to tell.

More than a month had passed since the man called Gingles had telephoned his mandate to leave town. When he failed to follow up on his order I could not decide whether the almost constant presence of Ron Dudman discouraged him or perhaps someone he trusted had advised him I was harmless to his enterprise. I asked René Lim for an answer and she was equally puzzled. Because Gingles's Place was such a popular rendezvous for transient international pilots I wondered if my first mistake had not been in failing to tell him a pilot's way of life had once been mine—my fault then for inadvertently giving him the impression there was something phony about my behavior. But then why had he been so menacing, what was he hiding, and why did he think I might interfere? Only one thing about my brief relationship with Gingles was very real. There was no guesswork about the phone call to my room and the tenor of his voice when he ordered me out of Hong Kong. In good fiction every story has a satisfying ending. Alas, in real life we are often left holding only one end of tantalizing threads.

It was not until I began writing the novel *Soldier of Fortune* that I realized Gingles had done me a favor. Regardless of his intentions, his place and the atmosphere he created provided one of the most colorful settings in a book which became a best-seller, was selected by the book clubs, and was translated into all the major languages.

The questions posed by Gingles's behavior were to remain an enigma, for he died not long after the book was published. Likewise did I wonder at my own fortunes, since after so much bounty the inexorable counter-weighting of *yin* was obviously at work.

On my return to Pebble Beach and what passed for the family hearth I found Eleanor in sagging health. Various ailments including a suspected ulcer further aggravated her arthritis. Even so her iron spirit showed little deterioration; while her fixation on doctors and her slavish response to their sundry recommendations remained unchanged, she still led an active social life and welcomed her errant husband warmly.

With such grace as I could muster I tried settling into the Pebble Beach environment. We entertained variously and were likewise hosted by pairs of tweedy, pleasant, and well-behaved people who knew Eleanor well and regarded me as a curiosity. It was understood that I wrote books, that my name appeared frequently in Herb Caen's San Francisco *Chronicle* column, and that my father was known as a "character" deserving of considerable respect. Our evening social occasions never varied in their Anglo-Saxon tribal rites, but the degree of etiquette reflected the cultural heritage of the particular locals as well as the changing American social scene. Guests invited to appear at seven o'clock were greeted heartily at the door and escorted to the living room where all remained standing in embarrassment for approximately three minutes. This programmed interval was always noisy, as simultaneous comments on the physical well-being of hosts and guests were exchanged. The "you look wonderful" salutes were fired regardless of the subject's actual appearance.

Once this amenity had been observed, a significant pause followed whereupon the host would clap his hands together and inquire, "What will everybody have to drink?" or "How about a little something to warm the cockles?" Guests were then supposed to signify their preference, which in the Pebble Beach area leaned heavily toward Scotch and soda or martinis. Bourbon whiskey, somehow categorized as the hand-laborers' choice, was rarely mentioned. A request for beer would have raised eyebrows all around and would probably prove unsuccessful.

Even in Pebble Beach, servants were to be found only in the homes of the older inhabitants. Spending the last of their fortunes, they did employ a man, a couple, or, very occasionally, as many as three servants to attend their house and needs. The young and middle-aged had already accustomed themselves to domestic chores and had learned to value the resulting privacy.

Depending largely upon the composition of the invited party and the enthusiasm of their host, the pre-drinking interval lasted for as little as thirty minutes or as long as two hours. A dinner was then served which featured the gastronomic specialty of the hostess and her wedding-present silverware. All wives present were obliged to praise the principal dish regardless of its quality and confirm their approval by asking for the recipe. Unlike Midwestern gatherings of similar economic status, wine was normally served and did much to raise the decibel count of the evening.*

These affairs usually concluded with no more than an hour's post-dinner conversation, which was dominated by the most powerful extrovert present. We were almost invariably the first to express our gratitude for the hospitality and leave. These early departures were agreeable to Eleanor since she wearied easily and upon arriving home went at once to her medicine chest, where she remained closeted until ready for bed. Now I was beginning to worry anew about her long disappearances and particularly the ever-growing array of potions accumulating in her bathroom. Other problems, however, pressed for my more immediate attention and caused me to neglect the most insidious of all.

In Pebble Beach—a locale dominated by the rich and very, very rich, an area totally without smog or any sort of pollution, a community joined with Carmel where our children attended a fine school—our daughter Polly, who had not been sick a day in her life, developed tuberculosis. The consequence was nearly a year's confinement to her room. Son Steven was also afflicted with a series of illnesses. Son George totaled his car, fortunately without damage to himself. As father and husband I could not seem to shake a sense of harassment. My own father's eyesight was failing rapidly, and now, during our weekly luncheons together, I found it necessary to guide him to the table and help him avoid the slightest obstacle.

These were the *yins* and in reaction I set a stern routine for myself. I rose before dawn and did calisthenics for twenty minutes followed by a mile's fast walk and run. Then after shaving and dressing I made breakfast in company with George and Steven if it was a school day. I wrote without pause until eleven o'clock, then took a twenty-minute break. If Eleanor was having a "good day" she was usually up and about by midmorning, but

---

* Acceptance of wine as an attribute to a principal meal did not prevail for most Americans until the 1960s. Californians, close to the grape, had long indulged themselves.

if it was a "bad day" I took fruit, tea, and toast to her bed, and always included a flower to decorate the tray. This little ceremony was at least one positive note in my otherwise dubious marital behavior.

Precisely at eleven-twenty I returned to work and kept at it until one. Then, exhausted physically as well as mentally, I emerged from my cage and made a light lunch. Sometimes Eleanor felt well enough to join me, but there were an increasing number of days when she remained in bed until later afternoon. If alone I read throughout the luncheon period, despairing of ever learning enough. Afternoons were spent at tennis or riding. Afterward for an hour or so I answered the ever-growing volume of mail from readers. This routine continued seven days a week and within six months I had completed *Soldier of Fortune.*

Much of the sense of accomplishment generated by the continuing success of *The High and the Mighty* was now shared with my constant companion, a magnificent fawn Great Dane named Ceares. She reminded me frequently that I had little to do with the wild enthusiasm created by both the book and the movie and suggested it was the haunting theme music written by Dmitri Tiomkin which kept the public interested long beyond normal duration. Now, as if to test my equilibrium, *Soldier of Fortune* rose rapidly on the best-seller list, while Lester Linsk held intense movie interest at bay. I asked Ceares to remind me frequently how lightning can strike twice in the same fashion and that heavy rain was sure to follow. "Remind me of other golden boys," I begged her, "and how they always seemed to forget their parachutes."

The continuous series of telephone calls and letters I received from Thayer Hobson at Morrow and others of the New York publishing world now indicated I had become a valuable "property," but sometime during this period I lost all notion of how much money was accruing to my name, a financial laxity which appalled my father. His unbounded pride in the fame and fortune which now came cascading down upon his son was touching to behold and often embarrassing. The public attention which my father so enjoyed made me cringe and invariably caused me to stampede for the nearest exit. To this end I bought a used sailboat, an open sloop of the Mercury class and named her *Black Watch* after the Scottish regiment whose exploits I admired. Sharing my love for the sea with George, these hours of sailing together in the sparkling waters of Carmel Bay became pure joy. As soon as George was capable of handling *Black Watch* by himself I gave her to him and bought a small yawl of twenty-eight feet. She was the *Thetis,* a little masterpiece of wood, whose builder had taken eight years to achieve perfection. Now George and I ranged even farther along the California coast and there were good and special days when the twins and even Eleanor joined us.

Bill Word, a flying comrade from my Trans-Ocean days, lost his life when his DC-6 apparently exploded between Wake Island and Honolulu. I was saddened, for I had admired him greatly and it seemed I had lost far too many friends to flying. Just on my own line there had been Pedley and Carpenter, Stoner, Dale Dryer, Bobbie Gay, Cooper, Hill, Hunt, Watkins, Harry Charleton, and recently Swain, Jeberjahn, and Job. Altogether I had known and shared the skies with more than a hundred airmen whose luck had not been as favorable as my own. Now it seemed to me I was another man from the one who had filled the line of logbooks still within reach of my desk. Yet I knew no urge to return, for the sea had become an obsession and I longed for some way to make it a greater part of my life.

Usually I avoided answering the telephone, but one afternoon while Eleanor was in San Francisco on one of her regular pilgrimages to the doctors, I obeyed its summons and said, "Hello."

"This is Clark Gable. Dannie Winkler gave me your number."

"That was careless of him," I said blandly. All right, I thought, if someone wanted to play a silly game I would humor him. Dannie Winkler was a Hollywood agent I knew only casually since he had at one time been associated with Lester Linsk. "What can I do for you, Mr. Gable?" I wanted to hear the payoff line and get back to the sea and sailing.

"I'd like to talk to you about *Soldier of Fortune.* It's a good book."

A pause. Whoever was on the other end was a fine

mimic, for the voice had the same vigorous tones I along with millions of other ticket-buyers had been listening to for twenty years.

"Where are you?" I asked cautiously.

"Right here in Pebble Beach. Could I come see you?"

"Why not?" Thinking to see the game through, I offered directions to Island in the Sky. And I made a private vow to delay my departure for the *Thetis* no more than fifteen minutes.

I held a brief conversation with Ceares on the matter of practical jokers and then strolled outside to the parking circle where the steep approach from the main road terminated. I waited only a few minutes before I heard a car climbing the grade. An ordinary rental-type sedan rounded the final curve and stopped before me. Clark Gable emerged with a smile and a "Hi."

I also said, "Hi."

During the next three hours Gable said "Hi" to the children as they came home from school one by one. Then Eleanor arrived from San Francisco and he said "Hi" to her and accepted our invitation to stay on for dinner. By this time he had reduced my gin supply considerably without apparent effect upon himself. Despite my determination to let him do the drinking for both of us until the sun was on the horizon, an exciting rapport developed almost instantly between us and by the time I poured my first Scotch we had shared our views on Hollywood, movies, marriage, children, women, and outdoor life in general. Since we were already waxing philosophical and Eleanor was finding Gable's charm hypnotizing, I suggested we get on with the dinner before I gave him *Soldier of Fortune* for nothing. Now I knew why so many millions of women as well as men placed Clark Gable above all other Hollywood stars, for certainly he was one of the most likable men I had ever met. We seemed to share everything but his passionate interest in money. "This is my bible," he laughed while slapping his knee with a pocket-sized Standard and Poor's stock index.

Thus that evening did Clark Gable persuade me that the only place for *Soldier of Fortune* was at Twentieth-Century Fox, where he had a commitment for one film. I could not conceive of a more perfect actor to portray the leading character in the book, and before noon of the following day Lester Linsk had closed the negotiations. He also committed me to writing the screenplay and momentarily there was joy unbounded.

The euphoria was soon soured by my accountant Walter Joe, who scratched at his bristle of hair and groaned, "Oh, you velly big man now. You payee Uncle Sammee much taxes. You buy him battleship all by self." I was not overly interested in the array of figures he scribbled on long yellow sheets and then passed to me for my inspection. Rather I would become lost in the scroll painting behind Walter Joe's head, a waterfall of mystic quality with surrounding mountain ranges rendered in faded blue. There was a small gazebo perched on one of the mountaintops wherein sat a man I judged a scholar and I envied his apparent lack of complication.

"You velly important to government now," Walter Joe insisted in his imitation accent, "you too big for Walter Joe." Then for the hundredth-odd time he tried to be rid of me and once more I stoutly refused to take my numbers elsewhere. Yet it was obvious that something must be done, or nearly all the money I would earn writing the screenplay would go for taxes.

Lester Linsk found a Hollywood lawyer, a man so steeped in the serpentine involvements of his profession that his monologues became almost totally unintelligible to me. Yet he represented many of Hollywood's great stars and his manner was so awesome, erudite, and forthright, his promises so glowing, I could only conclude that I had been quite honored by his entry into my affairs. Before I knew quite what had happened, I had been transformed from an individual into something called the Falcon Corporation, which was joined in partnership with Twentieth-Century Fox for the purpose of making a movie called *Soldier of Fortune*. In return for the rights to my best-selling book, the Falcon Corporation (me?) would receive twenty percent of the film's profits and I (me?—the corporation?) would be paid separately for writing the screenplay.

With Gable playing the lead there seemed little question the film would make millions. And since a corporation was taxed at a lower rate than an individual, some of the money might eventually find its way to the man whose writing had initiated the whole project.

I knew a moment's hesitation when I remembered Gable's keen interest in money and his easygoing assurance that he wanted but little salary and only five percent of the film's *gross*, but why should my share be any less if all my new associates (and incidentally, officers of the corporation) were so satisfied?

Innocence is the nourishment of the venal.

A part of the agreement was the usual provision that I need not work in Hollywood. Buddy Adler, a bright and enthusiastic man recently appointed head of production at Fox, suggested only that I meet occasionally with David Brown, the studio story editor. I found him a delightful man, very alert, well-read and possessed of an incredible memory. In my eyes he stood as a blessing; his manner, way of thought, and even his rather ivy league clothes were so totally un-Hollywood I could not have asked for more sympathetic company.

I shared the news with my father and he questioned me happily, detail for detail. What I did not understand, I made up, to augment his obvious pleasure in any complicated business arrangement. At last his only son was involved in something which at least sounded impressive and therefore was no doubt stable. He made church steeples with his fingers and spoke profoundly of corporate structures, leverage, annual statements, budgets, and voting stock, all of it giving him such satisfaction I hadn't the heart to remind him that my true position was that of just another screenwriter whose employment would cease abruptly if he failed to deliver what was needed. Nor, at this late date, could I bear to tell this man I so loved and admired how corporate financial statements had always left me totally bewildered. How was it, I continued to wonder, that no corporation ever seemed to make any money? Every report I had troubled to examine revealed the assets to be exactly even with the liabilities, which at best seemed to me to be just breaking even.* My own logic insisted it was much better business if I wrote my heart out every day and discovered a check at the end of the week which amounted to more than the cost of ink and paper.

For the moment at least the principal stockholder of the Falcon Corporation seemed in little danger of losing

---

* I am still waiting for a sensible explanation.

his job. Adler, Brown, Gable, and all concerned with *Soldier of Fortune* expressed enthusiasm for the script. During one of my periodic visits to a fancy office the studio held for me I was greatly flattered upon discovering it decorated with pine trees and filled with artificial fog created by the special effects department. "To make you feel at home," Adler smiled. "We want you to be comfortable here."

I was touched, but not persuaded, and once progress on the script had been reviewed, I vanished in a northerly direction, there to join all the fishermen, pilots, artists, sailors, and bon vivants of all categories with whom I felt at home. One moonlit night with Gidley and a suitable company of amateur pirates I joined in the pleasure of stealing a ferryboat. It did not lessen my joy to know the vessel was under a movie charter to William Wellman, who had spurned *Soldier of Fortune*.

Except for sailing with son George I seemed incapable of similar appreciation for my days at Pebble Beach. Gable came often to drink my gin, and when in Hollywood I tried to get even on his fine Scotch, yet because of my low tolerance my effort was relatively puny. When the script was completed Gable went off to Hong Kong for the filming and more than a year passed before we clinked glasses again. Meanwhile, I had further developed a relationship with quite a different sort of actor—and man.

Just after World War II ended, Russell Holman, then a Connecticut neighbor and vice president of Paramount Pictures, introduced me to Sterling Hayden, a magnificent giant recently returned from a wild real-life war performance. Hayden hated acting, but was resuming his career because he needed money, a requirement I understood very well. He was a fine sailor with a love for ships and the sea like mine and he possessed a collection of maritime books and periodicals from all over the world. He also had files on sailing vessels for sale in various ports, and a drafting table for studying their plans and photographs.

Hayden was generous with the sharing of his treasures and I was like a drunkard given the key to a saloon. *Soldier of Fortune* was obviously a tremendous success and the Falcon Corporation was bound for staggering profits once the film had paid off its production cost. I longed for a tall ship and Hayden, a student of every large sailing craft still surviving, brought out temptation after temptation from his files.

One of the vessels was the schooner *Albatros,* then operated as a training ship in Holland by the Royal Rotterdam Lloyd Steamship Line. "I hear she might be available," Hayden said with a leer I thought suitable to a sultan's procurer. "She's a lovely thing, isn't she?"

I left for Pebble Beach the next day, taking Hayden's photos of the *Albatros* with me. There, I spent hours trying to pick out details with a magnifying glass, dreaming of the impossible, and wondering how I might arrange even a visit to the schooner *Albatros.*

The tremendous power of suggestion depends upon the most subtle self-preparation, a process often commencing long before the final critical moment of surrender.

Chapter 37

While I would never forget Rikki or our adventure together in Germany, I had long since given her up for dead. I supposed she was either a casualty of the bombing of Holland or, knowing her spirit, supposed she had been involved in the Dutch underground and not survived. It had been sixteen years since we last communicated. Now, incredibly, not three days since my return to Pebble Beach with Hayden's photos, a letter arrived from Rikki. It had been addressed to Connecticut, forwarded to the Washington Street home in San Francisco, and relayed once more to Pebble Beach.

The letter was brief and rather formal. She was well, hoped the best for my family, and she finished with a weather report. Nothing more.

I sent off an immediate reply explaining I was still married to Eleanor, and had enjoyed some success as an author. The letter concluded with a request. The next time she passed through Rotterdam would she trouble to look for a vessel called the *Albatros*? I described the schooner as best I could from the photo.

Hardly more than a week passed before a second letter

arrived—also very brief. "I have been aboard your ship. She is waiting for you. I speak with the owners this very day and she is for sale."

The critical moment which ultimately would so change my life had come, disguised as I could not possibly have imagined, and I succumbed almost instantly. Eleanor was enjoying a spell of good health, which made it easier to leave for Holland the following morning.

If we are properly attuned then we can persuade ourselves of the logic in almost any enterprise. All of the necessary elements were present in Holland to transform a preposterous dream into reality. I was currently fat of finance and lean of excitement. My confidence in future work was nearly absolute—I saw no reason why I could not continue writing bestsellers one after the other and I gave no thought whatever to the mental and physical drain involved.

A more mature Rikki, now a charming Dutch lady who had somehow managed to preserve her extraordinarily buoyant spirit, became my loyal interpreter. In my eyes the *Albatros* was a serene beauty waiting only for my hand to lead her toward the bounding main. Nervous at such an easy gathering of factors I forced myself into a quick survey of available vessels in Denmark, Spain, and the Balearics—hoping almost wistfully I would find something better.

By the time I had finished crawling over a score of bedraggled and rotting hulks in Spanish waters I could hardly wait to see the *Albatros* again. Returning to Rotterdam I bought her for thirty thousand dollars and a guarantee from the steamship company that they would put her in first-class shape. My indifference to sensible finance was now so complete that I did not hesitate even momentarily when I learned why such a large steamship line had sold the *Albatros*. They could not afford to maintain her. I could . . . of course.

The steamship people were as good as their word in at least trying to make the *Albatros* seaworthy, but she had been built in 1921, her auxiliary engine was the weary relic of a First World War German U-boat, and the best of paint could not entirely hide her aging. Obviously she had seen better days, but my eyes saw only her graceful lines, heavy and powerful gear, and peculiarly warm personality. I valued even the depressions in her wooden decks—worn by the seaboots of thousands of cadets. Her steel hull passed survey with surprisingly high grades and I sensed the beginning of a great new adventure. During my very occasional moments of sanity I did suppose there might be a story in the *Albatros* which would pay for her, but such justifying was only temporary. A party celebrating my bigamous union with a sailing ship was held aboard and I was overwhelmed with wedding presents from a boisterous crowd of Dutch friends.

Now the main event was at hand; the *Albatros* must be sailed to California, a voyage I contemplated with the same innocent enthusiasm I might have had for a weekend cruise. I had not the faintest idea what I would do with such a vessel when and if the long voyage was ever completed.

The Dutch seamen who had manned the *Albatros* as well as the steamship officials were aghast at my resolve to employ only one professional—a cook. I had endured more than enough amateurs in *Story II,* and Rikki found one Charles Roverts, a young Dutchman who had manned the galleys of several tugboats. The balance of the crew I intended to make up from American sailing buffs. Returning briefly to California, I began an immediate enlistment program and at once encountered problems I had never considered.

While I knew the compatibility of shipmates was all-important, I did not reckon with the realities of other people's lives any more than I had with my own. It had never occurred to me that so-and-so's wife might not be enthusiastic about her husband disappearing for months just to join an old sailing vessel—which was, of all things, *not* a yacht. Too often my favorite candidates for a berth aboard had financial obligations they could not escape, and others could not afford the airfare to Europe. The rich were too committed and the poor unable. Recruiting progressed so slowly I began to wonder if I would eventually resort to shanghai-ing. I had thought people would be fighting for a part in such an adventure and was dismayed to find so few volunteers.

Somehow through most of our married life there had always been a third person present who became not only a friend of the family, but a kind of guest-in-residence.

I was never quite sure why these arrangements began or matured, but I found them pleasant, and everlasting friendships resulted. These individuals were particularly helpful to Eleanor when I was away and to the rest of us when her health prevented full participation in household affairs. Sometimes these quasi-family members slept in the guest room if we had one, but more often they lived independently and appeared only to share our evening meal. We valued and enjoyed their company and were utterly unguarded in their presence. This social phenomenon continued for years and developed wherever we lived, but never in any sense became a *ménage à trois;* rather, it was a need fulfilled by the right people who happened along at just the right time.

The first of these people was Gaillard Fryer, my sometime roommate at the Yale Drama School. He was possibly one of the most agreeable humans ever born, and during our earliest days became the confidant of us both, the man who did things no one else could find time to do and chief sympathizer to Eleanor during her times of crisis. Yet one day he simply vanished and was never seen or heard from again.

Next was Paul LaFrenier, who had so often flown as my navigator during the Second World War. He was a deeply religious man, strong in all his convictions, and particularly clean of mind and habit. I often told him he should have been a priest and his answer was always a smile and a hint that he someday might take the cloth. He became like a godfather to the children and his company was treasured by us all. Yet in time he too went his own way.

Next was a young woman, a neighbor who lived in Carmel, yet spent much of her time at Island in the Sky. She was Sherry Henderson, who became sort of an older sister to the children, and often took over the kitchen when Eleanor was confined to her bedroom. She was a saucy girl, very bright and fun-loving. She answered the telephone, discouraged the curious, helped entertain valued visitors, and shared our joys and woes.

It was Sherry Henderson who solved one of the *Albatros*'s crewing problems. A keen sailor herself, it was inconceivable she should be denied some part of the voyage so we decided she would join ship in Curaçao after the Atlantic crossing had been completed. Yet I was convinced that one female in a shipload of males was not a healthy situation no matter how careful or diplomatic the woman. A pair, I thought, would be the best solution, but where to find an outdoor girl who would be free and willing to go?

"Dodie Post," Sherry suggested.

I sent her at once to the telephone, for I had a vivid recollection of a mountainside in Squaw Valley where George and I had gone for skiing. Our previous experience at Alta and Aspen had met with less than dignified results. George was uninterested in learning how to turn and was consequently obliged to schuss straight down from wherever the lifts hoisted him. Inevitably, he ran into a tree, which shook him up but failed to modify his audacious technique. I broke an ankle at Aspen and was carted down the mountain ignominiously.

At Squaw Valley I thought a few lessons might cut down our hospital bills and was further persuaded of their value when I spied a girl instructor working the "bunny" slope. She was a petite brunette who carried herself with a jaunty air I decided was extraordinary even from a hundred yards distant. Inspired by her dashing manner I went at once to the lodge office intending to book lessons for both George and myself.

"We would like to take lessons from that girl instructor ... the one in dark blue on the bunny slope."

"Dodie Post? Sorry. She's booked for the rest of the year."

Strangely disappointed, I signed in for lessons with a Hans something-or-other, a powerful skier and ruthless instructor. He made me feel as if I were a clumsy dwarf who deliberately delayed proceedings by plunging headlong into the nearest snowbank. He had some cause for impatience each time we descended the bunny slope, for I always found reason to pause—a loose binding, a smudge on my sunglasses, some excuse to further my long-distance appreciation of the girl instructor. For a wild moment I wondered if I could disguise myself as a moppet and qualify for her class. I could not understand why I was so captivated when I had never been close enough to hear her speak a word. Determined to solve the riddle, I asked our hostess Jean Geisen to invite her for dinner.

That evening I discovered I was far from alone in admiration of Dodie Post. She was very much a star in the skiing world, a recent captain of the U.S. Women's Olympic Team, an event winner everywhere she skied, and a champion gatherer of friends male and female wherever in the world skiers gathered.

Everyone, it seemed, knew Dodie Post except George and myself. She appeared to be perpetually surrounded by a bodyguard of big handsome fellow instructors who obviously discouraged strangers. Our lowly status as relatively duff skiers was further inhibiting, but before the evening was over she made us feel comfortable. Both father and son succumbed easily to her charm, the result, I thought, of her novel indifference to tradition. I found her absolute directness and avoidance of cant highly refreshing.

During the drive back to Pebble Beach George and I fell to talking of women and discovered such similarity of opinion that I found it difficult to believe a generation separated us. Although we were unwise enough to generalize on a subject defying specifics, we did agree that Dodie Post's blooming health and vitality were invaluable attributes in the sort of companion we idealized. Secretly, I knew my own appreciation was in direct reaction to the unfortunate woman who had been my wife for so long. I became determined to scuttle such disloyal thinking and deliberately forgot Dodie Post.

Yet now when Sherry Henderson suggested her name as a candidate to join the *Albatros,* I had no trouble whatever remembering her.

It took much longer than I had thought to assemble a crew, but the final roster seemed sufficient to the task. Old friend and Rockland County neighbor Bigelow agreed to come as first mate, Oliver, ex-RAF and still of Wake Island, came to serve as second engineer, although he knew not a cylinder from a flywheel, and Johnson, an ex-bomber pilot from Carmel, also joined the crew. There was Dick Still, a Monterey doctor, and Yates, whom I had known since we were children in Lincoln, Nebraska. Friend Frank Warren came from San Francisco. McDaniel, who had sailed in Irving Johnson's famous *Yankee,* came as second mate, and for "Pully-haulys" Bigelow conscripted four ivy league college students:

Brownell, Stone, Davis, and Cellis. Son Steven, now an accomplished sailor in his own right, completed our company. My one regret was George's inability to join us. He was now in the California Maritime Academy having, at last, after exposure to both elements, decided to make the sea rather than the sky his career. Thus, including Roverts the cook and myself, there were fourteen souls on board, all of whom I was obligated to feed regularly and deliver alive to a distant shore.

Crossing an ocean in a modern sailing craft is no great feat if hurricanes and typhoons are avoidable, but physical discomfort is the twenty-four-hour regime and only a masochist regrets his first sighting of intended land. We were a sluggish forty-three days from Holland to Curaçao, missing by three days the great hurricane which brought disaster to Barbados. Despite our laggard sailing performance I was proud of our overall record for the passage. The only injury had been suffered by Steven, who met with a Portuguese man-o'-war. Seated in a bosun's chair swung from the yardarm, he was enjoying a dunking in the cool sea until he collided with the venomous creature and was stung most painfully. He remained in shock for most of the day.

In Curaçao our company changed and multiplied. Since the passage to Panama was routinely easy, Eleanor came along with daughter Polly and Sherry Henderson. Dodie Post arrived on schedule. I hardly recognized her in tropical clothes. Bigelow, Yates, our Doctor Still, and all the ivy league except Brownell departed for home, but their bunks were soon occupied by a new brace of volunteers, Cordrey and Gratiot, a doctor, and Cordrey's wife.

An unexpected addition announced himself soon after I delivered our ship to the Curaçao dockyard, where various unproductive attempts would be made to cure the *Albatros* of her endless mechanical frailties. Along with most of the crew I had indulged in a hotel room until the *Albatros* would be ready for sea again. The telephone by the bed rang and a man who said he was Ted Helprin announced he was reporting for duty. Only then did I remember inviting an enthusiastic young sailor I had known in Riverside, Connecticut. I had really not expected he could join us so late in the year. Delighted, I asked him to come to my room for proper welcome.

Minutes later I opened the door to behold a short white-haired man. He smiled and held out his hand.

"Hi. I'm Ted Helprin."

The Ted Helprin I knew was barely twenty. I was confused.

"My boy was killed. An auto accident. I came to take his place." He spoke so simply I knew at once this man must be a mountain of courage. Yet there was a long moment before I had the grace to welcome him. I was embarrassed, unequal to the shock and I fumbled for words to express regret. We talked of mutual acquaintances in Connecticut and I discovered with considerable relief that *this* Ted Helprin was a veteran sailor. Later I wondered what I was going to do for topmast hands since Helprin explained he could hand, reef, and steer, but was too old to go aloft.

Once we were at sea again any worries I held about Ted Helprin, the father, vanished. He was indeed a veteran sailor and most worthy on deck, but best of all was his nobility of character, a quality expressed incongruously in gravelly Brooklynese. We were to sail together four years in the *Albatros;* he became as my right hand whether we were underway or moored, and his priceless counsel again and again transformed problems into solution. Ted Helprin proved the finest of shipmates and most stalwart of friends.

After an easy crossing of the Gulf of Mexico, Eleanor, Polly, and Steven left the *Albatros* in Panama. The rest of us began the long slog north, predictably against winds and current. One hundred and nine days after sailing from Rotterdam we slipped through heavy fog in the Golden Gate and emerged very suddenly into a brilliant full moonlit night. A glittering San Francisco lay on our starboard hand, the smooth waters of the bay allowed the *Albatros* an unfamiliar peace. George and three of his shipmates at the Maritime Academy had joined us in San Diego for the final leg up the California coast. All was well aboard and even the rat which had pestered us for two thousand miles was dead. My cup, I thought, is very full, for I had returned to the place where two other lives had been lived. There, just abeam, were the same docks I had once patrolled as a strike-bound fisherman. Overhead, then unheeding of the great bull foghorns now grunting their warning. I had flown so many times to Hawaii and Japan as captain of much faster vessels.

I could not understand how these diverse things could be, nor could I conceive how there might be more. When we broached the rum I raised my glass to Dodie Post, and said, "To whatever comes next. Good luck."

Chapter 38

With the long voyage successfully completed, the *Albatros* was laid up in Sausalito while I took stock of my overstrained resources. After some debate with the immigration people I was able to keep the priceless Freddie van Heusen aboard, for I dreamed of further voyages, and good sea-cooks were extremely scarce throughout the world. Deep within Freddie there lurked some marvelous quality which served to draw women to him in throngs. Young, middle-aged, and old adored his blond tousled hair, delft-blue eyes, ready smile, and unaffected desire to please. Yet his ever-willingness and reputed prowess at stud was his frequent undoing; women who had once become intimate with Freddie adopted him as their personal property and his generosity kept him weaving and dodging until he could do little else. During his "rest" periods he was inclined to refresh himself with more drink than he could handle and, hoping to salvage his talents and protect him from the wrath of jealous husbands, I persuaded Victor Gotti of Ernie's, San Francisco's most renowned restaurant, to take Freddie on as a "student chef."

Freddie did not stay entirely out of mischief, but his chances of being shot at were reduced and his culinary skill was greatly augmented.

My own affairs had suffered while I had played the sailor. *Soldier of Fortune* with Clark Gable and Susan Hayward was a tremendous success, or so it seemed. The reviews were excellent and long lines tailed to the box offices. I inquired confidently about my share of the profits and was assured it was simply a matter of time—"The picture was very expensive and there are still some expenses to pay off." Even astute Lester Linsk believed this to be true.

I divided my time between visits to the *Albatros* and Pebble Beach, where I did my best to re-assume the role of husband and father. Eleanor's health remained variable with good days and unpredictable bad ones. Something had to be done about our now very high daily expenses so I launched full-tilt into the writing of *Twilight for the Gods,* not surprisingly a novel about a sailing ship and her stubborn captain as he fought for survival against the advent of steam vessels. Now able to foresee a certain level of sales for my books, Thayer Hobson allowed me a fat advance, which I thought sufficient to carry our domestic load until *Soldier of Fortune* paid off. With customary disregard for the facts of finance, I at once arranged for the *Albatros* to be converted into a brigantine—a very costly rigging change.

By now I had resigned myself to the unhappy profession of writing and my work habits had become as fixed as such an intangible labor permits. A now permanent quirk in my writing system was the need for an exceptional secretary to translate my convoluted scribblings to the typed page. I found it imperative to stand back and see clearly what repairs had to be made, and a faltering typist, unfamiliar with the phrasing or technical vocabulary I often used to lend authenticity, could not handle the job regardless of her goodwill. I needed intelligence rather than word-per-minute speed so I asked Dodie Post if she would forsake the winter slopes and give it a try. She was willing but had first to fulfill a more exciting commitment managing the Women's Olympic Ski Team during the winter games at St. Moritz. I said she was worth waiting for without really knowing if she was.

Twilight for the Gods demanded a tremendous amount of research and as usual I became lost in the one facet of writing that is pure joy. The timing for such a book could not have been better, for many of the old salts who had served in the last days of sail were living their own last days. I found them out and listened to the winds and the crashing seas of their words, enraptured. They were a very special breed of men and once aware of my project poured their hearts out, for they were all in love with their boisterous youth when fiercely independent men paced wooden decks and defied gales, steam economics, and even God to sink them. When I had finally gathered a mountain of material and had nearly foundered in my enjoyment of all things maritime, I knew the penalty box could no longer be avoided.

I took a last long look at the kind of life normal people lead, gathered what courage and confidence I had remaining, and locked myself back in the early part of this century. There I remained as a detached spirit for more than six months.

When her assignment with the Olympic Team was over Dodie Post came to work as my secretary.

The full-scale onslaught upon *Twilight for the Gods* left little time for any other endeavor, but already committed to rerigging the *Albatros* I could not bear to cancel the project. As a consequence I slept little, played hardly at all, and became a very dull fellow. A dream, common to many men, drove me relentlessly as I began to envy the fictional sailing ship captain with whom I lived every day. I wrote of him sailing the South Seas, and I had never been there. It is wrong then, I told myself. An author *must* know and experience the deeds of his characters. This was a handy excuse, and it became imperative that the *Albatros* sail for the South Seas. I wrote like a man possessed to speed the sailing date.

Almost one year from the day I became her master, *Albatros*, now a brigantine (or hermaphrodite brig), sailed for Honolulu. Several of the crew were new to the ship, but a strong cadre of the faithful had signed her articles. Both sons, George and Steven, were aboard, which gave me enormous saisfaction, and the irreplaceable Ted Helprin had come to join the little ship he loved as much as I. George Yates of Carmel signed on for a second hitch. Sherry Henderson and Dodie Post once more joined ship and Jean McDowell, wife of Harvey, who had once fished the *Mike* for the long-dormant Western Ocean Fishing Company, made a third woman aboard.

Harvey McDowell himself, a tall pebble-kicking stalwart, had agreed to come along as first mate. We had a fine doctor in John Gratiot, a surgeon from Monterey. Charlie, worn thin and considerably subdued by his romantic adventures would be dispensing an Ernie's restaurant-style cuisine from a glistening new galley on deck. While I had little patience with luxury yachts, and all of the accommodations aboard *Albatros* remained spartan, I saw no reason to eat salt horse and weeviled biscuits as my predecessors had done. Jim Durst, a recent honors graduate of the California Maritime Academy and friend of George's, came along as second mate. Knowles Hall, a sailing neophyte, was signed on as an ordinary seaman and George Atcheson, an ex-Navy frogman, took the third mate's berth.

Altogether we were a fine ship's company and once *Albatros's* new rig was properly shaken down I thought we might try for a record passage to Honolulu. Instead we were so frequently becalmed I once launched the little jolly boat a thousand miles from the nearest land and went for a row while my shipmates swam about their lethargic vessel. We were twenty-two days to Honolulu, a dismal performance we avoided mentioning among other sailors.

More realistic obligations removed several of our ship's company in Honolulu, including my sons, who returned to school. The rest of us carried on for the next five months through the Tuamotus, Polynesia, finally returning to Honolulu via the Marquesas. In Papeete, Charlie erred by mixing alcohol and motorbikes and, colliding with a cement bridge with such force, he was nearly a month in the hospital. While waiting out his recovery I took a house in Punaauia almost next door to where Gauguin had lived and painted. There I worked on rewriting *Twilight for the Gods* and realized, to my dismay, that I was deeply in love with Dodie Post.

There would come a time of reckoning, we knew, but there seemed to be no way of halting or even sidetracking the relation which had grown very slowly and steadily between us.

It was at first reminiscent of my strange relationship with the lock merchant in Shanghai during my time as a "student" of telephony. Every weekday morning my office-bound rickshaw-puller would pause at a busy intersection waiting for a chance to skip through the traffic moving at right angles to our own course. And every morning the lock merchant would be established at the same corner, squatting in the dirt which fringed the curbing, his cheap padlocks, door locks, box locks, and baggage locks together with their matching keys spread out before him on a ragged cloth. I never saw him selling his wares, and if he actually sold any then his supply was inexhaustible since there were always the same number on display, row upon row. The lock merchant was small and frail, but I knew on first sight he was more than a businessman, for in a tin can on one side of his ragged cloth was a fresh flower—a tiny and brave oasis amid a desert of dust, noise, and almost suffocating fumes. My embarrassment at being hauled about the streets by the physical strength of another human was somewhat eased by the presence of this seller of locks, because he saw me looking at his flower on the very first morning and then again the next and the next until finally our eyes met in mutual appreciation and I knew he understood my admiration for his spirit. Without exchanging a word, without touching each other or making any gesture save a gentle smile, our friendship began and endured through all the time I remained in Shanghai.

Both Dodie and I came from the same nineteenth-century moralistic background, with conveniently built-in consciences designed to prevent physical adultery and condemning even platonic attachment if even one party was married. Both of us had a world to lose.

Sarcasm was helpful, but no real cure. Seeking to avoid reality we would fall back on the most worn clichés, repeating in arch tones, ". . . this is bigger than either of us," ". . . where there's a will there's a way," ". . . when things are too tough for everyone else it's just right for us. . . ." We knew even while uttering such nonsense that we had fallen into an ancient entrapment and our efforts to chide ourselves or make light of our relationship only cemented it more firmly.

Time and again I went off by myself, determined to discover a rationale behind our steadily increasing dependence upon each other. Certainly Dodie had no need of a middle-aged married man with an ailing wife and three children. Her skiing career had won her a full court of dashing young men and she had not wanted for several invitations to become the wife of one of them. While I was eleven years her senior, I decided that might be barely acceptable, but what about my solitary habits and almost psychopathic need for privacy, faults Eleanor had long ago learned to tolerate? Furthermore, I was a wanderer, likely to hike over the horizon on a whim and not return until I wearied of whatever had drawn me away originally.

The more I counted the reasons for Dodie not having anything to do with me, the more reasons I found that she should. We laughed easily and much together. We saw things through the same eyes, be it the intricacies of a snowflake or the purple nose of a wino. Although our relationship had neither begun nor held because of physical passion, which I thought a very good thing, we were both devoted to the physical outdoors. Dodie, an instinctively feminine person, would rather play baseball than bridge, and I would far rather ride a horse or sail a boat than think of money or play poker. We were both rich in friends, but disliked large social gatherings. Except for a disdain of Communism we were apolitical and there lingered in us only faint traces of the racial bias which had been our heritage. Our appetites for the exotic extended in every direction; we shouted our mutual joy at what we thought a superb work of art and our enjoyment of fine food came very near to being religious. We were day people, finding little enjoyment in keeping late hours. We were fastidious of our bodies and incapable of sloth. We awakened almost instantly in the morning with laughter and renewed enthusiasm for life. The ritual of morning showering and scrubbing was accomplished in high glee. We were the antithesis of the do-not-speak-to-me-until-I've-had-my-coffee people; for us the time just after dawn was the most delightful of the entire day. Best of all, Dodie was a giver and I was hard put to match her endless generosity.

We rented a pair of motorbikes in Papeete and made frequent picnic expeditions to various sites around the perimeter of Tahiti. We sketched and made water-colors together, we ate ravenously and drank good fresh wine. We spoke only joyfully in each other's company, never sourly of anyone, for our happiness obliterated all else. I knew now I had found the sort of woman I had always desired, but my emotions were tangled in the realization that I was deserting a fine woman who in her own way had done her

521

utmost to be a traditional good wife. Worse, her health was far from robust and I kept telling myself that my place was not roving the seas with or without a woman I loved, but at Eleanor's side. Alas, I thought, a story as old as time is being written before my very eyes and I am the unmistakable villain.

When we returned to Pebble Beach almost five months later, Eleanor remained true to the lady's code she so treasured. She ignored the situation and went on as if Dodie were a necessary employee to be tolerated as long as she could be kept in place. Thus, during her bad periods she would summon Dodie from her typewriter and detail the household orders of the day; so-and-so was coming to dinner and the wine should be chilled or allowed to breathe. The carpenter should be called about the leak in Steven's window. The subscription to the Monterey *Herald* must be renewed, the grocery bill must be paid immediately, and there were medicines at the drugstore to be picked up. A check must be made for the gardeners who were bringing new plants, and please talk to Polly about straightening up her room and closet since she simply would not listen to her mother.

Dodie lived in her own house more than a mile away and yet her daily life became oriented around Island in the Sky. If Eleanor was feeling poorly, she would instruct Dodie to cook the evening meal. If guests were expected, she was told to play the hostess. To my dismay there were even times when we all dined and laughed together as a family unit and other times when Eleanor and Dodie went for long walks and returned apparent friends. All three children now accepted Dodie as a working member of the family and even my father sometimes included her in gatherings at the big house. I completed the final draft of *Twilight for the Gods* while waiting for the roof of the little greenhouse in which I worked to fall in.

Twilight for the Gods was greeted with fine reviews, two book club selections, a position on best-seller lists, and a bountiful contract for the paperback edition. My euphoria led me off on wild spending sprees in which no one was spared. There were new cars for everyone in the family and some considerable remodeling Eleanor had been wanting for the house. As a sop to my continuously needling conscience I built her an elaborate greenhouse, complete with all the heating and spraying devices she wanted to facilitate her orchid-raising hobby. She also made extensive and expensive revisions to the landscaping about Island in the Sky. I once counted five people, including an almost steadily employed pair of gardeners, on my payroll full-time, and eight part-time, a fair load for an enterprise vested only in paper and pen. I cared little. The cornucopia of wealth brought by my combined works was sufficient to the day and it never occurred to me that the flow might cease. Only my share of the movie *Soldier of Fortune* remained zero. I protested frequently for an accounting and was always put off with mumbo-jumbo about the need for "recouping the negative cost," an obvious stall in view of the box-office proceeds. The people I had known at Twentieth-Century Fox were gone or, like Buddy Adler, dead; now the Byzantine-minded Spyros Skouras commanded the company and a straight answer was almost impossible to obtain. Or so my Hollywood lawyer claimed when I suggested that the company was allocating every cost in the studio to the film, not excepting paving the streets and the salaries of the gate guards.

It was difficult to pursue this dubious affair with proper resolution while Lester Linsk was arranging yet another bonanza—this time of nearly incredible ramifications. First, he sold the book *Twilight for the Gods* to Universal Pictures for a fat price. Next, I would be paid handsomely to write the screenplay. In addition, I would share in the gross of the film and I would furthermore have approval of cast and director, an unheard-of privilege for a writer.

As if this were not enough, Universal also agreed to charter the *Albatros* as the ship in the film and employ me as her sailing master. Since the story demanded that the ship appear to be falling to pieces at sea, they further agreed that she would be restored to her original beauty once the film was completed. Old-timers on the Hollywood scene shook their heads in wonder at such bounty for a mere writer and I went to work soaked in privilege. Incredibly, the financial foolishness I had begun in Holland was going to pay off handsomely. Other gambles remained less certain of outcome.

By the time the filmscript was finished I learned once more how Hollywood is like an iceberg, concealing the largest proportion of its menace and evil far below the surface. While I was grateful for the high pay, I soon discovered my special perks were not as valuable as promised. Somehow the stars I had envisioned playing in the film were always "unavailable" to the studio. The reasons given were vague and casual—so-and-so could not sign for a film now because he was getting a divorce, another was committed elsewhere for a year, and another was poison at the box office.

Everyone concerned with the production was very "nice"; Gordon Kay, the producer, was a nice man and we were nice to each other. Joseph Pevney, another nice man, was finally chosen to direct in spite of his almost total lack of empathy with the sea. Rock Hudson, a very nice man, was chosen to play the desperate alcoholic captain, although he was the last actor in Hollywood I would have chosen for such a tough and uncompromising role. Cyd Charisse, a very nice lady, was signed to play the female lead, a prostitute on the run from involvement in a murder. She did the best she could with a role quite out of her field.

Everyone was so nice that it remains a Hollywood mystery why the film turned out as well as it did. Only Jim Havens, a resourceful, vitriolic ex-Marine who really understood ships and the sea, represented the type of casting I preferred. He took over the conversion of the *Albatros* in Honolulu and directed the actual scenes at sea, which all the nice people agreed were superb.

For a while I enjoyed my slight participation in the actual making of the film, and was amused at how I had been type-cast by both the cast and the crew. I was an author and therefore entitled to a certain respect not commonly tendered a straight screenplay writer. On the set I was always greeted cordially and even with enthusiasm, but of course was not expected to know anything about filmmaking. Sometimes when I was politely shunted out of the way so the knowledgeable could get on with this mysterious work, I thought of my days at Ray-Bell where I had learned nearly every job in the business and of my time as a stock and Broadway actor. But I saw no reason to reveal my past to such nice people. They were trying to broaden my education, and I knew they would if I simply smiled and kept my peace.

Is there a stranger always at our side, a forceful presence who with total disregard for our readiness is capable of exchanging our happiness for unhappiness? Upon my return to Island in the Sky my then-current euphoria was as suddenly and completely erased as if it had never been.

I found Eleanor in sorry straits. Her once-lovely hands were swollen and knobbed and I knew they must hurt dreadfully. Her ankles were swollen and her face puffed. Worst of all, she seemed to be of unstable mind, vague and withdrawn as if in a trance. Then, within an hour, she would become nearly hysterical. Watching her apprehensively, I remembered how, long before she was stricken with arthritis during our happier days in Rockland County, she had often expressed a desire to become a grand old lady who would punctuate her multitude of demands by stomping her gold-headed cane. "I will be a female curmudgeon," she had insisted, "I will tell my chauffeur, 'Everyone out of my way.' "

Now, shocked and almost unbearably remorseful over my absences, I wondered if earlier wish could bring about later actuality. I was determined to do something about her condition since all but one of the legion of doctors supposedly attending her needs had been unsuccessful. The exception was the eminent Kuzell of San Francisco, a man so recognized in the field of arthritic afflictions that he often lectured before his peers at international seminars. When we had lived in the Washington Street house he had been Eleanor's favorite; now, irrationally, she would have nothing to do with him and I could not discover why. It was Kuzell who recommended that I take Eleanor back to Baltimore for a thorough examination by a renowned team at Johns Hopkins.

Part Four

LIVING

THE TRAIN FROM PUERTO LIMÓN

Our little engine has taken to an anxious-sounding humming now that we are in the high altitudes of Costa Rica. It is abnormally quiet, with the car wheels seeming to slither along the track; the clicking sound as we pass over the rail joints is not so determined.

The old hag who was sitting opposite me is gone. She deposited a final glob of her spittle on the floor and disembarked at one of the shorter halts back down the line. Since then, two young Costa Ricans have taken her place. They are very young. She wears a thin wedding ring and a look of apprehension; he is very solemn and straight of spine, as if expecting some kind of important announcement. They are holding hands and I like to think their mutual reassurance will continue for the rest of their lives, for I know only too well the world's happy society is made up of pairs, and loners have a tough time of it.

The flight computer now returned to my shirt pocket has told me more than I really wanted to know about certain developments in my existence, but where is the crystal ball to finish the job? I could have used one that Sunday in spring when I left the little chalet in Switzerland to meet Darryl Zanuck in Paris.

Once arrived at the Paris airline terminal near the Porte Dauphine, I tossed my rucksack through the open window of the nearest taxi and told the driver to make for the Hotel Prince de Galles. It was a lovely afternoon and I was only disappointed when I caught a glimpse of my favorite bistro on the Avenue Bugeaud. I was hungry and it was closed.

As I paid off the driver he cursed the laxness of the gendarmerie who allowed any idiot to park as he pleased on Sundays. He lamented his inability to drop me directly in front of the Prince de Galles's main entrance as two vacant cars occupied the hotel's normal parking space. I said it was of no matter, the difference was only a few steps.

He smiled, drove away, and I squeezed between two parked cars to the deserted sidewalk. I went directly to the hotel's main entrance, registered, handed my rucksack to a waiting bellman and followed him to the elevator. It was now twenty-five past one and I was famished.

My room proved to be on the third floor and on the front side of the hotel. The bellman unlocked the door, stepped aside, and waved me past him. The room was stuffy, so I inquired about more ventilation. At once the bellman obliged by pulling apart a pair of long drapes revealing a double glass door leading to a balcony. He threw open the doors and their curtains quivered slightly in the resulting draft.

"Anything else, Monsieur?"

"No. Merci." He accepted my ten-franc tip with a slight bow and a wish for a pleasant stay. I turned, stepped out onto the balcony, and breathed deeply of the soft Parisian air. I remained on the balcony for approximately twenty seconds, a period of time later verified by the bellman, who was just leaving the room.

I turned back into the room and was one step inside when the world exploded. Even when servicing cannon as an artilleryman I had never felt such a fierce concussion. I stood witless, staring at the bellman while he also remained motionless, his mouth agape.

As the thunderclap subsided I heard the tinkle of broken glass beyond the window, and waited, half expecting a second explosion.

The bellman cautiously re-entered the room. I was equally discreet about returning to the balcony, but once able to see beyond its railing I remained fixed in disbelief.

The façade of the building next to the Prince de Galles was in ruins. The wide street was littered with glass and every parked auto within sight, even those on the far side of the street, had fractured windows.

"Monsieur," the bellman said apologetically, "it is the Algerians again. The office of their newspaper was in the next building. It is the Algerians and their terrible plastiques."

I knew of the current Algerian troubles and of the bombs known as plastiques, but I hardly heard the bellman. I was totally absorbed in the two overturned cars and a great chunk of masonry now joined in a crazy shambles upon the exact spot where I had stepped out of the taxi.

As the hooting sirens of vehicles bearing gendarmes and pompiers echoed along the empty street I glanced at my watch. It was one twenty-eight.

"Anything else?" the bellman asked, as if for an encore he might reproduce the fall of the Bastille.

"Yes! Bring me a magnum of Mumm's. A '59 if it's already chilled."

"Oui, Monsieur," As he left I lingered on the balcony watching but not really seeing the fast-growing groups of uniforms milling about uselessly in the street below. They are after the fact, I thought, and so had I been . . . almost.

With my second glass of champagne I took out my notebook and on a blank page put down the following figures.

(Exact)	13:10 Arrive Porte Dauphine Terminal
(Approx)	13:12 Into taxi

(Exact)   13:17 Arrive hotel
(Exact)   13:27 Boom!

It was the last figure juxtaposed with the next-to-last which held me spellbound. At twenty-seven minutes past one I was still very much alive. Had the identical preceding events taken ten minutes longer I would unquestionably now be very dead.

The young Costa Ricans on this train are obviously expecting certain things to happen when they reach their destination. The plastique in Paris among other experiences has taught me they are in for various surprises; the development may not be at all as they suppose. Right now they are in limbo—transiting from A to B. Waiting. Their status reminds me again of that glorious night we sailed the Albatros into San Francisco Bay. I stood with Sherry Henderson atop the wheel-house while we were picking our way through the fog. Then an event of long duration was nearly over and we questioned what would follow; for our time on earth does permit hesitation, even though we are not allowed a true halt until the ultimate event.

Now the young Costa Ricans are also near the completion of a journey. Will this adventure become a major event in their lives, remembered forever when they return to their village? Will they do something quite different next year, or once returned to their habitude simply flow with the happiness of each day until both are too old to argue with their destiny?

I refuse to accept passivity. Now aging like rum in a barrel, I want to know why my hours have been so lightened and darkened by enough events to fulfill twenty lives? The questioning eyes of the little black boy way back in the hamlet of Mary and Jesus still haunt me. Why his destiny—why mine?

Perhaps this journey has been revealing even though while lost in hopeless riddles I have missed most of the scenery. I can see how so many past events were interrelated; some because of my help and others totally independent of my influence. And it is now clear how all events, regardless of their origin, have a way of coming full circle. They cling together with marvelous tenacity lest the thread be broken, and since the form is now very apparent anyone can simply erase the names and events

*I have revived and substitute those provided by their own
existence. Basically, the summation must be the same.*

*We are rattling along the flat plains at high speed now.
The relatively cool air and open landscape have activated
my fellow passengers like puppets. They are bouncing up
and down, swaying to and fro in rhythm with the train,
their faces expressionless as dummies employed in some
Einsteinian experiment with speed and time. Only the
hand-holding pair seem alert to our progress, their eyes
are wide with wonder as they wait for the unknown. Now
I understand why they can never return to their village
exactly as they departed, nor would any of a subsequent
series of calamities and triumphs have left me the same
person.*

Chapter 39

We sat in the conference room, a sunlit place with wicker
furniture. At first only one of the doctors appeared and
then another and another. They were all pleasant and apparently forthright, although given to the special patronizing air of doctors trying to explain clinical matters to a
layman. Eleanor was still in her room on a different floor
of the hospital where she had been under observation for
a week. This was the day the medicine men were to deliver their conclusions. During the week I had taken a
hotel room where I wrote in the mornings, then would
spend as much of the afternoons with Eleanor as the elaborate series of tests permitted. I had filled her room with
the flowers I knew were so important to her morale and
listened patiently to her complaints about the doctors
"who don't seem to know what they are looking for." She
was very unhappy with them and the discomforts of the
tests and I saw she was very weary and discouraged and
did my best to cheer her. The doctors, I assured her, were
the best in the land. Now we would at least have a program to fight this terrible disease. I also told her she
would not fight alone.

Dodie was at Island in the Sky keeping house for the
children. I missed her very much, but was now so
anguished at Eleanor's condition I could not regard our

relationship as anything but a real-life soap opera certainly structured for a disastrous ending.

"The trouble with your wife," the first doctor said in obvious embarrassment, "could be you."

"I'm not surprised," I answered miserably, while quickly reviewing my many absences, infidelities, and almost total disregard of social convention. I vowed to change my ways. "What can I do to fix that?" I asked.

"Stand guard and help her get off the junk."

"I don't understand you."

"Your wife has rheumatoid arthritis, but not at all to a crippling degree. There is no reason why she cannot lead a normal life, or at least one with very few limitations. Her general health is good, but it won't be for long if she continues as she has been."

"You've lost me."

"She has been taking several times more than the customary dosage of cortisone, codeine, barbitals, and various sedatives. Her body cannot tolerate such a program much longer. Someone will have to put a stop to it."

That someone, I knew, had to be me, and I was greatly relieved to learn there was a tangible enemy to be conquered. If Eleanor's mind was clear again, perhaps we might return to our old understanding. And if I had been one of her involuntary enemies, then I intended to become friend.

Once Eleanor had been told offiicially that she was not destined for a wheelchair or even a gold cane, she made a remarkable recovery. I took her home to Island in the Sky and together we went straight to her bathroom. There, we filled three wastebaskets with bottles and vials of medicine and I was so overjoyed at her attitude I gave no thought to how she might have obtained so many lethal drugs. Later I dumped the lot in the garbage can without troubling to read the labels. I should have.

Eleanor was now on a very minimal dosage, one cortisone derivative pill a day and half a sleeping pill at night. The puffiness left her face, her movements greatly improved and the delusions of grandeur faded. She was able to think and speak rationally. I thought to slay any leftover antagonists by taking her to Europe. Dodie again took charge of the children and Island in the Sky while we toured England, France, and Switzerland. The trip was a success from every standpoint and Eleanor joined me in every activity except skiing.

With most of my personal troubles at least temporarily allayed I was able to concern myself more with the outside world, and one shocking exhibition, the testing of atomic bombs in the Pacific, I believed to be the ultimate insult to our planet. Ex-*Albatros* chief mate and dear Quaker friend Bigelow, also deeply disturbed, attempted to sail his little boat *Golden Rule* into the bomb area in protest, but was arrested for his pains and spent time in jail as punishment for his clouded thinking. The more I researched the whole disgraceful performance, the more convinced I became that the Atomic Energy Commission was much too powerful and autonomous and therefore a dangerous dagger pointed at our American way of life. By now I had become very conscious of another power— that of the pen when wielded right—and I sought to do what I could with mine.

I began a novel about an atomic testing site on an island in the Pacific and called it after the name of a typhoon which demolished all the evil works man had imported to a former paradise. Meteorologists named the storm "Lazy Ethel" because during the first days of its development it rarely moved. I called the book *The Trouble with Lazy Ethel* and wrote at it furiously for five months. I did not as yet know that fury, no matter how genuine, is no guarantee of a good book.

I wrote mornings and some nights trying to finish the book before my next project, which also demanded much attention. George Atcheson, who had sailed with the *Albatros* to the South Seas and subsequently taken care of her for the year she lay in Honolulu, now brought her to California for the promised rehabilitation by Universal Pictures. As if on cue, an experienced sailor, Chris Sheldon, made an offer to buy her, and since the amount nearly matched what I had invested in her I finally agreed she could be his. Yet I knew there would never be another vessel like her in my life and I insisted on one provision. He must take possession in Europe six months hence, and I would deliver her there. Until then she remained mine. The appropriation of a concubine, I remembered from a certain night in Peking, was a most delicate business.

Eleanor had always been a competent woman and now seemed restored in spirit as well as body. She had once again taken over the reins of the household, almost too firmly at times, I thought, because she was turning into a sergeant-major. Yet even with her ordering people about I was delighted to be assured of her capabilities and renewed energies; with my husbandly conscience clear for a change I took what time I dared from writing and began the necessary preparations for a final voyage in the little ship which had become my symbol of freedom.

Universal Pictures lived up to their word and at great cost restored the bedraggled *Albatros* to pristine beauty. As a side issue we would take the film *Twilight for the Gods* to London for its premiere. We were scheduled to sail first around to New York, then to England, and, for a final fling with my nautical love, to Scandinavia. Finally we would deliver her to new owner Sheldon in Portugal.

I asked my two favorite shipmates to sail with me again. Ted Helprin accepted without hesitation, as did Dodie, who had by now become my right arm. Weary of tinkering with the endless mechanical problems inherent in any aging vessel, I hired Yutaka Tamura, a Japanese-American who had handled *Albatros*'s engine room so efficiently during the filming in Honolulu. He was a splendid man and our friendship would endure long after others had drifted away. Another addition was one George Ptatnik, an American-Mexican-Czechoslovakian. A graduate in English literature, he came along as the paid cook to replace Charlie, who had returned to Holland. The balance of the crew was a mixed lot and unpaid except for their keep.

The passage from California to New York was accomplished with only two stops and all went well. While the *Albatros* was moored in New York I retreated briefly to Island in the Sky where I found Eleanor busy and content with her orchids and landscaping. She listened politely to my recounting of the passage, but I knew she was not really very interested. Likewise I had trouble finding excitement in tales of the latest orchid show. We did laugh together as she so frequently recited the outlandish Latin names given certain orchids and I suggested she refrain from using such language in mixed company. Our respect and affection endured, although we both knew the gap between us was widening.

During my brief visit, dinners at the big house were command performances, but I preferred taking my father to lunch at his favorite haunt, the Beach Club. He was greatly mellowed, but his rapidly failing eyesight was very apparent. He explained without hint of self-pity how the world now appeared to him as it might through the bore of a rifle, and the caliber was becoming smaller every day. It was now necessary to take his arm when any change of position was involved, and I marveled at his ability to maintain his sense of humor about all things.

I was very glad of our closeness during these long lunches; he sent me off to my own problems and adventures with new heart. I did not know it would be the last I would see of him.

Before leaving Eleanor I slipped into her bathroom and checked on the contents of the medicine cabinet. It was nearly empty, much as we had left it on returning from Johns Hopkins. We parted, rather formally for a pair who had been married so long, and she said, "You must lead your own life," words I considered very noble of her.

The Atlantic crossing in the *Albatros* was rough, tough, and bitterly cold. Gales and high winds drove us often to the ship's hull speed and the limits of our own endurance. Only eighteen days from Greenwich to Land's End, we came very near breaking the record, but it was a passage none of our exhausted crew was anxious to repeat. Our arrival in England was also a minor triumph, with more than two thousand people watching as we came to a mooring off the Tower of London. We were escorted up the Thames by two boatloads of reporters and more clambered aboard once we had secured to the buoy. I did my best to play the author returned from the sea, and since *Twilight for the Gods* had just been published in England and the film was premiering, both publishers and Universal Pictures were happy with the reams of publicity. Again I viewed my overflowing cup with apprehension.

Along with Dodie, son Steven, and his friend Dean Rowe, we bicycled from the outskirts of London to the channel coast near Portsmouth. Two weeks later with the same crew except for one who had drowned himself in the bottle, we sailed to Sweden, Norway, Denmark, and

Germany. Everywhere our welcome was exhilarating, for we purposely entered under sail whenever we could and now after so much practice were able to put on the kind of exhibition only the most venerable locals could remember. In Hamburg I was overjoyed to meet Leo Hochstetter, the roguish Fox Face of Culver Military Academy days. He was fat now, brilliant as ever, and worth his weight in platinum to the Motion Picture Export Association, which employed him to collect their monies in Europe and the Middle East. When I asked him how he, a Jew, managed in the Arab countries he chuckled and said, "Nothing to it. I carry a portable foreskin." I was greatly relieved to know a treasured schoolmate had not changed in the slightest.

In September we sailed from Hamburg to Portugal where the *Albatros*'s new owner would take her from me.

As we rolled before the dun-colored seas of the English Channel bound southwest for Ushant off Brittany I thought to radio Jack Sullivan, who had done so much in London promoting both the book and movie of *Twilight for the Gods*. He was an ebullient man, quick and dry of wit, and I hoped a few words with him would relieve the strange melancholy which held me ever since we had sailed on the final leg of the voyage. I rarely used our radio, disliking it perhaps because my years in the air had demanded so much radio chatter, and I could not understand why I should feel the need to communicate now. After four years I was losing the ship to which I had given so much and taken even more and perhaps like a man in the throes of divorce I wanted to confide in someone.

There was something different about Jack Sullivan's voice when the marine operator found him at his office. The lilt was gone and I thought his subdued response to my greeting was a distortion of the radio. He asked our location and I told him we were in the Channel just east of the Isle of Wight.

Then he said, "I've been trying to reach you. I'm afraid I have some very sad news for you. Your wife called . . ."

I held my breath. "Go ahead, Jack."

"Your father passed away four days ago. I'm very sorry. . . ."

"Oh . . . thanks. Thanks, Jack."

Stunned, I hung up the microphone and switched off the radio. Several of the crew had been nearby, unavoidable witnesses to what they heard from the loudspeaker. They were silent as I passed by them, their faces ill-defined as I fought to control my tears. I turned around the deckhouse and made my way very slowly along the deck until I passed the galley door where Ptatnik started to smile until he realized something .was wrong. I went on to the foredeck and passed the heavy structure of the anchor winch and came finally to the butt of the jib boom. I leaned against it with one hand on the bulwark rail and listened to the rhythmic sloshing of the seas as the bow of the *Albatros* rose and fell. The sun, pale and grimy behind a ceiling of haze, was a little past the zenith, and now, I thought incongruously, I will have missed taking a sight at local apparent noon.

Ahead the seas rolled on a carpet of gray-sepia, not at all pretty even when the sun touched them with brass. The waves chased after each other until they melted into the distant haze and I thought well, well . . . we were making good speed anyway, say about eight knots. That would be much faster, I recalled, than the great battleships of Nelson and the French and Dutch fleets would have made with the same winds. And let's see, if this wind held it would take us ten, twelve days to . . .

Suddenly I could hold back no longer. I sobbed until I thought my body would break and beat my fist upon the bulwark's steel caprail. The great gentleman was gone. With him also had gone an era and I sorrowed almost as much for the loss of the American style he represented as for those of us who had loved him well.

Swashbuckler, indeed! Perhaps I had been no more than ordinarily afraid when the oceans and skies were hostile, but now I had no one left in whose shadow I could hide when things went wrong, and a new loneliness nearly bent me to my knees. I stood a weeping coward, alone with my anguish, alone in a forbidden forest with my little-boy self.

I knew without turning around whose hand touched my shoulder. Dodie was silent because she understood, and I could think of nothing to say except, "Well . . . well . . ." several times over. Then I tried to make the same silly statements a man is inclined to make when he is in shock. "I suppose he has two good eyes now and can read a book a minute . . ." and I faltered as I deserved and finally surrendered my head to Dodie's shoulder allowing her to hold me until I was done.

When I had recovered wit, I called for a course change and we put in to the nearest port, Cowes on the Isle of Wight. My shipmates, including Dodie, said their solemn farewells, put me ashore, and I watched them weigh anchor and sail away for Portugal in the violet dusk. In all of my life I had never felt so alone.

———

A brace of well-dressed, eloquent lawyers were awaiting my arrival in Pebble Beach and I thought it very considerate of them to come all the way from Chicago just to extend their sympathies. They had established themselves most comfortably in the plush Del Monte Lodge and I found their knowledge of my father's affairs much superior to my own. They would be pleased, they offered, to take over the tiresome business of settling his estate, thereby sparing me, as executor, no end of bother. I was touched by their admiration for my father and appreciative of their voluntary efforts to soothe my stepmother, whose emotions, always at high key, made the necessary practicalities difficult. Eleanor did what she could to assuage my own sense of loss, but my thinking was distracted and much of my scarred spirit was aboard a sailing vessel still at sea and bound for Portugal.

There were countless expressions of sympathy from friends of my father, but none more attending and faithful than the pair of Chicago lawyers. We met daily on the porch of Island in the Sky while they explained most patiently the details of the will and what must be done to satisfy the tax collectors, my stepmother, others mentioned in the will, and, finally, the soul whose graceful signature stood at the bottom of his final testament. I tried very hard to concentrate, but kept watching the sunlight flickering across the azure sea, and I heard the distant pounding of the surf better than the carefully modulated phrasings of the lawyers. Listening to them, it seemed to me that the necessary legal procedures would be extremely complex, and weary of their explanations I found it easier to accept their so gently expressed suggestions;

if I would authorize them to proceed with settling the estate all I need do was fix my signature to a few papers.

The lawyers closed their briefcases with definitive clicks and departed for their Chicago offices before I could properly express my thanks for their solicitude, and when I had tried to determine their fee their answer had been sympathetic smiles. "It is too early to establish any exact amount. Don't worry, it will be very reasonable. Your father was our friend."

I was somewhat taken aback when I received a bill from the uninvited lawyers which not only included their round-trip first-class airfare from Chicago, but also the cost of several days of what must have been very high living at the Del Monte Lodge. I did not understand that their fees were only the preliminary bid to a grand slam.

As soon as I could depart in decency I hastened to Portugal where Dodie, George Atcheson, and Yutaka Tamura, all that was left of the *Albatros*'s crew, awaited me. We cleared the ship of our personal effects and, not daring to look back, Dodie and I boarded a little freighter bound for Denmark. There, I had already initiated a new project I hoped would fill my sense of emptiness.

With the money from the sale of the *Albatros* I hoped to finance the building of a dream boat, a sixty-foot ketch to be christened the same proud name as the little sloop I had given son George, *Black Watch*. My intention was to sail for Iceland, the fjords of Greenland, and to the sub-Arctic, regions for which I had developed an unaccountable affection during World War II. Therefore the ketch was to be of extraordinarily heavy wooden construction, deep of draft and broad of beam. After taking bids from many shipyards I finally selected a yard in Frederikssund, Denmark. Dodie took complete charge of the galley design and her separate office cabin forward, while I, in a sort of last-stand defense of my precious independence, designed a separate cabin aft.

What confidence in my literary ability I had managed to build suffered a rude shaking-up with the publication of *The Trouble with Lazy Ethel*. Only one book club took it and very much at their price. Sales to the stores were lethargic and the reviews mixed. I kept reminding myself how every author had his failures, and I fell temporarily into the usual author's division of blame—Thayer Hobson had died and what remained of his publishing house did not know how to sell books. Later, I faced the truth and admitted that my mind had been on too many other matters.

Hoping to recoup, I outlined a disciplined plan for the time *Black Watch* was building and I received a powerful assist from an unexpected source. Eleanor wrote to Dodie: ". . . please do not bring him home here for Christmas. The house is all torn up with remodeling, there are endless distractions . . . and he would not be able to work here. . . ." I could not help wondering if Eleanor was not deliberately helping me hang myself.

Seeking a locale where disturbance was unlikely I asked my Norwegian publisher, Per Mortensen, for a possible recommendation. He found a chalet in a village named Ustaoset, halfway between Bergen and Oslo. With the possible exception of Outer Mongolia in wintertime, there was probably no more isolated place on earth. Dodie and I packed long underwear, bought skis and rucksacks, and headed for the hills. During the years we had sailed in the *Albatros,* nearly two thousand people had for various reasons been our guests. Now solitude seemed ever more precious.

The window alongside the wooden box I used as a writing desk was filmy with hoarfrost and through it Dodie appeared to be a little doll moving slowly up the sloping hill. She was returning from her morning trip to Ustaoset. There were barely a dozen people in the village and the chalet in which we were trying to keep warm was on its outer fringes, as isolated from all other humans as the most devout misanthropist could wish.

Using her skis and poles with the rhythmic ease of an expert, Dodie was bent far forward against the gusting wind and was sometimes nearly obliterated in swirling snow. The thermometer outside the window stood at minus 10 degrees and I knew that with the wind, the true temperature must be brutal. I saw the heavy rucksack on her back, full of groceries and a bottle or two of wine plus the mail, and I knew it would have taken at least half an hour of steady plodding to come uphill from the village. Yet I was also certain she would arrive all pink-cheeked and laughing, with never a complaint of her burden or the cold, and she would go off to the freezing kitchen to ready a fine lunch for the time when I could write no longer. Once, thinking I had led her into unnecessary hardship, I had suggested, "Why don't we go down to Oslo and take a plane for Africa. We could warm our toes in the Mediterranean."

"If you're inviting me to a hot country," she frowned, "I prefer ski boots to sandals and the sight of my breath to perspiration."

Actually, we were reasonably comfortable, although the unheated outdoor toilet was hardly a place for relaxation. The chalet was situated at the crest of a plateau with the highest mountains in Norway forming a heavy barricade across its limits. We had been cautioned not to ski very far in that direction. "If anything happens you won't be found until summer."

On clear days the sun appeared at about ten, and by four o'clock the twilight softened the desolation. At dawn the distant mountains took on an iron-red patina made all the more dramatic by their draperies of snow. The plateau itself became violet and then lavender and finally a soft crimson in a spectacular series of color changes. I always found it difficult to leave such an exciting show for my daily toil at the typewriter. How dare I presume that I am really an author, still echoed across my morning thoughts and I wondered frequently how I dared continue. This time the situation was made even more difficult by my determination to change publishers, for no one in that distant New York world was even aware I was working. And cared less, I thought.

Wearied of literary invention I now proposed to write a nonfiction book using my career as a pilot of the line as a framework upon which I could hang numerous portraits of those great characters who had been my comrades and mentors. To avoid fictionalizing, I resolved to rely strictly on the logbooks which detailed my working hours aloft, and I found it surprisingly easy to recall most flights as they had actually been. The people involved once more came to life until they seemed passing visitors to the chalet. Then one day I realized how many of them had perished in the line of duty and how often I had experienced very narrow escapes. Why, I wondered, had others lost their lives while I, certainly no better a pilot, had survived to be writing in the middle of Norway? I knew the technical reasons for their misfortune and I knew the men intimately. Why were Charleton and Watkins killed, when I had been doing exactly the same job and had come away unscathed? And Miller, and Bob Gay, my old roommate in training school, and Toby Hunt, and nearly a hundred others? Luck had obviously been in control, and the exploration of its power became the underlying theme of the book. I called it *Fate Is the Hunter* and had no idea it would become a classic in the aviation world if only because there had never been a similar treatment of the subject.

The routine at Ustaoset was oriented entirely around my completing a first draft before the coming of summer, when I hoped the *Black Watch* would be ready. On both estimates I missed considerably. At Ustaoset we rose long before light and I was at work by dawn. At one o'clock we had lunch, then made for our skis and an exploration of the surrounding countryside, unless the weather was particularly severe. At three we usually managed to be down in the village to watch the only train of the day pause briefly on its way to Bergen. Sometimes our rendezvous with the train held special interest, for my publisher in Oslo would be sending a half dozen bottles of Bardinet rum, unobtainable in Ustaoset. Food as well as liquor was often a problem; we learned to spend an hour before dinner plucking fresh ptarmigan, and reindeer meat was a frequent staple. In the evenings we read or played chess or watched the stars gather against the black abyss of unadulterated sky. On those nights while the Aurora Borealis marched and countermarched across the heavens we listened to the majestic Sibelius and envied no man or woman their entertainment.

The *yin* was just around the corner. When I had finished about two thirds of *Fate Is the Hunter* a letter from my San Francisco lawyer advised that a long-pending case with the Internal Revenue Service was now scheduled for resolving and that my presence was required. ". . . Of course if you do not wish to return I am sure they would be willing to settle out of court. . . ."

"Settle, hell!" I told Dodie. "We'll go back and fight!"

Reluctantly, we left Ustaoset, paused briefly in Denmark to assess the slow progress of the *Black Watch,* and returned to Pebble Beach, where it seemed we had never been away at all. Eleanor was in good health and genial. I had feared that too long a separation from the children would make us near-strangers, and I set about making repairs only to find that all middle teenagers are strangers to anyone except their peers. George, now serving out his Naval Reserve time on a minesweeper out of Long Beach, had long ago passed through the difficult stage, and our reunion was as of two solid and loving friends.

If I had been troubled by my disagreement with the Internal Revenue Service, I tried secretly to thank them for flushing me out of the seclusion of Ustaoset where, given no cause to leave and utterly content in hibernation, I might have lingered too long. There was yet to be a culminating reward when I determined on going to court rather than "settling," as my lawyer was prone to recommend. "Either I owe them money or I do not owe them a penny!" I insisted. "There is no middle ground and I have nothing to hide. Justice will win out!" My pose during these orations was that of a martyred Patrick Henry, patriot to the core, and a few times I caught myself reaching instinctively to place a hand over my heart. Meanwhile, awaiting the federal judge who would try the case, the lawyer fretted uneasily and warned of the extra cost if the judgment should go against me. My more cynical friends smiled tolerantly and spoke in hushed tones of the IRS as if they represented some invincible combination of Gestapo and OGPU, capable of clamping any American into chains. The more I was cautioned, the more stubborn I became. "I don't care if it takes every last penny. I intend to fight until the end!"

This was the first time I had ever engaged in such bravado and I found some trouble maintaining it in the face of the direst predictions from friends, who announced quite openly I had lost my mind.

The judge came at last, complete in black robe and dignity. A battery of IRS lawyers—paid, I thought sourly, by taxpayers like myself—arrived in the courtroom with swollen briefcases. One had the gall to smile at me as we passed in the corridor and I was distressed to see my lawyer return a smile on my behalf. "Who the hell's side is he on," I muttered. "This is not a clubby gathering of legal brothers, it's war."

After the IRS team had its say, the judge put me on the stand for the better part of an hour. I began with a direct attack on the basic reason for this wretched occasion and my belief that I owed all the money claimed by the IRS or none. The enemy fired a barrage of objections at the end of every statement I made; the judge denied them every time and began questioning me himself. Soon I began to hope and before fifteen minutes had passed I felt victory was possible. The crux of the matter was an advance I had received from my publisher for *The High and the Mighty*. Was it "constructive" income or not? I explained how no publisher could foretell the success or failure of a book, no matter what elements were involved, and how an advance was subject to deduction from royalties until the book earned it back. Through a fusillade of objections by the lawyers, I accused the IRS of unashamed extortion, callously attempting to "suck as much as the traffic would bear" and adjusting their demands for tribute at just enough to discourage an all-out fight from the average taxpayer. "This system is a mockery of our basic law, because a taxpayer is considered guilty until he can prove himself innocent."

Some of my speechmaking must have struck a responsive chord in the judge. From the beginning it had been no contest, and the increasingly feeble objections by the IRS lawyers took on the sound of retreat. When their turn came to question me I found them ill-prepared in spite of their fat briefcases, and their queries were surprisingly clumsy.

The judge excused us all just before noon and said there was no reason to return. When we passed the IRS lawyers in the corridor this time, it was my turn to smile.

Months later, when the judge reached his decision, official victory was complete, and the case became legal history to the benefit of all American authors. Winning cost me considerable time when I should have been earning (and of course paying taxes on the earnings), plus my lawyer's fee. It was worth it and more, for I was reassured that my country still allowed David to slay Goliath.

Chapter 40

As *Fate Is the Hunter* progressed, I began to realize my very great obligation to the multitude of real characters who populated the book. Suddenly I saw the work to be a unique document of flight; a technology which was rapidly changing the lives of all mankind. Too many of my friends had died in the pioneering of this new and tremendous force; I knew my pen must stay absolutely honest lest I insult their memory. I had lived and earned my living among these men; now I brooded on their deaths and my own survival. Was it intuition of danger, reactions to some invisible stimuli? I found the physical universe almost totally unexplored and wondered if some men were in greater harmony than others with threatened danger. Were warning messages generated in their brain transmitted to the spinal cord or was it the other way around?

I went to Washington, where like an unwilling ghoul I prowled through the official accident investigations involving my friends. All the technical data were there, but the conclusions were almost always the same. The dead pilot, who could not answer for himself, was to blame. Knowing the men, I did not always agree with these verdicts, and I did my utmost to discover the true answers. I dismissed religion early in my speculations, for I knew that the virtuous had died side by side with the immoral, and the exit of both atheist and godly had been obviously haphazard. Secretly frightened by what I was attempting to prove, I gathered Dodie, my logbooks, records, old flying photographs, plus all my resolution, and returned to Frederikssund, Denmark. There, in a four-hundred-year-old house with cockeyed floors and a roof of heavy thatch, I completed the first draft of *Fate Is the Hunter*.

The ketch *Black Watch*, building in a shipyard twenty minutes by bicycle from the house, was finished almost at the same time. I must, I decided, stay the pace of things, for my energies were now drained to the bottom—fatuous nonsense, I later admitted, only a limp excuse to drop my pen and return to sea.

It was too late in the season for comfortable sailing, but we went anyway. When the winds of October screeched out of the North Sea and caught us one awesome night in the shallow waters of the Kattegat, Dodie and I were nearly convinced that the final penalty for our relationship was then to be paid. Yet thanks to the stout *Black Watch* we survived and put in gratefully the following morning to Hundested. After sleeping out our exhaustion and making light of our very real fears, we proceeded down the estuary to Frederikssund and laid up the *Black Watch* for winter.

From there I returned to the United States with considerable trepidation, for there were dragons on every hand. If I had thought there was some sort of "understanding" of my behavior on Eleanor's part, then I had been additionally guilty of self-deception and proved once again my limited knowledge of the feminine psyche. Eleanor wrote of her social embarrassment because of my travels with Dodie and I could not blame her. There was also a professional blot on my reputation, for a book which flops as resoundingly as had *The Trouble with Lazy Ethel* is remembered in the publishing world almost as vividly as a success, and the author's worth suffers accordingly. Wondering if any publisher would now be interested in *Fate Is the Hunter,* I knew only two places to seek an audience. I liked the sound of Random House and had admired from a distance the sparkling Bennett Cerf who led that enterprise in a most flamboyant fashion. I also remembered my father's ranching companion, Max Schuster, who had been so gentle in rejecting my very first book.

I waited in New York while both men read the book and was astonished by their enthusiasm. Cerf insisted I have lunch with him immediately, which I declined because I had always preferred to keep the solemn business of eating separate from the crass discussion of my own books.

I was very grateful for Cerf's blandishments and the excitement of his company, yet I knew he was not the sort of publisher I sought. He was such a performer himself, I feared his influence might steer me wrong during the necessary rewritings.

The equally notable M. Lincoln Schuster (Max) was

less of a personal showman, but far more the sentimentalist. I found his continuous aphorisms amusing and his puns intolerable, but there was such true heart behind his rumpled vest I was soon his for the asking. Best of all was his turning me over to a brilliant young editor, Robert Gottlieb, who at first I thought an incongruous choice and later came to treasure. Gottlieb, who claimed to be terrified of flight, somehow understood precisely what I was trying to say and led me firmly to it.

Fate Is the Hunter became an almost instant success and was chosen as the solo selection of the Book-of-the-Month Club. It was published in all the major languages and was used in the Reader's Digest Book Club. Lester Linsk proved his skill by selling such an unlikely book to the movies. The reviews were embarrassing accolades, but I was far more rewarded by letters, phone calls, and telegrams from a world I had forsaken. The surviving men with whom I had flown, sweated, and shivered side by side approved. Except for one, I had used their real names throughout and all agreed I had put down the barren truth.

One morning, soon after my return from Denmark, Eleanor escorted me to the sundrenched porch of Island in the Sky and explained that she wanted a "legal separation." Since I was by now nearly paranoid at even the hint of lawyers on the horizon, I inquired if she was talking about a divorce.

"No. It's not the same."

There followed an interminable silence and I knew not whether to weep or be relieved. We were now separated by light-years of emotion and I wondered why this had happened to two such well-intentioned people. It was not my attachment for Dodie, because the division between Eleanor and me was growing long before I ever met Dodie. It was not finances, the rickety platform for so many marital disagreements, and certainly it was not lack of understanding. We had known each other for thirty-five years and had been married for twenty-eight, which in itself should have formed an unassailable bond. I did not want a divorce. Eleanor was hedging in using another label, and for one critical second I considered refusing to leave. Perhaps if I stayed we could rescue ourselves and refute whatever accusations had been left unsaid. Yet our WASP heritage did not permit either argument or rebuttal. We could not throw things at each other or even shout to vent our emotions. This, I was acutely aware, was known as the "civilized" approach, and though I longed to explode in anger at my own delinquencies and communicate with a woman I still held dear, the ethics of my upbringing were all against such behavior. Even Eleanor, who was quite capable of a tantrum, remained politely reserved.

As if I were sitting alone in an auditorium and was only a spectator, I listened to our talking in clipped sentences, two actors playing out an obligatory scene.

"I'll go away for a while. You can think this over."

"You've been away. My lawyer will call you."

"Your *lawyer?*" I caught at my temper. Thirty-five years and we needed a stranger to translate what we might say? "You don't need a lawyer. You know very well I intend to take care of you for the rest of our lives."

Another silence followed, which I broke with a deliberate groan. Old, old, this story—so very old it reeked of age and anguish.

I stood up and made the pitiful little speech which I somehow thought necessary. The voice emerging from my throat did not sound like mine any more than the stilted phrasing. A stranger was talking to a stranger.

"This is your idea, not mine. I think it's crazy. I admit to not being the best of husbands, but I had hoped our marriage would last forever. If you change your mind, let me know. Meanwhile, be sure you will be well taken care of."

I thought it a measure of Eleanor's remaining trust that we had never once mentioned the children. George of course was on his own in the Navy, but the twins were still in college. Their future Eleanor knew full well was in good hands and I was dismayed she apparently felt so insecure about her own that she would feel the need of a lawyer.

I packed a few things, and took a small Gordon Grant marine painting, which had long been my favorite. It was as if I wanted to take with me one token of the domestic life I had known and which now lay in ruins all about me. I was stunned. Eleanor had turned away from me with a final smile of such sourness that I made no attempt to follow her into the bedroom. She had spoken of her injured pride and I remembered how important the regard of others was to her. A thousand whispers, guarded hints, and not-so-guarded insinuations, uttered by people, had in accumulation finally crowded Eleanor into a corner. If we had been differently bred and raised then I might have broken down the door and through a barrage of shouts and tears perhaps convinced her there was more strength remaining in our union than she had let herself believe.

We were not that kind of people. We cried within, not without. Thus, I took what I thought would be a last look at the ebony carving of a voodoo figure I had bought in Haiti, the Hunter Wood marine of a cod fisherman on the Grand Banks I had bought on installments during the long-ago when we could not afford such frills, and the round dining-room table, also bought when our bank balance was usually to be reckoned in two figures. The table was scarred with the marks of innumerable plates and utensils and beneath its polished surface was locked the warm affections of a man and his wife, the shouts of children's glee, the wisdom of countless distinguished guests, and the continuous joys and sorrows of an American family created, existing, and now gone forever. I kept telling myself this was happening to someone else, not to me.

I left Island in the Sky without looking back, because I could not see my way to drive.

George Jansen had been a bombardier during the Second World War and I thought he might therefore understand me better than others in his trade. He worked alone rather than as a soldier in a squadron of names, and I knew that what I wanted to do must be done right.

Resentful at even entering a lawyer's office I frowned at the traditional decor of leather-bound legal volumes lining the walls and promised myself to depart within five minutes. What I had come for, I knew, was so simple it should not take longer.

Jansen's appearance and manner cut instantly through my stiff reserve. His face was that of a droll hound, his eyes were extraordinarily alert despite their cradle of bags and his nose might have been a monument to Cyrano de Bergerac. He smoked continuously and his voice rasped with the unmistakable music of a man who enjoyed overindulging himself. A friend had told me that among his other accomplishments Jansen played saxophone in the Bohemian Club's Dixieland band. If there had to be a lawyer involved in my troubles, I decided, then he must be unconventional enough to make things easier.

I took approximately one minute to relate what had happened after so long a marriage, and quoted Eleanor exactly as wanting "a legal separation."

"I don't know what that means," Jansen said blowing smoke at his library.

"I think she means a divorce," I said.

"Do you want one?"

"No."

"Then what's the beef?"

"Pride."

"Ah . . ." Jansen pulled at his great nose and mouthed smoke from his cigarette. "Divorces are not my business. They are unpleasant, people get mad, and I get depressed." He stared unhappily at the ceiling and for a moment I thought he had forgotten me.

I said, "This should be very simple. I have a lot of money and a great many things. I want to give her everything. I'll sign whatever is necessary and start all over again."

I had rehearsed the speech hundreds of times in my gloomy thoughts of the last two days and my resolve had hardened each time. I would begin anew and prove to Eleanor that her lawyer was unnecessary since there would be no more to be gained. "Lock, stock, and barrel," I said, "I want it all to be hers."

Jansen's silence rather surprised me. His ears were a matching pair to his nose and although he ignored me otherwise, his ears seemed like radar disks waiting for a signal from me.

"She has done nothing wrong. The whole mess is my fault and I want it over with as soon as possible." Strange, I thought, how a man needed a lawyer to give part of his life away.

Jansen's silence continued as he pulled a top drawer

out of his desk, braced his shoes against it and tipped his chair back at a dangerous angle. Then he clasped his hands behind his head and sighed heavily. Even if he is a lawyer, I decided, here was a man I would like to know better.

The silence held for perhaps a full minute before he said very quietly, "I won't let you do it."

"That's the way I want it."

"Then get someone else."

"As I understand community property, everything is half hers anyway. She might as well have it all and save a lot of bickering.'"

"You want me to call her lawyer and tell him that? Look, mister. I don't know you and I've never met your wife. I assume you are sincere, but I assure you no lawyer is going to believe me when I offer such a proposal. He'll be sure you're hiding something."

"But I'm not." I had listed all my assets on a single piece of yellow paper and now pushed it toward him. He glanced at it, then shook his head.

Black Watch? What's that?"

"A boat. Tied up in Denmark now. She is the one possession I'd like to keep but since I can't maybe you could make some arrangement for me to buy her back if my new book is a success."

"Too bad we can't saw a boat in half."

Suddenly I knew an almost overpowering depression. How very far we had come from the sprightly young lovers we once had been. The Chicago days, the New York days when an evening of beer and sauerbraten at the Zumbrauhaus was considered an extravagant outing, the flying days when the two new gold stripes on my uniform meant true prosperity, the Washington Street days in San Francisco when we lived as no fisherman ever lived—and now we were plucking at the spoils. Despite my resolve, I found myself wanting to rescue the boat which had become so much a part of me.

"Everything goes to her," I insisted, more to choke off any weakness than argue with Jansen.

"Let's wait and see."

That night I telephoned Eleanor and gave her Jansen's number. I also told her of my intention. There was no reaction whatsoever. I said good night to a total stranger.

The orbiting path of chance was rarely more apparent than in those circumstances which led to my acquiring the establishment in Sausalito. Now, very temporarily, Sterling Hayden stepped into the scene again, although he became visible only to trusted accomplices. His own marriage having terminated in a particularly stormy contest, Hayden had felt compelled to abduct his own children and sail away to the South Seas in his schooner *Wanderer*. Now, if he could be found he might be technically guilty of a crime and might soon be put in irons. When Hayden had accomplished his purpose he did in time return to the United States, being careful to keep his whereabouts secret. Our mutual friend "Spike" Africa, a true-life version of Popeye the Sailorman, gave me a telephone number where Hayden could be reached. Thinking it better to smother my own troubles beneath his far more ugly ones, and longing for talk of the sea, I called Hayden and suggested we meet for dinner.

Hayden's complicated directions were intriguing.

"Do you know Sally Stanford's place?"

Sally Stanford had been a storybook San Francisco madam whose original emporium I had never been fortunate enough to attend. With the rise of sexual promiscuity came the relative decline of the professional all over America and plush bordellos faded one by one into oblivion. Sensitive to the time, Sally opened a fine restaurant in Sausalito and graced it with her abrasive voice and a parrot who sat croaking on her shoulder. As a woman of countless friends and insignificant enemies she was unquestionably the best-known female in Northern California. She was indeed the tough one with the heart of gold, and though she opened her purse grudgingly and recited incantations against persons who failed to repay, she always opened it.

I told Hayden I had known Sally Stanford's restaurant Valhalla when it was a hangout for fishermen and the only drink sold was bourbon straight up.

". . . climb down to the beach from Sally's. Walk south around Hurricane Gulch and keep going until you pass under two houses built on concrete pilings. There will be a ladder there waiting for you. Climb it and I'll be at the other end."

"What about the tide? You know I'm a lousy swimmer."

"It'll be dark. If you drown no one will know."

Fortunately the tide was out and the loom of lights from San Francisco was enough to ease my way along the beach. I came to the concrete pilings, saw a ladder, and climbed to a wooden porch. Hayden opened the door and took my hand. When our ho-ho's subsided he led me into a unique world.

"What a hideout! How did you find this place?" I stood enthralled, looking directly across the bay at the glittering lights of San Francisco. It was like being on the bridge of a ship come to anchor. Hayden told me that the proper entrance to the place was via a small cable car which descended on tracks from the main road. It was well over a hundred-foot drop and thus the isolation was complete.

As Hayden mixed our first drink, an inbound fishing boat passed, her red port running light tracing a bounding pattern across the glass doors. In a moment the wash from her passage made a sloshing noise below the floor and I thought this place must be the Fiddler's Green I had once written about.

Hayden told me the house belonged to a man named Fraser and he thought it was for sale. I thought of my resolve to become a temporary pauper and had trouble conquering desire. "I'm broke or soon will be," I explained, "but my credit is good, maybe . . . ?"

Two weeks later, with a Wells Fargo bank loan against-an-advance-against-a-book-I-intended-to-write, I was able to offer a small down payment on the Sausalito house and I waited in some trepidation for Fraser's reaction. I feared he might remember me all too well, for impulsive acts have a way of coming back to bite the protagonist and one night during World War II, while over the North Atlantic, I had summarily ordered an intruder from my flight deck. He was only trying to perform his duty as a check navigator, but I believed that my navigator, who had successfully guided so many flights, did not need harassment by wandering superiors. The man had no choice but to obey the captain's command. Although I later regretted my arrogance, I had not the grace to apologize and upon arrival in

Scotland we parted with cold indifference. Now fifteen years later I discovered that this man was the same Bob Fraser who owned the house I coveted.

While George Jansen was still trying to dissuade me from giving everything to Eleanor except the new and heavily mortgaged house, the first papers arrived from her lawyer. I read his accusations in disbelief and could hardly believe my lifemate for so long had approved them. Plodding through the legalese, I found myself described as a fiend of incredible malevolence. Three pages of wild allegations, portrayed me as Beelzebub's mentor in cruelty; an ogre, scoundrel, and shiftless vagabond. Oddly, no mention was made anywhere of my very real transgressions.

There followed three additional pages of financial and property demands which I barely glanced at. I had told Eleanor she would have everything I owned except what little remained of my father's legacy, yet plainly my simple word was not enough. Now a total stranger proposed to divide according to his fashion the bounty from my years of flying, the remnants of my father's life labors, and half the rewards both present and future of my work as an author. Something broke within me as I marched to the telephone. Now I remembered the expression in George Jansen's eyes when he stared at the ceiling of his office and said, "I won't let you do it."

"George," I said into the telephone, "that oath of poverty thing I wanted to do . . . forget it."

"What happened?"

"I've just received a communication from Eleanor's lawyer."

"Ah . . ." His knowing sigh was unmistakably sad.

"I still want Eleanor to be more than adequately taken care of, and for the rest of her life. She should not be obliged to change her lifestyle in the slightest. But as for that lawyer and his demands—"

"I understand perfectly," George said.

There followed two years of vindictive bickering, painful exchanges, depositions, and accusations which collectively drained us all and left me almost indifferent to the final outcome. As if ordained by some special god, I fell in with fascinating company and thereby directed my principal energies toward more productive channels. The full bag of characters who came to enrich my life was due to *Of Good and Evil,* a book I determined to write about both varieties of people.

Chapter 41

The writing of *Of Good and Evil* began with my proposal to Tom Cahill, then chief of San Francisco police. I told him I hoped to portray his men differently from the current stereotype police with their hands in the apple barrel or cigar box between bouts of brutality. Once Cahill understood that I meant to write an objective novel about law enforcement he allowed me the total freedom of his department and often took a personal hand in my further education. Soon I was attending police school, then spent various periods as an observer-inspector in homicide, fraud, vice, burglary, intelligence, theft, pickpockets, and missing persons. Every morning at nine I was present in the auditorium for line-up and soon learned to recognize the habituals from the just plain unlucky. I spent time helping to process prisoners in the jail and much more time in the crime lab learning the more common techniques of detection. I went to court with the arrested and sat with those who had done the arresting and I patrolled the busy street corners at Christmastime watching for pickpockets. I spent countless nights in patrol cars and marveled at my partners, who after years of encounter with the dross of humanity could still have faith in anyone at all. I learned to spot a "Kronkie" situation from a safe distance and made very real progress toward developing that special sense of knowing something is wrong which is so necessary to any good policeman.

Being a policeman is a dangerous business for the unlearned and I needed a mentor. Inspector Bob Kane, an Irish Catholic of impressive physical mass, was selected. He was an easygoing man and the butt of much badinage about his diet versus his tendency toward corpulence. Kane had a fine singing voice and was in much demand at police weddings and funerals.

The chore of nursing an author through the life of a policeman was regarded as a coup by many of Kane's fellow inspectors; temporarily at least he would be spared wrestling with female drunks, who were feared by all policemen, and it would be understood if he failed to make overmuch haste to apprehend some drug-hungry hold-up man willing to kill for his needs.

Kane's eyes were very large and blue and it was his habit to roll them toward the sky when asked if he would not prefer a return to his regular duty in the Chinatown squad. "Oh lordy, no!" he would intone. "This is much more interesting." The word "interesting" was uttered facetiously, for it had been his impression that the care and feeding of an author included keeping him as far from the scene of any trouble as possible. When he discovered that my intentions were exactly the opposite, he shook his jowls in disapproval. His chief had given him difficult orders; let him see what he wants, but don't let anything happen to him or you'll be walking a beat at Hunters Point.*

One of my first lessons taught me that crime is eternal and that those who live by it are dedicated to their ways. Most habitual criminals scoff at do-gooders who would "rehabilitate" them; they *like* their mode of life even if it may occasionally be interrupted by misfortune and a consequent spell behind bars. Most habituals are disturbed and at the same time ignorant, but they also develop the cunning of a predatory animal and know almost instinctively when danger in the form of police is a threat. Although Cahill knew that no one can successfully predict or halt the amateur criminal, he hoped to thwart the professional variety with the creation of the so-called S-Squad, a group of volunteers who would patrol the most crime-prone areas of the city in unmarked cars. Our very first activity with the S-Squad gave the usually imperturbable Kane some very nervous moments.

The S-Squad was composed of a dozen teams, mostly elite inspectors who liked their work and the overtime money. Patrols were on duty from 8:30 p.m. through 3:00 a.m., the peak hours of trouble. Each car was

---

* A notoriously tough and troublesome area.

manned by two plainclothesmen who might be involved in support of the regular patrol car crews if needed, but who were mainly instructed to anticipate and halt more serious crimes. The S-Squad operated only two nights a week and the scheduling was deliberately staggered to confuse the enemy. Briefings began at eight in the Hall of Justice and included necessary information on wanted persons, armed and dangerous individuals still at large, hot cars, and special information on possible trouble areas. I attended my first briefing with all the earnest attention of an overeager fighter pilot bound on his first mission. At least I had enough sense remaining to smile inwardly at my tendency to play everything to the bloody hilt. I wore an old trench coat for this first expedition, a traditional Aquascutum I had bought long before in London, and with a hat tipped far down on my forehead had convinced myself I might be taken for a dashing combination of super-sleuth and international spy.

In his wisdom Cahill had ruled out my being armed, which left me rather miffed. All the big boys carried a gun. Fresh from police school I thought I knew how to disarm an opponent whether he stuck a gun in my face or back and how to put him in cuffs afterward. Kane and my instructor at the school had been very careful to explain how a physical contest with a criminal rarely developed in the convenient way I had been practicing and the best thing for me to do was run in the opposite direction from even a hint of combat. This sly reference to my masculine prowess hurt, but if the occasion arose I would show them how a sailor hardened now by long ocean passages could surprise them. They had taught me how to knock a man down with my elbows and render him immobile by slamming my heel down hard on the arch of his foot. I knew how to break weapons away from an opponent's hand, grasp his fingers in a "come-along" to make him go where I wanted him to go, and with a grab at his hair crunch my knee to his chin, either to knock him unconscious or break his jaw or both. All I needed was about one hundred pounds of Kane's heft to conquer the most desperate individual, and I took great comfort in observing that some of the S-Squad appeared to be no more physically formidable than I.

When the briefing was done we joined Jim Hardy, a

dark-haired alert Irishman who moved like a leopard. I was pleased to notice we were nearly a physical match, but humbled almost immediately when we descended to the underground police garage to pick up our car. Obviously following orders from on high, Kane escorted me to the back seat, then joined Hardy in the front. My sense of being a full-fledged partner was temporarily lost. Why was Cahill so insistent on babying me?

Hardy drove out of the garage, checked the radio with police communications center, then turned south on Montgomery Street. There were only a very few people about as we cruised slowly through the financial district. Kane said night people were rare in the area, and since this was a Monday it would probably be a very dull ride for the next several hours. "But you never know," he added easily. "Sometimes these nights turn out to be hotter than a full moon. You never know what gets into individuals to make them misbehave the way they do. Some say it's the moon, others say it's all in the stars. . . ."

Kane's voice drifted off and Hardy said, "Individuals who are going to be naughty know goddamned well they can't win, but they don't care. They got their own idea how things should be . . . moon or no moon."

I had already caught myself using "individual" to denote a suspect on the wrong side of the law. It was an impersonal identification without accusation or vengeance. It was a professional term. It fit on a typewritten form and the form fit in a file.

"The subject individual was apprehended at oral copulation in the public toilets. The individual had stuck his penis through a hole in the partition between . . ."

". . . an eight-year-old caucasian female was found wandering the street alone at midnight. She had been beaten with an unidentified instrument. Subject individual was taken to the juvenile center. . . ."

". . . 30 years old, black male fired his .38 at me as I ordered the individual to halt. . . ."

I longed to encounter someone who had been naughty and whom I could refer to, most casually, as an "individual."

We continued along Montgomery Street until we came to a red traffic light at Market. Obediently, Hardy brought the car to stop and while we waited to proceed

Kane placed his arm on the back of the front seat and turned to look at me. "I hope to God you're not going to write one of those police books where the guys are always going through the streets at ninety miles an hour and sirens screaming," he said. "Sirens are okay for the fire department, but we don't like to scare away the individuals we're after."

I told him I would try to avoid the usual and just tell things as they were.

"This is usual. Waiting for a stoplight like everyone else. Of course we get paid for waiting but you don't have to mention that."

Hardy drove across Market Street and continued on until he reached Third. Here, situated behind the mercantile façade of San Francisco, was an area common to most American cities, a conglomeration of gummy-windowed cafes, cheap hotels, pawnshops, and quiet saloons wherein the patrons were usually too drunk to utter more than a garbled moan. Scattered along the street, weaving their way hesitantly between the mosaic of light cast from one neon sign to the next, were the winos, only a few at this early hour, but maintaining their own hapless patrol of territory they considered home. They were the concern of the regular patrolmen, who would eventually round up the farthest gone to keep them from dying in doorways or being run over in the gutters. After they had spent a night in the slammer, a judge would hear their obligatory toothless promising that they would never again swallow anything but heaven's liquid. They knew the judge would turn them loose once more, and they knew that one by one they would be dying and no one would care whether their name had been Richard or Sylvia or Henry.

This nether world was not a ghetto; there were no families in residence for miles and there was no real attachment to the rest of the city. The people who lived hereabouts knew each other, but they had no mutual attachment whatsoever. There were very few prostitutes because no one had any money for anything but alcohol, and no interest in anything save its consumption. Therefore there were fewer customers to be mugged and fewer pimps to take their booty.

All of this represented an area of very little interest to

men of the S-Squad, if only because there existed an undeclared rivalry between the cars patrolling wherever they thought the most action might be. A team that consistently brought in serious troublemakers was respected, as are the experts in any other profession, and the inspector partners within the car were most likely to attract the notice of their superiors. A team that spent the night cruising or sipping coffee in a pleasant cafe was likely to acquire a record for returning empty-handed and would find the lucrative overtime of the S-Squad no longer available to them.

Action thought worthy of an S-Squad team was rarely available on Third Street and Hardy turned along it only because it led south toward better hunting ground. He slowed in the middle of the first block, then I heard him say softly to Kane, "Well I'll be dipped in shit."

He pulled the car over to the curb and stopped. I saw they were watching the corner where three men stood outside a bar. Two looked like Filipinos and one was caucasian. They were talking and gesticulating, apparently in disagreement.

"I think I make the white guy," Kane said to Hardy. Then turning to me: "You're looking at a Kronkie situation. A perfect example."

From my time in police school I knew the word "Kronkie" was derived from a similar Yiddish expression denoting "sick," a vague way of saying something was not quite right. Experienced policemen could spot a Kronkie situation almost instantly, and combined their curiosity with a catalogue memory for the faces, names, assumed names, and records of known criminals. Recognizing a habitual offender was known as "making" the individual.

"He's a pimp," Kane said flatly, and I knew without question he was referring to the white man. I did ask what they had seen to indicate a Kronkie situation.

"One white man who's obviously sober carrying on an argument with two Filipinos would be Kronkie even if the son of a bitch wasn't a pimp. As it is we'll just take a closer look."

Apparently forgetting my presence, they were out of the car before I knew what had happened. After a moment of indecision I slipped quickly out of the back seat, slammed the door, and ran after them. I had not the faintest idea what I should be doing, but couldn't bear being only a spectator. They were less than twenty paces ahead of me when I saw Kane seize the white man from behind and hustle him to the side of the building. Hardy moved in just as quickly on one of the Filipinos and shoved him against the wall. To my astonishment the other Filipino ran right into my arms. In clumsy imitation of my companions I hustled him to the wall and spun him around until he faced it. I wanted to tell him to put his hands flat against the wall but the fierce flow of adrenalin so affected my voice I could barely squeak.

There had not been time to fight. Hardly a minute had passed since I had left the car and now I was bullying a total stranger who had so far offered no resistance. I heard him breathing hard as I began to frisk him. When my right hand came to his coat pocket I gasped and found my voice again.

"Hey, Bob! This guy's got a rod!"

I pulled out a short .38 caliber revolver as if it were a rattlesnake and stood numbly, wondering what to do with it. Only seconds passed before the weapon was grabbed from my hand and all of Kane's poundage intervened between the Filipino and me.

"Jesus Christ!" Kane said as he shoved me all the way to the curbing. I saw he was both exasperated and frightened and I was sorry for somehow displeasing him. "Please, stay right here. Don't move. Please to Christ, stay out of this."

I was chagrined. Hat and trench coat do not make a cop, I realized, but couldn't I have handled my first "individual" alone?

With nothing better to do I checked my watch and noticed it had been only ten minutes since we had left the Hall of Justice. Ho-ho! I thought, how convenient. The entire affair had been carefully staged for the benefit of an author who would hopefully write nice things about policemen. He should witness these heroes at work. Nothing too dangerous, mind you, just enough to give him the feel of things. I became even more suspicious when it developed that the only weapon possessed by the three men was on the person of *my* individual.

I sauntered along behind as Kane and Hardy herded

the three men to the car and called B.I. (Bureau of Identification) to check their records. The white man was wanted on a 402 (violation of parole) and my Filipino on a 301 (vice charge). As a parolee he would also be booked for possession of a weapon. Sure, I decided, the master stagers of this event had thought of everything. They should be staging TV shows in Hollywood.

The other Filipino was "clean" and was released. He lingered until the paddy wagon arrived and asked if he could accompany the others on the ride to the Hall of Justice. I was surprised to hear Kane refuse him. Were they going to break up the cast before paying them off?

Regulations called for the arresting officer to be present at the booking of suspects, so we followed the paddy wagon. Two uniformed officers escorted them to the elevators, which lifted us all to the fifth-floor jail. I stood aside during the paperwork and fingerprinting, resentfully the observer, disappointed in Kane, for whom I had already developed a considerable fondness. I was not really his partner, obviously, and never could be. I was simply an assignment like any other on his record. I must be coddled and deceived by all who came in contact with me until my brain was thoroughly washed with the dye of police blue.

An hour passed before we were back in the S car again, this time driving toward the Embarcadero, where muggings were more than occasional. Hardy drove slowly, his head always turning lest he miss life in any shadow. Kane was singing very softly to himself, an Irish air I would have found entrancing if in a different mood. Finally I could bear my sense of having been patronized no longer.

"That was some show," I said, "but too pat."

Kane stopped singing and turned back to me. He was smiling and asked what I meant.

"You should have built things up more. We were less than ten minutes from the Hall and you went right into the main event. It's going to be hard to top that act."

Kane stopped smiling and pressed his lips tightly together. "You bet your ass it will be. If he felt like it that little runt would as soon kill you as fart."

"Oh sure."

"He has a record starting at age fourteen and going

561

straight through to thirty-seven, which he is now. He's not a nice fella. The white guy is relatively a sweetheart."

Every morning before line-up it was my self-appointed duty to enter Cahill's office and listen to him read and pass opinions on the list of the previous night's activities. The process took half an hour and became a marvelous education in the sordid. Rape, sodomy preceding murder, child torture, burglaries, robbery and senseless beatings of eighty-year-old women, whores beseeching their pimps for fixes and slicing their faces to ribbons when refused, lesbians tearing and gouging at each other in what they described as a "family fight" (damaging enough to take both to the hospital), a homosexual tied spreadeagle fashion to a brass bed then whipped and beaten until dead complete with photographs of the gore, six muggings, two fires of suspected incendiary origin, and eleven drunks in the tank. A reasonably quiet night, Cahill commented, and then speared me with his pale blue eyes. I noticed a twinkle in them so kept my ease, but there was no question of his displeasure.

"Listen you," he began, in his gentle brogue, "I don't want any dead authors around here. It's not that I care about you, be sure, but what would the mayor be saying and the commissioners. A dumb cop they'd say I was if I let harm come to ya, so please don't be so eager."

The twinkle left Cahill's eyes and I knew very suddenly that the incident I had been involved in had not been staged. Two days later my impression was confirmed when I heard a judge remand both the white man and my individual over to a higher court for sentencing. Meanwhile they were held without bail. When I apologized to Kane he rolled his eyes to the ceiling and took on the look of the sorely tried. "The instant I heard you yell this guy's got a rod," he said, "I could see myself back in uniform patrolling Butcher-town. I thought you'd have sense enough to stay in the car."

By the end of three months I was better qualified to handle a Kronkie situation, but less inclined to participate. Wiser by far, I realized the policeman's lot is an unhappy one, full of frustrations and contradictions, and sometimes extremely dangerous. I attended police funerals and police weddings and was accepted as a member of the family. Ignorant of Catholic ritual I went several times to mass because so many policemen were present and I enjoyed watching George Hall, a great hulk of a man acting as altar boy. The lump formed by his gun was always visible beneath his white lace shawl. With Kane and other inspectors I lunched at least twice a week at the famous North Star restaurant, a gathering place for policemen and a few judges where the food was excellent and served in festive amounts. I rode with the horse patrol in Golden Gate Park and was most pleasantly surprised at the quality of their mounts. I spent more time in the morgue than I really desired and I helped Kane during his annual performance as Santa Claus to the children of Chinatown. Little by little my various companions dropped their reserve and confided in me their anxieties, woes, and special pleasures. When shyness was gone I was invited to their homes and introduced with pride to their families as a man who wrote books and yet understood their life. And with Cahill I became a lasting friend and likewise with Kane and Hardy.

Anxious to saturate myself in the police story I nearly allowed my enthusiasm to break me. I had not realized the weight of my eighteen-hour days until one morning, feeble with exhaustion, I simply could not rise from my bed. Dodie made my excuses to Cahill and kept me resting in Sausalito for a week.

There were other demands on my thoughts and time. Having sold *Fate Is the Hunter* to Twentieth-Century Fox, Linsk also sold me to write the screenplay. In his Chinatown office Walter Joe was pulling at his brush of hair trying to assemble all the facts necessary for income tax time as well as responding to the continuous demands of Eleanor's lawyer, who had apparently persuaded himself I had buried treasure all over the western hemisphere. I called Eleanor frequently on the telephone hoping to dissuade her from going through with a divorce and trying to convince her of my financial integrity and firm resolve to keep her handsomely. Her voice sounded muffled and at times she became strangely irrational, but I blamed the division between us and thought it unnecessary to investigate further. When she asked if I would finance a trip around the world to attend orchid conferences, I wished her a happy journey and assured her an open ticket would be mailed the same day.

During all of my involvement with the San Francisco police I had returned each night to Sausalito and recorded the day's events on a tape recorder. These recordings were augmented with bundles of handscribbled notes and a small library on criminals and the law. Now I decided there was enough accumulated material at hand and within my head for a book, but I knew an immediate start would be unwise. I had to get away from anything to do with the subject until the swollen river of recently acquired knowledge subsided and I could sift the unimportant from the essentials. I resolved to make as complete a change in atmosphere as possible and the impending need for a screenplay on *Fate Is the Hunter* was pressing. Darryl Zanuck, the producer, was now domiciled in Paris and since I would have to confer with him during the writing I thought Europe would provide a logical change of environment.

I rented the Sausalito house, Dodie packed our skis and the material for *Of Good and Evil* in two grocery boxes, our feisty dog Felix in another box, and we flew off to Switzerland. There, Swiss friends who had sailed with us on *Black Watch* had found a small chalet perched precariously on the side of an alp near a place named Verbier. The chalet was much simpler than the one in Norway and quite as poorly insulated against the cold, but the view of the valley almost six thousand feet straight down and the towering mountains beyond was breathtaking. It was like living in a free balloon and we fell in love with the place on first sight. No locale could have been better for our health and rejuvenation from the trials of California; it was half a mile of steep climb and descent to the post office and general store, and the surrounding ski area was recognized as one of the greatest in the world. There was no telephone.

Here in the silence of the snowclad Alps we settled in for a long winter and I had never known such deep content. As in Norway, my mornings were spent writing, my afternoons in the outdoors, and evenings in the most simple pleasures of food, wine, books, chess, friends, and, when there was time, painting.

My occasional trips to Paris for conferences on *Fate*

Is the Hunter were unwanted diversions, but not because of Darryl Zanuck. His dubious reputation as a tyrant and generally offensive Hollywood mogul of the old school I found entirely erroneous. He always treated me with the utmost courtesy and consideration, and when I began to flounder because of my overenthusiasm for the subject matter Zanuck skillfully put me back on track. He was an excellent editor, succinct and clever in the most difficult transitions, although his wild imagination too often produced absurd story suggestions likely to throw the entire script out of key. He liked working long hours and sometimes it was ten at night before we would halt for dinner, but I enjoyed his company greatly and his forthright opinions most of all.

By the time the alpine winter had faded I had completed the first draft screenplay of *Fate Is the Hunter* and begun on the novel *Of Good and Evil*. With little distraction except for the always inviting mountains and snow I found it incongruous although not difficult to write of a city and a seamy environment so far distant. As the snows melted and the wildflowers came to Verbier, I often took pen and notebook to the even greater heights looming behind the chalet and wrote from early morning until noon. Then I would see Dodie, a miniature figure far below, working her way slowly upward, traversing the steep slope with the steady pacing of a mountain person. Following her, an almost imperceptible white dot against the flank of the mountain, would be Felix, the gimpy orphan dog of unknown lineage who had possibly traveled more than any other animal in the world. He had flown the ocean four times, sailed the Atlantic, the North Sea, the Mediterranean, the Aegean, and the Ionian, all of which he detested, and he had sired a son in Greece after there establishing himself as the toughest mutt who had ever squirted urine along the ancient waterfront at Piraeus. We loved him very much despite his occasional ill-temper brought on by pain in his gimpy leg; then he might even nip at us.

On Dodie's back I knew would be a rucksack containing cheeses and bread for our lunch and a bottle of the exquisite Valais wine to wash it down. I watched her always with anticipation and a sense of enormous gratitude to fortune or whatever beneficent power had brought her to me. Her conduct throughout the recent most difficult times had been impeccable and her concern for my peace of mind seemed a responsibility she accepted without question. She knew I was doing my utmost to provide a splendid way of life for several people while employing only the simple instrument in my fingers. She knew how it taxed the spirit and the body to live with a subject twenty-four hours of every day and face an empty page every morning. It had been seven years since I first spied her on a mountain now far away.

Dodie would also be bringing the day's mail, which followed us everywhere, and there would be bills and bills from the United States, all necessary in their way I supposed. I found it amusing how consistently the living expenses of the man who paid the bills and his secretary were far less than those of the rest of my family. Dodie would write checks for the bills on the morrow and type out the answers I scribbled along the margins of the letters, then type the previous day's writings so I could revise once again, all the while preparing three meals a day and keeping the chalet orderly. It was my pleasure to tease her sometimes, implying she had too much leisure time.

"What do you do all day while I'm up here writing my heart out?"

"I lie around reading French novels and eating chocolates. What else?"

"Don't you realize idle hands lead a girl to mischief?"

"I've always wanted to go to mischief. Where is it?"

"Beyond yon mountain . . . somewhere."

"Can Felix go too?"

"Of course. But I need a haircut before I'd be presentable even in mischief."

"Maybe I can squeeze you in tomorrow afternoon between typing what you've done today, your French lesson, my trip to the post office, and cooking the goulash!"

There was a letter in the mail from George Jansen. It saddened me. Eleanor's lawyer was insisting that the *Black Watch*, now wintering in Greece, be included in the spoils of divorce. I wondered if she intended to hire a crew and sail away the vessel I so loved with herself in command. When my bitterness subsided I took a more objective view. "That sort of vindictiveness doesn't sound like the Eleanor I knew. It must be her lawyer or . . ." I hesitated as an even more disturbing thought struck me, ". . . or she must be sick."

Chapter 42

With Boswell in hand and Ted Helprin to keep us company we sailed the Hebrides that summer. Our voyaging was touched with hidden melancholy because it seemed reasonably certain that the pleasures offered by the *Black Watch* would soon be denied. As autumn came we sailed her down to Portugal and moored her in the exact same berth where four years previously the *Albatros* had passed into other hands.

It was very difficult for Dodie and me to regard the empty space where the *Albatros* had been without once more speculating on the inexplicable turns of fortune which spared us while capriciously taking others to their forevers. Christopher Sheldon, who had bought the *Albatros* from me, was a fine sailor. So was his wife, whom he had met when sailing around the world in Irving Johnson's famous brigantine *Yankee*. George Ptatnik, our cook during our last voyage in the *Albatros*, had elected to stay with her rather than accept our invitation to man the galley aboard *Black Watch*. His last letter had reached us when we sailed down to Greece from Yugoslavia. It was full of enthusiasm for the *Albatros* and her crew of students on the current voyage.

Only two days later a letter from another friend reported an almost incredible tragedy. While sailing in the Gulf of Mexico the *Albatros* had been caught, all standing, by a white squall. A vicious freak wind rolled her over until she could not recover. She went down in seconds, trapping Sheldon's wife, Ptatnik, and four students below. The rest managed to escape. Those on deck, including Sheldon, survived to spend less than two days in one of the lifeboats before they were rescued by a Dutch freighter. After the wind passed, the sea was relatively calm again, an eerie heartbreaking aftermath of the ocean's unpredictable power. I wept for Sheldon, realizing his torment as the responsible master, and I longed to stretch out a hand to him and say it could have happened to me. In the letter of condolence I wrote him I thought it inappropriate to question why it had not.

Now, rationalizing to the limits of my ability, I could not discover a satisfactory explanation for my repeated evasion of doom. Why Sheldon? Why all the many others I had known? Where was the balance?

Henry Simon, brother of Richard Simon, who, with Max Schuster, had created the publishing house of Simon and Schuster, became the editor on *Of Good and Evil*. He was a good man, of great sensitivity and tenderness, albeit more inclined to fuss over one of my dangling participles and split infinitives than to question how well I had told the story of big city police. Henry Simon was woefully thin and smoked incessantly despite warnings from his doctor on his frailness. I worried more about him than I did about the book and I was right in being concerned for both.

Just why *Of Good and Evil* proved disappointing to me and was not an outstanding success was impossible to ascertain, but I could not honestly accept Simon's opinion that it *was* a success. I concluded that the timing, the most essential element in any book launching, was wrong.

When I returned to the United States to tend my affairs, one of which was trying to promote the sales of *Of Good and Evil,* I found the influence of a relatively few Americans exaggerated beyond my comprehension. A spirit of defiance and senseless revolt prevailed. The assassinations of the Kennedys, the apparently senseless Vietnam involvement, and the erratic eruptions of the civil rights movement had brought my country into an era of continuous unrest. It seemed as if I had returned to a population gone mad, and I was astonished to see the so-called flower people, yippies, and assorted opportunists treated as folk-heroes and even the hope of a new America. It was a drug culture glorying in rejection of everything I believed made my country the greatest in the world. In an orgy of self-debasement and conformity, our young people were clothing themselves in sackcloth and ashes. Self-indulgence was the order of the day among the young and those middle-agers who tried to behave as if they were still undergraduates, but except for vague references to tearing down the establishment I failed to discover what they hoped to accomplish. At last it was the tragic killing of students at Kent State University that finally sobered Americans of all persuasions and at least began a trend toward more objective thinking.

This was also a time of youth worship; black or white, the young could do nothing seriously wrong and punishment was rarely laid upon their arrogant heads. Other inhabitants of earth had cause to wonder why a people who had more than they had ever dared dream of were so discontent. Only the Soviet headlines were joyous; American behavior as typified in our own press proved the decadence of a rotten system.

If there were to be heroes among those who spit on and burned their national flag, then there had to be villains and the press was quick to appoint the police. Suddenly "police brutality" became the battle cry rolling across the country from the streets of New York's Harlem to San Francisco's Haight-Ashbury. It echoed and re-echoed in print and on television until the average American wondered wistfully why he was being taxed to pay men whose only activity was beating up innocent and perfectly law-abiding citizens. The natural antipathy of most Americans for police of any sort was now compounded to such a degree that a policeman found it extremely awkward to earn his keep without violating someone's civil liberties. As a consequence many lost heart and let crime go its way.

Unfortunately for the book *Of Good and Evil*, it failed to portray policemen as merciless beasts addicted to torture and the oppression of minorities. It described them as they were, both the fit and unfit, mostly ordinary men addicted to the unfashionable habit of earning a living.

I finally realized that the atmosphere of the times was wrong for such a book and was grateful it at least could not be marked down as a total failure. It did hover for a while on various best-seller lists, and did extremely well in other countries, where apparently police were regarded more objectively. Once again Lester Linsk sold it to the movies and with the bounty received I bought the house next to the one I already owned in Sausalito, an action which spurred Eleanor's lawyer into a frenzy of activity. A divorce settlement had still not been reached and whatever I earned he considered at least half his to supervise. Apparently he was convinced I might be jeopardizing his client's future by making a poor investment.

I saw Eleanor once during a brief visit to California. The judge demanded my presence during the routine ceremony of filing for a divorce. I arrived in the courtroom early along with George Jansen and saw Eleanor enter on the arm of a friend. She could hardly walk and ignored me. I knew a moment of almost overwhelming pity for her and then recovered, for I knew that only a few days before she had attended a social function in apparent good health. Yet I still pitied her and so, obviously, did the judge. He accepted the lawyers' declarations, set the amount of my temporary alimony (at half what I had first proposed), and, as if dipping the flag before two swordsmen, advised the lawyers to have at each other until a final settlement was reached.

En route to this prodigal return, I had taken as much of my children's time as their busy lives allowed. Polly was at Georgetown University studying for the foreign service. Her schedule suffered while we joined with her host of friends and took in all of the best Washington had to give. I found Polly as vivacious as ever, a young lady of striking beauty and keen intelligence, altogether the sort of daughter a father loves to spoil. We had a wonderful time together and I hoped my pride was tolerable.

Steven greeted me with far less enthusiasm when I stopped to visit him at the University of Oklahoma. He was polite and reserved and yet obviously resentful of my behavior. There were long silences between us and I wanted desperately to hear him say he at least understood if he could not forgive, but I saw he was only counting the hours until I departed. When I did leave we shook hands, he pretending he wished me well with his hollow "Good luck," and I pretending his mother had not won away our son. When I was finally in the little commuter airplane and out of his sight, I wept without tears for the awesome gap between us. I had been judged, found wanting, and knew not how to make repairs. Maybe this was the balance?

George, now out of the Navy, his sword traded for an able seaman's berth in a Chevron Oil tanker, restored my spirits on the eve of the very same day. We had a joyful reunion at his house in Belvedere just across the bay of Sausalito from my own houses. He made me believe I was the father I so wanted to be, and I marveled at the unique relationship between us. Every matter of interest to George was of interest to me and he seemed to feel the same. We talked of airplanes until a hint of the sea would crisscross through our conversation, whereupon we would talk of ships until our eyes drooped. He took me to his small study beneath the house where he built museum-worthy ship models and I followed his constructions piece by piece with avid enthusiasm. We had long before begun our separate marine libraries and pounced upon any rare publication with the unswerving devotion of dedicated collectors. A prize found anywhere in the world was then a joy to be shared with the father or the son; in the flash of a page we could become lost in the intricate rigging of an eighteenth-century sailing ship.

My pride in George was unashamed and based on more than blood, for I should have been proud of any young man who would voluntarily forsake the relative comforts of a Navy lieutenant's berth and begin his career in tankers—first, according to regulation, as an ordinary seaman, and soon as able-bodied. With a little more sea time he was reasonably certain of a berth as third mate, then time and attrition should one day see him master. Married to Karen Galassi (daughter of my telephonic mentor in Milan so long ago), he had sired a daughter, Allysonne, who promised great beauty.

For the two days we had available, George and I prowled the San Francisco waterfront, calling on Captain David Saunders, who had steered him to the Chevron Shipping Company originally, Jack Dickerhoff, who had rigged the *Albatros,* and the inimitable "Spike" Africa, who was particularly fond of George and a yarn-spinner extraordinary. I wallowed in this maritime environment, pleased beyond measure to be recaptured by the same sirens I had first introduced to my sons. Both boys had sailed with me since they could remember anything at all, they had been teethed on stories of the sea, and I was delighted one had chosen a maritime career. I was also a little puzzled by George's apparent maturity. Quick to laugh, energetic, and exciting in mind, he was also unusually wise for his age and I found myself asking often his counsel.

"What do you think I should do about your brother? I admire his independence but I can't get through to him. He thoroughly disapproves of me and not just in the normal patronizing way so many young men regard their male parent."

"He'll get over it."

"What do you think I should do about the *Black Watch?*"

"There will be many other boats in your life."

As we departed in different directions our correspondence resumed its steady flow.

In Hollywood I paused briefly to confer with another extraordinary young man, Richard Zanuck, son of Darryl. He was George's exact age and I thought it fitting he should be in the movie business. Now he had taken over the production chores on *Fate Is the Hunter,* and where at first I had been alarmed at such a flagrant display of nepotism, I was soon reassured. While my sons were learning of the sky and the ocean, the younger Zanuck was learning about movies.

In spite of young Zanuck's fresh and vigorous story mind and my own renewed energies, we were having trouble translating *Fate Is the Hunter* to film. I took the remnants of the screenplay's first draft back to Switzerland and rewrote it, but I knew I was compromising. Struggle as I might, there seemed to be no rescue, and the realization that it was entirely my own fault distressed me even more. There followed a series of conferences with both Zanucks in Paris, but the basic story kept skittering away from us. I was not surprised when production plans were shelved. Meanwhile Robert Cohn, who intended to make a film of *Of Good and Evil,* was also encountering script troubles. It seemed that my fruitful association with Hollywood had run hard aground, and I found myself not caring.

My pen had not been given rest for twenty years: every day, if I was not actually flying or sailing, some small part of me oozed out on paper and now I wondered if the supply had not been entirely drained. I resolved to let my brain lie fallow for a while and allow my eyes and hands to satisfy an apparently ceaseless urging to create. Joyfully I took up my paint brushes and began to revive the skills my mother had taught me. The results were some rather inept oils of the surrounding alpine scene and one acceptable portrait of my neighbor Marcel, but my satisfaction in once again bringing life to canvas was out of all proportion to the worth of the paintings. Someday, I thought, before my pen becomes even more uncertain, I must detour into a different line of work. I vowed to keep honest and faithful company with my easel until such prospect stood a decent chance of achieving reality.

During my escape from writing, Dodie, upon my urging, accepted an invitation to make a cross-alpine ski tour with a pair of our Swiss friends. It was a significant honor for an American woman, a recognition of her expertise among the finest skiers in the world, and I was very proud of her.

George and Loli Firmenisch, Dodie, and their guide, chartered a Pilatus Porter aircraft to deposit them on one of the highest alpine glaciers. The dog Felix and I rode along, saw them away until they became minute figures trailing veils of powder snow, then flew down with the pilot to the green valley of the Rhone. Already uneasy without the woman who had cared for us so long, Felix and I set out in a Volkswagen for a Swiss settlement near Berne known, to my pleased sense of the ridiculous, as Belp. There, I intended to indulge in soaring, a sport I had long enjoyed.

I qualified for my "Carte d'élève—Pilote d'avions et de planeurs" in the first day and from then on was not once disappointed in the environment. One afternoon, sashaying back and forth along the gray face of an approaching front, I was able to maintain the glider's maximum cruise speed for two hours without losing a meter of altitude. The next day in lovely smooth air my barograph recorded a free ascent from 800 meters to 2,000 in less than twenty minutes, a most satisfying if hardly spectacular performance.

Yet I was not out to break records, much less find

myself pinned like a butterfly against an alp. I allowed the soft hiss of the slipstream to soothe my thoughts and since powerless flight is a retreat into unreality there were times when I ceased to care if I ever came down. These peaceful afternoons, alone in a body-tight cocoon, lofting as a bird and so utterly removed from fellow men, were an invitation to contemplating my lot. One afternoon after landing I lay on the cool grass with Felix pressing tightly against me and found I was unexpectedly troubled. Damn, I thought, I must be homesick.

If so it was unforgivable, for certainly we had enjoyed the very best of exile. In Switzerland we were welcome in the homes of many friends, a rarity for foreigners. Dodie's log in which she kept track of our activities listed elsewhere in Europe additional friends and acquaintances until a small army of names filled the pages. Everywhere from Ustaoset to Malta and from Athens to Lisbon, with a hundred way-points in between, we knew people who would willingly share their time with us.

And how very stiff-necked we had behaved! Indeed, our conduct still bordered on the farcical; it was as if we were a pair of frightened survivors of the Victorian era, for it had been our custom during our continuous wanderings always to take two hotel rooms, on different floors if available. This nonsense still persisted even if we went to Geneva for a weekend. I decided most people who knew us must be laughing their heads off at our pretensions.

While I watched the cumulus clouds fade with the afternoon I realized the source of my present dissatisfaction had nothing to do with Dodie, or even with my lingering affection for Eleanor, which I refused to let the legalese of her lawyer destroy. I was fifty-two years old and had thus far spent my lifetime as a gypsy. Although I owned two houses, both were rented to strangers and could hardly be considered to be permanent homes. I was as comfortable in Venice or Geneva or Copenhagen or Lisbon as in any American city, a metamorphosis I took as a disturbing sign. So many years of this wandering had slipped away, I had become a tourist in my own country, an unnatural role for an apple-pie American born in Nebraska.

The next day, high over Belp, with the sun shafting

blue steel rods down through the broken overcast, I decided the moment of final choice had come. Dodie and I could remain in voluntary exile gradually forgetting our heritage and the ways of our countrymen, or we could return and call America home.

Returning to America in spirit as well as body was not as easy as I had supposed. Once surrounded by multitudes of my fellow citizens, it seemed to me the whole temper of our country had changed. The cities appeared to be far more crowded, the country landscape troubled and tortured by a monstrous and ugly program of visual defilement. Freeways were everywhere and still abuilding as altars for the national worship of the automobile. The yippies were already passé, but hippies in far greater numbers remained omnipresent. They were particularly numerous in Sausalito, the once gentle little fishing village where I had resolved to establish a genuine home. I was shocked to see what they had done to the community and for a few disheartened days considered resuming exile. The gracious little waterfront park was closed—that gentle place where the elderly bronzed paisanos formerly sat all day, taking the sun's warmth to their toil-worn bodies and gossiping of the nation's politics and more importantly of the abundance or lack of fish in the near waters. A wire fence now surrounded the park and the melodious bubbling of the fountain was no more. The authorities had been obliged to close the oasis because the hippies had claimed the space for their own. There, zonked out on every variety of drug, they had moved in bag and baggage, male and female, sleeping, fighting and fornicating, eating and defecating on the once well-groomed grass, taunting passersby with their naked exhibitionism.

When the little park was no longer available to anyone, square or twisted, the hippies took to the single street which runs along the waterfront. The continuous spectacle provided by their colorful costumes and ways of life then generated a counter-phenomenon which transformed the sleepy little community I had known into a bustling fair. Square tourists came from all over the world to observe the hippies, who obligingly behaved like inhabitants of a zoo and exploited the tourists in all manner of new shops, peddling junk souvenirs, shawls, "earth" food, and horoscopes. To this sorry circus I returned in some dismay.

Although I kept assuring myself I would become accustomed to this new America, I felt at peace only when the little cable car jiggled down its steep descent to the water. There in the house on stilts with the waters of the bay beneath the floor, I found the privacy and tranquillity I so enjoyed. The second house, somewhat smaller, I intended to use as an office-studio. Eleanor's lawyer was now certain I was deliberately squandering money which should belong to his client. Incredibly, he was still in frequent argument with Jansen. Since Eleanor was very well taken care of, and I had not wanted a divorce in the first place, I tried to ignore the situation. Instead I called Eleanor for a report on her world tour, which I gathered she had enjoyed. We discussed our children, their doings and their needs, almost as normally as if two years had not slipped away since our separation. Finally, she told me of winning prizes in an orchid show and our conversation ended with my congratulations. We never mentioned her lawyer or the status of our pending divorce. It was like talking with a phantom from some long-lost time.

With the book *Of Good and Evil* fading rapidly from the best-seller lists, *Fate Is the Hunter* shelved, and my share of *Soldier of Fortune* profits still zero, my professional life was floundering. Before our departure from Europe, Roger Peetzer, an eccentric Hollywood producer of low-budget films, offered me a staggering sum to write something he was determined to call *The Aviators*.

Once I had agreed to work with Peetzer I regretted it. He was tall, dignified, white-haired, and capable of considerable personal charm when he wanted something; he was also very intelligent and energetic. We had met first in Bermuda, then London, and now Hollywood had become his forum. I wondered why he had hired me when a dictaphone would have served him as well and I had begun to estimate how soon he would drive me out of my mind.

Possibly Roger Peetzer was the cinematic genius he apparently thought himself to be and that was why any exchange between us was a conference in name only. While I sat for hours listening to his haranguing he would pace the room at a near-jog, all the while waving and slashing at the air with a symphony conductor's baton. Meeting after interminable meeting I watched his one-man show from whatever furniture I could find to support my restless body. I kept reminding myself how very well I was being paid to attend these performances. Once he pointed his conductor's stick straight at my eyes and waggling the end of it delivered a tirade on my latest cinematic perfidies and utter lack of respect for the story that he visualized. I was tempted to grab the stick, break it over my knee, and advise him exactly where he could shove both story and stick, but held my fire because I realized he was of the old Hollywood school, in which a writer was expected to behave like a servile hyena.

Yet Roger Peetzer was actually a Jekyll and Hyde whose arrogance and bullheaded conceit deserted him the instant we would pause in our wild professional debate for a glass of sherry, lunch, or tea. Then his delightful wife would be asked to join us and he became at once an amusing and gracious host capable of listening as well as orating. These redeeming transformations kept me from despair.

By the time I had completed the first draft of *The Aviators* I knew it was doomed to gather dust in the MGM story department where Peetzer had mined the money to pay me so handsomely, and this experience convinced me I had wasted too much valuable time on a medium where the writer was an eighth-class citizen. As a consequence I declined invitations to write the script for *Of Good and Evil* (which was a mistake) and to perform yet another rewrite on the script of *Fate Is the Hunter* (a second and much more serious mistake); the former was eventually burdened with a script bearing almost no resemblance at all to the book, and the latter was so confused and twisted in production that it ultimately scored as one of the worst movies ever made, indeed so ridiculous that I insisted Twentieth-Century Fox completely remove my name from it.*

* They obliged and as a result I deprived myself of the TV residuals, a medium in which the film played interminably.

Throughout all of this, Jansen continued his ceaseless exchange with Eleanor's lawyer, who I supposed would soon be upset when told of a new depredation upon my financial resources. I had bought a rowing dory for exercise and one afternoon instead of pulling toward the Golden Gate I aimed the dory in the opposite direction and after a mile or two came upon a scene which held me spellbound. Resting the oars, I watched a seaplane practicing landings and take-offs at the upper end of the bay and I thought it shameful I had never flown one. Later I found Bill Hardsaw, who managed the little seaplane operation, and I asked for lessons from Russ Donald. After one take-off and landing I was hopelessly hooked on flying off the water. Where had I been all this time? An airman-sailor's life was made to order for me. The taste of this new elixir filled me with the same ecstasy I had known at first solo. Overjoyed to be back in the air I envisioned aerial voyages to the most remote places in the world.

Once a man becomes committed to a life in contest with the elements he cannot ever again ignore them. Thus do old sailors and aviators continue to observe the constant changing of the sky, sniffing at the winds, eyeing the texture and formation of clouds, the quality of visibility, and all the other nuances which in the past have been familiar and have helped him survive. Likewise, seamen and pilots are inclined to view the tools of their trade with more than passing interest. Sailors haunt the waterfronts of the world lest they miss something new or different in ships; pilots, almost without exception, cannot resist watching an airplane overhead, landing, or taking off. At the little seaplane base in Sausalito I finally returned to the fold and soon nothing would do but I must have my own flying boat.

I found a used but not too abused twin-engined amphibian for twenty thousand dollars and in spite of my declining fortunes easily persuaded myself I could afford it. Using the same conveniently twisted rationale I had employed when buying the *Albatros*, I became the owner of a Piaggio Royal Gull, an Italian aircraft designed for military use. Therefore, as frequently as possible, I took off with Dodie for such true wilderness as we could find in Nevada and Mexico. One day this same airplane would bring us to quite another life.

Renewed association with the sky and airmen inspired me to undertake another flying novel, this time a tale of air combat during the First World War. I thought to call this book *In the Company of Eagles* and began with more than usual trepidation because I knew the subject had been much overwritten and anything I might produce risked a literary yawn. Against this possibility I resolved to be more than ever meticulous in my research, and since I had been much too young to participate in the real event my facts must be dug from extensive prowling through records of the time. As always I soon became so lost in the details of research, I nearly forgot that some order must be made of them and a book produced.

A man in love is a dangerous man, at least to himself, if only because he is likely to forget his limitations. Just before commencing the actual writing of *In the Company of Eagles,* Dodie and I accepted an invitation to ski at Vail with the Taylors, long her friends and experts on the slopes. Trying to follow Dodie through deep powder snow I caught a tip of one ski and tore my Achilles tendon clean through. Result: two months in a wheelchair and the next two on crutches. When I reckoned the cost of my clumsiness in work time, I lost all further interest in skiing.

By the time I was so adept with a wheelchair that I could stop precisely on target, spin around and take off in a new direction at high speed without damage to others or the furniture, I was also charged with impatience. There was much to be done about the new book and I was, according to my apparently inflexible average of two pages a day, now more than a hundred and twenty pages behind schedule. I wrote on schedule because it was the only reliable bastion I knew against the decline of interest in a work which must be sustained for at least a year and sometimes very much longer. For the most trying part of a writer's life is the enormous mental distance between first conception and the printed book hard in the hand. I had come to regard my books as written by someone else. On those few occasions when I had been tempted to read even a few pages of my latest creation I found only embarrassment. The good passages must have been written by someone I had never known and the bad stood out like rocks at low tide. Every author sets out from the beginning to write a masterpiece, else he could not continue to the end; much later, when he discovers how wide he is of the mark, discouragement can be overwhelming.

Now, partly because of my accident, I knew a haunting experience which undoubtedly affected the ultimate quality of *In the Company of Eagles*. The major part of the story was set in the "bloody April" of 1917, a time when the English and French were engaged against the Germans in a final struggle for command of the skies over the trenches. I thought it necessary to visit the exact area where my characters were supposed to be playing out their destinies, and with Dodie lugging our rucksacks while I crutched behind, right leg still bundled in a cast to the hip, we took off for France.

So many years had passed I had not expected to see anything left of the battlefields around Verdun where the most terrible trench warfare in the history of mankind had been waged.

What I did behold was a shock, and for the first time I realized that the dates I had chosen for this visit coincided exactly with those I had long ago selected for the story's principal action. More remarkable, the weather proved to be identical to that of the story's long-ago April. Every gloomy wind-driven meteorological detail matched the old photos I had studied and even the moon was the same. As if these eerie coincidences were not enough, we found that the battlefields had hardly been touched since the combatants finally laid down their arms in November of 1918. The trenches were still there, only slightly eroded in profile and softened by grass; the thousands of shell holes created by four years of almost continuous bombardment and the ruins of buildings were everywhere. I could not believe the French government would have left so much real estate untouched until I saw a French helmet hanging from a tree. It was not fifty feet from the road and even as I told Dodie to stop the Volkswagen I saw why the helmet would not become my souvenir. Now I took time to translate the warning signs posted at frequent intervals along the road. DANGEREUX!

PELIGROSO! The signs warned of mines still implanted everywhere, live ammunition of unknown caliber and location, tank traps, and other discouragements to exploration. Our curiosity was further sobered when we came upon a series of simple crosses scattered at some distance from each other. Each commemorated the sudden demise of a souvenir-hunter, and some were of very recent date.

Henry Simon edited *In the Company of Eagles* and proclaimed it a success. It did float in the middle of the best-seller lists for longer than I expected, was a book club selection, and did reasonably well in foreign language translations and the paperback edition. Lester Linsk, however, had no luck selling it to the movies and I chided him for this blot on his otherwise incredible record. My own greatest satisfaction from the book came from several letters I received from men who had actually flown in the First World War. Each made much the same inquiry. Since I had obviously been one of them, what outfit had I flown with? I could only hope they were not too disillusioned when informed I had known only seven years of life by 1917.

Now, at last, the divorce Eleanor had asked for became final. Numbed by the relentless actions of her lawyer, which included such theatrical and totally unnecessary ploys as hiring a "messenger boy" to hand-deliver papers disguised as a present, I was surprised how little I cared that the seamy business was finally done. A life I had once known had sunk out of sight, now to be only vaguely remembered, and I was beginning to question if someone long ago had mixed up my basket with another. For I did not feel at all as old as chronology determined, and I found it hard to believe so many things could possibly have happened to one man.

All I wanted now was peace, a fancy which held for about a month while George and I had numerous fine sails on the bay together, chattering like the fast friends we were of ships and the sea, the books we had read, and his prospects for the future. He had risen rapidly in the tanker fleet and was now a second mate with his first mate's license already won. There were times when our rambunctious enthusiasm and laughter was so hearty even the seagulls were frightened away.

George was also a frequent guest at the Sausalito house where invariably at dinner he shared what they called a "common bowl" with Dodie. Setting a wooden bowl of exotic salad between them they would pluck away at the contents with their fingers, claiming that any utensil would spoil the taste. It was a custom they had established when we all sailed the Aegean in the *Black Watch*, the same environment where they had formed a lasting affection and friendship for each other. My own love for both of them became more precious than life. Every time I watched George's tanker sail out the Golden Gate I felt diminished, and my need for Dodie, now ten years at my side, made me wonder if our fear of ruining a beautiful friendship by marrying was not imaginary.

As if to prove I could get along without her and also that my domestication was still far away, I was the only man to raise a hand one night at a San Francisco meeting of the Quiet Birdmen. Freddie Walts, a Pan American captain known as the President of the Pacific Ocean in spite of "Spike" Africa's claim to the same title, asked if anyone present cared to volunteer as a captain for Polynesian Airlines out of Western Samoa. I felt my hand rise as if some irresistible force dared me deny it. I knew absolutely nothing about the job, had never heard of the airline, and had only the vaguest idea where Western Samoa might be.

Walts pointed his finger at the solitary hand he saw. "You'll be flying DC-3s out of Apia for Tonga, Fiji, Rarotonga, and God only knows where else. The pay is a skimpy six hundred dollars a month, so expect your true reward in heaven."

Volunteers, I remembered, too often wind up in heaven. And six hundred dollars a month would not begin to pay my alimony, let alone Dodie's expenses and the payments on the Sausalito houses. I hoped, wistfully, that Eleanor's lawyer just might develop an ulcer because of this latest caper. Since his client now owned in addition to Island in the Sky, my boat, insurance policies, plus a further ownership of half of my royalties past and future, I was unenthusiastic about writing. What I had once volunteered was now demanded.

Dodie drove me to the airport and bade me farewell with such composure I nearly turned around on the spot.

She had nothing to go on except my promise to send for her once I had settled. Until then her only duty was to look after the Sausalito houses and pay the continuous parade of bills from what funds I had remaining.

"Felix and I will miss you."

"Just think—you can sleep till noon."

"Write when you feel like it. And paint some pretty pictures."

Long pause. Our eyes met at last, I embraced her momentarily and thought, if she weeps I will not be capable of leaving, and if she fails to shed a tear it will be what I deserve. Goodbye, fool. Stalwart, steady men are standing in line to replace you.

She was smiling when I gathered the nerve to look at her once more. So it was easier for me to say so long and finally turn away, more alone than I had ever been since Dodie Post had joined the brigantine *Albatros*. I went off trying to persuade myself the separation was good for us both.

Western Samoa had just emerged from the benign protectorate of New Zealand and become an independent nation. The airline I would be flying for was created as the national flag carrier, and operations under the direction of New Zealanders had barely commenced with a single DC-3. Arriving in Apia, said to be the scene of Somerset Maugham's *Rain*, I took up residence in a small cottage, part of the hotel run by the renowned Aggie Grey. She proved to be a fascinating personality, part confidante, part housemother to the permanent guests of her establishment. Unfortunately, Polynesian Airlines' sole aircraft was grounded with a bad engine in faraway Rarotonga and the demand for my services was nil until a new engine arrived by ship. Hence for a week I rode my bicycle over the pot-holed road along the shore, drinking in the lush beauty of the island and admiring the dignified ways of the unspoiled Samoans. Evenings I drank in the little bar beneath the porch of Aggie Grey's hotel, slurping down an extra gin and tonic against the heat I found as oppressive as the dreary New Zealand-type food served in the dining room. Afterward I would paint for a while, trying to revive my limited skill with water-color. The results were disappointing. I had not the technique to capture the extraordinarily colorful scene now a part of my daily life, and all my creations looked like cheap post cards.

Weeks passed, with the flag carrier of a newly proud nation still grounded for lack of a single working engine. Restless with inactivity I asked for leave to return home until the situation resolved itself. For once my timing was perfect. The airline had just ordered a second DC-3. When it was ready I could ferry it back to Apia.

Dodie was waiting for me. And Felix. Our reunion in Sausalito was happily prolonged by delays in fitting out the elderly DC-3, which now became the *Savaii,* after the second island of Western Samoa. I was greatly revitalized by the San Francisco climate. There my son Steven and I spent a day together which I thought went reasonably well—considering. He was now in the Green Berets and stood very tall and handsome. He brought a girlfriend to the Sausalito house and there were moments when he seemed to let down his reserve, but I was wary of hoping for too much. Every time in the past I had thought we might assume an open father-son relationship I had been rebuffed. Something I could not identify always slipped between us and clanged down the barrier again. Or was it someone?

During this happy interlude I sailed with George frequently and brought Polly to the only home I knew. Like George, she thoroughly approved of Dodie and I watched happily as their friendship, so firmly established in Pebble Beach when Polly had been stricken with tuberculosis, continued to flower. The three of us flew frequently in the Piaggio and I was so impressed with Dodie's ability as a co-pilot that I decided to take her along to Samoa in a like capacity.

It is a long way from San Francisco to Western Samoa in a DC-3, fifteen hours and thirty minutes to Honolulu and then another fifteen plus forty minutes to Apia. As long as the engines remained faithful I had feared exhaustion might be our greatest danger, but I had underestimated the comforts of a solid DC-3 of any age. While we exchanged duties there was room to stretch out on the floor for a quick nap and the inexplicable weariness of pressurization was not ours to fret about. For a whiff of bracing fresh air all we need do was open a window.

It was altogether a delightful flight and we arrived in

Apia precisely on schedule, a proud accomplishment in the eyes of the officials and horde of well-wishers assembled to greet us. A few years hence I would write about this nostalgic flight in a story called "On the Beak of an Ancient Pelican," and properly give credit to our navigator, a New Zealander named George Washington.

I had now to make a difficult choice and knew I might have weighed the options differently if I had not so recently returned from long exile. I could stay on in Western Samoa, a sort of Rip Van Winkle aviator twisting between tropical cumulus in an antique flying machine until retirement age, and I could ask Dodie to settle down with me on an island where the relatively few caucasian women were expected to play bridge, fan themselves, gossip discreetly, and do little more. While she found the Samoans delightful and liked the island, we shared a mutual antipathy for such heat. Our spirits drooped with the daily rise in temperature and we had both seen too much of the slow but certain deterioration of white women long resident in the tropics. We were Nordics and it seemed our blood would never run thin enough to accommodate the heat.

The other choice was a return to Sausalito where I could at least attempt to make a living without writing. I knew the rules of seniority would make it impossible for me to return to any major airline, but perhaps there was something else?

We left Western Samoa reluctantly, for even in a short time we had made friends and the unspoiled, easy-going atmosphere captivated us. I had even made plans to resume a long-distance chess match with Lester Linsk, after exacting a promise that during this exile he wouldn't seek the secret assistance of restaurateur, his Imperial Highness Mike Romanoff, renowned as one of the most skillful players in the world and responsible for my continuous defeats while living in Switzerland.

Once I returned to Sausalito, friend Johnnie White helped me to find a unique job—"flying" the experimental British Hovercraft, which were to go on trial as possible ferries about San Francisco Bay. I was not involved when the first Hovercraft capsized, fortunately without injury to her abashed crew, but the incident was indicative of problems to come. The Hovercraft were sometimes close to unmanageable in high winds, and leaving the water they stirred up a terrible fuss of noise, dust, and loose debris. I was about to solo on one of these things when Lester Linsk called with a handsome offer to write a series for television. Since I would be paid a salary and not royalties subject to sharing, I immediately agreed and did not look back when I defected from the Hovercraft.

Once again with more income than outgo I still knew a feeling of deprivation. No matter how pleasant Bill Self, who was in charge of the television project, made my work, I snobbishly resented writing for television when I could be writing a book.

As with all television projects, there was a plethora of meetings and discussions joined by all manner of characters, each of whom must speak his piece lest his presence be eventually considered superfluous and the desk where he had tried to look busy be occupied by someone else. Only Bill Self expected himself from this obligatory shin-kicking and thus spared time and patience. Everyone and anyone is convinced he can write for television, and often does, which at least partly accounts for its quality. Network vice presidents, along with their minions, are the incapacitating venereal disease of creative writing and there is no known cure for its ravages. For a change I saved the money I was paid, thus being able when the project rolled over and died (as I suspected it would) to launch a second "back to the land" campaign. The first, I vividly recalled, had been attempted with Eleanor when I had left Manhattan and settled down writing in Quizz Marcum's barn. Perhaps a second five-year plan would do as well.

Dodie's serene performance during the Polynesian episode had left me convinced I could not live happily without her, so this time I inquired if she would mind returning to a very simple life instead of telling her she was going to be uprooted whether she cared to be or not. My plan was a typical masterpiece of incongruity, certain to be ridiculed by Walter Joe, who could add two and two, and would possibly be cheered by Eleanor's watchdog lawyer, whose ulcer, to my great disappointment, had not yet blossomed. We could fly the Piaggio northward until there was more wilderness than people and cement —British Columbia, I thought, might be about right. During the brief spell when I had been flying fishermen to Alaska I had flown over British Columbia only at night and knew nothing of it except as a part of Canada.

"I thought you wanted to live in the United States," Dodie said flatly.

"Well, Canada . . . is sort of different. Pine trees, wild-life, trout for breakfast every morning, elk, deer, cari-bou . . . Royal Northwest Mounted Police . . . sweet-smelling air."

"Doesn't it rain all the time?"

"What's a little rain? It freshens the soul . . . provides the abundance we need to live off the land."

"Do you know some land that will grow alimony? It's a crop you have to raise every month."

"It is my pleasure," I said grandly. Then I explained how, if we lived in a more frugal way, even half the royalties of a good book would be sufficient. "We will buy an old tugboat, run her up on a beach somewhere and presto . . . there is our instant home complete with steam heat."

"How can you afford a tugboat?"

"An old one can't cost much. We'll sell these homes, let the hippies have Sausalito to themselves, and breathe fresh air once again."

Chapter 43

I was shocked to see Vancouver was as large and busy as San Francisco. What kind of wilderness was this and where were the grizzly bears? We did find a few old tugs, all in advanced stages of rot and very expensive. Then a young real estate agent captured my imagination with the idea of buying an island. We climbed in the Piaggio, flew the length and breadth of Georgia Straits and in-spected several islands. The agent, I knew, was im-pressed with the Piaggio's fancy new paintwork and, since an identical aircraft* was owned by Aristotle Onassis, had obviously concluded I was several times a

* Onassis's son was later killed in it.

millionaire. Ten books could not pay for any of the islands he pointed out to our longing eyes.

Discouraged, we returned to Sausalito. There was a second flurry of television activity with the same negative results, but I did gather enough extra funds to inspire even more trouble.

"We've got to establish ourselves in the wide open spaces. Life is slipping by. Are we going to spend the rest of our days as cliff-dwellers . . . breathing the noxious gases of a city . . . paying these outrageous taxes?"

My last complaint was the most honest. Taxes on the Sausalito houses had been doubled in a single year. Unnoticed, except by students of the economy, inflation in America had begun to accelerate.

"We ought to sell out and buy a productive ranch. Now there's a life for a man and a woman! Back to horses and manure . . . flapjacks for breakfast . . . quiet except for the howling of an occasional coyote . . . good solid beef to eat free of charge—"

"I didn't know you knew so much about ranching," Dodie said.

"By God, it will be fine to mount a horse again," I said not hearing her.

We did have rancher friends, the Roths of Montana, and they tried their best to keep us unencumbered of some of the disaster real estate we were shown as "ranches." We looked at so many prospects I sometimes forgot whether we were in Montana, Colorado, or Nevada. At least Dodie had the good sense to wonder why so many were for sale. I have developed my own reservation; all were too far from the sea, and I doubted very much if I could live happily without being near salt water.

"How about Ireland?" Dodie suggested. "Everything there is close to the sea and we could raise donkeys."

"No. That's exile again. And sure enough I'd buy an Irish hunter, a big fellow . . . say seventeen hands . . . and break my neck jumping those stone fences. Very bad for writing."

Keegan Low, a friend in the real estate business, is a patient man and as our guest for dinner was one night obliged to hear out my determination to head for the woods. There were islands off the coast of Washington, he suggested, and he knew someone there who might have the answer to the difficult mixture of cattle and salt water.

Again the Piaggio bore us northward, but this time only as far as Seattle. Then north again for an additional eighty-five miles to an island named Orcas. All the time of our looking the weather was heavy with low clouds and so lacking in light even at high noon I wondered why we had ever left the California sun. "Heathcliffe!" I yelled, to the embarrassment of the real estate agent, "where are you?" At night Dodie claimed she heard the hounds of the Baskervilles.

Later, when we thought to inspect a nearby island known as San Juan, the weather turned even worse. The Piaggio became obstreperous when I tried to land on the little strip at Friday Harbor in a forty-knot wind. The rain sped past on the horizontal all day long and the small ranch we had come to see had only recently been bought by the very real estate agent who now displayed other "opportunities."

Now thoroughly disappointed, I thought to take Sam Buck the real estate man aloft as some recompense for his time and effort. By chance alone, we flew over the center of the island and he pointed out a farm which *might* be for sale. It was just over one hundred acres. I circled the farm once, more to oblige him than satisfy myself. Then, as if I bought land every day, I said casually, "Buy it if you can."

Two weeks passed and I had nearly forgotten where San Juan Island was when Sam Buck telephoned.

"Okay. You own a farm if you send the earnest money."

When I told Walter Joe I had bought a farm I had never set foot upon he said he would light special incense for me. "Wise man never throw money out of airplane windows. He keepum money until he feel fat of pig."

I was undeterred. Deliberately sketching independently of each other, Dodie and I began making drawings of the way we thought the little farmhouse looked inside. We also had the gall to sketch alterations we supposed would be necessary and planned for a return to the island within a week.

There was a delay. A friend in Pebble Beach called to

tell me Eleanor was ill and had been taken to the hospital. I left early the following morning and went straight to the hospital. She refused to see me. Worried, I resolved to stay nearby until she became more willing and to that end began sending a variety of presents and flowers to the hospital and arranged with the hospital office to pay all medical charges.

I took a room at a Carmel hotel and spent my waiting time in nostalgic little expeditions through the empty shell of a former life. I walked the hills of Pebble Beach where I had once so enjoyed riding with my father and I thought how pleased he would be if he knew I was the proprietor of a genuine farm. Later, with the new owner's gracious permission, I stalked the grounds of my father's house, saddened by the neglect of the gardens my mother had so loved, the more so when I saw that the lily pond in which so many guests had dropped coins for good luck was now filled only with withered leaves. The peacocks and pheasants were long gone from the wooded areas and most of the magnificent woodwork and splendid floors of Spanish tile in the house had been painted a bright pink. The stables where so many lavish parties had delighted the born host in my father were now rented as a residence and there was not a horse in sight. The land around it was about to be sold and together with the polo field transformed into a housing development. I spent one pleasant yet wistful evening with my stepmother, who had moved into a tidier house in the Del Monte Forest.

Driven by curiosity I ventured into the grounds of Island in the Sky and found there the same gardeners maintaining the exquisite beauty of the place. They joined with Eleanor in a commercial orchid business and were apparently delighted to see me. After a conducted tour of their beautiful landscaping they let me into the house, assuming, I supposed, it was my right. Sometimes it was difficult even for second-generation American-orientals to understand our divorce laws.

I stood motionless in the living room, vaguely uncomfortable. There was new furniture all about and a few lamps I could not recognize. The couch, worn to an overly weary look when I had last seen it, had been recovered. Several of my books were still on the shelves, but none I had written. The carved figure I had bought in Haiti was still in place. There was a new display of silver along the sideboard in the dining room and I remembered that Eleanor's beautiful mother had come to live for a while and I thought she must have brought the family silver with her. She had not long survived her stay. She had been among the very last of the clique my own mother and father had played with during the Roaring Twenties and I had always been very fond of her.

I saw that the carpet was new. Feeling like a burglar, I went to the porch and saw that the little cannon I had bought in Portugal and brought back to Eleanor was still on a side table. A small magnifying glass over the cannon's touchhole could be adjusted in combination with the azimuth of the carriage, causing the cannon to fire precisely at local noon. It was made in the seventeenth century and I had thought very highly of it. Why had I bought such an unfeminine gift for a woman like Eleanor? I should have known it would not interest her in the slightest.

I stood for some time watching the play of sunlight on the seas rolling into Carmel Bay adding the *yang* and subtracting the *yin* I had known since I last stood exactly so.

Later, reluctant but compelled, I entered the bedroom, moving almost on tiptoe as if fearing discovery. The bed was made up and all was orderly—the cleaning lady, I supposed, but she had left the sliding door to the long hanging closet open. I saw a multitude of dresses, far more in numbers then Eleanor had ever had when we were together. It pleased me to believe they must be giving her pleasure until I noticed several that had never been worn. The size and price tickets were still in place. Puzzled now, I entered the bathroom and saw at once what I had long suspected. The array of pill bottles was back, row upon row of pain-killers and sedatives and patent medicines for several varieties of ailments. I wondered how any sane doctor could have prescribed such an abundance of panaceas for a single patient. Checking the labels I discovered that several doctors had been involved, and that most of the prescription dates were recent. Nor were all of the drugs from the same pharmacy.

I left the house quickly and with melancholy, realizing I had made a mistake in returning to Island in the Sky. You cannot go back, I thought, you cannot revisit scenes of happiness lost and expect anything but disappointment. Unnoticed, the fruits of those times had been rotting for too long and I wanted desperately to look away now they had been exposed.

There was a message at the hotel: Eleanor would see me. I went at once to the hospital, where I found her sitting up in bed and looking much better than I had feared.

"I'm sorry to be so much trouble," she said cheerfully as I entered the room. Then she pointed at the four-foot stuffed panda bear I had sent as an ambassador. "You're crazy, but I love it," she said. "Do you mind if I give it to some child?"

"Why not keep it around for a while to remind you I care what happens to you?"

"And the flowers . . . the cymbidiums are lovely."

"Haven't I always warned you about using such language in mixed company?"

I saw a half-smile cross her face and then there fell a month of silence between us. I sought desperately for something to say that would be innocuous and I was sure she was doing the same thing. It seemed another era when we had met on the occasion of daughter Polly's elaborate wedding to Sam Fry, a young foreign service officer in Washington, and yet another age since Eleanor's dramatic entry into the courtroom. Now an ocean of petty grievances stood between us. Did I dare ask her how she managed to obtain so many drugs? And where were all the doctors whose names appeared on the bottles?

I studied the room, which faced on a green lawn. The usual clinically depressing atmosphere of a hospital had been cleverly disguised. "If you must be ill, this is certainly a pleasant place to be," I said lamely.

"It's lovely. And they're taking excellent care of me."

Since this was the first time I had ever heard Eleanor speak favorably about any of the innumerable hospitals in which I had sat beside her bed, I thought she must be feeling much better. I asked when she expected to leave.

"Not until Steven arrives. He will look after me."

"But he's in the Army."

"He's getting compassionate leave. It's all arranged."

"Oh . . . well . . . well . . ." My voice fell away with my thoughts. I had been allowed into this room as a stranger and it was obvious I would leave as a stranger. Neither my help nor company was wanted. Pride ruled all. I left soon afterward, marveling at my naïveté in expecting a more enthusiastic welcome.

It was almost another month before Dodie and I could return to the archipelago we had already begun to think of as home, although we had yet to set foot on the place we had bought. Spring had come to San Juan Island. The green fields so like rural England seemed to throb with the trilling of larks, and wildflowers in profusion were everywhere. Gordon Buchanan, the heavy-shouldered, gruff-voiced farmer who now held a fat mortgage for his land, welcomed us into our new domicile and poured a glass of his homemade mead. We sat talking in the kitchen as all good farmers do and Lorena, his wife, occasionally slipped a chunk of wood into a stove which had held a fire continuously since anyone could remember. The farm was very old and in need of repair, all of which I managed to ignore in my anxiety to commence a new life. The house was small, simple, and within it proved to be almost exactly as we had imagined. The Buchanans were frugal people; Gordon made almost everything he needed for the farm in his shop or smithy and advised us that his cash expenditure the previous year had been just over two hundred dollars.

An unexpected dividend of our new acquisition was the sweeping view of a lovely valley, with fields stretching to the distant Strait of Juan de Fuca. Beyond the iridescent water stood the snow-mantled Olympic Mountains. The magnificent panorama framed by dignified and fat old oaks held us enthralled. Would this paradise at last be home?

Wanting proper entry into paradise we soon recognized there were problems we had not taken into consideration. San Juan Island had a loosely estimated population of twelve hundred souls, most of whom were either related to each other or knew each other since childhood. Now we were planning to live in their midst and wanted least of all to be considered "off-islanders," which to the natives meant any visitor. The majority of islanders were simple, God-fearing people, fishermen, farmers, and small merchants—their numbers augmented in summer by a scattering of summer residents and tourists. In essence the island way of life was that of America in the thirties, an atmosphere we found as quaint as the low price of land. We longed to join these pleasant people without allowing our different backgrounds, and particularly my peculiar occupation, to form a barrier.

The solution was easier than we had thought. I took a job flying the archipelago for the small air-taxi company, heaving baggage, produce, and packages into little Cessna 172s along with the few passengers. It was two months before a Seattle paper caught on and printed a long featured story about the world-renowned author who was said to be the "richest pilot since Howard Hughes." Fortunately, I had by then been accepted as just another island newcomer trying to make a living. When my neighbors refused to believe such preposterous nonsense I knew I had been accepted.

Dodie made even better progress by taking a line job in the fish cannery. When the whistle blew she took off for long hours of standing in rubber boots and apron while stuffing cans with salmon. It was not the most pleasant work and the local ladies who worked in the same assembly line soon acknowledged her as one of them. In a few short months we had come as close to becoming "islanders" as any man or woman born elsewhere could become.

Once our new course was set I decided we should adjust our personal situation before our arrival on the island. One night in Sausalito while still packing for our grand exodus, I asked Dodie to make me a formidable martini. After much clearing of throat and waffling around the subject I broached a perilous matter.

"We are about to move into a different society. They are good people who read the bible and go to church on Sundays. Friday Harbor is a small town . . . we do not want to start this new life with our neighbors talking behind our backs. I don't think they will understand. . . . "

"Understand what?"

"Our relationship." I gulped a long swallow of the martini. "We've been together eleven years now . . . what would you say if I asked you to marry me?"

"You mean—?"

"In a church. All the trimmings." I was finding it difficult to breathe.

Dodie said, "I'll have to ask my mother."

I bowed very low from the waist and in my most formal tones declared that such a procedure would be appropriate. At last that good woman, who had fretted so long over the fate of her daughter, would be content.

Instinctively, we reached for each other and in our total silence we said all there was to say.

The ceremony took place in a small white church in Minden, Nevada, and was preceded and followed by events uncommon to most nuptials. Polly came west for the occasion, but George was at sea and could not officiate as best man. Lester Linsk was recruited to serve in his place. Dodie, surrounded by gushing bridesmaids, several of whom were worrying about the first hint of gray in their hair, was kept out of the prospective groom's sight. Polly, serving as a combination bridesmaid and sort of smiling field referee, kept assuring me I was "doing the right thing by our little Nell."

It was going to be a long day. I had hardly slept the night before from a mixture of excitement and anxiety; although I obviously had the approval of George and Polly, what about Steven who was now supposedly looking after his mother?

By noon the heat promised to set a Nevada record. Already perspiring in rivers I checked my watch so often the gesture had become a nervous twitch. Lester Linsk and I were sitting on a park bench not far from the hotel where the wedding party was quartered. He reached for my pulse. "You'll survive."

"Tell me about Hollywood. Tell me anything. I need distraction."

Casually, he began telling horror stories of his own recent divorce. As he intoned grim detail after detail, I closed my eyes and tried to recount all the wonderful qualities of my bride-to-be.

"Stop!" I cried out. "Shut up until it's all over. Just make sure you don't lose the ring. What time is it?" In spite of my watch-checking the actual time had not found a place in my crowded thoughts.

"One-thirty. Two hours and a half to zero hour."

"Dear God." I was thinking of the traditional pre-ceremony meeting Dodie and I had endured with the minister who would officiate. He was much younger than my children, but seemed unaware of any generation gap. At first both Dodie and I had some trouble controlling our amusement when he pointed out that it was beneficial to know the chosen mate well before joining in holy matrimony. We thought we qualified. When he began talking about our responsibility to each other as partners in life, I saw that Dodie's eyes were overwet and soon I found it necessary to wipe at my own. Finally he escorted us to the door, looked me straight in the eyes and said, as gravely as he might to an eighteen-year-old, "You realize this is a very serious step you are taking?"

"Oh I do, I *do!*"

The temperature stood at one hundred and two when the best man and his melting groom arrived at the church. Through the open doorway I heard the soft tones of an organ and I thought, my God is someone just practicing or are we going to have music along with everything else?

"Steady," Linsk cautioned as we entered the church.

The rest of the day became a contest between what little self-control I had retained and my emotions now stretched to their outermost limits. Never had I loved Dodie more than when I heard the voice I knew so well catch ever so slightly at her willingness to accept me as husband. I had intended my own response to be so strong it might rock the church, but my "I do" came out as an almost unintelligible squeak. When the young minister pronounced us man and wife and the organist struck up the wedding march with what sounded to me like wild abandon, I lost nearly all contact with the outside world. On the lawn outside the church I saw, through my tears of laughter and relief, the bride's bouquet tossed and caught by Dodie's mother, who outflanked the much younger spinsters present and clutched her prize with the determination of a Notre Dame end.

The official reception dinner lasted until darkness, which was a long time coming. When the last toast had been made we returned to the hotel where my eyelids drooped until I was nearly blind. Exhausted from such unique excitement I begged to be excused from any further festivities and retired to the same little single room I had occupied hours before as a bachelor. By chance Dodie had run full tilt into one of her old skiing comrades, a handsome fellow with the look of a true outdoorsman about him. Along with Lester Linsk and Polly they entered the hotel's gambling room and that was the last I saw of my bride until the following morning.

My turn came then as the pitiful remnants of our wedding party climbed into the Piaggio for the flight back to Sausalito. Dodie, somewhat the worse for a very late night, inquired if I regretted yesterday's main event. I reassured her with the flat statement that it had been the happiest day of my life. And thus began our new lives.

Chapter 44

Hemoglobin, 14.1. Hematocrit, 4Y. Red blood count, 5,100,000. No evidence of anemia. White blood count, 8,000. Thyroid function with a T-4 of 5.8. Alkaline phosphatase at 2.1 and blood cholesterol, 279. These were certain values governing the carcass in which I arrived on San Juan Island, where, almost at once, I began to see the rest of the world through different eyes.

As workmen began the remodeling of the farmhouse to meet our more sybaritic needs, I urged a venerable Stinson into the dawn, heading across the bays and channels of the archipelago toward Anacortes where the mail for the islands would be waiting. The aircraft was almost identical to those we had used for training twenty-eight years previously and the little Cessna 172s we flew on other missions throughout the islands were certainly not overpowered for the job. Unaccustomed to bush-flying, I tried to console myself with an ancient Chinese proverb, "When a blind cat meets a dead mouse . . . there you are."

When ten years previously I had been hanging from the *Albatros*'s mainmast seventy feet above deck and a supporting piece of rigging broke without the slightest warning, why had I not plummeted to my end? If I had not, within the micro-second of mortal time remaining, stabbed the middle finger of my right hand through a hole in a metal flange, then would George Ptatnik, the wonderful sea-cook I had not yet met and who later went down with the *Albatros,* still be alive? The hole was only a few millimeters larger than the circumference of my finger and it was doubtful if standing safely and securely on a steady base I could have hooked it so accurately. That perfect physical reaction which enabled me to hang on long enough to regain security with a turn of line around the mast had kept me alive to accomplish many things—one of which was the hiring of Ptatnik, who was soon dead. God, I thought, like so many great artists, is often a bad manager.

I knew these things happened in one form or another to everyone—it was only a question of time and recognition —but were we like the performers in the flea circus at Copenhagen's Tivoli Gardens? I came to know the mistress of that circus well because there had been considerable newspaper to-do upon our Copenhagen arrival in the *Albatros* and of all things she happened to be a reader of my books. When I attended her show she recognized my face and nothing would do but I must report to her little dressing room backstage after the performance. She had saved every clipping and displayed two of my books, one in Danish, of which she disapproved, and one in Spanish, her native tongue. Eventually she told me of fleas, and I returned several times in fascination. I learned how her performing fleas would act just about as expected, pulling tiny golden carriages and lifting incredible loads, until they would suddenly become temperamental and refuse to do a damn thing. My friend, a bosomy, dulcet-voiced lady with a tendency to philosophize, claimed that her fleas were just like people. "Every one of them thinks he is the only flea in the circus. They get the big head, you understand, and think they know everything."

While I was bush-flying for Roy Franklin, the genial proprietor of the little air-taxi-mail line, I tried to remember I was only another flea in his circus.

Remodeling the farmhouse took more than six months, nearly all of my bank account, and most of my patience. At last the day came for me to carry Dodie over the threshold, a ceremony heavy with sentiment and her frequent warnings to "be careful of your back!" Then in spite of having devoured a small library of agricultural books I thought it best to hire someone who really knew a heifer from a steer. He was a good and kind man, an ex-railroader, miner, carpenter, mechanic, clock-fixer, and farmer. He worked furiously, accomplishing more in four hours than most men in eight. Unfortunately for the first twenty animals I bought, he shared a reverence for the clock common with many ex-railroad men. He knew to the split second when noon and five o'clock arrived. He was never one minute late to work nor did he work thirty seconds overtime, a routine not always compatible to four-legged creatures. Yet he stayed on for three years rebuilding most of what we now called Red Mill Farm, repairing where it was crumbling, securing where it might blow away in the local strong winds. Gradually, as I could afford it, we bought more brood cows and by the time he decided he had enough of farming and of me, we had a small herd. I had not only learned the difference between a heifer and a bull, but how to pull a calf if necessary. I had also learned that my "live off the land" program was an impractical dream and I had best return to more lucrative work before it became a nightmare.

I wrote in a small wooden structure built of cast-off pieces from the old island schoolhouse. It had been used as a chicken brooding house and was up to my apparently inevitable specifications for an author at work, therefore being much too cold in winter and almost unbearably hot in summer. I first began a book of drawings which expired beneath my pen before I had finished. Alarmed at the ever-rising cost of a farm which I had so innocently believed would at least pay its own way, I asked for an advance from Simon and Schuster and began *Song of the Sirens*, a book about the seventeen boats I had owned. I dedicated the book "To son George, true man of the sea and stalwart shipmate."

Unfortunately, Henry Simon had fallen gravely ill and could not make his usual editorial improvements, but other less identifiable factors kept the book from becoming as complete a success as I had hoped. This time I did not blame myself; for once I believed the work well written, an opinion reinforced by the reviews. But Simon and Schuster were the wrong publishers for a book of its nature, they did not understand it and consequently were incapable of promoting it.

I was of little help in publicizing the book. During the past few years the obligations of all authors were changed by a new and onerous twist known as the television talk show. Suddenly authors who were anxious to promote the sale of their work were expected to become performers. They were asked to sit in a plastic chair while a television personality with, at best, a cursory acquaintance with the book, interviewed them between the praising of deodorants and laxatives. I found that the majority of television people behind the camera were like movie crews, solid and pleasant workers who treated visiting guests with the utmost consideration. "Personalities" before the camera were, in contrast, among the most insecure and arrogant people I had ever met. The single exception was Bob Cromie in Chicago.

I had long held to the belief that authors should be read and not seen or heard, for in exhibiting themselves they are bound to destroy illusions. At the urging of Simon and Schuster, who knew that television appearances sold books, I bounced from city to city becoming progressively disgusted with the forced jollity of talk shows and the snake-oil selling atmosphere which seemed to smother work to which I had given a fair portion of my life and much of my heart.

My subsequent refusal to continue as a performing bear was not helpful to the sales of *Song of the Sirens*. Even so it did well enough and my overall disappointment was eased by George, who was delighted with the work as were his many shipmates. Volunteering their professional opinion they agreed that the man who had written of their element had been there.

A vital key in the human regenerative process is our tendency to preserve the ways of our ancestors; though often unrecognized or even violently rejected, the continuity is always there and through the living generation is passed on to the newly born, making of the whole a timeless cycle. The son who proclaims he is not in the least like his father is lying to himself, and the rebellious daughter who vows she will become nothing like her mother is fighting an impossible battle.

As the relative tranquillity of island life combined with

the refreshing delight of marital happiness, I became aware of various developments within myself while the carcass remained almost the same. I forgave more easily and made conscious effort to view the problems of others from their perspective, rather than my own. These were habits of my father and my mother. The mellowing of age was not a factor; there had not been enough time. In fact the swift passing of four years on the island involved an opposite reaction. On impulse I bought a highly versatile aerobatic aircraft, a Bücher Jungman biplane used long before in training the German Luftwaffe. Powered with an American engine capable of sustaining flight while upside down as well as right side up, it became my wild joy to climb for the heights over Red Mill Farm and for an hour or more tear up the atmosphere in aerobatic maneuvers I had not attempted for thirty years. These aerial waltzes were especially satisfying in the late northern afternoons when the sun lingered just above the horizon and tinted the billowing swells of an overcast just below my wings a pale yellow ochre. Then, rolling, climbing, and diving, hanging from the security belts until my blood throbbed through my head, I was rejuvenated.

Although the slipstream provoked a cutting chill to my exposed hands and cheeks, my exertions combined with the changing positive and negative gravitational forces warmed my torso and aroused near-sexual satisfaction in vital parts. There were moments aloft during the very last of the twilight when I knew sheer ecstasy. Breathing deeply of the high wilderness I would whisper my gratitude for the skill still remaining in my hands, and for eyes capable of seeing into infinity though my brain could not comprehend it. Below in the dusk and soon to be joined was the woman of my very good life and there were moments when I knew such contentment I was tempted to shout in rapture.

I was never anxious or brooding when aloft; always it was as if I had come home to regions I knew as surely as the city-dweller does his block, the shepherd a side of a hill. The Bücher trembled and snarled when I commanded the more violent maneuvers, yet I never knew fear as I had occasionally as a pilot of the line. This was freedom known to only few men and I deeply regretted each time it had to end. Separated from the planet by a deck of cloud, utterly alone with sky and machine I felt a new peace, as if all that had happened to the carcass now sitting on a hard parachute pack and strapped so tightly to the Bücher's frame had been but a prelude to a life continuing indefinitely.

When I returned to earth just at darkness I would shut down the engine and sit for a few minutes without moving. I would pull off my helmet and rub at the places where my goggles had pressed too hard and rub my hands together to restore circulation. I sat waiting for my spirit to rejoin me on earth, because always it seemed I had left it on some cloud and I would listen to the tinking metal of the engine as it cooled and wonder at my extraordinary good fortune. For a little while at least I had forgotten my concerns about what the Vietnam war was doing to my country, the writing of books, Eleanor's unpredictable health, and the apparently never-ending need for me to keep working.

Once returned to the solid earth of Red Mill Farm and the welcome of Dodie and the durable Felix, I would find further relaxation in reading books rather than in writing them, a direct heritage from my father. Like him, I kept a large supply handy and constantly replenished my library. One night I came upon an archaeological report on Masada by Israel's redoubtable Yigael Yadin and at once became lost in the Judean desert. I had never heard of Masada, where nineteen hundred years earlier the Jews of Palestine had made such a gallant stand against the Romans.

Longing to know more about the mountaintop of Masada I encountered a series of frustrations. I queried several of my Jewish friends who had "heard of" Masada, but were vague about its significance. A search of the Seattle library revealed almost nothing about Masada except relatively brief mention of its siege and the subsequent mass suicide of the defenders as described by Josephus, a Jewish general who had previously defected to the Romans. Later I discovered that Josephus's report on these tragic events was to be valued as little more than hearsay since he had never been to the mountain and confessed to gathering his facts from two old women who supposedly had survived the final debacle.

Now with my curiosity thoroughly aroused I went to

602

New York where I met with Peter Schwed, Simon and Schuster's publisher, who *had* heard of Masada, but was as fuzzy as all the other Jews I had questioned about the details. "What do you think," I asked Schwed and his assembled colleagues, "of a goy writing the Valley Forge of the Jews?" A ripple of polite laughter followed and no one present voiced any of the objections I had expected, such as recommending I mind my own business and leave such grand tales to my betters—say Herman Wouk or Leon Uris.*

I could hardly believe my research when I found that no one had ever before thought to novelize a story so saturated with drama. All of my instincts were now bristling as I followed the spoor of a story which left me in such awe of my inadequacy I nearly retreated to Red Mill Farm. I was not overworried about my ability to handle the besieger, Roman General Silva, and his legions; there would always remain those heavy marks on my brain inflicted by reading Caesar in Gaul in Latin at the impressionable age of twelve and my subsequent studies of Roman civil and military life during my years as a cadet. But the Jews! How could a WASP possibly reflect their culture and thought with any integrity? The obvious solution was to learn a great deal more about Jews than my superficial experience had offered.

First I immersed myself in Hebrew literature and history until I had finally assembled a small yet respectable library on the subjects. Then I booked passage for Dodie and myself on an immigrant ship bound for Israel, thereby participating in one of the craziest voyages ever to sail out of New York harbor.

The ship was the ex-*Kungsholm*, a former luxury liner once under the Swedish flag. Now the *Olympic*, she was required to return to Greece for maintenance and inspection by Lloyd's. The owners thought to make a profit by transporting American Jews who had decided the time had come for their permanent return to the Promised Land.

The owners were apparently determined not to spend one more drachma than necessary out of their native land and as a result the *Olympic* sailed in woeful condition. She

* Uris later switched the switch by writing of the Irish in his book *Trinity*.

was very short on victuals for either of the two dining rooms and the Orthodox Jews complained that the kosher food was not always so kosher. She sailed short on fuel, which caused a reduction in speed to maximum economy cruise and forbade the drag of her stabilizers. Thus she rolled along abominably at twelve knots, hardly more than a steel barrel adrift upon an ocean perversely inclined to turbulence.

Once well at sea, where the passengers were less likely to mutiny, the travesty of a relaxing sea voyage commenced. The magnificent Scandinavian woodwork, which had so distinguished the very ship in which my father had cruised extensively in her grander days, had been preserved. Now, preparing for Lloyd's inspection, a "wrecking gang" of a half-dozen crewmen would herd passengers aside and remove a mahogany panel from behind their heads, a carved balustrade from a staircase, or a part of the ceiling. When lifeboat drill was called we reported to our assigned stations with the utmost dispatch, and I thought, . . . with good reason.

Yet the general chaos was peaceful in comparison with the more lively days in the ship's synagogue where daily classes in Hebrew were given to those immigrants who could speak only English or Yiddish. When I asked if Dodie and I could attend the classes we were welcomed and I was given a black skullcap to conform with synagogue custom. The instructor was a bright young man paid by the Israeli government to teach the national language now lost to most American Jews, and thereby ease their immigration adjustment. He was beset with problems from the first hour of the first class, and we thought his patience with his often obstreperous pupils magnificent.

Hebrew is a difficult language for Westerners if only because the Semitic syllables are pronounced deep in the throat and the sounds bear no relation whatever to Nordic- or Latin-based diction. Everything—grammar, tense, pronunciation, even rhythm—is so different, the beginner must start as a baby learning to express first desires. For me it took longer to learn the correct pronunciation of a single word in Hebrew than a whole sentence in French, German, Italian, Spanish, or even Japanese. Challenged, we were determined to excel and after strict attention during the morning classes in the synagogue we spent the afternoon practicing our homework. The majority of our classmates took a different attitude, ranging from argumentative clashes with the instructor to silent despair. Many were elderly and had great difficulty in forsaking their accustomed Yiddish for a language they had hitherto thought buried in the Talmud or Torah. Another group of middle-agers were from Los Angeles and spent most of their time arguing among themselves or correcting the instructor's English despite the very obvious fact that it was better than their own.

There was only a handful of young people, all very bright and serious. With them we sometimes practiced the most elementary conversation. "It is a nice day . . . I would like a glass of orange juice."

On the last day in the synagogue Dodie and I took the written examination and later the oral. We were immensely proud to have achieved the highest marks of any students in our class. I was very touched when I handed my little skullcap back to the instructor and he said he would like me to keep it as a graduation present.

I knew it would be impossible to learn even elementary Hebrew in two weeks, but my brief exposure did give me some flavor of the people for whom Israel had been home ever since the first Diaspora and it seemed to keep me in key with ancient Palestine during the writing of *The Antagonists*.

There are uncertainties and surprises in any literary adventure. I wanted to fly from Jerusalem to Masada, thereby gaining a buzzard's-eye view of the Judean desert and the general relation of the mountain itself to the rest of what had been Roman Palestine at the time when Eleazar, the Jewish leader, defied General Flavius Silva. After some trouble I was given the telephone number of a charter outfit in Tel Aviv, Wings of Israel.

I called from our hotel room and was immediately taken aback by the voice on the other end of the line.

"Hi, y'all!"

There had obviously been a mistake. The hotel operator must have plugged me into an overseas call to someplace in Mississippi.

"Do you-all do charter flying?" Wings of Israel, indeed.

"Sho 'nuff. Where y'all wanta go?"

"Masada."

"Where?"

"Masada. Don't tell me you've never heard of it."

"Oh . . . yeah. That's where they swear in our Air Force officers."

"It has also been the scene of a few other important events."

I told him my name, spelling carefully. There followed a long silence.

"Y'all ain't the man who wrote *Fate Is the Hunter?*"

I was so touched that I confessed. Modesty is too easily buried by authors recognized thousands of miles from home base.

Next morning, Dodie and I, with rucksacks containing lunch for three, waited at the rarely used Jerusalem airport.

At nine o'clock I saw a Cessna 172 land and soon afterward a man eased himself to the ground. He was wearing cowboy boots and a ten-gallon hat and, as we shook hands, a most warming smile. "Wal I'll be jiggered," he said. "I didn't really think y'all was real."

Jerry Renov offered to let me do the flying and I accepted instantly because I wanted to experience landing an aircraft thirteen hundred feet below sea level, at the lowest point on earth. About an hour later I put the Cessna down on a strip running parallel to the shore of the Dead Sea, thus automatically qualifying as one of Renov's "submarine aviators." When the engine was shut down the silence of the desert became so overwhelming we found ourselves talking in near-whispers. There were no structures of any sort along the airstrip and, it appeared, no other humans in the desert.

Shouldering our rucksacks we began a hike I could easily visualize as having been made by Flavius Silva's legionnaires nineteen hundred years before. The scorching heat was already creating mirages to the south and the hard Judean hills seemed to shudder beneath the hammering of the sun. Masada, looming majestically by itself, stood gray-ochre on the horizon, a massive rock apparently on skids, for half an hour's hiking brought it no closer. I tried to forget the baking heat by parading my recently acquired knowledge before Dodie and Renov—finding it easy to let them believe I knew much more than I did. I told them how Cleopatra had offered to seize and present this land to her lover Mark Antony and how Herod had built a palace atop Masada as a refuge to cool himself in summer while at the same time creating an impregnable fortress should the very real prospect of his subjects' rebellion mature.

At last we came upon the base of the mountain and paused at a hostel for refreshment. The place was now deserted except for a single girl who waited behind a snack bar. There the glorious moment I had been waiting for presented itself. Making sure Renov could not miss a syllable, I ordered in Hebrew three orangeades. When the girl promptly brought out the drinks I could not bear to remove the look of respect from Renov's eyes by confessing how little more I knew of his national tongue.

After a short rest we felt the terrible power of the sun again as we commenced the long ascent of Masada's eastern face via a route known as the snake path.* Over these very stones, I thought, followers of Eleazar had once ascended to their doom. With pauses for breath and to wipe the sweat from our eyes we were nearly two hours ascending to the summit.

Once on top I found everything as I had pictured it, thanks to Yigael Yadin's masterful research and book. Yet a further dividend awaited as we put down our rucksacks and began chewing thoughtfully on our sandwiches. For some unknown reason, perhaps the season and time of day, we were the only humans visible on Masada and the silence was broken only by the soft brushing of the wind and our own slight movements. Where I had expected guides and chattering groups of tourists there was nothing but the eloquent ruins and a few buzzards riding the thermals high overhead. Far below, outlined by rubble and preserved by the desert climate, were the camps of General Flavius Silva, who had disappeared from history once Masada had fallen. The great attack ramp he had caused to be built by multitudes of Jewish slave labor was still a mountain itself. With my eyes wide open I could see the Roman catapults being dragged up the ramp and assault troops of the famous 10th Legion moving upward protected by their "turtle-backs." I could hear Eleazar calling down insults to Silva and the

---

* Fortunately for my purposes, the teleferic had not yet been constructed.

Roman's haughty reply, just as clearly as the acoustical phenomenon had been said to be. All the rest of the day while we prowled the ruins of Herod's palace, later converted to the uses of Eleazar's zealots, I was haunted with a sense of not being alone.

The eerie dreamlike trance I seemed incapable of breaking continued until the sun mellowed and disappeared in a final conflagration behind the western hills. Throughout the crumbling ruins, the baths, and great cisterns which had supplied ancients with water, I felt accompanied, not by a specific person, but by a constantly changing series of specters who were trying to tell me something. Again and again I denied the sensation; it was utter nonsense of course, a fringe of madness brought on by too much exposure to the sun and an overworked imagination. Yet it was there, undeniably, and it held with me as at last we descended the snake path, now cooling in shade.

I brooded all the way back to the aircraft and declined Renov's offer to fly. I wanted only to think about the great mountain behind us, the Roman camps occupying the surrounding terrain, and the last-minute appearance of a guard who charged us a few dollars for the visit and handed us tickets in return. It was he who had been unreal.

The Antagonists did very well in all the usual categories and drew only one condemnation from a female reviewer in Boston who was furious because a Gentile had written the story of Masada. Once again I was persuaded into a nationwide television tour and soon took an oath in my own blood I would never do it again. Then just as I returned to the tranquillity of Red Mill Farm I had a phone call from my son Steven. The continued use of various drugs had caused a failure of the lymph glands and his mother was dead.

Chapter 45

With the passing of Eleanor's life there went a part of my own. Nor could I escape a sense of guilt, despite our now long separation. If I had refused to leave when she asked and perpetuated the sham of our marriage would she still be alive? I lamented not for myself, but for a woman I thought had been accursed since the earliest days of her existence. Her father had been killed flying an airplane, when, at fifteen, she had perhaps needed him the most. Her brother killed himself with a gun. The son who was the last of her children had lived only a few days. She was afflicted with innumerable physical debilities culminating in the terrible disease which killed her. She had only beauty and intelligence—not enough in my opinion to balance her fortune. Where now was the proof of my long-nurtured theory that every joy bore a penalty and every penalty a joy?

I sat between my sons George and Steven at the funeral. There were some twenty other people attending; the majority I did not know. At least the ceremony was minimal, which I knew would have pleased the woman we had come to honor. I grieved for all of us who were so suddenly face to face again with our mortality. A day, a month, another ten years—who knew how long? To distract my morbid thoughts I kept trying to weigh Eleanor's life, and each time failed. Perhaps, I thought, there were compensations unknown to me or others I had failed to recognize.

The tremendous contrast between Eleanor's life and my own now obliged me to take new inventory, the better, I hoped, to form a scheme for future conduct. I had always seen God in the manifestations of nature, the droplet of dew in the throat of a flower, the emergence of a butterfly from a cocoon, the return of the hummingbirds, and the echoing and reechoing hoots of the owls resident on my farm. I had always seen more of the divine majesty in the hammering of a thunderstorm than in any religious structure or graven image. For the one life we each enjoyed I did not believe we should be grateful to some vague father-figure in a beard and white robe, yet my yearning to express gratitude, generally aimed for lack of surer direction at the sky, was usually unsatisfying. Should I look up at a cloud and whisper, "Thanks for preserving me one more day," or should I look down at the roots of a mighty tree which I believed was just as alive as anyone else I knew? Now, stepping ever more gingerly, seeking answers I knew would never be entirely revealed, I tinkered and fussed with the general scheme of things until I became convinced that all of us live in the outer pavilions of heaven and hell and whether or not we pray to our private divinity is of no consequence to the pattern. In an exchange of letters with Bill Sloane on my esoteric researching, I wrote, ". . . I am not talking about predestination or anything of the sort. But it strikes me as fascinating how so often my own rather rousing life has been influenced by even momentary contact with certain individuals . . . why was it the DC-3 I flew to Western Samoa without incident crashed six months later killing the three crew members who were on a training flight? The door came off. . . . I believe these things (in different ways of course) happen to everyone and I find myself wishing I were several thousand people so I could prove it."

Sloane, true as ever to the target, responded, "Your last letter is full of sentences which read, *all of this marks any man's or woman's life*. Of course it does . . . It is a truism of almost thunderous banality in certain hands and perhaps misused. If you mean by some of this philosophical disquisition that in retrospect certain scenes and events have a clarity of presentation on the screen of memory, I will agree to that . . . some of the things we have forgotten and do not come to mind when we are thinking back have been proved to have as much power over the shaping of our lives as anything that can be brought easily into the light. Believe me, the headshrinkers live off this simple fact."

Before this kind of brooding got me into deep trouble I saw a chance for a complete change of mental gears and went to it with wild enthusiasm. Two friends, both encountered by chance, led me to the entrance—this time to NASA's Apollo program. They were the incomparable Bob Hoover of North American Rockwell, who was (and still is) one of the greatest pilots the world has ever known, and the buoyant Walker Mahurin, World War II and Korean War ace. Both men worked for the same giant corporation then engaged in manufacturing the rocket engines and many other components for the Apollo program, and both understood I was a frustrated astronaut.

While I would gladly have given ten years of my life to go to the moon I had seen thirty years too many to qualify. Thus I was obliged to be content with simulation, a restriction which did not keep me from becoming lost in space for the next two months. For that period of time I forsook sailing terms like *luffing, jibing, wearing,* and *tacking,* put aside aviation's *side-slip, whip-stall, aileron, elevon,* and *empennage,* and larded my vocabulary with *nano-seconds, translunar injection* (TLI), *coeliptic sequence initiation,* and a host of acronyms to save spittle and another fracture of my jaw. Thanks to Dr. Thomas Paine, ex-submariner and then chief of NASA, I was allowed to "fly" the simulators of the command module and the Lunar landing craft. I suited up in Neil Armstrong's standby suit and walked vicariously on the surface of the moon. Before Apollo 13 finally roared off into space with Lovell as commander and Haise beside him, I told friend Jack Swigart, the command module pilot, I would be suited up and standing by on the gantry when he slipped on the banana peel I had placed in his path to history.

I was unbelieving when someone predicted I would cry at the actual launching of the world's greatest firecracker. Thanks to Ben James of NASA I stood as close to the towering Saturn as anyone was allowed to go. While presidents and kings watched from miles away, the press (apparently considered expendable if anything went wrong) was close enough to feel the physical impact of the sound and cringe at the incredible forces driving Apollo 13 out of sight. I actually wept and gasped for air, a stunned mite of a man trying to believe I was the same human who had flown in the time of helmet and goggles and now beheld a brave penetration of our universe. When Apollo 13 ran into trouble while well on the way to the moon I fretted all through the days and slept uncertainly until the crew was safely back on earth. Astronauts were the last of our heroes aloft and we needed them all.

The solitary working life of a writer had always pleased me, for to be alone is a privilege, the impossible becomes possible and the dreams of those unhampered by the opinions of others may soar without limit. A person who cannot find stimulation and company in the characters created or recorded by his pen is bound to have such trouble as a working author that the production of anything worth reading is unlikely. The only honest collaborator is faith in self, an attitude best maintained when alone.

Unfortunately, the physical inactivity necessary to writing has often been prolonged torture for me. I have tried everything to lose the psychosomatic afflictions which homestead in my carcass whenever a writing project is in work. If it is not my aching back it is my legs, or my wrist, arm, ears, even nose. My eyelids quiver. I grind my teeth. My toes hurt and in the middle of a difficult paragraph I may become as horny as a satyr. Trying everything to alleviate these symptoms I write standing, tipped back in a leather chair, bent over my desk, very upright in a resurrected barber's chair, and sitting on the floor. I cannot dictate even a sensible letter and find that a typewriter, despite my touch system ability, is an agreeable tool only for certain subject matter. It seems easiest to write longhand in notebooks and hire some resourceful, clever, and patient girl to transfer my scrawling to a typed page. And still the physical complaints continue, ceasing miraculously once a project is completed.

I have made various attempts to curb my rebellion against the forced confinement obligatory for any author. At one time I tried chaining myself to a chair, securing the links with a padlock and pitching the key to the other side of the room. The physical effort involved in scooting the chair across the room provided exercise and discouraged attempts at escape. One day I threw the key with too much force, and it bounced off the arm of a chair and vanished. Later, when I needed to go outside and relieve myself I clambered around on my hands and knees searching anxiously for the key. Since the chair was still attached to my backside I hoped no one would intrude. When I had nearly decided I would be wearing the chair until a locksmith could be summoned, I found that the key had somehow dropped through the grill of a floor ventilator and was just within reach.

Every six months my need for physical relief became so overwhelming, something had to be done regardless of the current literary endeavor. Various options were usually available and upon accepting one invitation I came to Clovis, New Mexico for the first time. Near Clovis was Cannon Air Force Base, where a squadron of F-III fighter-bombers was stationed. They were the first "variable geometry" aircraft made operational in our Air Force and, for reasons no one could determine exactly, had acquired a grim reputation.

"What? You're going to fly an F-III? Have you checked your will lately?"

"I wouldn't if I were you."

"No one will ever get me in one of those swing-swing things."

These were typical encouragements to the venture, and they were made all the more disturbing because they were offered by pilots whose judgment I respected. Yet when I asked if they had ever flown an F-III or even seen one, the answer was always negative. At that time the F-III was the fastest aircraft in the world and such a thorn in the backside of the Soviets that they did everything they could to damage its reputation. All of these factors demanded my better acquaintance with such a controversial and scandalous device, even as a beautiful woman with one unexplained black eye becomes irresistible. When Colonel "Chuck" Francis, commander of the 27th Tactical Fighter Wing, explained I must first attend school before I would be allowed to fly in such exotic company, I volunteered to become his servant for as long as necessary.

Despite my hours in aircraft powered with reciprocating engines I had very little time in jets, let alone an 80,000-pound behemoth with two engines and retractable wings. At Cannon I settled into ground school and flew the F-III simulator under the tutelage of Tom Wheeler, a patient, brave lieutenant colonel who had known the aircraft since it had first been in production. He was tall and blue-eyed, quiet-spoken and dedicated. He also possessed the magic quality of inspiring confidence and said he felt he knew me. When I asked why, he explained he was a very good friend of my ex-navigator and commercial fishing partner Paul LaFrenier.

As warming-up exercise I flew the T-33, a single-engine jet trainer of rather sedate ways, and then, with a red-hot young major riding along as flight instructor, the F-100, a projectile shaped vaguely like an airplane and wearing wings of so little dimension I wondered if most of the machine had not been left in the hangar. While I had done very well with the lazy T-33 I was always seconds behind the F-100 and never did manage to keep the wings continuously horizontal. I was told how in time I would get the hang of it; meanwhile I was relieved to be transferred to a very much larger aircraft, the much-maligned One-Eleven.

A chill prairie gale swept across the flatlands surrounding Cannon Air Force Base and the pale New Mexico sky looked more like sheet-iron than a blue heaven worth the vaulting now at hand. I had been briefed for an hour on our mission, which would consist of demonstrating the One-Eleven's capabilities first hand.

Although I had already spent hours studying the controls and systems in the One-Eleven cockpit and was reasonably familiar with its profile, the great brown and green bird looked much larger to me on this morning. It seemed to be hunkered down on its very belly, a creature of enormous power waiting to make a clown out of a Rip Van Winkle aviator. As we mounted the ladders to the cockpit I could only think how this long sword had cost the American taxpayers eighteen million dollars. And where would I hide if I put a dent in the blade? Although I could not detect any increase in my pulse rate I did behave with the elaborate casualness of the hopeful but uncertain as we strapped ourselves in our seats. Tom Wheeler went through our emergency procedures once more. Parachutes were not worn in a One-Eleven, which contributed greatly to the physical comfort of the two-man crew. If disaster seemed imminent, an explosive charge could be activated; the entire control capsule then separated instantly from the main body of the aircraft and, floating under its own parachute, would descend gently to earth.

"Or so it is supposed to be," Wheeler said with a grin.

During taxi for take-off I relaxed. The One-Eleven was a big aircraft with its wings extended, yet it handled like a baby carriage. The take-off was reasonably accomplished, thanks to Wheeler's soothing voice leading me through all the procedures I had memorized and now forgot as the tremendous power of the afterburners left me mentally still on the runway while we were climbing through five hundred feet. I recovered soon enough to retract the wings and climb to the north on a steady course. I found the flight controls almost sensual and the One-

Eleven's smooth response as lively as my little Bücher. It was difficult to believe my movements were only feed for a computer which instantly calculated all the parameters of weight, speed, altitude, and balance, and supplied the necessary movement to the external control surfaces.

New Mexico sank into the haze. I leveled off at twenty-two thousand feet, made one circle, and was so pleased with the One-Eleven's docility I asked Wheeler if I might try a slow roll.

"Why not?" Wheeler, I thought, was absolutely nerveless. He seemed to be laughing within himself.

I took a deep breath hesitating at even the idea of rolling over eighty thousand pounds around the sky. Why could I not have been content with a nice little tourist flight?

On the first roll I lost nearly three thousand feet. "Sorry about that," I said into the intercom.

"Try another."

The second roll went much better, the third erased my shame, and the fourth was so pleasant and reassuring I wanted to continue for the rest of the morning.

"This is like popcorn. I can't stop."

Wheeler smiled in understanding. He was a man sharing a love with another of his stripe. There are few more intimate moments between men.

"I'd like to try a four-point roll."

"Go . . ."

I rolled to the vertical, hesitated, continued to full-inverted, hesitated, and repeated the performance around until the sky and the earth were returned smartly to their proper places.

"How about an eight-point?"

"Go."

I repeated, this time hesitating at eight points around the circle, amazed at the sweet behavior I found in a strange aircraft. For good measure I did a few Cuban-eights and said at last I had enough.

"Take a breather then. Will go TRF." Wheeler engaged the complex autopilot and we began a long descent for the distant Sangre de Cristo mountains. We had been aloft less than an hour and I already felt at home. As the state of New Mexico rose rapidly toward us my relaxation was soon to be shaken.

The feature of the One-Eleven most disliked by the Soviets was its ability to intrude at high speeds and very low levels—a hundred feet and even lower—making it difficult to pick up on radar, and defending fighters would have trouble overtaking it without diving into the ground. During low-level attack the autopilot took over the controls, a device so sensitive to its on-board radar it could avoid even such relatively small objects as fences, powerlines, boulders, and bridges. One-Eleven crews staked their lives on their TFR—Terrain Following Radar. Now it was my turn and I had been promised free martinis in the officers' club if I successfully resisted reaching for the controls.

Minutes later the eastern slopes of the Sangre de Cristos were rushing toward us. Imitating Wheeler I took a deep breath and folded my arms. I noted the airspeed—480 knots (555 miles per hour). I became fascinated with our rapidly decreasing altitude—one thousand, eight hundred, four hundred . . . it was a bad dream I had sometimes known when I overindulged in Mexican food! The rusty surface of the mountains filled the windshield and, I thought, squirming uneasily, would be in my lap after ten more seconds.

I longed to haul back on the stick, but glancing at Wheeler saw him yawn. At two hundred feet the One-Eleven magically leveled itself and began a climb to match the rising terrain. We dipped into a canyon and rose again. Barn-sized boulders flew past. Just as I decided no martinis were worth this strain and thought to suggest a higher altitude I saw Wheeler take out a worn Esso road map of the vintage we had flown with in open cockpit days. He held it before his face like a newspaper and pretended to study it anxiously. He could not possibly see ahead.

"What the hell are you doing?" I asked in shock.

"Trying to find out where we are."

"We're sitting on millions of dollars' worth of navigational equipment and you have to use an Esso map? Let me out of here!" I remembered all the failures of automatic pilots I had known. Now my helmet suddenly weighed a ton and my interest in the martinis became lost in the fast-moving panorama ahead. Yet in front of Wheeler I could not betray my uneasiness. When I saw a trace of a smile about his mouth I felt better. The Esso map was an act inspired by Chuck Francis. They were going to give this tenderfoot's nerves special attention and I became more determined than ever to make them pay for my martinis. I formed my dry lips into a whistling position and pretended to enjoy the all too immediate scenery.

With uncanny accuracy the One-Eleven climbed the side of a great mountain, surmounted the crest, then started down the other side into a narrow valley. The sensation of being aboard a roller coaster with an invisible genie in charge was now so stunning I no longer cared if the next hump in the terrain was obviously not going to move out of the way. If I must die in New Mexico I had no particular objection; seen from a greater distance it might be nice country.

"I suppose you get used to this sort of thing?"

"Not at night when it's raining. Then sometimes I wish the mission was over."

West of the Sangre de Cristos we sped over open country. Wheeler suggested I take the controls. We would climb to forty-five thousand feet and begin the high-speed run. New Mexico sank again.

We were over Albuquerque when I dipped the One-Eleven's long snout to the vague horizon and leveled off. Wheeler added more power and the instruments quivered slightly as we passed through the speed of sound. The mach meter rose with the One-Eleven's skin temperature. We passed Mach One point three, point five . . . eight . . . nine . . . Mach Two . . . two point one . . . and paused at two point three—approximately 1,270 miles per hour. Because of our height there was no sensation of great speed; the earth slid past below at only a slightly faster pace than when seen from an ordinary jet. When the skin temperature reading approached the red line maximum Wheeler told me to cut back the power. Clovis was already in sight as I began descent.

Once over Cannon I spent the balance of my time with the superb One-Eleven doing touch-and-go landings and take-offs. I found it easy going. Because of the One-Eleven's forgiving nature all went extremely well and I finally taxied to the ramp with the very special sensation known only to aviators who have had a perfect day.

Chuck Francis had assembled a small crowd that embarrassed me with congratulations. I demanded my free martinis and was very jolly indeed until a burly, hard-jawed crew chief approached me. Pointing up at the One-Eleven's huge tail he growled unhappily, "Look what you done."

I looked up at the tail and groaned. The very fancy logo of the 27th Fighter Wing was torn and scorched until it was barely recognizable. This was how I repaid the generous hospitality of my new friends? I had held supersonic speed too long and the resulting friction between air and aircraft skin had built up so much heat the logo had nearly burned away.

"Oh, I'm damned sorry . . . terribly sorry. Can I buy a new one? What can I do?"

The crew chief let me stew in remorse for a long moment. I could only think I had made an unforgivable error. People would be polite of course, because they were gentlemen and wanted me to write nice things about the aircraft they believed the best in the world, but I would be known as the man who had carelessly burned their proud standard and reasons would be found for my early departure.

I started a further apology when the crew chief placed his hand on my shoulder. And I saw he was grinning mischievously. "Don' worry yourself, man. It happens every time these birds go supersonic. It's only a decal and we have a hangar full of them."

I came very near embracing a crew chief.

These were the perks of an author, some compensation for his self-discipline and those countless hours when removed from his fellow man he must be his own advocate and judge. These were the minor diversions I usually covered in magazine pieces to ease a very real sense of guilt. Some irrepressible alter ego invariably appeared to gnaw at my spirit the instant I accepted a frivolous invitation. "I can only spare three days . . . a week from today I am due to . . . I'd like very much to postpone things until I've finished writing . . ."

The postman delivers a letter, the customs officer clears a ship, the seamstress mends a torn garment, all because of their being needed as individuals. Since their work is usually routine there is no conflict between what they have done and what has been left undone. They exist. Their jobs exist. Very well then, go to it and at the end of toil know the sleep of the needed.

One of the heaviest burdens of an author's life is the sneaking suspicion he is not professionally needed, much less his works. The world he observes when he dares venture afield is obviously smothering in books and why should anyone trouble to pay good money for his? This sense of emptiness turns to melancholy when a book fails to attract the attention its parent thinks proper, and if the author has any sense at all creates near-despair after the first exhilaration of acclaim. How can such bouncing success be repeated?

My somewhat erratic solution has been the seizing of escape whenever available. I flew the Goodyear blimp *Columbia* for thirty-three hilarious hours between Seattle and California. With Dodie and a great mixed company of lively souls, including Robert Fraser of the North Atlantic and the Sausalito "boat" house, I spent eight days threading the Colorado River on a life raft. I spent almost as many aboard the aircraft carrier *Constellation* living like a lord of the oceans and making four arrested landings. I have flown to Mexico's Scammon Lagoon to watch the whales breed and to Alaska's North Slope to observe the oil wells likewise proliferating. One summer, nostalgic for more exciting times over the North Atlantic, I entered the Great London–Victoria, B.C., Air Race with Dodie as my co-pilot. The eastbound flight to the starting line at Abingdon, England, was particularly satisfying because I could show the woman who now shared my life such locales as Goose Bay, the haunting fjords of Greenland, Reykjavik, and Scotland. During our approach to Narssarssuaq on Greenland's western coast the weather turned quite as foul as we so often found it during World War II. Using the same landmarks and methods we then employed, I worked our Cessna 310 up the correct fjord nicely sandwiched between a two-hundred-foot ceiling and very large icebergs. During this transit up the fjord, which I well remembered as nerve-wracking for first-timers, it amused me to hear my normally impervious wife address me as "Sir."

Lester Linsk had become a producer in his own right and hence was not involved in the sale of *The Antagonists* to the movies. I cheered his new career and missed his counsel. I was not interested in writing the screenplay, partly because much farther away another matter beckoned me to leave the peace of Red Mill Farm. An airliner had crashed on approach to Taipei, Taiwan. While many passengers were killed, a most unusual circumstance had occurred. The flight crew survived with only minor injuries. As if their miraculous escape were not enough, the Chinese government arrested the crew for criminal negligence—an unheard-of procedure, and as developed later, entirely without foundation. The professional flying world was horrified at such arbitrary arrogance and our fury mounted when it became known the crew were already under house arrest and stood a very real chance of going to prison for their "crime." Thinking I might bring my pen to their aid through international publication of their story, I took off for Taiwan and once again various lines in my grand diagram of events and people became joined. For I was welcomed at Taipei airport by none other than Tom Boyd, once of American Airlines, and his wife Helen, who had flown with me many times as a stewardess. It had been Boyd who had first introduced me to the DC-3 and Boyd in a major's oak leaves who first greeted me at Labrador's Goose Bay. Now Boyd was vice president of the line whose long and brilliant record had been marred by the recent crash. After our standard fare of insults on reunion he offered every cooperation.

Almost simultaneously more powerful swords joined the battle and I relinquished direct attack lest inadvertently I spoil their better plan. The International Air Line Pilots Association sent representatives to the Chinese government in London and to Taiwan objecting to the "criminal" charges. They backed up their objection with a threat of boycott unless the government changed its position and the "prisoners" were declared entirely free of further prosecution. While the Chinese officials dawdled, I discovered further unexplained crashes and learned of numerous near-misses from various line pilots who were flying into Taipei, and I became increasingly suspicious. When I went deeper into the local aeronautical scene I found that a series of reports on "anomalies" in the electronic approach facilities had been filed by Northwest, Pan American, Cathay Pacific, and other flight captains. A particularly common complaint was the reception of false signals from the low-frequency locator equipment.

As far as I could determine, nothing had been done by the Chinese technicians to rectify the alleged faults. I remembered the importance of "face" to the Chinese and speculated upon how that oriental idiosyncrasy might have influenced the aviation bureaucrats responsible. When I became better acquainted with the crew and heard out their story I was impressed with their sincerity and very genuine distress, not only at the unfortunate crash, but at their treatment as criminals. They were Americans long settled in Taiwan. They were proud of themselves and their skill. Their humiliation when required to stand trial in civil court had become a macabre torture when the prosecutor held gory photographs of the victims before their eyes and asked who was responsible.

Before leaving Taipei I developed a theory I thought might identify the real culprit, yet because the Chinese Republic was a police state I could not prove it. Thanks to Tom Boyd I had been able to study all the available information on the crash, but the part I thought most vital, a clear record of the Chinese government's failure to correct the apparent "anomalies," was not available to anyone.

Hampered by this lack of factual confirmation I could not organize the written attack I had originally planned and urgency was much diminished when in last-minute response to the threat of aerial boycott, the Chinese government rescinded all criminal charges against the crew and granted them permission to leave the country. I allowed the complexities of my findings to simmer for a while and finally decided to write the story as fiction. Thus began a novel I called *Band of Brothers*. It gave me no end of literary trouble.

My assembled research filled a large apple crate and I added more as the book progressed. Usually, when a work is almost half finished I send the first one or two hundred pages to the publisher for a reaction. Was I on the right track or in the blindness of creation had I drifted too far away from the original conception? For some unknown reason I waited this time until a complete first draft was finished, the work of more than a year. I sent it off to Peter Schwed at Simon and Schuster and was confident we had the structure and basis for a very good book. I was stunned when Schwed called to say he was disappointed and, joining with an assistant editor, recounted a long list of objections. Wondering how I could have gone so wrong I brooded for days, finally decided Schwed and his assistant had been right, and ceremoniously set fire to the entire manuscript. Since Simon and Schuster had given me a generous advance I was obliged to pay them back or deliver a book. Working at forced draft for a further eight months I did complete a very different version of *Band of Brothers* and saw it become a middling success in all the usual categories. Yet like the father of a bastard never to be met, I often wondered how the first version might have fared.

Meanwhile I was very glad to see the money earned by *Band of Brothers,* for I had found an even deeper well in which to pour what funds the taxman left me. In a repetition of the Western Ocean Fishing Company's twisted philosophy, wherein two boats should make a profit while one could not, Red Mill Farm had increased in acreage until it could now be classified as a genuine operating ranch. Similarly, our herd of beef cattle had multiplied to respectable numbers and our production of grains and grasses greatly increased. All of this promised well as I adapted easily to the eternal optimism of fishermen and farmers, the two categories of Americans least likely to become solvent.

Just as in fishing, however, there were rewards other than crass currency and I convinced myself that good management and hard work would eventually produce a modest profit. I hired Scott Jackson, a good cattleman, to keep me from making too many mistakes and when he left for greener pastures, Gregory Black, a marvelously energetic young Montanan and a throwback to the days of the great painter of the early American West, Charlie Russell. His very life was cattle and with the herd under his surveillance I was better able to enjoy what we had created from so very little.

Mornings, as always, were devoted to writing. On decent afternoons I would saddle Melody, my Tennessee Walker, and ride through the valley or down to the sea. I found great contentment in little things, the squeak of leather beneath my legs, the soaring of eagles above my fields, and the chimes of the little church on the fringe of the valley tolling out "Greensleeves." There were rabbits, of which we disapproved because they destroyed the land and ate the grasses we needed for cattle, and muskrats along the little creek flowing through our land. In summer the valley was full of wild canaries singing of their ecstasy, bees fertilizing our clovers, while quail and young pheasants rustled in the hedgerows. Ducks, deer, and geese would come to our ponds in the fall and knew somehow they had found safe refuge, for I would not allow hunting anywhere. Felix at age fifteen could no longer catch rabbits, but he trembled and yipped in his dreams as if still hard at the chase.

I rode through all of this as often as possible, proud of Melody, a roan with taffy mane and tail. Most of the time Dodie rode beside me, as much the mistress of her peppery Morgan as she had been of her skis. One day, holding our horses to a lazy walk, I told her, "We have so much it cannot last. It scares me so I'm almost afraid to go outside in a thunderstorm."

I knew we were living an anachronism, for we were the country squire and his lady. Our worries were almost non-existent and certainly not those of the average American citizen. We had continued to live "very high on the hog," as my father would have said, and I saw no possible threat to our future. There were times when my contentment with all about us was so persuasive and lulling to my senses, I forgot the inexplicable balancing of every man's affairs. I had almost become convinced there were no wild gods left on the loose.

This illusion was somewhat marred by the discovery that my carcass was complaining of the cruelty of time. I had thought the long and painful recovery from three collapsed vertebrae in the back had been enough reminder, but now it seemed my plumbing had gone awry and unless something was done real trouble was certain. Almost before I realized what license I had given to the surgeon, he sliced me in half across the belly and removed the offending gland. Pointing to the long wound, I told those who were interested I had attempted hara-kiri and had bungled the job. Recovery took an extraordinarily long time because extraordinary events occurred. Now, suddenly, the wild gods vent their wrath upon me.

Part Five

THE BALANCING

THE TRAIN FROM
PUERTO LIMÓN

The train is slowing now. We have passed through the suburbs of San José and the station must be somewhere near since my Costa Rican fellow passengers are gathering their mesh bags and little imitation leather suitcases and several are already standing in the aisle. Ahead the diesel engine is doing a great deal of horn-honking as we pass through intersections with the streets. Have I frittered away this whole day's expedition with thinking of matters better left to evaporate with time? Or have I disclosed certain clues which may eventually complete my now long-neglected exploration of a forbidden forest? I have made this junket to escape from writing and still various proj-

ects will not leave me in peace. Next year or the next I will go farther afield and fly my airplane around Cape Horn, thereby qualifying to spit to windward.* Next year? Who can predict what will happen five minutes from now, when this train is due in San José?

Where are we at this appointed time and place in relation to all that has gone before? The old wounds capable of healing are healed. Other wounds will never heal. Many of the blessings are still at hand; notably Dodie, and our love seems everlasting. Felix is gone; we put him to sleep to spare him blindness and deafness and agonized movement and we buried him in the shade of a tree on Red Mill Farm with far more ceremony than we intend for ourselves. I carved his headstone to OUR GALLANT COMRADE, a maudlin act I knew, but how else to salute his unswerving devotion?

Red Mill Farm continues to improve and the mortgage for a part of it is nearly paid in full. We have too many personal toys and apparently not enough time to use them properly. It seems less than once a week that I mount Melody and ride across the valley, and even less frequently take our little powerboat Strumpet for a cruise through the archipelago. Or anywhere else. We are surfeited with all manner of luxuries, our engagement calendar is as full or empty as we wish it to be; our only conceivable home is the island where we have now lived for ten years.

I have recently finished a book I hope may be a valuable contribution to aviation history, Flying Circus. Temporarily disenchanted with novels I decided to write about those airliners I thought had been most important to commercial air transport since its true beginning; not that I ever thought the subject would have wide appeal, but as some show of gratitude for what aviation had done for me. Flying buffs bought a good many copies and critical praise was very high. Writing such a specialized book, I knew my greatest reward would be in the extensive research, which joined me in fascinating hours with pilots of airliners all over the world.

Most of the friends I held dear are still mine to enjoy even if our reunions are sometimes infrequent. On those frustrating occasions when I pass through Hollywood try-

* Mission accomplished, January, 1977.

ing to discover whatever happened to The Antagonists, *or* Band of Brothers, *or* Of Good and Evil, *none of which ever reached the screen, I always spend enjoyable hours with Lester Linsk. I no longer bother to call the fancy Hollywood lawyers who were supposed to salvage at least a few dollars for my share of* Soldier of Fortune. *They did succeed in prying five thousand dollars out of Twentieth-Century Fox and their ultimate letter now hangs framed on the wall of the little chicken house where I still write.* ". . . *we are retaining these monies for our own account as attorneys' fees in this matter.*" *In my temper when the letter came I scribbled across it,* SIC SEMPER TYRANNIS, *when I actually meant* sic transit gloria.

Sometimes I dine with Richard Burton or David Brown in Hollywood or young Richard Zanuck, but his father seems to have disappeared from the scene. Valerie Douglas, long my champion and white huntress in the Hollywood jungles remains my confidante. I play chess with Duke Wayne and always lose. In San Francisco there is still Bill Kincaid, and Harvey McDowell of the Albatros, and D. K. Smith. Sloniger is long gone and Sterling Hayden lives in France. The Gotti brothers are still managing their superb restaurant, Ernie's.* Occasionally I have a delightful reunion with Tanya Mifsud-Bryant-Cutler-Dobbs, who is apparently almost spared the marks of time.

Somewhere, I suppose, I have enemies, but they do not openly declare themselves so I cannot make amends for wrongs I may have done. I enjoy a host of flying friends everywhere and I am pleasantly surprised at their rate of survival. Bill Oliver lives well in Honolulu, Tom Boyd buys me lunch in New York whenever I can out-hesitate him, and he always sees me off. I have kept touch with a multitude of people in spite of my physical isolation, which is the way of life I prefer. Therefore I am among the most fortunate of men since I have not lacked love, friends, accomplishments, laughter, or health. There has only been the terrible balancing.

---

* Named after their father. My only connection is as a paying customer.

Chapter 46

The winds of December are harsh in the archipelago. They swing wildly from the southeast to the southwest, bringing the rain horizontally, whipping the stark deciduous trees mercilessly and bending the evergreens in abject obeisance. During these gales the perimeter of our valley is often illusory, apparently expanding and contracting in the fog while the straits and the mountains beyond are lost in low rushing cloud. There is no real daylight until nine o'clock and the glower of twilight is upon us at four. By five it is dark. The damp winds of December create a chill factor out of all proportion to the recorded temperature. Yet this kind of weather is strangely invigorating for those who like walking in the rain, well protected against the gusts, and accompanied by a shaggy dog.

One afternoon I walked with Judy, daughter of Felix, intending to check the volume of water in the stream while simultaneously rebuilding my strength from the recent session in the hospital. The dull overcast was not higher than one hundred feet, the visibility hardly a mile, and I thought it might be nearly dark before I returned to the house again. The wind was very hard, but sheltered by the double row of hawthorns flanking the gravel road I was only aware of the general sound of distant lashing trees and the low thrumming of the telephone wires. I was counting my resources, trying to decide if I could afford to buy an additional fifty-five acres, which would improve the efficiency of Red Mill Farm. I fell to wondering why I cared about the farm and allowed it to absorb so much of my energy and money. The all too recent hospitalization had reminded me once more of the forbidden forest (it seemed more like a jungle now), and the old American tradition of passing the family farm on to the children hardly applied to our situation. The State Department had transferred Polly and her husband to Oslo and by no stretch of the imagination could she be considered even a potential farm girl. Steven was not interested in any of my affairs. George's career was now assured. He had passed his Master's Certificate for all tonnages and was presently chief mate of a very new tanker, the *Chevron Mississippi*. A new ship, scheduled to be his first command, was already abuilding. In public at least I tried to restrain my pride in his remarkable progress and was delighted with his current master, a relatively young captain, Cyril Pemberton.

A Chevron port captain had confided in me that the pair were considered the best team in the fleet and as a consequence had been assigned to the most recently launched tanker. I remembered how the best pilots were always selected to fly the new types of aircraft. There were always problems with any untried vessel whether airborne or seaborne and the most resourceful crews are expected to ease the break-in period. I knew the *Chevron Mississippi* had more than her share of birthing pains because both Pemberton and George had given me an escorted tour. Seamen prefer to be proud of their vessel—they were not.

She was a prime example of my country's growing lack of interest in producing a superior product, and I found it disturbing that the oil companies, who are hardly suffering from economic distress, would join the common compromise. Even a landlubber might look askance at some of the work turned out by the ship's builders. Among many other crude deficiencies was the ship's main exhaust stack. Viewed from astern it was obviously out of plumb approximately five degrees. All of the navigational equipment had also given trouble. A long series of minor deficiencies and failures were recorded in the logbooks, but Pemberton and his chief mate kept telling themselves the shoddy workmanship could eventually be conquered if they just persisted. They would have preferred more benign waters for the difficult teething period, but a multimillion-dollar ship must start earning her keep immediately, and soon after commissioning the *Chevron Mississippi* was assigned to the Alaska run.

I had no doubt such a stalwart pair would soon have the minor faults of their vessel corrected even if the cockeyed stack must remain a disgrace to American shipbuilding. Yet the more I studied their great ship the more offended my eyes became. She was eight hundred and ten feet long. I wondered how much her lack of aesthetic appeal influenced my opinion when I saw that her stern had been sawed off just where buoyancy should have begun. Although I was not a naval architect or a tanker man I had been to sea more than long enough to know something about the importance of buoyancy. After congratulating the Captain and his mate on their fine new ship and the considerable improvement in their spacious quarters from the older tankers, I decided to venture my objection.

"That stern. I would think any kid carving a boat for his bathtub would know better than to cut off the stern like that. I would guess when it starts down in heavy wave action it will keep going down for a long time before it comes up again. There is no flare, nothing to stop the wrong end of the teeter-totter. Why would an architect send something like that to sea?"

They gave me some quick and grumbling answers.

"The architects don't have all that much to say."

"In construction costs it saves about a million dollars by chopping off the stern."

I understood. In every enterprise of magnitude there are always little men involved who would draw attention to themselves by reciting numerical chants across the polished mahogany of board-room tables. Their voices almost always dominate the courageous few who want the best available of anything.

Whenever he reached port George made it a habit to find a booth along a pier and telephone Red Mill Farm. There were always so many things to discuss—the progress of his latest ship model, restoration of the one-hundred-year-old schooner *Wanderbird* in which we both had an avid interest, my latest flying caper, and a considerable exchange of opinion on the current books we were reading. Why had Nelson made certain maneuvers at Trafalgar? We both kept a record of our readings and were quick to recommend or condemn from the current supply. We did a great deal of laughing during these conversations because we trusted each other so absolutely, our interests were identical, and robust ho-ho-ing was the nature of our kind. There were times when Dodie said we sounded like a pair of pirates prying open a treasure chest.

George called me when I was in the hospital and again when his ship put into Seattle shortly before Christmas. Now striding along with the December wind at my back I thought about our last conversation. I had asked if he would be in San Francisco at Christmas and he had said, "Yes, I think so. I don't see how we can miss because we have to go into the shipyard for so many things. The ship is falling apart . . . nothing fundamentally serious . . . just little things one after another. It's driving us all crazy."

Later I learned there had been a last-minute change in sailing orders for the *Chevron Mississippi*. George had said to Bos'n José Lopez, "Guess what? We won't be home for Christmas. We're going north instead of south." And Bos'n Lopez had groaned unhappily, for he knew what the Gulf of Alaska was like in December.

At the end of the gravel road I passed through one of our cattle gates and walked upward along a gently sloping pasture. I had walked altogether hardly more than a mile and was already weary, for the operation had left me with a further complication. Trying to regain my strength too rapidly I had overdone things and somehow ruptured myself. It seemed certain I would have to be operated upon again and I was trying to accept the necessity with such humor as I could manage. As long as they kept their knives away from my brain, I thought, I was bound to recover. But if "they" started subtracting from the two-cylinder mechanism behind my eyes I was in real trouble. Walking, I made a noise like a one-cylinder "make and break" engine and found childish relief in the soft repetition of spasmodic explosions.

It was nearly dark when I approached the top of the pasture and saw to my puzzlement Greg Black waiting for me at the small horse gate. Now in the half-light the cowboy hat he rarely removed made him look all the more like a figure stepped from a Charles Russell painting. I wondered, idly, why he was waiting since the ranch work was done for the day. I said, "Hi . . ."

"Hi . . ." Greg's voice had always been gentle for so powerful a young man.

"What are you up to?"

"Well. . . ." He hesitated. "I'd like to walk up to the house with you. Something I want to tell you."

We walked the few hundred yards side by side in the gathering darkness. I sensed he was nervous and hoped he was not going to tell me he was leaving for a better job. I dismissed the idea he might wish to confide some family trouble, for Dodie and I had but two days before shared a jolly Christmas dinner with him, his wife Patty, and their three young sons.

"What's on your mind?"

"Well . . ." Again the same hesitation. We were approaching the small outbuildings surrounding the main house. "Well . . . I have to tell you, your son has been lost at sea."

I heard him without hearing. My mind rejected his words as meaningless nonsense. I continued walking without losing stride. There was some mistake, of course. It would all be set right and proved but another exaggeration of the news—as soon as I could get to a telephone.

We entered the house. Dodie stood waiting for me and I saw she was weeping. And suddenly I knew how the God of the Christians had felt.

Numb with grief, I attended the Coast Guard hearing in San Francisco. Key members of the *Chevron Mississippi*'s crew had been brought down from Alaska to testify, for not only was my George lost, but also Captain Pemberton and a seaman, Mario Romersa, had been killed. A nearly incredible series of circumstances combined to make this one of the most tragic and unnecessary losses in the long annals of the sea.

Two days after Christmas, southbound from Alaska, the *Chevron Mississippi* had run into heavy weather which gradually increased until the winds became Force Ten to Eleven and the swells twenty to thirty feet high. The great ship labored in such agony it became necessary to reduce speed. During the night several fifty-gallon oil drums lashed on the chopped-off stern came adrift and took up a lethal dance in response to the ship's motion. Some drums contained fuel oil to power the ship's small boats and emergency generator, others carried chemicals used in regular ship's maintenance. In a ship eight hundred and ten feet long, the designers had been unable to find any other place to stow the barrels.

Just after dawn, after he had been relieved of his regular watch on the bridge, George led a party to the afterdeck where they began the tricky business of capturing the heavy drums and securing them. William Diggs, the very young third mate, now stood watch on the bridge and was alerted to the working party aft. He was joined shortly after breakfast by Captain Pemberton, who surveyed the furious ocean and made a slight course change. Then he said he would go aft himself and see what progress was being made with the maverick barrels.

As they continued to struggle with the barrels and new lashings Bos'n Lopez was surprised to see the Captain himself appear at his side. He said, "What are you doing back here, Captain?"

"Just thought I'd see how you're getting along."

They were his last words. Suddenly, the chopped-off stern started down and kept going down. A great wave engulfed them all. The stern rose, the sea cleared and a second great wave followed almost immediately. Bos'n Lopez managed to cling to some rigging. When at last the stern rose he saw both his captain and his chief mate in the sea and far behind the vessel. Seaman Romersa was prone on the deck, apparently unconscious.

Precious minutes were lost before Lopez could telephone the bridge and advise young Diggs of the situation. Then the alarm sounded and Second Mate Snyder, whose experience at sea was not much more than Diggs's roused himself from his bunk to take command. It was a terrifying responsibility and immediate decisions were mandatory. As he ordered the great ship turned back he wondered if he should compound the disaster by ordering a boat overside to effect a rescue if and when the missing men could be found.

Even before the *Mississippi* had returned to the general area it was obvious that the launching of a small boat would be extremely hazardous even if volunteers could be found to man it. While they were still searching, Seaman Romersa appeared to be dying and no one could find the key to the medicine chest.

Some two hours later, it was all over. Seaman Romersa was dead. Captain Cyril Pemberton had been floating head down in the water, his arms stretched over a partly submerged oil barrel. He could not have been alive. George was never seen again.

A fraction of my grief was alleviated by my anger at the conduct of the Coast Guard hearing, a disgraceful exhibition by a representative of a service dedicated to safety of life at sea. The officer in charge sought repeatedly to divert any blame for the tragedy from the ship or her owners, nor did he once ask any of the crew present on that terrible morning for recommendations which might prevent similar losses in the future.

Yet rage and bitterness are but temporary salves and when weeping becomes dry, only bewilderment remains. As a neo-pagan I was unable to find solace in formal religion: could any priest or minister convince me it had all been God's benign will and tanker men were needed in the heavens? I felt only that three fine men had been lost because a giant corporation had somehow been persuaded to save a few dollars in the design and construction of a supertanker. As a consequence, two women were widowed and several children fatherless. I had lost not only a son, but the dearest friend I had ever had in all my worlds.

———

I had first taken the very young George to sea and we had been shipmates on countless occasions. I had encouraged him to make the sea his career. Since his loss I felt more than ever compelled to find my way through the dark scheme which permitted me, now long past my prime, to stalk this earth while younger men with lives still to be fulfilled were slain. It was outrageous, this way of things, I decided, and should not be accepted meekly as some inexplicable deed of a convenient Almighty.

As the train slides to a halt at San José station my ignorance continues to vex me. Why are we as incapable of comprehending our individual destiny as we are the true measure of infinity? Why should a gate clang shut and the most brilliant minds be brought up short at these ageless riddles? Our inability is so absolute we are not even permitted exploration beyond the frontier.

I was not born the small boy who stared me down so many hours ago when the train paused at the hamlet of Mary and Jesus. Another life has been mine, yet because no man on earth is removed from any other by more than fifty cousins I would like to ask the small boy what he expects of the coming years and what he hopes for his fortune. And he would not really know the results of the next five minutes. Then I would like to explain to him, gently, how all of us are little men, naked to our enemies. And I would like to assure him somehow that along with his inevitable calamities there will be joys in equal degree; perhaps then he can better resist the frightful blows which may otherwise lead him to bitterness.

In the eons of time since our emergence from the Pleistocene Age we have learned to prolong our lives, but no one lives to be hundreds of years old. This is undoubtedly a very good circumstance. As long as we are aware of our mutual nakedness, as long as we find humor in reminding ourselves how cockroaches have a greater resistance to radioactive poisons than humans, then our opportunities to enjoy our given lives are multiplied to infinity.

All we are permitted to know of our destiny is how the complex scheme begins with the half-stifled grunts and gaspings emitted by a male and a female. The passionate echoes of procreation and the sobs of mourning are our entrance and exit to a forbidden forest.

KEEP YOURSELF IN
SUSPENSE...
from
BALLANTINE BOOKS